THE TRUE CHURCH

THE TRUE CHURCH

The Path which Led a Protestant Lawyer to the Catholic Church

PART 1 CHRISTIAN THEORY

PART 2 DOCTRINE AND DISCIPLINE

Peter H. Burnett

With a foreword by

Kevin Starr PhD

State Librarian of California

Edited by ***Dominic Colvert***

Solas Press

Antioch

2004

First Published in 1860 by D. Appleton & Company New York under the title *The Path which Led a Protestant Lawyer to the Catholic Church*

Permissions Dept.
SOLAS *Press*
P.O. Box 4066
Antioch CA 94531
USA

SOLAS Press web site www.solaspress.com. E-mail info@solaspress.com

Library of Congress Cataloging-in-Publication Data

Burnett, Peter H. (Peter Hardeman), 1807-1895
The true church : the path which led a Protestant lawyer to the Catholic Church / Peter H. Burnett ; with a forward by Kevin Starr
p. cm.
Rev. ed. of : The path which led a Protestant lawyer to the Catholic Church
Includes bibliographic references and index
ISBN 1-893426-74-2
1. Catholic Church – Doctrines. 2. Catholic Church – Controversial literature. 3. Apologetics. 4. Catholic converts. I. Title: Path which led a Protestant lawyer to the Catholic Church. II. Burnett, Peter H. (Peter Hardeman), 1807- 1895. Path which led a Protestant lawyer to the Catholic Church. III. Title.

BX1751.3.B87 2004
282 – dc22

2004056547

PREFACE TO THE 1860 EDITION

I was once a Protestant, and I became a Catholic. The main reasons which led to this change will be found substantially stated in the following work. There are several topics that I have not noticed for want of room. It is also true that several authorities are referred to that were not then read; and several that I read at the time which were not noticed, because they were not assessable. My quotations of Scripture are generally from King James's translation, mainly for the reason that this was the one used by me in my pursuit of the true Church.

My parents were Baptists; but until the age of thirty-two, I was not a believer in the truth of Christianity. My own observations of men and things, as well as the arguments of others, at length satisfied me that the system was divine; and I at once acted upon my convictions, and joined myself to the Disciples, in 1840. In 1843, I removed with my family to Oregon. After my arrival and while I was temporarily located at Fort Vancouver, I attended High Mass as a mere spectator, on Christmas, at midnight. I had never witnessed anything like it before, and the profound solemnity of the services -- the intense, yet calm fervor of the worshippers -- the great and marked differences between the two forms of worship -- and the instantaneous reflection, that this was the Church claiming to be the only true Church, did make the deepest impression upon my mind for the moment. In all my religious experience, I had never felt an impulse so profound, so touching. I had witnessed very exciting scenes in Protestant worship, and had myself often participated, and was happy. But I had never felt any impulse so powerful -- an impulse that thrilled my inmost soul. I gazed into the faces of the worshippers, and they appeared as if they were actually looking at the Lord Jesus, and were hushed into perfect stillness, in His awful presence.

As I knew nothing of the reasons upon which the Catholic theory assumes to rest, I soon thought I saw errors that I could not sanction. And then there came a painful revulsion in my feelings, as if the flowers of Paradise had been almost within my reach, and had been suddenly withdrawn from sight and I had found it to be but an illusion and a mistake. But still I can never forget the holy impulses of my soul at that deep moment.

My knowledge of the Catholic theory was exceedingly general and indefinite. I had never read a work in its favor, and had never heard but two Catholic sermons, and they were not upon controversial points. I knew that the Old Church made what are called arrogant and intolerant pretensions; but in all my reading, in all my intercourse with men generally, and among my own kin, I had scarcely ever met with anything in her favor. From my limited opportunities, I had only learned that

"To love her was shame to revile her was glory."

In the fall of 1844, a Baptist preacher settled in my immediate neighborhood, who had the published Debate between Campbell and Purcell; and as the Catholic question was often mentioned, and as I knew so little about it, I borrowed and read the book. I had the utmost confidence in the capacity of Mr. Campbell as an able debater. But while the attentive reading of the Debate did not convince me of the entire truth of the Catholic theory, I was greatly astonished to find that so much could be said in its support. On many points, and those of great importance, it was clear to my mind, that Mr. Campbell had been overthrown. Still, there were many objections to the Catholic Church, either not noticed by the Bishop, or not satisfactorily answered; and I arose from the reading of that discussion still a Protestant.

My thoughts continually recurred to the main positions and arguments on both sides, and the more I reflected upon the fundamental positions of the Bishop, the more force and power I found them to possess. My own reflections often afforded me answers to difficulties that, at first, seemed insurmountable, until the question arose in my mind, whether Mr. Campbell had done full justice to his side of the question. Many of his positions seemed so extreme and ill-founded, that I could not sanction them. All the prejudices I had, if any, were in his favor. I knew that it was worse than idle to indulge prejudices when investigating any subject whatever. I was determined to be true to myself! and this could only be in finding the exact truth, and following it, when known.

My mind was, therefore, left in a state of restless uncertainty; and I determined to examine the questions between Catholics and Protestants thoroughly, so far as my limited opportunities and poor abilities would permit. In the prosecution of this design, I procured all the works, on both sides, within my reach, and examined them alternately, side by side. This investigation occupied all my spare time for about eighteen months.

I observed substantially the course of investigation pointed out in the introduction, and followed the rules of construction therein given.[‡] Besides this, I prayed humbly and sincerely, that I might first know the truth, and then have the grace to follow it wherever it might lead me. I examined carefully, prayerfully, and earnestly, until I was satisfied, beyond a doubt, that the Old Church was the true, and the only true Church.

"And I said, if there's is peace to be found in the world,
The heart that was humble might hope for it here"

In this I was not mistaken. I found her, as holy Cyprian of old had said, "The house of unity and peace." I mean to live and die in her communion.

[‡]Burnett is referring to the six principles given in Part 1 Chapter I: 1. Inclusive reference rule, 2. Single author rule, 3. Meaning in context rule, 4. Principles apply in the widest sense rule, 5. Limitation of exceptions rule, and 6. Natural construction rule. Editor.

EDITORS NOTE

The first purpose of an editor is to excite in the reader the thoughts and emotions that the author intended. In this instance, there was also a challenge to make Burnett's work more readable and accessible to the modern reader. Burnett's full text and language is given to achieve the primary goal. To achieve the secondary goal a number of changes have been made to the 1860 edition. Where it seemed appropriate, the explanatory notes were incorporated into the text. Some infelicities in construction were removed through punctuation. Some conjunctions such as "now," "but," and "and," which might be associated more with an oral presentation were removed. We have endeavored to improve the section headings, and divided the work into two logical parts. Burnett's argumentation followed a logical progression, however, on many occasions he contented himself with headings such as "The same subject continued," and "Miscellaneous." Improving the headings helped to clarify the flow of the analyses. A list of authorities and indexes have been added to assist the reader.

Since Solas Press began the project to bring Burnett's work to the modern reader we have received encouragement, correction and helpful advice from a wide spectrum of persons too numerous to be mentioned. In addition to those who gave generously of their valuable time to review the galley copies and provide testimonials to the book's continuing relevance, we would like to note the contributions of Antoninus Wall, Tom Woodhouse, Peggy Cahill, and John Flynn. For any errors that remain despite the best of help I accept responsibility.

Dominic Colvert

CONTENTS

PART 1 CHRISTIAN THEORY

PART 2 DOCTRINE AND DISCIPLINE

FOREWORD

In 1860 the highly respectable New York publishing firm of D. Appleton & Company issued a most unusual book by Peter Burnett (1807-1895), the first civil governor of California. Entitled *The Path which Led a Protestant Lawyer to the Catholic Church*, Burnett's treatise was, most fundamentally, an exercise in apologetics: a lawyerly sifting of evidence and presentation of argument. As such, *The Path* would have been unusual enough; for the mid-nineteenth-century United States did not sustain – with the notable exception of Orestes Brownson – many laymen interested in, much less capable of apologetics. The more one examines *The Path*, however, the more distinctive this book becomes in the landscape of nineteenth-century theological discourse.

First of all, Peter Burnett was not only a layman devoid of a formal theological education, he was a convert, having entered the Catholic Church in 1846 while serving as judge of the Supreme Court of Oregon. Had Burnett been a layman with a formal education – a graduate of Harvard or Yale, for example, long resident in the Eastern states, well-traveled, living a privileged and intellectually enriched life – it would be easy to understand how he might have come, following his conversion, to write this book. But Peter Burnett was a hard-scrabble autodidact, born in Nashville, Tennessee, when it was barely a frontier settlement, raised in poverty on a Missouri farm, a clerk and bookkeeper as a young man working for subsistence wages before marrying and studying privately for the law.

There is nothing in his early life to suggest adequate preparation: no leisure, no formal education beyond a few years of elementary schooling, a self-taught lawyer with a practice – defending Mormons – that literally put his life in danger. Nor did Burnett turn to theological or other academic pursuits as he entered his thirties. He became, rather, an overworked district attorney in Missouri, plagued by debt from early business failures. Nothing thus far in his life, in short, would suggest the evolution of a writer capable by the late 1850s of a level of theological, scriptural, and historical exegesis that would have done honor to a privileged academic in the Eastern states, or even a protagonist in the

Oxford Movement in England that would bring such a paragon of learning as John Henry Newman into the Catholic Church.

The story becomes even more intriguing in 1842 when Burnett takes his wife and family to the Oregon Territory by wagon train. As far as a center of learning was concerned – a world of books, libraries, publication, and erudite discourse – Missouri was remote enough; but the Oregon of 1843 was on the edge of nowhere, sparsely settled, its legal status uncertain, its Native American population hostile and resistant. And if these challenges were not enough, Burnett, now in his mid-thirties, could look behind him to a record of business failures, a resignation from the district attorneyship, even a resignation as leader of the wagon train in which he brought his family West.

He had come to Oregon to help his wife regain her health. The trip, noted the Burnett family physician, would either kill or cure her. But he had also come West to improve his prospects, which eventually happened, with whatever mixed results. Everything in the life of Peter Burnett seems touched by ambiguity, by half-successes, by resignations from office once office was attained, by a pursuit of wealth when, inwardly, he turned out to be having so much else on his mind.

Burnett succeeded in Oregon, publicly at least, being elected judge of the Supreme Court and a member of the First Territorial Legislature. But something else happened as well in the Oregon Territory. He attended a Roman Catholic midnight High Mass on Christmas 1843 at Fort Vancouver. Born a Baptist, he had left Christianity behind as a young man; but now, that evening, he encountered; in the Latin, the vestments, the incense, the flickering candlelight, the intense concentration of the worshippers; the possibilities of another approach to the sacred. Within two years, the Supreme Court justice became a Roman Catholic. He was even more alone in his new identity (Burnett's wife did not follow him into the Church), more on the edge than ever, having joined a church that was still held under a deep cloud of suspicion by the vast majority of even the most well meaning Protestant Americans.

The next fourteen years of Peter Burnett's life, prior to the publication of *The Path,* is a case study in the fast-forwarding of history that was the California Gold Rush. In rapid order – indeed, almost simultaneously – Burnett moved to California (his family would join him later, arriving by coastal steamer), earned his grubstake as a working miner, became John Sutter's lawyer and business partner, prospered in Sacramento real estate, moved to San Francisco, entered politics, was appointed to the

Superior Tribunal of California by Military Governor Bennet Riley, led the crusade for statehood, was elected governor for the newly established civil government, served in that position for slightly more than a year, played an important role in organizing the new state, resigned, served a short term on the state supreme court, returned to his business interests in Sacramento, where he also served as a city councilman, and rejoined the supreme court (this in 1858). Sometime in the midst of all of this, he wrote *The Path which Led a Protestant Lawyer to the Catholic Church*.

Were *The Path* a mere pamphlet, or even a modest-sized book, it would be comprehensible that a busy frontier lawyer, judge, miner, real estate investor, inaugural governor, and supreme court judge might, just somehow, find time to produce a pamphlet bearing witness to his newly found faith. But *The Path* is not a pamphlet. Running to more than 700 pages in this new edition from the Solas Press, *The Path* is in reality among the most ambitious explications of Roman Catholicism to appear in the United States in the nineteenth century. Drawing upon scripture, history, the Fathers, and apologetics down through two millennia, it is also a vastly learned treatise, soaked through with a sense of history.

How did he research this book, much less find the time to write it? Although Burnett did spend some time in New York City in the late 1850s and thus can be expected to have used the libraries of the metropolis, much of his research must have been carried on in San Francisco and Sacramento as well. The sheer fact that Burnett was capable of at least partially researching and writing this book on the remote Pacific Coast in the first decade of its American existence, testifies, I suppose, to the presence of scholarly books on the frontier in terms of libraries and bibliography and, of equal importance, to the internal sense of culture that self-educated Americans could achieve in the nineteenth century on the frontier. (Abraham Lincoln comes immediately to mind.) Burnett does not write *The Path* as a frontiersman, nor even a provincial. Like the great Puritan divines of seventeenth-century Massachusetts, he writes with full authority and assurance, trusting his sources, unintimidated by the prestige of his intellectual opponents.

From a national perspective, *The Path* falls into the genre of formal debates between Catholic and Protestant protagonists that was such an intriguing feature of the nineteenth-century American religious landscape as the Protestant community became increasingly aware of the fact that Roman Catholics were becoming more numerous in the United States and that their social, institutional, and political presence was beginning to show a growing force. On the Catholic side of these debates, the highpoint was reached by Orestes Brownson in his *The American Republic* (1866), written to defend the compatibility of Roman Catholicism and the American political system and way of life. To align *The Path* equally with *The American Republic* would not be an honest thing to do; yet in its learning – especially its sense of the Fathers and the historical development of the Church – *The Path* can be said to occupy a lesser yet respectable niche in this literature of apologetics.

Considered in terms of its origins on the frontier, *The Path* becomes somewhat astonishing. It testifies to the rich interior resources brought to the frontier by so many pioneers: the interior beliefs and commitments that prompted Burnett and his colleagues to form a state, to establish libraries, to open schools and colleges, to preach learned sermons (this especially from the Protestant pulpit), to bear witness in season and out to the fact that the frontier did not represent a repudiation of learning, merely its translation to new shores.

Catholics can read *The Path* as apologetics and a case study of just how important a role converts have always played in the American Church. Historians of American religion can read *The Path* as an important point of Catholic-Protestant encounter in the mid-nineteenth century. Historians of the frontier, especially the California frontier, whatever their individual religious beliefs, can read *The Path* as evidence of the high-minded concerns that came West with the wagon trains and persisted amidst the hurly-burly of the first frontier.

Kevin Starr

Sacramento January 2004

SOME OF THE AUTHORITIES QUOTED

Ambrose, Saint (c. 340 – 397). He was the civil governor with his capital in Milan when, by popular demand, he was elected bishop. To this new office he brought courage, learning and administrative ability.

Archelaus. Died c. 278. Bishop of Cascar Mesopotamia.

Balguy, John (1686 – 1748). English controversialist. Among his many works is *The Foundations of Moral Goodness* 1727, in which he defended the views of Samuel Clarke. Clarke used Newtonian mechanics as a foundation for theological positions called the Newtonian Settlement (NS). The NS is thought to be a bridge from Deism to Atheism.

Baronius, Caesar (1538 –1607). Cardinal and Church historian. On two occasions, he was almost elected Pope. His major work is *Annales ecclesiastici a Christo nato ad annum 1198.*

Basil the Great, Saint (c.330 –379). He succeeded Eusebius as Bishop of Caesarea. He is a Doctor of the Church and one of the four Fathers of the Greek Church. He established Nicene orthodoxy over Arianism.

Beecher, Edward (1803-1895). Edward was one of thirteen children of the noted Presbyterian minister Lyman Beecher and brother of Harriet Beecher Stowe. He was a correspondent with Henry James. Among his many publications was *The papal conspiracy exposed, and Protestantism defended, in light of reason, history, and Scripture* (1855).

Bellarmine, Robert (1542 –1621). A Jesuit made a Cardinal because of his distinguished scholarship. He was involved in a great many controversies but in particular in those with the reformers. In this area his great work is entitled *De Controversiis.*

Blackstone, William (1723-1780). English jurist. He is author of the standard work *Commentaries on the Laws of England.* This was the first comprehensive treatment of English law and constitution.

Blandina, Saint. A Christian slave who suffered martyrdom in Lyons (Lugdunensis) in 177 A.D. She was tortured to wring evidence from her. When this failed she was exposed to wild beasts who failed to harm her. She was then subjected to more torture and killed.

Bossuet, Jacques Benigne (1627-1704). French Catholic bishop, historian, orator, and controversialist. He was elected to Academie Francaise in 1671. Among his prolific works his *Exposition de la doctrine de l'eglise catholique sur les matieres de controverse* was translated into English.

Boswell, James (1740-1795). He was a lawyer but his true interest was in a literary career. His great work *The Life of Samuel Johnson, LL.D.* (1791) established his reputation as perhaps the greatest biographer of Western Literature.

Breckenridge, John (1797-1841). He debated Archbishop John Hughes of New York on the subject of "Is the Protestant religion the religion of Christ." This was published as the *Hughes-Breckenridge Controversy.*

Bruyére, Jean de La (1645–1696). A quotable French philosopher, moralist, and author.

Burnet, Gilbert (d. 1715). Bishop of Salisbury. He came with William of Orange to England in 1688. He was noted for his anti-Catholic writings and for his *Bishop Burnet's History of His Own Times.*

Calixtus, Georg (1586–1656). German clergyman noted for his writings against Roman Catholicism.

Campbell, Alexander (1788-1866). He seceded from the Baptists and founded the Church of the Disciples. Campbell was a prolific debater and his controversies have continued to be of interest in apologetics. He debated Nathan Lewis Rice for eighteen days beginning November 15, 1843 in Lexington, Kentucky. He debated with John Baptist Purcell, Catholic Bishop of Cincinnati from the 13th to the 21st January, 1837 in Cincinnati, Ohio.

Campbell, George. (1719 – 1796) Scottish theologian. He published *Dissertation on Miracles (1762)* an answer to David Hume's *Philosophical Essays Concerning Human Understanding.*

Chillingworth, William (1602 – 1644). Anglican divine who from his discussions with the Jesuit John Fisher decided to become a Catholic. From further discussions with William Laud bishop of London, he returned to Anglicanism. He published *The Religion of Protestants and a Safe Way to Salvation* (1638).

Clement of Alexandria (Died c. 215). He was a convert to the Christian faith and became director of the Christian school at Alexandria about 190 A.D. He showed brilliance as a theologian and philosopher. His rule of faith is generally accepted, however, his style is difficult to interpret making it easy to see some of his doctrines as suspect.

Clement of Rome, Saint. He died A.D. 97. Third successor to Saint Peter. His First Epistle to the Corinthians is a very important document. He was pope from 88 to 97 A.D.

Cowen, Esek (1787-1844). Reporter of the Supreme Court of New York 1823 to 1829. Author of books and treatises including co-authorship of *A Treatise on the Law of Evidence.*

Cyprian, Saint. (C.200–258). As Bishop of Carthage he defended the church against the heretic Novatian, and was martyred in the persecution of Valerian.

Digby, Kenelm Henry (1800–1880). English antiquarian. His family history involved Catholic causes and he became a Roman Catholic. Among his published works are *The Broad Stone of Honor* (a manual for gentleman) and *Ages of Faith.*

Du Pin, Louis Ellies (1657–1719). A church historian whose work was opposed by Bossuet and others. He tried to effect a union of the French church with the Anglican Church and with the Russian Church in correspondence with Bishop Wake of Canterbury and Peter the Great.

Eusebius of Caesarea, also called Eusebius Pamphili (c. 260-c.340). Bishop of Caesarea. He was learned and a prolific writer. His most important work was *A history of the Church from the time of its Founder to the year 323.*

Faber, George Stanley (1773–1854). English theologian. He espoused evangelical views in his writings. Among his works are *A Dissertation on Prophecies* and *Difficulties of Romanism.*

Grotius, Hugo (1583-1645). A learned Dutchman. At age 15 he was received in France as the 'miracle of Holland.' As a theologian he worked for a new reformation which would unite the Christian churches, but this was not well received in Holland. International Law owes much to his work and to the principles of law that he based on natural law. His letters were collected by H. and J. de Groot in 1687.

Greenleaf, Simon (1783–1853). American jurist. He became a professor of law at Harvard University in 1833 and published many works including *Examination of the Testimony of the Four Evangelists....*

Hackspan, Theodoricus (1607–1659). German theologian who wrote in Latin.

Hale, Sir Matthew (1609-1676). English jurist and statesman, he studied classical law, history, the sciences and theology. His best-known work *The History of the Common Law of England* (1713) furnished Blackstone the basis for his *Commentaries on the Laws of England.*

Hallam, Henry (1777–1859). English historian. Author of the standard work *A View of the State of Europe during the Middle Ages.*

Hay, George (1729-1811). Widely published Catholic bishop who wrote on doctrinal issues and on political issues of his time. Among his publications is *The Scripture doctrine of miracles displayed.*

Hegesippus, Saint (died 180A.D.) Hegesippus wrote a 100 year history of the Church, from the passion of our Lord to the year 133 A. D. Only fragments of this work are now known, but Saint Jerome and Eusebius knew his writings. From his visits to all the churches of his day, he was able to testify that, despite the errors of some individuals, none of the episcopacies had fallen into error.

Hermas or Shepherd of Hermas. This is an early Christian document thought to be completed in the second century. Its author(s) is unknown.

Hermes, Georg (1775–1831). German Catholic theologian, he sought to establish the Christian faith on a rational basis. His orthodoxy was questioned later.

Horne, Thomas Hartwell (1780-1862). English bibliographer and author. Among his works is *Deism Refuted or Plain Reasons for Being a Christian* (1826).

Hoadly, Benjamin (1676–1761). Anglican Bishop and staunch Low-Churchman.

Hughes, John Joseph (1797-1864). See also Breckenridge. From 1850 Catholic Archbishop of New York. He founded St. John's College (later Fordham University) and St. Patrick's Cathedral. He was a powerful and influential figure in New York.

Ignatius of Antioch, Saint (died c. 110). As bishop of Antioch, he was condemned and sent to Rome to be executed. On his journey to Rome, he visited many churches and wrote seven letters. These letters provide a source of knowledge of the early Church.

Irenæus, Saint (120/140–200/203). Bishop of Lyon (Lugdunum) His work *Adversus Haæreses* (Against Heresies) was a refutation of Gnosticism. These writings were important for the establishment of the canon of Scripture and the delineation of apostolic succession. As a child, he heard and saw Polycarp who had known the Apostle John at Ephesus.

Ives, Levi Silliman (1797-1867). An American Episcopal bishop. Being deeply interested in the Oxford Movement he became a Catholic in 1852. He published *The Trials of a Mind in its Progress to Catholicism* (1854).

Josephus. Flavius Josephus (37-93). Jewish historian. His works are a first hand account of history of the Roman occupation of Palestine. He served as a commander in the Jewish revolt (75-79) and later became a Roman citizen.

Johnson, William (1769-1848). A reporter of cases in the New York Supreme Court from 1799 to 1823. His multi-volume work is known as *Johnsons's Digest of New York Cases.* He also translated *The Maritime Law of Europe* by Domenico Azuni from the French.

Johnson, Samuel (1709-1784). English author, literary figure and the foremost conversationalist of his day. With Joshua Reynolds he formed the literary club that included in its membership Oliver Goldsmith, Edmund Burke and James Boswell – his biographer.

His famous dictionary, with illustrative quotations, was published in 1755.

Justin Martyr, Saint (c. 100–c. 165). After his conversion he tried to convert others through philosophy. He opened a school in Rome, and was martyred under the Emperor Marcus Auerlius. His best known works are *Apology* and *Dialogue.*

Kenrick, Francis Patrick (1797-1863). Archbishop of Baltimore and apostolic delegate. When first ordained he taught in the college at Bardstown Kentucky. He published *The Primacy of the Apostolic See, and the authority of general councils, vindicated* (1838).

Kent, James (1763-1847). American jurist. .He was law professor at Columbia University and chief judge of the New York Supreme Court. He published *Commentaries on American Law* (4 volumes 1826-30). This work was enthusiastically received and went through six editions in his lifetime. Its influence in America is comparable with the work of William Blackstone in England.

Lactantius, Lucius Caecilius Firmianus. A rhetorician and Christian apologist of the 4th century. A large body of his writings are extant. Saint Jerome called him the most learned man of his time but observes that he had greater skill in refutation of error than in the establishment of truth.

Law, William (1686–1761). Fellow of Emmanuel College Cambridge. Clergyman and High-Church controversialist. In 1728 he published *Serious Call to a Devout and Holy Life.*

Leslie, Charles (1650-1722). Author of *A Short and Easie Method with the Deists.* It claimed to demonstrate the certainty of the Christian religion by infallible proof from four rules.

Leo the Great. Pope from A.D. 440 to A.D. 461

Madison, James (1749–1812). Fourth president of the United States. He is celebrated as an authority on the Constitution rather than for his executive ability.

Marcion. A second century Gnostic (sometimes referred to as a semi-Gnostic because his theology differed from Valentinus.) He thought there were two cosmic gods, one the angry creator of the world, the other the Father of Jesus Christ. His treatment of Scripture forced the Church to fix the approved canon. He was excommunicate by Pope Pious I.

Marshall, John (1755-1835). Renowned American jurist, fourth Chief Justice of the United States Supreme Court from 1801-35.

Middleton, Conyers. (1683-1750). English Divine who engaged in many controversies. In his book *Free Will* he attacked accepted doctrines on miracles.

Miller, William (1782–1849). Religious Leader. After a prolonged study of the bible he was convinced that the second coming of Christ would occur in 1843. He attracted a large following, called Millerites. After the failure of his prophesies, a group remained faithful to his direction and adopted the name Adventist. This group formed the nucleus of a number of religious sects.

Milner, John (1752-1826). English antiquary and Catholic bishop. Among his many published works was his *The End of Religious Controversy* (1818).

Mosheim, Johann Lorenz von (1694–1755). Protestant theologian. Chancellor of the University of Göttingen. He wrote several Church histories.

Nightingale, Joseph (1775-1824). English clergyman. He published on a broad variety of topics including portraits of Catholicism and Methodism. In *The Religions and Religious Ceremonies of all Nations* he discussed Christians, Mohammedans, Jews, Brahmins and Pagans.

Origen (circa 185-circa 254). Celebrated Christian writer, teacher and theologian.

Paley, William (1743-1805). English theologian and lecturer in moral philosophy at Cambridge and chancellor of the diocese of Carlisle. Among his many works is *A View of the Evidences of Christianity* (1794).

Porteus, Beilby (1731-1808). Bishop of London. Quotable writer of prose and verse.

Polycarp, Saint. 2nd century bishop of Smyrna (Izmir, Turkey). He was a friend of the older man Saint Ignatius. Because of his moral authority, his defense against heresy, and his quotations from Saint

Paul and the evangelists he is considered a link between the apostolic and patristic ages. He wrote the *Letter to the Philippians*. He was burned to death for his faith.

Pombal, Sebastião José de Carvalho (1699–1782). In 1750 he obtained the post of Secretary of State for Foreign Affairs. He rendered the weak king Joseph I of Portugal entirely subject to his influence. He was ruthless with those who ventured to obstruct his plans and his record is one of the bloodiest in Portugal. On the death of the king in 1777, he was banished, and all his orders reversed.

Pope, Alexander (1688–1744). English poet. He was noted for his didactic and satirical couplets.

Purcell, John Baptist (1800-1883). Bishop of Cincinnati. (See also Campbell.) He was noted for his founding of schools, orphanages, and academies. He also published a series of textbooks for use in schools.

Rice, Nathan Lewis (1807-1877). See Campbell.

Sherlock, Thomas (1678–1761). Bishop of London. Many of his sermons were published.

Spring, Gardener (1785-1873). Widely published American Protestant author. Among his publications is *A Dissertation on the Rule of Faith* (1844), first delivered as a lecture in Cincinnati.

Starkie, Thomas (1782-1849). English lawyer who authored standard works on evidence, slander and liable, which included *A practical treatise of the law of evidence*.

Stillingfleet, Edward (1635–1699). Anglican bishop of Worchester. He was noted for his liberal views and for his efforts to reach a compromise between Episcopacy and Presbyterianisn.

Story, Joseph (1779–1850). Justice of the Supreme Court of the United States. His writings were influential in molding American jurisprudence. In his constitutional opinions, he supported Washington and Chief-Justice Marshall.

Taylor, Jermy (1613–1667). Bishop of Down and Conner in County Antrim Ireland. His widely read *Liberty of Prophesying* was a defense of toleration. However, his treatment of the Presbyterians did much to move them to be an independent sect.

Tertullian. Quintus Septimus Florens Tertullianus. Born circa 155/160 in Carthage and died after 220 A.D. He received an exceptional education and after advanced study in Rome, he became a Christian. He is chiefly known as a moralist and wrote on almost every conceivable subject. His writings were influential, and he is considered the initiator of church Latin. In later life, he left the Church to found his own sect of strict observation.

Trajan. Roman emperor 98-117 A.D.

Valentinus. He studied philosophy in Alexandria, and was a baptized Christian. He moved to Rome c. 136 A.D. He left the Church when he failed to be made Bishop of Rome. He is considered the founder of Gnosticism a doctrine that has traces in every age to the present.

Vincent of Saragossa, Saint. Saint Vincent suffered martyrdom in the year 303 in Valencia Spain. His story is told in *The Passion*, a hymn of Prudentius, and in the sermons of Saint Augustine.

Volney, Count Constantin-Francois de Chasseboeuf (1757-1820). French historian and philosopher. He investigated the origins of civil society and saw revolution as the result of abandoning natural law, religion, equality, and liberty. His most influential work was *Les ruines, ou meditations sur les révolutions des empires.*

Vossius, Gerhard Johann (1577-1649). German classical scholar and theologian with Calvinistic sympathies. He was educated at Leyden and became a lifelong friend of Hugo Grotius.

Waddington, George (1793–1869). English divine. His writings included works on his travels and Church history.

Watts, Isaac (1674–1748). Pastor of the Congregational chapel in Mark Lane, London. He was also a popular writer of works on divinity, and of manuals of religious instruction and hymns for nonconformist congregations.

Webster, Noah (1758-1843). He was a proponent of the cultural independence of the United States. Webster's dictionary is the American standard.

Wheaton, Henry (1785-1848). American jurist and diplomat who made significant contributions to international law. His most important work *Elements of International Law* (1836) became a standard and was translated into many foreign languages.

White, José Maria Blanco (1775–1841). Born in Seville Spain he became a Catholic Priest. Later he emigrated to England and became an Anglican cleric. Unsatisfied with Anglicanism he became a Unitarian. Fluent in English because of his Irish father he wrote and composed poetry in Spanish and English.

Wiseman, Nicholas Patrick Stephen (1802-1865). He was rector of the English college in Rome and then appointed vicar apostolic in London. In 1836 he founded the *Dublin Review* with Daniel O'Connell. In 1850 when the Catholic hierarchy was restored in England he was made a Cardinal Archbishop of Westminster.

THE TRUE CHURCH

The Path which Led a Protestant Lawyer to the Catholic Church

PART 1 CHRISTIAN THEORY

LONG CONTENTS

PART 1 CHRISTIAN THEORY

CHAPTER I

INTRODUCTION

1. A proper method of inquiry

"The investigation of truth, the art of ascertaining that which is unknown from that which is known," says the profound and philosophic Starkie, "has occupied the attention and constituted the pleasure as well as the business of the reflecting part of mankind in every civilized age and country."[1]

This has resulted, not only from the ineffable beauty of the object sought, but also from the transcendent importance of this knowledge to our happiness. Inquiries into truth in no case can be so important as those that relate to knowledge of our duty, our destiny, and ourselves. For the knowledge of these truths that affect us in this life only, can bear no greater proportion to those relating to our future state, than does the limited period of human life to eternity itself.

To form a clear, accurate, and just conception of a subject is the legitimate end of all fair and honest investigation. And no end can be attained without the use of proper means, and no correct solution of any question arrived at, but by adopting the proper method. "The human mind is so limited," says Dr. Johnson, "that it cannot take in all parts of a subject; so that there may be objections raised against anything."[2] This being true of our limited capacity, it is only by confining our attention to one particular at a time, and carefully estimating its force, and then passing to others in succession, that we can arrive at any clear conception of a subject. The mechanic who constructs a chain, makes each link separately!

It is not only necessary to use the proper means, and pursue the proper method, but we should carefully remove all obstacles that may weaken the legitimate force of any argument that may be presented to the mind. Nothing is more important for this purpose than calm impartiality. All prejudices should be manfully cast aside, and no one should enter upon the investigation of any subject with any preconceived antipathies against it. He that has preconceived antipathies had better not investigate at all, for then he will at least save his labor.

THE TRUE CHURCH

The ingenious mechanist, seeking to invent a machine for a particular purpose, enters upon his project with a mind perfectly open to conviction. He is ready to adopt a good suggestion from any source. He knows that all his fond attachments to a particular theory, if wrong, will avail nothing. All the world may desire his success, and yet his machine will not go. He cannot force the laws of nature. Equally inflexible are the laws of truth–they cannot be forced. And so it must be with the inquirer after truth. He must be impartial, just, and determined, to be successful.

The great art of investigation is to begin at the beginning, to keep our minds attentively fixed, *in succession,* upon the main points of the controversy--those essential elements that make up its very essence. Then with impartially, and with just discrimination, apply the leading principles of the system to cases as they arise. In most controversies, there are certain great leading and essential principles, either conceded by the candid approval of both parties, or satisfactorily proven, which, if fairly and legitimately carried out will lead, by a certain and sure process, to the right conclusion.

It is well known to every jurist and lawyer, that almost every new and at first perplexing case, not governed by statutory law, arising in our courts of justice, is eventually decided by legitimate extensions and applications of well-known and familiar principles. The difficulty that exists is in the extension and application of the principle to new predicaments of fact. The judge who possesses discrimination and impartiality in the highest degree, is most certain to arrive at the correct conclusion. The power to discriminate between a just and a false application of a principle belongs to the highest order of mind.

All the parts of every system of truth must be perfectly consistent with each other. All the facts, and series of facts that have existed at any time from the beginning of the world to the present age, were consistent and harmonious in every particular. The existence of one does not displace that of another. They no more conflict with each other, than do the stars of heaven. Each occupies its place in the vast chain of events.

All the parts of a true system, as well as all facts, are not only thoroughly consistent one with another, but they all bear a certain relation to each other, more or less intimate. As all the events that ever did occur were connected with certain other events–with some as their causes, with others as their effects–so, all the truths of a true system are, in the same way, connected with each other.

INTRODUCTION

If in the investigation of a certain system, we can find its leading principle, then by patient and honest application and extension of this principle, we shall be led, step-by-step, to the discovery of other principles. And finally we shall be enabled to arrive at the whole truth.

Language is but a medium through which a writer or speaker conveys to his readers or hearers, such ideas existing in his own mind as he intends to communicate to them. The character of this medium, which is simply artificial and arbitrary, is fixed by *the existing usage at the precise time the words are written or spoken.* This usage may give the words a figurative or literal meaning.

The object of every fair writer or speaker is to place, in the minds of others, an exact copy of his own thoughts. In doing this, he selects words and phrases best adapted, in his opinion, to accomplish the end intended. If the writer or speaker understands the existing usages of the language he employs as a medium of thought, he selects those terms, which will most accurately convey his true meaning to others. For this reason, the construction put upon the words of a writer or speaker by his contemporaries, is generally the correct one. There are exceptions to this general rule, for the meaning may be misapprehended. These exceptions are special cases, to be judged by the special circumstances of each particular case.

The philosophic author Georg Hermes, has expressed his views upon this subject in the following beautiful terms:

> For what is conversation between man and man? ‘Tis a mutual intercourse of speaking and hearing. To the speaker, 'tis to teach; to the hearer, 'tis to learn. To the speaker, 'tis to descend from ideas to words; to the hearer, 'tis to ascend from words to ideas. If the hearer in this ascent can arrive at no ideas, then he is said not to understand; if he ascends to ideas dissimilar and heterogeneous from the speaker's, then he is said to misunderstand. What then is requisite that he may be said to understand? That he should ascend to certain ideas treasured up within himself, correspondent and similar to those within the speaker. The same may be said of a writer and reader.[3]

2. Inclusive reference rule, in interpreting Scripture

Construction should be upon the entire Scriptures, taken and construed together, so as to give free force and effect to all the passages.

THE TRUE CHURCH

The rule at law for the construction to be placed on statutes and written instruments is substantially the same as the construction to be placed on Scriptures, with one exception, which will be stated in its proper place.

> One part of a statute must be so construed by another, that the whole may (if possible) stand.[4]

> It is an established rule in the exposition of statutes, that the intention of the lawgiver is to be deduced from a view of the whole, and of every part of a statute, taken, and compared together.[5]

> The construction ought to be upon the entire deed, and not on any particular part of it. And such construction should be given, that, if possible, every part of the deed may be operative.[6]

The reasons for this sensible rule are very simple. It is presumed that the lawmaker intended something by each and every provision of the statute, and that he also intended to be consistent with himself. As a mere human legislator may, and often does, contradict himself, the courts will only give force and effect to the different provisions so far as possible. Such a limitation will not apply to the divine law, which is consistent, and not contradictory.

There are many examples in the Scriptures that show the necessity and propriety of this rule. In one place we are substantially told that we are saved by keeping the commandments–in another, by grace–in another, by the blood of Christ–in another, by baptism–in another, by faith. These different provisions are not at all in conflict with each other, and may, therefore, be so construed together as to give force and effect to all. The correct construction would be that we are saved by the agency of all these requisites taken together.

The violation of this fundamental rule has, perhaps, led to more errors than any other. We have a notable instance in the temptation of our Lord by Satan, when he said:

> If thou be the son of God, cast thyself down; for it is written, He shall give his angels charge concerning thee, and in their hands they shall bear thee up, lest at any time thou dash thy foot against a stone.

This proposition was very acutely made, and the quotation to sustain it seemed very appropriate. But the poor devil had forgotten that another passage of Scripture must also be construed with it, and, consequently, his learning was completely put down by the reply of our Lord: "It is written again, Thou shalt not tempt the Lord thy God."

3. Single author rule, in interpreting Scripture

All the texts relating to the same subject must be considered as written by the same person, having a perfect knowledge of all that has been written before, the reader making fair allowance for the difference in the style of the writer, and the different character of the existing circumstances.

The rule of law that requires all statutes relating to the same subject, though passed at different times, to be taken and construed together, is substantially similar to the above rule. The rule at law is based upon the presumption that the lawgiver was competent, and therefore acquainted with the state of the law as it existed at the passage of the act, and had the previous laws in his mind when framing the statute.

> These laws being in *pari materia,* and referred to in the one giving us jurisdiction, must be taken as one law. [7]

The framers of statutes may be, and are sometimes ignorant of the existing state of the law. This fact may possibly render the rule subject to exceptions in special cases.

But the rule I have laid down in reference to the proper construction of Scripture is not subject to such exceptions. The whole having been dictated by the same infallible Spirit must be held equally entitled to our confidence. The *prima facie* presumption of competency in a human becomes conclusive when applied to a Divine Lawgiver.

4. Meaning in context rule, in interpreting Scripture

Words of unlimited meaning are yet to be restricted by the general scope and intent of the system.

Among the examples to be found in the Scriptures, coming within this rule, it will be sufficient to mention the one found in the sixteenth chapter of Saint John's Gospel, where our Lord tells His Disciples that, "when he, the Spirit of Truth, is come, he will teach you all truth." The phrase all truth is exceedingly broad, yet it must be restrained by the general scope and intent of the system Christ came to establish. It was no part of His system to teach mere truths of science. The latter class of truths cannot be embraced in the phrase "all truth."

The rule is founded in the principles of sound interpretation. At law it is substantially the same. A statute may contain very broad and sweeping terms, and yet they are restrained to the scope and intent of the act. The provisions of the seventh amended article of the Constitution of the United States, which, in general terms, secures the right of trial by jury in all cases where the matter in controversy exceeds the sum of twenty dollars, is confined to trials in the Federal tribunal. It does not prevent the States from restricting the right of trial by jury to controversies involving a larger sum than twenty dollars.

5. Principles apply in the widest sense rule, in interpreting Scripture

When a general principle is laid down in general terms, and without exceptions stated at the time, or in any other portions of the Scriptures, it must be taken in its widest sense compatible with the general scope and intent of the system.

It is the practice of all lawgivers to state general principles embracing a whole class of cases, in general terms, and then to state the exceptions to the general principle specially. The form or manner of the statement of these exceptions is not at all material. They are often stated expressly as exceptions, and defined to be such; but they are often stated simply as special provisions in reference to special cases, without any express statement that they are express exceptions. In either case they limit the meaning of the general clause. There are some principles embracing all cases, and without exception; while there are other principles that embrace only a great majority of cases, and are, therefore, subject to some exceptions.

In regard to the latter class of principles, it is matter of convenience first to state the general principle in general terms, and then afterwards to state the exceptions specially. We will suppose that the general principle would embrace ninety-eight out of each hundred cases. It would then be very difficult to state each of the ninety-eight cases separately, while it would be very easy to state the two cases as exceptions.

6. Limitation of exceptions rule, in interpreting Scripture

When such exceptions to the general rule are stated in any part of the Scriptures, they are to be taken out of the operation of the general principle as exceptions, leaving the general principle to govern all the other cases coming fairly within the import.

This rule is properly but a branch of the fourth rule, but it will be found useful in practice. Both these rules are substantially the same as those applied in similar cases at law. There are often general statutes passed, embracing a great many cases, and yet liable to exceptions. These exceptions are often stated in the body of the act as exceptions--they are often stated in the same act, but not in the form of exceptions, but as provisions for particular cases, and they are often found in separate acts relating to special cases, which would otherwise come within the general principle. These special acts, as a general thing, have no express reference to the general act, but their provisions in their very, nature are special, and must be taken out of the general principle, because they conflict with it.

To state a case in point: There was a general act passed by the legislature regulating the Practice at Law. In this act there was a general provision requiring *all* process to be served upon the defendant by reading the same to him. There were many different forms of action, and in reference to one form of action, "Petition in Debt," there was a special act, and a clause in this act requiring the process to be served by delivering a copy of the writ to the defendant. There was no express reference in this special act to the general Practice Act, and yet there was no doubt as to the correct construction. In "Petition in Debt" the process had to be served by copy, and in all the other cases by reading.

Among similar examples in Scripture, it will be sufficient to mention one or two as illustrative of these two rules. It is said that we are saved through the merits of Christ. This is a general principle without any exception. Again, it is said that "All things are possible with God," but Saint Paul says that, "God cannot lie." This is a case of exception to the general rule. Consider also, "Ask, and you shall receive," and "You do not receive because you ask amiss."

7. Natural construction rule, in interpreting Scripture

The natural, simple, and literal construction is to be preferred, unless there be something, either in express words or in the context, to show a figurative meaning.

The rule at law is substantially the same. "The words of a statute," says the learned Commentator on American Law, "are to be taken in their natural and ordinary signification and import; and if technical words are used, they are to be taken in a technical sense."[8]

The rule I have laid down is founded upon the grounds of reason and experience. That construction which is most obvious, simple and natural, is generally the most correct in reference to any writer; and before this rule should be departed from, there should exist good reasons for such a departure. As every writer and speaker is supposed in simple justice to himself, his subject, and his readers or hearers, to select the most natural and simple terms, so the general rule must be in accordance with that presumption.

8. Consulting the Ancient Fathers of the Church

In every examination regarding any question of fact connected with the history of the early Church, we must necessarily consult the Ancient Fathers--the historians and ecclesiastical writers of that period. The Catholic Church does not esteem them as inspired. They are held to be simple, but authentic witnesses to matters of fact, to wit: what were the doctrines held, and the observances kept by the Church in their day? If the Church held certain doctrines, and kept certain observances then these are held to be true; and as to the historical fact, the testimony of the Fathers is heard.

In his debate with Bishop Purcell, Mr. Campbell said:

> Among Protestants, the reason and authority of religious belief and practice is, 'Thus saith the Lord.' It is not important to ascertain when any opinion or practice began nor who introduced it; but if it be not in the Bible, no matter how ancient it may be, it wants apostolic sanction for the apostles sanctioned only what was written and ordained before their death. Saint Clement and Saint Ignatius and Saint Irenaeus, and all the other Saints in the Roman Calendar, were born too late to sanction any article of faith or morals by their vote.[9]

In this extract Mr. Campbell assumes that the Bible contains all the Word of God now obligatory upon us, and that consequently, it is not important to know "when a practice or opinion began, nor who introduced it." And from this position it would seem that the authority of all preceding ages, even as to questions of mere *construction* of the written word, is wholly unimportant.

If the opinions and practices of former ages, especially of the early Church, were of any authority and force as to the true construction of Scripture, then it *is important* to know when any opinion or practice began. If on the contrary, the faith and practice of the Church in the days immediately succeeding the apostles were of no validity, when compared with the contradictory Protestant constructions of the Scriptures, then Mr. Campbell does take consistent ground.

If the authority of the ancient Church is consulted at all, and it differs from the Protestant construction a question arises. The issue must be met, whether the united construction of the early Church, possessing all her superior advantages, and tried as she was, in the fires of persecution, is superior or inferior to the individual and contradictory constructions of those living so many centuries later.

Such a question must come up in the minds of all sincere persons who seek the truth for its own sake. Admitting for the sake of argument only, that there is no infallibility in the Church, and that these gross errors could have been introduced into the early Church, and at the same time created no disturbances, no divisions. Conceding all this, still the question must arise, whose disputed construction *is most worthy of confidence?*

Who had the best opportunity to know? Who did the most for Christianity? Who suffered, labored, and accomplished the most? Who gave the most conclusive proofs of sincerity and heroic devotion? Who spread Christianity over the world, and who spread divisions? If the authority of the Fathers is to be admitted, even in questions of construction, the sincere inquirer must ask and answer these interrogations.

As to the position of Mr. Campbell that the saints were born too late to sanction any article of faith by their vote, he is right, provided he means to say that they had no right to create and make new additions to the law, and therefore could exercise no legislative power as to matters of faith or morals. Whether the vote he speaks of was to be given as legislators or as judicial officers, I could not tell.

But in his debate with Mr. Rice, some years later, in speaking of the Greek and Latin Fathers as visionaries, mystics and fond of old wives' fables, he says, "but I regard them as faithful witnesses of facts. I receive their testimony as honest men."[10] And when speaking upon the proposition that "Christian baptism is for the remission of past sins," he quotes extensively from the Fathers. He says, among other things,

> If neither the Bible, nor the Confession, nor the Greek and Latin Fathers are to be understood nor believed when affirming that baptism is for the remission of sins, what kind of evidence could satisfy him?[11]

And Mr. Rice is equally careful to call up the authority of the Ancient Fathers, when they are on his side of the question. In the debate regarding the baptism of infants, he says:

> For let it be distinctly understood, I appeal to the early Christian Fathers, not for their opinions, but I call them up as witnesses to a matter of fact, viz., that in their day, and as far as they know to the days of the apostles the baptism of infants was universally practiced.[12]

I could not but remark the gratification shown by each debater when he found himself in company with these "visionaries and mystics." Under such circumstances he failed not to breathe freer and deeper.

9. Four rules for consulting the Fathers on matters of fact

The question whether a certain doctrine was held or a certain observance kept by the Ancient Church, is simply a question of fact, and can be the subject of historical examination and proof. If the Ancient Church held a certain doctrine, is that fact *evidence* that the doctrine is true? If the infallibility of the Church is conceded, there can be no doubt. But if that is disputed, the great difficulty of introducing such a doctrine into the Church, under the received maxims she did then hold, and the vigilance, sincerity, and means of detection then existing, is certainly a most powerful and decisive proof with the Christian who admits that the Church started right.

Protestant writers, in defending Christianity, assume the ground taken by Dr. Paley, when he says:

> The success of a religion founded upon a miraculous history, shows the credit which was given to the history; and this credit, under the circumstances in which it was given–*i.e.*, by persons capable of knowing the truth, and interested to inquire after it–is evidence of the reality of the history, and, by consequence, of the truth of the religion.[13]

The learned Divine was right. The credit given to such a story by such persons is evidence of its truth. Applying the same correct principle to the case in hand, it would seem to be true that the success of certain doctrines and observances in the early Church shows the credit that was given to them. And this credit, under the circumstances in which it was given–*i.e.*, by persons not only capable of knowing the truth, but who did know it (because first well instructed), and interested to preserve it, and also vigilant in doing so–is evidence of the reality and truth of such doctrines and observances. For it seems clear to me, that if persons were interested in inquiring into the truth of this miraculous history in the first instance, then, after they did believe it, they were to be more interested in inquiring into and preserving the true faith as delivered.

As to the testimony of the Fathers, in reference to *matters of fact*, as distinguished from their individual opinions (when considered by persons inquiring for the true Church) it seems to me that the following positions are just and reasonable:

1. When a Father states a doctrine or practice without hesitation, and without any statement that it is his private opinion, he must be held to intend to give the faith or practice of the Church, unless there is something in the context to show the contrary.

2. That when a Father sanctions a doctrine or practice without contradiction of any other Father, then such doctrine or practice must be held as those of the Church, and the consent of the others presumed from their silence

3. That when a doctrine or practice is shown to be in the Church, for instance in the fourth or fifth century, it must be presumed, *prima facie*, to have been in the Church from the beginning, unless stated to be a new opinion or practice.

4. That though there may be seeming discrepancies in regard to a few points where one or two Fathers are apparently in conflict with the great majority; still the clear testimony of the great body of the Fathers must prevail over the doubtful language of the few.

In reference to the first rule, it would seem to be evident that no Christian writer would express a Christian truth without hesitation, when he meant only to be understood as giving his individual opinion. Dr. Paley, in speaking of the character of the testimony of the Fathers in reference to the New Testament, says:

> Whenever any thing now read in the Gospels is met with in an early Christian writing, it is always observed to stand there as acknowledged truth; *i.e.,* to be introduced without hesitation, doubt, or apology.

If uttered "without hesitation, doubt, or apology," it stands as "acknowledged truth;" that is, it shows the testimony of the writer that such was received Scripture.

In respect to the second rule, it must be conceded that the rule of law that says that one affirmative witness is worth more than several negative witnesses, is founded on common sense and general experience. This is especially true of the Fathers, who did not write upon the same, but upon different subjects. As a matter of course, they would generally speak only to the subject discussed.

In regard to the third rule, it may be remarked that the following is true. That it would be entirely unjust to suppose, that an honest historian relating a doctrine of practice as then existed in the Church–without hesitation, as an acknowledged truth, and as not stating it to be new, or giving any date when it was introduced,–is yet to be held as intending to state it is new. The law presumes every officer to do his duty.[14] And surely heresy is not presumed to be in the Church, contrary to the promises of Christ. And the *light* presumption that preceding authors would have mentioned the fact had it been true, is overcome by the *overwhelming* presumption, that when ever it was introduced, it would have caused such divisions as must have been mentioned by some writer. We have the time, place, and person given, in reference to the heresies of the day; and the acknowledged vigilance of the Church, taken in connection with the circumstances of the time, would always exclude such a conclusion. "Now omission," says Dr. Paley,

> is at all times a very uncertain ground of objection. We perceive it, not only in the comparison of different writers, but even in the same writer, when compared with himself. There are a great many particulars, and some of them of importance, mentioned by Josephus in his Antiquities, which as we should have supposed, ought to have been put down by him in their place in the Jewish wars. Suctonius, Tacitus, Dio Cassius, have all three written of the reign of Tiberias. Each has mentioned many things omitted by the rest, yet no objection is from thence taken to the credit of their histories.

These, and other remarks, the learned author makes in answer to the objection made by infidels, that the Gospels contradict each other, because one mentions many of the most important facts, omitted by all the others. For example, that stupendous miracle of Christ, the resurrection of Lazarus, and that most beautiful parable of the Prodigal Son, are each only mentioned in one Gospel.

In reference to the fourth rule, its justice would seem to be plain. If a court or jury were to reject the testimony of ten good witnesses, because of the doubtful contradiction of one, then we might reject all history where there is a single historian who may seem to dispute a single fact. As Dr. Paley very justly says: "The usual character of human testimony is substantial truth under circumstantial variety." The philosophic Starkie, and the accurate Greenleaf, have both adopted this position as true, and every lawyer and jurist knows it to be so, from most ample experience. "Dr. Middleton," says Dr. Paley,

> contends that the different hours of the day assigned to the crucifixion of Christ, by John and by the other evangelists, did not admit of the reconcilement which learned men had proposed, and then concluded the discussion with this hard remark: "We must be forced with several of the critics, to leave the difficulty as we found it, chargeable with all the consequences of manifest inconsistency." But what are these consequences? By no means the discrediting of the history as to the principal fact, by a repugnance (even supposing that repugnance be not resolvable into different modes of computation) in the time of day in which it is said to have taken place.[15]

The learned writer also notices several cases of apparent discrepancy between the New Testament writers and Josephus and the Roman historians, and between the New and Old Testaments. [16]

These discrepancies may be apparent and not real; but at this day we are not in possession, perhaps, of the true explanation. To reject, therefore, the great body of history, because of a few apparent or even real contradictions, would seem a very erroneous practice. And as in Scripture so in the Fathers, there may be apparent discrepancies in a few instances; but we must look to the particular circumstances under which they wrote, in order to do them justice.

---

[1] Thomas Starkie, A practical treatise of the law of evidence, preface.

[2] Cf. James Boswell Life of Johnson.

[3] As cited by Dr. Wiseman in his lectures upon the Real Presence.

[4] William Blackstone, Commentaries on the Laws of England, p 89.

[5] James Kent, Commentaries on American Law, vol. 1 p 461.

[6] William Johnson, Johnsons's Digest of New York Cases. Vol. 16 p 172. [Para materia is a legal term describing rules that relate to the same type of processes or proceedings, and should be construed together. – Editor]

[7] 6 Peters 720, also James Kent, Commentaries on American Law, vol.1 p 463.

[8] James Kent, op. cit. vol. 1 p 463.

[9] A. Campbell and J. Purcell, A debate on the Roman Catholic religion. p..277

[10] A. Campbell and N. Rice, Campbell Rice Debate on the Holy Spirit 163

[11] Ibid. 456

[12] Ibid. 406

[13] William Paley,. A View of the Evidences of Christianity (1794)

[14] Thomas Starkie, A practical treatise of the law of evidence. Part 1 p79

[15] William Paley, op. cit.

[16] For instance, as the "taxing" when Christ was born, the statement in the third chapter of Luke, "Now in the fifteenth year of the reign of Tiberius Caesar," the case of Theudas, Acts 5:36, and the case of Zacharias son of Barachias, in Matt 23:34.

CHAPTER II

THE LAW OF CHRIST

1. The infirmities of human legislation are not in God's law

The learned commentator on the laws of England defines municipal law to be, "A rule of civil conduct, prescribed by the supreme power in a State, commanding what is right and prohibiting what is wrong."[1] When he says, "Commanding what is right, and prohibiting what is wrong," he means, as *judged by* the theory of municipal law, of which he was speaking. As judged by the theory of civil government, and not by the law of God, or of abstract justice, the civil law always commands what is right, and prohibits what is wrong. As the civil law is often unjust, when judged by the principles of morality, the lawmaking power in political government could not rightfully require us to believe its enactments just.

As no power in such a government can know the thoughts and intents of the mind, unless manifested by outward signs, the civil law could only place crime in action. No mere intention however wicked, can constitute a crime under this theory. The intention is only one of the ingredients of crime. And as the civil law leaves belief and intention untouched, it could never form a moral code. It lacks the wisdom, power, and justice required; and must, therefore, be exceedingly imperfect in these respects. All that the law of the land can rightfully require us to do is to comply with its provisions by our *acts.*

But the infirmities necessarily incident to human legislation are not found in the law of God. That sublime code can rightfully require us to believe all its provisions to be just because they are, in point of fact, just; *and* we are only required to believe that which we may know to be unerringly true.

2. God's law governs intention as well as act

For the very reason that a fallible lawgiver could not rightfully assume to govern faith and intention, an infallible lawgiver should regulate both; otherwise, they would be left without government. And if faith and intention are left without control, there can be no pure morality, and no perfect obedience.

The wicked intention is the first element of moral wrong. To hold a free agent responsible for this first voluntary act, is the most efficient, and for that reason, the most merciful rule. To teach the party governed, that he is responsible for his evil thoughts and criminal intentions, is to check vice in its inception. Therefore, to teach him that he must believe the truth is to secure his love and reverence for it and his more ready and hearty obedience to it. For obedience will always be more faithful to a law believed to be just in itself, than to one whose justice is disputed.

We may safely conclude that whatever revelation God made to man, must have been just and true. If just, it must for that reason, constitute a rule of moral conduct; and if true, it must for that reason, be believed. A perfect law in every particular, has a right to demand our perfect obedience, in *thought, belief*, and *act*. It is reasonable that an Infinite lawgiver should be *just to Himself*, as well as others; and for this reason, have some eye to his own rights, and the respect due to His *real* character.

The human legislator prescribes his law, and says to the party governed; "I have given you the best law I could, but it is still imperfect. I do not, therefore, ask you to believe it just; and if I did, my limited powers would not enable me to reach your thoughts and intentions. But as the good of society imperiously requires government, and government must, of necessity, require obedience, you *must* obey my law in *act*-whatever you may believe and intend." However, an Infinite Lawgiver holds a different language, and says: "My statutes are just and true in every particular. I, therefore, require you to *think* right, intend right and act right; and I have the right, the knowledge, and the power, to enforce obedience in all these particulars."

3. Law is indifferent to the mode of its dissemination

The law governing any associated body of men, either civil or ecclesiastical, may be promulgated in different ways. Therefore, it may be either written or oral, or partly written and partly traditional. Speaking of the promulgation of law, Blackstone says:

> But the manner, in which this notification is to be made, is matter of very great indifference. It may be notified by universal tradition and long practice, which supposes a previous publication, as is the case of the common law of England. It may be notified, *viva voce* by officers appointed for that purpose, as is done with regard to proclamations, and such acts of parliament as are appointed to be publicly read in

> churches and other assemblies. It may lastly be notified by writing, printing, or the like; which is the general course taken with all our acts of parliament.[2]

As language, whether oral or written, is still but a sign or medium by and through which our intelligence communicates ideas to another, the *character of the law itself* is not affected by the mere manner of its publication. The will of the legislator exists without any regard to the *mode* of publication; and the publication is only *evidence* of that will. The different modes of publication only constitute different kinds of evidence to prove the *will* of the legislator. The *thing* to be proven is, in both cases, the same.

These two modes of publication have their respective advantages. A written code is more concise and portable, while a traditional code is more full and complete. A mixed code combines the advantages of both, and is most preferable in practice. The two parts of a mixed code mutually explain and illustrate each other.

The municipal law of England is divided into two kinds, the unwritten, or common law, and the written, or statute law.[3] The States of our Union with one exception, have adopted the common law, and have, therefore, mixed codes of jurisprudence. And in speaking of the unwritten law, Blackstone, the learned commentator on the laws of England, says:

> I would not be understood as if all those laws were at present merely *oral,* or communicated from former ages to the present solely by word of mouth. But with us at present the monuments and evidences of our legal customs are contained in the records of the several courts of justice, in books of reports and judicial decisions, and in the treatises of learned sages of the profession, preserved and handed down to us from the times of highest antiquity. However, I, therefore, style these parts of our law *lex non scripta* because their original institution and authority are not set down in writing, as acts of parliament are.[4]

Again the same learned commentator says:

> But here a very natural and a very material question arises, how are these customs or maxims to be known, and by whom is their validity to be determined? The answer is, by the judges in the several courts of justice. They are the depositories of the laws, the living oracles, who must decide in all cases of doubt, and who are bound by an oath to decide according to the law of the land....

> And, indeed, these judicial decisions are the principle and most authoritative evidence that can be given of the existence of such a custom as shall form a part of the common law. The judgment itself, and all the proceedings previous thereto, are carefully registered and preserved, under the name of *records*, in public repositories set apart for that particular purpose; and to them frequent recourse is had when any critical question arises, in the determination of which, former precedents may give light or assistance....
>
> For it is an established rule to abide by former precedents when the same points come again in litigation; as well to keep the scales of justice even and steady, and not liable to waver with every new judge's opinion, as also because the law in that case being solemnly declared and determined. What before was uncertain, and perhaps indifferent, is now become a permanent rule, which it is not in the breast of any subsequent judge to alter or vary from, according to his private sentiments. He being sworn to determine, not according to his own private judgment, but according to the known laws and customs of the land; not delegated to pronounce a new law, but to maintain and expound the old one.
>
> Yet, this rule admits of exception, when the former decision is most evidently contrary to reason; much more if it is clearly contrary to divine law. But even in such cases, the subsequent judges do not pretend to make a new law, but to vindicate the old one from misrepresentation.[5]

4. The advantages of a mixed code

To those who are engaged in the practical administration of the law, the advantages of a mixed system will become apparent. A written code can only conveniently embrace the leading principles of a system, expressed in general terms. It cannot be so full or complete as the unwritten law. In the application of a written system to particular cases, where it is not aided and illustrated by the unwritten law, the difficulties would seem to be great. It is very doubtful whether any complete system of written law, suited to the various wants of a civilized people, could be formed and practically put in operation, without the aid of the unwritten law. It would necessarily be either so concise as to be defective in omitting necessary provisions, or so voluminous and minute, as to become inconvenient for ordinary cases.

It must be obvious to those who have well considered the nature of all laws intended for the government of men, that a comprehensive principle may be adopted in a very concise form, and yet embracing a great number of cases under it. Or the legislator may himself extend the principle out into its various ramifications, so as to show its application to different classes of cases.

In the first instance, his law will be very brief in *form,* while in the second it will be very full. But whether the lawmaker adopts the concise or more detailed mode of enactment, or a combination of both, the result must be substantially the same in the end, or injustice must be done to the parties governed. Their wants are still the same, and those wants must be provided for, either by the law itself in full, or by the construction of the courts. The particular cases must be decided either by the specific provisions of the law, or by the extension of concisely expressed principles by the judgments of the courts.

Laws, as a rule, can only lay down general principles, expressed in general terms. One general principle may embrace a number of subordinate principles legitimately flowing from it. The subordinate principles, when not developed in the law itself, must be discovered and applied by the courts; otherwise there is a defect of justice. If, then, a written code be adopted, and the unwritten law excluded, the judges will find it more difficult to administer such a system, and they will be forced, either to pass by wrongs without a remedy, or they must take the responsibility of extending the principles of the statute to doubtful cases.

It would seem to be exceedingly difficult, in the nature of thing, to adopt an entire written code that will be sufficiently full and complete, so as to embrace all the cases demanding relief under civil government. It is by a combination of the two parts of written and unwritten law that the most just, complete, and convenient code can be formed. The statute law will then embrace all new changes, and also the more ordinary everyday provisions, while the unwritten law will contain the more infinite provisions necessary to be applied in critical cases. The Romans, Spaniards, and Swedes had a common law.[6]

As illustrative of this view I may refer to an experiment in France. "Though the French codes," says Chancellor Kent,

> digested under the revolutionary authority are distinguished for sententious brevity, there are numerous volumes of French reports already extant upon doubtful and difficult questions, arising within a few years after these codes were promulgated.[7]

The learned American commentator states in a note that these reports had amounted, in 1818, to fifty volumes and upward, and that "from the time of the French Revolution down to 1828, there were over one hundred volumes of statutory law made in France."

5. Tradition as a mode of transmission

It has been often objected that tradition is an unsafe medium of transmission; and those who urge this objection usually illustrate it by referring to the uncertain nature of general reports circulating in a community. That tradition is an uncertain medium of transmission when used for the preservation of unimportant matters, in which no one is particularly interested, is true; and it is apprehended that writing would not be sufficient to perpetuate the memory of that which no one cared to preserve. Besides this, such unimportant matters are not committed to any particular depository–no one is specially charged with their preservation and safe transmission.

But such is not the case with regard to *laws*. They are matters too deeply important to be neglected or forgotten, for the reason that they not only regulate the dearest interests of society, but they are of daily application and competent tribunals are made the depositories, as Blackstone says. That tradition, under such circumstances, and in reference to such important matters, is a safe, certain and efficient means of transmission, is demonstrated in the case of the common law of England. For after all the changes that have been made in that system and all that may hereafter be needed, the great mass of its provisions will most likely remain. And if we make a judicious deduction for unadvised changes, which rashness and ignorance have made in the name of reform, we shall be able to see how little has been accomplished in the way of genuine improvement upon that great traditional system of law.

The true character of laws is best seen and understood when they are practically administered. As the military commander that is the most consummate chieftain is he whose plans work out most beautifully upon the field of battle, so that system of law is the best which produces the most practical good. Our great judges our best law writers, from Lord Hale to Chief Justice Marshall, and from Blackstone to Kent, are almost, if not quite, unanimous in their admiration of the common law, and in their condemnation of all hasty and crude changes in the system.

If we look into the numerous and perplexing cases that have arisen in courts of justice in modern times, we shall find that the most difficult questions have been in reference to the construction of statutes. We shall also find that the most uncertainty and confusion have been produced by these frequent changes; and that of the two, the common law is the more uniform, consistent, and certain. "And" says Blackstone,

> it hath been an ancient observation in the laws of England, that whenever a standing rule of law, of which the reason perhaps, could not be remembered or discerned, hath been wantonly broken in upon by statutes or new resolutions, the wisdom of the rule hath in the end appeared, from the inconveniences that have followed the innovation.[8]

Mr. Justice Cowen, among other things, says:

> There is scarcely any branch of legal policy more worthy of being enforced than that which aims to keep the laws of a nation the same in all respects from one age to another, except in points where change becomes absolutely necessary.[9]

Lord Hale says:

> Time, is wiser than all the wits in the world, and the law which has been tried by it has the highest possible evidence in its favor. Time is the schoolmaster, which teaches law most effectually, and without which it cannot be generally known.

The same great judge calls this an "age when there is literally a mania for changing every law in some way." In this sentiment Chancellor Kent agrees when he speaks of "the rage for bold, reckless, and presumptuous innovation, so prevalent at this day, acting in contempt of usages and wisdom of the common law."[10] And Lord Hale says, "Such are the common laws of England; namely, the production of much wisdom, time and experience."[11]

If, then, a great system of law, so nearly approaching perfection, and, as Lord Hale says, "is vast and comprehensive," and "consists of infinite particulars" has been transmitted by tradition from age to age, in a form so fixed, certain, and uniform, upon what ground can we say that such a medium is unsafe in the transmissions of laws in the preservation of which every member of the association is so deeply interested?

The abstract objection against tradition as a medium of transmission is not only shown to be unfounded by the historical test in the case of the common law of England and other countries, but also by the history of the creation. God's early dealing with mankind was transmitted by tradition from age to age, for the space of two thousand years, until written out by Moses. Speaking of which, Dr. Spring say "Before his word was reduced to writing, these various communications were narrated, treasured up in the memory, and became a traditionary revelation."[12]

So far as abstract considerations go, they are not against the position that the law of Christ is partly written and partly oral; but for the reasons already given, and others that will be hereafter stated, they would seem strongly to support it. And it was admitted by Dr. Spring, in reference to this law of Christ that "there is no absurdity in supposing it to be partly oral and partly written, while both might be amplified and interpreted by one another."[13]

6. The written law of Christ

In the nature of things, before the mind can arrive at the conclusion that the Bible is inspired, there must be, sufficient proof of this fact. This evidence must either be found in tradition, or in the book itself, or in both combined.

If the point to be proved is simply the historical existence of the Scriptures, then the testimony of ordinary history will suffice. In other words, it will be competent to prove that the separate books, bearing the names of the writers, were in fact written by them; for ordinary history can show us that those books were in existence at a certain period, purporting to have been written by the authors whose names they bear; and this will, *prima facie,* prove their authenticity and genuineness, as the same kind of testimony would the authenticity of the works of any other writer. It will also prove. *prima facie,* the integrity of the writers, for this must be presumed until the contrary is shown. But when we prove the authenticity of the books of the New Testament–that they were in fact written by the persons whose names they bear, and at the periods mentioned, we have not established anything more than the *facts stated in each of the books themselves*. Moreover, if the fact of *inspiration* is not stated in the books we must of necessity, resort to other testimony, or admit the assumed fact without proof. In short, we must look to proof outside the record.

It is, indeed, insisted that the inspiration of Scripture is, in part, seen upon the face thereof, although not expressly stated in words. Thus the Rev. Hartwell Horne says: "The miracles *related* in the old and new Testaments are proofs that the Scriptures were given by inspiration of God."[14] And Dr. Spring says: "These books speak for themselves that they are not the work of men."[15]

It would seem somewhat difficult to understand how the miracles related in the Bible can be a proof of the inspiration of the books in which they are simply recorded. We can well understand how these miracles were proofs of the *character* and *capacity* of the persons by whom they were performed, but it is not so easy to see how they can constitute proofs of the inspiration of books written long after they occurred. The facts related may constitute proofs. This inherent capacity, as proofs, exists in the *facts themselves*, no matter when or by whom related, if they are duly authenticated. If, therefore, the same facts are related in any other book, and their simple relation proves the book inspired, then the history of Josephus is inspired, because true miracles are related therein.

It is not, then, the character or quality of the facts related that proves the inspiration of the historian. These facts may be related by an uninspired historian as well as any other class of visible facts. And when Dr. Spring says the Scriptures "speak for themselves that they are not the work of men," he does not mean to say that they state so in express words; but that the extraordinary character of the facts and doctrines stated is proof that the mind of man could not have originated the system therein recorded.

But this relates only to the nature of the matter recorded; and not to the inspired character of the record itself. That which assumes to be a deposition may contain important and true evidence, and yet this will not entitle it to be read. It must have been properly taken. And I apprehend that if an honest, yet uninspired historian, had been with Christ, and witnessed his miracles, and had, to the best of his ability faithfully recorded what he saw, and that this record had come down to us, neither Dr. Spring nor Mr. Horne could have pronounced as to its inspiration, simply because of the character of the matter related.

It may well be conceded that the human mind is competent to determine the extent of its own powers, and that, consequently, the system recorded in the Scriptures could not have originated with man. But this is not the only fact to be proven. We wish also to know whether the Scriptures contain *nothing but the truth;* and when we reach the conclusion that the record is inspired, we are satisfied that it contains no falsehood. The inspiration, when once established, is a conclusive guaranty that the record is true.

But how can the human mind assume the capacity to determine, from the face of the record itself, that there have been no additions or omissions? The capacity to decide upon the face of the record, that no changes have been made, must be equal to the capacity to originate. Suppose some texts omitted, and some interpolated, would the human mind be able to restore the mutilated text to its original form? And with a copy of the original Scriptures before him, would not the forger be able to make so good an imitation as to defy detection by a simple comparison of the two, when it was unknown which was the genuine record?

7. Were the authors of the New Testament inspired by God?

What then is the logical course of examination that will lead an original inquirer to the conclusion that the New Testament Scriptures are inspired? The point to be proven is that these books are all, and each, of them inspired records, containing *only* the truth, written by the authorized agents of God.

It is obvious that any being inspired by God, for a given purpose, must be His agent for the end intended. A principal, who, in virtue of his own nature, possesses a mass of powers, may delegate them in smaller or larger portions, at his pleasure. So, God can delegate inspiration and authority to one or more individuals for one specific purpose only, or for several specific purposes. In such cases, the inspiration and authority will be confined to the specific purposes mentioned in the commission.

It is also obvious to common sense that when power is delegated from a principal to his agent that the principal must himself give the evidence of that fact. It is true that the principal may appoint an agent, with the power to appoint subagents, but in that case the evidence of the original grant of power must flow from the principal, and is shown by his act.

Power and inspiration could not flow from God without His consent, and the evidence of such a delegation to another must necessarily come from him. His act alone can constitute such evidence. This evidence must be of such a character as to be apprehended by the persons to be affected by the acts of the agent; otherwise, the fact of agency could not be known to them.

With these principles in his mind the inquirer takes up the New Testament and any other history relating facts bearing upon the question. He regards them all as placed upon the same ground – *as simple, uninspired history*. He considers the New Testament writers as men, competent, without inspiration to state facts they witnessed, and relate discourses they heard. The genuineness of their works, and the integrity of the writers, are proved to him in the same way, and by the same evidence, as the works and integrity of the other historians he may consult.

The miracles of Christ were visible acts. So, His discourses were delivered in human language, and could be recorded as any other discourses. The inquirer becomes satisfied, from the testimony that the miracles related were in fact performed by Christ. From his knowledge of the more obvious and familiar laws of nature, he knows they could not have been the acts of men, and he draws at once the conclusion of Nicodemus that no man could do those things, except God be with him.[16] The performance of the miracles is established by the historical testimony, and the miracles, when proven, establish the character and capacity of Christ.

The inquirer is then prepared to believe Christ upon His word; for if he is God, He cannot lie; and if He were not God, but only an inspired agent, still he cannot lie as to the facts of his agency and inspiration. Whatever account, therefore, the divine or inspired person gives of his character and of his mission, must be believed, because God *by His own act*, has conclusively established the veracity of the person, in reference to those matters.

Whenever such a person assumes to act in his capacity as such agent, he must be believed. Then as to what Christ said, the same simple historical testimony relates to it. Matthew and John heard it, and have left their record. Therefore, the historical testimony equally proves the miracles, and discourses, and the acts of the apostles. The miracles performed by the apostles prove them to have been veracious and competent witnesses, and their testimony, as to the facts, must be true.

From the testimony of the New Testament, he learns that Christ said He would build His church, against which the gates of hell should never prevail-that He commanded His followers to hear this church-that He commissioned the eleven to teach all nations-that they did set up the Kingdom, the church, and put the law of Christ into practical operation. By the record he is informed how the church was practically governed-what was its character, what were its powers as then exercised, and that the whole deposit of faith was left by Christ with the Church.

His reason and common sense assure the inquirer that Christ, like any other founder of a government, would necessarily make the institution created by Himself the depository of the laws intended for its own direction. He finds it historically related as a matter of fact, that long after the organization of the Church, a difficult question arose among its rulers; that to settle this question the Council of Jerusalem was called. He finds that some of the apostles, as well as *other governors* of the Church, participated; that this body rendered a final and conclusive decree, declaring the law applicable to a particular case; that this decree was the act of the Church; and that, upon its face, it assumed to be the result of inspiration of the Holy Ghost. He finds, upon the face of the historical record of this degree, the evidence of Peter, Paul, and James, to the inspiration of the Church. He also finds Paul stating that this Church was the pillar and ground of truth.

Having thus arrived at the knowledge of the fact that the Church is an inspired witness, he finds, by examining her history, that she has attested the fact that the works of the New Testament authors, including those of Mark and Luke (who were not apostles), were the inspired word of God, originally deposited with the Church.

In this way the inquirer arrives at the conviction that the canon of Scripture is complete, containing all the inspired books, and only such. With him ordinary history proved the miracles and discourses of Christ and His apostles; they proved the institution and character of the Church; and the *Church* proved the inspiration of the New Testament writers; the chain of testimony is complete, and he has supernatural or inspired testimony to the fact of the inspiration of each writer, of each book, of the New Testament.

It would seem exceedingly difficult, if not impossible, upon any other authority, to establish the inspiration of all the books composing the New Testament, especially those of Mark and Luke. These writers perform no miracles so far as we are informed; and we have no testimony of Christ as to their inspiration, nor do any of the apostles tell us they were inspired, nor do the writers themselves claim any inspiration. So far from Mark or Luke saying they were inspired historians, the latter, in his preface, seems to write as an ordinary historian as he states he received the facts recorded from the witnesses who had delivered them to him. And if they had stated they were inspired, such a statement alone, made by persons whose veracity was not first divinely attested, could not have proven it to be true, as it would have been only that human testimony which any impostor could have given, without the fear of direct contradiction.

To prove the performance of miracles, or the delivery of discourses, which are external matters, cognizant by the senses, and seen and heard by a number of witnesses, who are mutual checks upon each other, the testimony of ordinary history is amply sufficient. But when we come to prove the higher fact of the secret and invisible communication of the Holy Spirit to the minds of Mark and Luke, we must have testimony as high as the fact to be proved–that of miracles, or of persons whose veracity has already been divinely attested. A man cannot prove his own inspiration by his own testimony, independent of that of God. The secret inspiration could not be known to others not inspired, and the ordinary historian could not give evidence of that which, from its nature, could not be known to him without the visible attestation of God.

8. The Unwritten law of Christ

From the simple history of the New Testament it is shown that Christ appeared among men as a lawgiver-that He promulgated his law orally, that He gave no command that His laws should be reduced to writing but having verbally instructed His apostles, that He commissioned them to act as His agents.[17] These inspired agents carried out the commission, and the kingdom was governed for many years before any part of the law was written. This unwritten law was the original law of the Church. It was given and practically administered in that form, and in that form was obligatory upon every member of the association.

This being the original and established form of the code, to substitute the written law for the unwritten, either in whole or in part, would require the affirmative act, either of the lawmaker Himself or of His lawful agents. Only in so far as the written includes the unwritten, can the former become a substitute for the latter, except it be expressly so declared. If, then, it is true, that only a part of the original law of Christianity has been written, the entire code must consist of both these parts, unless the unwritten portion has been expressly repealed.

When God gave a law to the Jews, He expressly commanded it to be written.[18] The tables upon which the law was engraved, having been broken by Moses, they were renewed.[19] The law was required to be read to all the people at the end of every seventh year, at the Feast of Tabernacles.[20]

If our Lord intended that the law governing the Church organized by Him should become a written code, it would seem very natural and reasonable that He should have made provision for that end, as was done in the case of the Old Law. It would seem difficult to understand why God, intending to accomplish the same end in both cases, should make express provision to secure the end in one, and not in the other. Upon the theory that He intended the code to be written in the one, and not in the other, we can well understand why God acted differently in both cases.

We meet with no intimation, either in the words of Christ or those of His apostles, that any such intention ever existed. And when we come to look into the books themselves, and consider their history, we shall see abundant reason to negate any such idea. We find that these books were the result, not of any direction of Christ that they should be written, but of casual circumstances.

Matthew wrote for a specific class of readers, and Luke wrote for a single individual. The epistles of Paul were evidently written to different churches and individuals, whom he could not visit at the time, and for the purpose of correcting some local corruptions or heresies. The very form in which the books of the New Testament are written, not being regular and methodical, shows they were not intended by their authors to form a complete code of law. Many of the most important doctrines mentioned by Saint Paul were very concisely stated, and introduced parenthetically, and as illustrations.

The apostles were expressly commanded to preach, and this mode of teaching became obligatory. But as to teaching by written instructions, there seems to have been nothing determined by Christ. The adoption of that mode was left discretionary-to be governed by circumstances. Hence, we find the apostles resorting to the written mode to communicate with particular individuals or churches as often as circumstances rendered it advisable. While absent or in prison, this was the only means available

As the unwritten law was the first law of Christianity, and the *only* law for many years; before the written law could become a part of the code, it would be requisite to establish its validity by some affirmative act. The mere fact that portions of the law were subsequently written, would not, of itself, show any intention to substitute those portions for the entire code.

If we go back to the earliest British statutes now extant, the fact of their existence as written law, and the passage of numerous statutes since, by parliament, will not afford the slightest evidence of any intention to abolish the common law. Except, of course, where it has been expressly superseded, or the statute is manifestly incompatible with it. It may be justly said, that the statutes themselves recognize the common law as a part of the law of the realm. It would seem to be equally true that the written, expressly admits the existence of the unwritten law as part of the Christian code. We will consider this in another place.

9. The written word is not the entire law of Christ

Those who insist that the written word contains the entire law of Christ, are bound it would seem, by every rule of sound interpretation, to show at least one of two things:

1. That the written law contains *all* of the original unwritten law; or

2. That admitting it not to contain all the original law of the kingdom, it has been by competent authority, expressly adopted as an entire substitute for it.

For unless one or the other of these positions can be satisfactorily proven, the presumption of law and right reason would always be, that the code consists of two parts, the written and the unwritten.

As to the first position, that the written includes all of the unwritten law, there is no satisfactory proof. The evidence seems clearly to establish the contrary fact. It is true that Saint Luke says, in the preface to his Gospel, that he had "perfect understanding of all things from the very first;" and in his Acts of the Apostles he says, "the former treatise have I written of all that Jesus began both to do and to teach." Yet these general expressions are not only limited by his own statements in other places, but are limited by the statements of other New Testament writers and by the facts recorded by them. Luke himself informs us that Christ was seen by the apostles forty days after His Passion, and speaking of the things pertaining to the kingdom of God; and this writer no where assumes to give these instructions of our Lord in full.

Besides, Matthew, John and Mark record numerous facts and instructions of our Lord not mentioned by Luke; and Saint John tells us that many other things Jesus did, which he does not himself record, and says, in strong hyperbolical language, that if they all should be written, every one, the world itself, he supposes, could not contain the books. And none of the subsequent books assume to contain all the instructions of Christ or of His apostles, Indeed this position is so clear, that I am not aware of any writer who maintains the contrary.

In reference to this matter, Dr. Spring says:

> The Savior appeared among men as a living teacher. We have no evidence that His personal instructions were delivered to the apostles in writing, or that the preaching of the apostles was in any other way than orally. On the other hand, we do not deny that both Christ Himself, and His apostles, uttered many and important truths that were never committed to writing....
>
> But there is no evidence that any of them (the instructions of Christ and His apostles), or even any of the books of the New Testament, were written until years after His ascension into Heaven.[21]

These are very important admissions, and while they concede no more than the simple truth, they give rise to serious and interesting inquiries.

Was Christ a lawgiver? As such, was He powerless, incompetent, or frivolous? In giving His law, did He so exhaust His powers that He made no provision for the preservation and perpetuation of His *entire code*? Or did He intend that the Christians of the first age should be governed by a full and complete code of law, while the Christians of all succeeding ages should be governed by a mutilated code, robbed of "many and important truths?" Did He intend that the Church, in the days of the apostles, should believe one system of faith, and His followers, in after ages, should believe another?

On the contrary, did not Christ build but *one* Church, for the government of which He gave but *one* law? And did He not intend that this entire code, as He delivered it, should govern this one Church, from the first even to the last period of her existence upon earth? Did not the Christians of the apostolic day live under the *same* dispensation and under the same code of law as we of the present? Were they not required to believe the same things?

Our Lord promised His apostles the Holy Ghost, who should "teach you *all* things, and bring to your remembrance all that I have said to you."[22] And after making this inviolable promise, He gave them that imperative command to "teach all nations to observe all things whatsoever I have commanded you."

This command was the last one given. It was to take effect and be put in force on and after the day of Pentecost. Therefore it included all things Christ had commanded the apostles to observe before that day, except the few commands specially limited to them, such as the command to tarry in Jerusalem. The command in the commission is general, and for a general purpose. It is not limited by any other text; and, according to our fourth rule, must be taken in its widest sense compatible with the general scope of the whole system.[23]

The apostles executed this commission for Saint Paul tells the elders of Ephesus: "I have not shunned to declare unto you all the council of God."[24] And the same apostle says to the Galatians: "But even if we, or an angel from heaven, should preach to you a Gospel contrary to that which we preached to you, let him be accursed." And so important did Saint Paul esteem this doctrine that he repeats it in the next verse, almost in the same words.[25]

If, therefore, the Gospel received and taught by the apostles was made up of certain requisites, no man is authorized to preach any other Gospel made up of any other requisites, either more or less. For if such a Gospel contain more or less constituents than the original, it is adulterated in the first, and mutilated in the second case, and it cannot be the *same,* but must be different. How, then, can the Gospel which does *not* contain "many and important truths uttered by Christ and His Apostles," as Dr. Spring admits, be the same gospel preached by the Apostles?

If we can omit "many and important truths" and the identity of the gospel be not destroyed, what limit can there be to such omissions? Would a mutilated statute, deprived of "many and important" sections, be the same as the original. Suppose we strike from the constitution of the United States, "many and important" provisions, would it still be the same constitution?

10. Has competent authority repealed the unwritten law?

The law of Christ was originally promulgated orally, and reduced to practice in that form. For many years the entire church was so governed-and as the *written* law is conceded not to contain "many and important truths"-before we can assume that the entire unwritten code has been repealed, the proofs should be of the highest and most conclusive character.

The intention thus to mutilate a great system of law, given for the government of the same *perpetual* institution, and given by a Divine Legislator, Who could make His law perfect at the beginning without the necessity of subsequent change, ought to be shown by proofs remarkably clear and full. For it would seem a strange anomaly, that a lawgiver of such a character should so defectively arrange His government, that His code should become incomplete in a very few years after its promulgation; thus leaving the subsequent subjects of His kingdom not so well governed as those at the beginning.

Such a result might well happen from the imperfect system of a human legislator, and contrary to his intention. But how the law of Christ could be thus crippled, contrary to His intention, is most difficult to imagine. For we cannot conceive why the "many and important truths" should have been uttered by Christ and His apostles, unless it was intended they should be preserved. Nor can we think that Christ and His apostles were idle or powerless-that they uttered truths to be forgotten-enacted laws not to be obeyed-and that they promulgated important principles, forming a part of one entire system of law, that they, nevertheless, intended should be lost.

It is true that Saint John says: "But these are written, that ye might believe that Jesus is the Christ, the Son of God; and that believing ye might have life through His name." But this he spoke of his own gospel only, as can be seen in the preceding verse. If the apostle intended anything exclusive in this statement, so as to show that his gospel was alone necessary and sufficient, independent of any other part of the law, then he intended to exclude, as well the other Scriptures, even his own Epistles and his Revelations, as the unwritten law itself. He does not seem to have that consequence in view; and as the text is general and not specific, we must look to other portions of the Scripture, which refer to this question, and construe and apply all together, and give force and effect to all.

11. Saint Paul's view of the written and unwritten law

Saint Paul in his Second Epistle to Timothy seems to place this subject in a clear light. He says,

> But continue thou in the things which thou hast learned, and hast been assured of, knowing of whom thou hast learned them.

This passage taken in connection with proceeding passages, especially those where Saint Paul tells him to "hold fast the form of sound words, which thou hast heard from me." and "the things that thou hast heard of me among many witnesses, the same commit thou to faithful men able to teach others also," as well as those regarding the manner of Saint Paul's teaching, inculcates upon Timothy the duty of continuing in the things which he had learned from the apostle verbally. And he is to commit the same to others in the same way. In other words, it is a commendation of tradition; showing that the law thus conveyed to Timothy was obligatory upon him and others in that *form.*

The apostle goes on to say in close connection with this passage:

> And that, from a child thou hast known the Holy Scriptures, which were able to make thee wise unto salvation, through faith which is in Jesus Christ.

Now the Scriptures here spoken of were undoubtedly those of the Old Testament, for Timothy had known them from when he was a child. These Scriptures are said to be able to make Timothy wise unto salvation; but the apostle qualifies this language by adding "through faith which is in Jesus Christ." The substance of this passage is an endorsement of the Old Testament Scriptures; and taken in connection with the preceding verse, which is part of the same sentence, amounts to a statement, that these Scriptures and the system taught by Christ, *when taken together,* were able to make Timothy wise unto salvation.

The apostle, having thus far spoken of tradition and the Old Testament Scriptures, commences a new sentence, and speaks of the character of *all* Scripture without distinction in this way:

> All Scripture is given by inspiration of God, and is profitable for doctrine, for reproof, for correction, for instruction in righteousness: that the man of God may be complete, equipped for every good work.[26]

Now, when Saint Paul says that *all* Scripture is profitable to produce a certain end, does he mean to say that it is *alone sufficient*? Does he mean to say to Timothy, "The Scripture is the only rule necessary, and that tradition which I have just commended, you may set aside?" In other words, is there anything *exclusive* in the form of expression used? I cannot so understand it!

On the contrary, the term profitable gives to the apostle's language a limited meaning, and shows that his intention was *not to exclude tradition*, but to include "all Scripture," as being profitable to produce the end stated. Two or more means may be profitable to produce the same given end, and we may, therefore, speak of each one separately, and say it is profitable for that purpose. The term, in this place, means useful, advantageous; and to speak of the sole agent in producing the indicated end, as being profitable, would seem not to be accurate. The word *able* or *sufficient* would express such exclusive meaning better.

We are told in Scripture, in one place, that we are justified by grace; in another, by faith. In one place that we are saved by hope; in a second by faith; in a third, by confession and faith; in a fourth, by baptism; and in a fifth, by keeping the commandments. We cannot say that these expressions, though much stronger than the word *profitable*, are intended to exclude all agents in justification and salvation, except one only, in each of the cases mentioned. On the contrary, we must understand that all these agents form *parts* of one entire system, and all combine to produce the result stated.

So we understand Saint Paul, in the four verses under consideration as *including* (1) Tradition, (2) the Old Testament, and (3) all Scripture, as composing but parts of the law, and *all* being profitable to qualify a minister for every good work. And he certainly does inculcate all these upon Timothy, and could not, therefore, have intended to exclude any one or more of them.

The language of Saint Paul, in portions of his other epistles, seems still more explicit. To the Corinthians he says:

> I commend you because you remember me in everything and maintain the traditions even as I have delivered them to you.[27]

To the Thessalonians he says:

> So then, brethren, stand firm and hold to the traditions which you were taught by us, either by word of mouth or by letter.... Now we command you, brethren, in the name of our Lord Jesus Christ, that you keep away from any brother who is living in idleness and not in accord with the tradition that you received from us.[28]

These passages are very much to the point, and give rise to very important reflections.

It must be conceded that the Thessalonians had been taught the entire law of Christ; and this entire law the apostle calls "the traditions," whether taught by word or epistle. That which was taught by word and that by epistle were equally obligatory; and they were both placed upon the same footing, and entitled to precisely the same confidence and obedience.

The law as taught to these brethren, consisted of two parts, the written and the unwritten, and in these forms, was obligatory upon them. Where have we any evidence that these oral teachings were reduced to writing? There is none by Paul, for the command to hold fast both, was given in his second and last epistle to the Thessalonians. If these oral teachings were so necessary to these Christians, why are they not so to us? The doctrines taught were true; and were the doctrines taught by Christ!

Where, then is the evidence in the Scriptures that the written superseded the entire unwritten law? The kingdom was for many years governed by the unwritten law, and by that only. And when the law was written, it was only in part, and upon special occasions; and we find Saint Paul mentioning *both* parts of the law, and commanding both parts to be held equally sacred, for the reason that they were *both the Word of God*.

Now in opposition to the general principle, that a body of laws once obligatory in a certain form, unless they are subsequently all written out, or partly written and those not written expressed repealed; and in violation of the clear language of Saint Paul commanding his brethren to stand fast and hold both; by what system of right reason can we assume to mutilate a great and sublime code of law, by leaving out "many and important truths" originally belonging to it? And if the apostles had so intended, would they not have told us so in terms not to be mistaken? Where is that authoritative act recorded, which every principle of sound law, and reasonable construction, requires to have been performed, in order to set aside an entire system of unwritten law, first authoritatively established and put in practical operation by Christ and His apostles?

12. The alleged incompatibility of the Bible and Tradition

In reference to the question of the incompatibility of the Bible and tradition, Dr. Spring has certain abstract positions that I examined with care. He says:

> To ascribe infallibility to any other standard of truth than the Bible, is itself casting the Bible into the shade. Two infallible standards of faith cannot be; since, if they differ, one must be wrong, and if they do not differ, they are the same thing.[29]

The imagination cannot conceive, not the tongue of man utter any encomium upon the Scriptures, as to their truth and sublimity, that they do not merit, for the simple reason, they are the Word of God. And, perhaps nothing can add to the beauty of the simple statement of Saint Paul, that, "All Scripture is given by inspiration of God." As to their sacred character, there is no question.

But is it true that the Scriptures contain the *entire* Word of God? And if they do not, how can it depreciate the written Word, to put the unwritten Word of God upon the same footing? Were they not both uttered by the same Infinite Lawgiver? Are they not both infallibly true? If so, how does it wrong either one to be just to each, and to both?

If we put the two parts of a machine together, to make it complete, is this a wrong to either part? And if you put two parts of an infallible code together, and thus make it complete, is this error? is this confusion? Or is it order–heaven's first law? I confess that I could not understand how putting both parts of a code together could depreciate either. It would seem that they were both honored, and the true intent of each was accomplished.

With due deference to the opinion of the learned Divine, I submit that the whole question is resolved into does the Bible contain the entire code as originally delivered by Christ and His apostles? and if not, was that portion of the unwritten law not recorded in the Bible repealed? If the Bible does not contain the entire code *now* obligatory, to say it is the *only rule*, is to do it as clear an injustice as that attempted towards Saints Paul and Barnabas, when the people wished to sacrifice to them as gods. And such a course would be equally unjust to Tradition, as withholding from it that which is its just due.

When the learned Divine, speaking of the incompatibility of Scripture and tradition, says, "Two infallible standards of faith cannot be" he seems to overlook his own clear language, uttered in the preceding page. Speaking of the Christian law he says, as already quoted: "There is no absurdity in supposing it to be partly oral and partly written, while both might be amplified and interpreted by one another."[30]

In addition, he seems to me to answer himself very fully, as to the supposed incompatibility of Scripture and Tradition in making a charge against the Catholic Church. "Romanists," Dr. Spring says,

> teach the doctrine that truth becomes truth *because it is believed,* and that it is first believed and then true, whereas, independently of its being believed, it has an unchanging and everlasting existence.

If truth has an everlasting and unchangeable existence, then all that Christ and His apostles did utter, whether written or unwritten, is equally true in *both* forms, and wholly consistent. All the facts that ever did exist – all the events that ever did occur – all the truths ever uttered by God, or man, were consistent with all others, and harmonious in every particular. How then can there be any contradiction or inconsistency in the words of Christ and His apostles -"those many and important truths," as the learned Divine admits, "that were never committed to writing," and those that were so committed?

When Dr. Spring says that if these standards "do not differ, they are the same thing," I understand him; but when he says that, "if they differ, then one must be wrong," I cannot see "whereunto this must grow." He himself has told us that "many and important truths uttered by Christ and His apostles were "never committed to writing;" and of course these truths "*never* committed to writing" must be different from those *written;* and yet he admits they were *truths*, and if truths, they must have an "everlasting existence" and, therefore, "must not be wrong."

Under the Catholic theory, the Scriptures and Traditions are held to be but constituent parts of one whole system of law, each part containing nothing but the truth, and both parts, taken together, only containing all the truth. There can be no theoretical contradiction or inconsistency herein; and there can be none, in point of fact, unless truths have been lost or error added to the system by one or both of these parts.

When Dr. Spring maintains that there *must* be an incompatibility, I must think him wholly mistaken. Or if not I must say, that the *first* part of Scripture which was written was itself incompatible with that portion of the truth not *then* recorded.

It is true that in systems of civil law composed of two parts, written and unwritten, there is always a provision, that where they conflict, the written law shall prevail as being the last will of the legislator. This provision is predicated upon the ground that human legislation is imperfect–that it may need amendment—that the lawmaker is actually fallible, and for that reason may contradict himself. Hence, such a provision becomes necessary.

But the same principle cannot apply to a system of law made by Christ. The same liability to imperfect legislation cannot exist. The nature and character of the Lawgiver, and, therefore, of His law itself, being as different from human legislation, as fallibility and infallibility from each other. This principle, so necessary to the fallible system, is, for that reason, inapplicable to the infallible.

When the learned Divine, Dr. Spring, asserts that "Romanists teach the doctrine that truth becomes truth because it is believed, and that it is first believed and then true," with due deference I must say, I could never find any verification of such a statement. So far as I have been able to discover the true teaching of the Catholic Church, he has precisely reversed her maxim, for she holds, not that "truth becomes truth because believed," but that it is believed, because it is truth.

True the Church lays down this rule in substance, that the fact of a certain doctrine having at all times been believed and taught by the Church, as a truth coming down from the apostles, is conclusive *evidence* to show that such a provision was proclaimed originally by Christ and his apostles. This belief of the Church is treated by Dr. Paley as evidence of the truth of Christianity itself, as we shall hereafter see.

Blackstone says, as we have seen, that the judges of the courts are the depositories of the common law-that they determine what it is -and that their decision is the most authoritative evidence that can be given of the prior existence of such a custom. But the learned commentator did not mean to say that such a custom become a law because of these decisions; for the judges are not delegated to pronounce a new law, but to declare and maintain the old one. The courts only declare the law-the legislative power makes it. The law was in existence before the courts so declared it.

So it is with the Catholic Church. Under her theory, she is the depository of the entire law, not delegated to pronounce a new law, but simply to declare and expound the old one. Her decisions do not create a law–do not make that law which was not before such–but are simply evidence of the law "once delivered to the saints."

The fact being undeniable and conceded, that "many and important truths uttered by Christ and His apostles were never committed to writing;" and, therefore, not to be found in the New Testament, it is difficult, upon any system of sound logic, to reject Tradition. Such a rejection leads to so much confusion and contradiction, that I was wholly unable to find any warrant, either in Scripture or common sense, to support it. It is derogatory to Christ, as a lawgiver, and to the Church as an institution founded by Him.

To maintain that God created anything in vain, is to impute to Him an infirmity, deeply disparaging to His character as Creator. We may not be able to comprehend the exact use for which portions of the Universe were designed, but we can see the purpose for which most portions of the visible creation were made; and the consistency and beauty of these portions should satisfy us that nothing was made in vain, though it be true that our limited intellects will not enable us to scan the entire creation at a glance, and designate the precise purpose for which each portion was made. So, if we say that Christ made any portion of His code of law in vain, we impute to Him an idle frivolity deeply disparaging to His dignity as a Divine Lawgiver.

13. The correct theory of Christ's lawgiving

It occurred to me that Christ being a Divine Lawgiver he would never make a system of law, and permit it to be either mutilated or lost. He never would have committed His law to the world at large–to aliens and strangers–to take its chances of preservation like the teachings of mere philosophers. He would perpetuate it whole either by His special superintendence, or by depositing it with an inspired and protected guardian. The latter method was not only most in accordance with reason and in accordance with his system of governing men, but with the express declaration of Scripture. And if He adopted either of these methods, the truths of the system, written or unwritten, would alike come down to us as originally given, that we might enjoy, if we would, the same advantages as the Christians of the early church.

I could not conceive why Christ should build a church against which the Gates of Hell should never prevail, and which Saint Paul declared to be the pillar and ground of the truth and yet not commit the very law intended for the government of this great institution to *its keeping*. The idea that Christ, as a Divine Legislator, should organize an institution, such as He and Paul described it, and yet it be incapable of *knowing* its own faith, and not a credible witness of the same–thus creating an association of living men, wide as the world, and durable as time, and yet so frail and unreliable as not to deserve the respect and confidence due even to ordinary civil institutions would seem, upon its face, to be wholly inadmissible.

It did seem to me that those who reject Tradition, under the idea of attaining greater certainty, did, indeed, increase the uncertainty; not only by destroying a part of the law itself, but by attacking the credibility of the only proper and reliable witness to the inspiration and authenticity of the entire canon of Scripture.

By conceding that "many and important truths" of the system have never been written, and must, therefore, be lost, because the testimony of the Church is unworthy of belief, the character of our Lord as a Lawgiver, and of His Church as a competent witness, is depreciated, and the whole subject left in irremediable doubt.

In the Catholic theory, there is a combination of all the proofs, as well as beauty, strength, and consistency. Every motive of credibility and every proof are therein preserved. In this theory "our Lord" as Mr. Campbell justly says, "anticipated the future in all his precepts, and spoke with an eye to it, as well as to the men of his own time.[31]

Knowing that the art of printing would not be invented for fourteen centuries, and that the great mass of men would always be unable to read; and that, therefore, all entire written law interpreted by each individual for himself in the last resort, would be impracticable, our Lord, for these, and other reasons, adopted a method that *must* be practical everywhere, and at all periods; and, therefore, promulgated His law orally. He commanded His apostles and their successors to do the same thing, leaving such portions of the law to be reduced to writing as after circumstances render prudent and advisable. And as the different modes of promulgation and transmission of laws by writing and tradition have each their advantages, a combination of both methods is most efficient and useful. So, the apostles and others, inspired by God, wrote parts of the laws of the early Church, and committed the same to the Church, as also the unwritten traditions, for safe transmission, attestation, and practical administration.

By this theory, the Church is the inspired depository, witness, and interpreter of the entire code left by Christ and His apostles. So that, no part of the law can be lost, and the code remains entire, without mutilation or change; and the work of Christ, and the institution founded by Him, remain perfect and complete, and worthy of the character of a Divine Architect.

14. Extracts from the Fathers

Of Saint Ignatius, the holy martyr, and disciple of Saint John, Eusebius says:

He warns them to be especially on their guard against the heresies just then springing up and increasing. He exhorts them to hold firmly to the tradition of the apostles, which, for security, he thought necessary, as a witness, to confirm in writing.[32]

Saint Irenaeus says:

So also Polycarp, who not only had been instructed by the apostles, and had conversed with many who had seen the Lord, but was also appointed by apostles, bishop of Smyrna, in Asia. Him we saw in our early youth....

The things which he had learned from the apostles, those he uniformly taught, which also he delivered to that church, which alone are true. To these all the churches throughout Asia, and they who to this day have succeeded Polycarp, bear testimony, being a witness of the truth more credible and more faithful than Valentinius and Marcian, and the rest of the perverse thinkers....

But the church also in Ephesus, founded indeed by Paul, but with which John remained until the days of Trajan, is a veracious witness of the tradition of the apostles.[33]

Therefore we ought to avoid them, but to cling with the utmost care to whatever is of the church, and to hold fast to the tradition of truth.[34]

But when, on the other hand, we challenge them [heretics] to that tradition which is from the apostles, *which is preserved in the churches, through the succession of presbyters,* they are adverse to tradition, saying, that being themselves not only wiser than presbyters, but even than the apostles, they have discovered the genuine truth.... Thus it turns out that, at last, they neither assent to the Scriptures nor tradition.[35]

In a fragment of the *Epistle ad Flavinum* preserved in Eusebius:

These dogmas are not in accordance with the church...these dogmas the presbyters before us, and who shone together with the apostles, delivered not to you.[36]

Saint Clement of Alexandria, G.C., says, among many other things,

Let him go the real light–to the truth, which in what is written, indicates the things not written.

But these were preserved the true tradition of the blessed doctrine directly from Peter, and James and John, and Paul, the holy apostles, having received it in succession, the son from the father, etc.

> There were some things delivered to the Hebrews without writing.[37]

> So he has ceased to be a man of God, and faithful to the Lord, who has thrown aside the ecclesiastical tradition, and plunged into the opinions of human heresies.[38]

Tertullian says:

> For these and such like rules, if thou requirest a law in the Scriptures, thou shalt find none. Tradition will be pleaded to thee as originating, custom as confirming, and faith as observing them.[39]

> That was different so it had been handed down; now that which has been handed down, that was true, as having been handed down by those whose it was to hand down.[40]

These are taken from writers of the second century, and are only part of their testimony. I might quote many from the third and fourth century to the same effect.[41]

I will make two extracts from Origen the learned Greek Father of the third century:

> We are not able to credit these men, nor to go out from the first and the ecclesiastical tradition; nor to believe otherwise than as the churches of God have by succession transmitted to us.[42]

> Which has neither been transmitted by the apostles, nor manifested in any part of the Scriptures.[43]

The testimony of the Fathers of the fifth century is equally full, to the same point. Such seems to have been the faith of the ancient church in the days of her mighty struggles to establish Christianity, when she had received the deposit of faith fresh from the apostles, and no one but heretics, such as Valentinius, Marcian, and Cerinthus, disputed the authority of tradition.

15. Maintaining the true apostolic tradition

Of the Ancient Fathers Dr. Spring says:

> The ancient fathers acknowledged the authority of the apostolic traditions, unwritten and written; but, as we shall hereafter show, they only never pretended that the church must blindly receive as apostolical traditions all that may be put upon them as such, but urged the obligation of bringing them to the test of the written revelation.[44]

According to the learned Divine, the *principle* of acknowledging the authority of the apostolical traditions, both unwritten and written, was the faith of the ancient church; but the church was careful not to admit everything that might claim to be tradition but brought them to the test of the written Word. That the church was careful to admit only true traditions seems clear, and that the Scriptures were used as well as other proofs to show what were apostolical traditions, is no doubt true.

But that a tradition was rejected simply because it *differed* from, while it did not *contradict* the Scriptures, is, I apprehend, an error, if such a position was intended to be advanced. It will be seen at once, that the unwritten must have differed from the written traditions – the Scriptures. To test them therefore, by the Scriptures could only be done in so far as they were alleged to be contradictory. Mere *difference* may not constitute contradiction. Every contradiction is a difference; but every difference is not a contradiction.

If additional facts be preserved by tradition these may not contradict the Scriptures, any more than the additional facts stated by Saint Luke, contradict the Gospel of Saint Matthew. It was only upon the ground that these additional facts were preserved by tradition, that the authority of tradition was admitted by the ancient church. There could have been no satisfactory reason but this.

It was by tradition that the Scriptures were attested, as a single extract from Origen will show:

> As I have learned by tradition regarding the four gospels, which are the only disputed ones in the church of God which is under heaven – that the first was written, etc.[45]

So far as I have been able to learn, the Catholic Church has never admitted, or contended that she must receive as apostolical traditions all that may be sought to be put upon her, as such; but she has been exceedingly careful not to admit any but such as were well attested by the church in all ages, and that she has always used both the unwritten and written law, to amplify and interpret one another.

She has ever held it to be alike her duty to reject spurious traditions, as well as spurious Scriptures. As Blackstone well says, the common law of England is not "at present merely oral or communicated from former ages by word of mouth." Similarly the traditions of the apostles are not at present merely oral, nor were they communicated from former ages by word of mouth only, but were reduced to writing soon after the days of the apostles; and are found in the testimony of the Fathers, and in the decisions of the Church. Thus in the first extract regarding Saint Ignatius, martyred about 106 AD, we see he had reduced a portion of them to writing, as stated by Eusebius.

The learned Protestant Bishop Montague says:

> There are hundreds of particulars which have been instituted by God in point of religion, commanded and used by the Church, of which we own that the Scripture delivers or teaches no such thing.[46]

I could never find the authority in the New Testament for keeping the first instead of the seventh day of the week as a Sabbath. The language of the Old Law is most explicit that the *seventh* day shall be kept. And not only is the language definite and certain, but the reason why God ordained that specified day is given; i.e., that the Creator himself rested on the seventh, and blessed the seventh day.[47] To say, in the face of so clear a provision, that the observance of any other day of the week is a compliance with the law, is to indulge a hazardous latitude with the explicit language of the lawgiver. But tradition informs us that the first was substituted for the seventh day of the week, by the apostles, in honor of our Lord's glorious resurrection.

It has been often objected against the traditions of the Church, that our Lord told the Scribes and Pharisees that they had made void the law of God by their traditions.[48] Our Lord certainly did condemn certain *specified* traditions, but how condemnation of particular traditions can be construed into a general condemnation of all traditions is certainly not obvious.

If our Savior had intended a general condemnation of all tradition as a medium of transmission He would not have used language specially confined to a particular class of traditions then in existence. His language, in such case, would have been general, so as to include the future, as well as the past and the present. As Christ expressly confined His condemnation to one class of tradition, by what rule of rational construction can we make general that which He chose only to make special? To expressly confine a provision of law to specified cases, *is to exclude the idea of generality*. When a lawgiver specifies a single error, and denounces that the denunciation cannot be extended to other matters not designated.

If we take it to be true, for the sake of argument only, that Christ meant simply to condemn the particular traditions alluded to, we cannot put into his mouth more appropriate words to express such intention, or language more definite and certain, unless we make him resort to useless tautology, a thing not usual with competent legislators. The quotation sustains the Catholic view, and is against the Protestant.[49]

It would seem that our Lord did not intend to condemn His own, and the subsequent acts of His apostles, in promulgating and administering a traditional system of law. He did not intend to give the Jews the occasion to say, with truth: "You condemn *all tradition*, and then enforced your own system in the same form." To say that because there were some false, that there could be no true traditions, would seem about as illogical as to say that we should reject all true history, and true Scriptures, because there has been false histories, and spurious Scriptures.

---

[1] William Blackstone.

[2] William Blackstone, *Commentaries on the Laws of England, Vol. 1 p*. 46.

[3] *Ibid*., p. 62.

[4] *Ibid, p*. 64..

[5] *Ibid. p. 69.*

[6] *Ibid*. 66, 74.

[7] James Kent *Commentaries on American Law* 1 468.

[8] William Blackstone, *op. cit*. 70.

[9] In the case of Douglass *vs*. Howard *24 Wendell's Rep*., 45-47.

[10] James Kent *op. cit*. 1473 note.

[11] *Ibid*. Cited by Kent 472.

[12] Gardiner Spring. *A Dissertation on the Rule of Faith 13.*

[13] *Ibid*. 12.

[14] Thomas Hartwell Horne, *An introduction to the critical study and knowledge of the Holy Scripture* Vol. 1 Introduction p. 204, 7th ed.

[15] Gardiner Spring *op. cit*. 28.

[16] Jn 3:2.

[17] There is no evidence in the record that He ever wrote anything, except what He wrote with His finger upon the ground.

[18] Ex 24:4 "And Moses wrote all the words of the Lord"

[19] Ex 31: 1-28.

[20] Deut 31: 10,11.

[21] Gardiner Spring *op. cit p.* 17.

[22] Jn 14: 26.

[23] *Cf.* Chap. 1 Introduction. Ed.

[24] Acts 20: 27.

[25] Gal 1: 8.

[26] 2 Tim 3:16-17.

[27] 1 Cor 11: 2.

[28] 2 Thess 2: 15, 3: 6.

[29] Gardiner Spring *op. cit.* 72.

[30] *Ibid.* 12.

[31] A. Campbell and J. Purcell, *A debate on the Roman Catholic religion.* 14.

[32] H.E., 1.iii.,c.36.

[33] Saint Irenaeus *Adversus Haeres.*, 1. iii., c. 3, n. 4, p175.

[34] *Ibid.* 1. iii., ch., 4, p 178-9.

[35] *Ibid.* 1. v., c. 20.

[36] Fragment *Epistle Adversus Flavium* t. i., preserved in Eusebius *History of the Church* .,m 1. v., c. 20.

[37] Clement of Alexandria, Saint *Stromateis*, 1. v., p 682-5.

[38] *Ibid*, 1. vii., p 890.

[39] *De Corona* p 101-2.

[40] *De Carne Christi* n. 2 p 308.

[41] *Cf.* From the third century – Saint Seraphian, G.C.; Caius, L.C.; Origen, G.C.; Saint Hippolytus, G.C.; Firmilian, G.C.; and Saint Cyprian, L.C.

From the fourth century – Eusebius, G.C.; Saint Julius, L.C.: Liberius, L.C.; Saint Hilary, L.C.; Saint Athanasius, G.C.; Saint Cyril of Jerusalem, G.C.; Saint Ephrem Syrus, G.C.; Saint Gregory of Nissa, G.C.;Saint Gregory of Nazianzum, G.C.; Saint Basil, G.C.; Saint Pacian, S.C.; Saint Damascus, L.C.; Faustinus, L.C.; Saint Siricius, L.C.; Theophilus of Alex., G.C.; Saint Epiphanius, G.C.; Saint Ambrose, L.C.; and Saint Jerome, L.C.

[42] T. iii. Comm. In Matt., n.46.

[43] T. iii. Comm. In Matt., 1.xiii. Ex Pamphil. Apolog.

[44] Gardiner Spring, *op. cit.* 17.

[45] T. iii. Com. In Matt. P440 Eusebius H., 1. vi., c. 25.

[46] Cited by Demetrius A. Galitzin, in "A letter to a Protestant friend on the holy Scriptures," published by F. Lucas, Jr., Baltimore. p. 396.

[47] *Cf.* Ex 20: 8-11.

[48] *Cf.* Mt 15.

[49] The very fact that our Lord was careful to condemn only a certain class of tradition, shows clearly that he did not intend to go beyond those mentioned. If He intended to make His condemnation general, then it would be idle to put it in a special from, and expressly confine it to certain specified traditions. Were a lawyer to quote a special statute to confute a general principle, he would be considered as establishing the general principle, and as confuting himself. To show exceptions to a general, only goes to establish it. So, to show that our Lord only condemned certain traditions, is to show that He did not intend to condemn other not mentioned.

CHAPTER III

THE VISIBLE CHURCH

1. The order in the Church flows from the character of Christ

If we concede that Christ was a lawgiver, then we must concede that He would necessarily organize His followers into a visible association. As He was the sole founder of the system, He would naturally establish a visible kingdom – not a republic.

All lawgivers intend their laws to govern associated, not dispersed, men. Each code of law is intended to govern one association only. When a just legislator founds a system, he always has in his eye the adaptation of his government to the condition of men united. For it is only in that state that men can be governed.

If Christ made a law to be practically obeyed by men on earth, he must have instituted a government *here*; and this government could not exist without a visible association of the parties governed. In addition, if he did found any system of government on earth, any kingdom, it, of course, must have been practical. It must be justly adapted to the wants of human nature, and possess in itself the elements necessary for success

Assuming that Christ was a Lawmaker, the organization of the visible church must logically flow from that character. It would seem equally clear that if He did organize a visible association of men called a Church, He must have intended that there should exist in this association perfect unity of faith.

2. Union is necessary for success

It must be obvious that no great goal is ever undertaken without the union of numbers. From a small village debating society, through every grade of organization, up to the mightiest civil government on earth, the first end to be secured is union of effort. The truth of this position is shown by the fact that where there is any great charitable, literary, or other objective to be attained, those who engage in it, at once unite themselves into a visible society. Success comes through unity of design and unity of effort.

If Christ intended the success of His system, He must have left sufficient means to attain it. If men who pretend to preach the same system of religion differ widely among themselves regarding what the system is, it at once produces confusion among all parties–both the teachers and the persons taught. It affords one of the most obvious and ready arguments against the truth of a system; an argument always applied with great practical success. All men seem to know at a glance, that two contradictory systems cannot both be true–that truth is, and must be, one and indivisible.

But union is not only necessary to success, but it is especially necessary to *rightful* success. There is no unholy ambition in the bosom of Christ; and the only success contemplated by him was success of the *entire truth*. The success of a mutilated or corrupted form of Christianity was no part of the Divine intention. Christ designed only the success of the system as He established it. To secure this success, continued unity in the same faith once delivered, was indispensable.

3. Discord fosters disbelief

I was myself for many years a Deist. I remember the weight the argument drawn from the divisions among Christians had with me, and how often I heard it in the months of all skeptics. At that time I knew nothing of the Catholic system, and nothing of the grounds upon which it assumed to rest. Had I been well informed in regard to it, I do not think I should ever have had much difficulty in believing the system of Christianity to be true.

The celebrated Volney, in his *Ruins* has put arguments into the mouths of the advocates of different systems of religion in the world, the Christian, the Mohammedan, and Heathen, each sustaining his own system, and attacking all others. After he makes them exhaust themselves in war against each other, he concludes that they are all wrong. Such conclusions result very naturally from man's impatience, and from his disposition to reject whatever is contradictory and confused.

The differences and consequent divisions among professed Christians have made more infidels than all other causes combined. If the diversity of views regarding different systems of religion have the practical effect of retarding the progress of Christianity in the world, how much greater must be the effect of the divisions among those who profess the same system! Most men who are infidels, neglect or refuse to investigate. They satisfy themselves by the easy and offhand reflection that there must be something radically wrong in Christianity itself, something not to be understood, or else the professors of the system would agree as to what it is. According to the impressions they take up, they must first go through the arduous labor of an investigation into the truth of the system, and after they have arrived at that point, they must then examine the still more complex question as to which of the five hundred divisions in Christendom is right.

The Mohammedan says to the Christian: "First agree among yourselves as to what your religion is, and when you have done that, then come to me. If you, who have studied this matter all your lives, do not understand it, how can you expect me to do so? You Christians preach so many different doctrines, and are split up and divided into so many parties, that you do not know yourselves what is right, and you are not, therefore, capable of instructing me. You had better confine your arguments to yourselves, until you come to some common conclusions to what you shall teach others."

The force of this reasoning is very readily apprehended by even ordinary minds, and makes a deep impression upon those persons who are naturally inclined to doubt. We unhesitatingly, and at once, draw the easy and ready conclusion, that there must be some great defect in a system that has provided no practical means of securing unity of faith, and about which there exists so wide a difference of opinion among those who profess both to believe and to understand it.

4. Infidelity is more pervasive than supposed

Teachers of Christianity are excluded, by their position, from the same opportunities enjoyed by men of other professions to learn the sentiments of the great mass of men. Other professions are necessarily brought in contact with the outside world. Many men because they care nothing about the system itself, or are yet in a state either of great doubt or confirmed infidelity, will very readily state to a teacher of religion that they believe the system, for the purpose of avoiding an argument,. You will scarcely ever hear a public speaker on the stump or at the bar say anything against Christianity. Most of them will pronounce eloquent eulogies upon it, when, in truth a majority of them are skeptical to the last degree. Most of the editors of our daily and weekly political and literary papers write beautiful articles in praise of Christianity, while very few of them believe in it with any confiding faith.

THE TRUE CHURCH

As already stated, I was for many years a Deist, and being sincere in my views, I was ready to admit them upon proper occasions. In my conversations with those who were not professors of religion, and while giving my reasons against it, I could not but observe how readily they were received by those who heard me. I found individuals, not members of any church, who candidly admitted their belief in the truth of Christianity. But these were few and only constituted exceptions to the general rule. It would seem utterly inconsistent for a man to believe in Christianity, and yet not embrace it. His faith must evidently be very weak, for upon a subject of such unspeakable importance, not many persons will act a part so ruinous to themselves. Whenever any man becomes sincerely convinced of the truth of a religious system, if he is not direct and positive enemy of himself, he will be very apt to act, and put his convictions in practice.

This infidelity as a general thing that exists even without any systematic effort on the part of infidels to propagate their views. They have very few public speakers who employ their time for that purpose, and their publications do not extend half so far as their opinions. You may go into many houses, where you will find the Bible and no infidel works; and yet most of the family will be infidels or skeptics, and show it, most conclusively, by their *acts.* This extended diffusion of unbelief throughout society is mainly owing to the divisions and disputes among Christians. This ready and forcible argument drawn from this most deplorable and melancholy state of things has produced this result. I can safely appeal to every intelligent man, at all conversant with the feelings and opinions of men, as to the correctness of this position.

I speak of the *practical* effect of these divisions, and not of the effect they should have, in right reason, upon the minds of men. But the difficulty lies here -- most men are prone, from motives of convenience, or feelings of indolence, or current interest, to judge of things pertaining to the future by some summary method. They like to judge of such things in one mass, and dispose of them in the same way. You must first almost convince them of the truth of a system, before you can excite them to investigation.

Mr. Campbell, in his debate with Mr. Rice very truly says:

> The land is full of infidelity.... The reason is, the gospel is blasphemed by discords, the variances, the hatred, and the strife engendered by your partyism.[1]

5. Scriptural proofs that Christ contemplated unity

It would seem, from a just and candid consideration of the reasons stated, that Christ must have intended a visible organization of His followers. Furthermore, it seems that such an organization was intended by design to have a continued unity in it. The latter deduction necessarily results from the former. If the organization was designed to exist at all, and was necessary, in the nature of the system and of the beings it was intended to govern it is clear that it was designed to continue so long as the system itself should endure.

If we pass from this train of reasoning to the positive testimony of Scripture, we shall find these positions most clearly sustained. Throughout the New Testament, when the general terms "the Church" are used, without being qualified by other words, or without being used in such a connection as to show a limited meaning, it is applied to the one visible universal church.

In Saint Matthew's Gospel Christ says: "Tell the church" – "if he will not hear the church" – "upon this rock I will build my church." In the third chapter of Saint Paul's first epistle to Timothy, the church he speaks of is plainly the visible church. In the second chapter of Isaiah, speaking of the future church, we find the prophet using these words:

> And it shall come to pass in the last days, that the mountain of the Lord's house shall be established in the top of the mountains, and shall be exalted above the hills, and all nations shall flow into it. And many people shall go and say, Come ye, and let us go up to the mountain of the Lord, to the house of the God of Jacob; and he will teach us of his ways, and we shall walk in his paths, for out of Zion shall go forth the law, and the word of the Lord from Jerusalem.

Here the church is most beautifully compared to a house on the top of the mountains, exalted above the hills. There is surely nothing contemplated in this sublime passage but a visible church, in which "the Lord will teach us of his ways," and in which "we will walk in his paths." Connect Isaiah's description with the fourteenth verse of the fifth chapter of Matthew, where Christ says to His apostles: "Ye are the light of the world. A city set on a hill cannot be hid."

That perfect unity in this visible organization was intended by Christ, not only follows from the reasons given, but it is shown by the written word. It is shown by the testimony of the Church in all ages, and by the admissions of Protestant writers themselves.

> And I have other sheep that are not of this fold; I must bring them also, and they will heed my voice. So there shall be one flock, one shepherd.[2]

> There is one body and one Spirit, just as you were called to the one hope that belongs to your call, one Lord, one faith, one baptism.[3]

> He is the head of the body, the church.[4]

> The household of God, which is the church of the living God.[5]

No comments could add anything to the force of the extract from Saint John: "There shall be one fold, and one shepherd." And Saint Paul says: "There is one body, one spirit, one hope, one Lord, one faith, one baptism." All these are closely connected in the same sentence, and have the same power: and as there can be no divisions in the "one spirit, one hope, one Lord, one faith, one baptism," neither can there be in the "one body" (the church), but there must be the most perfect unity in *all, or in none*.

Again, Christ is the "the head of the body, the church," and if the head is not divided, can the body be divided? Christ Himself laid down the general principle, that a "kingdom divided against itself cannot stand;" and the church of Christ is his Kingdom.[6] Again, could the church be "the pillar and ground of truth" if in her there was not a perfect union? And the "house" in which Timothy was instructed to "behave" himself, must have been *one* thing, and only *one*. There is nothing like the idea of division or disunion conveyed in any of these quotations, nor in the whole New Testament. The whole spirit of the system contemplates union. The whole drift of the New Testament seems to contemplate nothing less!

For what purpose would disunion be desirable? What good in proportion to the evil, could be accomplished by it? It is true, I have sometimes heard it suggested in private argument, that the divisions in Christendom were productive of good. They created a sort of rivalry among the different parties that naturally led to more industry, more research, and more activity. Consequently more was done. But such a state of things seems never to have been contemplated by the system. It was expected that Christians would do their duty from love of the cause, without being driven to it by party bitterness. The gentle and united system of Christianity never supposed that its followers would be guilty of the madness of the Jews who when besieged in Jerusalem by Titus, they wasted their strength in destroying each other–instead of uniting against the common foe. Surely no founder of any government intended to frame it so as to produce divisions. On the contrary, division is the very evil that law and all government were intended to prevent.

It may be true, to some extent, that divisions, for a time, may produce more activity and more exertion. But they produce more prejudice, more bitterness, and more hatred; and this activity and this exertion are turned, not so much against the common adversary as against each other. Mutiny in an army does not conquer the enemy.

6. Protestant views of the need for unity

I will now make a few quotations from Protestant writers, to show the importance they attach to the union of the visible church.

Dr. Spring says:

> On no principle can the Protestant Reformation be vindicated, or the reformers be held guiltless of the most uncalled for schism that ever rent asunder the visible church, if it be of minor consequence whether the oracles of God, or the decisions of Rome, be the rule of faith.[7]

Mr. Rice says:

> I agree with my friend Mr. Campbell that the union of all the disciples of Christ is an object greatly to be desired. I go for Christian union upon Scriptural principles as zealously as he, and so do evangelical denominations generally, so far as I know. We differ not concerning the importance of the object, but concerning the proper method of securing it…
>
> Concerning Christian Union, let me repeat, we are all most decidedly in favor of it. What is the union of which the apostle speaks? It is the unity of the faith, and of the knowledge of the Son of God.[8]

The writings of Mr. Campbell abound with many unanswerable arguments for union. In his debate with Mr. Rice, there are many fine bursts of eloquence upon this theme, only a few of which can be inserted here. Mr. Campbell says:

> In this sectarian and schismatic age, we have assembled for the purpose of discovering, if possible, the roots of discord and the seeds of schism which have unhappily alienated and estranged us from each other, that we may, peradventure, find some remedy for those wounds and grievances which have so disgraced our holy faith, marred its beauty, and impeded its progress in the world.

> But, my fellow-citizens, there is one point that cannot be too deeply impressed upon your minds–that the union of Christians is essential to the conversion of the world, both at home and abroad.
>
> What is the state of the case? We shall see that Christendom is at present in a distracted, agitated, disturbed condition, cut up or frittered down into sects and parties innumerable, wholly unwarranted by right reason, pure religion, the Bible–the God of the Bible. Before the high, and holy, and puissant intelligences of earth and heaven, this state of things is most intolerable.[9]

Mr. Rice may well say that: "The union of which the apostle speaks, is the unity of the faith, and of the knowledge of the Son of God." For the unity of the faith, and of the knowledge of the Son of God, is the unity contemplated by the system. In reference to these distractions in Christendom, Mr. Campbell's language is not less eloquent than true.

7. A Catholic view of unity

I shall close this chapter with the following beautiful extract from an eminent living Catholic writer, as it expresses my own views in language far more beautiful and appropriate than any I could select myself:

> Nothing can be more beautiful in the conception of a Christian Church, than a perfect unity of belief. Such an idea is beautiful to the imagination, because it is the consecration of the first and most essential principles, whereon society is based. For the social union tends to merge the feelings of each individual in the general mass, and leads him to embrace mankind rather than individual men. And in like manner does the principle of religious unity tend to excite your love towards them, no longer as brothers in the flesh, but as connected with you by a holier and diviner bond, and assists towards inspiring every member of the community with all that can be reciprocally felt, in the nearest ties and connections of our nature.
>
> And if the very idea cf a republic or government, in which men were united by such real or ideal bonds, as that they fought side by side or contributed towards the common weal, did seem to them of old so beautiful and heavenly, that the very conception of such a state, embodied under outward symbols, should have been deified and worshipped–what shall we say of that sacred union which holds men together. Not merely as constituents of a community, but as members of one mystical body; not cemented together by the sense of mutual want, or strung one unto the other by the ties of the flesh, or the interests of the world, but firmly united by the headship of One. One in whom the sublimest thought reposes, as in its proper sphere only

communicating through the circulation of vital influences, passing from one unto the other. Not contributing to the common stock the gifts or qualities of earth, but the fairest virtues, the most precious ornaments of our nature. Not directed in their views towards a worldly aggrandizement or a passing glory, nor linked in a battle field by a bond of hatred against a human foe, but looking upwards for their trophies and rewards to the peaceful smile of heaven, after they shall have contended together in the gentle strife of mutual and universal love.

Then add the reflection, how this influence stretches beyond the reach of any other known sentiment among mankind. For, outstripping all the motives of sympathy among men of different countries, it flies over mountains, and seas, and oceans, and puts into the mouths of nations the most remote, and the most dissimilar, one canticle of praise, and into their minds one symbol of belief, and into their hearts one sentiment of charity. And, thus professing alike, they kneel in countless multitudes before one altar, and from the soul of each proceeds the golden chain which joins them unto it, which God joins unto the rest, which He holdeth in His hand for in Him is the center towards which the faith of all converge , and in His truth it is blended into uniformity and oneness of thought. Surely this is the idea which you would wish to conceive, of the efficacy and of the effects of that rule, which has been given by God, to produce unity of belief.

But then also is this unity of faith subservient to another great end, to the evidence of our Blessed Savior's true religion. For He was pleased to declare that the unity observed among His followers should be among the strongest evidences of His heavenly mission. "And not for them only," He exclaimed, "do I pray, but for them also, who, through their word, shall believe in me; that they all may be one, as the Father in me, and I in thee, that they also may be one in us, that the world may believe that thou least sent me." And that this unity is not merely of the heart, through love, but also of the mind, in faith, His blessed apostle hath abundantly declared. For according to him, if we wish to walk worthy of the vocation wherein we have been called, it must be not only by "humility, and mildness, and patience, supporting one another in charity," but we must be "careful to keep the unity of the Spirit, in the bond of peace," so as to be "one body" as well as "one spirit" and to have "one faith" as much as "one Lord and one baptism."

Not surely that charity, the beautiful and the perfect, steps not beyond the circumscribing line of religious unity, or that her genial influences, like a flower's sweet odor, spread not abroad beyond the plant which first produces it; but universal as must be our love of men, this will be ever its noblest exercise, to wish and to strive that all be brought to that closer union and unity which is in and through faith." [10]

---

[1] A. Campbell and N Rice, *Campbell Rice Debate on the Holy Spirit.* p.905.

[2] Jn 10: 16.

[3] Eph 4: 4, 5.

[4] Col 1: 18.

[5] 1 Tim 3: 15.

[6] *Cf.* Dan 2: 44, Lk 1: 33.

[7] Gardiner Spring, a lecture delivered in Cincinnati and published as *Dissertation on the Rule of Faith. 1844.*

In this treatise, the learned divine has made many grievous and bitter charges against the Catholic Church. It is not written in that spirit of charity that should be found in every Christian writer. It is true, that while the course pursued by Dr. Spring would be most satisfactory to the prejudiced reader, it has involved him in many contradictions. It also contains many misrepresentations of the Catholic Faith. But while I am compelled to give this as my view of the general character of the lecture, I most cheerfully admit that there are many instances of candor displayed in different portions of it. In the quotation above, there is a very incorrect statement of the issue between the two parties. The Protestant rule of faith he makes the "oracles of God" and the Catholic "the decisions" of the Catholic Church. In the Protestant he leaves out the *construction* of the Written Word, and in the Catholic he leaves out the *law itself.* But in justice to D. Spring, I cheerfully admit that in other places he explains the Catholic rule more correctly.

[8] A. Campbell and N. Rice, *op cit. p.* 163, 770, 780.

[9] *Ibid.* :230, 783, 904.

[10] Nicholas Wiseman, *Moorfield Lectures* p. 77.

CHAPTER IV

THE GOVERNING POWER OF THE CHURCH

1. An association of men cannot continue without government

Christ organized His followers into a visible body of men, upon certain terms common to the association, and with the intent to accomplish a joint purpose. Therefore, it would seem to follow that some sort of government must have been instituted to keep the organization together.

It may be safely assumed as a correct principle, that any and all kinds of organizations among men that come together for some common end must do so upon *some terms*. Of necessity, there must be power placed somewhere in the association to settle disputes and questions respecting these terms. In other words, there must be government in every association of men, to which a law is given. The learned commentator on the laws of England well remarks:

> For when civil society is once formed, government at the same time results of course, as necessary to preserve and keep that society in order. [1]

This necessity exists in all associations and therefore must exist in the Church of Christ, as well as in all other collective bodies.

The invincible necessity for government results from the nature of man as an inferior being. Since it is the right and duty of the superior, to govern the inferior, and the correlative duty of the inferior to obey, that each may be kept in his proper sphere. That order may exist, it follows that such government ought to possess the requisite power to accomplish these ends. Order must exist in the system of Infinite Wisdom, and in everything proposed by Him to us. If, then, Christ formed a visible church, He must have given it the principles essential to its continued existence. We cannot upon principles of reason or experience, conceive of a visible Church without government.

2. Can the Church be a democracy

If these views are correct, it follows that one of two things must be true; either that Christ visibly presides on earth to exercise the judicial and executive powers of the Church, or He has delegated these necessary powers to others to be exercised by them as His agents or officers. Again, it follows that if Christ delegated this authority to others, He must have confided it to one man, to an order of men, or to the whole Church collectively. In the latter case, each member of the Church would have equal power, as a part of the whole.

A Democracy is a government in which the governing power is placed in the people; and a pure Democracy, is where the people meet themselves in council, and make the laws. A representative Democracy is where the people make and administer the laws through their agents. Now the Christian government is not a Democracy of either kind. It does not derive its just powers from the consent of the governed, nor is it in any manner founded by them. It is called a "Kingdom" not a Democracy. Christ was the sole founder of the system, and had the right to institute it in such form as seemed to Him best.

As the Church was intended for one united body, to extend undivided over the whole earth, and to exist for all coming time, the idea of placing the governing power in the hands of all the members, would seem inconsistent with the principles of government. That a lawgiver, supreme in virtue of His own nature, should promulgate a positive and fixed law for the government of a certain association of men, and at the same time confide the governing power to all the members, would seem evidently inconsistent with His rights as the founder of the institution, and incompatible with the end intended.

We are, then, thrown upon the other two positions, that Christ either delegated the governing power in the Church to one man, or to an order of men. It could not, I think, be supposed that Christ would create but one office in His Church, as one office would be clearly insufficient for the duties to be performed. It would, therefore, seem far more reasonable that our Lord would create several offices, in due subordination to each other, and confide the government of His Church to them.

3. Sovereignty resides in Christ

It may be proper to remark that the officers of any government among men only exercise *delegated* authority. The proper and only source from which this power flows, is the rightful founder of the government. The officer acts, not for himself, but he represents the sovereign power of the government, whatever that may be.

If the people institute a civil government, then, according to the theory of that government, the sovereign power resides in them, in their collective capacity. For the same reason, if Christ instituted any government among men, the sovereignty of the institution resides in Him, and every officer of such government must represent Him and Him only. It would, therefore, seem to follow, that, in delegating the necessary powers to govern the Church, it would be very unphilosophical to suppose that Christ would confide these powers to each and every member of the association—the very parties, and the only parties to be governed.

It then seems to me clear, that as Christ was a lawgiver, He must have organized the church, and that when organized, government in the church became inevitable. This government, to be government at all, must be supreme, and have jurisdiction over all questions arising under the law. Since Christ does not visibly exercise these powers on earth, Of necessity He must have delegated them to others who act as His agents.

4. The extent of governmental powers in the Church

It is a fundamental principle, that whatever power has the right to found a government, it has a right to say in whose hands the governing power shall be placed. Men, who, in the beautiful language of the Declaration of Independence are all "created equal," institute civil governments. The just powers of civil government are immediately derived from the "consent of the governed," though ultimately from God.

The people of the United States had the political right, in forming their Constitution, to frame their government in any shape they pleased. They could have united rather than separated the legislative, executive, and judicial powers. With reference to the Christian government, it may be said, that while it is derived, not from the consent of the parties to be governed, but from Christ alone, it still possesses certain great, leading, and essential features, common to every system of law, intended for, and adapted to, the government of mere men.

When a mere fallible power founds a government, it would be very unwise to attempt to frame a complete and full system of laws in advance, and thus to leave out the legislative power. This is for the plain and simple reason, that the founder of the government could not foresee all the circumstances that might exist in the future, requiring an enlargement or modification of his code. Hence the fundamental or constitutional provisions of civil governments are, from their nature, confined to the more general principles of the system.

But it is rational to suppose that an Infallible Legislator should, at some period, form a full and complete system of laws, to operate through all coming time. Christ did form a new code of law at the beginning of the new dispensation, embracing all the necessarily permanent portions of the system, and leaving no legislative power in the Church, except as to matters of discipline. Disciplinary laws could not have been very well made at the beginning, since changing circumstances might require a change in these mere disciplinary regulations.

The other indispensable powers of government—the executive and judicial—in the very nature of the powers themselves, could not have been exercised in advance. Laws are rightfully prescribed (which means both to make and publish) in advance of the commission of crimes. Commands must be given before they can be obeyed or violated! Before the judicial power is required to act there must be a violation of law, and this power must be exercised as often as cases may require. Therefore it must continue in operation so long as the Church itself shall exist in the world. The same may be said of the executive power. The occasion must arise before it is required to be used.

5. Succession must exist of necessity

If the Church was intended by Christ to exist for a greater period of time than the lives of those to whom the power to govern the church was originally given, there must be a succession of officers, or there would be an end of the institution. In other words, if certain offices were created in the Church by Christ, having attached them to certain powers, and certain persons placed therein, and these offices were intended to continue, so long as the Church itself should exist, it is plain that succession must follow. It is so in all governments. The officers die--while the offices live on. Government must be based on practical principles!

A civil government usually exists for several centuries, but the Christian government is intended to continue to the end of time. If certain permanent offices are necessary to the existence of the church, then when one incumbent dies, another must come to fill the position, and this constitutes succession. So long as the officer must die, and the office must exist, so long the principle of succession must be acted upon. There is no other mode of continuing the institution. This is the case in all political governments, and must be so in all governments intended for men, where the offices are to be filled by men,

Whatever government Christ did adopt for His Church, must have been consistent with human nature. He could not be supposed to form a government for men that would only answer for some other race of beings. Any government instituted by Christ must possess all the elements of a perfect system, one part having a due dependence upon another, so as to constitute a fitness and harmony in all its parts, that the combined whole may be practical, simple and efficient.

6. The true task of reason

It must be conceded that, while Christ never intended to suppress reason, the noblest attribute of man, He did intend to confine it within its legitimate limits, and to its appropriate objects. Like every other attribute belonging to inferior beings, it must be subject to rules and restrictions. It could not, therefore, be a true guide in reference to everything, and under all circumstances. But while it is limited and restrained, it must be competent within those limits. And though all truth must be strictly consistent and reasonable in itself, portions of it must, in the nature of things, be above the powers of limited reason.

The faculty of reason, when fairly exercised, must be competent to act decisively upon *some* portions of truth; otherwise it has been given in vain. If it is not to be relied on *in any case*, it ceases to be useful, and fails to accomplish the very purpose for which it was given. It would seem to be a just conclusion, that every system of truth must possess some plain principles, readily comprehended by the fair exercise of reason, and some more complex and difficult, either entirely beyond the reach of reason, or requiring the utmost exertion of its power.

The fair exercise of reason would lead us to admit that in a supernatural system, there would be mysteries necessarily above the comprehension of reason. By the exercise of reason we can examine the proofs of Christianity, because these are external matters, coming legitimately within the jurisdiction of reason. From these proofs we can know the character of Christ; and from His Word we can ascertain the plain facts and principles of the system; and these will lead us to the institution founded by Him as the competent guide of all, in all things, mysteries included.

THE TRUE CHURCH

The laws of nature have been open to the observation of mankind from the beginning. While we can, and do know the plain and more familiar laws of nature, so that we can pronounce with certainty that a particular effect or event, happening under a given state of circumstances, was a clear violation or suspension of these laws; yet we do not know, and may never know, all the laws of nature. We could not, therefore, be competent to speak decisively as to the true character of some events that have occurred, or that may hereafter occur.

The first principles of the science of mathematics, the most certain of all the sciences, are so simple that they can be readily understood by the infantile mind. Yet the higher problems, which are mathematically demonstrable, and are, therefore, equally true and equally capable of being conclusively shown to be so, are so complex that it requires the utmost effort of the best intellects to understand them. And we may well suppose that there are mathematical truths that never will be known to man.

So, the first principles of the science of civil government are simple and easily understood, while there are others exceedingly difficult of practical applications. The same observations are applicable to most, if not to all, the sciences. If it were not so, the powers and works of the great Creator would be limited to the entire comprehension of reason, and the creature would be equal, at least in intelligence, to his Creator. It is well said by the great Dr. Johnson:

> *"Whose prose was eloquence, by wisdom taught,*
> *The graceful vehicle of virtuous thought,"*

that "the human mind was so limited, that it cannot take in all parts of a subject."[2]

The same inseparable features must belong to Christianity. Many of its truths are plain, simple, and easily understood, while some are difficult, and hard to be understood. To establish the truth of the system itself, the appeal must, in the first instance, be made to reason in some form. We can only predicate our faith upon testimony. Testimony must be fairly tested by reason, and founded upon experience, before we can believe it.

Now, among the matters that can be best known to man, is the true character of human testimony. Men all possess the same essential nature and are in constant daily association and intercourse with each other. Therefore, they must be held competent to estimate the force and value of the evidence given by themselves. The gifted and accomplished young Judge Jones, upon his deathbed, used this language: "I have never been an infidel. I had examined the positive evidences for Christianity, and they greatly preponderated in favor of its truth; and taken in connection with its appropriate fitness to man's wants and nature, it was, as a lawyer would say, a plain case upon the face of the papers." And Dr. Johnson has said that no honest man could be a Deist, "after a fair examination of the proofs of Christianity."[3]

Among the matters that must be within the legitimate sphere of reason, and that must be well known and understood, are the plain, practical and luminous principles of government--those foundations upon which society itself is based. Men have been under government, in some form, from the earliest times, and must, therefore, be competent to understand the plain principles of that science, if there be any such in the system.

Proceeding upon these grounds, it has been my object to show the considerations, drawn from reason and experience that naturally led me to form some idea of the leading and most apparent features of that government actually instituted by Christ. For it was plain to my understanding, that while governments must differ from each other in those respects that constitute them different governments, they must agree in those fundamental respects that constitute government itself.

7. Governing power derived from Christ's teaching commission

In the last verses of Matthew's Gospel, before our Lord ascended into Heaven, and while he was with the eleven disciples in a mountain in Galilee, He said to them:

> All power is given unto me in Heaven and in earth. Go ye, therefore, and teach all nations, baptizing them in the name of the Father, and of the Son, and of the Holy Ghost; teaching them to observe all things whatsoever I have commanded you: and lo, I am with you always, even unto the end of the world.

The first part of this wide commission is, "Go – teach all Nations." This commission was first addressed to the eleven disciples, and constituted the office of teacher. They were to teach the nations to observe all things that Christ had commanded them to observe.

This right to teach is the most essential attribute bestowed upon the governing power in the Church. In the nature of mere civil government, as I have attempted to show in a previous chapter, the legislator could not rightfully require faith in the justice of his laws, for he would require a belief in what might be a falsehood. But in a government constituted by Christ, it is reasonable that faith should be required, as well as simple compliance in acts. Obedience will be more perfect when we believe in the unquestioned justice of a law; and Christ intended to create a closer union among the members of His church than exists among the citizens or subjects of a civil government,--faith was necessary for this purpose. If we obey a law because we are forced to do so, whether we think it just or unjust, we render but a reluctant and unwilling obedience. This is not the kind of obedience that an infinite lawgiver would require. He would rightfully require perfect obedience to a perfect law.

Faith, then, being required, the necessity of a power to teach becomes evident. This commission plainly distinguishes between two separate and distinct classes of men – teachers and persons taught; for while one class is commanded to "teach," the other class is commanded to "observe." In the reason and nature of things, there could not exist teachers without persons to be taught. The two classes must exist, or there could be no employment for either. The only command here given to the eleven was to "teach and baptize"--the nations were to "observe." The commission was addressed to them as teachers, constituting a separate and distinct class of men, to whom the power to teach and baptize was given; and it was only as teachers, and in the duties as such, that Christ promised to be "with them to the end of the world." Christ first tells them, "go teach," etc., and then in the same sentence immediately adds, "and lo, I am with you," only connecting His promised assistance with their teaching. He does not, *in this place,* promise to be with them in any other capacity, but *as teachers.* The words "Go teach," first constituted them teachers, and all that followed after those words was addressed to them only in that *capacity.*

In the tenth chapter of Saint Luke our Lord said to the seventy disciples,

> He that heareth you, heareth me; and he that despiseth you, despiseth me; and he that despiseth me, despiseth Him that sent me.

Now, although this is said to the seventy sent upon a *special* mission, it shows one thing, and establishes one important principle. It shows that they were first invested with authority by Christ, and when so invested, that they acted as His agents. Any insult to them, in their capacity *as His agents,* was an insult to Him, and to his Father who sent him.

8. Testimony of Saint Paul on the governing power of the Church

Saint Paul, in the tenth chapter of his Epistle to the Romans, says:

> How shall they call on him in whom they have not believed? and how shall they believe in him, of whom they have not heard? and how shall they hear without a preacher? and how shall they preach except they be sent?

Although this language is in the interrogative *form*, yet under a well-known rule of construction, there are four affirmative facts asserted in this extract. The apostle having stated in the preceding verse that "whosoever shall call upon the name of the Lord shall be saved," assumes the four positions so distinctly stated in the passage. It was clear that the preacher could not preach unless he was sent --that he could not send himself; and it is equally clear that the party to hear and believe was not the preacher sent. In other words, there were two classes --teachers and persons taught. Saint Paul does not here give us any statement as to the manner of sending preachers or as to who sends them. These matters are stated in other epistles.

The same apostle in his first epistle to the Corinthians, says:

> And God has appointed in the church first apostles, second prophets, third teachers. Are all apostles? Are all prophets? Are all teachers?[4]

This is explicit as to the fact that, in Saint Paul's time, a certain order of men had the right to teach, and that all had not. Saint Paul uses this clear and explicit language:

> Remember your leaders, those who spoke to you the word of God, consider the outcome of their life, and imitate their faith.
>
> Obey your leaders and submit to them; for they are keeping watch over your souls, as men who will have to give an account. Let them do this joyfully, and not sadly, for that would be of no advantage to you.[5]

It is difficult to conceive of language more explicit and more to the point than the foregoing extracts. The following points are distinctly stated:

1.That a certain order of men had the *rule* over the church.

2. That this order of men was those who "had spoken unto them the word of God."

3. That the Hebrews were commanded to *"follow the faith"* of them who "had the *rule* over them."

4. That they were commanded to obey those who "had the rule over them," for the reason that those rulers "watched for their souls, as they that must give an account."

Now it is evident that those who had the *rule* over the church were one class, and those who were commanded to *obey* were another and a distinct class. The rulers had the right to rule, as to matters of faith, for those commanded to obey were to *"follow the faith"* of those who had spoken to them the word of God. Now connect this with the commission "Go teach," and it is plain that teaching was one of the leading powers of government bestowed upon the apostles and their successors, *as teachers,* and that those who had the rule over the church had the right to teach authoritatively, in Christ's name, in matters of *faith*. And as those who have the rule over the church have the right to teach faith, there is a great responsibility resting upon them, because they "watch for the souls" of those over whom they have the rule, as *"they that must give an account."* It is a just principle, universally adopted, that where great powers are given great responsibility is imposed, and the officer is held to a strict account.

Saint Paul says to his Hebrew brethren, "Remember" --an expression always denoting great earnestness and calling particular attention to what follows. He first tells them to remember them who have the rule over them, and then tells them how they are to remember them, and that is by following *their* faith.

In the second extract he is equally emphatic. He first says, "obey them that have the rule over you," and as if this was not sufficiently strong and clear, he adds, "and *submit* yourselves" and then gives them the reasons why they should obey and submit.

Now the terms rule, obey, and submit, can mean nothing in this connection but government and obedience. The word *rule* here means government; and to govern is to "control the will and actions of others, either by arbitrary power and authority, or by established laws." The rule or government that those orders had over the Church was the power to control the will and actions by established laws. The word *obey* here means "to comply with the commands, orders, or instructions of a superior." To submit is "to be subject; to acquiesce in the authority of another."

THE GOVERNING POWER OF THE CHURCH

In the fourth chapter of the Epistle to the Ephesians we find this language:

> And he gave some, apostles; and some, prophets; and some evangelists; and some, pastors and teachers; for the perfecting of the saints, for the work of the ministry, for the edifying of the body of Christ; till we all come in the unity of the faith, and of the knowledge of the Son of God, unto a perfect man, unto the measure of the stature of the fullness of Christ. That we henceforth be no more children, tossed to and fro, and carried about by every wind of doctrine, by the sleight of men, and cunning craftiness, whereby they lie in wait to deceive. But speaking the truth in love, may grow up into him in all things, which is the head, even Christ: from whom the whole body, fitly joined together and compacted by that which every joint supplieth, according to the effectual working in the measure of every part, maketh increase of the body, unto the edifying of itself in love.

This is one of the most clear and distinct passages found in the writings of Saint Paul. It contains a great many particulars in the same long sentence, all closely and beautifully connected, and as consistent as that *unity* of the faith, and *knowledge* of the Son of God, of which he speaks.

Saint Paul speaks of a certain order of men, consisting of several grades -- apostles, prophets, evangelists, teachers, and pastors. All these are given for certain specific purposes, namely: "for the perfecting of the saints, for the work of the ministry, for the edifying of the body of Christ," *i. e.* the Church. The immediate end of this authoritative labor, this perfecting of the saints, this work of the ministry, this edifying of the Church, was, that the members of the Church might "all come in the unity of the faith and of the knowledge of the Son of God." In addition, this unity of faith and knowledge must be perfect, "unto the measure of the stature of the fullness of Christ." The legitimate result or effect of this unity in this perfect knowledge of the Son of God is, that "we henceforth be no more children, tossed to and fro, and carried about by every wind of doctrine." "But speaking the truth in love, we may grow up into him in all things, which is the head, even Christ;" so that every part of this body, the Church, might be "fitly joined together and compacted." Thus, being fitly joined and compacted, the "effectual working of every part" might make "increase of the body," thus answering the prayer of Christ for the unity of His followers, that the world might believe that the Father had sent Him.

In this epistle to the Ephesians, the apostle tells us that there was a certain order of men given for certain purposes, and in the Epistle to the Hebrews, he tells us to "follow the faith of those who have the rule over us," and these are they "who have spoken unto us the word of God." Now put these passages together, and do not these results follow?

1. That the "rule" of government of the church was given to a certain order of men.

2. That among the powers granted, was especially the power to "teach."

3. That this order of men taught *authoritatively,* for the Hebrews were expressly commanded to *obey and submit to them by following their faith.*

4. And by following implicitly the faith of this order of men, as they were commanded to do, we can most readily understand how the ancient Christians could come to the "unity of the faith." And that while they followed the faith of those who had the rule over them, they would be certainly guarded against being "tossed to and fro, and carried about by every wind of doctrine."

5. That the legitimate result of all this would be the perfect and harmonious action of the Church, which would "make increase" of its numbers, and edify "itself in love."

9. Testimony from Saint Paul's epistles to Timothy and Titus

The Epistles of Saint Paul to Timothy and Titus, were addressed to them in their capacity as teachers. The whole drift, spirit, and language of these Epistles show that Timothy and Titus had "the rule" over their respective churches.

To Timothy Saint Paul says:

> As I besought thee to abide still at Ephesus, when I went into Macedonia, that thou mightest charge some, that they teach no other doctrine.... This charge I commit unto thee, son Timothy.

Speaking of bishops, among other things he says:

> One that ruleth well his own house, having his children in subjection, with all gravity, (for if a man know not how to rule his own house, how shall he take care of the church of God?)

After mentioning many things, the apostle tells Timothy:

> These things [do thou] command and teach....
>
> Let the elders that rule well be counted worthy of double honor, especially they who labor in the word and doctrine....
>
> Let no man despise thy youth....
>
> Neglect not the gift that is in thee....
>
> These things give in charge, that they may be blameless....
>
> These things teach and exhort.

Speaking of certain false teachers, the apostle says to Timothy:

> From such withdraw thyself....
>
> O! Timothy, keep that which is committed to thy trust....
>
> Wherefore, I put thee in remembrance, that thou stir up the gift of God which is in thee, by the putting on of my hands....
>
> Hold fast the form of sound words, which hast heard of me, in faith and love, which is in Christ Jesus. That good thing which was committed unto thee, keep by the Holy Ghost, which dwelleth in us....
>
> And the things that thou hast heard of me among many witnesses, the same commit thou to faithful men, who shall be able to teach others also.

To his son Titus, the apostle says:

> For this cause left I thee in Crete, that thou shouldest set in order the things that are wanting, and ordain elders in every city, as I had appointed thee....
>
> These things [do you] speak, and exhort with all authority. Let no man despise thee....
>
> A man that is a heretic after the first and second admonition [do you] reject.[6]

Now these quotations show that Timothy and Titus, *as ministers,* had the right to "command and teach" "with all authority;" and in thus doing, they would but carry out the original commission given by Christ to His apostles. Saint Paul tells Timothy "to charge some that they teach no other doctrine." The term *charge* implies authority, and the apostle uses it in this sense when he says, "this charge I commit to thee...." He compares the ruling of a household to "taking care of the church." Now to know what is meant by the phrase "taking care of," we need only to refer to the seventeenth verse of the fifth chapter, where he says, "Let the elders that rule well be counted worthy of double honor, *especially* they that labor in the word and doctrine." So that "to take care of the church" means to rule the church; as is still further shown from the fact that "taking care of the church" is compared to ruling a family, where the father does speak with *authority.* "These things command and teach." The words "command" and "teach" imply nothing but authority. If Timothy had the right to command and teach, and it was made his express duty so to do, then it must have been the duty of some one to obey.

Speaking of certain proud and perverse teachers, the apostle tells Timothy, "From such withdraw thyself." Now it is plain that Timothy was to decide who these teachers were. The apostle gives him a description of such a class, in general terms, but leaves Timothy to decide the question whether a particular individual came within the definition. In other words, Paul, the inspired apostle, as such, laid down the law to Timothy, leaving Timothy to construe the law, and administer it in each particular case as it arose. "Let no man despise thy youth."

The apostle, after stating to Titus that "there are many vain talkers and deceivers," commands Titus to "rebuke them sharply, that they may be sound in *the faith.*" He further commands Titus: "These things speak, and exhort, and rebuke with all authority." Now here was the most explicit authority given Titus to "rebuke sharply," and then "*with all authority;*" and the object of these sharp and authoritative rebukes was, that those thus rebuked might "be sound in the faith." The authority of Titus did not stop here. He was not only to "rebuke, exhort, and speak with all authority," that those thus rebuked, exhorted, and taught might "become sound in the faith" but he was expressly commanded to "reject a heretic, after the first and second admonition."

These commands were given to Titus *as a minister*, having the rule over the church at Crete. *He* was first to decide who were the "vain talkers and deceivers;" *he was* then to "exhort and rebuke them sharply, and with all authority," that they might become "sound in the faith;" but if they persisted after the first and second admonition, *he* was to reject them as heretics. Titus was the judge, who was to decide whether certain opinions were heretical, and *he* was to reject the heretic. *He* had the authority to rule or govern. Paul says to him, "Let no man despise *thee*:" that is, in the discharge of thy duties. In other words, let no man despise thy authority. This is clear from the words going before, as well as from the fact that the whole Epistle is *addressed to Titus in his capacity of teacher*, and regards him in that capacity, and not as an individual; having no official authority.

Among the powers conferred upon Timothy and Titus were the following:

1. The power to command and teach, rebuke and exhort, with all authority.

2. To ordain elders.

3. To reject heretics.

And these powers were given them by the laying on of the hands of the apostle, and were to be exercised by them, and not by the members of the church at large. These powers were most full and ample. Putting all these passages together, as well as taking the general drift and spirit of the whole system, how readily we can see the *manner and the means* by which the members of the church were brought to "the unity of the faith."[7]

The process was most simple and beautiful, efficient and rational. Christ organized His followers into a visible Church, which is a united body of living men. In this church He instituted a certain order of men, to whom He delegated the governing power of the Church. According to the laws governing this institution, *faith was required of each member.* The power to "teach" faith "with authority" was therefore necessary, and was the principal power of government to be exercised by this order of men. They taught as the *agents* and *officers* of Christ, the founder of the institution. The members of the church were required to "follow the faith" of these teachers, and to obey them; and when a member refused to do this, he was "rejected as a heretic."

In this way "the unity of the faith" was kept pure in the church. As often as a member became infected with improper opinions, he was rebuked, exhorted, and admonished twice, and if he still persisted, he was rejected. This process was pursued towards others as often as occasion might require. It is obvious that there could be left *in the church* nothing but "the unity of the faith" spoken of by Saint Paul. There could be no process more simple and efficient than this. It accords with all the laws of reason, with human nature, and with the first and most essential principles whereon all governments of law must be based.

The power to expel for heresy is a necessary incident to the power to teach, given by Christ in the commission; and the power to expel for heresy necessarily includes the power to determine what heresy is, and what it is not. It is one of the plainest principles of law, that when power is given to the agent to do a certain thing, the *means* necessary to accomplish the end are inseparable incidents; otherwise, the grant of power would be idle. To say to the agent, "Do this," and yet give him no means wherewith to do it, would be wholly useless. *Titus* was commanded to admonish and to reject the heretic; and whatever may be the definition of heresy, it was a crime against the law of Christ, and must be *judged by that law*. If Titus was to reject the heretic, *he* must, of necessity, decide what was heresy, as defined by *the law* making it criminal. In other words, *he* must construe the law, and determine authoritatively the question arising under the law.

Now those who were commanded to admonish and reject heretics were those whose faith the early Christians were commanded to follow. From the Scriptures alone, the mode of teaching, the powers of the teachers, and the duties of the members taught, may be stated concisely thus:

1. The lay members of the church were to "*obey*," "*submit to*," and "follow the faith" of their teachers who had "the rule over them." This secured unity of faith between the teachers and the persons taught.

2. In case of any serious difference among the teachers themselves, as to any point of faith to be taught, a council was called, and the question therein settled, both by *argument*, and the aid of the *Holy Ghost*. This secured unity in the college of teachers.

3. The united effect of both these was unity in the entire body, the church.

10. The offices of government in the Apostolic Church

This was the process of governing the Church in the days of the apostles. There was a certain order of men that had the rule over the church. They taught, they ordained elders, they expelled heretics, and they, in a word, exercised all the powers necessary to govern the institution as it was then constituted. The acts of government that we know were then exercised by that order of men, were all that the nature of the institution required.

The question then arises whether this order of men had succession, and still exists in the church. There can be nothing more plain and palpable than this, that if Christ did organize any visible church, and institute any government for it, and, therefore, did create *offices* to be filled by men, and these offices were intended to continue so long as the church itself should last, either the first incumbents were to live while the church existed, or there must be a succession of officers. It follows also, that so long as the church remains unchanged, the successor must have the same powers as his predecessor. It is the office that gives power to the man, and not the man to the office.

Christ organized and perfected the Christian government and made the permanent Christian code of laws for its guidance. The system came from Christ and His apostles possessing certain characteristics or constituent principles. It would have been a strange anomaly, indeed, if Christ had created no offices for the government of His Church. It would have left the system exceedingly imperfect.

That He did create certain offices is shown from the extracts already given, and from the language of Saint Paul in his first Epistle to Timothy. There Saint Paul speaks of "the office of a bishop" and "the office of a deacon;" and the only question to determine is, whether those offices were intended to continue in the church while the church itself should last. If Christ did create certain offices in the church, and there is no limitation as to the duration of the office, either by the mere temporary nature of the duty to be performed, or by the express words of the law creating the office, then the intent would seem to be plain, that the existence of the office would be commensurate with the existence of the system itself.

The Constitution of the United States organized a government. It is not stated in the instrument how long the system was intended to continue; and yet it was intended to be perpetual, for the reason that *no limit is given.* When a corporation is created, and no limit put to its existence, it must be held to be perpetual; for while the law will presume the death of a *natural* person after the expiration of a certain period of time, it will not presume the death of an *artificial* being which may live on.

By the U.S. Constitution, the executive power is vested in a president, and the judicial power in one supreme court, and such inferior courts as Congress may establish. It is not stated in express terms that the office of president shall exist so long as the Constitution endures; yet this is the palpable intent, because the office is created as a part of the system, and must necessarily continue so long as the government itself shall last. If an office be created in the organization of the government, unless its duration be limited as before stated, the intent of the founder is plain, that the office must continue as a *part* of the system.

That our Lord did create certain offices, the duties of which were not temporary but perpetual, and not limited in their duration by express words, or by the acts of those who put the system into practical operation, there would seem to be no doubt. Knowledge cannot be inherited, but must be acquired, and each succeeding Generation must be taught as was the proceeding one. For this reason the duty of teaching is perpetual, because the system to be taught is so.

11. The power to teach was not personal to the apostles

That the commission constituted the authority of the apostles, and empowered and required them to teach all things whatsoever Christ had commanded them to observe, cannot be disputed. The only question is, whether the power thereby conferred was a power personal to them, and therefore temporary; or whether, this commission created the office of teacher, and the power given to the office itself. In the latter case the apostles were merely appointed the first officers and their powers continue down to their successors through all time.

If the commission only gives authority but to the apostles there could be no authority to teach after the deaths of those to whom it was first given. If, on the contrary, it was intended to create perpetual offices there must be a succession of officers having the *same powers* as their predecessors.

The command to teach, and the promise, "Lo, I am with you always, even unto the end of the world," are so closely connected together, that the existence of the one must be commensurate with the existence of the other. If Christ then commanded the apostles and their successors to teach, He equally promised to be with them "always, even unto the end of the world"; and He does not promise to be with them any longer than they have authority to teach. If this promise extends to the successors of the apostles, the command to teach does also.

The power to baptize is also given in this commission, and forms a portion of the mass of inseparable powers bestowed upon the apostles as teachers. The power to teach is first given, and then the power to baptize those taught, which is only carrying out the power to teach, and forming a part of it; and therefore, the power to teach and baptize must stand or fall together. If, therefore, the power to teach did not come down to the successors of the apostles, in virtue of the commission, the power to baptize did not. Thus, in so far as the commission is concerned, there is no power in the Church, since the days of the apostles, either to teach or baptize; and we must look to other portions of the Word of God for such authority, if it exist in the visible church at all.

12. Meaning of the phrase 'end of the world'

Then what is the true meaning of the phrase "end of the world," as it stands in the commission? Does it mean the term of a person's natural life? There is not a single instance in the New Testament, where this phrase has such a meaning. It was a very common expression with our Lord: and, whenever used by Him, has one invariable meaning.

The only passage that can be brought to give plausibility to the phrase meaning 'the term of a person's natural life,' is found in the twelfth chapter of Saint Matthew. There our Lord, speaking of the sin against the Holy Ghost, says: "It shall not be forgiven him, neither in this world, neither in the world to come." Now, might not the word *world* in this connection mean the period of a person's natural life, during which this sin shall not be forgiven? It cannot. The expression is general and the sentence is antithetic, having the same substantive *world* in both members of the sentence, and the word must have the same power in both. One is this world, and the other the world to come. They both signify opposite states. The world to come cannot signify the term or duration of a natural life, but clearly signifies a future order or state of things. And therefore, "this world" must signify the present or existing order.

The provision of the law is general, while one case is put for all. In the contemplation of Christ, there are but two states, this world and the world to come; and He meant to lay down the general principle, that the sin against the Holy Ghost would not be forgiven in either state. The practice of putting one case for all, and of using the masculine for both the masculine and feminine genders, was very common with our Lord, as it is with all lawmakers. "He that believeth and is baptized." &c. "Except a man be born of water..."

In every instance in the New Testament in which this phrase occurs, it means the end of the present state. In this sense it occurs in the thirteenth of Matthew: "The harvest is the *end of the world.*" "So shall it be at the end of this world." This phrase has the same meaning, where the disciples ask Christ what shall be the sign of *His* coming, and of the "end of the world." If, then, Christ promised to be with the eleven to the end of the existing state of things, one of two things must be true: either that the apostles were to live to the end of the world, or the promise extends to their successors, and was so intended.

13. Protestant theories interpreting Christ's commission

Mr. Rice, in his debate with Mr. Campbell, says: "We know that the apostles were authorized and commanded to baptize and teach. But this is not all; *the promise extends to the end of time.*" This extract clearly supports the view I have taken.

Mr. Campbell says:

> For by every role of interpretation, I must apply every work of the commission to the apostles; because it is addressed to them only.

He then quotes the commission, concluding it with, "and lo, I am *with you always*, even to the conclusion of this state, or to the end of the age or world."[8]

Now I understand Mr. Campbell to have meant by the phrase "conclusion of *this state*" the end of the present state of existence or being. In other words, the end of time.

Understanding him in this sense I could never put these two positions together. Christ knew that His apostles would not live beyond the period of human life; and, in the contemplation of this theory, the command and promise contained in the commission were *personal* to the apostles, and both expired with them, and our Lord is made therefore to promise His infallible aid beyond the period when it would be needed. I could never understand why our Lord should make an idle and gratuitous promise of assistance, when He only intended to afford it for a very small portion of the time fixed by the promise itself. The promise itself extends to the end of time, and yet the performance of it is limited to the days of the apostles. How then could our Lord redeem His promise to be with the apostles after they were dead?

The promise was to infallibly assist them in the duty of teaching. The work to be done was to be accomplished in *this* world, and the promised aid was to be given *here*. He did not permit them to live to the limit fixed for the promised aid, and how did He keep His word according to this theory?

The different Protestant theories concerning the commission lead to irreconcilable contradictions.

1. The theory of Mr. Campbell, *if I understand him correctly,* makes Christ forfeit His word for the mere purpose of doing an idle and vain thing.

2. Those who insist that the phrase "end of the world" does not mean the end of this state, are forced to reject the sense in which Christ had always used it, and to give to it a new and unheard of meaning, exceedingly unnatural and awkward.

3. Those who concede that the promise extends to the end of the existing state of things, and that Christ does keep His promise, are compelled to admit, either that the aid of Christ fails to accomplish the end intended by Him, or that there is now an infallible *teaching* authority in the church.

The Catholic theory, that Christ first constituted a college of teachers, and then addressed His command and promise to them in that capacity, is the only one compatible with the character of Christ as a Divine Lawgiver; and the only one commensurate with the scope and intent of such a system.

But conceding that I have misunderstood Mr. Campbell, and that he only intended to maintain that Christ promised His assistance during the lives of the apostles, the difficulties of this theory are almost as great as those of the other.

The only things that Christ commanded the apostles to do, (*in this commission,*) was to teach and baptize. The system established by Him was permanent, and, therefore, required permanent teaching. The duty of teaching was continuing. Each separate individual, in all coming time, had to be taught. Nothing of faith or knowledge could be inherited. It is, then, most singular, that the *first* teachers, instructed *personally* by our Lord Himself, should still require this infallible assistance, while *future* teachers, teaching the *same* system, could do without it. The duty to be performed was the same; and yet assistance is given in one case, and refused in the other. The teachers after the apostolic day could not learn their duty more fully than the apostles did under the instructions of Christ. This infallible assistance, in the very nature of the system, was needed, and, therefore, promised, at all periods from the beginning to the end of the institution.

But besides this, the words, "I am with you" occur very often in both Testaments; and in no case (so far as I am advised,) where the promise was *personal*, were the words added, "always, even to the end of the world." And the reason why they are not added in cases where the promise was confined to the individual to whom it was made, would seem to be obvious.

If we take the theory to be true, for the sake of the argument only, that the promise was personal to the apostles, then, all that Christ need have said was, "Lo, I am with you." The command and promise *always* being commensurate with each other, this would have expressed all the sense contended for by Mr. Campbell, and those who think with him.

But is it not unaccountable that our Lord should add words not required to express His meaning, but also use them in a sense wholly contrary to the sense in which He Himself had always used them *before*? It would seem that the very reason why our Lord added to the promise, "I am with you" the words "always, even to the end of the world," was to qualify the promise itself by showing that it was not personal but continuing. Unquestionably, the duty of teaching was not personal to the apostles. They were simply the *first*, but not the *only*, teachers. The command and promise must exist or expire together. They are inseparable.

14. The correct interpretation of Christ's commission

It may be contended that the use of the pronoun "you" restrict both the commission and the promise to the apostles, to whom our Savior addressed Himself orally. However, this construction would be in direct conflict with the promise, if I have given the correct definition of the phrase "end of the world."

It must be evident to the most casual reader of the New Testament, that the larger portion of the instructions given by Christ were given in terms *personally* addressed to the apostles. We read in the first chapter of Acts, that Christ was "seen of the apostles forty days, and speaking of the things pertaining to the kingdom of God." Now these instructions were given to them personally, so far as we can judge from what is said. The instructions given by Christ, as recorded in Saint John's Gospel, from the thirteenth to the seventeenth chapters inclusive, were given in terms personal to the apostles. “A new commandment I give unto you, that you love one another.” At the last supper, our Lord, addressing the apostles in terms personal to them, said, “Do this in remembrance of me.” The pronoun *you* is here used in all these cases, and in many others, when Christ was addressing His chosen apostles alone, no one being present but them; and are these commands applicable to the successors of the apostles, or not? Were succeeding Christians required to love one another? Were they required to “do this in remembrance” of Christ? If so, why are not those who come after the apostles required to “go teach,” as well as they? Why confine the meaning in one case, and not in the others? Was there no need of teachers after the apostles?

The fact that the larger portion of the instructions given by our Savior was given in terms personal to the apostles is evident; and the fact that these instructions are applicable to us, unless they are limited, either by express words or by the nature of the command itself, is equally clear. Thus, for instance, the command given to the eleven to tarry in Jerusalem until the descent of the Holy Spirit, does not apply to us, for the command was but temporary, and could not extend beyond the event mentioned as its limitations. It was not a general *continuing* command, but local and temporary. It could not be fulfilled again and expired by its own limited character.

The reason and truth of this rule will be apparent, I apprehend, upon a little reflection. Christ selected twelve apostles to be with Him during His ministry. They saw all His miracles -- heard all His discourses, which were mostly given in terms personal to them, and received His last instructions, and saw Him ascend into heaven. The last thing He said to them was, "Go teach... teaching them to observe all things whatsoever I have commanded you." He had instructed them personally for more than three years, and now he commands them to teach others to observe that which He had previously commanded *them* to observe.

This commission applied the teachings of Christ, given in terms personal to the apostles, also to their successors. They were commanded to "tarry in Jerusalem until they were endowed with power from on high." When so endowed, they were to commence teaching. The date, therefore, when the commission was to take effect, was the day of Pentecost. Whatsoever Christ had, previous to that day, commanded them to do, they were to teach others to observe. Now, on that day, one of the things Christ had previously commanded the eleven to do, was to "teach all things whatsoever he had commanded them;" and this made it their duty to teach others to teach what they had been themselves commanded to teach. In other words, the phrase "all things whatsoever I have commanded you," would embrace all commands given before the time when this command was to be put in force, and would include in the words " all things whatsoever" the command "Go teach."

The phrase "all things whatsoever" is exceedingly general and would include all commands. But according to the fifth rule of construction I have given, a general rule may be limited by a special clause. And it is upon this ground that I lay it down as a principle of construction, that all commands given by Christ in personal terms to the apostles, descend to, and are obligatory upon us, unless they are limited by express words, or by the temporary nature of the command itself. Unless the general clause "all things whatsoever" be limited by some other clause, or by the nature of the command itself, its meaning remains unrestricted; and "all things whatsoever" Christ commanded His apostles observe or do, are obligatory upon Christians in all ages. The limitations upon the general clause will not restrict it only in so far as may be required by these exceptions of limitations, leaving the remainder of the clause to have full effect.

But these commands are only obligatory upon future Christians in the proper *capacity*; namely: If Christ commanded the eleven, in their *capacity as teachers*, to teach, then the same duty would devolve upon their successors in the office of *teacher*, and upon them *only.* If He commanded them, as individuals, to love one another, then this command would be obligatory upon *all* Christians, in all ages. If He commanded them, as individuals, to eat the Lord's Supper, and as ministers, to administer it to others, then their successors in these two different capacities must obey the command, "Do this in remembrance of me."

Whenever associated men are divided, as they must be, into different orders, and the distinctions of those different classes, first separately and specifically pointed out, then any general direction must, by every rule of construction, be applied to each in his proper position. As a lawgiver, our Lord would consistently begin with the first and simplest elements of His system. And as all Christians, both lay and clerical, are still individual members of the Church, and bound, as such, to discharge all the duties of that capacity, our Lord would first teach His apostles their duties as simple Christians, and afterwards their duties as officers. And He would logically give them the commission in the close of His ministry, and in terms sufficiently general to include all that had been embodied in His permanent code.

It is a rule that instructions from a superior to an inferior, acting in a certain capacity, are necessarily confined to him in that capacity, unless there be some express statement to the contrary.[9] And so it is with persons filling official positions. One man may fill several offices, where the duties are not incompatible with each other, and the same superior officer may supervise the inferior in all these different capacities; and, in giving him instructions, would address him at the beginning in the capacity for which the instructions are intended. So it is in the commission. Christ addressed the eleven in their capacity as teachers. He first constitutes them such, and then the instructions and promise are applied to them that capacity only.

There is another sufficient reason why the use of the pronoun “you” in the commission, could not restrict the command and promise to the eleven apostles. Let us assume, for the sake of the argument only, that our Lord, in the commission, created, for the first time, a body or college of teachers, having perpetual succession; and that He addressed them in their collective capacity as teachers. Then, it is clear that the use of the personal pronoun would have been proper in that case. We find such to be the usage of Scripture, as well as at law, and in common practice.

In the first Epistle to the Corinthians Saint Paul, speaking of those Christians who are to be living at the end of the world, says: "and we shall be changed."[10] He says the same thing, in substance, in the fourth chapter to the Thessalonians. The pronoun “we” is here applied to those Christians who shall live many ages after the writer, although the pronoun is in the first person. But all Christians, in all ages, in the contemplation of the theory of Saint Paul, constituted but one collective body or corporation, always existing, and always present, from the beginning to the end of the Christian era, and the use of the pronoun personal was strictly proper. So, when he says, “till we all come in the unity of the faith," he includes all the Christians of the future as well as of the then present time.

In the same way, and for the same reason, Christ constituted a perpetual college of teachers. In the contemplation of His theory, this college was then present, and would continue to be to the end of time, and the use of the pronoun was strictly proper, and His promised assistance to the end of the world was in just accordance with it. When instructions are given to the proper organs of an artificial being, they are given to the being itself, *through its organs*, and are applicable at all times, unless expressly limited in words, or by their temporary character.[11]

It would then seem plain, that if Christ intended to limit the commission to the apostles, He would appropriately use the pronoun "you;" and that, on the contrary, if He constituted them a college of teachers, having perpetual succession, he could have used the same pronoun with the same propriety; so that the use of this pronoun is entirely compatible with either view. But it is not so with the phrase "end of the world," which could not be used in the sense required to limit the promise to the apostles themselves for the reasons already given.

15. The apostles by their appointments show succession was intended

There is another mode of deciding the question, whether this commission extends to the successors of the apostles or not. When we see how the apostles put the system into practical operation, we may be able to arrive at a correct conclusion.

If Christ intended by this commission to create a certain *office*, having attached to it certain powers and duties, and this office was to continue while the church should exist, the question of succession is very simple and plain.

What powers did Christ bestow upon the apostles by the commission? What powers did He give to them in their capacity, as teachers? The power to "teach all things whatsoever I have commanded you," and the power to baptize. Now what incidents does the power to teach necessarily include?

1. The right to decide what construction they would give the law – in other words, what the law required, as of faith, and practice.

2. The duty of those taught to obey. “He that believeth not shall be dammed.”

3. The right to reject heretics.

These powers are inseparable from the power to teach. There would seem to be no question on that point. Now if we find that those who succeeded the apostles –those whom the apostles appointed to govern the church --exercised the same powers necessarily included in this commission, is it not clear, that this commission was intended to extend to the successors of the apostles?

What result could possibly be more plain and palpable than this? It ought to be remembered that the power belongs to the office, and not to the man, that the man must die, the office not–that all officers, as such, act only from mere delegated authority, and not of themselves – they are but agents and agency ceases with death.

Now what powers did those exercise, who succeeded the apostles in the government of the church?

We hear Saint Paul say to the Hebrews:

> Remember them which have the rule over you, who have spoken unto you the word of God: whose faith follow, considering the end of their conversation....
>
> Be not carried about with divers and strange doctrines....
>
> Obey them that have the rule over you and submit yourselves; for they watch for your souls, as they that must give account.[12]

From these passages it is plain that there were certain persons who had the rule or government over the Hebrews. It is plain that these persons were they that had spoken unto them the word of God –that is, those persons, who had obeyed the command "Go teach" –and whose faith the Hebrews were commanded to "follow" that they might not be "led away by diverse and strange teachings." Again the Hebrews are told to "Obey your leaders and submit to them."

Those persons that had the rule over the Hebrews, certainly did exercise all the powers given in the commission. They had the right to teach, and when they taught, the Hebrews were commanded to follow *their faith*; and if they did not follow the faith of those teachers, these rulers must have had the necessary power to reject. For if they had not power to enforce their teachings upon the *members* taught, they could have had no rule over the Hebrews at all.

When Christ commanded the apostles to "Go, teach," He added, "he that believeth..." and "he that believeth not..." The persons taught were required to believe their teachers. So, when Saint Paul tells the Hebrews to "obey them that have the rule over you and submit yourselves," he also tells them to "follow *their* faith." How very similar is the command in the commission to "believe" and in the Epistle to "follow the faith." The hearers in both cases are substantially commanded to do the same thing. Now were not those who were to be believed in each case, invested with the *same* authority to teach that which was equally required to be believed by the persons taught? It would certainly seem so.

The apostle, in these extracts, certainly speaks of others besides the apostles, to whom the commission was first given. The language is too general to admit of any other construction; nor can we suppose the apostle would find it necessary to command the Hebrews to obey the other apostles.

The epistles of Saint Paul to his two sons in the faith, Timothy and Titus are still more explicit. The passages have been already quoted.

The apostle, after stating that he had left Timothy at Ephesus to "charge some that they teach no other doctrine." Compares the rule of a bishop over the church to the rule of a parent over "his house, having his children in subjection;" and, after mentioning many things as true, he says to Timothy: "These things [do you] command and teach." Is not this as strong language as that used in the commission "Go teach"? Christ had first taught His disciples certain truths, as Saint Paul had taught Timothy; and then both gave command to teach to others the *same* things taught to them, and the things taught in both cases were the same. And in his capacity, as a teacher, Timothy was not only to teach the things mentioned in the verses preceding the one containing this command, but he was to teach the entire system of Christianity. This is shown by the general drift of the two Epistles to him, but especially by the fourteenth and succeeding verses of the third chapter of the second Epistle. There the apostle speaks of the truths taught orally, and those found in Scripture; so that Timothy, as a teacher, carried out the command "Go teach," as well as the command of Saint Paul, "these things command and teach."

The apostle, after stating "there are many unruly and vain talkers and deceivers," commands Titus to "rebuke them sharply, that they may be sound in the faith."[13] He further commands Titus: "These things speak and exhort, and rebuke with all authority. Let no man despise thee."[14] "A man that is heretic, after the first and second admonition [do you] reject." Here was the most explicit authority given to Titus to do certain things in the church, and with *all authority*. The persons mentioned as unruly and vain talkers and *deceivers*, were heretics, because not "*sound in the faith*;" and as to *these* Titus was first to rebuke and exhort with all authority, and if these rebukes did not have the proper effect, he was to reject the heretic. Unless he had the power to reject or expel the heretic—the vain talker and deceiver—from the church, the right to rebuke would have been wholly idle, because the evil would have still remained *in the Church*, without any efficient remedy.

These directions were given to Titus as a minister. He himself was first to determine who were the "unruly and vain talkers and deceivers;" *he* was then to "exhort and rebuke them sharply;" but if they persisted, *he* was to reject them as heretics. Titus was to decide the question whether certain opinions were heretical. This being *his* right, it was the corresponding *duty* of the persons rebuked and admonished, to obey him who had the rule over them, and to submit themselves.

Compare the powers exercised by Timothy and Titus with those given in the commission, and are they not the same? Were not they but carrying out the commission? From whom did they receive their powers, and by what means? God, the Father, constitutes the original fountain from which this stream of authority flows. Christ says to His apostles: "As the Father hath sent me, so send I you." "He that receiveth whomsoever I sent, receiveth me, and he that receiveth me receiveth Him that sent me." Saint Paul received his authority from Christ, and Timothy and Titus received their authority from Saint Paul.

After giving Timothy a description of the qualifications of certain officers in his first Epistle, Saint Paul, in the second goes on to say:

> Wherefore I put thee in remembrance, that thou stir up the *gift* of God, which is in thee by the putting on of my hands....
>
> That *good thing* which was committed unto thee, keep by the Holy Ghost, which dwelleth in us....
>
> And the things that thou hast heard of me among many witnesses, *the same* commit thou to faithful men, who shall be able to teach others also.[15]

To Titus the apostle says:

> For this cause left I thee in Crete, that thou shouldest set in order the things that are wanting, and ordain elders in every city, as I had appointed thee.[16]

The apostle also speaks of "a bishop" as the "*steward* of God... holding fast the faithful word as he hath been taught, that he may be able by sound doctrine both to exhort and convince the gainsayers."

The "gift" mentioned in the first passage is the "good thing" stated in the second. And the "good thing committed" to Timothy is the *same* which Timothy is commanded to "commit to faithful men, who shall be able to teach others also." These things committed by Saint Paul to Timothy, and directed by him to be committed by Timothy to others, were the power to teach, and the things to be taught, contemplated in the commission. For we find that Timothy was only to commit the *same* things he had heard of Paul to "faithful men who shall be able to teach others also" and that Titus was commanded to "ordain elders in every city." It appears also that bishops were "as the stewards of God," whose duty it was to teach others what they had themselves been taught.

If we keep constantly in view the powers exercised by Timothy and Titus, we can most readily understand how the power passed down from the one to the other by *succession.* They had received them by the ordination of Saint Paul. They were directed, the one to "commit to faithful men," and the other to "ordain elders," (which means the same thing.) The same things that Timothy had heard of Saint Paul, he, in turn, was to commit to "faithful men," who were also to teach the "*same things.*"

Could the commission, "Go teach all nations," be more beautifully and faithfully carried out? Here was a perfect system, and perfect order. Here we have four links in the chain of succession, and as all the links in the same perfect chain must possess the same power, it is all that can be required. From God to Christ, from Christ to Saint Paul, from Saint Paul to Timothy and Titus, and from them to others to whom they were to commit the same things. As, in every treatise upon arithmetic, we have the rule first given in words, and then a few examples of the application of the rule in practice, and we are then left to apply the principle to other questions, so it is here. Christ gives the general principle in the commission. A few examples in practice are given in the cases of Timothy and Titus, and those they were commanded to ordain, and we are then left to apply the general principle to other cases.

16. The shepherd metaphor shows the bishops were successors

In the tenth chapter of Saint John's Gospel, our Lord spoke the parable of the Sheepfold, in which the door and the shepherd represent Himself, and the sheep His followers. In speaking of the relation that the elders bore to the churches over which they respectively had the rule, the apostles Paul and Peter apply the comparison of an under-shepherd over the flock. Thus Saint Paul, addressing the elders of the church at Ephesus, in their capacity as such, said to them:

THE GOVERNING POWER OF THE CHURCH

> Take heed therefore unto yourselves, and to all the flock over which the Holy Ghost hath made you overseers, to feed the church of God...[17]

The apostle also speaks of wolves not sparing the flock. The word *overseer* is defined to be "a supervisor—superintendent;" and superintending is defined as "care and oversight for the purpose of direction, and with authority to direct."[18] A mere spectator or looker-on is not an overseer, nor is a mere equal, who inculcates his views by argument alone.[19]

In this extract the Church is called the flock, and the elders are commanded to feed the church. Although these elders are here called overseers, those they superintended were called "the flock;" and the duties these elders were to perform were compared to the feeding of a flock.

In the fifth chapter of the first Epistle of Saint Peter, he exhorts the elders to "feed the flock of God which is among you, taking the oversight thereof... and when the chief shepherd shall appear, ye shall receive a crown of glory that fadeth not away."

In this extract from Saint Peter, the same idea is conveyed, but more explicitly. Christ is here called the "chief shepherd," and the church "the flock of God;" and the relation that the elders bore to the flock and to Christ, was that of under-shepherds.

Now what relation exists between the shepherd and the flock, as shown in the parable? The shepherd was to call His sheep, to find the, or lead them out to pasture; to protect them from wolves, and to lay down His life for the sheep; and the sheep were to know the shepherd, to hear His voice, and to "follow Him." An under-shepherd is simply a shepherd subject to the "chief shepherd," acting for Him , and discharging the same duties, but in a *subordinate* capacity; and as the under-shepherd, is only exercising authority delegated by the Chief shepherd, and does not act in his own right, the sheep are to "hear his voice," and also to "follow him," for "he that heareth you heareth me," says Christ.

Now, if these elders of the ancient church, as well as the apostles, bore the relation of under-shepherds to Christ and the flock, then it would seem clear that they equally derived their authority from Him; and that, therefore, the laity were bound to know them, to hear their voice, and to follow them. Hence we hear Christ say: "Hear the church," which, being a corporation, can only speak through its proper organs—

these under-shepherds. So also, we hear Saint Paul say not to aliens but to *his brethren*, "know," "obey," "submit to," and "follow the faith" of "them who have the rule over you, who have spoken unto you the word of God," "who are over you in the Lord, and admonish you." Christ says in substance: "My sheep know me, hear my voice, and follow me;" and Saint Paul says to his brethren in substance: "Know your under-shepherds, obey them, and follow their faith." How similar is the language in the two cases, showing that there is the same train of authority and relationship running through both.

It is true, that the under-shepherds do not possess *all* the power and authority of Christ. He was the *door*, as well as the *shepherd*. He exercised the legislative power, and only left to them that power which still remains to be exercised, so long as the flock remains to be fed.

17. Scriptures that appear to conflict with the governing powers

I will now proceed to examine certain texts which may at first seem to conflict with the view taken in the preceding sections.

> 1. "Submitting yourselves one to another in the fear of God."[20]
>
> 2. "The elders which are among you I exhort .... Feed the flock of God, which is among you, taking the oversight thereof, not by constraint, but willingly; not for filthy lucre, but of a ready mind; neither as being lords over God's heritage, but being ensamples to the flock."
>
> 3. "Likewise, ye younger, submit yourselves unto the elder. Yes all of you be subject to one another, and be clothed with humility."[21]
>
> 4. "Who art thou that judgest another man's servant? to his own master he standeth or falleth."[22]

In reference to the first and third extracts I will remark that, in the places where these passages occur, the *manner* in which we are required to submit to each other, is not fully pointed out. Therefore we must look to other portions of the Scripture to see whether the manner in which these general clauses are to be put into practical effect, is specially stated.

Keeping in our view the first, fourth, and fifth rules of construction, I think it will be easy to find the true meaning of the apostles. Both the apostles tell wives to submit to their husbands, servants to their master, and Paul tells children to obey their parents, and his lay brethren to obey, submit to, and follow the faith of those who had the rule over them. Paul also tells his brethren who are strong, to indulge the weak brethren in reference to meats, and keeping certain days which were matters indifferent.

Now did these apostles or either of them, mean to say that husbands, masters, parents, and those who had the rule over the Church, were, in their *turn*, to submit to their wives, servants, children, and "the flock"? And that this submission should be in reference to the *same* matters regarding which those wives, servants, children, and lay brethren were themselves *specially* charged to submit to, and obey, others respectively? Did Paul mean to say, husbands submit to your wives, and wives to your husbands? Did he mean to say to his Hebrew brethren, obey and follow the faith of them that have the rule over you and submit yourselves, and they, *in turn*, shall obey you and follow your faith, and you, in that same respect, shall the rule over your rulers? In other words, were the higher official orders required to submit to the lower, and in those very respects which constituted the difference in the orders themselves? If A be required to follow the faith of B, and B to follow the faith of A, then, in so far as they differ, it would be a mere exchange of faith. This could not have been the meaning of the apostles.

These extracts are what are properly termed general clauses, and are subject to being limited and applied by more specific and special provisions. When therefore Paul tells wives to submit to their husbands, children to their parents, servants to their masters, the strong to the weak brother, and the lay members to those who have the rule over them, these specific and special directions, by every rule of construction, must have their full force and application. They but point out in detail, and with more minute accuracy, how, and in what manner, and in reference to what matters, we are to submit to one another. In this way we can give force and effect to all the texts without any conflict. If, on the contrary, we say that a superior order in the church was as much required to obey as an inferior, then we annihilate all rule over the church whatever. The specific and special commands of Saint Paul to obey, submit to, and follow the faith of those who had the rule over the church, would be entirely abrogated, by these merely *general* clauses.

The second extract was addressed by Saint Peter to the elders as such, and points out, not only *what* they were to do, but also the *manner* of doing it. They were to "feed the flock, taking the oversight thereof," and this they were to do, "not by constraint, but willingly; not for filthy lucre, but of a ready mind; neither as being lords over God's heritage, but being examples to the flock."

They were first told to feed the flock, and take the oversight of it, which was clearly the exercise of authority; and does then the phrase "neither as being lords over God's heritage" take away this authority? Was this part of the passage aimed at the existence of the authority of the elders, or was it intended to apply simply to the manner in which is should be exercised? Clearly to the manner of its exercise; for the apostle tells these elders to take the oversight, willingly, with a ready mind, and not by constraint, nor for filthy lucre, nor *as* being *lords* over God's heritage, but as examples to the flock. They were not to act as lords over the heritage. Who is the *lord* over a heritage? The owner of it is lord. "The lord of that servant." "The lord of the vineyard." The elders were not to exercise their authority, which was but *delegated*, as if they were the lords or owners of the heritage; but they were to exercise their powers, not as of their own right, but as the "stewards of God," as Saint Paul has it, and as under-shepherds, as Saint Peter has it.

The fourth extract is taken from Saint Paul's Epistle to the Romans. The apostle first tells his Roman brethren to:

> receive him that is weak, but not to doubtful disputations. For one believeth that he may eat all things; another, who is weak, eateth herbs. Let not him that eateth despise him that eateth not; and let not him which eateth not judge him that eatheth; for God hath received him.

Then follows the extract given; and in the fifth verse the apostle continues: "One man esteemth one day above another; another esteemeth every day alike. Let every man be fully persuaded in his own mind."

Now, it is clear that the passage quoted is confined to the matters spoken of in the preceding two verses, and the verse that follows. For in the second verse of the chapter, the apostle expressly commands those who eat and those who eat not, neither to despise nor judge one another for eating or not eating. And he gives as a reason why they should not judge one another, that these things were not evil in themselves, but were only evil to those who thought them so.[23] So, in like manner, in reference to keeping certain days, he says, "Let every man be fully persuaded in his own mind." The act itself being indifferent, and the sin, if any, consisting only in the belief of the party that it was wrong at the moment of its commission. The rulers were very properly restrained from judging a member in reference to such matters.

But in reference to acts that were wicked in themselves, or in regard to matters of faith, did the apostle mean to say that members should not be judged? If they were fully persuaded in their own minds it was right to walk disorderly, or be guilty of heresy, that therefore they could be guilty of these offences, and yet be as innocent as if they eat meat or not? Did the apostle mean to say that Timothy ought not to receive and try an accusation against an elder, or that Titus ought not to reject a heretic, if in these cases the accused would only say he thought he was in the right? And even if Timothy and Titus had possessed the power to look into the secret hearts of men, and had been satisfied that the accused was sincere, were they not bound to reject the member, unless he repented in the one case and recanted in the other?

Was mere *sincerity* ever held as a good excuse for the willful violation of a positive law commanding this and prohibiting that? And especially a positive rule requiring faith as well as works? Because, in reference to certain matters expressly stated to be *indifferent,* members are not to be judged, does it follow, that in other matters expressly stated to be *material*, they are also not to be tried? On the contrary, does it not legitimately follow, that because in matters indifferent they were not to be judged, that in matters material they should be judged? The manifest difference in the two cases leads to a manifest difference in the treatment of each. "In matters essential, let there be unity—in matters non-essential, liberty—and in all things, charity," is one of the most noble, rational, and Scriptural sentiments ever uttered.

18. Objections from Saint Paul's epistle to the Corinthians

Saint Paul, in the first chapter of his first Epistle to the Corinthians, says:

> Now I beseech you, brethren, by the name of our Lord Jesus Christ, that you all speak the same thing, and that there be no divisions among you, but that ye be perfectly joined together in the same mind, and in the same judgment.

From this direction being given to the members of the church at Corinth generally, and especially, in this case, to the lay members, does it not follow that the persons addressed were to arrive at such unity of faith from their own individual researches exclusively —and not from any obedience to the elders of the church? It does not.

The apostle would not have given this command to those brethren if there had existed no means, by the fair and just use of which they could have arrived at this unity of faith. The apostle states to his brethren what they are to arrive at. But he does not, in *that* place, point out the means or the manner, except as to those special instances mentioned in the next verses.

If this passage stood alone in the New Testament with no other text to point out the manner and the means by which they were to arrive at this unity of faith, we would therefore, be left to infer them ourselves. Then perhaps we would be justified in concluding that, since the command was given directly to them, they could arrive at the truth without following the faith of those that had the rule over them. However, this text must be construed with reference to other texts relating to the same subject –and unity of faith. Such construction must be given with a harmonious force to all. When Saint Paul tells his brethren to "speak the same thing," he does not mean to contradict other portions of this same epistle, nor his other epistles to other churches. He intended to be consistent with himself.

After laying down the general principle that they must come to the unity of the faith, the apostle, as one of their teachers, goes on to point out, not in general terms, but in very precise language, certain particular errors, which he condemns in express words. But the general principle he had laid down related to and embraced the necessity of unity, not only in reference to the questions specially mentioned, but to all other material questions. In reference, then to other questions that might come under the general principle, the apostle did not say to his brethren, in that place, you must arrive at the unity of faith by this means or that means, or in this manner or in that manner. He leaves the means and the manner to be stated elsewhere. Consequently, in the very same epistle, we find him saying to these same brethren, in the same conciliatory language:

> I beseech you, brethren, (ye know the house of Stephanas, that it is the first fruits of Achaia, and that they had addicted themselves to the ministry of the saints,) that ye submit yourselves unto such, and to every one that helpeth with us, and laboreth.

Now it is plain that Stephanas, and "*everyone* that helped and labored with "Saint Paul in the "*ministry*," had the rule over these brethren in *some* respects. That they were bound to "submit themselves to such" in the same way they submitted themselves to Saint Paul, in his capacity as teacher; not only because they are expressly so commanded, but because these men helped and labored with Saint Paul in the same ministry.

Now in reference to the unity of the faith, were these brethren not bound to submit to Stephanas and the others that labored with Saint Paul? Does not that command to submit to these men embrace all the preceding matters mentioned in this epistle? It would seem so. But supposing this not sufficiently clear from this epistle, whatever we find in Saint Paul's other epistles, or in any other part of the Scripture, relating to the same subject, must be taken and construed with these texts. We must suppose that whatever part of the system had been included in other epistles had also been intended for these brethren, and that they had been well instructed.

Saint Paul then tells these brethren, in substance, that they must arrive at the unity of the faith. Of course, some adequate means existed by which they could do this. What were these means? The same apostle very explicitly answers that question. He says that some apostles, some prophets, some evangelists, and some pastors and teachers, were given "for the perfecting of the saints, for the work of the ministry, for the edifying the body of Christ, till we all come in the unity of the faith and of the knowledge of the Son of God."

Now the ultimate *end* to be attained by the labors of these different orders, was the arrival of Christians "in the unity of the faith and of the knowledge of the Son of God;" the very same end that Saint Paul commanded his brethren at Corinth to attain. And he here tells his Ephesian brethren that it was for *this* purpose Christ gave these different orders. These were the *means* given to attain the end. As to the *manner* in which the brethren were to use these means, the same apostle is not less explicit. He says to his Thessalonian brethren, "Know them that labor among you, and are over you in the Lord, and who admonish you." To his Hebrew brethren he says, "Remember them and submit yourselves;" and to Timothy and Titus, "Command, teach, rebuke, and exhort with all authority and doctrine, withdraw from perverse teachers, try elders, expel heretics," and perform other duties of teachers.

Now put these together, and are not the *means*, and also the *manner* in which they are to be used, for coming to "the unity of the faith," the same mind and judgment" most distinctly stated? If the Corinthian brethren obeyed them that had the rule over them, and implicitly followed their faith, they would certainly speak the same thing, and be of the same mind and judgment; and in this way most explicitly obey the command of Saint Paul. But if, instead of doing this, they had followed their own faith, they would clearly have violated very plain and repeated commands; and not only so, but it is exceedingly difficult to see how they could, in this illogical way, have ever come to the same conclusion.

19. The position of Mr. Breckenridge examined

In reference to the ministerial authority of the Reformers, Bishop Hughes, in his controversy with Mr. Breckenridge, asked this question: "Had the Reformers themselves, and if not, could they transmit to their successors any *ministerial authority*?"

To which Mr. Breckenridge replied: "that whatever authority your church possessed in this way, was imported to them."

Bishop Hughes answered: "But our church recalled this authority, in their suspension and excommunication, and a new supply was necessary."

To this Mr. Breckenridge replied: "The proper answer to this question turns on the settlement of a previous question, to wit: had the church of Rome the right or the power, in this case, to withdraw their ministerial authority?"

After giving some reasons, Mr. Breckenridge takes this distinct ground:

> Then the principle is plain, that when a church deposes ministers of Christ for refusing to preach ruinous errors, and refusing to submit to oppressive usurpations, the deposing act is null and void. If a minister of Christ be deposed for refusing to sin, the deposition is null and void. [24]

This position of Mr. Breckenridge, in its essence and in its practical effect, denies all government in the Church.

It is true Mr. Breckenridge puts in a condition. The act of the church is only null and void when made for reasons not allowed by the law of Christ. But of the sufficiency of these reasons, who is to judge? Is it the tribunal making the deposition, or the person deposed? Some one must determine the question before the conclusion can possibly be reached, that the deposition is null and void. The power and right to determine this important question must rest somewhere. If this power resides in the

Church, it does not reside in the minister. It cannot equally reside in both. The right of ultimate decision must remain with only one of the two. Mr. Breckenridge gives this right and power, in his theory, not to the church, but to the person deposed.

What sort of theory is that which makes the decision of the highest tribunal in the government practically null and void upon the objection of the very person it tries and condemns? The Senate of the United States must try all impeachments. Suppose that body should try an impeachment of the President, find him guilty, and depose him from his office. And suppose his counsel should then take the novel and bold ground that the deposition was null and void, because contrary to law, and oppressive and tyrannical. In such case had not the counsel better return to the study of his profession?

When the Supreme Court of the United States makes a decision, who can declare that decision null and void, because given upon grounds alleged not legal and just? In the theory of our government that exalted tribunal is bound to decide according to law, and in this same theory, it always does so decide. That tribunal, in the contemplation of the Constitution, cannot err. If the Legislature thinks that an Act of Congress has been misconstrued, the act may be amended; and future cases will come under the new Act. If, in the opinion of the people, that Court misconstrues the Constitution, they can amend that instrument, and make it plainer.

Suppose A and B, having a controversy, should go into a court of justice and say "May it please the Court, we have a matter we wish to submit to the decision of this Court, upon the condition that the decision shall suit us." The Court would promptly reply: "This Court cannot sit here to receive idle and insulting propositions."

In another place Mr. Breckenridge says:

> We believe in a visible Catholic (not Roman) church, to which appertain the ministry, the oracles, and ordinances of God, which is to continue to the end of the world; to which the Holy Spirit is promised as an abiding gift; against which the gates of hell shall not prevail; and which is at last to fill the world.[25]

Now I cannot put the two positions of the learned controversialist together. They seem to be in direct conflict. He holds a visible Catholic Church, which is to continue to the end of time, to which all the powers of government are given, and their exercise guaranteed by the Holy

Spirit; and yet when this divinely protected Church ordains a minister, and afterwards deposes him, that deposition may be null and void. Here is a church to which the Holy Spirit is promised as an "abiding gift," and against which the gates of hell "shall not prevail," and which at last is to "fill the world" that cannot even depose a minister without the liability of error. A Church thus divinely protected, that may still command her ministers "to preach ruinous errors" and "to sin." It would seem a most singular theory, that gives the church the abiding gift of the Holy Spirit, and guards her against the gates of hell at all times, and yet deserts her in the exercise of her highest functions –the very and only end of her creation. Surely, if the Holy Ghost should aid the church at all, this aid should be effective; and if effective, it must be in making her decisions, and in administering the law of this kingdom.

According to the theory of Mr. Breckenridge the church ordains a minister, and then, for causes judged sufficient by the ordaining power, deposes him. Yet this sentence of deposition, though made by the highest power in the church on earth, is not final, not conclusive, in the contemplation of his theory. The alleged decision has no force, unless the deposed submits. He may say it is null and void, and if he does say so, there is no power on earth to decide that question against him.

Is there any government in a Church, whose alleged decisions may be set aside by the party condemned, or by any other party? What sort of government is that, whose assumed decisions, in the contemplation of the theory of the government itself, are entitled to so little respect, that they can be disregarded by its own citizens or subjects? That which we call government is alone, it would seem, predicated upon the idea of supremacy –the right to make a final and binding decision in each particular case. Without this supreme and exclusive right placed somewhere in the governmental institution, there can be no government at all; and the organization is powerless, and must fail to accomplish the very end and purpose of its creation.

It may be that the learned divine is suitable to his own Church, and in strict accordance with her true character; but I am wholly unable to find any intimation in the New Testament that the Church of Christ was ever liable to these painful infirmities, and that her decisions might be null and void. I might as well expect to find such an intimation in the Constitution of my country regarding the decisions of the Supreme Court of the United States; or in the British Constitution with reference to the decisions of parliament.

---

[1] William Blackstone, *Commentaries on the Laws of England* vol.1 p. 48.

[2] James Boswell, *Life of Johnson.*

[3] *Ibid.*

[4] 1 Cor 12: 28, 29.

[5] Heb 13: *7,* 17.

[6] These sentences being elliptical, I have put in brackets the words necessary to fill them up.

[7] How forcible and beautiful is that expression of Saint Paul, "The unity of the faith."

[8] A. Campbell and J. Purcell, *A debate on the Roman Catholic religion.* 52.

[9] For example: I may act in several different capacities, under several different superiors, or under one superior, who has the rightful supervision of different inferiors, acting in different capacities. I may be agent for A. B., and also for C. D., having the power to appoint sub-agents under me in both cases.

We will suppose that I appoint E. F. sub-agent for both these parties, and that I write him letters of instruction in both these parties, and that I write him letters of instruction in both cases. In the first case I address my letter to him in this way: "Mr. E. F., Sub-Agent of A. B.: You will," &c., giving him instructions, without again mentioning the name of A. B. In the same way I address him as the sub-agent of C. D., and give him my instructions accordingly. Now, it would be a violation of all rule and of all usage for E. F. to do for A. B. what I had instructed him to do for C. D. Having addressed him in a certain *capacity*, instructions are confined to that capacity.

[10] 1 Cor 15: 52.

[11] If we once admit that the promise extended beyond the apostles, then we are forced to concede that the form of expression used can only be compatible with the fact that our Lord first constituted them a college of teachers, and then addressed them *as such.* The pronoun personal can only be applied to persons real or artificial. You may well address the organs or members of a corporation as you would the corporation itself. You may also address a permanent college of teachers as a person destined to live throughout all coming time.

This is what our Lord did. He first created the college by addressing all the apostles collectively, and imposing upon them duties that only the whole combined could perform. They were to teach all nations all things which He had commanded. For our Lord to say that He would always be with them to the end of the world, and yet they not be members of a continuing college of teachers, destined to live as long as the promise itself was to continue, would seem to be entirely erroneous. As the promise itself was continuing, and yet the pronoun personal was used, there must have been a college of teachers then organized, the apostles being the first members of the college.

[12] Heb. 13: 7, 9, 17.

[13] What does this term *unruly* mean? Webster says it means "ungovernable; licentious; disregarding restraint, turbulent."

[14] That large body of Protestant ministers who claimed the right to rebuke Congress for passing the Nebraska bill a few years ago, adopted this, among other resolutions:

"1. *Resolved*, That the ministry is the divinely-appointed institution for the declaration and enforcement of God's will upon all points of religious and moral truth; and that as such, it is their duty to reprove, rebuke, and exhort with all authority and doctrine."

The language of this resolution is certainly very clear and strong. The ministry is not only the "*divinely-appointed institution* for the *declaration* and *enforcement* of God's will," but it is "their *duty* to reprove, rebuke, and exhort with all *authority and doctrine*."

Of course, if it be their *duty* to declare and *enforce* God's will, and with *all authority*, it would seem to be someone's bounden duty to *obey*; and that some means must exist for practically enforcing their decisions, otherwise the power to declare and enforce amounts, at last, to no power at all, except in mere name. How the powers claimed by these ministers can be reconciled with the assumed right of private interpretation in the last resort, it is most difficult to conceive. Unless we hold, in plain contradiction to the powers claimed, that this divinely-appointed institution is, *after all,* absolutely *inferior* to the very persons reproved, and in reference to the very things for which the reproof was given.

The theory of these Divines is strangely mixed. God creates an institution for the *very* purpose of declaring and enforcing His will; and yet, in the contemplation of this *same* theory, God has done a very idle and useless thing, for each member rebuked has only to appeal to himself to defeat the assumed judgment of this "*divinely-appointed*" yet fallible institution. As the decision, in the contemplation of the theory itself, is as fallible as the judgment of the person rebuked, it cannot, of course, ask or demand any respect or obedience while the institution is arbitrarily and painfully compelled, *by duty*, to assume and exercise this frivolous authority.

But these ministers not only claim the right to rebuke the members of their own churches, but they go beyond the Catholic theory, and claim this right over aliens and strangers. Saint Paul's directions to Timothy and Titus had reference to the members of the Church. It did not refer to aliens from the kingdom, over whom the Church had no jurisdiction to do anything more than to simply to *declare* the truth, and not to *enforce* it, and who would perish because they were out of the Church, as the people perished because they were out of the ark.

[15] 2 Tim1: 6, 13, 14; 2: 2.

[16] Titus 1: 5, 7, 9.

[17] Acts 20: 28.

[18] Webster.

[19] Though the language of Saint Paul, as translated, seems to confuse the figure, as he is made to speak of "*feeding the church*" by "*overseers*," his meaning is still clear. The elders addressed had thc rule over the church as Ephesus, and it was their *duty* to exercise it.

[20] Eph 5: 21.

[21] 1 Peter 5: 1-5.

[22] Rom. 14: 4. In reading the Epistles of the apostles one cannot but be struck with the kindness of the form and manner of their instructions, even when giving the most positive and inflexible commands. Saint Paul says: "I beseech you brethren that you all speak the same thing"—"that you submit yourselves to such." (1 Cor 1:10, 16:16.) "Rebuke not an elder, but entreat him as a brother." (1 Tim. 5: 1.)

The under-shepherds were taught to use the same gentleness towards all men, but especially towards the flock. "The servant of the Lord must not strive; but especially towards the flock. "The servant of the Lord must not strive; but be gentle…" (1 Tim 2: 24.) But while as to the mere manner of teaching, they were to be as gentle as their Divine Master, they possessed *actual* authority as He did, and were told to command and teach with all authority, to rebuke sharply, to reject heretics, to withdraw from perverse teachers, and to let no *man despise them in the exercise of their authority.*

[23] Ver. 14.

[24] John Hughes, Hughes-Breckenridge Controversy p. 294, 443.

[25] *Ibid.* p. 61.

CHAPTER V

THE INFALLIBILITY OF THE CHURCH

1. Governments must provide a tribunal to determine the law

Man is competent to live in society, and the object of political government is to regulate his conduct while in that state. Hence, laws are made to secure the peaceful union of a great number of individuals under one government, and courts of justice are instituted to explain them. Law being a rule prescribed by a superior to an inferior, which the inferior is bound to obey, there must, of necessity, be a tribunal to declare and administer it. The very idea of government supposes the formation of a competent tribunal to determine what the law means.

If we look around us through the world, we shall readily find that no great object is ever undertaken without the union of numbers. From a small village debating society, through every grade of organization, up to the mightiest civil government on earth, the *immediate* end to be secured is *union of effort*. Men seem to be so aware of the importance of this union, that they never fail to make some provision for it. In the constitution of every society, there is some tribunal to decide all matters of difference that may arise. All men seem to act under the clear consciousness of the invincible necessity of some judicial tribunal to decide what the law means; for to what end was any law given unless it is to be *practically* administered? And how can this be done without a judiciary?

Among the great number of visionary schemes of government put forth by different writers, not one, to my knowledge, ever advanced so wild a theory, as to make each individual governed the judge of the law in his own case, and dispense with the judiciary. So extravagant a theory was never proposed anywhere, and certainly never reduced to actual operation. Therefore, since the very idea of law presupposes this judicial power to exist in the government, the idea of union among a number of individuals cannot be rationally entertained without it. There can be no continued union among men, without some competent means to preserve it!

The Constitution of the United States, and the constitutions of the several states, distribute the powers of government among three departments, namely the Legislative, the Executive, and the Judicial. The powers conferred upon each of these three departments, are all equally necessary to the continued existence of the government. But whether the judicial power be separated from the others or not, of necessity it must exist. Even the absolute monarch either administers his own laws himself, or through judges acting for him.

All positive laws intended for the government of men must be construed; and as they constitute a rule prescribed by a superior, they cannot, in the nature of the case, be construed in the last resort by the inferior, the very party to be governed. The power and right to make the laws in the first instance, and construe them in the last resort, must be placed in the hands of the superior. A right of ultimate construction in the inferior, would defeat the entire purposes of the legislator. Every government must furnish its own tribunal to administer its own laws. Every association of individuals must contain, in itself, some competent power to determine controversies, or it will be divided against itself. No association can permit a foreign tribunal to administer its own laws over its own members. Every society of men must have the power lodged somewhere, to construe the law independently of the individual opinion of its members. This vital principle is necessary to the very existence of any sort of government.

2. These principles apply the Christian association

The question then arises, are these clear, luminous, and practical principles, which are inherent in the nature and necessities of government, applicable to that "rule of moral conduct, and measurer of faith" prescribed by God to man? Did God in making a positive law for mankind, intend to institute any sort of government among them? Or did He intend there should exist any *union* among those who obeyed His law? If so, has He provided any competent *means* to preserve this union? Did He provide any efficient means to administer that government through agents authorized by Him for that purpose? Or does He Himself visibly administer and construe His law from time to time as occasion may require. Is there the same or *even greater* necessity that men should know with certainty, the meaning of the law of God, as there is that they should know the meaning of the "municipal law"? If so, must there not be efficient means to produce that end?

In making a comparison between the Divine and municipal law, it is necessary to keep our attention steadily fixed upon the point of whether the two systems agree substantially in *those* respects that render the establishment of some tribunal to decide controversies indispensable. If they do, the conclusion becomes invincible that, in the nature of things, there must exist such a tribunal in the association brought together and kept in existence by the law of Christ.

In relation to the municipal law, it may be remarked, that it is almost wholly taken from the Divine. There is scarcely a crime prohibited by Divine law that is not prohibited by the municipal law. All the great leading features of the municipal law are borrowed from the Divine law. No Christian, as such, can violate the municipal, without violating the law of God, except in those rare cases where the two conflict. This never happens, except where the powers of civil government are usurped, or perverted from their legitimate ends. In the concise and beautiful language of one of our earliest law books:

> In every law positive well made, is somewhat of the law of reason, and of the law of God; and to discover the law of God, and the law of reason, from the law positive, is very hard.[1]

The civil law then is based upon the Divine. It derives its force and efficacy from the *permission* of the divine law to establish political government; and from the express command in the Gospel, to obey those in lawful authority.

It must be obvious to common sense, that all laws must be similar in those general respects requisite to constitute law itself. There must be certain constituent principles to make up every law. It could not be a law at all without constituent principles. I, therefore, lay down these two positions as true:

1. All systems of positive law must agree in those essential elements necessary to constitute law itself; otherwise, they could not be laws at all.

2. They must differ in certain *other* respects; otherwise, they would be the same.

These positions being true, in what great and essential respects do the municipal and the Divine law resemble each other?

1. They are both based upon the fundamental principle that some government is indispensable to man's condition.

2. That there is some right to make laws, and some corresponding duty to obey, placed somewhere.

3. They are both positive laws, promulgated in human language; and both must, therefore, be construed and administered.

4. They are both intended for *men*, and have in view the same immediate end -- the union of numbers, and the preservation of peace among those united.

5. They both have penalties attached.[2]

They are, therefore, alike possessed of the essential principles that must constitute every positive law.

3. The necessity of a judicial tribunal in Christian government

It is indispensable for the just administration and success of the municipal law, that there should be a living, speaking judiciary, plainly accessible to all, whose duty it is to decide what the law is, and what it means. Is it not also plain and palpable that there should be a like institution to determine the true construction of the Divine Law, so as to preserve unity and peace among those whom it governs, by keeping the construction of the law always the same, throughout every part of the association? To my apprehension this conclusion must follow from a just and fair consideration of the nature, end, and object of all law.

It is true that the Divine law is derived immediately and the municipal law but mediately from God. But the mere source from which the law immediately emanates does not divest the system of the inherent characteristics of all law. The mere fact that the Divine law was put forth by God in the form of a positive code, does not obviate the necessity for the continued existence of some tribunal to determine what the law means. This is for the plain reason that this law is intended, like the municipal code, to govern men, to unite men. It is addressed to men, in man's imperfect language, and must, therefore, be construed by someone; and there is thus the same, if not greater necessity for uniformity of decision, to obtain peace in the association, and success in the system. The fact that this association was intended to embrace all Christians everywhere, in all ages, under one law, in one united government, is the strongest possible reason for the organization of one tribunal of the last resort.

4. The role of a tribunal in prescribing law

One of the most forcible reasons why God should have made a direct revelation to man, is that He could not justly punish men, unless he first "*prescribed*" His law. From the same reason it follows that it is the duty of the lawmaker to create a competent tribunal to construe the law. For without such a tribunal, the *publication* of the law is very imperfect, and does not afford that reasonable means of certainty that every just system should supply.

We will suppose a legislator to put forth a code of laws, drawn up with all attainable accuracy while we are forced to convey our ideas thorough so changeable and imperfect a medium as human language, and addressed to so frail a mind as that of man. Further, suppose that he should have constituted no tribunal to determine what he meant, and should leave the people to whom this code was given for a great number of years, and should then return and call them up in judgment before him. What a strange medley of opinions he would find regarding the construction of his laws! He would say to them: "You have misconstrued and violated my laws, and I must punish you." They would answer: "That is a hard case. You did not treat us fairly. You gave us no authorized tribunal to decide for us, whose decisions from time to time would have settled difficulties, and upon which we could have relied for a correct interpretation of your law. You left each one to interpret for himself, at his own peril; and as we are so differently constituted, with different powers of mind; and as our opportunities of information were so widely different, we could not but come to different conclusions. Immediately after you left, difficulties of construction arose, and have been constantly arising ever since; and had there existed a tribunal, they could have been all settled from time to time, as often as they arose. The idea of giving the same law to so great a variety of persons as necessarily compose every community, requiring each and all to think and act *alike*, without giving them the *some* tribunal, *equally* competent to construe the law for *all*—the learned and the ignorant, the rich and the poor, the high and the low—is to our minds unfair. We think you ought not to punish us. One thing we do know, and that is this, we have been wholly unable to agree in the construction of your law, and you left no means to secure this agreement."

To such unanswerable logic as this, what could the legislator justly reply? In vain would he say: "My law is plain, simple, and easily understood. It scarcely needs construction." They would reply: "Truly and verily, the wisest men among us, while they declare it plain, differ most essentially as to what it means. They cannot all understand *plain* alike. And as for most of us, we are plain, illiterate men, and the law is not plain to us." The Greek language may be plain to him who understands it, but it is still Greek to us. And had it been your deliberate purpose to so arrange your system as to involve the very best of us in unwilling violations of it, you could not more successfully have accomplished such a design, than you have done by leaving us in the confused and destitute situation you did."

Is it not, therefore, reasonable that the Divine law, which comprehends the whole duty of man, should provide a tribunal to construe it, and thus to settle all disputes in the association respecting it? If such a tribunal be necessary in political government, it not even more so in the Christian system. If there be truth in Christianity, it is surely more important to know its law with *certainty* than to correctly understand the law of the country. And can associated men remain united without some competent authority to settle disputes? If so, what sort of union can it be? Is there any living, perpetuating principle in a system without such a tribunal? Is there any thing like *system* in a code which provides no court to decide what it is? Is there, or can there be, any government at all in any association of men, without a judiciary? If so, what sort of government is it?

It may be said that the *ultimate* end of the municipal law is to produce *temporal*, and that of the Divine, *eternal* happiness; and, therefore, the necessity for such a tribunal which exists in the former, does not arise under the latter system. But this would seem to be no answer to the argument. It is true that there is a vast difference between temporal and eternal happiness; but this fact only renders it the more necessary to understand the Divine law, and proves the greater necessity of a competent tribunal to construe it in the last resort.

Besides this, it is still happiness, and happiness of the same being that constitutes the ultimate end of both systems. Temporal and eternal happiness differ in degree and duration. Government is only a means and not an end. The immediate end proposed by both systems is the practical and continued union of men. It does not matter that the ultimate ends of these different systems are not the same in degree and duration, while they are the same in substance. If the means used are substantially the same, these means must be subject to the same general laws.

If our Lord resorted to a visible association of men to accomplish the union of His followers, and the united, and, therefore, successful spread of His system, this association of men must, in itself, possess all the requisites that enter into, and constitute all associations, and render them practically efficient to accomplish the purpose intended. To suppose that our Lord would adopt means of a certain character, and yet take from them the vital and inherent principles essential to render such means efficient, would seem to be clearly unjust to Him. When He used language as a medium of communication with men, He did not rob it of its established character.

5. Law must achieve finality

As the municipal law only assumes to control our outward acts, and does not reach our mere belief and intentions, a man may believe all the falsehood, and intend all the wrong he pleases, and still commit no offense against that code. But it is not so in the perfect law of God, which controls us in belief, intention, and act.

The law of Christianity goes so much further than the municipal code, requiring so much more to be forborne, believed, and done. Its punishments and rewards are so much greater and more enduring, These facts that render it the more important that there should be union and peace in the Christian association; and that for this end, it is still more necessary that some tribunal, perfectly *competent* to determine all controversies, should be found in the Christian government.

If union among men be necessary for any given purpose, the preservation of that union becomes equally important, so long as that purpose continues to exist. The union cannot be accomplished unless some fair and adequate means be provided for this end. It may be laid down as an unerring principle, that union, in any association of men, cannot continue to exist without peace; and that peace cannot be preserved without competent means to end disputes. The happiness that men expect to obtain by entering into society cannot be enjoyed without peace. If peace cannot be had in an association the end and objective of the association will fail. If the design of all law and of all government be to form and secure peace among the members associated, and if it be necessary for these ends that a tribunal be established to decide controversies, it follows, as a matter of course, that the determinations of such a tribunal must be full, final and conclusive. If not the decision must fail to accomplish the end intended and thus amount to no decision at all. The decisions of a court of last resort must be final; otherwise they amount to nothing, and no end to the dispute.

6. Judicial infallibility is found in political governments

If we go into the appropriate apartment of the Capitol, at Washington City, we shall find in session an august tribunal, before whose bar the most learned and gifted men of the nation display their reasoning eloquence. This great court is composed of a very few judges, whose equals, if not superiors in mental and moral qualifications, are found among the great lawyers who stand before it and among the learned judges who sit in the state courts. Yet its decisions are conclusive upon all. Its adjudications not only control the course of decision of the inferior Federal tribunals, but are binding upon the state courts, and are competent to annul the acts of the President and of Congress.

Before this lofty tribunal, honor, titles, wealth, and fame are powerless. Nothing but pure legal justice is presumed in contemplation of law, to govern and guide its conclusions. No armed bands of soldiers throng its halls to protect it and enforce its decisions, and yet this court settles questions involving the dearest rights of millions of civilized and enlightened men. This venerable tribunal is the Supreme Court of the United States, and upon it the Constitution of our country has conferred judicial infallibility.

The framers of that great instrument, the Constitution of the United States, were men of preeminent ability, and they gave to it all the certainty attainable by them.[3] And yet they knew it would be idle to make a constitution and laws under it, and not organize courts for their construction. They also knew that it was useless to have courts, unless their decisions could be made final, and for this purpose they provided for the organization of *one* supreme court, with appellate jurisdiction. They gave Congress the power to provide for the creation of inferior tribunals only. They had it not in their power to confer upon the Supreme Court *actual* infallibility, for this is an attribute belonging alone to God, and only communicated by Him to whom He pleases. In the very nature of all governmental or social institutions, such is the invincible necessity for infallibility of some sort to reside in some *one* of their tribunals, that when *actual* infallibility cannot be conferred, judicial infallibility is given.

In the contemplation of our Constitution, the Supreme Court cannot err. There is no legal power anywhere to question its decisions. All must submit. It is not in the power of the President, the Congress, and all the State courts combined, to set aside one of its decisions. Yet it is generally conceded that the court has actually rendered incorrect decisions. That court sustained the constitutionality of the *Alien and Sedition Laws*, which decision is now almost universally held to have been erroneous. But admitting that the Court has not yet actually erred, it must be conceded that it may. The framers of the Constitution were compelled to bestow upon this tribunal judicial infallibility, because they could bestow no other, and some sort of infallibility was indispensable. So necessary is peace, it is a much less evil to submit to an occasional erroneous decision than to have no decision at all. In every government, in every association of men who are to be governed at all, there must be infallibility of some kind, placed somewhere, or there can be no end of disputes, and no peace, and no union, and no success of such an institution.

7. The Christian association must have actual infallibility

If there be any union required by the law of Christ, and any tribunal to decide disputes, is it not clear that such tribunal must, of necessity, possess infallibility of some sort, or else the institution will be totally defective and insufficient? If there be no infallibility in the association of men, formed in accordance with the law of God, then it is more defective than mere political governments, and cannot possibly possess any living, perpetuating principle. For what purpose does a tribunal decide if its decision is not final, or cannot be made final, by an appeal to a higher court? What is the object of a decision? To end disputes; and if not final, it does not end the controversy, and is simply idle. That which is not competent to make a final and binding decision, cannot be properly called a judiciary.

If God did establish such a tribunal, could He, in reason, give it mere judicial infallibility? Would He make it as defective as mere human institutions, when He possessed the wisdom and the power to make it perfect? Does God do His work in that way? It is true, that if God implicitly required all the members to submit to the decisions of such a tribunal, the association might continue, but it would not continue the same pure association. The tribunal being actually fallible, and only judicially infallible, must actually err, sooner or later, and God would thus be requiring implicit submission to erroneous decisions. The idea of a tribunal only clothed with mere judicial infallibility, deciding finally upon a law dictated by actual infallibility, would seem to be clearly erroneous. And the idea of a tribunal of the last resort deciding upon a law given in human language, and such decision not being final, would seem equally inadmissible.

Had the framers of political constitutions possessed the power, they no doubt would have bestowed upon their judiciary actual, instead of mere judicial infallibility. But as God possessed the power and the wisdom, and, therefore, did make a perfect law, would He not necessarily create a tribunal competent to construe such a law? And is not a actually infallible tribunal, in the nature of things, indispensable to construe a law made by the Divine lawmaker? Could the great ends aimed at –the mighty purposes intended –be accomplished without this?

It is a just and generous mode of reasoning, to take the theory under investigation to be true, *for the sake of the argument only*, and then submit it to a fair and impartial test, by a legitimate extension of its principles into all their logical results. For this purpose I will suppose that our Creator made man and placed him upon the earth and that He bestowed upon him the faculty of reason, and its necessary incident, free will. Further, suppose He gave to this free agent a direct and positive law prescribed by Himself. The immediate end of this law was to bring all men of good will into one association of pure faith and virtue, to be governed by this one law and this law was given in human language, and must be construed. In this collective body of men under the law, God does not Himself visibly preside for the purpose of deciding controversies. For this end, He organized a tribunal in the association, and delegated to it power and authority to decide, with infallible certainty, all questions regarding His law that may arise from age to age, and in succession, *as they arise*. This association is a visible body to whom all men may join themselves, if they will; that communion with this association is a practical and sure test of faith, and that this institution is but *preparatory* to that enduring institution in heaven.

Is there anything in this theory inconsistent, unjust, or unphilosophical? Is it incompatible with the attributes of the Deity? On the contrary, is this not a rational theory, beautiful to the judgment, and consolatory to the heart? It would seem to possess every element of a perfect system, harmonious, practical, and just, in every feature.

8. The extent of the judicial power of the Church

The Constitution of the United States organized a government, possessing certain defined powers, and intended to accomplish certain great national objects. In the theory of the system, this instrument is the fundamental and, until amended in pursuance of its own provisions, unchangeable law. From the nature of mere human systems, and the limited capacity of men, and the constantly varying circumstances of the people governed, the legislative power could not all be beneficially exercised at the beginning. It is left, in part, in the government, to be exercised from time to time, within the limits prescribed by the Constitution. The powers of this government are divided between three departments, the legislative, the executive, and the judiciary. Together these embrace all the powers communicated to the system. In reference to the extent of the judicial power, Chancellor Kent has said:

> The judicial power in every government must be coextensive with the power of legislation. Were there no power to interpret, pronounce, and execute the law, the government would either perish through its own imbecility as was the case with the old Confederation, or other powers must be assumed by the legislative body, to the destruction of liberty.[4]

While the legislative power in the Christian government could be exercised in advance, in reference to all the material and permanent features of the system, the executive and judicial powers, from their nature, could not, as already stated be exercised in advance. These must continue in the Church, and be exercised as often as occasion may require. Therefore, it would seem plain that the governing power left by Christ in the Church must have jurisdiction over all cases embraced within the law governing the institution. In other words, if Christ gave to His own institution a law for its government, "commanding what is right, and prohibiting what is wrong;" then, whatever governing power He placed in the church, must embrace whatever is commanded or prohibited by the law. The code is mainly intended for practical application in this world, and is, therefore, given for a certain end. There are two kinds of obedience required by the system, instead of one only, and as they are both vitally important to reach the end aimed at by the lawmaker, whatever power was left in the church to construe and apply the law must extend to both these particulars, or the institution must "perish through its own imbecility."

Every violation of the law is an offense, more or less aggravated according to its nature, as defined by the law itself. Heresy may be defined as the willful disbelief of an essential article of faith, or the willful belief of an essential false doctrine, by one who professes to be a Christian. Therefore, it is an offense against the system, for the reason that the law requires correct faith, and prohibits a false one. Thus Christ says: "He that believeth not shall be dammed" and Saint Paul speaks of heresies as offenses against the law of Christ; and in the fifth chapter of his epistle to the Galatians he says:

> Now the works of the flesh are manifest, which are these; adultery, fornication, uncleanness, lasciviousness, idolatry, witchcraft, hatred, variance, emulations, wrath, strife, seditions, heresies, envying, murders, drunkenness, reveling, and such like; of which I tell you, as I have told you in past times, that they that do such things shall not inherit the kingdom of God.[5]

The language of the apostle is clear and explicit, that those offenses exclude the guilty party from the Kingdom of heaven; and heresy is classed with idolatry, murder, and the other offenses mentioned. If the judicial power of the Church extends to any one of these offenses, it must extend to all. For to give to men a law, and a judiciary to construe it, and yet to restrict its jurisdiction to part of the code, would seem to be a solecism in government.

9. The Gospel must consist in the sense of Scripture

In the mind of Christ there was no confusion. All was unclouded, intellectual day. When He came to convey His will through so imperfect and changeable a medium as human language, addressed to so frail a mind as that of man, it would seem that certainty could not possibly be attained under the circumstances without an infallible interpreter.

All intelligent writers are agreed to the imperfect and changeable character of language. Its imperfections are most fully understood by statesmen, jurists, and lawyers. Before courts of justice, where the rules of investigation are the most rigid, and searching, the true character of this medium is best understood –"Such is the intrinsic imperfection of all human language, that it frequently becomes impossible, from the mere words alone of any writing, to ascertain the meaning of the parties."[6] James Kent says:

> But such is the imperfection of human language, and the want of technical skill in the makers of the law, that statutes often give occasion to the most perplexing doubts and discussions, arising from the ambiguity that attends them.[7]

The learned Protestant bishop Walton is cited in John Milner's *End of Religious Controversy* saying:

> The word of God does not consist in mere letters, whether written or printed, but in the sense of it; which no one can better interpret than the true church, to which Christ has committed this sacred pledge.

"Let us be persuaded," says Saint Augustine, "that the gospel consists not in the words, but in the sense."

Christ's law is the most extensive and wonderful code ever given to man. It embraces not only plain and simple truths, but truths of the most sublime and abstruse character; revelations of awful import; a code regulating in the most perfect manner; all our duties in all the multiplied relations of life, and our whole duty to God. It reveals to us the nature of angels and spiritual existences; giving us glimpses of that heaven where the inspired Paul heard words unspeakable. And it requires us, not only to understand and perform all duties enjoined, but to believe, with unfaltering faith, all these high and holy words of mystery and truth.

10. The Scriptures are in some cases obscure

It is a common error to suppose, that because all truth, from its very nature, is consistent and but a unit, it must be very simple, and easily understood. It may be assumed as an axiom that truth is never confused as error generally is. But it does not follow from this unity and consistency that it is always easily understood. It does not follow anymore than it follows that because the first mechanical powers are simple that a clock or steam engine is not a complex machine. In a perfect, but complex machine, there is a *combination* of a great variety of mechanical contrivances, all operating together in perfect harmony. So, every great system of law, embracing a multiplicity of subjects, must consist of many truths, all united by some leading, harmonious principle.[8]

Christ's law is a supernatural system, revealing truths that we never could reach by the, mightiest efforts of unaided reason, and prescribing a perfect morality far above all our natural conceptions of justice, and embracing so many interests, both temporal and eternal. In the nature of such a system we must expect to find many truths and duties of a plain and simple character, and some most difficult.

If a system be extensive, and assume to regulate many interests it must, of necessity, be more complex, or otherwise it must be incomplete. A system of law requisite to governing a wandering race of men may be very simple, for the reason that they have few rights to protect. They have no merchants and they need no bills of exchange; they have no lands, and need no land law; they have little or no property, and need no law to protect that; they have no mechanics, and need no law of lien; they have no steamboats, no railroads, no telegraphic lines, and need no laws to regulate that which they have not. But the moment a people take to a new branch of business, they need, and must have, a law to protect it. As their employments increase, their code of laws must also be extended, and in proportion as the code is extended to new objects, so is its complexity increased. Each new subject gives rise to a new law, and each new law gives rise to some difficult questions. The Legislature is therefore compelled, either to leave interests unprotected, or to enact laws from time to time, as these interests increase.

When we examine the written word of God, we find many things in it easy to be understood, and some things hard to be understood. The narrative portions, as a general thing, are plain and simple, but the doctrinal portions are more difficult. Let any calm, sincere, and clear-headed reader examine the New Testament carefully, without any preconceived system of faith in his mind, and he must find some things hard to be understood. He will find this fact apparent upon the face of the record.

For example, in the twenty-fourth chapter of Saint Matthew, our Lord predicts the destruction of the Temple and many other things, and then says in the twenty-fourth verse:

> Verily I say unto you, this generation shall not pass, till all these things be fulfilled.

This same obscurity may be found in the thirteenth chapter of Mark.

In Luke we find this passage put forth in the form of a command:

> And I say unto you, make to yourselves friends of the mammon of unrighteousness; that when ye fail, they may receive you into everlasting habitations.[9]

In the twenty-second chapter of Luke our Savior commands His disciples to sell their garments and buy swords. They brought two swords, and He said, "it is enough;" but when Peter had used one of the swords, our Lord reproved him, saying: "Put up again thy sword into his place; for all they that take the sword, shall perish by the sword."

The accounts of the genealogy of our Lord are difficult portions of Scripture. These are found in the first of Saint Matthew, and third of Saint Luke.

When the reader has passed from the Gospels and the Acts of the Apostles to their Epistles, he will find passages hard to understand, especially in those of Saint Paul. In particular, I have often read that Epistle to the Romans attentively, and I confess there are some things in it hard to understand, even after all the explanations that have ever been given. In the third, fourth, seventh, eighth, and ninth chapters, the apostle seems to preach predestination, and justification by faith only; and especially when, in the ninth chapter, he compares God to the potter, and man to the clay.

In the Old Testament many passages occur that are obscure. The sixty-eighth Psalm and the last chapter of Ecclesiastes are so. In the twelfth chapter of Exodus we are told that the children of Israel "borrowed jewels of silver, and jewels of gold, and raiment, and spoiled the Egyptians."

These are only portions of the obscurities of Holy Writ. They are undeniable, and no man among Protestants has more clearly and forcible expressed himself than Dr. Balguy, a learned English Divine, of the established Church:

> But what will you reply is all this to Christians? –to those who see, by a clear and strong light, the dispensation of God to mankind? We are "*not as those who have no hope. The day-spring from on high hath visited us. The Spirit of God shall lead us into all truth.*" To this delusive dream of human folly, founded only on a mistaken interpretation of Scripture, I answer in one word: open your Bibles; take the first page in either Testament, and tell me, without disguise, is there nothing in it too hard for you to understand? If you find all before you *clear* and *easy*, you may thank God for giving you a privilege, which He has denied to many thousands of sincere believers.[10]

11. A Protestant theory of 'clarity in all essentials'

But while this learned and candid Divine makes these truthful admissions, which militate so much against the entire theory of Protestant individual interpretation in the last resort, Bishop Porteus, Chillingworth, Dr. Spring, Mr. Rice, and most other Protestant writers, insist that the Bible is clear as to all essential matters.

To sustain the fundamental principle of private interpretation it is indispensably necessary to take the position that Christianity is predicated upon a few simple facts and commands, and that the Bible containing these is clear and plain. Christ certainly revealed but *one* system of truth intended to be believed and practiced by *all.* He made no distinctions in His code between one essential truth and another, but He commanded His apostles to teach *all things whatsoever* He commanded them, and then said that "he that believeth..." and "he that believeth not..." Under a system of individual construction, the inexorable laws of logic compel its advocates to reduce the truths of faith to the fewest number, and those of the most general and simple character. The Scriptures, as a matter of course, must also be held entirely simple, so as to be understood, in all needful particulars, by all persons.

But in opposition to this leveling process, cannot the same end be accomplished by elevating the judgment and capacity of each individual by the aid of the same infallible interpreter? Whether, plain, or hard do be understood, this theory places all persons of every grade of intellect upon the same footing. It elevates all to the same infallible standard of interpretation, and to the same conceptions of the sublime truths of the system, without violating any rule of logic, justice, or common sense, and without being in conflict with the evident character of the Scriptures, and their own express words.

It is true that we must first understand a proposition before we can either believe or disbelieve it! However, there is a marked difference between understanding and comprehending. A man may understand the point settled by a decision of the Supreme Court of the United States, and believe it just, simply upon the ground of authority, without comprehending the reasons given to sustain it. We know that we exist – that we have the power of voluntary locomotion –that our mere will puts our bodies in action; but we cannot comprehend why this is so. So, if the doctrine of the Real Presence be admitted for the sake of the argument, the simplest capacity can understand the simple proposition, "this is my body;" while the greatest intellect cannot comprehend the nature of the mystery. As our Lord required *belief*, and not comprehension, when we understand simply the truth proposed and believe it, we fulfill the law, whether we comprehend the reasons for it or not.

Dr. Spring says: "The Bible is a plain book, and easily understood."[11] "We agree," says Mr. Rice, "that the Bible, especially on all important points, is a plain book."[12] But is this true? Is it compatible with reason, the nature of all law, or the Bible?

It is a little difficult, I apprehend, upon principles of sound reasoning, for men to show that what they do not understand is unnecessary to be understood. Professing to take their faith and morals from the Scriptures in the sense each individual puts upon the written law, and coming upon undeniable difficulties which they are forced to admit, they presume to make a distinction between those portions that are material and those not material. In doing this, each one makes his individual capacity to understand or not to understand the Scriptures, the *standard* by which to measure the materiality or immateriality of the different provisions of this inflexible and positive code of law.

If the Scriptures contain the entire code now obligatory, with this assumption, it would seem as though it must have all been written with the intent to be understood. Otherwise there was no necessity for its being written. But conceding, for the sake of the argument, that portions of the Bible are idle and immaterial, it is assuming an awful responsibility to decide what portions are material and what not.

But it must be apparent to every sensible reader of the Bible that the most difficult portions are those relating to doctrines that must be believed, and to moral duties that must be put in practice. We are not left alone to arrive at this conclusion from the numerous instances of obscurity that exist upon the face of the Scriptures; but we are plainly told by the Apostle Peter, that such is the fact with reference to material portions of the Written Word. The apostle, speaking of the epistles of Saint Paul, says:

> In which are some things hard to be understood, which they that are unlearned and unstable, wrest, as they do the other Scriptures, unto their own destruction.[13]

Dr. Spring says, "easily understood," and Saint Peter says, "hard to be understood." Which is right—the apostle or the Protestant? So, Mr. Rice says plain, while Saint Peter says otherwise.

If any portions of the Scripture are plain, they are the narrative portions; for the reason that a narrative of facts is the most simple form of composition. Now the apostle here asserts two simple facts: first, that there are some things in Saint Paul's Epistles *hard to be understood*; and second, that the unlearned and unstable wrest these things hard to be understood, as they do the other Scriptures, to their own destruction. And these things were not only hard to be understood, but they were important and *necessary to be believed*, because, if wrested from their true meaning, they led to *destruction*, just in the *same way* as did the misconstruction of other portions of Scripture. So far from the apostle making any distinction between material and immaterial portions of Scripture, he does make a distinction between those *easy*, and those *hard* to be understood, and conclusively establishes the *materiality* of *both*.

That the great and overwhelming majority of men, in every age and country, who rely alone upon their individual judgment belong either to the class of unlearned or unstable, would seem to need no proof. If it did, it is conclusively, shown among Protestants, from the fact of so many different parties existing among them, who can never understand the plain Bible alike. Whatever may be their worldly and literary knowledge, they are not learned and stable in the sense of the apostle; otherwise there could not exist the five hundred different sects in Protestant Christendom. The more earnestly and emphatically they contend that the Scriptures are plain and easily understood in all important points, the more powerfully do they condemn themselves for those divisions so utterly inconsistent with right reason and the united and consistent law of Christ.

12. The causes of obscurity and the need for infallibility

There are many causes for obscurity of the Scriptures such as:

1. The *extent* and *sublime nature* of the system of law therein contained.

2. The mysterious nature and uncertain language of prophesy in general.

3. The peculiar customs and modes of speech common among the Hebrews.

4. The peculiar style common with the sacred writers.

5. The absence of scientific arrangement, in the admixture of simple narratives of fact, with statements of the most difficult doctrines.

These causes of obscurity are mostly peculiar to the Scriptures, and are not generally found in other writings.

In addition, there exists a difficulty in the construction and application of the Scriptures that must, in the nature of things, exist in every code of law, however extensive or limited it may be. This difficulty is greater in the Christian than in the civil code, for the reason that the former embraces a much larger sphere of duties, contemplates ends much more important and enduring, and relates to objects more sublime, varied, and difficult. This difficulty cannot be avoided by any possible accuracy of language or scientific arrangement, although it may be modified by such accuracy to some extent. But after all the possible clearness and accuracy in the statement of the provisions of such a code, and, indeed, of every code, there must arise great and serious difficulties in the *application* of the principle to cases that come up for adjudication.

The great leading principles of the law of the land are expressed in language as accurate and certain, as centuries of discussion and examination by the most acute and powerful minds in the world, could possibly enable them to select. These principles are as familiar to our courts as time, experience, and study could make them. And yet, it is a well-known fact, that new cases of the most perplexing character arise in our courts every day, that are ultimately determined by the legitimate application and extension of these old and familiar principles. This difficulty arises, not from the want of certainty in the statement of a principle; not from any avoidable ambiguity in the language; and not from ignorance of the principle itself; but it arises from the uncertainty whether a given state of case comes within the principle. Is a certain act, or a certain state of case, a violation of a certain principle, or of several principles combined. This is the difficulty![14]

This difficulty arises from the nature of all law, the imperfection of the human mind, and the new and varied circumstances constantly arising in the progress of human affairs. Constitutions and codes of law, from their nature, can only lay down principles, and cannot specify the circumstances of each particular case. As a general thing, several classes of cases are embraced under each principle.[15] It often happens that a case must be determined by the legitimate and harmonious application of several different principles; and although the principles themselves are clearly laid down and well understood, yet to apply them to these new cases is, indeed, a very serious task. Statute laws go more into detail than written constitutions. They are more full and minute, but still they are at last confined to a mere statement of principles, which the courts can only apply to cases coming within the principles laid down in the statute.

For instance, men of the most eminent ability and of the most unquestioned integrity framed the Constitution of the United States. They were great jurists, lawyers, and statesmen, and they gave to the instrument all the certainty and accuracy attainable by them. Yet, immediately after the adoption of the Constitution –a very able work – the Federalist, was written by Mr. Madison and others, for the purpose of rendering its provisions more clear. Many thousands of pages have been written by the most eminent men of the nation, to explain the meaning of a short instrument of nine or ten pages; Mr. Justice Story's commentaries upon the Constitution, fill thirteen hundred pages. Discussions in Congress, in the Supreme Court of the United States, and in the Courts of every State in the Union, and by the greatest men of the country, have still left many questions in painful doubt and uncertainty. This diversity of views has not arisen so much from any avoidable ambiguity in the language of the Constitution, as from the difficulty of applying its provisions to the new and complicated cases that have arisen from time to time.

Among the many provisions of that instrument, which is stated in language as definite and certain as any that could, perhaps, be selected, and yet has given rise to many decisions and conflicting opinions among legislators and jurists, is that part of the tenth section of the first article, which provides that "no state shall pass any law impairing the obligation of contracts." The word, contract, as a legal term, is very accurate, and well understood. And yet the Supreme Court of the United States has been compelled to decide many acts of the Legislatures of different States unconstitutional under this prohibition. New questions arise under this provision and the acts of the State Legislatures continually, and will, most probably, for many years to come. The varied cases arising under this single provision of the Constitution, which apparently seems so clear and simple, go to show what every jurist and lawyer knows, that one of the chief difficulties in the constructions and administration of law often arises in the application of a familiar principle. And these new and difficult cases must continue to arise, with diminished frequency, so long as the government lasts.[16]

If we take up the New Testament, and exclude the narrative portions of the Gospels and the Acts, and the local and argumentative portions of the Epistles, and all repetitions in each, we shall find a very small space occupied by the provisions of the written law of Christianity. Yet this code embraces much more than any human system and so concisely are its leading principles stated, that they occupy a very small space. If a careful selection were made of all the doctrinal texts, and they were put together, it would be apparent that a very small volume would contain a very extensive code.

The Christian code embraces a more extensive range of duties than any municipal code; and, like all other codes only lays down principles, and does not attempt to decide each case in detail. Therefore, it would seem reasonable that we must expect as great, if not greater difficulties to arise in the application of its great principles, than those we meet in the practical application of the laws of civil government. We would naturally anticipate that the pride, the ingenuity, the ambition of men, as well as the honest mistakes of a zeal not according to knowledge, would bring up many questions of the most perplexing character. Thus, in the absence of some common and competent tribunal to decide all questions for all parties, it would give rise to a great variety of views

If we take up, and carefully examine, the New Testament narrative concise as it is, we shall find, that even at that early day, difficulties arose at every step, in the application of its principles. While the twelve were with Christ, we find our Lord often upbraiding them for their want of faith, and their slowness to understand. Repeated explanations were given by our Lord to His apostles, who heard all His instructions, and witnessed all His miracles. They did not even understand that He was to rise again from the dead, until after the happening of that event. We are surprised to find this proneness to unbelief, and this dullness of apprehension, in the chosen apostles, after all they had seen and heard; and we are very naturally inclined to pay ourselves the happy compliment to think that we should have been, under such wonderful circumstances, much more docile, confiding, and apt to understand. But in coming to this conclusion we show a very imperfect appreciation of the difficulties that must attend the individual investigation of a system so mysterious and sublime; and we exhibit a very inaccurate conception of the weakness and frailty of the human mind. For, after ages of experience, and after the greatest critics have written more upon the construction of this small, but wonderful volume, than upon any other one subject in the world, the same difficulties in the way of individual examination still exist; and not only so, but they increase with time; so that those who rely upon their individual construction, are divided into more numerous parties than ever.

We find that notwithstanding the apostles were commanded by Christ to "go teach all nations," as Saint Matthew has recorded it, or "go into all the world and preach the gospel to every creature," as Saint Mark has it, it required a special interposition of Providence to induce Saint Peter to admit Cornelius, the Gentile, into the Kingdom of Christ. There were Jews resident in every country in the known world, and the apostles construed the commission as only extending to them; and up to the time of the conversion of Cornelius, although thousands of Jews had embraced the faith, no uncircumcised person had been admitted into the church.

The question that arose about circumcision, and led to the Council of Jerusalem, was a judicial question, and the difficulty existing in the case, was the application of admitted principles and facts. None of the apostles assumed to have had any direct and special inspiration in reference to the particular case. This instance is one which shows that cases may often be decided by logical conclusions, drawn from facts previously existing. Many most important doctrines of Scripture are formed from a patient and logical application and extension of several different principles. Thus, for example, the doctrine of the Trinity can only be deduced from the comprehensive and harmonious interpretation of different passages combined. We shall have occasion to speak more at length of the decision of the Council of Jerusalem in another place.

We may remark here, that the *conciseness* of a code of law will not render its construction easy, unless it embrace but a very *few subjects*. As we have before stated in substance, the *extent* of a just code of law, depends upon the number of rights protected, and interests regulated. However concise the *form* in which the code may be delivered, the wants of the people governed will remain the same; and, if these wants be *numerous*, the more concise the form of the code, the more difficult it must be to carry out in practice, as a general thing. A radical principle may be laid down, embracing a number of subordinate principles flowing from it; and in such cases, this principle must be extended in practice, to meet the circumstances of each particular case. Thus our Lord said that all the law and the prophets hung upon *two* commandments; yet other commandments were necessary.

From these, and other examples that may be found in the New Testament, we can show that in the days of the apostles numerous difficult judicial questions arose at intervals. These occurred in the application of conceded principles to particular cases, requiring the decision of the governing power of the church to settle them. And if we follow down the stream of events, after the days of the apostles, we shall find new questions often arising from age to age, requiring the application of the law to the facts and circumstances of each new case as it arose.

We are informed, that in the days of persecution many of the early Christians yielded to the tortures and denied the faith. Afterwards they repented and wished to return to the Church. Two questions arose under the new state of things; whether they could be received again into the Church under any circumstances? and if received, whether they were to be re-baptized?

Between that time and the Reformation, many other questions arose for the *first* time. At the Reformation and after that event, many new questions appeared. In the future it is likely that many question will arise. All these multiple questions must be decided by the extension and application of pre-existing principles laid down in the law.

Let it be conceded or proved, that whatever governing power was left by Christ to be exercised by the officers of the church, must embrace whatever was commanded or prohibited by the law of this institution; and that certainty as to the true construction of the code is indispensable; and that the Scriptures contain obscurities peculiar to them, as well as those common to every code of law; and that those things hard to be understood must still be understood. Then does it not follow most logically that there is the same necessity and propriety for the judicial power of the church to be guided by the same infallible Spirit that guided and controlled the legislative power necessary to complete the code? In other words, in constituting and administering a government for a vast collective body of men, intended to embrace all nations and kindreds, and tongues, and exist in perfect unity, in all ages, and for all time to come, should not the exercise of the legislative and judicial powers of government should be guided alike by the same infallible Power?

13. The right of revolution cannot exist in the church

The people who found a civil government constitute the sovereign power. They are the source from whence all the powers of the institution immediately flow. Being the founders of the government, they give to it such form and powers as in their wisdom they deem best. When instituted, the government is only *their agent* to act for them. In organizing the same, they act in their *collective* capacity.

The lawful and valid acts of a democratic form of government are the acts of the people, in their united capacity. Hence an individual citizen or subject cannot lawfully resist the execution of a law in his individual capacity. Nor can any number of individuals, separately or combined, do this lawfully, so long as the system shall last. The same power that created the government may amend it, either in the mode pointed out by the fundamental law, or they may do so by exercising the right of revolution in extreme cases. But in both cases the right rests in the fact that the sovereign power exists in the founders of the government. They who created may destroy or change, when sufficient reasons exist therefor, and the sufficient reasons they have the political right to determine. The founders can resume the powers they originally conferred upon their agent whenever there exists, in their opinion, a sufficient cause for it.

This right of revolution does not and cannot exist in the Church. Christ was the sole and only founder. It is compared to a kingdom, not to a republic. The right to institute this government was not, therefore, derived from the consent of the governed. The consent of the governed can properly be required only when the parties governed constitute the sovereign power. In other words, when partners institute a government for themselves, the consent of a majority is requisite, but this is not so when a superior being institutes a government for an inferior. Whatever laws Christ gave His Church, and whatever powers of government He bestowed upon Her, must remain unchanged, unless changed in pursuance of some provision of the law itself. And if no such provision exists, then such change cannot be made.

14. Unity is fractured under Protestant theory

Civil government is properly a political partnership, in which each person is equal as a *partner*; and not equal as an independent individual. Partners are always bound by the acts of each other in that capacity, and when they act as such partners their acts affect their co-partners. When they act as partners they act for the society. Hence, in the contemplation of the theory of political government, the right to institute it resides with the majority as the organs of the whole, and the minority must submit, whether they think it best to institute government or not. Such is the theory. In practice there are exceptions; for the law of force is often resorted to, and the minority constitute the government and control it.

When civil government is formed, and offices created, the powers of the government are exercised by these officers, who, in the contemplation of the theory, act independently of the will of individuals. Consequently, individuals, whether many or few, so long as the government remains unchanged, must submit to the decisions of the admitted tribunals. There is no such thing known in any sort of government as the right of the individual governed to construe, in the last resort, the law intended for his own government. Such a right in individuals at once destroys all practical, as well as theoretical government. The two never can coexist. I cannot form a conception of any *possible* system, in which individuals can be governed, and yet construe the law for themselves in the last resort.

The relation that Protestants bear to each other, and to the law of Christianity, under the logical application of their fundamental rule, is very different from that which individuals sustain to each other, and to the laws, under civil institutions. For if the relation was the same, the independent and personal right of private interpretation in the last resort could not exist. The will of the lawmaker, as determined by the officers created by Him, would govern. The whole question, under any logical view of it, resolves itself into this: Was Christ a lawgiver, and did He organize a visible, perpetual, united, and universal church, and give to it any law, and *any* powers of government? If so, those powers of government of necessity must be supreme over individuals, and the right to construe and apply the law must be among the powers given.

Most Protestants admit that there is a positive law given for the government of Christians. This admission, taken in connection with their fundamental rule, makes the relation they sustain to each other and to the law the same that independent sovereignties bear to each other, under the law of nations. The law of nations is a code admitted to exist in theory, by each civilized nation. But there being no *common tribunal* to construe and apply it, each sovereignty is left to construe for itself. The result is, as we might readily suppose, that while in theory this code is admitted by all, there is no uniformity of decision, and the code becomes necessarily powerless to settle disputes, and ceases to be a code of law in fact. The main practical effect has been to mitigate the mode of war, not to prevent it; consequently, civilized, as well as semi-civilized and barbarous nations, carry on war with each other, to the extent of their means and power. War is an expensive game in blood and treasure; and civilized nations have not only warred to the extent of their existing means, but nearly all of them have anticipated the means of posterity, and have, therefore, created burthensome national debts, which they will leave entailed upon their successors.

Among Protestants, their theory being substantially the same, the practical results have been the same. Their wars have generally been wars of words and ill feeling, of discords and divisions –the very kind of wars intended to be prevented by the law of Christ among the professors of His system. Whereas Christ designed but *one* organization; from the beginning of Christianity to the present time, including all the different sects, more than one thousand separate and distinct organizations, differing in doctrines and discipline, have existed. To such a melancholy and deplorable extent have these ever-increasing divisions been carried, that in the eloquent and indignant language of Mr. Campbell, "before the high and holy, and puissant intelligences of earth and heaven, this state of things is most intolerable."

15. The laity are the party governed

If Christ had left the governing power in the Church to be exercised by mere fallible men not guided by the Holy Ghost, and had commanded His followers to obey these officers without any condition or reservation, then the right of revolution was left *practically* in the Church. For these officers, who were to be implicitly obeyed, would be liable at any time to err, and in the end, would err. Thus the system would change in many of its essential features. If, on the contrary it is supposed, Christ left the governing power with conditions and reservations to be *judged of by the parties governed,* the same imminent practical power and danger of revolution would exist in the institution. The liability to err, and the danger of error would, in the latter case, be only transferred from the fallible officers to the fallible parties governed. Indeed could such could be called government at all!

Christ tells His followers to "hear the Church." In addition, Saint Paul, acting for Him, commands his brethren to "obey, submit to, and follow the faith of them that had the rule over them." If, for example, in these cases there were not express, but yet implied conditions and reservations to be judged of by the parties who were *themselves* thus commanded to hear and obey others, is it not clear that the right of revolution would practically exist in the lay members of the Church? Did Christ mean to be understood as saying, in plain language, "hear the Church, so long as *you* think she speaks the truth?" In other words, "hear yourselves." And did Saint Paul mean to say, "obey, submit to, and follow the faith of them that have the rule over you, if *you* think they are right?" That is, obey *yourselves*, and follow your *own faith*.

The idea of a reserved right in the party governed to decide whether the officer placed over him by Christ and acting solely as the agent of Christ, construes the law correctly or not, is utterly incompatible with every principle of government. For even in political government, the right of the citizen or subject to decide thus in his capacity as the party governed, does not exist. Only the whole people, or a majority of them, acting in their sovereign collective capacity, may remodel the government they themselves created.

In the kingdom of Christ, no lay member can act in any other capacity than that of a party governed. He is under government, if there be any in the Church at all. The officers of the Church are equally under government in their individual capacities. So, the Pope, as an individual, is required to do all that any other individual member is required to do. In our political theory, the President as an individual is equally subject to the law of the land.[17]

16. The duties of the judicial power

It is the duty of the judicial power, in every government, to construe the law and apply it to particular cases. The legislative power makes the law, and the judicial power only construes and applies it. The difficulties are about as great in the exercise of one power as in that of the other, and it requires about equal capacity to attain perfection in each. What then is the necessity of a separate judiciary? What are its advantages? Cannot the lawmaker express his intentions as clearly as a tribunal constituted *by him* for that purpose?

That a lawmaker, possessing the same capacity, could use language as correctly as the judge who decides the law, is clear, and must be conceded. But the two are placed in very different positions. There is a wonderful difference between making a law in advance and afterwards construing it.

All laws are made in advance, and before any case can arise under them. They are intended to govern future, not past actions. Hence it follows that law can only lay down principles, but cannot apply them to particular cases that arise after the law is made. Law must, in the very nature of the fact, deal in principles, embracing a variety of cases under each principle. Law never speaks but once. It never changes its language, although the meaning of its terms may be changed by usage. Under any and all sorts of perversion, it says no more. It adopted no new illustrations, suited to the particular question raised, and the capacity of the party. It decides no particular case. All it can do is to lay down principles. It cannot enumerate in advance the incidents that will make up each particular case that may afterwards arise, and pronounce the proper judgment.

But it is not so with a living, speaking judiciary. A particular case comes up before it. The question is, does this particular case come within a certain principle? The tribunal says yea or nay. It does not leave the party to construe the law, and by comparison and rational deduction to arrive at the intent of the lawmaker, but says to him plainly, "in this case you are wrong," or "you are right," as the case may be.

Many of the disputed passages of Scripture are only subject to one of two opposite constructions, one of which being condemned, the other must stand. "This is my body" admits of but one of two opposite constructions. How easy would it be for an authorized tribunal to settle the construction! A tribunal confines its decision to a single point at a time, and adapts its language to the precise state of particular misconstruction. Though it is the general character of language, as a medium of thought to be deficient in precision, there are still certain forms of expression too plain to be misunderstood. The tribunal could take the very words of the proposition and say, "this is wrong." Suppose we had the Council of Jerusalem still with us, could not that tribunal settle the questions now in dispute as it did the one before it?

The decisive advantages of a living, speaking tribunal are:

1. It decides after the difficulty has arisen, and adapts its language to the precise state of the particular case.

2. It can repeat its explanations until it must be understood.

3. It is always prepared to meet every new difficulty, as occasion may demand.

A Court, as each new case arises, makes a construction of the law in reference only to that case. As all cases consist of a certain number of incidents, when one case is decided in a certain way, all cases afterwards arising, having the same incidents, come under the principle settled. If the decision is misunderstood, the Court is always in being, ready, able, and willing to correct any misconstruction of its opinion.[18]

17. How Christ produced certainty in the Church

The law of Christ has to contend against all the vices –all the local prejudices of nations and races –all the changes and novelties of each and every age –and all the vicissitudes of every condition in life. The duties to be performed and the truths to be believed are "hard to flesh and blood." The kingdom takes a wide sweep. It is only bounded by the limits of the habitable earth, and includes the entire race, and extends through all time. The perfect sphere of its duties includes all the virtues our race can possess, and the elevated circle of its faith, the highest and sublimest truths they can believe. Everything morally good must be believed and practiced, and everything evil must be hated and avoided. The Christian is to live for the bright future more than for the tempting present. He must leave to God the revenge of his wrongs and the reward of his merits. The man that injures him, he must pray for –that hates him, he must love. And not only must all these things be believed and done, but the consequences are as enduring as the system is boundless, and as eternity is endless. A few short years of pleasure constitute not its rewards, the temporary terrors of the scaffold, not its punishments.

The perfection of the system –the perfect faith and obedience required –render it still more necessary to know the proper construction of its law. The truths are supernatural, and therefore difficult enough to be believed, and the duties difficult enough to be performed, when they are known with infallible certainty. But how much more difficult would it be, if each individual must construe the entire code at his own peril, without the aid of any authorized interpreter!

There are only, as I conceive, three possible ways in which Christ could produce certainty in the construction of His law:

1. By an inspired personal revelation of the true construction to each individual, as often as occasion should arise.

2. By the institution of an infallible tribunal.

3. By enumerating in advance all the exact incidents of each particular case, and pronouncing the proper judgment as to each.

By far the most simple, logical, and consistent method is the second one. The first is liable to many serious objections. It does away with the necessity of teachers, and of all government in the church, and besides, the inspired persons might know themselves that they were right, but others would have no test by which they could determine between the true and the pretending believer. Each individual asserting, as a matter of fact, resting in his own individual knowledge, and not, therefore, to be disputed, that his interpretation was inspired, the confusion produced would be endless. The third effort would have required an amount of labor at the beginning too extensive and difficult.

18. The Apostolic Church exercised judicial power

Did the teachers of the early church exercise any judicial power? Did *they* construe and apply the law in the last resort? or did each member of the church construe for himself?

In the first chapter of Saint Paul's first Epistle to the Corinthians, verse ten; he lays down the principle of the unity of the faith. He then goes on to construe the law of Christ, and apply it to particular individual cases of heresy then found in the church at Corinth. No one could ever imagine that those particular questions would arise, and the apostle did not know of them until informed by "them of the house of Chloe." The apostle points out, in detail, each particular heresy, and condemns each. He gives them the reason for his construction of the law, assuming as a fundamental principle of the law already taught, that Christ could not be divided. From this position, and the fact that they were all baptized in the name of Christ, he concluded that, under a proper construction of the law, they could only be "of Christ."

Now suppose the apostle had only laid down the point of law in the tenth verse, requiring them to all believe the same thing, and had not specified the particular heresies mentioned. Would that have corrected these errors? The tenth verse contains doubtless but the restatement of a principle already understood, for our Lord had prayed for the unity in faith of all those who should believe in Him. This restatement was made for the purpose of applying it to the particular cases mentioned. If Saint Paul had only made this restatement, which inculcated only the *necessity* of unity, the further question as to which of the four parties were wrong, would have been left wholly unsettled. The brethren would have remained still divided, just as the five hundred Protestant sects all admit, and insist upon, the necessity of unity, while each as strenuously contends that all the others are wrong in their construction of a conceded law. The question having being undecided, those "of Paul" would have said not us, and so of all the others.

Who shall decide when members disagree? Saint Paul said, in substance, I will decide this matter for you. You that say you are "of Apollos," and "of Paul," and "of Cephas," are each and all of you in the wrong; and you that say you are "of Christ," are in the right. This was explicit. No law, made in advance of the existence of these particular errors, could have been so explicit, without going into the full detail of all the circumstances of each particular question.

The question as to the necessity of circumcision for the Gentile converts already alluded to, is another noted instance of the construction and application of the law to a particular case of error. The facts and circumstances of that case were remarkable. They have already been stated, in part.

The apostles, being the first incumbents, appointed to fill the office of teacher, performed all the duties as such, until the disciples so multiplied that it became necessary for them to appoint other teachers. After their appointment *the appointed teachers* taught. At Antioch there were certain prophets and *teachers,* among whom were Barnabas and Saul. All these men are classed together as teachers and prophets, and when Paul and Barnabas went upon a special mission, "they ordained them elders in every church." Now it is plain that all the persons mentioned, namely, Barnabas, Simeon, Lucius, Manaen, and Saul, were all teachers, and carried out the commission "Go teach."[19]

Until the question regarding the circumcision of the gentile converts arose, it was not deemed proper or necessary to decide it. When it did arise, it was among the members of the college of teachers; and so wide was the difference of opinion, that it became necessary to convene a council to consider the question.

Christ had promised the protection and guidance of the Holy Spirit to the apostles and their successors in their corporate capacity as a college of teachers. Hence "the *apostles and elders* came together to *consider* of this matter." When Peter speaks, he argues from certain admitted facts and principles, that circumcision was not required. He contends that, as God bestowed upon the uncircumcised Gentiles the same gifts as on the Jews, and put no difference between them, therefore it followed that circumcision could not be required. If the same *end* could be attained without circumcision, than it was clear that, under the system, it could not be necessary. Peter having taken this ground, and referring to the case of Cornelius, concluded by saying, "We believe that through the grace of the Lord Jesus Christ we shall be saved even as they."

The arguments of Paul and Barnabas consisted of the simple statement of the "miracles and wonders God had wrought among the Gentiles by them." Peter had referred to the single case of Cornelius. But Paul and Barnabas went into other and more numerous cases and proofs to establish the same fact; to wit: that God made no difference between Jew and Gentile –between circumcision and uncircumcision. All of which went to show, by the most rational deduction, that circumcision could not be required by the principles of the law already promulgated, when the *end* in view by the law itself was fully accomplished without this rite. James argues upon the same ground, as well as upon the additional ground that this had been predicted by the prophets of the Old Law; and that, therefore, when the New Law came into existence, it extended to the Gentiles; and that, as it extended to them, it did not require of them circumcision.

That this decision of the Council of Jerusalem was only the judicial construction and application of the law (long before that time promulgated) to this particular case of heresy, is not only shown by the facts and reasons already given, but also by the language used, and the names given to the decision itself. They "came together to *consider* of this matter." The usual form of a judgment is, "It is therefore *considered* by the court." Saint James calls his decision a "sentence." The decision of the whole council is called "decrees," which Paul, Silas, and Timotheus delivered to the different churches to keep. They were called "*decrees* which were ordained of the apostles and elders which were at Jerusalem." Now these terms, "sentence" and "decrees," when both used to designate the *same* thing, can only be applied to the judgment of a judicial tribunal. The language of the Jews to Saint Paul, on a subsequent occasion, conveys the same idea. When speaking of the decision of this council they say:

> As touching the Gentiles which believe, we have written and concluded that they observe no such thing.

The words "*we* have *concluded* that *they* observe no such thing," can only mean, in this connection, to have formed a final judgment; to have ended.

It will be observed that none of the apostles claimed any personal inspiration in reference to this particular question. No one who spoke, attempted to put down the friends of circumcision by the statement that Christ had ever *expressly* mentioned the subject, or that the law, as promulgated at and after the day of Pentecost, had ever *expressly* made any provision upon this exact point. We find nothing in the New Testament history, previous to this decision, that distinctly settled this question. To determine it, required the authoritative judicial application of the conceded principles and facts of the system of law *before* that time promulgated, and for years put in practical operation.

Had the question not been raised until *after* the deaths of the apostles, would there have been no authority in the church to settle it? It seems clear that there would have been such authority.

It is certain that the Council of Jerusalem was the organ of the entire Church. It is certain their decrees bound all the members of the association. It is equally certain that this council was not held by the apostles *alone.* "The *apostles* and *elders* came together to consider of this matter." The elders participated in the discussions. They formed part and parcel of the council. They united in the decrees, and they were aided by the Holy Ghost as well as were the apostles. The elders as well as the apostles said: "For it seemed good to the Holy Ghost and to *us*." Then whatever was done in and by this council, was done by the *joint* act of the apostles and elders, each one participating in the act, and performing his appropriate part of it. And the *decisive conclusions* that inevitably flow from the simple facts recorded of the proceedings of this council, are these:

1. That the judicial power of the church passed to the elders; and that they, together with the apostles, composed this council, and with the apostles exercised the judicial power.

2. That the assistance of the Holy Ghost promised in the commission descended also to the elders, and was *not confined* to the apostles.

It cannot be said that this was a consultation, and no more. A consultation is defined to be "deliberation of two or more persons with a view to some decision."[20] The consultation had in this case resulted in a decision, so that there were *both* a consultation and a decision. When a court is composed of a plurality of judges, it is usual for them to consult with each other, before the decision is made. The decision is the *binding act*, and may or may not follow a consultation, and may also be rendered *without it.*

It may be urged that the apostles and elders did not alone compose the council, as it is said that "it pleased the apostles and elders, with the whole church, to send chosen men..." and "the apostles and elders and brethren send greeting..."[21]

If these expressions stood alone, they would show, *prima facie*, that the council was composed of apostles, elders and others. But taken in connection with other passages, and it would seem plain, that the council was only composed of apostles and elders. It is stated in verse second, that "they determined that Paul and Barnabas, and certain other of them, should go up to Jerusalem unto the apostles and elders about this question;" and in verse six it is stated that "the apostles and elders came together to consider of this matter." The question was agreed to be referred to the apostles and elders, and *these* came together to consider of the matter; and, in the sixteenth chapter, verse four, it is said that the "decrees were ordained of the apostles and elders." The apostles and elders composed the ordaining power, because *they* ordained. No doubt the decision gave satisfaction to the whole Church at Jerusalem, and they no doubt contributed the means to send the messengers, and these facts constituted the reason for mentioning the facts stated. Saint Paul commences several of his Epistles in the joint names of himself and others.[22] But in these same Epistles, he afterwards speaks in the first person singular.

The law governing the Apostolic Church received many instances of judicial construction and application to particular cases of heresy, or other violation of the law. These are only two among the many instances.

19. The judicial power still exists

From the simple narrative of the New Testament it appears certain, that in the days of Christ, whenever His previous words were misconstrued, He was ready to explain; and that after His ascension, the means were still left in the Church to reach the same result. The disciples were not left to get at the proper construction of the law the best way they could, according to the learning, condition, and circumstances of each individual. There existed in those happy days an infallible tribunal to construe and apply the law in the last resort. Disputed constructions of the law were settled decisively, and controversies ended. The disciples of that day saw that the same Holy Spirit guided the Legislative and Judicial powers of this government. These most fortunate disciples could well rejoice for the consolation, when they read the epistle from the Council of Jerusalem. They could dispense with the yoke sought to be imposed upon them, without the slightest risk of being deceived. They had the endorsement of the Holy Ghost. It was the voice of God, speaking through His agents. There was no mistaking the decision. It mentioned the particular heresy in the very words of those who maintained it, and condemned it by the most explicit language, applied to that individual case alone.

THE INFALLIBILITY OF THE CHURCH

The immeasurable distance between a fallible and infallible tribunal is apparent to the simplest mind. Well may Mr. Campbell say:

> We sooner or later all discern, that between the fallible and the infallible, there is a gulf, into which the universe might be hurled, without at all reducing the chasm. Finities and fallibles are weak authorities, when heaven and immortality are at stake.[23]

The practical superiority of such a tribunal may be shown by a very simple but conclusive test. We will suppose that a council could be called at a given time and place, fully empowered to determine all controversies existing among Protestants, with infallible certainty; and that Protestants conceded that fact. How easy it would be to harmonize all differences, and condemn all errors among them. There could exist not the slightest difficulty in understanding the council. Each particular error could be enumerated and condemned. The decisions could be made as plain as the decision of Paul, or that of the Council of Jerusalem. The council could take the definitions of each particular error as made by the party maintaining it, and say: "this we condemn," or "this we approve." Adapting the form of the decree to the error condemned, certainty could be attained.

This was the course pursued in the Council of Jerusalem; for in their decree they say, among other things:

> Forasmuch as we have heard, that certain which went out from us here have troubled with words subverting your souls, saying, Ye must be circumcised and keep the law, to whom we gave no such commandment.

In the case of Luther, when he submitted his work to the Pope, there were some forty-two propositions stated by Luther in his own words. These propositions, as stated by him, were condemned by the Pope; and so plain was the decision that Luther at once understood what was intended.

But according to Protestants no such tribunal can now exist. Faith then rests in the fallible construction of each fallible mind. The written code, by which alone they profess to be guided, makes no further answer –gives no further explanation –names no particular error. Under any and all sorts of perversion, it is silent. Having once laid down general principles, it ceased, and remains mute. Having once spoken, it speaks no more. It allows no one to interpret its language with unerring certainty, as it gives no infallible guide for such a purpose. If this system of uncertainty is the true character of the government of Christ since the days of the apostles, we are truly unfortunate. It had been better for us to have been born in those days of purifying persecution, but of absolute certainty. Better to suffer any amount of temporal inconvenience, than thus be left as mere

"restless wanderers after rest."

But it is true that Christ and His apostles exercised the judicial power during the short period of their lives, and yet intended that this power, which, in its very nature, is a part of the system, and should exist while the law is to be practically enforced in *this* world, should then cease? That therefore, the Christians of that favored day should have and enjoy all the advantages of such a tribunal, and that all subsequent Christians should be governed by a crippled system of law? Was the exercise of the judicial power in the apostolic church idle and useless? If so, why? If useful, then why are we deprived of it? Why is a great system of law, made by an Infallible Lawmaker, and purporting to be permanent, thus shorn of one of its most consolatory and practical elements?

It is a melancholy truth, if it is so. We cannot "rejoice for the consolation," as did the Gentile converts. If this is true, God now speaks through no living agents. He has now no agent on earth who can speak with any authority. Each individual does that *now* for himself, that which was *then alone* done for *all*, by those who could say with *authority*, "*it seemed good to the Holy Ghost and to us.*" One of the most consolatory and beautiful features and conservative powers of the early Church has been lost, when it would seem to be as much needed now as at the beginning.

Instead of possessing the perfection the institution did in the beginning, it has lost its infallible judiciary. According to this leveling and destructive theory, it is now a mock government, not possessing the genuine powers of government, because its judiciary has no infallibility, either actual or judicial. It therefore can make no final and binding decision –a system without a parallel in any social institution. A law intended to govern a united people, and yet each individual governed is to construe the law alone for himself in the last resort. An association whose shadowy tribunals make decisions in mere *form*, that no one is bound to obey; for the reason that the decisions, in the contemplation of the *theory itself*, are not *evidence* of the true construction of the code. They are idle, for they settle no question, as did the decisions of the Apostolic Church. When she spoke through her organs, she was heard.

When she gave her construction of the code, it was final. She was, in fact, *a Church.*[24]

The Protestant theory does leave the Church, since the days of the apostles, in the most deplorable condition. She is still charged with all the duties of teaching that devolved upon the apostles. She is required to teach the same truths –no more, no less. But while she is thus bound to construe and apply the very same code of law, she is denied, by this theory, the very powers and qualifications found *necessary*, in the days of the apostles, in order to do the very *same thing*. If the judicial power was necessary, and did exist, and was exercised in the Apostolic Church, can any logical mind conceive or give any substantial reason why the same power should not always exist? If certain given powers and qualifications were necessary to administer the law at one time, is it not so at all times, when the same thing has to be done?

20. Scriptural proofs of the infallibility of the Church examined

Has this retrograding change expressed by Protestant theory come over the system? Is it true that we are now left without any infallible tribunal in the Church? Is it true that questions of construction can arise from age to age, and accumulate from century to century, and still remain undecided till the last day of the institution on earth, for want of power in the Church to settle them? Is the Church, founded and built by Christ, so imbecile as that? Is *His* own work, *His* own institution, so unworthy of any confidence? Is this the best that a Divine Founder of an institution could do?

However, what were His promises to His Church? What did His chosen witnesses say of her? Did they speak of her as weak and sickly, tottering and mutable? Did they give her a perishable, temporary character?

Before we proceed to examine the texts in reference to that institution which Christ called "*His church*," and the apostle Paul "*The Church*," it is necessary to inquire whether this Church was visible or invisible.

It is difficult to conceive how an invisible church could exist as a church at all. It can hardly fill Lindley Murray's definition of a noun, for it seems not to be "the name of any thing that exists, or of which we can form any notion." It is an intangible, indefinable, and imaginary body, about which no distinct idea can be formed, and for the existence of which no tolerable reason can be given. It is difficult to divine for what purpose, and to what end it was instituted. It being invisible, no one can see it, and it cannot exercise any authority.

The powers of government given to the church were given to the visible church, as we already proved. When Christ tells us to hear the church, He certainly means the visible Church. And when He speaks of one fold, He must refer to the visible Church. When we are told that the "Lord added daily to the Church such as should be saved," we are informed that they were added to the visible Church. And the church in which Timothy was to behave himself, was the visible Church, "the pillar and ground of the truth." The duties inculcated upon Timothy and Titus were to be discharged in the visible Church. The Council of Jerusalem was held in the visible Church, and they issued visible decrees.

It seems to be clear that whatever powers of government Christ bestowed upon the Church, were to be exercised by the visible Church, and the Holy Ghost guided this exercise in the days of the apostles. If those powers and this guidance were intended to be temporary, and to last only for the first few years of her existence, and then to cease forever, of course the exact limits of their duration are plainly marked! Otherwise it would be very difficult to determine, from the Scripture, the period when they did cease, or whether they were to cease at all. But no such limits are set, and we find the promises accompanied with expressions that refer to all coming time. We cannot, therefore, without the utmost violence to the language, and the whole drift and spirit of the system, decide them to have been temporary in their character.

In Gospel of Saint Matthew our Lord said:

> If he shall neglect to hear them, tell it unto the church: but if he neglect to hear the church, let him be unto thee as a heathen and a publican.[25]

When Christ tells us to hear the church, He speaks of but one Church –the Church He instituted. He says the *Church* in the singular. He does not refer to the *church* as existing in this or that age, in this or that country, but He refers to the corporate institution as existing in all after ages. The Church is viewed as an artificial person or corporation, that never dies, and that can speak through her proper organs. He says "hear the church." It is the Church that speaks, not the individual members in their own right. The teachers that speak, speak for her, and as her organs only. What she does through her organs, she does herself.

But not only does Christ say that the Church can speak, but He commands us, without any reservation, to "hear the church." There is no exception made. The command is general and imperative. Would He command us to hear, without any reservation or exception, a mere fallible tribunal? In such case we should be compelled to "hear the church," whether she spoke the truth or not. Again our Lord says explicitly:

> Upon this rock I will build my church, and the gates of Hell shall not prevail against it.

The Church is here viewed in the light of a visible structure, founded upon a rock, and that is the reason why Saint Paul afterwards calls this Church the "house of God." Now the phrase "my church" –the phrase "the church" –and the phrase "house of God," unquestionably refer to one and the same thing precisely; namely: the visible Church.

When, therefore, Christ tells us that the gates of hell shall not prevail against this church, His promise regards the entire Church of all ages, in the same way that the command to hear the church does. The promise is as general and unlimited as the command; and they either must stand or fall together. They both regard the Church as existing through all coming time.

Christ establishes the Church as a decider of controversies arising under the Christian law; and then says, in another place, that the gates of hell shall not prevail against her. This promise has relation to the command to hear the Church. As the Church possessed the power to decide controversies, this must be one goal of its institution. The power was given for a great and beneficial purpose. If she failed to exercise this power correctly, she would so far fail to attain the purpose of her creation.

Nothing would seem more consonant with reason and Scripture than this: that teaching the truth was the leading end to be accomplished by the visible church, and that the power and duty of teaching must include the right and duty to determine what shall be taught, and what is contrary thereto. If the church failed in this main purpose of her creation, then the gates of hell would have prevailed against her. For it must be evident, that the moment the governing power of the church failed, she must fail, and subvert the souls of those who are commanded to hear her. What more could the gates of hell desire than that this Church should fail to do her duty, and thus defeat the mighty purpose of her creation?

It would seem also clear that the temporary errors of particular teachers, would not subvert the entire Church, any more than the errors of those who insisted upon the necessity of circumcision, or of those unruly teachers alluded to by Saint Paul, or the errors of inferior courts would subvert civil government. They are spots upon the sun, and spots only. When the entire governing power of the Church is subverted (wherever that power is held to be placed), then the gates of hell would surely prevail against her. Such a result would be in plain violation of the promises of Christ.

21. Other views in regard to an infallible Church

Mr. Rice in his argument to sustain infant baptism, quotes largely from the Ancient Fathers to show the practice of the Church and says:

> In conclusion I offer one more argument. It is this: if it should turn out that infant baptism is unscriptural, and that Mr. Campbell's views of immersion as the only valid baptism are true, then we are forced to the conclusion, that for several centuries there was no true church.... We are obliged to believe that the Savior's promise has failed; and the 'gates of hell' did prevail against his church.[26]

I certainly cannot dispute the argument and conclusion of Mr. Rice. However, it would be very difficult to show any reason against applying the same argument to other alleged errors, charged to have been introduced into the Church. If she failed because she taught the alleged error of infant baptism (conceding it to have been an error, for the sake of argument) then she equally failed when she taught the doctrines which the Protestants allege as errors, if in fact they were such. I am constrained to think that the argument of Mr. Rice, when fairly and legitimately carried out, would prove one of two things very clearly:

1. That these alleged errors were truths handed down from the apostles; or

2. That the promises of Christ did fail – His Church did fail – and there is no true Church in the world.

If we say that the Church has ceased, or will cease, to exist at any period before her prescribed course has been run, then we must concede the failure of the promises of Christ. Such a failure would be in direct conflict with His clear and most explicit promises –"lo, I am with you always, even unto the end of the world" –"the gates of hell shall not prevail against it." In addition, His promises would have failed because the continued existence of the Church is necessary to accomplish the great and beneficent purposes of His mission. The Church having been constituted by Him, His teaching agent, it was but just to all ages, that this same teaching authority should be always in existence, and always visible. If we regard the Church as a visible corporation (and we can form no conception of an invisible corporation composed of visible men) then her continued existence must follow, or she must die to exist no more on earth. The promises of Christ to her were unconditional, and not conditional, as were His promises to individuals regarding matters of their own. Her unfailing existence and continued purity, as a teaching agent, are absolutely necessary to accomplish the great ends contemplated in her creation. If we once concede that the Church can fail, then we concede that Christ was fallible, weak, and impotent, and only created an institution like himself.

Our Savior commanded us to hear the church, and pledged Himself for her continued purity and unfailing existence. When creating the office of teacher, and appointing the first members of the college, and commanding them what they should do in *that capacity* He also said that He would be "with them always, even unto the end of the world." Before that time He had promised them that the Father would give them the Comforter to "abide with them forever."

What did our Lord mean by the expression, "I am with you –abide with you?" Christ very often uses these expressions, which mean the same thing, and in every case the meaning is invariably the same; namely: "I am with you to aid you with my power." It always means that the persons to whom the promise was given were to be guided and protected by him. The presence of the Holy Ghost did the same. Of course, our Lord would not be with them for a mere idle purpose, and He could only be with them to enable them to accomplish the end proposed. Therefore, the effect of this promise is always limited to the objects for which it was given. When Christ constituted a college of teachers, and promised to be with them to the end of the world, He only promised to be with them in the office He created, and for the purposes of the office. Hence we find the Holy Ghost abiding with the Council of Jerusalem, and guiding that tribunal to a correct construction of the law.

It can be said, that as all men possess free agency, and no one is compelled to be a Christian it is possible that in some one or more ages of the world, there would be no Christians on earth, and no Church; and that Christianity might afterwards revive. It is true, that such a state of case is abstractly possible. Our Lord did promise that the 'gates of hell' should not prevail against His Church. How then, could he positively make this promise, and yet leave free agency untouched? If the 'gates of hell' should prevail *at any time* against the Church, the promise that it should never happen, would fail.

The answer to this is very simple. Our Lord foresaw the future. Therefore he adapted His system and promise to the actual state of things, and not to bare possibilities. The personal free agency of all men He left untouched; and yet he could safely promise that the 'gates of hell' should not prevail against His Church. He foresaw that among the millions of human beings existing in all ages, there would always be a sufficient number believing in His name to form the Church.

The Church, being a continuing corporation, with numbers indefinite and variable, and being his own institution, created as His own agent, He has the right to control this artificial being while assuming to teach His own law and doing His own business. Although He has not the right to force any one to join the Church, yet after they did so voluntarily, and while voluntarily remaining members, He has the right to control the collective whole while the whole assumed to act for Him as His agent. Most errors in reference to the Church will be found, when thoroughly examined, to be essentially based on the error of not distinguishing between individuals, acting for themselves, and the corporation or Church, acting for Christ. When a man joins the Church, he acts for himself, and not as an agent for Christ. In reference to his own business his free agency is untouched. The Church is not an individual, but the combined whole. It is the corporation that our Lord infallibly aids, when she assumes to teach as his agent, and in His name. He might well promise His unfailing protection and His overruling assistance to an institution that he foresaw would always exist by the voluntary acts of His creatures. Knowing that here would be believers in every age, who of their own free will become such, He could well upon this existing basis predicate His promise that this existing institution should always teach the truth as He delivered it.

The words of Saint Paul are very emphatic and clear. Speaking of the visible Church, he calls it "the church of the living God, the pillar and ground of the truth." Observe the certainty and force of the expression, – the Church – the pillar and (the) ground of the truth – the house – the living God. There was one God, one house, one church, one pillar, one ground, and one system of truth referred to, and *only one*.

The apostle had ample reason for saying so. He commanded brethren to "obey, submit to, and follow the faith of them that had the rule over them," and had himself been at the Council of Jerusalem, and had witnessed that tribunal guided by the Holy Spirit to a final decision. He might well call the Church the pillar and ground of the truth. Now as Saint Paul regarded the Church not only as the pillar, but also as the ground of the truth, how could such an institution be anything but infallible?

The distance between the fallible and infallible being so great, as so eloquently described by Mr. Campbell, how could such glorious things be affirmed of a mere fallible tribunal? Nothing, it would seem, could fill the description of the apostle, but an infallible Church. How could a church teaching essential error be the pillar and ground of the truth? In such case she would be the pillar and ground of error, and not of truth. It could not be denied, except by an unbeliever, that whatever Christ promised He would perform. It would seem impossible for a Church to which such magnificent promises were given, to be fallible as mere human institutions.

If we consider the visible Church in regard to its founder, the nature of such an organization, and its history we reach the irresistible conclusion that it is guided by the Infallible Spirit. Its founder was of the perfect character and unlimited power. Our Lord commanded His followers to hear the Church and promised to found it upon a rock, and protect it against the gates of hell, and to be with His teachers to the end of the world, and to send them the Holy Ghost to abide with them forever.

To achieve its end it has to contend with the nature of all governments of law over associated bodies of men; including the inherent defects of all language, the obscurities peculiar to the Scriptures, and difficulties even in the application of well understood principles to particular cases. In addition, this great institution had obstacles to be overcome, arising from the extent of its empire, the long period of its existence, the variety of races, manners, habits, and national prejudices, and the perfection of faith and practice required.

We then see what Christ and His apostles did, how our Lord first taught His disciples, and then appointed them as teachers, and they in turn did the same thing, and commanded those they appointed to appoint others. History also shows how the teachers had the rule over the apostolic Church, their faith was to be followed, and they were to be obeyed. Then see how Christ carried out his promises by guiding the decision of the Council of Jerusalem to infallible certainty, making the Church the pillar and ground of the truth in fact. To use the touching language of the noble Saint Paul, we "think on these things," and sincerely, and without prejudice, calmly put them all together, and fully appreciate the combined force of all, then it is that:

Truth bursts upon us with resistless day.

The conclusion becomes irresistible, that Christ was the Divine founder of a perfect system. We conclude that the permanent code was made perfect at the beginning, not only because He possessed the power and the wisdom to make it so, but that all His subjects in all after ages, might be alike governed by the same law. We conclude that as the necessary judicial power to secure this permanent end, could not be exercised in advance, He confided it to His agents, whom He qualifies and guides from age to age, with the same Infallible Spirit that dictated the code itself.

In reference to the infallibility of the Church, Dr. Spring says:

> We grant that there are promises of divine guidance made to the church, but we do not grant that there are any promises of infallibility. That the true and spiritual community of the faithful have the promise of preservation from essential and fundamental error, no one can question, because such preservation is indispensable to its existence as a true church.[27]

The distinction between infallibility and that "divine guidance" sufficient to preserve the Church from essential error, is, I apprehend, not very apparent. I understand that infallibility may well be conferred upon a corporation for a certain given purpose, and limited to that purpose, in the same way that limited jurisdiction may be conferred upon a particular court.

The infallibility bestowed upon the apostles was confined to Christianity. They were not any wiser as to science. So, when divine personal protection was promised to Saint Paul, it was specially confined to that purpose.[28] So, the infallibility promised the Church may well relate to faith and morals -- to the judicial construction and application of the Christian code; and if that infallibility embraces these objects, and preserves the Church free from error, it does no more than the "divine guidance" spoken of by the learned divine Dr. Spring. The amount and measure of aid to the Church is the same, producing the same effects, in both cases, and is equally divine in both. The only difference, it seems, is this, that Dr. Spring contends that this divine guidance was given to the invisible Church, which is, therefore, the invisible pillar and ground of the truth and the invisible house of God; while I contend it was given to the visible Church, for the visible exercise of its powers of teaching. It was certainly as easy to bestow it upon the visible, as upon the invisible Church, and far more useful in practice. The writer states on page 33:

> The true Church of Jesus Christ is a spiritual community. While the church visible, may contain the church spiritual, they are by no means identified.

The language of Mr. Rice, and that of Mr. Breckenridge, as already quoted, seems clearly to give the promises to the visible Church. They seem too sensible to believe in that intangible and imaginary thing, called an invisible Church.

I could never find any evidence that Christ ever did build more than *one* Church; and as it is *conceded* that He did establish the visible Church, I never could see any reason for the creation of any other. There certainly is only one Church mentioned in the New Testament. Christ said, "My church," and Saint Paul said, "The church."

It would also seem evident from the very nature of mere delegated authority that this protection from error only extended to the apostles and their successors in their official capacity. Thus in their personal capacity they are left as other individual members of the Church. As agents and officers of Christ, they were guided by the Holy Spirit because their acts, in that capacity, were *His acts*. When they assumed to act for Him, He did not permit them to err in His name. If they had the power to err as His agents, then we could not know that the facts stated by them as His chosen and inspired witnesses were infallibly true. Christ then guaranteed their official not their personal, conduct. When they acted for themselves, as individuals, their free agency was left in full force. It could not have been otherwise, without a violation of the great principle of personal free agency. Their official power was one thing, and their personal virtue was another. They were not *compelled* to become the agents of Christ; and when they did voluntarily become so, He had the right to control them in reference to His "Father's business," as much as any man has the right to control His own agent, in reference to his own business.

Hence, all the apostles personally sinned while they were with Christ, and under His immediate visible eye. Peter and Paul were guilty of dissimulation long after the day of Pentecost. What was true of the apostles was true of most of the patriarchs, prophets, and priests of Aaron's line. Being *men*, they sinned even after all they had seen and heard. Moses was not allowed to enter the promised land, because of sin. But these personal transgressions of the law did not render void their official acts. Christ also spoke to the multitude and to his disciples:

> Saying the Scribes and Pharisees sit in Moses' seat. All therefore whatsoever they bid you observe, that observe and do; but do not ye after their works: for they say and do not.[29]

The case of Caiaphas is a remarkable illustration of this clear principle, concerning which Mr. Campbell says:

> Even the wicked Caiaphas was vested with an oracle. The spirit came upon him, and he prophesied, being High Priest that year. He was then a good High Priest, although a wicked man.[30]

Zacharias was punished for not believing the angel Gabriel, yet he was afterwards filled with the Holy Ghost and prophesied. Even the thief and traitor Judas Iscariot, was sent with the other apostles to preach the gospel, heal the sick, and cast out devils.[31]

22. The tribunal under the Old Dispensation

In the debate with Mr. Campbell, Mr. Rice maintained this position:

> The church then is the same under the Jewish and Christian dispensations.[32]

Under the Jewish dispensation there existed a tribunal to determine all questions arising under the law of God.

> And behold Amariah the chief Priest is over you in all matters of the Lord; and Zebadiah, the son of Ishmael, the ruler of the house of Judah, for all the king's matters: also the Levites shall be officers before you.[33]

These tribunals are also spoken of in the seventeenth chapter of Deuteronomy. The sentence was *final*, for the Israelites were told "not to decline from the sentence to the right hand not to the left." Josephus also states that the "High Priest sacrifices to God before other priests, guards the laws, and *determines controversies*."[34]

It will be perceived that there were two Presidents of the Court, one the High Priest for ecclesiastical causes – "matters of the Lord;" and the other for civil cause – "the king's matters;" and that the penalty for disobedience was death. God himself gave the code of law, which this ecclesiastical tribunal was empowered and required to construe and administer. From its decisions no appeal could be taken, and all the Israelites were to submit implicitly. The right of private interpretation in the last resort did not exist under that system. There was conclusive authority in this court. It was limited, however, in its jurisdiction and duration.

Now, was the infallibility bestowed upon this tribunal actual or judicial? From the fact that its decisions were not to be questioned, and that it was its duty to expound and administer the express law of God, it would naturally follow, that it possessed actual infallibility. That God should communicate an express and positive law to His chosen people, prescribing the worship due to Him, and at the same time direct them to obey implicitly a tribunal created by Him, but still fallible and erring, would hardly be in unison with the evident intent and object of giving the law itself. This tribunal was intended to endure for many ages, and if liable to err, would almost certainly depart from the pure spirit of the law, sooner or later, and thus defeat the intention of the lawmaker.

We know that the wicked Caiaphas was enabled to prophesy, because he was High Priest that year. The gift was attached to his *official character*. It is true; Christ reproaches the Pharisees with having made void the law of God, in certain specified respects, by their traditions. But this does not seem to be directed against the decisions of this tribunal, (which our Lord had expressly commanded His disciples to observe,) but against the opinions of individuals. It is clear, that the opinions of individuals could not destroy the character of the tribunal itself. Christ Himself clearly distinguishes between the decisions of this tribunal, and the acts of the Scribes and Pharisees, "for they say and do not."

It is alleged that there was a tradition among the Jews, that Christ would be a temporal sovereign. Was this ever so decided by this tribunal? The existence of this tradition, or opinion, among the mass of the nation, would not prove that the tribunal had ever made any decision upon the question. Again, was the question regarding the true character of Christ's then future kingdom upon carth, a matter material to be understood and believed by the Jews? The Pharisees believed in the resurrection of the dead, and in the existence of spirits; while the

Sadducees rejected both. Had any one of these questions ever been decided by this tribunal? I am not aware that any such decision was ever made.

But if it was a matter of faith with the Jews, that Christ's kingdom should not be temporal, but spiritual, and it was matter of fact that this tribunal had decided to the contrary, then it would follow, either that its decisions were not final, or that God required the Jews to obey erroneous decisions. If the determination was not final, then, who was to question it and how was it to be done? Both the law and the tribunal for its administration, were expressly made and organized by God himself; and no human power could set them aside, but they must be obeyed until their termination.

I am therefore forced to conclude that this tribunal was infallible in fact, and guided by God, who created it. I cannot see any evidence that such was not the fact; but on the contrary, every circumstance confirms this view. I know it is very forcibly and justly said, that in rejecting Christ, as this tribunal did in his condemnation, it clearly erred. Nothing can be clearer than the fact that this tribunal did err in that case. Now were the people bound to submit to its decision, and reject Christ? Most clearly not. They were bound to reject the decision. Then, if they were in this *particular* case, not only at liberty to reject the decision, but bound to do so, upon what ground can we claim infallibility of *any* kind, for this erring tribunal? Why should men be required to obey such a tribunal? And on the other hand, why should men have the right, first to ask the decision of a tribunal, and then to set it aside, if it happened not to suit them?

There must be some fair and just way to settle and adjust all these apparent difficulties. The very fact that the *only* conceded error in the decisions of this tribunal occurred in the close of its duration, if not afterwards, is conclusive proof to my mind, that it did possess actual infallibility up to the period when this protection was withdrawn. When did this tribunal err before this period? During the many ages of its existence, under every variety of change and trial, if it did not err, then it must have been protected.

In the law creating this tribunal, it was limited in jurisdiction, and in duration. It was only to continue until the new dispensation came in. Before Christ appeared, the only living tribunal to expound the law of God, was the one created by God Himself. The people could look to no other. But in the very law itself, it was shown that Christ should come.

This tribunal had always so held. After our Lord appeared, they were bound to know that this tribunal was superseded in all things opposed to His teaching. Our Lord was then present a living, visible teacher, to whom they could appeal.

As to the *exact* period at which this divine protection was withdrawn, it is not material for us to know. From the command of Christ to His apostles, and the prophecy of Caiaphas, it would seem clear that it was not withdrawn at the commencement of our Lord's ministry. It may be than when our Lord ate the Passover for the last time, that He closed the law. Or it may be, that as the period of our Lord's earthly ministry was one of preparation for the incoming dispensation, and was a period of transition, that this protection was gradually withdrawn; especially in reference to Christ and His then future kingdom.

But conceding, for the sake of the argument only, that this tribunal was never under the Divine guidance at any period of its existence. Then the state of the case, and the natural result flowing from it, would be this: that God had made an express law for the government of His chosen people, intended to exist for many ages, and had Himself created a tribunal for the administration of His law, from whose decisions no appeal could be taken; and yet He left it as fallible as if it had been a mere human institution. But such was the invincible necessity for the existence of some visible and accessible tribunal to construe and administer the law, that even so fallible a court was much superior to the right of individual interpretation in the last resort –so necessary are uniformity and peace in every association of men. If this position be correct, that the court possessed mere judicial, and not actual, infallibility, this tribunal did make void the law of God by its decisions; and yet the people had no right of appeal from its decisions, but were bound to submit implicitly. From which it would seem clear, that even a mere fallible tribunal is better than no tribunal at all!

Why, then, does not this *same* Church under the new dispensation, have also a tribunal to decide controversies arising under the law of Christ? If it be the same Church, as Mr. Rice contends, it ought to possess equal privileges with the Church under the old and mere preparatory dispensation.

But if the position be true, that this tribunal was protected by the divine guidance up to the termination of its legal existence, then, by what process of reason can we arrive at the conclusion, either that our Lord left no tribunal in His Church, or that its decisions can fail before its destined course is run? While Christ was on earth, He was a present, living, and supreme Sovereign, to whom application could be made in all cases; but since His ascension, if there be no tribunal in the Church, there is no government, and no certain mode to terminate any controversy. Now, either give us Christ present and visible, or give us some tribunal to act for Him. Leave us not in a worse condition then the Jews of old. The code of law given to them, was certainly as plain and as easily understood, as the law of Christ. If they needed a tribunal, even though actually fallible, do we not also? The end of the new dispensation has not yet arrived. Christ has not appeared the second time. Before He does so appear, let us have some tribunal whose judgments cannot fail. And if we cannot have an actually infallible tribunal, let us have one that we may *safely* follow –right or wrong. It would, at least, be much better than that confused and illogical theory which requires *unity*, while it leaves us no means to attain it, but makes ever member of that which is called a Church, the judge of the law in his own case in the last resort.

From Mr. Rice's position one of two things must follow: either that the church under the new dispensation has such a tribunal, or that she has lost a most important part of her constitution, and is nothing now in unity, efficiency, and symmetry to what she was of old. She has lost the great conservative element that she possessed while confined to the Jews, now that she embraces all nations, and for that very reason, seems to need it most.

23. Claims of private interpretation in the Apostolic Church

In this connection it will be necessary to examine certain texts and reasons, which are relied on by Protestant writers to show, that even in the days of the apostles, the right of private interpretation existed in each member independent of the church, and not in subordination to it. If such right existed in that day, as a matter of course it existed ever after. If, on the contrary, it did not exist then, it never existed afterwards.

It is difficult upon principles of sound reasoning, to understand how this right could exist in the individual members of the church when so many persons were forced by her decisions to change their construction, and others were expelled because they refused to do so. It is difficult, I apprehend, to reconcile the strong and clear commands of Christ, of St. Paul, and of the Council of Jerusalem, with the alleged right of private interpretation in the last resort.

The following passages are most usually relied upon:

THE INFALLIBILITY OF THE CHURCH

1. "You search the scriptures; because you think that in them you have eternal life; and it is they that bear witness to me..."[35]

2. "Now these Jews were more noble than those in Thessalonica. for they received the word with all eagerness, examining the Scriptures daily to see if these things were so."[36]

3. "Beloved, do not believe every spirit, but test the spirits to see whether they are of God..."[37]

4. "Not that we lord it over your faith; we work with you for your joy, for you stand firm in your faith."[38]

5. "If any of you lacks wisdom, let him ask God, who gives to all men generously and without reproaching, and it will be given him."[39]

6. "All Scripture is inspired by God and profitable..."[40]

The ground taken by Protestants is, substantially, that these texts establish two points:

1. That individuals were allowed to read the Scriptures and were commended for so doing.

2. That as they were permitted to read, of course they were permitted to construe.

If we take these and other texts and construe them together, so as to give force and effect to all, we shall find but little difficulty in arriving at a just conclusion. It will be seen that the first two passages relate to persons outside the church –to aliens from the Kingdom. They had never come within the jurisdiction of the Church, and she could not inflict upon them any ecclesiastical punishment. All she could do to persons in their lost state was to place before them the truth, which they could either accept or refuse. If they refused, she could do no more. No affirmative act, on her part, was required to change the relation they sustained to her. They simply remained where they were before. She had no power or jurisdiction over them, any more than a political government can have jurisdiction over aliens not within its territory. They had never received any thing from the Church, had contracted no obligations to her, and she had, of course, nothing to withdraw. Therefore, the right of individual construction existed in aliens from the Church, (in the same way that such right exists in aliens from political government,) because they were such, and only acted and spoke *as such.* If they remained in that state of alienage, *they* were the sufferers, not the Church.

But in reference to *members*, who bore another and a very different relation to the Church, the rule was *different.* Hence Christ said those of His fold –the Church –would hear His voice and follow Him. He told *members* to hear the Church; and Saint Paul commanded members to obey the rulers of the Church; and Saint Peter exhorts his *brethren* to submit to their under-shepherds; and Timothy and Titus and were to rebuke and expel members, not strangers.

Conceding for the sake of the argument only, that the teaching authority of the Church, in the days of the apostles, permitted the lay members to read or hear the Scriptures as one means of instruction. Then the essence of the objection is that the right of the church to construe the law in the last resort is incompatible with the reading of the Scriptures by individuals. But is this true? The true explanation is this: that the individual construes in the *first instance*, and the church in the *last resort.* These rights are perfectly compatible with each other, and exist in every system of law. For the very reason that the individual under every system of government is allowed to construe in the first instance, he is not allowed to construe in the last resort.

The object of the just lawgiver is to place in the mind of the party governed a perfect knowledge of his will. The written or traditional code –the words of the legislator –are mere evidence of his will, which is the higher and ultimate object sought by the party under government. Suppose that for this purpose the lawmaker places in the hands of each one of his subjects, the volume containing his law, and at the same time they are informed by him and by the book itself that there is a tribunal to construe in the last resort; is there anything illogical or contradictory in this? If so, then all the great legislators and jurists of every civilized country in the world have long acted upon a very illogical system.

The great statesmen and jurists of the United States, from the days of Washington to the present time have all, with one accord, urged every citizen to read and study the Constitution of his Country; and yet the Constitution itself informs everyone that the right of *ultimate* construction rests with the Supreme Court of the United States. The Senate of the United States has had purchased, for gratuitous disposition, some thirty-five thousand copies of Hickey's corrected copy of that instrument.

Now suppose an individual to whom Mr. Webster had sent a copy, to have addressed him thus "Sir, you have sent for my perusal and study a number of Hickey's Constitution; and yet, I find, upon examination of the instrument, that there is a judiciary to construe the Constitution and other laws in the last resort. Therefore, for what purpose have I read it? since my construction is but subordinate, and not final. Is it not absurd to recommend a man to read and study an instrument which, at last, will be construed by another tribunal, without any regard to what he has done? We can well imagine the surprise with which the great constitutional expounder would have received this plausible, but wholly erroneous objection.

The Constitution and laws of our country contain many plain provisions, easily understood, and some hard to be understood –as Saint Peter says of Saint Paul's Epistles. The reader, therefore, can learn a portion, and this will be profitable to him. He can learn those plain provisions that teach him he is under government; and that while he has the privilege to read and construe the law in the first instance, the ultimate right of construction is vested in the Judiciary.

If there can be any real incompatibility in the existence of a subordinate right of construction in *one* party, and the superior right of exposition in *another*, then it is most difficult to perceive it. The Old Law was required to be read at the feast of tabernacles to all the people, and yet they were implicitly bound by the higher construction of the tribunal established by God Himself.[41] Now there is no difference, so far as the point of present inquiry is concerned, in reading and hearing read the law. In one case the *words* are conveyed by sight, in the other by hearing, to the mind; and in *both* the *words* of the law must be *construed.*

Now if there be no incompatibility in permitting each citizen to study the Constitution himself, while his construction is but subordinate and not final, how then does it follow that the ancient Christians could not read the Scriptures unless they, and each of them, were allowed to decide the construction in the last resort? The passages quoted, nowhere lay down any such principle. They establish the proposition that individuals were commended for reading the Scriptures. But cannot this be true, and yet perfectly consistent with the ultimate right of the church to construe in the last resort? The individual could be profited and edified, and yet hear and obey the church. They but exercised a subordinate privilege that exists in all governments. These texts do not annul the clear and specific provisions of the code, requiring us to hear the church, and obey, submit to, and follow the faith of them who have rule over us.

The practice of the apostles and elders of the church in their day was perfectly consistent with this view. They intended to make the system consistent with itself. They did not intend to give commands that were not to be obeyed. When we look into Saint Paul's Epistles we find that a large portion of them is taken up in giving his construction of the code, and his reasons and proofs to sustain it; and hence he refers often to the Old Scriptures. In these Epistles we find him mentioning certain particular errors in different churches, and distinctly condemning them. The brethren to whom he wrote had misconstrued the law, and we find Saint Paul overruling their construction. The Corinthian brethren had erred in this way. So, the Jewish teachers who insisted upon the necessity of circumcision for the Gentile converts, had misconstrued the law, and the Council of Jerusalem overruled their construction, just as a higher Court would the construction of an inferior tribunal.

Christ had appealed to His miracles as proofs of His character. The Pharisees relied upon the Scriptures, and our Lord referred them also to those Scriptures, at the same time telling them, in substance, that they misconstrued them, and that if they would search and construe properly, they would find that these Scriptures testified of Him. But in thus referring to the Old Testament, did our Lord intend to say to the Jews that His Miracles were no proofs of His mission? He only referred to additional, but not contradictory proofs. And when the noble Bereans searched the Old Scriptures, they did not neglect the proofs that Paul and Silas gave them, independent of these Scriptures.[42] So, when Saint Paul said the Scriptures were profitable, he did not mean to say: "You must not obey, submit to, or follow the faith of them that have the rule over you." Nor did he intend, when he commanded Timothy and Titus to command, teach, exhort, and rebuke with all authority, to ordain and try elders, and reject heretics, that these persons thus rebuked and rejected, should construe the law for themselves, independent of Timothy and Titus. These persons were in duty bound to obey and submit, not to govern and decide themselves. When Christ told his followers to hear the Church, He did not mean to say that they should construe the law independent of her.

The quotation from Saint John, where he tells his brethren to "try the spirits whether they are of God," is far from being against the view I have taken, but would seem to support it. The apostle gives his brethren two rules by which they were to test the spirits to know whether they were false teachers or not, for many false prophets had gone out into the world:

1. "Every spirit that confessed that Jesus Christ had come in the flesh was of God, and every one that denied it was not of God.

2. "He that knoweth God heareth us: he that is not of God heareth not us.

Hereby know we the spirit of truth and the spirit of error."

The spirit that confessed Christ was a true spirit; and the test, as to whether a particular individual confessed Christ, was the fact whether he heard the apostles or not. This was saying, in substance, that the false prophets were they who refused to hear the church; for when they refused to hear the proper organs of the church, they refused to hear the Church itself. This was a very simple test by which to detect these false prophets. The apostle first tells his brethren what they must do, and then tells them how they can do it. So the apostle Paul, when he commanded the Corinthians to speak the same thing, and be united in the same judgment, tells them to submit themselves to those of the house of Stephanas, and to all such.

The fourth extract, where Saint Paul says he had not dominion over the faith of his brethren, was intended simply to state that that apostle acted in a subordinate capacity, and not in his own right. Dominion is defined to be "sovereign or supreme authority."[43] No one could have dominion over faith but God. The right of a subordinate officer to decide the proper construction of the law, and to say what was faith as defined by it, does not give him dominion over the faith. To have dominion over faith is to say what it shall be, not what it is. It is the power to create, not the power simply to declare. The Council of Jerusalem did not claim any dominion over the faith, but only the right to declare what it was as previously established by a higher power. So it was with Paul and Barnabas when the people wished to sacrifice to them as Gods. They declared they were not Gods – that they did not act for themselves, but as subordinate agents. The apostle certainly did not assume to *create* faith, while he as certainly did assume the right to declare what was, and what was not, of faith. He did not mean to say to these same brethren, whose errors of construction he had expressly condemned in his first Epistle, that he had usurped authority not granted to him.

In the fifth extract the apostle tells those of his brethren who lack wisdom, how they can obtain it. The prayer of faith is, no doubt, one means of obtaining Christian wisdom; but it is not the only means pointed out in the law, and is not exclusive of those other means mentioned in other portions of the Written Word. The existence of this means is not incompatible with the existence of the others. It is said in one place that we are saved by faith; in another, by baptism; in another still, by grace. One does not exclude the others. We must put them all together, and give force and effect to all, so that all may stand, and the will of the lawmaker be consistently carried out in all things, as He unquestionably intended to accomplish some good purpose by each and all. The apostle James did not intend to contradict his own practice in the Council of Jerusalem. Nor did he intend to contradict the command of Christ to hear the church, nor those of Saint Paul to obey the rulers of the church nor those of Saint Peter to follow their under-shepherds, nor the test given by Saint John, that they who heard not the rulers of the Church were false prophets.

But this wisdom was only promised to the *prayer of faith*. If the member did not pray with faith, he could not obtain the desired wisdom. In that case, had the Church still no power to expel him as a heretic? If the Church had such power, by what *test* or *standard* was she to ascertain the fact? She could not see into his heart, and know his secret intentions, except from the fact *that he did not hold the proper faith.*

If the failure to pray with faith only affected the individual himself, and not the association in any material respect, then the right to judge and expel him as a heretic would not be necessary or useful. But *one* of the objects of expelling heretics was to preserve the faith of others. Heresy is a crime that, in its very nature, affects the integrity of the institution itself. For while the party is allowed to speak *as a member*, and at the same time to set the authority of the Church at defiance, his power of evil is much greater than it is after he is condemned as a criminal, and left only to speak *as such.* That theory cannot be true, which permits each *member* to determine for himself, in the last resort, whether he has prayed with faith, and has received the requisite wisdom. If that theory be true, then how could Timothy and Titus have tried and rejected those unruly and vain talkers and deceivers –those factionists, who created divisions by preaching a false faith? When called upon, each could have said: "I have prayed for wisdom with faith, and have obtained it." How could Timothy and Titus have determined whether this statement was true or false, except by testing their faith by *the law*, as construed by the *proper* authority? Using *this test*, they could well say: "Your faith is not true, and, therefore, you could not have asked in faith for true wisdom."

In reference to the sixth passage, it will readily be seen that it does not at all conflict with the ultimate right of the church to construe the code for all. The Scriptures may be profitable to the individual reader, who is allowed to construe in the first instance. A very large portion of them is taken up in the simple relation of the most touching incidents connected with God's early dealings with His Chosen people –of signal displays of mercy, and the infliction of punishment. There are numerous biographical sketches, (or history teaching by example) of renowned and faithful servants of God. The New Testament contains the simple narrative of the birth, life, death, and resurrection of our Savior, and the history of the labors and suffering of the early saints. Besides the historical portions, there are many plain and simple commands, and many edifying instances of faith and humility. But after all the plain portions of the Written Word, there are some things hard to be understood that must still be understood.

24. A passage from Isaiah on obscurity

The prophet Isaiah, speaking of the future way of holiness, uses this language:

> And a highway shall be there, and a way, and it shall be called the way of holiness; the unclean shall not pass over it but it shall be for those: the way-faring men, though fools, shall not err therein.[44]

Now, is it not evident that the *way* spoken of by the prophet is plain, and so plain, that a fool shall not err therein? And if the Scriptures alone constitute this way, it follows that they must also be plain, otherwise the way mentioned could not be plain. But if the Scriptures are plain and easily understood in all needful particulars, was not Saint Peter plainly mistaken when he plainly asserted the contrary? How then shall we reconcile these apparently contradictory passages? Is there any necessary contradiction? May not the way itself be plain, and the scriptures still contain some things hard to be understood? There must be some way left to arrive at a just conclusion.

I suppose the path of duty may be plain to a citizen of the United States, although the Constitution and laws of the country contain some things hard to be understood. And this path is plain, for the reason that the same Constitution provides means to make the *application* plain, of that which is not plain of itself. And may it not be so in reference to the Scriptures, conceding for the sake of the argument only, that they contain the entire code now obligatory? The law may not all be plain in itself, but the application of it may be made plain to the *party governed*, by judicial decisions.

Now does not the theory that assumes the existence of an infallible tribunal for the construction and application of the law, perfectly reconcile these merely apparent discrepancies, and leave all the passages in full and harmonious force? Is it not the only theory that does produce this result? or that can produce it? The prophet did not assert that the Scriptures were plain. He only asserted that the *way* was plain.

We have endeavored to show that the true character of Scripture, as of every system of law, is simplicity in many things, and obscurity in some. Among the most simple portions of Scripture are the historical narratives, and some of the commands and promises. If then, these plain portions lead the honest and diligent inquirer, aided by common sense, experience, and natural reason, as well as by other proofs from history, to the infallible guide provided by the system itself, the *way is plain*, although the Scriptures are not *entirely so*. If the Scriptures be plain in *those* respects which lead the inquirer to the competent tribunal, then it is clear that the way is plain, whether all the Scripture be plain or not.

Any way is plain with a competent guide. When the Eunuch could not understand the Old Scriptures without a guide, the way was made plain to him when he selected Philip as his guide, and followed him. The way for the Corinthian brethren was made plain by the aid of Saint Paul, when he construed and applied the law to the particular cases of error existing among them. He said to them plainly –Paul is not the way –Cephas is not the way –Apollos is not the way, but Christ is the way. And when the Gentile brethren were so much distressed in regard to circumcision, the way was made plain to them by the decision of the Council of Jerusalem. The Council said plainly –circumcision is not the way.

It must be apparent, that the existence and authority of this infallible guide, would fully carry out the prediction of the prophet, and yet not contradict Saint Peter. The guide being accessible to all, and equally competent to give the *same* information to all, we can well understand how even a fool should not err in this way. A way that is furnished with a competent guide along its whole route, may well be called plain. This guide places all travelers upon a perfect equality. They have all the same means of finding the way. This guide equalizes all the differences in the natural powers and opportunities of each.

In reference to this guide, Bishop Porteus very confidently says:

> Romanists themselves own that men must use their eyes to find this guide; why then must they put them out to follow him?

Truly, they should not put them out at all; but surely, they should *only* employ them in following their guide. If one needs a guide and finds him, he had better follow him. The very idea of a guide, shows a man cannot, with his own eyes, find the way. A man may be very competent to find a good lawyer, a good physician, or pilot, without being himself competent to discharge the duties of these professions. It must be conceded by every candid mind, that the way of the Christian faith and duty should be plain to the inquirer who is faithful and true to himself. For while he is true to himself, he cannot be false to any other being, or to truth itself.

If we take the Scriptures as construed by each individual for himself in the last resort, as the sole way, then the inexorable rules of logic require us to assume that the Scriptures are plain and easily understood by all of every grade of capacity. This crippling and mutilating theory does the utmost injustice to the lawmaker by forgetting that his code must be complete, while the way is plain. The system must attain the great, and extensive and perfect ends sought; and this cannot be done by a code containing so few and so simple provisions, as to be perfectly plain to all unaided capacities, under all circumstances. The code must be complete by containing all the provisions necessary to reach the perfect ends sought; and this cannot be done except by the aid of an infallible tribunal.

To assume that a supernatural system should contain nothing but plain truths, equally within the unaided reach of all, is substantially to assume that God could not reveal any high and sublime truths to man, and that his revealed law could contain no mysteries. On the contrary, it would seem plain to good sense, that if God made any direct revelation to mankind, He would reveal many truths of so sublime a character, as to fill and test the highest capacity of the human mind; not only for the purpose of giving us some idea of the character of infinite wisdom, but some conception of the blessedness of that state which is to come.

The Catholic theory is the only one that makes the way plain, while the code is left complete and full, in every particular. It makes the way plain, not by mutilating the law, but by elevating the minds and judgments of all to the same infallible standard of construction. This theory unites and combines, in harmonious consistency, every element of a plain, but full, complete, and perfect system, in every respect.

The Christians in the days of the apostles, had the same means of arriving at the true interpretation of the words in which the law of Christ had been promulgated, as the citizens of the United States, and of all the civilized governments of earth, have of ascertaining the correct construction of the laws of their country. This is shown in reasons and authorities given in the preceding pages. When the Christians of those days misconstrued the law, their construction was overruled by those who had the rule over them; and, when the misconstruction arose among the teachers themselves, a council was called to consider the matter, and their error infallibly corrected. Nothing could be more consistent and logical than this efficient process, founded and based, as it is, upon the simplest principles whereon all society must rest. When a teacher of science is instructing his pupil, he puts into his hands a treatise upon the science intended to be taught; and yet he overrules all misconstructions of the student. Nothing could be more simple and reasonable than the question asked by the Eunuch of Phillip. The latter had asked the former this question: "Understandest thou what thou readest?" The Eunuch answered "How can I, except some man should guide me?"

25. A passage from Saint Peter on obscurity

In this connection it becomes necessary to notice a very clear passage from the Second Epistle of Saint Peter. This passage seems conclusive proof of the correctness of the position we have taken; namely: that the right of private interpretation in the last resort, does not, and cannot exist in the Christian system, any more than it does or can exist in any other system of law.

The apostle after telling his brethren that they would do well to take heed to the sure word of prophecy, says:

> Knowing this first, that no prophecy of the Scripture is of any private interpretation. For the prophecy came not in old time by the will of man: but holy men of God spake as they were moved by the Holy Ghost.

The prophecies to be interpreted were those of Scripture. The word "interpretation" is one of the most definite and certain in the language. When applied to prophecy, it is defined to be, "the act of expounding or unfolding what is not understood or not obvious."[45] So, the word private in this connection, that is "private interpretation," is equally definite and certain, and must mean "individual, personal; in contradistinction from public or national."[46] The phrase "private interpretation," would seem too plain to be misunderstood: and, therefore, the apostle denied the right of interpretation to individual members.

It cannot be said that the context shows another meaning; because we cannot resort to the context, when the words are clear and definite, and need no explanation. When we look to the context, we can see nothing to change the clear significance of the terms used.

When we look into the whole spirit and drift of this Second Epistle of Saint Peter, it will be seen that the great leading object the apostle had in view, was to strengthen the brethren in the faith –to point out the danger of heresy, the character of those who would introduce it, and how it might be avoided. For these purposes, he first speaks of the character of the true faith and its blessed consequences. Then he gives them the proofs of its divine origin by referring to the testimony given of Christ from heaven on the Holy Mount. He also gives the testimony of the holy prophets; and that they might know how to use this testimony properly cautions them against the errors of those he afterwards describes. He tells them, "knowing this first, that no prophecy of Scripture is of any private interpretation." He then gives them the reason why it is not so – because it did not come by the will of man, but of God, and being His Word, was not the subject of private interpretation as if it were the word of man. But it was subject to the interpretation of His authorized teachers, in the same way as the doctrines of the new dispensation, which the apostles and elders taught.

Pursuing the same train of reasoning, he then tells them of "false teachers, who privily shall bring in damnable heresies." He tells them "they are presumptuous and self-willed" –that "they speak evil of the things that they understand not" – that "they allure those that were clear escaped from them who live in error" –and "while they promise them liberty, they themselves are the servants of corruption." How well this description of these false teachers agrees with that of Saint Paul where he speaks in his Epistle to Titus of the "unruly and vain talkers and deceivers, whose mouths must be stopped." The apostle Peter then goes on to say, that his object was to remind them of the words of the holy prophets and of the "commandment of the apostles" –the teachers of the church. And in the close of his Epistle, he gives them an instance of the evil of private interpretation in those "unlearned and unstable" persons, who wrest the Scriptures to their own destruction.

A friend has sent me the following passage(as quoted, if I am not mistaken,) from the translation of George Campbell, thus:

> Knowing this first, that no prophecy of Scripture is of any private impulse, for never at any time was prophecy brought by the will of man; but holy men spake, being moved by the Holy Spirit.

The difference between the two translations is most palpable. Perhaps no two terms in the language could convey to the mind more different ideas than those of *interpretation* and *impulse* in the connection in which they stand. The first is the act of the individual in expounding or unfolding prophecy; the second is not the act of the individual at all, but "force communicated" or "influence acting on the mind."[47]

As to the merits of the different translations, I cannot speak from any knowledge of the original. But if this new translation be correct, I must say it seems rather remarkable, that the Catholic, and nearly all the Protestant translations, should agree in their rendering "private interpretation." Catholic writers from the beginning of the Reformation have relied upon this passage, as translated. And all Protestant translators were fully aware of the force of the passage against their theory of private interpretation. It is certainly remarkable that the error in the translation of so decisive a passage was not discovered before. Besides this, the translation seems incorrect upon its face. If this new translation is correct, then it was intended by the apostle, in this part of the passage, to put the phrase "private impulse" in contrast with that of the Holy Ghost. The term *private* would not be accurate, as it would not exclude public interpretation or public impulse. The word "human," in that case, would only be correct.

But this most material difference in the translation of so important, and it would seem, so plain a passage, must cause a feeling of the most painful uncertainty in the mind of every sincere believer who trusts to his own interpretation, without any guide but that of translations so liable to err. Nothing could more forcibly show the invincible necessity of some infallible tribunal, than this very case of gross error. Or if it be not a gross error, then of the extreme uncertainty of human language, and of the extreme danger of relying alone upon a medium so imperfect, when eternity is at stake. Our Lord and His apostles promulgated the code in only one or two languages, when the system was intended to embrace all kindreds and tongues of all ages; and if we must rely upon mere fallible and disputed translations, and constructions of those translations, then we lean upon a feeble reed. The mistranslation of a single word may entirely change the sense of the most important passage. The present case is a good illustration.

26. The one visible Church is a preparatory institution

Christ established but *one* church, intending there should exist perfect unity in it as a necessary means of its purity of faith, and of its rightful success in the world, and He gave but *one* law for its government, and *one* infallible tribunal for the interpretation and application of the code. Given this it follows, that this visible Church is but a preparatory institution on earth through which men must pass to the church triumphant in heaven. It would seem plain that Christ could not be the author of confusion, or the founder of an imbecile institution; and that truth must ever be a unit, and not contradictory and confused, as error often is. Whatever system He did establish must have been but *one.* The whole reason, drift, and spirit of the system, show its perfect *unity of design.* The Eternal Mind could never build a house divided against itself.

When we turn from reason to the express testimonies of Scripture, they are equally explicit. Our Lord speaking of the Church, says, "*One fold, one shepherd;*" so that the fold must be one and only one as the shepherd is one and only one. He also prayed for those who should believe in Him "that they might be one." And Saint Paul says of the Church: "So we, being many, are *one* body in Christ, and every one members of another."[48] So, he also says: "One body, one spirit, one hope, one Lord, one faith, one baptism."[49]

In addition to these explicit texts, when we come to look at the practice of the apostles and other early teachers of Christianity, we shall find it in perfect accordance with this sentiment. They gathered into the Church all whom they were willing to call and treat as members of the true fold. Furthermore, we are told that the converts made on the day of Pentecost "continued steadfastly in the apostle's doctrine and fellowship;" and that "the Lord added to the church daily such as should be saved."[50] These passages are very explicit. Such persons as should be *saved*, were *added* to the Church. Why does Saint Luke couple salvation with *addition* to the Church, if such addition was not material, and salvation could be found outside the Church?

We also find the different apostles deploring divisions in the Church as one of the greatest of evils, and Saint Paul delivering Hymeneus and Alexander unto Satan, that they might learn not to blaspheme.[51] The whole history of the Apostolic Church, shows that it was ever regarded but as one, and that they who expected to reach heaven, must do it through this one Church. Christ said distinctly, after first commanding *all the truth* to be preached, "He that believeth not shall be damned." Saint Paul is similarly explicit when he says, "Without faith it is impossible to please God." He tells his Corinthian brethren not to keep company or to eat with any man called a brother who was guilty of certain offences mentioned. Saint John, the apostle of charity, forbids the faithful to receive him into their houses, or even to bid him God speed, who "bringeth not this doctrine of Christ."[52]

27. Is this theory intolerant?

Is not this theory intolerant? Is it not illiberal? It may be so. But was there ever a system of just law, or of truth, in the universe, that was not inflexible and intolerant? Must that which is true yield to that which is false?

How could Christ make any law but that which is just? And how could He fail to execute a just law? Is He not bound by the irresistible force of His own attributes to execute justice? Has he not pledged, in advance, His eternal veracity, that not one jot or tittle of the law shall fail? How can a lawgiver, after he has said, "you must do this, and you must not do that, and this shall be the consequence of your disobedience," fail to fulfill his word, unless he is not to be believed?

For what purpose is government instituted? Is it to indulge and excuse men who will not learn? What sort of system would it be, that had so little truth in it, and so little claim to respect, that, after laying down positive rules in positive terms for both faith and act, still did not require those rules to be believed and obeyed? The laws of civil government require every man to know the law. "Ignorance of the law excuseth no man," is the fixed maxim of the code. And if ignorance of the law did excuse a man, who would care to know the law? The law favors the diligent and obedient, not the idle and disobedient.

When we refer to the laws of nature, we find them equally inflexible, except when God Himself pleases to suspend or overcome them. If a man ignorantly violates the laws of nature, he must suffer. It is his duty, his interest, his business, to learn; and he has the means of doing so. He cannot expect to escape, when others do not. No man can lift himself above the laws of nature or of truth, except at his own peril.

"Shall gravitation cease if you go by?"

With respect to the perfect law of Christ, why should it not require the same implicit obedience? For what noble purpose was this law given, and why is it impossible without faith to please God, if the law is not to be believed? Heaven being the free gift of God, He had the right to fix the terms upon which it should be attained. He had the right to determine what acts and belief he would consider as merit, although they were not meritorious in themselves, but only so when judged by a system established and given through grace.

That it is but reasonable and just that God should govern the universe, there would seem to be no doubt, unless we can deny that He created it. And when He makes known His law, and gives men sufficient evidence of the fact, and they refuse to believe and obey, ought they to be rewarded for this? So far as the government of God is concerned, heresy is just as much a sin as any other, though it may differ in degree.

As to liberality, it is like taste. It is a thing not found in law, which assumes to be predicated of justice, not of liberality. Liberality has no measure or limit but the ideal standard of each individual. The infidel thinks it remarkable hard that he cannot be permitted to enter heaven, when he believes the system, which promises it to be a cunningly devised fable. The gay, the worldly-minded rich, the proud and vain, think any system that requires any personal sacrifices of them in this life, and in default of which debars them of heaven in the next, exceedingly illiberal; and especially do they think that system illiberal, which permits the suffering, humble, and pious poor to go into heaven before them. They desire the best in this world and the best in the next; both of which may be very natural, but not very just, and therefore, not very likely to succeed with the Just Judge. And so the Universalist thinks that it is exceedingly illiberal not to admit all men into heaven, sooner or later. And so of every other class in the world. As the acute Calhoun once said in the Senate of the United States, "there is no accounting for taste in this world." The same is true of liberality. It is a thing as indefinable as the ten thousand opinions regarding it. All states and all heads can conceive something concerning it, but no two heads can ever understand it in the same way. "My doxy is heterodoxy with you, and your doxy is heterodoxy with me." So long, then, as men make their ideas of liberality the standard of truth, they never can arrive at any unity of faith or belief.

There is no illustration more often used by latitudinarians than this: that we are all traveling different roads to the same point –we all aim to get to heaven, and only go there by different paths. But, unfortunately, there is but one way mentioned, and he that climbeth up some other way is not entitled to enter, because he is a "thief and a robber." There is not only but one way, but that way is straight and narrow, and few there be that find it. There cannot be two or more, as only one *straight* way can exist between two points. From one place to another, in this world, there may be many devious ways,

"But 'tis not so above."

God made both earth and heaven, and opened up the only way that leads from one to the other; therefore, who ever reaches that happy abode, must travel this provided way.

Is not that theory of mere apparent mercy, in itself, the most delusive cruelty? There is nothing, perhaps, in this world that has done more injury than mistaken mercy. The jury that acquits the guilty culprit, through mistaken sympathy, and turns him again loose upon society, commits a cruel act. It is mercy to the guilty, and cruelty to the innocent. It is a confusion of all just distinctions, or rather, a reversal of all just distinctions.

To assume that the way to heaven is wider than it really is, must be the greatest of all mistakes. It is certain that such assumption, however flattering to our pride and vanity, will not widen the way, *in fact*. It forever remains as narrow as before, and the same prediction still inexorably exists –"few there be that find it." The more men are taught to believe that Christianity consists mainly in good conduct, and not in both faith and works, the more faith is degraded from its due importance in the system, and the more God is robbed of the homage due to Him, the more infidelity and disunion are encouraged and propagated. It is a very flattering and insinuating, but delusive thought, that Christian perfection consists mostly of good conduct –that we can believe almost anything. We are deluded if we believe that there are numerous roads to heaven, suited to the convenience, prejudices, and tastes of different travelers. We are deluded if we believe that God not only gave His only Son to die for us, but has given us a wide latitude of belief, and made so great a variety of ways to heaven that all can be suited – and not only so, but that these ways are easy, and lead through the flowery vales of earth to the:

"Sweet fields beyond the swelling flood."

After all that has been, or can be, said it must be apparent, at last, that every system must have some fundamental principles. Principles that, in contemplation of the theory itself, must be inflexible. Otherwise, the theory must dispense with *faith entirely,* and only require sincerity and good conduct. The whole matter resolves itself into two question: is *any* faith required and *in what* is it required.

It must be obvious to the reflective mind, that if a system of religion requires faith at all, it is just as rational to require it as to all, as to a part. The system depends entirely upon the right and authority of him who founds it. When established by God His authority is conclusive. All we desire to know is His will. This must be obeyed. It is, then, just as reasonable that we should all be required to believe the same things, and join the same Church, as to believe any other article of faith, or do any other act required by the law. These requirements are not unreasonable, but are logical and sensible in the very nature of Christ's one kingdom.

The idea that there may be many visible Churches, each differing from the others in doctrine, discipline, and church government, and yet that salvation can be found in more that one, is, in its practical results, a cruel and mistaken theory for two reasons:

1. This assumed liberality will not , in point of fact, widen the way.

2. It leads to discords and divisions, and these impede the progress of religion in the world; and in the end, actually diminish the aggregate number of professors.

A logical, united, and exclusive system is in conformity with a true system. Such a system will always provide the greatest ultimate results, and for that reason is the best for humanity. If a man is made to believe that he can be saved almost anywhere, with almost any sort of faith, he naturally becomes indifferent to such a theory that is indifferent to itself. He consults his tastes, and mere personal partialities, and joins those whom he likes best as friends and neighbors. Religion, with him, becomes a secondary consideration. It sinks down in his estimation, and ceases to command his genuine reverence and respect. A chameleon theory and a gum-elastic conscience are inconsistent with truth and justice.

Another reflection is this –from the nature of this *permanent* system, wherever limits are fixed, they must have been so fixed at the beginning. So they must continue unto the end. Whatever was required to be believed at the beginning, must be required to be believed now and at all future times. The limits of faith cannot be extended or contracted, to suit this or that one. For if this were done from time to time, there would soon be but the shadow, and not the substance of faith left.

This exclusive and rigid system is the Catholic Church. It is based upon the idea that Christ never did establish but one church. And that church was the visible church –that more than one true church never was, and never could be required, and was never contemplated by the Divine Founder of the institution. As a general rule, salvation must be found in that one church. The theory admits one exception made by the law itself. In the case of invincible ignorance, where a baptized person, without prejudice, and with true humility and perseverance, has faithfully sought for the entire truth, and, for want of opportunity, has failed to find it.

28. Testimony of the Fathers

I will now quote from the earliest of the Ancient Fathers, those only of the first and second centuries, in support of the positions advanced in the preceding pages. The first quotation is from the Holy Clement, bishop of Rome. It is taken from his Epistle to the Corinthians, written in the first century and during the life of Saint John the Evangelist. The occasion of this epistle, was a schism existing in that church.

> It is shameful, my beloved, it is most shameful, and unworthy of your Christian profession, that it should be heard that the most firm and ancient church of the Corinthians, on account of one or two persons, is in a sedition against the priests.
>
> Do ye, therefore, who laid the foundation of this sedition, submit yourselves to the priests, and be instructed unto repentance. Bending the knees of your hearts, learn to be subject, laying aside all proud and arrogant boasting of your tongues; for it is better for you to be found in the sheepfold of Christ, little and approved, than, thinking yourselves above others, to be cast out of His hope.

How very similar is this language to that of Paul, when the apostle tells these same brethren to "submit themselves unto such, and to every one that helpeth with us and laboreth." And the holy Bishop alludes to this very Epistle of Paul when he says:

> Take up the epistle of the blessed Paul the apostle. What did he first write to you at the beginning of the Gospel? Verily he did by the Spirit, admonish you, both concerning himself, and Cephas, and Apollos, because that even then ye had formed partialities amongst yourselves....

The *means* pointed out both by the blessed apostle and the holy bishop, for healing divisions, were the same *–submission to them that had the rule over them.* Unfortunately these brethren had not all obeyed the command of the apostle, and had not submitted to Stephanas and the others, and this departure from his explicit commands led to further divisions, and these rendered necessary this epistle of Clement, the disciple of Paul. The effect of this epistle was to produce the unity contemplated by the gospel.

The following extracts are from the Holy Martyr and Bishop Ignatius, the friend of Saints Peter and John, and the disciple of the latter:

> It becomes you to concur in the mind of your bishop, as also ye do. For your famous presbytery, worthy of God, is knit as closely to the bishop, as strings to a harp.
>
> Let no man deceive you; if a man be not within the altar, he faileth of the bread of God...
>
> Let us take heed, therefore, that we do not set ourselves against the bishop, *that we may be set under God.*
>
> For whomsoever the Master of the house sendeth to his own household, we ought to receive, as Him that sent him. It is plain, then, *that we ought to look to the bishop, as to the Lord Himself.*[53]
>
> ...but, as wise men in God, *submitting to him*[*the bishop*]; *yet not to him, but to the Father of Jesus Christ, the Bishop of all.*
>
> For inasmuch as you are *subject to the bishop as to Jesus Christ*, you seem to me to be living not according to man, but according to Jesus Christ....
>
> Guard against such men (heretics); and guarded ye will be, if ye are not puffed up, nor separated from the God Jesus Christ, and from the bishop, and from the regulations of the apostles. He that is within the altar is pure; but he that is without, is not pure: that is, he who does aught apart from the bishop and presbytery and deacon, he is not clean in conscience.[54]

> Apart from the bishop do nothing: keep your flesh as the temple of God: love unity: avoid divisions: be ye followers of Jesus Christ, even as He is of his Father.[55]
>
> Let that be esteemed a sure Eucharist, which is either under the bishop, or him to whom he may commit it. Where the bishop is, there let the multitude (of believers) be; even as where Jesus Christ is, there is the Catholic church.[56]
>
> Give heed unto the bishop that God may hearken unto you. My soul for the soul of those who are in subjection to the bishop, presbyters, and deacons, and may my portion be with them in the Lord.[57]
>
> It is fitting that you should, by all means, glorify Jesus Christ, who hath glorified you; that by a uniform obedience ye may be perfectly joined together in the same mind and in the same judgment, and may all speak the same about the same thing, and that being subject to the bishop and presbyters, ye may be sanctified in all things.
>
> I exhort you that you would all concur in the mind of God; for Jesus Christ, our inseparable life, is the mind of the Father; like as the *bishops, who have their stations at the utmost bounds of the earth, are after the mind of Jesus Christ.*[58]
>
> Neither attempt ye any thing that seems good to your own judgment; but let there be, in the same place, *one* prayer, *one* application, *one* mind, *one* hope, in love in joy undefiled. There is *one* Jesus Christ, then whom nothing is better. Wherefore haste ye all together, as unto the temple of God, as unto *one* altar, as unto *one* Jesus Christ, who proceeded from *one* Father, and in *one*, and to *one* returned.[59]
>
> Be not deceived, my brethren; whosoever followeth one that createth schism, he inheriteth not the kingdom of God.
>
> Wherefore I did my part as a man fitted for the preserving of unity. For where is division and wrath God dwelleth not. The Lord forgiveth all who repent, if their minds be turned unto God's unity and the council of the bishop.[60]

From these extracts the following points are, among others, clearly established as the faith of the church in the days of Ignatius, so far as his testimony could establish any thing:

1. That the bishops over the world held the same faith and that Jesus Christ was found in this Catholic Church.

2. That these bishops were held as the servants or agents of Christ, and were for that reason to be submitted to and obeyed in accordance with

the statements of Christ: "He that despiseth you despiseth me. He that heareth you heareth me."

3. That the means provided by Christ to produce the unity of faith, was submission to the rulers of this Catholic Church.

4. That nothing could be done without their consent.

5. That perfect unity must, and did exist, in the Catholic Church.

6. That in this Church salvation was to be found.

7. That they who resisted thc rulers of the church, were heretics. And unless they repented and returned to the unity of God, they could not be saved.

One cannot but observe the strong resemblance between the language of the old Martyr and that of Saint Paul, in his first Epistle to the Corinthians, first chapter. Ignatius exhorts his brethren to "be perfectly joined together in the same mind and in the same judgment," that they "all speak the same about the same thing, and that being *subject* to the bishop and presbyters, they may be sanctified in all things." Saint Paul uses the same language in part, and inculcates the same subjection to the household of Stephanas and others.

In these epistles of Ignatius, there is to be found nothing like the principle of private interpretation independent of the church. The duty of submission is inculcated as clearly and as forcibly as it could be done. The principle of government in the church is, in very strong language, distinctly and repeatedly asserted. The most powerful reasons are given for it. It is because the rulers were only the agents of Christ, and acting for Him, and in His name.

In reference to the succession of officers in the church, Saint Clement, bishop of Rome, says:

> Preaching through countries and cities, they (apostles) appointed their first fruits—having proved them by the Spirit –bishops and deacons of those who were about to believe.
>
> So also our apostles knew, through the Lord Jesus Christ, that contention would arise on account of the episcopacy. And for this cause, having a perfect foreknowledge, they appointed the aforesaid, (bishops and deacons,) and then gave direction in what manner, when they should die, other approved men should succeed them in their ministry.

And Ignatius says:

> I exhort you, that ye study to do all things in a divine unanimity, the bishop holding presidency, in the place of God; and the presbyters in the place of the council of the apostles; and the deacons most dear to me, intrusted with the service of Jesus Christ.[61]

And the holy martyr and bishop Polycarp, the disciple of Saint John, of whom Saint Irenaeus says "he was instructed by apostles, and lived in familiar friendship with many who had seen the Lord," says:

> In like manner, deacons blameless in the sight of His righteousness, as the ministers of God in Christ, and not of men.... Wherefore it is necessary that ye abstain from all these things, being *subject to the presbyters and deacons as unto God and Christ.*[62]

Saint Justin, in commenting on Psalm forty-four verse seven, says:

> And these words also proclaim that the Word of God (addresses Himself) to those that believe in Him –as being one soul, and one synagogue, and one church –as to a daughter, to the church, that is, which is derived from, and partakes of, His name; for we are all called Christians.

Saint Irenaeus, the disciple of Saint Polycarp, the disciple of Saint John, among others gives these testimonies:

> There being such proofs to look to, we ought not still to look amongst others for truth, which it is easy to receive from the church. Seeing that the apostles most fully committed unto this church, as unto a rich repository, all whatever is of truth, that every one that willeth may draw out of it (the church) the drink of life. For this is the gate of life; but all others are thieves and robbers. Therefore we ought to avoid them, *but to cling with the utmost care to whatever is of the church, and to hold fast to the tradition of truth.*
>
> An ordinance to which many of the barbarous nations who believe in Christ assent, having salvation written, without paper and ink, by the Spirit, in their hearts, and sedulously guarding the old tradition.
>
> For before Valentinus there were no Valentinians, nor Marcionites before Marcion, nor, in fact, any of the other malignant sentiments enumerated above, before there arose inventors and beginners of each perverse opinion.[63]
>
> Wherefore we ought to obey those presbyters who are in the church, those who have a succession from the apostles, as we have shown, who, with the succession of the episcopate, have received, according

to the good will of the Father, the sure gift of truth. But the rest, who depart from the principal succession, and assemble in any place whatever, we ought to hold suspected, either as heretics, and of an evil opinion, or as schismatics and proud, and as men pleasing themselves; or, again, as hypocrites doing this for gain's sake, and vain glory.[64]

And, indeed, the preaching (or, public teaching) of the church, in which one and the same way of salvation is set forth throughout the whole world, is true and firm. For to this (church) has been intrusted the light of God, and on this account is the *wisdom* if God, through which He saves men, proclaimed in the gates; in the streets she acts confidently.[65]

Having, as I have said, received that preaching and this faith, the church, though spread over the whole world, guards (it) sedulously, as though *dwelling in one house.* And these truths she uniformly holds, as having but *one soul*, and *one* and the same *heart;* and these she proclaims and teaches, and hands down uniformly, as though she had but *one mouth.* For though throughout the world, the languages are various, still the force of the tradition is *one and the same.* And neither do the churches founded in Germany, nor those in Spain, in Gaul, in the East, in Egypt, in Africa, nor in the regions in the middle of the earth, believe or deliver a different faith. But as God's handiwork, the sun, is one and same throughout the universe, so the preaching of the truth shines everywhere, and enlightens all men that wish to come to the knowledge of the truth. Nor does he who, amongst the *rulers in the churches,* is more powerful in word deliver a different doctrine from the above, (for no one is above his teacher;) nor does he who is weak in speech weaken the tradition. For the faith being one and the same, neither he who has ability to say much concerning it, hath any thing over, nor he who speaketh little, any lack.

The whole church has one and the same faith throughout the whole world, as we have explained above.[66]

...but the public teaching of the church (is) everywhere uniform, and equally enduring....[67]

But He will also judge all those who are *out of the truth, that is who are out of the church.* But He will be judged by none.

Therefore, in every church there is, for all those who would fain see the truth, at hand to look unto, the tradition of the apostles made manifest throughout the whole world. And we have it in our power to enumerate those who were, by the apostles, instituted bishops in the

> churches, and the successors of those bishops down to ourselves; none of whom were taught or knew any thing like unto the wild opinions of these men. For if the apostles had known any hidden mysteries, which they apart, and privately taught the perfect only, they would have delivered them, before all others, to whom they even intrusted the very churches. For they sought that they whom they left as successors, *delivering unto them their own post of government*, should be especially perfect and blameless in all things; whose upright discharge of their *office* would be of great profit, as their fall would be a great calamity.
>
> By this order and by this succession, both that tradition which is in the church from the apostles, and the preaching of the truth, have come down to us. And this is a most complete demonstration, that the vivifying faith is one and the same, which, from the apostles, even until now, has been persevered in, and *transmitted in truthfulness.*[68]
>
> For everywhere is the church *distinctly visible*, and everywhere is there a wine-press dug; for everywhere are those who receive the Spirit.[69]
>
> If a man believe in God… he will *first hold to the head.*[70] Then, afterwards, also every discourse will be clear to him, if also he read the Scriptures *diligently with those who are presbyters in the church,* with *whom is the apostolic doctrine,* as we have demonstrated.[71]

In these extracts, Saint Irenaeus states substantially that "the church was a rich repository, into which the apostles *committed*" all the truth. He states that all may learn this truth of this church, which is the "*gate of life*":

1. That the barbarous nations sedulously guarded the old tradition, and held the true faith.

2. That the brethren ought to obey those presbyters who have a succession from the apostles, as *they* have received the *sure gift* of truth.

3. That the *public teaching* of the church *is the same* throughout the *whole world.*

4. That to this church has been entrusted the light of God, and *on this account*, the *wisdom* of God, through which He saves men, is proclaimed

5. That the church having received the faith, though she was spread over the world, guards it *sedulously*, as if dwelling in *one* house, as having but *one* soul –*one* heart, and proclaims and teaches as though she had but *one* mouth.

6. That the whole church held *one* and the *same faith* throughout all the world.

7. That her teaching was everywhere *uniform and equally enduring.*

8. That God will judge those who are out of the truth, that is, those who are out of the *church.*

9. That the tradition was handed down by succession from the apostles in truthfulness.

10. That the apostles delivered to those they appointed *their post of government.*

11. That the church is everywhere distinctly visible and.

12. That if a man held to the head, Jesus Christ, and then read the Scriptures diligently *with the presbyters* in the church, every discourse would be clear, as with these *presbyters* was the apostolic doctrine.

In short, the saint and martyr gives a most beautiful historical description of an infallibly governed, and for that reason, a universal and united church, in whose communion salvation was to be found.

In reference to the universality of the church in his day, Saint Justin says:

> But there is no race of men –whether of barbarians or of Greeks, or, in fine, bearing any other name, whether because they live in wagons, or are without a fixed habitation, or dwell in tents, leading a pastoral life –among whom prayers and eucharists are not offered to the Father and Maker of the universe, through the name of the crucified Jesus.[72]

And Saint Hegisippus says:

> But in each succession (of bishops) and in each city, it is just as the law proclaims, and the prophets of the Lord.

He proceeds to name several heretics and their sects, as Simon, Menander, Marcion, Valentinus; and observes:

> Each of these introduced of himself, and different from all the rest, his private opinion. From these sprang false Christs, false prophets, false apostles, who severed the unity of the church with counterfeit teaching against God and His Christ.[73]

And Saint Clement of Alexandria gives this testimony among others:

THE TRUE CHURCH

> The way of truth is one: but other streams run into it from various quarters, as into a perennial river.[74]
>
> The one church is then associated to the nature of the One; which church these men violently attempt to divide into many heresies. In substance, in sentiment, in origin, in excellence, we say the ancient and Catholic Church is alone....
>
> But the excellence of the church, like the principle of every thing concrete, is in unity, surpassing all other things, and having nothing similar or equal to itself.[75]
>
> Christ looks upon His only church.[76]
>
> And she remains rejoicing unto all ages. It is called the kingdom of God, the heavenly assembly of love, the holy church.[77]
>
> The church on earth is the image of the church in heaven.[78]
>
> An excellent thing the city and the people...governed by law, as, by the word, the church is governed, which is a city on earth, impregnable, and free from oppression, the divine will on earth, as (it is) in heaven.[79]

Speaking of Marcion, and Prodicus, and other heretics, Saint Clement says:

> But it would have been well for them if they had been able to hear the things which had been previously handed down....
>
> For that they made their human assemblages *later* than the Catholic church, there needs not many words to show.[80]

From Tertullian:

> These things being so, it is manifest, that out of the primordial and most true church, these after-born adulterate heresies have been formed, by innovation, as also those that, later still, have come after them.[81]
>
> The apostles having obtained the promised power of the Holy Ghost for miracles and utterance, first having throughout Judea borne witness to the faith in Christ Jesus, and established churches, next went forth into the world, and promulgated the same doctrine of the same faith to the nations, and forthwith founded churches in every city. From *which (churches) the other churches thenceforward borrowed the tradition of the faith,* and *the seeds of doctrine, and are daily borrowing them that they may become churches*: and for this *cause they are themselves also accounted apostolical, as being the*

> *offspring of apostolical churches.* The *whole kind* must needs be classes under *their original. Wherefore these churches, so many and so great, are but that one primitive church from the apostles, whence they all sprang.* Thus all are the primitive, and all apostolical, whilst all being one, prove unity....[82]
>
> Now what the apostles preached, that is, what Christ revealed unto them, I will here also rule, must be proved in no other way than by these same churches which the apostles themselves founded; themselves by preaching to them as well *viva voce*, as men say, as afterwards by epistles. If these things be so, it becomes forthwith manifest that all doctrine which agrees with the apostolic churches, the wombs and originals of the faith, must be accounted true, as without doubt containing that which the churches received from the apostles, the apostles from Christ, Christ from God. But that every doctrine must be judged at once false, which savoreth things contrary to the truth of the churches, and of the apostles, and of Christ, and of God.[83]
>
> To sum up, if it is certain that that is truest which is most ancient, that most ancient which is even from the beginning, that from the beginning which is from apostles. It will in like manner also be certain that that has been handed down by the apostles, which shall have been held sacred by the churches of the apostles.[84]
>
> For although Marcion rejects his (John's) Apocalypse, nevertheless, the succession of bishops, counted up to their origin, will stand by John as the author. Thus also is the noble origin of the other churches recognized.[85]
>
> But if any (heresies) dare to place themselves in the midst of the apostolic age, that they may therefore seem to have been handed down from the apostles, because they existed under the apostles, we say: let them then make known the originals of their churches. Let them unroll their line of bishops, so coming down by succession from the beginning, that their first bishop had for his author and predecessor some one of the apostles, or of apostolic men, so he were one that continued steadfast with the apostles. For in this manner do the apostolic churches reckon their origin.[86]

To answer the plain and simple argument of Tertullian, the separatists in his day took the ground that the apostles were not fully instructed in all truth. Alleging Saint Paul's rebuke of Saint Peter, they argued that the churches founded by them were not reliable witnesses, because they were some of them rebuked by the apostle Paul, as the Galatians and others. To this ground Tertullian replies, among other things:

> Well, then; be it that all have erred; that the apostle also was deceived in the testimony which he gave (in favor of some). Let it be that the Holy Spirit had regard to no one of them (the churches) so as to *guide* it *into* truth, although for this sent by Christ, for this asked of the Father, that he might be the Teacher of truth. That he, the Steward of God, the Vice-regent of Christ neglected his office, suffering the churches the while to understand differently, so believe differently, that which he himself preached by the apostles. *Is it likely, that so many churches, and so great, should have gone astray in one faith?* Never is there *one result among many chances. The error* in the doctrine of the churches must needs have *varied.* But what is found (one and the same) amongst *so many*, is not error, but tradition. Let any one, then, dare to say that they were in error who delivered it.

Speaking of the general characteristics of heresy and heretics, he says:

> They huddle up a peace also with all everywhere. For it makes no matter to them, although they hold different doctrines, so long as they conspire together in their siege against the one truth. All are puffed up; all promise knowledge. The catechumens are perfect before they are taught.
>
> In these works alone do they act humbly, and smoothly, and submissively; but they know no reverence even towards their own chiefs. And this is why there are commonly no schisms amongst heretics; because, when there are any, they appear not; for schism is their very unity. I speak falsely if they do not differ among themselves, even from their own rules, seeing that each forthwith moulds, according to his own pleasure, the things which he hath received, even as he, who delivered them to him, framed them according to his own pleasure. The progress of the matter is a confession of its nature, and of the manner of its birth. The same thing was allowed to the Valentinians as to Valentinus, the same to the Marcionites as to Marcion –to change the faith according to their own pleasure. Finally, all heresies are found, when thoroughly examined, differing in many things from their own founders.

---

[1] *Doctor and Student*, 1 Dialogue, 1. 4.

[2] The reason why God did not prescribe any positive form of political government, is that such government is a *present necessity;* and this necessity, like the laws of nature, would practically vindicate itself. And as the effects of political institutions are but temporary, men can create governments competent to attain substantially the end intended, namely: the preservation of the race. But, conceding the immortality of the soul, and the consequent existence of a

future state of rewards and punishments, the necessity of a direct revelation of God's will to mankind, become at once apparent. We may well be able to bear the evils incident to mere human institutions; since, if we *first* fulfill the law of God, these temporary evils are but trifling; but to leave *eternal* consequences to hang upon uncertainty, would be equally unjust to God and to man.

[3] The following beautiful lines are from the pen of our native poet, Bryant:

"Great were the thoughts and strong the minds
Of those who framed, in high debate,
The immortal league of love that binds
Our fair, broad empire, State with State
"The noble race is gone – the suns
Of sixty years have risen and set,
But the bright links those chosen ones
So strongly forged, are brighter yet."

[4] James Kent *Commentaries on American Law* 1, p. 296.)

[5] *Cf.*1 Cor. 11:18-19,

[6] *Wheaton's Law of Nations,* 3rd Ed. p. 77,334

[7] James Kent, *op. cit.* 1, p. 461.

[8] The truths of science are not all simple and easily understood. It has been said by competent persons, that it requires a man of more than ordinary intellect to understand the discoveries of Sir Isaac Newton to their full extent.

[9] Luke 16: 9.

[10] *Discourses*, 133.

[11] Gardiner Spring *A Dissertation on the Rule of Faith* p. 36.

[12] A. Campbell and N Rice, *Campbell Rice Debate on the Holy Spirit*, p. 132.

[13] 2 Peter 3:15, 16.

[14] Is a certain act, or a certain state of case, a violation of a certain principle, or of several principles combined? This is the difficulty! One of the most remarkable instances of the difficulty met in the application of the provisions of a statute, drawn up with consummate ability and great care, is to be found in the celebrated Statute of Frauds, passed by the British Parliament in the reign of Charles II. It is a statute containing very few sections, and one of the sections that has given rise to so much difficulty in its application to cases coming under the principle, is as follows:

"Sec. 17. That no contract for the sale of any goods, wares, and merchandises, for the price of ten pounds sterling or upwards, shall be allowed to be good, except the buyer shall accept part of the goods so sold, and actually receive the same, or give something in earnest to bind the bargain, or in part payment, or that some note or memorandum in writing of the said bargain be made and signed by the parties to be charged by such contract, or their agents thereunto lawfully authorized."

The different questions arising under this section would surprise any one not acquainted with legal proceedings, and the difficulty of applying very plain language to cases as they arise. My limits will not allow any notice of all the various questions raised and decided under this section. What constitutes a *signing* of the note or memorandum would seem to be the plainest question that could arise under the section. Still, very difficult questions have arisen regarding the *signing*. A memorandum in the defendant's handwriting, beginning "I, James Crockford, agree to sell, &c., but not subscribed by him," was held to be good under the statute. "A bill of parcels, in which the name of the seller was *printed*, and that of the purchaser *written* by the seller, was held a sufficient memorandum to charge the seller." (*Long on Sales*, 37)

[15] The Supreme Court U. S. decided that a Constitution, from its nature, deals in generals, not details. (2 Con. Rep., 190.)

[16] A new and very perplexing case arose a few years since. If I remember correctly, in negotiating the treaty of Washington, in reference to the power of the President and Senate to make a treaty affecting the boundary of a State; and it was thought at least more safe to obtain the consent of the State whose boundary was in question.

[17] I remember a striking illustration of the principle, that an insult to the agent or officer is an insult to the power he represents. I was a practicing lawyer at the time, and the judge who presided was an upright officer, and has since been a member of the United States Senate. An ordinary man had taken a personal dislike to the judge for some imaginary cause, (as dislikes and enmities among men mostly arise from prejudice and imagination,) and therefore he committed a contempt of Court by some insolent conduct, intended as an insult to the judge personally. He was arrested and brought before the Court. When he first appeared before his Honor, he seemed to be quite stubborn and malicious. The judge addressed him briefly, but in very noble language. "You have," said he in substance, to the culprit, "insulted this Court, and not the judge personally. I act not for myself. I am but an agent of the State. For myself individually I ask no protection from insult, but I do ask it for my country –for the sovereign State, whose servant I am. You have not insulted me, but you have insulted your fellow-citizens –the people of the whole State, of which you are also a citizen. You have insulted your country, and it is my duty, by the laws of the State, to protect her dignity and her Honor from insult and contempt. But as you have acted under a mistake as to the object of your contempt, the Court will only impose upon you a small fine."

I never saw a man so mortified as the poor culprit. For the first time in his life he understood the distinction between an individual and an officer.

[18] Thus, in the great case of Colonel Fremont, lately decided by the Supreme Court of the United States, there were two questions raised as to the construction of the Mexican colonization laws, and the Act of Congress organizing a Board of Land Commissioners, and laying down the principles under which land claims, in the State of California, should be decided. One of the questions had arisen in many cases, and had been decided adversely to the claimants by the board, and by the United States District Court. The Supreme Court reversed the decisions of the inferior tribunals, and what, *to them*, was uncertain before, has now become fixed and certain. Now all the cases possessing the incidents of this case, and those incidents only, must come under this decision.

Before this decision was made, the judges of the inferior tribunals, and the attorneys, had labored with intense application to find out the correct construction of the law. They had before them all the laws. There was no difficulty as to the *identity* of these laws. It was only a question of construction, and no more. As to that question, they arrived at different and precisely opposite conclusions. But the moment the supreme tribunal decided, there was one unanimous consent as to what was the proper construction, and their labors, as to that matter, were past. Now will any man say that the same unanimity could have possibly been attained, without such authoritative construction of the law? If so, he must take a singular view of things.

It is true, that while all must admit that this decision is legally right and judicially infallible, many will doubtless think that the decision ought to have been different. But suppose that Court had possessed actual, instead of mere judicial infallibility, what perfect unanimity would have resulted from such a decision –not only unanimity of submission, but also of relief. In such case no man, admitting the existence of this actual infallibility, would ever question the correctness of the decision, in argument or theory. All would have been perfect unanimity in the two elements of act and belief.

[19] Acts 13,14.

[20] Webster's Dictionary.

[21] *Cf.* Acts 15:22, 23.

[22] For example, 2 Cor., Philip, Coloss., Thess., and Philemon.

[23] A. Campbell and N Rice, *Campbell Rice Debate on the Holy Spirit*, p. 764. Mr. Campbell continues: "And the moment that B propounds his synopsis with the slightest air of authority, in the way of exacting obedience, or acknowledgment, that moment there is something in human nature that whispers in A, Who is this brother B? A fallible like myself! A great man he may be; but he is fond of his own opinions, and prides himself upon his superiority. I will

not lay a victim upon his altar, nor burn incense at his shrine; I too am a man, and will yield to none the right to dictate to me."

But most unfortunately the theory of Mr. Campbell provides no remedy for the evil he mentions. The supposed question between A and B was simply one of construction of a conceded written law. A is most fully justified in rejecting the fallible interpretation of brother B; but while he does so, he only falls back upon his own equally fallible interpretation. He is just as apt to be fond of his own opinions as brother B. True, it may be flattering to the pride of brother A –to that "something in human nature" –to be allowed to interpret for himself in the last resort. But as his *sole* and *only* object should be to arrive at the true will of the lawmaker, whose system never did flatter human pride. He might rely, with just as much *chance* of being right, upon the fallible interpretation of brother B, as upon his own equally fallible construction. So, after all the eloquent, the beautiful, the true language of Mr. Campbell, as to the difference between the fallible and the infallible, he leaves his brother A still resting alone upon "finities and fallibles," those "weak authorities when heaven and immortality are at stake."

[24] It is true that the apostles acted in two perfectly distinct capacities. They were *witnesses* and *teachers*. But it is equally true that they had the infallible assistance of the Holy Spirit in *both.* And as the duty of teaching is *perpetual*, (and not temporary, as was the duty of witnesses,) there must, of necessity, be the same powers and qualifications to teach in every age. Who can form any conception of a system requiring a great duty always to be performed, and at the same time denying the necessary powers and qualifications to accomplish it?

[25] Matt 18:17

[26] A. Campbell and N Rice, *Campbell Rice Debate on the Holy Spirit.* p. 421.

[27] Gardiner Spring *A Dissertation on the Rule of Faith.* p. 34.

[28] Acts 18: 10.

[29] Matt 23: 2, 3.

[30] A. Campbell and N Rice, *op. cit.* p. 309.

[31] Luke 1, Matt. 10.

[32] A. Campbell and N Rice, *op. cit.* p. 285.

[33] 2 Chron. 19.

[34] Lib. 2 *Contra Apionen.*

[35] Jn 5:39.

[36] Acts 17:11.

[37] 1 Jn 4:1.

[38] 2 Cor 1:24.

[39] Jas 1:5.

[40] 2 Tim 3:16.

[41] Deut. 31: 9-12.

[42] *Cf.* Acts 17:10.

[43] Webster's Dictionary.

[44] Is 35:8.

[45] Webster's Dictionary.

[46] *Ibid.*

[47] *Ibid.*

[48] Rom. 12: 5.

[49] Eph4: 4, 5.

[50] Acts 2: 42, 47.

[51] 1 Tim.1: 20.

[52] Mark 16: 16, 1 Cor. 5: 11, 2 John 1: 10.

[53] Letter to Ephesus.

[54] Letter to Tralles.

[55] Letter to Philadelphia.

[56] Letter to Smyrna.

[57] Letter to Polycarp.

[58] Letter to Ephesus.

[59] Letter to Magnesia.

[60] Letter to Philadelphia.

[61] Letter to Magnesia.

[62] Letter to the Philippians.

[63] *Adversus. Haereses*. 1, iii., c. iv.

[64] *Ibid.*, 1. iv., c. xxvi., n. 2.

[65] *Ibid.*, 1. v., c. xx., n. 1.

[66] *Ibid.*, 1. i., c. x., n. 1—3.

[67] *Ibid.*, 1. iii., c. xxiv., n. 1.

[68] *Ibid.*, 1. iii., c. iii., n. 1—4.

[69] *Ibid.*, 1. iv., c. 30.

[70] Col 2: 19.

[71] *Adversus. Haereses.*, 1. iv., c. xxxii., n. 1, 2.

[72] *Dialogue with Trypho*, n. 117.

[73] Eusebius of Caesarea. Ecclesiastical History, 1. iv., c. xxii.

[74] *Stromateis*, 1. i.

[75] *Ibid.,* 1. vi.

[76] *Ibid.*, 1, i.

[77] *Ibid.*, 1. ii.

[78] *Ibid.,* 1. iv.

[79] *Ibid.*, 1. iv.

[80] *Ibid.*, 1. vii.

[81] Tertullian. *De Praescriptione. Haereticorum*

[82] *De Praescriptione. Haereticorum.*, n. 20.

[83] *Ibid.*, n. 21.

[84] *Adversus. Marcion*, 1. iv., n. 5.

[85] *Ibid.*

[86] *De Praescriptione. Haereticorum.*

CHAPTER VI

THE PRIMACY OF SAINT PETER

1. Executive power must exist in the visible Church

If we concede that Christ was a Divine Lawgiver Who prescribed a fundamental unchangeable law for the practical government of men while in this state of being, we are then forced by the plainest and clearest principles whereon all governments intended for men must rest, to concede that His subjects were intended to be governed in unity, and not in discord. The moment we concede the character of Christ as the author of a *practical* system, we are also forced to concede that in the government He instituted, there must exist those necessary elements, without which government itself cannot exist.

That the executive power must exist in every practical government is as clear as that the legislative and judicial powers are required. We can as readily conceive of a government without the legislative, as without the executive and judicial powers. There cannot be a law prescribed without legislation. Nor can it be a law at all unless intended to constitute a rule for the parties governed; and it cannot be a rule, unless intended to be practically administered. This practical administration cannot be attained, unless the executive and judicial powers both exist in the system. I cannot form a conception of a visible association of men, governed by a positive unchangeable law, without the existence of the executive and judicial powers placed somewhere in the institution. Nor can I conceive of any practical and efficient system of government, wherein the executive and judicial powers are not coextensive with the actual exercise of the power of legislation. For what purpose do they exist but to enforce all those portions of the law intended to be put in practical operation?

If it is true that executive power exists in the Christ's system, that power must have been placed somewhere, either in the hands of an individual and his successors, or in the hands of several. The Catholic theory holds that our Lord conferred this power upon a single individual and his successors.

"The idea of supremacy" says Cardinal Wiseman,

involves two distinct, but closely allied, prerogatives: the first is that the Holy See is the center of unity; the second, that it is the fountain of authority. By the first is signified that all the faithful must be in communion with it, through their respective pastors, who form an unbroken chain of connection from the lowliest member of the flock, to him who has been constituted its universal shepherd.

We likewise hold the Pope to be the source of authority; as all the subordinate rulers of the church are subject to him, and receive directly, or indirectly, their jurisdiction from and by him. Thus the executive power is vested in his hands for all spiritual purposes within her; to him is given the charge of confirming his brethren in the faith; his office is to watch over the correction of abuses, and the maintenance of discipline throughout the church; in case of error springing up in any part, he must make the necessary investigation to discover it and condemn it; and either bring the refractory to submission, or separate them, as withered branches, from the vine. In cases of great and influential disorder in faith or practice, he convenes a general council of the pastors of the Church; presides over them in person, or by his legates; and sanctions, by his approbation, its canons or decrees....

The supremacy, which I have described is of a character purely spiritual, and has no connection with the possession of any temporal jurisdiction. The sovereignty of the Pope over his own dominions is no essential portion of his dignity; his supremacy was not the less before it was acquired: and should the unsearchable decrees of Providence, in the lapse of ages, deprive the Holy See of its temporal sovereignty, as happened to the seventh Pius, through the usurpation of a conqueror, its dominion over the Church and over the consciences of the faithful, would not be thereby impaired.[1]

2. The scriptural proofs of the primacy of Peter

The first passage which bears upon this question, is taken from the first chapter of Saint John's Gospel, verse forty two:

> And when Jesus beheld him he said, thou art Simon the son of Jona; thou shalt be called Cephas, which is by interpretation, a Stone.

According to the Douay Bible, "thou shalt be called Cephas, which is interpreted Peter." In his work upon the primacy of Saint Peter, Bishop Kenrick says that Cephas is a Syro-Chaldaic term that signifies rock.

It had been a practice with God, on particular occasions to change the names of his servants when bestowing upon them some signal pre-eminence. For example, when God made a great covenant with Abram, he changed his name to Abraham, and that of his wife from Sarai to Sarah.[2] Also, when Jacob wrestled with the angel and refused to let him go without a blessing, the angel blessed him and said: "Your name shall no more be called Jacob, but Israel, for you have striven with God and with men, and have prevailed."[3] The moment Christ saw Simon he said, "Thou shalt be called Cephas."[4]

Christ was no idle lawgiver. He always had, in His eye, His Father's business. What He did ever tended to that end. He did not give a surname to all the apostles. His practice was not general, but special. Special reasons must have existed to justify special acts. It would seem clear that Christ had some important object in view, when He gave Peter his name. It is not mentioned at the time it was given, but it does not matter when or where the reason for the change of name is given, provided it is given. In the sixteenth chapter of Saint Matthew's Gospel we have the explanation:

> He saith unto them, "But whom say ye that I am?"
>
> And Simon Peter answered and said, "Thou art the Christ, the Son of the living God."
>
> And Jesus answered and said unto him, "Blessed art thou, Simon Bar-Jona for flesh and blood had not revealed it onto thee, but my father which is in heaven. And I say also unto thee, that thou art Peter, and upon this rock I will build my church; and the gates of hell shall not prevail against it. And I will give unto thee the keys of the kingdom of heaven: and whatsoever thou shalt bind on earth shall be bound in heaven: and whatever thou shalt loose on earth shall be loosed in heaven."

It will be observed that both the powers to bind and loose were conferred on Peter. The one power without the other would have been as idle as the power to remit, without the power to retain sins. The power to open, without the power to shut, the gates of the Kingdom, would have been equally idle. If the power to loose, was the power to open the gates of the Kingdom; then, the corresponding power to bind was the power to shut.

According to the half-complete theory of Mr. Campbell and others, the gates were only to be opened by Peter *once* to Jews and Gentiles – were always after that to remain open – and there is no more use for keys. But when did Peter ever shut the gates? At the time the keys were given to him, the gates were closed. If after been once opened, they were always to remain open, the power to bind was wholly useless. By this theory, our Lord is accused of doing a very senseless thing –by conferring the power to bind on Peter when it never will be used.

There are four facts that clearly distinguish Peter's case from that of the other apostles:

1. He is the only rock –foundation

2. The power was separately delegated to him

3. He was the only one to whom the whole flock was committed.

4. He was the only one to whom the keys –the symbol of supreme command –were given.

These facts are most important and full of meaning. They are of a conclusive character when legitimately considered and applied. It must be conceded that this is one of the most emphatic passages to be found in the four Gospels, and must teem with meaning of the greatest importance.

3. The primacy of Peter based on being the foundational rock

The first question that gives rise to a difference of opinion, is whether Peter is the rock upon which the Church was to be founded. Many Protestant authors concede that he was. Others contend that the truth revealed to Peter was alluded to by our Lord as "this rock." All Catholic writers, whose works I have read, insist that the clear meaning of the passage is, as if written, "Thou art a rock, and upon this rock I will build my church." Mr. Campbell, in his debate with Bishop Purcell, gives this reading:

> Thou art stone, and upon this rock (on this great truth which flesh and blood has not revealed to thee) I will build my church.

Of the merits of the different translations I am not competent to speak. There are circumstances that seem clearly to refute the interpretation of Mr. Campbell. Our Lord had previously given Simon the surname of Peter, without giving him any reason for it; and now, in the commencement of His reply, He simply calls him Simon Bar-Jona, and then gives him the reason why he is blessed, because the Father had revealed to him this great truth. Then following the blessing, and the reason given for it, our Lord uses that most emphatic affirmation: "And I say also unto thee, that thou art Peter." When our Lord first called him

Cephas, His language was not so emphatic. It was simply "thou shalt be called Cephas."

It is true, that our Lord, in the first sentence of his reply to Peter, alluded to the truth confessed by the apostle; but He does not there designate that truth as a rock, and if He did not call Peter a rock, how could He afterwards say, with any propriety, *this* rock? Had our Lord intended to make the truth confessed, the rock upon which the Church should be built, He would have naturally expressed Himself substantially in this form:

> Blessed art thou, Simon Bar-Jona: for flesh an blood hath not revealed it into thee, but my Father which is in heaven; and upon this truth I will build my Church, and the gates of hell shall not prevail against it.

He would have put the promise to building in close connection with the foundation, in the place where the foundation is *first* mentioned, and not in a distinct sentence. Why our Lord should have given Peter the most emphatic confirmation of his name immediately before His promise to build the Church, and closely connect the promise and the confirmation together in the same sentence, when they had no relation to each other, it is most difficult to conceive. According to the theory of those who deny that Peter was the rock, the promise to build is closely connected with what is not the foundation, and disconnected from that which is –thus reversing all the rules of correct usage.

Now for what purpose and for what intent, did our Lord use this emphatic language? The phrase is too emphatic to be idle and meaningless. Besides, our Lord never did an idle thing. He must have had some end to signify. What was it? I could never find a Protestant writer who could give any plausible reason for the use of that emphatic statement. "Thou art Peter" and yet deny that he was the rock.[5] What conceivable purpose could Christ have had in view, but to make that the basis of that which immediately followed –"and upon this rock I will build my church."

The true and simple view of this passage would seem to be this: Our Lord, at the beginning, gave Simon his surname, without stating to him any reason for the act. God, the Father, afterwards reveals to Peter the divinity of Christ. Our Lord called out the confession of Peter, not that He needed to be informed of the facts inquired after, but for the purpose of affording Him a fitting opportunity of constituting Peter the foundation of the Church. Peter had been favored by a special revelation, and our Lord knew this fact. When Peter had confessed our Lord reaffirmed the name Peter, for the purpose of letting him know that he was not only a rock, but the rock upon which the Church should be built, and then He states the character of the Church.

This view gives force and effect to every part of the reply of our Lord to Peter, and does not leave the emphatic affirmation "thou art Peter," to stand in such close connection with "and upon this rock," etc., and yet be idle and meaningless. The very reason why our Lord at first only called him Simon, was to reserve the affirmation that he was Peter, for the purpose of putting it in close and immediate connection with "this rock."

The opposite construction cannot be true, because it breaks the chain of unity running through the whole passage. Everything in it has a connection with Peter. He is the first pronounced blessed –he is then told that he is Peter, and that the Church should be built upon him, and then he is promised the keys. That the promise to build the church was connected with Peter, is further shown from that which follows. Why should our Lord continue His promises in this form, "And I will give unto thee the keys…" unless both promises related to Peter? There are three sentences contained in our Lord's reply to Peter, and they all relate to him and matters connected with him. The first and third confessedly relate to Peter. Why does not that in the middle have relation to Peter also? If we concede that the church was founded on Peter, we can readily see why Christ defined the character of the structure to be built on Peter. The character of the Church necessarily qualified the prerogative of the apostle. The promise to build would not be definite, unless the character of the thing to be built was also given. So, when our Lord promised the keys, He at once states what they will enable Peter to do.

It was objected by Mr. Campbell, as well as others, that Peter could not be the rock, because Christ said "Thou" in the second, and "this" in the third person. "To have addressed Peter in the second and third persons as both present and absent, in the same breath, is wholly unprecedented."[6]

But with all due deference to the opinion of the learned debater, his objection seems more plausible than sound. Our Lord first tells Peter that he is a rock, and after that, so long as He speaks of Peter under that symbol, He very properly uses the third person. But when He comes to speak of Peter, not as the rock, but is the earthly head of the Church, holding the keys, then our Lord uses the second person. I cannot see any violation of correct usage in this. The use of the third person in one case, and of the second in the other, was in strict accordance with the figures used by Christ. Having first declared Peter a rock, so long as He kept that symbol in his eye He would regard him in that light, and speak of him accordingly. The interpreter of a dream, of a parable first tells you that he will give the interpretation, and after that he proceeds to use language in a positive form – "the reapers are the angels, the harvest is the end of the world."

Bishop Kenrick says:

> Bloomfield a recent Anglican commentator, observes that every modern expositor of note has abandoned the distinction between Peter and the rock as untenable. Bishop Marsh, quoted by him, says that "it would be a desperate undertaking to prove that Christ meant any other person than Peter." Rosenmuller the German rationalist coincides in this critical judgment. "The rock," says he, "is neither the confession of Peter, nor of Christ painting out Himself by His finger, or by a shake of the head (which interpretations the context does not admit), but Peter himself."[7]

The learned author says on the next page:

> In Gerhard's *Institutes of Biblical Criticism,* is contained the following just observation –Canon 511: "The most obvious and natural sense is to be set aside only when it is absolutely contradictory to something plainly taught in Scripture." [8]

Gerhard then remarks that "the opposite way has been taken by all sects;" and, quoting the 18th verse of the 16th chapter of Saint Matthew, observes:

> Building on Peter is explained, by some, as contrary to the faith that Christ is the only foundation as given in One Corinthians chapter 3, and as favoring, the succession of Peter and his successors. But the connection shows that Peter *is here plainly meant.*

Such is the language of this text-book of so many Protestant colleges and theological institutions, both in this country and in England."

Mr. Thompson of Glasgow, in his *Monatessaron*, concedes that "Peter was the rock on which Christ said His church should be built." The same author states that, "Protestants have betrayed unnecessary fears, and have, therefore, used all the *hardihood of lawless criticism* in their attempts to reason away the Catholic interpretation."[9]

It has been often objected, as it was by Mr. Campbell that Peter could not be the rock upon which the Church was built, because this would be a contradiction of other portions of Scripture.[10] In the third chapter of first Corinthians it is said: "For other foundation can no man lay than that is laid, which is Jesus Christ." And in the second chapter of Ephesians the apostle says, alluding to the faithful: "And are built upon the foundation of the apostles and prophets, Jesus Christ Himself being the chief cornerstone."

The term foundation has several meanings, one of which is "the basis of an edifice; that part of a building which lies upon the ground, usually a wall of stone which supports the edifice."[11]

It is evident that the apostle used the word with reference to this sense, as he speaks of foundations as having been laid. And were we to adopt the principles of criticism urged by Mr. Campbell, we should make the apostle contradict himself; because, in the first extract the apostle speaks of Christ as the foundation, and does not mention that apostles and prophets composed it in part as he does in the second. I am not aware of any text in which our Lord was ever spoken of as constituting the foundation, in whole or in part, that does not speak with reference to a foundation laid, not selected.

The term has another and a wider signification, "the basis or ground work of any thing; that on which anything stands and by which it is supported." A rock is "a large mass of stony matter, either bedded in the earth, or resting upon its surface."[12] A rock, upon which a building is based, is "bedded in the earth." It was with reference to this sense that Peter was called the rock. Our Lord, when He spoke of building His church upon a rock, used the word rock in the same sense He did when speaking of the wise man, whose house "fell not: for it was founded on a rock." That must be a foundation upon which an edifice is founded.

The different figures used in different portions of the Scriptures, are all perfectly consistent with the Catholic view, and with each other. The same thing may be a fit symbol to illustrate different parts of the same system, when contemplated from different points of view. Thus Saint Paul calls Christ the Spiritual rock. He speaks of Him under the symbol of a rock from which flowed the water that saved the perishing Israelites in the desert.[13] The rock of Horeb was in the apostle's eye, and he did not intend in this passage, to compare Christ to a foundation. When God the Father speaks of himself as a builder He says: "Behold, I will lay in Zion for a foundation stone," where the foundation stone alluded to was

Christ. When the everlasting firmness of Christ is represented, He is called the 'rock of ages.' So, when our Lord spoke as a builder He said, "Thou art Peter, and upon this rock I will build my church."

4. Peter's primary role is a continuing power

If we concede that Peter was the rock, then we concede that he was superior to the other apostles, who were not the rock, but only a part of the foundation as laid by Christ. In what then did this superiority consist? The Catholic theory holds that superior official power was conferred on this great apostle. Protestants deny this. The most plausible ground that can be taken (after conceding that Peter was the rock) to defeat the Catholic construction is that the promise to build the church on Peter was fulfilled by his being the first sent to convert both Jews and Gentiles, so that in some sense, the Church might be said to rise from him.

But this explanation would seem to be entirely too narrow, and in conflict with the plain and obvious figure used by Christ. It would seem to be about as erroneously restrictive, as that narrow construction which sought to confine salvation alone to the Jews, when the wide commission was, "Go teach all nations…" – "Preach the Gospel to every creature."

The simple facts that Peter stood up with the eleven on the day of Pentecost, and was the only one who spoke on that day; and that he afterwards was the first to receive a Gentile into the Church; does not show he had more official power than others. The first president of the United States had no more official power than the second. How could the first president, as such, be properly called the rock upon which the political fabric rests?

According to the Protestant view, Peter was only the *first* to exercise a power given alike to all the apostles. In this case how then can it be said with any propriety that he was the rock upon which the Church stood. This would not seem to be in keeping with the magnificent promise of Christ.

The rock upon which an edifice is built, is contemplated as continuing in the same permanent state it was in at the precise time when the building was erected. If we say that our Lord first created the office of Supreme head of the Church on earth, as He did the office of teacher in the commission, and afterwards addressed Peter in his official capacity, then we can see how Peter could be appropriately called the rock upon which the church was built. The power and effect of the office would always be the same as at the first, and the Church might well rest upon it. Christ regarded The Church as a permanent structure, and the rock or foundation upon which it is built, must have been viewed by Him as equally continuing. The permanency of one must have been commensurate with that of the other.

That this is the correct view would seem to be clear from the fact, that the stability of the Church is but the consequence of this foundation. When our Lord said the foolish man built his house upon the sand and it fell, we must conclude that it fell because of the insecurity of the foundation. This conclusion is shown to be correct from the fact, that when our Lord spoke of the wise man who built his house upon a rock, He said "it did not fall, because it had been founded on the rock."[14] Here the cause of the stability of the house was its rock foundation. So, when Christ says, "and on this rock I will build my church, and the gates of hell shall not prevail against it," the relation of the structure to the foundation is so close, that we must say the stability of the building is the consequence of the stability of the foundation. Christ made Peter the rock, and the stability of the rock came from Christ, its Creator.

How the mere personal privilege of being the first to exercise an official power, shared in common with other then existing equals, could give this permanent stability to the Church, is difficult to see. The cause is wholly inadequate to produce the effect. There is no due proportion between them.

Our Lord gave to Peter the keys of the kingdom, and the consequence of this possession of the keys of the entire kingdom was the Supreme power to bind and loose. In other words, the power to bind and loose was but a consequence flowing from the keys of the entire kingdom, and was a power supreme over all. Observe the clear and explicit language of our Lord: "And I will give unto thee the keys of the kingdom of heaven; and whatsoever thou shalt bind on earth, shall be bound in heaven: and whatsoever thou shalt loose upon earth, shall be loosed in heaven."

Mr. Campbell and others have insisted that the keys were only give to Peter to enable him to open, once and for all, the gates of the Church to Jews and Gentiles. But with all due deference, it seems that this explanation is too narrow and diminutive. If I am correct in holding that the power to bind and loose was but a result flowing from the possession of the keys, then the construction must be erroneous. For the power was not only to loose but also to bind *–to shut.*

I have never been able to find any instance in which so small a consequence could be give to such a symbol. The delivery of keys has always been a symbol of supreme command.[15] In the 22nd chapter of Isaiah, God, speaking of His Son, says: "And I will commit my government into His hands… and the key of the house of David will I lay upon His shoulder: so he shall open, and none shall shut; and he shall shut, and none shall open." Therefore, in the first chapter of Revelations, the keys mentioned in verse eighteen, were symbols of supreme command. So, at law, where the delivery of personal property is necessary to pass the title, the delivery of the key of the warehouse in which the goods are stored, is a symbolical delivery which is regarded as equivalent to an actual delivery, and passes the command of the property to the purchaser.

This is so in the usage of all nations. In the very nature of the symbol it can mean nothing else. The delivery of the keys of a fortress or walled city to a conqueror is a surrender of the same into his possession. This very act yields up the command of the place by one party, and passes it to the other. When, therefore, our Lord gave Peter the keys of His kingdom, what else could He mean, but to give him, to whom He committed the keys, the supreme command? And that our Lord created an office by this act, would also seem clear. His system itself was permanent. The gates and keys of this kingdom were part of this permanent kingdom. There is no limitation put to the duration of this power in this permanent kingdom, any more than there is to the office of President of the United States, in our Constitution. But our Lord says, without any limitation as to the time, "I will give unto thee the keys of the kingdom of heaven."

Our Lord used the symbol of the keys, in the same sense in which his Father used it when speaking of Him as the future Messiah. The Father committed the government to His Son by delivery of the keys of the house of David, that is the Church. The Son committed the same to *His* servant by the same symbol. As the Father constituted Christ his agent, so Christ constituted Peter his agent. God the Father is the original source of authority, and governs the kingdom through His Son, Jesus Christ. All power in heaven and earth was given to our Lord, who in turn, committed the government to His subordinates. He governs through His agent Peter, and sub-agents appointed by Peter.

By the delivery of the symbol, Peter had the power not only to loose, but also to bind. The power to do both was necessary as the Church must be often opened to some and shut against others. These powers were permanent by the nature of things. They are needed at all times during the existence of the institution.

The kingdom meant is the visible church, whose gates require to be often opened, and then shut. Do the gates of the city, after being opened for the first time, always stand open after that? And to all persons? If so, of what use are the gates? The very idea of keys and gates, presupposes the utility of opening to all who are entitled to enter, and of shutting against all who would enter improperly. True, the keys were necessary to open the gates for the first time; but they were equally necessary to open and shut, at intervals, through all coming time. The prophet said Christ should open and no man should shut, and no man should open. Christ was to do both; and what He does by His agent, He does Himself.

5. Peter was given superior jurisdiction

Those who concede that Peter was the rock, and yet deny his supremacy, insist that the same power was afterwards conferred to all the apostles, thus making them equals.[16] But if this conclusion, drawn from the facts, be true, why did Christ do an idle and vain thing in conferring the power *separately* on Peter? Our Lord had some motive in making this separate delegation. What could it have been but to give him superiority over the others, to produce unity in all?

The facts conceded, taken in connection with other examples in the New Testament, constitute a very strong argument to sustain the Catholic view. For example, when our Lord conferred the power to bind and loose upon all, He did not promise them the keys, as he did separately to Peter. This is a marked and most material difference in the two cases. Besides this difference, other instances mentioned in the New Testament show what was intended. Our Lord required all to *follow* Him. Yet, when He addressed Peter, Andrew, and Matthew individually, and said, "Follow me" He required them to follow him in a distinct and peculiar manner.[17] So also, when it is said that John was the *beloved* disciple, is it not clear that he was more beloved than the others, although our Lord loved them all most tenderly?[18] So also, the apostles were all commissioned to teach all nations, yet Saint Paul and Saint Barnabas were sent on a special mission. Was there nothing peculiar in the missions of Paul and Barnabas?

Putting these examples together, they show our Lord was not an idle lawgiver. When He conferred a power separately upon a certain person He intended by the very act, to give him a peculiar vocation, although the same power was conferred upon others collectively including the person upon whom it was separately conferred. In the case of Peter this is made clear by the following extract:

> So, when they had dined, Jesus said to Simon Peter, "Simon son of Jonas, lovest thou me more than these?"
>
> He saith unto him, "Yea Lord; you know that I love thee."
>
> He saith unto him, "Feed my lambs."
>
> He saith to him again the second time "Simon son of Jonas, lovest thou me?"
>
> He saith unto him, "Yea Lord; thou knowest that I love thee"
>
> He saith unto him, "Feed my sheep."
>
> He saith unto him the third time, "Simon son of Jonas, lovest thou me?"
>
> Peter was grieved because he said unto him the third time, Lovest thou me? And he said unto him, "Lord, thou knowest all thing; thou knowest that I love thee."
>
> Jesus saith to him, "Feed my sheep."[19]

The expression "more than these" is elliptical. Mr. Campbell construed it to mean: "do you love me more than these fish, of these victuals?"[20] The Catholic interpretation is: "do you love me more than these disciples?" In support of his view, Mr. Campbell insisted that Peter could not have answered such a question, because he could not know how much his companions loved his Master. However, this suggestion seems more plausible than just.

Whether or not Peter loved our Lord more than the other disciples loved Him, he certainly gave the most conclusive evidence that he did. In the very chapter in which the passage occurs, the moment that he knew it was our Lord, he cast himself into the sea, while the others remained with the fish, and he only returned to them after our Lord commanded to bring some of the fish they had taken. Besides, the construction of Mr. Campbell is shown to be erroneous by the form of the answer of Peter. For the construction of Mr. Campbell to be correct Peter would have answered: "Lord, thou knowest that I love thee more than I love these fish or these victuals." No amount of delicacy could have influenced him in such a case. And no motive of delicacy could have influenced our Lord, as such a feeling is not indulged by lawgivers at the expense of truth.

Our Lord knew the answer Peter would give. The form of the answer shows that Peter was governed by motives of humility and delicacy, while our Lord was not. In justice to the other disciples, we cannot suppose that they would be hurt by the act of their master, while they might object to an act of Peter in determining that he loved their Lord more than they loved Him. It was not necessary for Peter to state that he loved his Master more then the others, because out Lord knew the fact as well without a statement as with one. Peter in his answer, appeals to this knowledge. Our lord in his question did not settle the matter as to the one who loved him most, and Peter did not determine it, but referred the matter back to the knowledge of Christ. The object of our Lord, in asking the question, was to make a fitting opportunity to commit His whole flock to Peter. In doing this our Lord himself answered the question in the affirmative. Peter did love him more than the rest.

The answer of Peter is not fully responsive to the interrogative, and when given he did not know what our lord intended. His Master at that precise point of time left the question as to the one who loved Him most, an open one. The humility of Peter, and his knowledge that Christ knew all things, prevented him from assuming to determine a question of delicacy between him and his companions. Therefore, he simply answered that he loved his Master who knew all things, and referred the measure of this love, as compared with the love of his companions, back to our Lord. This view makes the conduct of Peter intelligible. It explains the reason why our Lord did not reprove him for an apparent evasion of His question. Upon the theory of Mr. Campbell, Peter evaded the question propounded without any reason for doing so.

Aside from this question, the passage, when fairly considered, is very clear support of the primacy of Saint Peter. It is true that Mr. Campbell and others object to the interpretation of sheep as bishops, and lambs as laity. But while they make these objections they do not help us any by informing us what Christ did, in their opinion, mean by this distinction. He must have meant something; otherwise the distinction was idle and useless. What then did he mean?

In the tenth chapter of Saint John's Gospel, when Christ speaks of His entire flock, as separated from the world, He simply called them sheep.

But when he comes to speak of them as distinguished among themselves into two classes, He calls one class lambs, and the other sheep.

That this meaning is correct would seem plain when we consider that Christ called Himself the Shepherd, and Saint Peter afterwards called Him the Chief Shepherd. There cannot be a Chief Shepherd without under-shepherds. The apostles Peter and Paul, as we have already seen, keep up the comparison of the sheepfold. That the laity are, meant by lambs would seem clear from the fact that the lambs accustomed to follow the sheep: and Saint Paul tells his brethren to obey, submit to, and follow the faith of them who had the rule over them.

Whether this distinction is correct or not, one thing is clear, that the two classes, lambs and sheep, did comprise the entire flock, and they were all committed separately to Peter. This being true, Peter bore to all the others the superior relation of under-shepherd, next in authority to Christ; and he must of necessity, have had superior jurisdiction over those who bore to him the subordinate relation of sheep to their shepherd. To say otherwise would destroy the unity, of the whole figure; for the commission to feed is always a commission to govern and direct, as may be conclusively seen, by an examination of other passages. [21]

That the whole flock was committed to Peter, is further shown by the twenty-second chapter of Saint Luke's Gospel:

> And the Lord said, Simon, Simon, Satan hath desired to have you (in the plural), that he may sift you as wheat; but I have prayed for thee, that thy faith fail not: and when thou art converted, strengthen thy brethren. (in the Douay Bible, confirm thy brethren.)

It is conceded by all that the pronoun "you" referred to all the apostles. Why then did our Lord pray separately for Peter, and, when he is converted, he is charged to strengthen or confirm his brethren? We are not informed that He prayed separately for any one or more of the others.

If this passage stood alone, it could perhaps, be explained upon some other hypothesis. But taken in connection with the fact that Christ promised the keys to Peter, and afterwards committed His entire flock to him, both lambs and sheep, the most simple and natural conclusion is that Christ used Peter as His superior agent to confirm the others.

6. Objection from our Lord saying "Get thee behind me Satan"

It has been often objected, that after Christ had promised to found His Church upon Peter, He said to him, "Get thee behind me Satan." This text has been much perverted; but Mr. Campbell conceded that our Lord did not call Peter, Satan, but simply opponent.

> The word *Satanas*, signifies adversary. Jesus calls him not *ho satanas*, Satan, but simply opponent. Stand aside, thou who opposest me in this matter. Thou dost not understand these divine things.[22]

The fact that Peter erred from his love of his Master, does not show that he was not afterwards qualified to the Supreme head of the Church on earth. On the contrary, Mr. Campbell, while denying the existence of the office, clearly proved his eminent fitness for such a position.[23]

7. Objection from Peter and John being sent to Samaria

It is stated in the eight chapter of the Acts that the apostles *sent* Peter and John to Samaria. It is objected that this conflicts with the Catholic theory. Mr. Campbell thought, "This fact spoke volumes against the pretended successors of Peter."[24]

But is this true? Suppose we take, for the sake of argument only, the theory of Mr. Campbell, that all the apostles were independent equals. Then how could all the apostles together have the right to send a portion upon a mission without their consent? Equals have no right to command equals. However, if we say that Christ created a college of teachers, making the college superior to each member, then we must concede that this college is perpetual. We are forced to admit succession.

The sending of Peter and John is entirely reconcilable with the Catholic theory, and in strict accordance with it. The act of sending was the act of the college, including the Head, Peter. He, like any other individual, could act in different capacities, under mere delegated authority. In Catholic theory, he was the equal of the other apostles as teacher under the commission, "Go teach." He was superior to them under the separate delegation of power in virtue of the keys. Therefore, the college, with Peter at its head, was superior to Peter in his capacity of teacher under the commission. The act of the college was the concurrent act of all, including Peter. With his consent, he could well be sent with John. As Peter filled different capacities, one supreme, and the other subordinate, he had the exclusive right to determine in the first instance the capacity in which he would act. When he had done this, and consented to act in a subordinate capacity he was subject to the whole college. There was nothing incompatible with the Catholic theory in the act of the college sending Saint Peter with Saint John.

This same objection against Peter's headship will also lie against Mr. Campbell's theory. Take the example of the teachers who insisted upon the necessity of circumcision who were the inferiors of Saint Paul. Yet we are told that, "*they* determined that Paul and Barnabas, and certain others of them, should go up to Jerusalem unto the apostles and elders about this question."[25] Who are *they*? Is it not certain that the pronoun *they* included these teachers as well Paul and Barnabas? How then, will Mr. Campbell reconcile this with the principle upon which his objection is based? With due deference to the opinion of the learned debater, I must say that "this fact" is more difficult of reconciliation with his theory than with the Catholic theory.

8. Objection from the conflict in accepting Gentile Christians

After Saint Peter had admitted Cornelius into the Church, it is stated in the eleventh chapter of the Acts that, "they that were of the circumcision contended with him." Mr. Campbell thought this fact was, "still more humiliating to the successors" of Peter. But is Mr. Campbell right?

The act of Saint Peter in admitting Cornelius into the Church was an official act, performed under the assumed authority of Christ. Though an official act, it was not performed by him in his capacity as head of the Church. It was performed in his capacity as teacher under the commission. Any other teacher could have performed the act of admitting individuals into the Church. The thing done belonged to an inferior capacity. In addition, the question was new, and had never been authoritatively determined, and Saint Peter had acted without the knowledge of the other teachers.

The objection also proves too much. The fact is just as difficult to reconcile with Mr. Campbell's theory as with the Catholic theory. The critics were not apostles, and under any theory they were inferiors to Saint Peter. When well considered it will be seen that under any theory we can only account for the conduct of these critics upon the ground that they admitted themselves to be inferiors. As such, they asked for reasons for the act of their superior, and Saint Peter gave them the facts as his justification. An inferior may well contend with a superior without a violation of duty when the latter permits it. It amounts to no more than a statement that the inferior endeavored, by argument, to sustain his view before the superior. Conceding the Catholic theory to be true, Saint Peter might well permit these men to contend with him about a new question not authoritatively settled.

9. Objection based on Saint Peter's role in Council

It is insisted by some that the conduct of Saint Peter in the Council of Jerusalem was inconsistent with the theory that he was head of the Church on earth. It does not appear in the narrative of the fifteenth chapter of the Acts, who called the council, or who presided. The fact that Saint Paul, Saint Barnabas, and other teachers "determined to go to Jerusalem unto the apostles and elders about this question" shows only that they determined to "go up" –not that a council would be called.

Agency can be affirmed by subsequent assent of a principal, as well as by his prior act. Whether the council was called by Peter, or not, it is certain that it was called with his consent. This consent would give it his sanction. Under the Catholic theory, those at Antioch might well determine for themselves to submit a question to the council, but they could not compel the council to sit. This is not at all in conflict with the authority of Saint Peter as Head of the Church.

It must be conceded, that the history of the council is concise –not full. We do not know from history that anyone did, or did not, preside. It is most reasonable to suppose that some one did preside, and if anyone did, it certainly is most probable it was Peter. It is also certain that there had been much disputing in the council until Peter spoke. After he spoke, the friends of circumcision were silent. Not a voice was afterwards raised in support of this error.

The fact that he spoke in the council is not at all inconsistent with the theory of his primacy. Conceding that he presided, he had the right to speak. The Speaker of the House of Representatives has the right to speak and vote.

The fact that Saint James was the first to propose the exact form of the decree is nowise contrary to the Catholic theory. The Pope may or may not speak in council. He must constitute a part of every council, either in person or by his legates, and must himself sanction their decrees to give them effect.

The objection is based on an inaccurate and confused conception of the Catholic theory. It appears certain that Saint Peter was always at hand, and always forward and prominent on all great occasions. Whether he was constituted Head of the Church on earth, or not, his conduct was consistent with that character.

10. Objection from Paul's confrontation with Peter

It has been objected that the conduct of Saint Paul in withstanding Saint Peter to his face, for a personal act of the latter, was inconsistent with Saint Peter's alleged official superiority.[26] Those who make this objection seem to forget that Saint Peter was an individual member of the Church. As such, he possessed personal free agency, and could sin as others would. In his private capacity he was no more than any other member. Saint Paul had the right to reprove him for his personal dissimulation. It would seem from the statements of Saint Paul, that Saint Peter admitted his error, since he made no reply to the objection.

Saint Paul himself seems to have afterwards fallen into the same error, when he purified himself in the temple.[27] If it be said that Saint Peter's error was official, not private, then it is difficult to understand why Saint Paul had the right to call in question the official act of an individually infallible apostle.

11. The objection that Peter did not claim the primacy

It is objected by Mr. Campbell, that Saint Peter in his epistles nowhere expressly assumes to speak as Supreme Head of the Church, and that this silence is inconsistent with such a capacity. However, omission is a very weak argument. One affirmative witness is worth many negative ones. Omission is the main ground upon on which the Infidel relies to show contradictions in the four Gospels, and is one of the positions that Dr. Paley confutes in his *Evidences of Christianity.*

Saint John writes his Epistles simply calling himself an elder. In his Epistle to Philemon, Saint Paul simply called himself a prisoner. In his Epistle to the Hebrews he does not mention that he was an apostle. Saint James commences his Epistle by calling himself a servant. Several of Saint Paul's Epistles are commenced as if written jointly with others. Now these omissions do not prove that the several authors were only entitled to fill the positions mentioned, and none others.

It is true that Saint Peter simply calls himself an apostle, an elder, a servant. It is equally that he was all of these, and could have been Head of the College. There is nothing in either Epistle that required Saint Peter to state or to assume to act as Supreme head of the Church.

As head of the Church, the Pope rules the Church through his subordinates. If they fail to do their duty, they can be reached directly by him. The individual members are primarily responsible to their immediate pastors, with the right of appeal to the Pope.

Conceding, for the sake of argument, the truth of the Catholic theory, there is nothing inconsistent in the silence of Saint Peter with this theory. All that he said he could well say in a subordinate capacity. This being the fact, his admitted humility fully explains his silence.[28]

It will also be observed that Saint Peter gives his testimony to facts he has seen and heard as a chosen witness of Christ. Neither of these capacities belonged to his office as Head of the College. The apostles were the only chosen witnesses. This fact made it proper for him to state that he was an apostle when giving testimony in his Epistles.

He also records certain prophecies he made. He was also writing part of the Scriptures. The gift of prophecy and the inspiration of a scriptural writer were special gifts not confined to the apostles. These special gifts did not belong to the office of Supreme Head of the Church, and therefore, there could have been no propriety in his assuming to act in that capacity when writing his Epistles.

12. The objection that a Supreme Head is not Scriptural

Mr. Campbell insisted that the office of Supreme Head of the Church, being an important office, should have been clearly defined in the Scriptures. Its not being so specified he insisted was a strong argument against the existence of the office.[29] In support of his position, he read certain portions of the Constitution of the United States relating to the office of the President.

This objection would be entitled to great weight if all of several things were true:

1. That Peter's superiority is not plainly stated.

2. That the scriptures contain all of the code of law.

3. That the Scriptures assumed to be regular and methodical.

4. That the right of the Church to determine authoritatively all questions arising under the law was not clearly stated.

That Peter was the rock upon which the Church was built seems very plain to my mind. This fact once conceded, his supremacy follows as a simple logical consequence. Mr Campbell seems to be sensible of this result, as he put his denials in the right place to be *apparently* consistent. An entire negation, however false, is still consistent with itself. Mr. Campbell, therefore, denies that Peter was the rock. But with all due deference, it would seem that he did not deny enough. He should have insisted that there were no gates and no keys; for the reason that they were perfectly idle and useless in contemplation of his theory.[30] They were used but once; and a simple opening in the wall, or no enclosure, would have better suited his theory. The idea of a wall, gates and keys to be used but once, and that at the beginning, is not very intelligible.

Mr. Campbell's position proves too much. If it were applied to other portions of the Scriptures, it would be seen how unsound it is. There are many of the most important tenets not more plainly taught. The authority for observing the first, for the seventh day of the week, is not very easily found in Scripture. The same may be said of the authority for not washing feet, contrary to the command of Christ as stated in the twelfth chapter of Saint John's Gospel. It would seem that Mr. Campbell's rule of criticism would ruin his theory of Scripture alone. If there be any things in the Scripture plainly taught, the power of the Church to decide all questions is, in my best judgment, one of them.

13. Objection from the need for the greatest to be a servant

In Luke's gospel it is stated:

> And there was strife among them, which of them should be accounted the greatest. And he said unto them, the kings of the Gentiles exercise lordship over them, and they that exercise authority upon them are called benefactors. But ye shall not be so; but he that is greatest among you, let him be as the younger, and he that is chief, as he that doth serve. For whether is greater, he that sitteth at meat, or he that serveth? is he that sitteth at meat? but I am among you as he that serveth.[31]

It has often been insisted that this passage is in conflict with the Catholic theory. But is this true?

It appears from facts stated in other portions of the Gospels, that at the time the strife occurred the apostles believed that the coming kingdom of Christ would be temporal. Hence, their natural pride prompted them to contend as who should be the greatest in this earthly kingdom. It was to correct this error in judgment, and to reprove their pride, that our Lord used the language quoted.

Our Lord states in substance, that that He did not come to establish such temporal authority as the Gentiles exercised. Therefore, in that respect they were not to be distinguished one above another by *His Law*. To prevent them from construing this general language into a prohibition of all distinction, He expressly states that one should be the greatest, and one should be the chief. To restrain all pride in the exercise of this pre-eminence, He tells them that the greatest shall be (not the younger) but *as* the younger; and the chief *as* he that serves. Then He compares the state or position of that one with his own, saying that He was among them *as* he that served.

As our Lord was among them *as he that served,* and yet He was the greatest in power and authority; so the one that was to be chief, should be as one who served. The example of the superior authority of Christ, and the laborious and humble manner of its exercise by Him, was expressly held up to them as a pattern for the one that should be chief among them after He was gone. If Christ Himself could be among them *as he that served*, so the one that would be chief could retain authority and be among them as he that served. The chief would be but the agent of Christ, acting for Him, and in His stead. His authority was to be exercised by him, as laboriously and as meekly as his Master had exercised the same authority before him. The office was to possess power; but the power accompanied with the greatest labor and humility.

Now if Christ intended that such an office should exist these are the features he would bestow on it; He would unite power, labor, and humility. This would be in harmony with the whole scope and spirit of His system. Power was indispensable to enable the officer to accomplish the great ends intended, labor and humility were necessary checks upon pride and ambition. It was a beautiful combination of all the efficient, yet safe, features of an office.

This passage far from being in conflict with the Catholic theory, it is, when justly considered, a very strong support of it. Had Christ ended by saying in general terms, "But ye shall not be so," then His meaning would not be clear. He does not stop there but goes on to point out another kind of distinction that should exist among them. He fixes clearly the character of that distinction, and the manner of its exercise; He compares the situation of the "chief" with His own. When a lawgiver first lays down a principle in general terms, and then is careful to make an express exception, this fact shows more clearly his true intent.

14. Objections from prophecy

The third proposition of Mr. Campbell in reference to the Catholic Church was that, "she is the Babylon of John, the Man of Sin of Paul, and the empire of the Youngest Horn of Daniel's Sea Monster."[32] It must be conceded by calm and dispassionate men, that the language of prophecy is obscure. There are good and sufficient reasons why it should be so. It was not the intention of God to touch the free agency of individuals, but to leave it untrammeled. It was his purpose to keep His children always vigilant and hopeful. To have made the prophesies in clear and distinct language would have defeated the evident purposes of the Deity in making them. There may be some exceptions to this general rule; but if so, they only prove it to be true.

Those who take the giddy and perilous position of Reformers of the Christian world are necessarily compelled to exhibit some plausible ground upon to which to justify their conduct. If they can find nothing in the past or present, that will clearly sustain their pretensions, it is quite natural, if not a necessity for them to plunge into the unseen future where the imagination has ample room to revel. He who cannot rely either on the past or the present to sustain his views must necessarily give them up, or drew upon the credit of the future.

He who cannot sustain his positions by the plain testimony of Scripture, would necessarily retreat to the obscure language of prophecy. It has been so with the Protestants. Ever since the days of Luther and Calvin, the prophesies of the Old and New Testaments have constituted a most extensive field of labor among them.

Mr. Campbell put forth his interpretations of prophecy in 1837. The celebrated Miller put forth his later.[33] Miller had put his views together in a very plausible manner, but the event did not transpire at the period predicted. If I remember correctly, the world was to have been destroyed in 1843 according to his theory.

The theory and illustrations of Mr. Campbell were plausible, but there were several objections quite apparent. Like Miller, he was candid enough to fix the time when, according to his interpretation, the Catholic Church is to be destroyed. He said, "The continuance of the Little Horn is therefore twelve hundred and sixty years." The Man of Sin, he states, "was a young man full twenty-one" in 606. Putting these together, the period fixed by Mr. Campbell is 1866. Time, as Lord Hale has it, is wiser than all the wits in the world, and which,

"upon the far shores of Existence
Counts each wave-drop swallowed by the sand,"

will soon give Mr. Campbell his proper position as an interpreter of prophecy.

So confident was Mr. Campbell in the correctness of his interpretation that he went so far as to say: "Such a catastrophe is even feared in Rome itself." After giving some reasons in support of his statement, he says, "It has been said by the most intelligent in the internal affairs of Roman Catholic countries, that it would not be the most unexpected event if the present incumbent of the Papal chair should be the last of the Popes of Rome."[34]

It was in 1797 that Pius VI was seized and taken prisoner to France. There he died after two years, at the advanced age of eighty-two. The city of Rome was in the hands of the French, the cardinals were scattered, and there appeared no possibility of their uniting to elect a successor. The enemies of the Old Church everywhere said, "The Papacy is destroyed, another Pope can never be elected." But another Pope was elected. In addition, Gregory, who was Pope when Mr. Campbell spoke, had a successor.

Among the various interpretations which Protestant ingenuity has given rise to is that of a Presbyterian minister in Kentucky.[35] It is, perhaps, as much to the point as any other:

> Saint Paul says, "the mystery of iniquity already worketh;" but you know, my friends, that Protestantism –in its present form and shape – did not exist until many centuries after his time; *therefore*, he must have meant the Catholic Church, or "popery," by the "mystery of iniquity."

The minister seemed perfectly willing to concede the non-existence of Protestantism in the days of Saint Paul, provided that, by doing this he could annihilate the Catholic Church.

Upon reading Mr. Campbell's interpretation I could see some objections that seemed to me to upset his theory.[36] However, I have no confidence in these interpretations for other reasons:

1. These numerous interpreters differed among themselves most materially.

2. They also failed that great test of truth – time. Time had proved their interpretations to be false, in all cases where the period fixed by them had expired.

3. Many of the most candid and enlightened Protestants condemned these interpretations.

4. The most fanatical sects and individuals had generally been the most ardent and expert at these interpretations.

5. In proportion as others failed, each new interpreter seemed the more confident. They all agree the Catholic Church was the thing foretold, and as each expositor failed, each succeeding one seemed to consider his chances of success that more enhanced.

6. These continued failures proved the truth of the remark of the great Bossuet, speaking of the false interpreters, "that they suffer themselves to be transported beyond all bounds, and without enlightening the understanding, seek only to kindle hatred in the heart."[37]

7. The inevitable tendency of the licentious abuse of the word of God was to bring it into disrepute.

Anyone who will calmly and dispassionately reflect upon the monstrous abuses of private interpretation of the prophesies, will see the wisdom of the statement of Saint Peter, "that no prophecy of Scripture is of any private interpretation," and that they who licentiously violate this plain prohibition are but, "blind leading the blind."

Mr. Campbell, near the close of his remarks upon these prophesies, said, "I did not intend, indeed, I am sorry I proposed, an argument of this kind before an assembly, limited as I am at present to an hour or two at most, to complete it."[38] It must certainly be conceded that Mr. Campbell would have been wiser, had he kept his first resolution.

15. Testimony of the Fathers

It is well said by Mr. Allirs, a late learned Protestant writer of the established Church:

> So long as the Church was engaged in a fierce and unrelenting conflict with Paganism and despotism of the empire, she could hardly exhibit to the world her complete outward orgnization.[39]

I shall only make a few extracts from the ancient Fathers. I refer the reader to the late able work of Dr. Ives for a full and clear statement of their testimony, and a most able answer to the main objections of Protestants writers.[40]

The letters of Saint Clement, bishop of Rome before the death of Saint John the Evangelist, and of Saint Ignatius his disciple, are not without weight in considering this question. Though their testimony is not so positive and clear as that of Saint Irenaeus.

Certain divisions existed in the Church at Corinth. Even after the two Epistles of Saint Paul, Saint Clement sent an embassy to that Church. It is not certain that an appeal had been taken to Rome, but it is certain that the embassy was sent from Rome, for Saint Clement says in his epistle:

> Those who have been sent to you by us – Claudius Ephebus, and Valerius Bito , together with Fortunatus also – send back to us again, with all speed, in peace and with joy, that they may the sooner acquaint us with your peace and unanimity so much prayed for, and desired by us, so that we also may rejoice at your good order.

In the epistle of Saint Ignatius, when addressing the Church of Rome, there is a marked peculiarity deserving of notice:

> Ignatius which is also Theophorus, to the church which hath found mercy in the majesty of the Father most High, and of Jesus Christ his only Son. (To the church) Beloved and enlightened in the will of him who willeth all things, which are according to the love of Jesus Christ our God, and which (church) has foremost station (or presided) in the place of the Romans, all-godly, all-gracious, all-blessed, all-praised, all-prospering, all-hallowed, and having first place (presiding) in love, with the name of Christ, with the name of the Father, which (church) I greet in the name of Jesus Christ….

Saint Irenaeus, the disciple of Saint Polycarp, the disciple of Saint John, says:

> But as it would be a very long task, to enumerate in such a volume as this, the succession of all the churches; pointing out that tradition which is the greatest, and the most ancient, and universally known church, founded and constituted in Rome, by the two most glorious apostles, Peter and Paul, --derives from the apostles, and that faith announced to all men, which, through the succession of (her) bishops has come down to us. We confound all those who, in any way, whether through pleasing themselves, or vain glory, or blindness, and perverse opinion, assemble otherwise than as behoveth them. For to

> this church, on account of a more powerful principality, it is necessary that every church, that is, those who are on every side faithful, resort, in which (church) always by those, who are on every side, has been preserved that tradition which is from the apostles.[41]

It will be seen how very explicit and clear the later portion of the extract is –it was necessary that every church resort to that of Rome on account of her more powerful principality. Those who did so were faithful.

Tertullian says:

> Was anything hidden from Peter, who was called the rock whereon the church was to be built, who obtained the keys of the kingdom of heaven, and the power of loosing and binding in heaven and on earth.

Tertullian again says:

> Come now, thou who wilt exercise thy curiosity to better purpose. Run over the apostolic churches, in which the very chairs of the apostles, to this very day, preside over their own places, in which their own authentic writings (letters) are read, echoing the voice, and making the face of each present. Is Achaia near thee? Thou hast Corinth. If thou are not far from Macedonia, thou hast Philippi, thou hast the Thessalonians. If thou canst travel into Asia, thou hast Ephesus. But if thou art near Italy, thou hast Rome, whence we also have an authority at hand. That church how happy! on which the apostles poured out all their doctrine, with their blood. Where Peter had a like passion with the Lord. Where Paul is crowned with an end like the Baptist's. Where the apostle John was plunged into boiling oil, and suffered nothing, and was afterwards banished to an island. Let us see what she hath learned, what taught, what fellowship she hath had with the churches of Africa likewise.[42]

It has been objected that because salvation could be had equally in all the churches referred to by Tertullian, that, therefore, they are all equal in authority with that of Rome. This does not follow. Two things like a third thing are like each other. Any number of churches resorting to the Church of Rome, as Irenaeus has it, and in communion with her, would necessarily have the same faith – teach the same truth – administer the same sacraments – and of course, the truth and salvation would be found equally in all. For the reason that they would all speak the same thing, believe the same thing, and be united in the same mind and judgment –as Saint Paul hath it.

The very same law, with the same interpretation of it is administered in the district Courts of Maine, Florida, Texas, and California. The simple reason is that they are each under the one Supreme Court of the United States, at Washington.

Saint Cyprian speaking of Cornelius having been made bishop of Rome says he was made bishop "when the place of Fabian, that is, when the place of Peter, and the rank (grade) of the sacerdotal chair, was vacant."[43]

Again Saint Cyprian in his epistle to Carnol says:

> Moreover, after all this, a pseudo-bishop having set up for themselves by heretics, they dare to sail, and carry letters from schismatics and profane persons, to the chair of Peter, and to the principal church, whence the unity of the priesthood took rise. Nor do they consider that the Romans are those –whose faith was praised in the preaching of the apostle – to whom faithlessness cannot have access.

In the same epistle he says:

> Peter, on whom the church had been built by the Lord Himself, one speaking for all, and replying with the voice of the church, says, Lord to whom shall we go?

Origen says:

> What in a previous passage (Matt 16:19) was granted to Peter alone, seems here (Matt 18:18) to be shown to be granted to all who have addressed their admonitions to all sinners, in order that, if they be not listened to, they may bind on earth the person condemned to be a heathen and a publican, since such a one is bound in heaven. But, as it was fit – even though something in common was spoken of Peter, and of those who should thrice admonish the brethren – that Peter should have something peculiar above those who should thrice admonish. This was previously ordained separately respecting Peter; thus, I will give to thee the keys of the kingdom of heaven, before (it was said) and whatsoever thou shalt bind on earth, and what follows; and truly, if we solemnly attend to the evangelical writings. Even in them we may discover – with regard even to those things which seem to be common to Peter and to those who have thrice admonished the brethren –much difference and pre-eminence in the words spoken to Peter, beyond those spoken in the second place

Origen evidently considers the giving of the keys to Peter, before our Lord had said "and whatsoever thou shalt bind" etc. gave him a pre-eminence over the others – that the power to bind was the power to expel from the church, a member who had been admonished and who refused to submit.

---

[1] Nicholas Wiseman *Morefield Lectures*, p. 226.

[2] *Cf.* Gen. 17:5-15.

[3] Gen. 33:28.

[4] It is true that our Lord surnamed James and John "Boanerges." (Mark 3:17) It is equally true, that the history of the labors of these apostles, is but sparingly given in the New Testament. If we had this history in full we should no doubt be able to understand the reason for this change of name. But because the reason for the surname of the apostles does not appear upon the face of the record, it will not justify us rejecting the explanation therein given for the surname of Peter. In civil governments, a man has no right to change his name without the consent off the government.

[5] Mr. Campbell does indeed intimate that the name Peter "was most probably occasioned by the fact that Daniel spoke of the kingdom of the Messiah under the figure of a stone cut out of a mountain" (A. Campbell and J. Purcell, *A debate on the Roman Catholic religion.* p. 112). But it is very difficult to understand how Christ could have intended to say to Peter, in substance: "Thou art my Kingdom."

[6] A. Campbell and J. Purcell, *A debate on the Roman Catholic religion.* p. 94.

[7] Patrick Kenrick, *The Primacy of the Apostolic See, and the authority of general councils, vindicated.* p. 29.

[8] The reference may be to Gilbert Gerard, *Institutes of Biblical Criticism: or Heads of the course of lectures on the subject: read in the University and King's College of Aberdeen* –Editor

[9] Cited from Patrick Kenrick, The Primacy of the Apostolic See, and the authority of general councils, vindicated. p. 31.

[10] A. Campbell and J. Purcell, *A debate on the Roman Catholic religion.* p. 95

[11] Webster.

[12] Webster.

[13] 1 Cor 10:1-4

[14] Matt 7:25.

[15] Rev 3:7.

[16] Matt 18:18.

[17] *Cf.* Jn 8:12; 10:4; Mark 8:38.

[18] *Cf.* Jn 13:1; 15:12,15.

[19] Jn 21: 15-17

[20] A. Campbell and J. Purcell, *A debate on the Roman Catholic religion.* p.86.

[21] *Cf.* 1 Kings 17:4; 1 Kings 22:27; 1 Chron. 11:2; 1 Chron. 17:6; Ps 28:9; Ps. 78:71; Is. 40:11; Jer. 3:15, 23:4; Ezek. 34:2, 34:23; Nahum. 3:18; Mic. 7:14; Jn. 10:1-3; 1 Pet. 5:2-4; Acts 20:28.

[22] A. Campbell and J. Purcell, *A debate on the Roman Catholic religion* p. 97.

[23] *Ibid.* p. 86, 87.

[24] *Ibid.* p97.

[25] Acts 15:2.

[26] *Cf.* Gal. 2:11

[27] Acts 21:20-26

[28] *Cf.* Greanleaf. *Evidence of Four Evangelists.* "Peter's agency in the narrative of Mark is asserted by all ancient writers, and is confirmed by the fact, that his humility is conspicuous in every part of it, where any fact is or might be related to him; his weakness and his fall being fully exposed, while things which might redound to his honor, are either omitted or slightly mentioned." p. 45.

[29] A. Campbell and J. Purcell, *A debate on the Roman Catholic religion.* p.*111*

[30] *Ibid.* p. 85.

[31] Luke 22. See also Matt. 20

[32] A. Campbell and J. Purcell, *op. cit.* p. *224*

[33] Mr. Campbell put forth his interpretations of prophecy in 1837, but I did not read them until 1845. In the mean time, the celebrated Miller put forth his, which I read in the winter of 1842-43.

[34] A. Campbell and J. Purcell, *op. cit.* p. 233

[35] As related in Dr. Spalding's *Life of Bishop Flaget*, p. 258.

[36] The prophetical number 666 was the number of a man, and the name given by Mr. Campbell was improperly written – as he conceded. Then the words "The Latin Empire," which in Greek agreed with the number, was not he name of a man, and much more probably meant Pagan rather than Papal Rome. The name itself was that of Pagan Rome. Besides, I found after wards, that ingenious Catholics had found that the Latin name of Martin Luther contained the number. So also of many other individuals.

The Man of Sin more probably referred to an individual. The prophecy could not refer to the Catholic Church, because the Man of Sin was to *exalt himself above* all that is *called God* or that is *worshipped.* It seems plain, that this character must *claim* superiority over all, admitting his inferiority to none. This he could not do, while he admitted himself to be an inferior, and was himself a worshipper of one higher than he.

It is true that Mr. Campbell to get over this great difficulty, insisted that God in this passage, might mean a magistrate or king. But this could not be, for the God mentioned was clearly God Almighty since the apostle says the Man of Sin should exalt himself above *all that is worshipped.*

[37] Jacques-Benigne Bousset, *Variations of the Protestant Churches.* Bk. viii. Sec. 27. For a masterly discussion of this question the reader is referred to Book viii, where he will find the subject very fully noticed.

[38] A. Campbell and J. Purcell, *op. cit.* p. 248.

[39] Cited in Patrick Kenrick, *The Primacy of the Apostolic See, and the authority of general councils, vindicated.* p. 18.

[40] Levi Ives, *Trials of a Mind in its Progress to the CatholicFaith.* p 158.

[41] *Adversus Haeres.*, 1. iii, c., iii n. 2.

[42] *De Praescript. Haeret.*, n. 32- 6

[43] Epistle iii ad Antoni

CHAPTER VII

CATHOLIC MIRACLES

1. Preparatory remarks

Since the whole system of Christianity is founded on miracles, it must be conceded by every Christian that the Almighty has the same power to perform miracles now as in the days of the apostles. Consequently a miracle, in its nature, is still a miracle, whether performed in this or that age – no matter how, when, or where it is performed. A miracle then by its nature, is no more surprising, because it happens today, than would be a miracle that occurred a thousand years ago. Both are still miracles; and as such, are surprising and wonderful events.

It must also be obvious to him who reflects, that one kind of miracle is just as easily performed by God as another – that the least miracle in the eyes of men, is a as great in the eye of God as the most stupendous displays of His power, as estimated by us. It is just as easy for God to raise a dead man to life as to resuscitate a dead fly, and both are equally impossible with man.

Has God attested the faith and sanctity of the Catholic Church by miracles? This question, from the very nature of the case, demands a careful consideration. It is of the utmost importance to showing one of two very great results, either:

1. That miracles still continue in the church.

2. Or the Church makes the most unfounded and arrogant claim to that which she does not possess, and that she supports this false claim by the greatest mass of unlimited fraud ever found among mankind; and especially among civilized men.

For it may be said with truth of the Church's claim, that it is wholly unparalleled for its extent, duration, and character, in the annals of the world.

The question of miraculous intervention is then, deeply interesting to the Christian and the philosopher. For the result of such an investigation will satisfy the candid and unprejudiced inquirer either that God has performed miracles as claimed by the Catholic Church, or that man is a creature possessing a wonderful capacity to delude and to be deluded – that he possesses but few powers of resistance, to protect himself from imposition. The result of such investigation must teach the patient inquirer a great lesson of faith, or a great lesson concerning human nature.

In prosecuting such an enquiry, it is necessary to make ourselves acquainted with the grounds taken by Infidels, Protestants, and Catholics. When we do this, we can then see clearly the main leading features of all. We can see wherein they all differ, and whether these respective grounds agree in any thing, or whether any two of them have any affinity in essence and substance.

2. The theory of the Infidel

The infidel admits those results legitimately flowing from the existing constitution of nature. He rejects all alleged special interpositions of Providence in violation of the established order of nature.

In support of these opinions, the most celebrated and acute of the English Infidels, David Hume, has assumed this comprehensive position: "A miracle," he says,

> is the violation of the laws of nature; and as a firm and unalterable experience has established these laws, the proof against a miracle, from the very nature of the fact, is as entire as any argument from experience can possibly be imagined.

The language of this proposition, if taken in its strict literal sense, is stronger, perhaps, than Mr. Hume intended, and does not convey his idea clearly. The assumption, as stated, that a "*firm and unalterable* experience has established" the laws of nature is too broad, for the reason that, if taken strictly, it illogically assumes the falsehood of the question in debate without proof. His position, in effect, would then stand thus: "A miracle is the violation of the laws of nature, and therefore, no man has ever witnessed it." It assumes, in substance, that a miracle is *impossible*, and of course it never happened.

He who takes the position that a miracle is impossible, must assume one of two things to be true, either:

1. That there is no Creator.

2. Or admitting the existence of such a Creator, in creating the world and giving to it and its inhabitants certain properties and laws, He resolved in

advance, never, for any purpose, or any occasion, to interfere, in any manner, with the legitimate effects of this order.

In assuming the first position to avoid the possibility of any violation of this order, the party must also assume the eternal existence of this order of nature; for if it were the result of chance at any time, this same chance may certainly undo what it had done. If mere chance could possibly originate a system of any kind, surely it could modify or destroy it.

The same may be said of God. If He created, He surely can modify, destroy, or suspend, unless He had resolved not to do so. If the second position is assumed –that God has resolved, in Himself, not to interfere with the regular operation of what we call the laws of nature – it being an affirmative proposition, he who assumes, must prove it!

A miracle, abstractly speaking is a violation of the laws of nature; but a miracle *known* to us must be a violation of the *known* laws of nature. The exception to this rule is when we are assured by an inspired person (whose inspiration is first proven) that a particular matter is a miracle, which we could not know to be such from our own knowledge.

It occurs to me as clear, that our knowledge of the laws of nature is limited, and, therefore, it does not include a knowledge of all. Yet we have a certain and positive knowledge of some of these laws, or indeed, we have no certain knowledge of anything! If we have a certain and positive knowledge of the operation and effect of the more familiar laws of nature, under a given state of circumstances, then we can determine with certainty, when a sensible violation of these known laws of nature, occurs under the same circumstances. There is, therefore, a plain distinction between an event merely new, and one directly in violation of a known law of nature. A miracle may not be new in its kind, because similar miracles may have occurred before, and may occur again.

However, I do not understand Mr. Hume as intending to assert that miracles are impossible. His objection lies against the competency of the testimony offered. I understand him as assuming, substantially, that as a miracle is a violation of the laws of nature – and as the general uniform operation of those laws has been proven by general experience, the proof against a miracle is "as entire as any argument drawn from experience." But does he intend to maintain that an argument, drawn from experience, is conclusive and not, therefore, to be rebutted? or only *prima facie* true, and therefore, liable to be overcome by competent and sufficient testimony?

The strong language he uses, – that a firm and unalterable experience had established these laws of nature, and that the argument, drawn from them is *entire* – will bear the construction often given to his words. Yet his illustrations, taken in connection with the statement of his general proposition seem to show a different intent, and that it was not his purpose to assume an argument drawn from experience to be *conclusive*.

When a writer is ambiguous, and his language may be construed in different ways, the honest and generous rule, is to give his language that construction which will best support the general scope and intent of his argument. Mr. Hume, then, as I understand him, intended to assume this ground: that the proof against miracles, drawn from experience, is *prima facie* true; and that the testimony of men is not competent to rebut this proposition.

If, then, a miracle were possible, it may have occurred; and if so, it surely may be proved in some way. The existence and operation of these laws are proven by human testimony, founded upon human experience; and if this evidence is competent to prove the existence and operation of a certain law of nature, cannot the same class of testimony establish the fact of its violation? It would seem that the same character of testimony, given by the *same beings,* would be competent for both purposes.

As a miracle is possible, and may have happened, we will suppose for the sake of the argument only that it has occurred. How, then, would Mr. Hume have proven it, under his theory? To say that a visible and palpable fact may exist and be known to men, and yet that reason and philosophy deny all competent evidence of such a fact, is to degrade reason and philosophy, and would seem to be manifestly erroneous.

It might be said that the testimony of all mankind has proven the existence and effects of the known laws of nature, and that the testimony of only the few goes to sustain the existence of miracles. Then, the argument continues, "as the testimony of the few is in necessary and direct conflict with the testimony of the many, therefore, we must believe the many, and disbelieve the few – for we must disbelieve one or the other." I reply: that although we are not compelled to believe the many, and disbelieve the few in all cases, still, in this case, the argument would be conclusive if it were true that the testimony of the few, from the nature of the case, was in *necessary* conflict with the testimony of the many.

But is it necessarily so that the testimony of the few is in conflict with the testimony of the many? Before we can say there must, of necessity, be a conflict of testimony in such a case, we are compelled to assume that miracles are impossible. For if possible, they may have occurred, and if they did occur, they can be proved, and if proved, the witnesses are certainly not in conflict with any other true witnesses. Upon the hypothesis that miracles may have existed, and, therefore, may be susceptible of proof, there can be no necessary contradiction in the two classes of witnesses. One class proves the general rule, the other the exception.

When Mr. Hume gives as a reason – in substance, – that experience has proven the general uniform operation of the laws of nature, and the same experience has also shown that men will sometimes lie; and therefore, it is more reasonable to believe that men lie in regard to miracles than that these laws have been violated; I am constrained to say, that he overlooks the fact, that God can only make a revelation to mankind through miracles. The probabilities and reasons why miracles should sometimes occur, are as great, if not greater, than those against them. For without going into the subject at large, it occurs to me as the genuine dictate of pure reason – that as the properties infused into matter, and the instincts given unreasoning animals are so different from the laws enacted for the government of rational free agents, they must be communicated in a different manner. While the effect of the properties and instincts would be uniform, and, for that reason, not require any new and additional interference, the effects of free agency would be variable, (though still confined within the limited powers of the rational creature). For that reason the laws for rational free agents would require the special interposition of the Creator at some period or other, and, perhaps, at different periods.

Mr. Hume also overlooks the fact, that, although experience has shown that some men will lie, under the influence of certain motives, others will not under any known temptation. And for that reason, that human testimony may be credible to the highest degree of moral certainty. I believe that London exists, and I believe it with the same certainty that I do any other of the most certain facts. This I believe purely upon human testimony. Now why should I adopt an arbitrary rule, and say that a miracle may occur, but there can be no testimony to prove it? Did the laws of any country ever admit the possible existence of important facts, and yet propose to reject all testimony to prove them? The facts had as well not exist at all.

Mr. Hume seems to have become so sensible of the arbitrary and sweeping nature of his general position that he puts in this limitation. He says:

> I beg, the limitations here made may be remarked, when I say that a miracle can never be proved so as to be the foundation of a system of religion; for I own that otherwise there may possibly be miracles or violations of the usual course of nature of such a kind as to admit of proof from human testimony.

Upon which the profound Starkie has these remarks:

> In what way the use to be made of a fact when proved, can affect the validity of the proof; or how it can be that a fact proved to be true, is not true for all purposes to which it is relevant, I pretend not to understand. [1]

Mr. Starkie is surely right. This limitation of Mr. Hume cuts up his general position by the roots. All that he had said before about "a firm and unalterable experience," and the "entire" argument drawn from it against miracles, is at once unsaid by admitting that a miracle may exist, and may be proved by human testimony. His limitation is like a proviso repugnant to the purview of the statute itself; as if a statute granted a piece of land to A, provided such person does not exist.

The candor and manliness of Hume must be conceded, because he conceals none of the consequences of his theory, but lets us know distinctly the reasons which impel him to adopt his arbitrary rule for the exclusion of human testimony. He recommends his readers "to form a general resolution never to lend any attention to the testimony, (for miracles in favor of religion,) with whatever specious pretext it may be covered." The reason he gives is because "those who are so silly as to examine the affair by that medium, and seek particular flaws in the testimony, are almost sure to be confounded." [2]

The extent of this concession is certainly very great. How distressed must be the condition of that reasoner, who, to sustain his position, is compelled to shut out all proof! But it must be conceded that this system is effectual. It is as much so as the maxim of pirates, that "dead men tell no tales." Mr. Hume does not kill the witnesses. He only closes their months by refusing to hear them. His means of suppressing testimony may be more merciful, but fully as arbitrary and irrational.

The best result of my reason and reflection is this – that a miracle is possible, and, therefore, not incredible – that the question whether a particular miraculous event occurred, is purely a question of fact, to be established by testimony – that to prove an event contrary to the order of nature, requires more testimony, or stronger proof, than to establish an ordinary event; because it requires a greater weight of testimony to rebut and overcome the *prima facie* presumption against miracles than to establish a general case, in the first instance. He who assumes to overcome a *prima facie* presumption against him, must necessarily bring a greater amount of proof than he would be required to produce, if no such presumption stood in his way.

3. Protestant theories

The views of Protestants on this subject, as on many others, have undergone great changes. Protestant writers generally, if not entirely, up to the period of the publication of Dr. Middleton's flippant "Free enquiry," admitted the existence of miracles *after* the days of the apostles. They disagreed as to the period of their cessation, some bringing it down as late as the fifth century.

In attempting to fix this period, these writers were involved in great perplexity. Dr. Middleton, therefore, assumed the bold ground that miracles ceased with the apostles. Most Protestant writers since that period have followed Middleton, so far as I am advised. This is now the more general Protestant theory on the subject.

This ground, like that of an invisible true Church, avoids old difficulties, but gives rise to many new difficulties. Those who assume this ground must necessarily give some criterion, by aid of which we may distinguish between the miracles of apostolic days, and those alleged to have happened since. Dr. John Douglass, bishop of Salisbury, published a treatise upon this subject.[3] After this, the celebrated Dr. Paley published his *Views of Christianity* in which he cites Dr. Douglass frequently as an authority. I do not have access to the treatise of Dr. Douglass. Therefore, I shall confine my attention mostly to the views of Dr. Paley.[4]

4. Dr. Paley concerning the competency of witnesses

In a professed treatise upon evidences of Christianity by a Protestant, it was necessary and proper to lay down the marks that are alleged to distinguish the true miracles of the New Testament from the so-called false Popish miracles. In the outset, the learned Divine lays down these propositions:

> 1. That there is satisfactory evidence that many professing to be original witnesses of the Christian miracles, passed their lives in labors, dangers, and sufferings, voluntarily undergone, in attestation of the accounts they delivered, and solely in consequence of their belief of these accounts; and that they also submitted, from the same motives, to new rules of conduct.
>
> 2. That there is *not* satisfactory evidence that persons professing to be original witnesses of other miracles, in their nature as certain as these are, have ever acted in the same manner in attestation of the accounts which they delivered, and properly in consequence of their belief of these accounts.

It will readily appear that these two propositions regard the competency of witnesses. They do not regard the sufficiency of the testimony itself. The distinction between competency of a witness and the sufficiency of the testimony is a very plain one. If a witness is incompetent, his testimony is not to be considered. If he is competent, he will be heard; but the testimony he gives may be sufficient or insufficient to prove the truth of the allegation. The facts proven by a competent witness may not be sufficient to prove the proposition sought to be established.

5. Concerning Dr. Paley's first proposition

The requisites, as laid down by Dr. Paley in his first proposition, to constitute the competency of an original witness are:

1. He must have "voluntarily passed his life in labors, dangers, and sufferings."

2. These must have been undergone in attestation of the accounts he delivered, and solely in consequence of his belief of these accounts.

3. That the witness submitted, from the same motives, to new rules of conduct.

It is clear that the witness to be competent under this rule must possess all and each of the requisites laid down. This is conclusively shown by the terms of the second proposition, which rejects the testimony of witnesses not possessing the same requisites.

I will examine these requisites separately. The first requisite excludes all persons, however honest, reliable, and sincere, unless they have voluntarily passed their lives in labors, dangers, and sufferings. If then, the witness happened to live in an age and country where no persecution exists, he could not testify. For the dangers and sufferings intended by the learned Divine are not those ordinarily incident to life, but those additional ones incurred in attesting the truth of the miracle itself. If then, a miracle should happen in a country where no one would persecute the witnesses, how could such a fact be proven under such a theory? It would be of no concern what the number and character of the witnesses might be – this arbitrary requisite excludes them all.

The second requisite is still more exclusive. These labors, dangers, and sufferings must be undergone in *attestation* of the accounts the witness delivers

Note it would not seem quite correct to say, that the *apostles* endured the sufferings in *attestation* of the facts of miracles. It would be more proper to say, that they suffered, not solely because of their attestation, but also because they taught the system of the Lord Jesus.

For instance, Peter and John were arrested after healing the cripple, because the priests, and the captain of the temple, and the Sadducees were "grieved that they taught the people, and preached through Jesus the resurrection from the dead."[5] When they were examined and discharged they were "commanded not to speak at all nor teach in the name of Jesus." It was not the simple fact alone that they gave their testimony to the miracles of Christ that brought upon then them the sufferings and dangers.

The Jews themselves attested the miracles of Christ. They said they were performed by the aid of Beelzebub. They also conceded the miracle performed by Peter. Nevertheless, the Jews did not draw the same conclusions from the facts admitted. Had the apostles simply said, "We saw the miracles performed by Christ – we saw him after He had risen from the dead – we are compelled to state these facts when asked concerning them; but we do not pretend to know by what power these were performed – we draw no conclusions from what we heard – we found no religion upon that basis." Then it is apprehended that no persecution would have followed.

Those Christians who were not the original witnesses of Christ's miracles were also persecuted. All who believed the system and openly professed it were persecuted. The apostles were more persecuted than others because they were the first teachers, and claimed to have been commissioned by Christ.

A second aspect of the second requisite, is by far the most important. This branch requires these voluntary dangers and sufferings to have been undergone "solely in consequence of the belief" of the witness *in the testimony he gives*. The witness must not only undergo the sufferings, but this must be done from the belief of the particular facts related by him as an original witness. This is to be his sole motive.

From the third requisite if the witness is a Christian before he saw the miracle, he cannot testify unless he ceases to be such, and "submitted to new rules of conduct." In other words, if his belief of the miracle changed his belief in Christianity, and he submitted to new rules of conduct, he could be a witness under Dr. Paley's rule of competency. But if he remained a Christian his mouth must be closed. This result is not only clear from the proposition, but is insisted on in considering the second proposition.

6. Concerning Dr. Paley's second proposition

The learned Divine, when he comes to discuss his second proposition, makes two distinctions, "those relating to proof, and those relating to the miracles." Under the first division relative to 'proof' he lays out several classes of cases. His seventh class he gives in these words:

> We have laid out the case, those accounts which require no more than a simple assent; and we must now also lay out the case those which come merely in *affirmance* of opinions already formed. This last circumstance is of the utmost importance to notice well.

What an emphasis the learned Divine lays upon "this last circumstance!" The learned author, after further remarks in reference to this class of exclusion, says:

> No part of this description belongs to the ordinary evidence of Heathen or Popish miracles. Even most of the miracles alleged to have been performed by Christians, in the second and third century of

> its era, [are wanting] want this confirmation. It constitutes indeed a line of partition between the origin and progress of Christianity.

If therefore, a man is a Christian before he witnessed a miracle in favor of Christianity he cannot be a competent witness, because as the Dr. says:

> men may not only receive a miraculous account, but, may act and suffer on the side and in the cause, which the miracle supports, yet not act or suffer for the miracle, but in pursuance of a prior persuasion.

7. The implications of Dr. Paley's propositions

That the learned Divine intended his two propositions as fixing the competency of witnesses is further shown by his subsequent remarks:

> I apprehend that, when we remove from the comparison, the cases which are fairly disposed of by the observations that have been stated, many cases will not remain. To those which do remain we apply this final distinction: that there is not satisfactory evidence that persons pretending to be original witnesses of the miracles, passed their lives in labors, dangers, and sufferings, voluntarily undertaken and undergone in attestation of the accounts which they delivered, and properly in consequence of their belief of the truth of those accounts.

Surely the learned Divine is right in his opinion, that if he erred in his enumeration of the different classes of cases excluded by his first and embraced by his second sweeping proposition, that a mere repetition of the second proposition would most effectually settle all those cases he might have omitted.

After having placed all Christian witnesses to miracles occurring in the progress of Christianity, in a position such that they could not possibly possess the requisites of competency that he lays down, he may well and safely say, "there is no satisfactory evidence" that they did possess these *impossible* requisites.

This is the essence of Dr. Paley's two propositions. When they are taken and considered together, no persons – however numerous, honest, and reliable they may have been – who were Christians at the time they saw the miracles performed, and remained Christians afterwards, can be competent witnesses to prove the facts they saw.

The laws of every civilized country require testimony to be given by competent witnesses. Similarly, Dr. Paley puts forth certain requisites to constitute competency. These requisites are of such a character that it is impossible for witnesses who lived after the days of the apostles to possess them.

The learned Divine was bound, from the nature of his subject, and his views as a Protestant, to make the dividing line between the miracles of the Scriptures, and those not recorded therein. As he disbelieved the alleged Catholic miracles, he was necessarily obliged to adopt some rule that would effectually exclude them. If he excluded the witnesses to these miracles, as a matter of course these alleged miracles could not be proved. It will be seen by the attentive inquirer how studiously his propositions are framed to accomplish this result.

It must be conceded, that his rules of competency wholly preclude all investigation. Nothing certainly can place the advocates of Catholic miracles, more completely at fault. There is not a spot of earth left to them, upon which to rest the soles of their feet. They can only allow room for their graves. Their witnesses cannot testify because they remained true to the faith. They are incompetent witnesses because they did right. They believed before they had seen; and although our Lord pronounced such blessed, they are rejected for that reason. Is it the legitimate effect of Christianity to destroy a man's integrity? Are his senses prostrated? Can he still not see?

When the learned author says, that most of the miracles of the second and third centuries, were given in affirmance of a religion already established, he does not mean to admit that a portion of them can be proved. "This description," he says, "constitutes , indeed, a line of partition between the origin and progress of Christianity." His first proposition regards "Christian miracles;" and his second (which embraces all those excluded by the first,) includes *all others*. "Christian miracles" are only those found in the Scriptures. As he says, in the beginning of the first chapter, that "Christ, his associates , and immediate followers, acted the part which the first proposition imputes to them;" and that "they did so in attestation of the miraculous history recorded in the Scriptures, and solely in consequence of the belief of the truth of this history."

So when he says that "no part of this description belongs to the *ordinary* evidence of Heathen or Popish Miracles," he does not mean to say, that any of the so-called Popish miracles are not rejected by his first proposition. When he uses these expressions of seemingly limited meaning, he does so in reference to only one of the *requisites* he lays down. Even in reference to this, we cannot see how any witnesses to any miracles alleged to have occurred after the "origin of Christianity," could possibly possess that requisite; except those who changed their faith by ceasing to be Christians.

The sweeping rule of exclusion is very much like the assertion of Bishop Watson, in his third letter in reply to Mr. Gibbon. "We see," he says, "the pretension of the Romish priesthood to miraculous powers, and we know them to be false." There is no disputing the assertion of a gentleman when he says he *knows* a thing! even though it be a negative – that most difficult of things to prove. Dr. Paley does not use language quite so strong. He does not say, "I know the alleged Catholic miracles to be false," but he says, "I deny that there can, in the nature of the case, be any competent testimony to prove them."

But with all due deference for the logic of Dr. Paley, is his rule true? Does he mean to assume that miracles in affirmance of Christianity are impossible? Or if possible, does he mean to say that there can be no competent witnesses to prove such miracles? Since they may have happened, we will suppose for the sake of argument they did occur. How then under Dr. Paleys's first proposition could they be proven? It is impossible for the witnesses to possess all the requisites. Under his rule of competency, a stupendous fact may exist which was performed by God for a great purpose, yet this purpose cannot be attained, simply because those who witnessed the fact were then believers in God Almighty's truth.

There are many instances where miracles were performed during "the progress" of the Old Dispensation. These were simply in affirmance of truths already revealed.[6] How would Dr. Paley dispose of such miracles under his theory?

8. The similarity of Dr. Paley's and Mr. Hume's positions

Dr. Paley's position is about as conclusive as the position of the Infidel. He would not hear any proof of miracles from a Christian because his testimony would establish his own system. He would not hear any testimony from an unbeliever because he was not honest; otherwise he would have been converted by the miracle. As both classes of witnesses were incompetent he would not hear testimony at all.

Are not the respective summary positions of David Hume and Dr. Paley based on the same fundamental ground? Are they not both the embodiment of the same radical error – distrust of human veracity? Are they not both alike arbitrary? Are they not both partial? Is not the effect of both the same – to close the mouths of honest and reliable witnesses? Do they not both exclude all investigation into alleged facts conceded to be possible. What essential difference is there between the Infidel and the Protestant?

Mr. Hume had so little confidence in human testimony that he would not receive it at all to prove a miracle, "so as to be the foundation of a system of religion." Dr Paley has so little, that he will only receive the testimony of men of one particular generation, and for one purpose only. The only difference between the Infidel and the Christian Philosopher is that the former rejects human testimony in the *origin*, and the later in the *progress* of Christianity. Mr. Hume set out to reject Christianity. Dr. Paley set out to reject the alleged Catholic miracles. Each accomplished the end intended with about equal ability and success.

The remark of the learned Starkie, in reference to Mr. Hume's position is equally applicable to that of Dr. Paley. "Estoppels," he says, "are odious, even in judicial investigations, because they tend to exclude the truth; in metaphysics they are intolerable."[7]

9. The fear of bias in Dr. Paley's position

The reasoning of the learned divine in support of this excluding rule regarding witnesses, is based upon the ground that men more readily receive accounts of facts which go to confirm them in their existing opinions, than they do those which require them to change. He says:

> The miracle like any other argument which only confirms what was before believed, is admitted with little examination. In the moral, as in the natural world, it is change which requires a cause.

There can be no doubt of the truth of such a general principle in reference to the mass of mankind. But there are circumstances connected with the first witnesses that must be taken into account.

The learned author says, "This people, (the Jews) with or without reason, had worked themselves into a persuasion that some signal and advantageous change was to be effected in the condition of the country, by the agency of a long-promised messenger from heaven. Afterwards, in speaking of the belief and conduct of the apostles and early Christians he anticipates an objection. He answers it in this way:

> If it be said that the sure promise of a future state would do all this; I answer, the sure promise of a future state without any evidence to give credit or assurance to it , would do nothing. A few wandering fishermen talking of a resurrection of the dead, could produce no effect. If it be further said, that men easily believe what they anxiously desire; I again answer, in my opinion, the very contrary of this is nearer to the truth. Anxiety of desire, earnestness of expectation, the vastness of the event, rather cause men to disbelieve, to doubt, to dread fallacy, to distrust, to examine. When our Lord's resurrection was first reported to the apostles they did not believe, we are told, for joy. This is natural, and is agreeable to experience.

That the Jews expected and desired the advent of the Messiah there can be not doubt. That the time in their opinion was at hand when Christ appeared, would seem equally clear. Christ came, not to establish an entire new antagonistic system, but to fulfill and end an old one, and also establish the new in pursuance of the old dispensation itself. The differences between Christ and the Jews regarded not the fact that a new kingdom should be set up, but the character of this new kingdom, and the identity of its founder.

The desirer for immortality, and the desire for the advent of Christ, must have had some effect upon the mind of men. Dr. Paley thinks it would have made them more cautious. I cannot quite agree with him in the form in which he states it. My observation and experience lead me to a modified conclusion. I believe the desire for immortality would predispose the great majority of men, to a certain extent, to believe a system promising what they wished. I think the promise of immortality would induce the majority more readily to believe Christianity, than if they did not desire immortality at all. It is only upon the ground that desire will, to some extent, predispose men to believe a religion, that we can account for the fact that the great mass of mankind have believed false religions without sufficient testimony.

But the effects of this desire upon the majority of men, in both cases, is limited. It would not induce men blindly to receive the most extraordinary accounts of visible miracles, without competent proof. Also, while desire would have the effect mentioned upon the majority, it would have a contrary effect on a minority – the prudent and cautious. These would distrust and examine more carefully, because of the intensity of their wish.

That the vastness of an event such as a miracle, would make men more cautious than they would be in reference to an inferior matter, I think there can be no question. But I cannot understand why this character of an event should have effect more at one time than another. The Jews were just as well prepared for miracles as the Christians in after times. They had the miraculous pool with them, and also their Scriptures, were full of miraculous accounts.

The learned divine makes a distinction between the effect of a desire to acquire something new, and a desire to preserve that which is already possessed. He assumes that the effects in the two cases are precisely opposite. When the Jews desire immortality, this made them cautious and distrustful. When the Christians, in after times, desired the same thing, this made them more credulous. The desire for immortality was the same in both Jew and Christian. I confess, I cannot see why, if the wish is father to the thought in one case, it was not equally so in the other.

I could not understand how all this could affect the witnesses of miracles. The desire of immortality was equally strong in the witnesses in one age as in another. Man is always the same, and will desire the same good. Could such a desire induce the witnesses to commit perjury? I should think not.

Concede for the sake of argument only, that men would more readily believe a miraculous account affirming a system promising immortality, than they would the same account, establishing the prior theory. Still this would only affect the *hearers*, and not the witnesses. It would only show that impositions might be more easy in one case than in the other. But this would not affect the competency of the testimony itself. If then, an unbeliever investigates this testimony, the relation he sustains to the testimony establishing the first miracles of Christianity, or those occurring afterwards, is precisely the same. And it would seem to be so with the Christian

10. The true rule for competency of witnesses

As to the competency of witnesses, the law lays down the true rule. The witness must be able and willing to state the truth. He must know the facts, to be able; and he must be honest, to be willing. In reference to the witnesses of miracles the only proper inquiry must be in regard to these two points.

Dr. Paley lays down certain tests that no witness can possess except those who lived in the origin of Christianity. These tests are local, partial, and confined from their nature to the witnesses of the first miracles. For the sake of illustration, I will suppose two witnesses. The first is a witness of the origin miracles; the second is a witness of subsequent miracles. If they are both equally honest and able, there must be some means to show this in *both* cases. If not, of what avail are the ability and integrity of the second witness?

The facts to be proved are the same in both cases – miracles. The sufferings undergone by both witnesses for Christianity we will suppose are equally great. For the Christians in the ages subsequent to the age of the apostles suffered all the persecutions they did. These two witnesses then give the same evidence of sincerity. If the first witness testifies falsely, he gains no immortality. His testimony only establishes a false system, in which he can have no interest in the future. He incurs punishment in the present. If the second witness testifies falsely to affirm the system, he forfeits heaven, and has therefore, no more interest in sustaining the system than the first had to establish it.

If I were I going to lay down an arbitrary rule for the exclusion of witnesses of miracles I would exclude the first and admit the second witness. The first witness, supposing the system to be false, knew that fact. In giving his testimony he would not be influenced by any hope or fear of the future. All he would dread would be the infliction of punishment in this life. The second witness would give his testimony under three tests:

1. The fear of present punishment.

2. The fear of future punishment.

3. The loss of a happy immortality.

The first witness would give his evidence only under one test – the fear of present punishment.

Far be it from me to lay down any such test of the competency of witnesses to miracles. Christ has laid down none such. As to the competency of witnesses, the law lays down the true rule. The witness must be able and willing to state the truth. To be able he must know the facts; and to be willing he must be honest. In reference to the witnesses of miracles, the only proper inquiry must regard these two points: is he able? is he willing? If he is both able and willing, he must be a good witness.

After all the reflection I have been able to bestow upon this subject, there is but one just and righteous rule in my opinion – is the witness able and willing. As to his integrity, that may be shown by sufferings, services, pious and exemplary conduct, or in any of the many ways by which an honest man may prove his integrity and establish his character. It does not matter what his particular views may be, or what his religion, if he is honest, and the facts he stated are of such a character as to preclude reasonable grounds for mistake.

11. A possible reason for Dr. Paley's extraordinary rules

The sweeping and summary position of Dr. Paley gives rise to a very serious and important reflections. Is it possible that the proofs of the alleged Catholic miracles are so direct and strong, and the miracles of such a conclusive character in themselves, that an intelligible line of partition cannot be made between them and the Scripture miracles, without the adoption of a rule so extraordinary? Was the learned Divine compelled from the inexorable necessity of his case, to adopt a principle essentially the same as that of Hume.

Is it then necessary for the defeat of Catholic miracles to impeach the veracity of all men except those who lived in one period of time? Are men still men or have they degenerated into beasts? Have they no integrity left?

Was the natural effect of Christianity to make men more the dupes of imposition? They were expressly told to be wise as serpents while they were harmless as dove. To mark this line between Scripture and Catholic miracles, are we driven to the melancholy and miserable conclusion that since the establishment of Christianity men have grown worse instead of better? If so, it must be so! But it is a humiliating and painful conclusion.

Are we honest ourselves? Can we know the facts? If we can and do know the truth, is there no means by which we can show it to others? If we are honest can we not speak the truth, and when we speak the truth should we not be believed? What we claim for ourselves shall we not accord to others? Shall we be just?

12. The theories of Dr. Middleton

In reference to the views of Protestants before his time, Dr. Middleton says:

> The prevailing opinion of Protestants, namely, of Tillotson, Marshall, Dodwell *et cetera,* is that miracles continued during the first three centuries. Dr. Waterland brings them down to the fourth, Dr. Berriman to the fifth. These unwarily betrayed the Protestant cause into the hands of its enemies: for it was in these primitive ages, particularly in the third, fourth, and fifth, these flourishing times of miracles, in which the chief corruptions of Popery, monkery, the worship of saints, prayers for the dead, the superstitious use of images, and the sacraments were introduced.... We shall find, after the conversion of the Roman empire the greater part of their boasted miracles were wrought either by monks, or relics, or signs of the cross, *et cetera*: wherefore, if wc admit the miracles we must admit the rites for the sake of which they were wrought: they both rest on the same bottom.... Everyone may see what a resemblance the principles and practices of the fourth century, as they are described by the most eminent Fathers of that age, bear to the present rites of the Popish church.... By granting the Romanists but a single age of miracles after the times of the apostles, we shall be entangled in a series of difficulties, whence we can never fairly extricate ourselves, till we allow the same powers also to the present age.[8]

It will be seen that Dr. Middleton takes the distinct ground that no miracles have been performed since the times of the apostles. Although, from his first extract we might infer that he did not intend to deny the alleged miracles of the second century as he particularly specifies those of the third, forth, and fifth. The last extract is very full to the point, and excludes all miracles after the days of the apostles. The reason is well assigned by Middleton, that the admission of miracles after the times of the apostles involves the Protestant theory in a series of difficulties.

Has not the theory of Dr. Middleton also its own "series of difficulties?" How does he get around the evidence of alleged miracles since apostolic times?

Dr. Paley adopts the arbitrary principle that the witnesses are incompetent. Dr. Middleton takes the bold ground that the testimony is false and the witnesses perjured. He says:

> It must be confessed that the claim to a miraculous power was universally asserted and believed in all Christian countries, and in all ages of the church till the time of the Reformation: for Ecclesiastical History makes no difference between one age and another, but carries on the succession of its miracles, as of all other common events, through all of them indifferently to that memorable period.... As far as church historians can illustrate anything, there is not a single point,

> in all history, so constantly, explicitly, and unanimously affirmed by them, as the continual succession of these powers, through all ages, from the earliest Father who first mentions them, down to the Reformation; which same succession is still further deduced by persons of the same eminent character for probity, learning, and dignity in the Romish church, to this very day: so the only doubt which can remain with us: is, whether church historians are to be trusted or not: for if any credit be due to them in the present case, it must reach all or none: because the reason for believing them in any one age will be found to be of equal force in all, as far as it depends on the character of the persons attesting, or on the thing attested.... When we reflect upon the surprising confidence with which the fathers of the fourth age affirmed, as true, what they themselves had forged, or knew to be forged, it is natural to suspect that so bold a defiance of the truth could not be acquired or become general at once, but must have been gradually carried to that height by the example of former ages.

It must be confessed that the language of Dr. Middleton is candid and emphatic, definite and certain. The meaning is palpable. He does not seek to avoid a difficulty by an evasion of his true position. He states it manfully and takes the consequences. He does not equivocate as if:

"Willing to wound, and yet afraid to strike."

He admits what no candid man, it would seem, can deny, that the historians who record these alleged miracles were persons of "eminent character for probity, learning, and dignity." He does not quibble and say, their testimony is not direct and full to the point. He admits that. He does not say they were deceived – that they were dupes of others. He does say plainly, they were all liars and cheats, from the first to the last.

He does not say these were pious impositions, arising from honest but mistaken zeal; as if there could be an honest rogue, or a pious cheat. He takes the consistent ground that the "things attested" were matters about which men could not be mistaken, and that the "persons attesting, affirmed as true what they themselves had forged, or knew to be forged."

Bishop Watson in his third letter to Gibbon takes the same ground. He says,

> We see the pretensions of the Romish priesthood to miraculous powers, and we know them to be false; we are conscious that they at least must sacrifice their integrity to their interest or their ambition.

Mr. Breckenridge also takes the same ground. In reference to the rites and ceremonies of the Catholic Church, he says, "and sustaining them by such barefaced impostures called miracles."[9]

13. Gibbon's historical analysis

In reference to the opinions of Protestants, as to the period when miracles are alleged to have ceased, Gibbon says,

> The conversion of Constantine is the era most usually fixed by Protestants. The more rational divines are willing to admit the miracles of the IVth, while the more credulous are willing to reject those of the Vth century. [10]

Among the secondary causes assigned by Gibbon, for the rapid progress of Christianity, he sets down, "the miraculous powers ascribed to the primitive church."[11] In speaking of this cause, he says:

> But the miraculous cure of diseases of the most inveterate or even preternatural kind, can no longer occasion any surprise when we recollect, that in the days of Irenaeus, about the end of the second century, the resurrection of the dead was very far from being esteemed an uncommon event; that miracle was frequently performed upon necessary occasions, by great fasting and the joint supplications of the church of the place, and that the persons thus restored to their prayers, had lived afterwards among them many years.
>
> The Christian church from the time of the apostles and their first disciples, has claimed an uninterrupted succession of miraculous powers, the gift of tongues, of vision and prophecy, the power of expelling demons, of healing the sick, and of raising the dead.

In another place he says:

> Dr. Middeleton observes that as this pretension (the gift of tongues) of all others was the most difficult to support by art, it was soonest given up. The observation suited his hypothesis. Every age bears testimony to the wonderful events by which it is distinguished, and its testimony appears no less weighty and respectable than that of the proceeding generation, till we are insensibly led on to accuse our own consistency. If in the eight or twelfth century we deny to the venerable Bede, or the holy Bernard, the same degree of confidence, which, in the second century, we so liberally granted to Justin of to Irenaeus. If the truth of any of these miracles is appreciated by their apparent use and propriety, every age had unbelievers to convince, heretics to confute, and idolatrous nations to convert. Sufficient

motives might always be produced, to justify the interposition of Heaven.

14. Dr. Middleton's rule is arbitrary and incredible

The facts attested and conceded, and the ground taken are certainly very important! In my investigations upon this subject, I have always believed, because I found it always asserted by Protestants, and because I had not known what were the alleged proofs, that the alleged Catholic miracles were spurious. These facts and this testimony did make a most powerful impression upon my mind. I had been a lawyer for some years, and had given much attention to the subject of human credibility. I did not dream that the testimony to support the alleged Catholic miracles was so strong – direct – certain – long continued – so often repeated, and by so many witnesses – in so many different places – in so many continuous ages – and these witnesses "persons of eminent character for probity, learning, and dignity," as Dr Middleton candidly admits, and as Gibbon testifies. Nor did I dream that, to overcome this proof, Protestants were forced to adopt rules so arbitrary, or so acrimonious.

When I looked into the matter carefully, I found that Dr. Middleton had not admitted too much, when he says, "As far as church historians can illustrate anything…" From Dr. Middleton's admissions, the testimony of Gibbon, and from the earliest records and monuments of the church it is clear that what Dr. Middleton asserts is true also of the second century, the days immediately succeeding the apostles. These earliest church historians were most of them holy martyrs, who sealed their faith, and their testimony by their voluntary blood.

The rule laid down by Dr. Middleton, and followed by most Protestant writers since his day, gives rise to very momentous reflections. It is certainly one of the most formidable and extensive wholesale charges ever preferred against human nature. It concedes all the Infidel could desire to enable him to defeat Christianity itself. The charges on their face are indeed most extraordinary.

There is an amount of calm, dispassionate, cool, calculating, continued, successful forgery and falsehood, joined to the most consummate and life-long hypocrisy, in persons who gave the greatest possible proofs of integrity under circumstances which insured it, that has, I apprehend, no parallel among mankind. The mind sickens, and staggers, and sinks, under such a mighty mass of unlimited fraud. One cannot tell what to think of the vice and stupidity of poor human nature, even in its best aspect. Nor can the mind find where to rest.

This stupendous charge of human delinquency, involves among others, these clear difficulties:

1. An implausible association of dishonest persons.
2. An unbelievable combination of falsities to be established.
3. The existence of vice where heroic virtue is to be expected.
4. That the diligence of the apostles could be impeached.
5. That such imposters were confined to the Catholic Church.
6. That Christianity itself fosters fraud and delusions.

15. An implausible association of dishonest persons

Dr. Middleton assumes a combination is so extensive, embracing so many persons, in places so widely separated from each other, and in so many distinct ages, and for so long a time, that one cannot conceive how it could be possible. We know from many proceedings in our courts, that combinations of villains are broken up every day – that they cannot last long. Dishonest men fall out. Men without principle, change with changing circumstances.

16. A unbelievable combination of falsities to be established

The combination events assumed by Dr. Middleton is not only incredible, when considered with reference to numbers, places, and duration. The falsehoods to be established by false proofs, were of such an extraordinary character as to preclude the possibility of success.

They were plain, palpable, public facts, cognizant by the senses. They were alleged to have been performed in the presence of numbers – subject to every proper test, and were so fully proven that they were "universally asserted and believed." The most inveterate physical diseases are alleged to have been cured – men raised from the dead. The patients in these latter cases remained afterwards among those who knew them most intimately. Many of these alleged miracles were performed in answer to prayers of whole churches and witnessed by great numbers. As to the character of alleged miracles considered abstractly, they were just as varied and credible in themselves as the Scripture miracles.

It is true that false miracles, like false coin, were asserted to have been performed, but they were confuted and exposed. The very fact that false miracles existed is proof that true miracles also existed. A false coin is always but an imitation of the genuine one. Had there never been a genuine coin there could not be a counterfeit. The fact that false miracles have been detected and exposed by proof is strong confirmatory evidence that those not thus detected and exposed *are true*. It marks the dividing line between the false and the true.

17. The existence of vice where heroic virtue is to be expected

The ground of Dr. Middleton is not only incredible on account of the character of the alleged combination, and the notorious and visible nature of the false 'facts' to be established by it. But it imputes vice and stupidity, of an extraordinary character, to men of an age and reputation where we should expect the most heroic virtue and the greatest Christian knowledge.

That vice of the most extensive and iniquitous kind should be found among men of such eminent character for probity, learning, and dignity - as Dr. Middleton has it – is surely most extraordinary. That the immediate successors of the apostles had among them so much fraud, and at the same time so much stupidity, is also most astonishing. For this stupendous system of fraud is alleged to have originated with those appointed by the apostles themselves, and was imposed upon those they had themselves taught and converted by their own labors.

Not only so, but it had its origin in the days of persecution, when it would seem that most men could not have professed Christianity, but from honest motives. For we know, if there be any truth in history at all, that persecutions, general, bloody, and cruel, were often repeated against Christians from the days of Christ, until 312 A.D. These persecutions were as cruel as human ingenuity could well make them. Every description of insult and affliction awaited the Christian. The church had short intervals of rest, only to be followed by renewed persecution. In the simple and beautiful language of the author Diognetus, who wrote about 130 A.D., and who states that he "was a disciple of the apostle," the Christians:

> loved all men and were persecuted by all. They were unknown and yet condemned.... They were treated with dishonor, and by dishonor are made glorious; their integrity is ensured by the insults they suffer; when cursed they bless, and reproaches they pay with respect. When

> doing good they are punished as evil-doers; and when they are punished they rejoice as men raised to life. By Jews they are treated as aliens and foes; by Greeks they are persecuted; and none of their enemies can state a ground for their enmity.

"Their integrity was ensured by the insults they suffered." Upon its face, is not this statement the most reasonable that could be imagined? For if we cannot find integrity among twelve millions of martyrs who suffered in these persecutions, and among those who incurred but escaped from the dangers, where shall we look for it? Shall we seek it among those who never gave any such proof of it?

These men of eminent character, who are alleged to have committed these innumerable forgeries and frauds, *who were they*? Were they Christians? Could they be such? Were they, under this supposition, anything else but Atheists, cheats, and liars? What else can we justly call them? Were they not hypocrites, who wore masks all their lives, and died with them still on? Did they not go about, *lying to teach virtue?* Did they not seal falsehoods with their voluntary deaths?

The members of the church who believed these things, *who were they*? Were they not simple, stupid dupes, fit victims of dishonesty? Had they lost all their senses? Were they honest? Did not all these things happen in a most enlightened age of Rome. Did it not happen in the Augustan age of orators, poets, historians, and philosophers?

What adequate motives could have influenced these men? Men do not commit great crimes without great motives. It is a weary thing to wear a mask through life. How it goads the wearer! How ill it fits! And what greater tests of sincerity did the apostles undergo, than those endured in the second, third and fourth century. The persecutions were the same, the honors no more. The Christians of those centuries had before their eyes the same infamy, tortures, and death. In both cases their "integrity was ensured by the insults they suffered." If the love of fame could possibly be supposed to have produced such a result, then Christ and his apostles had greater motives to put forth false statements than their immediate successors. For this reason, there is more glory in founding an institution than in sustaining it afterwards.

18. That the diligence of the apostles could be impeached

The position of Dr. Middleton impeaches the diligence and capacity of the apostles themselves. If miracles were to have ceased with the apostles, why did they not so inform those they themselves taught? Did *they* know it. It was certainly a very important matter – none scarcely more so. Far from telling us so, they speak of miraculous powers, as they do any other permanent thing in the church.

Suppose, on the contrary, they did well instruct the bishops whom they appointed as well as the elders and members generally. If they informed them that miracles would cease with their lives, where do we find the slightest evidence of such?

These bishops and elders must have been very incompetent and unworthy men. The apostles must have made very bad appointments. The people they taught must have been very poorly instructed.

Dr. Middleton's ground is that the whole Church so widely diffused, containing such numbers in her communion, and in the days of stern trial; immediately after the apostles, and contrary to their express instructions, would unanimously affirm, and assume to believe in the continued existence of miracles, contrary to the truth and the fact. The idea, is so unreasonable in itself, that I confess I cannot believe it to be true. And the idea that the apostles neglected to teach them properly, I cannot admit. Nor can I understand how it could be possible to find in that honest and enlightened period, so much corruption and stupidity in the Church.

19. That such imposters were confined to the Catholic Church

We must ask what it means if some combination of events such as those discussed were possible, and deception did take place, and has continued in successful operation for about eighteen centuries. That it is the case the great and overwhelming majority of professed Christians, in all ages, have been its dupes and victims.

Is it not most remarkable that none of the thousand sects of ancient and modern times have made and sustained any such pretensions? They could not, each and all of them, have been the true church. They were often reproached because they could not perform miracles. Were they too honest to make such a pretension? Where was Marcion, who mutilated the Scriptures to sustain his own views? Was he too honest to attempt a fraud so practical and easy, and so much needed to support the pretensions of his theory? Why did not some other party try this *successful* experiment? Successful experiments never want for imitators and competitors. The originators are never "left alone in their glory." Others are certain to "take up the tuneful lay."

I am not aware that such a claim to a continued succession of miraculous powers, of the same or similar character, is made by the adherents of any other religion in the world Mohammedan or Pagan. Dr. Paley says:

> Mohammed did not found his pretensions upon miracles properly so called; that is, upon proofs of supernatural agency, capable of being known and attested by others.[12]

The powers claimed by the ancient magicians and the Eastern jugglers bear no comparison, either with the Scripture or Catholic miracles. As Christianity is unlike any other religion in the world in regard to the time and proofs of its origin. So the claim of the Catholic Church to so long a succession of such miraculous powers, is without parallel, I apprehend in the history of mankind.

20. That Christianity itself fosters fraud and delusions

If as Dr. Middleton has it the, "prevailing opinion of Protestants that miracles continued during the first three centuries unwarily betrayed the Protestant cause into the hands of its enemies," I apprehend his position, when fairly and logically considered, "betrays the cause" of Christianity itself "into the hands of its enemies." For this position of his assumes as true a state of practical fraud and delusion, on the part of the primitive Christians, that destroys all confidence in their discretion and veracity.

If true, the position undermines all confidence in human integrity itself. It amply sustains Mr. Hume's position, that men are not competent to prove a miracle for any religious purpose. The logical mind cannot understand why we should believe miracles of one age upon the testimony of witnesses and refuse to believe the miracles of a subsequent age, proven by the same kind of testimony – miracles of the same visible, palpable, public character, and established by a succession of witnesses, more numerous, and equally credible.

Nor can the logical mind understand, if the alleged miracles of the second, third, and fourth centuries were false, and still universally claimed as true, and received as such, when the Church was so much more extended and contained so many more members, why the original miracles could not have been palmed upon the converts of the apostles. Dr. Milner asks:

> For if all the ancient Fathers and other writers are to be disbelieved, respecting miracle of their times, and those which they themselves witnessed, upon what grounds are we to believe them, in their report of miracles which they had heard of Christ and his apostles, those main props of the Gospel, and our common Christianity? Who knows but they may have forged all the contents of the former, and the whole history of the latter?[13]

The reasoning mind will ask this obvious question: "If these false pretensions to miracles as great, visible, and public, as the alleged miracles of Christ an His apostles have been so successfully maintained and believed by such numbers in all ages, why could not the early Christians and others have been deceived by like false pretensions?

I cannot understand upon what rational ground Dr. Middleton, as also all Protestant writers, in sustaining Christianity against unbelievers, should quote and rely upon the testimony of these *"eminent" false witnesses*. For the unbeliever may well say: "You cannot expect me to believe witnesses that you admit are perjured. Surely you do not intend to mock my understanding by asking me to believe the testimony of the very witnesses whom you, yourselves, have been most careful to impeach? For if they would lie to sustain Christianity in one way, surely they would lie in any other way that was practical and efficient. And you have saved me the trouble of proving two important points, namely:

1. Fraud and falsehood on the part of the leaders among the early Christians.

2. Delusion on the part of their followers; for you have, indeed, assumed both. Nobody recorded your apostolical miracles but Christians; and you have given them just such a character for fraud and delusion as would make them fit subjects for impostors and victims.

Mr. Gibbon in his *Decline and Fall,* chapter fifteen, has seen and stated the advantages the Protestant position gives the infidel. In speaking of the period when miracles were alleged to have ceased, he says:

> Whatever era is chosen for that purpose, the death of the apostles, the conversion of the Roman Empire, or the extension of the Arian heresy; the insensibility of the Christians who lived at that time will afford a just matter of surprise. They still supported their pretensions after they had lost their power. Credulity performed the office of faith, fanaticism was permitted to assume the language of inspiration, and the effects of accident or contrivance were ascribed to

supernatural causes. The recent experience of genuine miracles should have instructed the Christian world in the ways of Providence, and habituated their eye (if we may use a very inadequate expression) to the style of the divine artist.

Certainly there is great force in Mr. Gibbon's remarks if, for the sake of argument only, we take the Protestant position as true. It is surely very astonishing that the very men who were best acquainted with the true, should be the most readily deceived by the false miracles.

In vain will Dr. Paley insist upon his assumed distinction between the competency of witnesses of miracles performed in the origin of Christianity, and those performed afterwards, in affirmance of the same religion. It is a distinction without any substantial difference.

Everyone must see that the end of all tests is to show the ability and integrity of witnesses. As to ability, their senses and opportunities will show that. As to their integrity, it does not matter by what means you prove it, so they are satisfactory. Voluntary death and voluntary sufferings are not necessarily evidence of the correctness of the sufferer's religion, but they do prove his sincerity. If, then, the religion itself, for which he thus voluntarily suffers, plainly teaches him that falsehood forfeits all its rewards, and incurs all its punishments, he cannot die with a lie in his mouth. It may be assumed as certain, that no sincere Christian can give false testimony as to the facts, about which he cannot be mistaken.

We believe the apostles because their conduct and character proved the sincerity of their belief in a system that promised them no competent earthly reward. We can find no adequate motive then for perjury. Upon the same ground, we should believe the testimony of witnesses, whose labors, sufferings, and deaths, or other evidences, proved their sincerity in the belief of the same system. It promised them no title in this world, and threatened them with forfeiture and punishment in the next, for the same kind of vice. It does not matter whether Christianity be true or not, the witness who firmly believes it, whether in the beginning or at a subsequent time, must be equally honest and equally credible.

If it were said that the works imputed to the Fathers of the second and third centuries were forged by those of the fourth, and thus palmed upon the Christian world as true, this solution creates new difficulties equally great. These various writers were men of eminent character and widely known. Their works are referred to and quoted by each other in so many ways, that such a forgery is impossible. If these works were forgeries, and published, not as new works, but as works written when they purport to have been written, how did they succeed in deceiving the world? The first time these books appeared they must have created great astonishment.

If these numerous works could be the forgery of a subsequent age so could the Scriptures. The New Testament Scriptures are not referred to by a single writer, Roman or Greek, until after the apostles were dead. In fact, if this position be assumed, it at once answers Leslie's celebrated *"A Short and Easie Method with the Deists.* The ground he takes would be completely answered by such a position.

In reference to these writers, Dr. Paley very justly says:

> It may help to convey to us some notion of the extent and progress of Christianity, or rather of the character and quality of many early Christians, of their learning, and of their labors, to notice the number of Christian writers who flourished in these ages. Saint Jerome's catalogue contains sixty-six writers within the first three centuries, and the first six years of the fourth; and fifty-four between that time and his own; viz., A.D. 392.
>
> Jerome introduces his catalogue with the following remonstrance: "Let those who say the Church has had no philosophers, nor eloquent or learned men, observe who and what they were who founded, established and adorned it; let them cease to accuse our faith of rusticity, and confess their mistake." Of these writers, several, as Justin, Irenæus, Clement of Alexandria, Tertullian, Origen, Bardesanes, Hippolitus, Eusebius, were voluminous writers.[14]

21. The numbers and character of early Christians

As to the number of Christians in the primitive ages, Dr. Paley says:

> Justin Martyr, who wrote about thirty years after Pliny, and one hundred and six after the Ascension, has these remarkable words: "There is not a nation, Greek or Barbarian, or any other name, even those who wander in tribes, and live in tents, amongst whom prayers and thanksgivings are not offered to the Father and Creator of the Universe by the name of the crucified Jesus."
>
> Tertullian, who comes about fifty years after Justin, appeals to the governors of the Roman Empire in these terms: "We were but of yesterday, and we have filled your cities, islands, towns, and boroughs, the camp, the Senate, and the forum. They (the heathen

adversaries of Christianity) lament, that every sex, age, and condition, and persons of every rank also, are converts to that name."

I do allow that these expressions are loose, and may be called declamatory. But even declamation has its bounds. This public boasting upon a subject which must be known to every reader, was not only useless but unnatural, unless the truth of the case in a considerable degree, correspond with the description. At least, unless it had been both true and notorious that great multitudes of Christians, of all ranks and orders, were to be found in most parts of the Roman Empire.

The same Tertullian, in another passage, by way of setting forth the extensive diffusion of Christianity, enumerates as belonging to Christ, besides many other countries, the "Moors and Gætulians of Africa, the borders of Spain, several nations of France, and parts of Britain – inaccessible to the Romans the Samaritans, Daei, Germans, and Seythians. And which is more material than the extent of the institution, the *number* of Christians in the several countries in which it prevailed is thus expressed by him, "Although so great a multitude , that in almost every city we form the greater part, we pass our time modestly and in silence."

Clemens Alexandrinus who preceded Tertullian by a few years, introduces a comparison between the success of Christianity and that of the most celebrated philosophical institutions: "The philosophers were confined to Greece and to their particular retainers. But the doctrine of the Master of Christianity did not remain in Judea as philosophy did in Greece. It spread throughout the whole world, in every nation, and village, and city, both of Greeks and Barbarians; converting both whole houses and separate individuals; having already brought over to the truth not a few philosophers themselves. If the Greek philosophy be prohibited, it immediately vanishes; whereas from the first preaching *of our* doctrine, kings and tyrants, governors and presidents, with their whole train, and with the populace on their side, have endeavored, with their whole might, to exterminate it, yet doth it flourish more."[15]

Dr. Paley also gives an extract from Origen to the same effect.

When we come to consider the number and character of the early writers and Church historians, as also the Christian clergy of the day, and the members of every age, sex, condition, and capacity, are we prepared to say, that a large part of them were base and infamous imposters, and the remainder simple and stupid dupes?

If the whole Christian world could so deceive and be deceived, in the period when "kings and tyrants, governors and presidents, with their whole train, and the populace on their side, endeavored with all their might, to exterminate Christianity," who can believe *anything* depending upon human testimony?

Look at the amount of labor these alleged imposters performed. Did they not conquer the world for Christ? Who but they, after the days of the apostle, put down the idols and temples of the Heathens, and established Christianity in every part of the Roman Empire, and even in the barbarous countries beyond it? Should not imposters be made of viler stuff?

Is not that professed Christian in a most painful and melancholy position, who concedes that miracles did once happen – that they are still *possible*, but who to sustain his own particular views, is forced to accuse all the most holy eminent, and dignified Christians for the last eighteen centuries, of an incredible combination to cheat and defraud all mankind?

This most dark, gloomy, and terrible theory, even the bold and reckless Middleton seemed to wish somewhat to mitigate and soften. He says, "It is natural to suspect that so bold a defiance of truth could not be acquired or become general at once, but must have been gradually carried to that height by the example of former ages." But it is exceedingly difficult to see how this explanation could help the matter, or be reconciled with the other statements of the Doctor.

It is true, it somewhat excuses the lying Fathers of the fourth century because they followed the example of former ages. It somewhat excuses the lying example of the former ages because they were not quite so general. If, as he asserts and admits, the claim to such a power was *universally* asserted and believed in all ages, I cannot understand how there could be less falsehood and imposition in these former ages, than in the fourth, in proportion to numbers. The claim was the same – the imposition the same – the delusion the same – and there must have been the same "bold defiance of truth" in these "former ages" as in the fourth century. This attempted explanation is about as effectual in softening the charge, as for one person to say to another with exceedingly polite air, "Permit me sir, if you please, to call you a liar."

22. Not everyone is converted to belief by miracles

It may be asked why, if the proofs of the Catholic miracles are so strong and full, have not all professing Christians believed them? In answer to this, it might well be inquired why have there been any heretics in the world? Is it not true that the great majority of professed Christians in all ages have believed in the continuance of miraculous powers in the Church? The many have believed, the few have disbelieved.

The same objection is urged by Infidels against Christianity. They allege the fact that the majority of persons in the ages and countries, in which Christianity first appeared, rejected it. They ask, why all the Jews and Gentiles who witnessed the stupendous miracles of Christ and His apostles, did not believe it? They had ocular demonstration, and are said to have admitted not one, but many miracles. Yet they were not converted.

Dr. Paley, in his *Evidences of Christianity*, notices this objection and devotes a chapter to its confutation. He admits the fact that a majority rejected Christianity in the apostolic day and gives the most conclusive reason why they did. He divides his answer into two parts, one regarding the Jews and the other regarding the Gentiles. In speaking of the latter, he says:

> The infidelity of the Gentile world, and that more especially of men of rank and learning in it, is resolved into a principle which, in my judgment, will account for the inefficacy of any argument, or any evidence whatever, *viz*.: contempt prior to examination....
>
> This contempt prior to examination is an intellectual vice from which the greatest faculties of the mind are not free. I know not, indeed, whether men of the greatest faculties of mind, are not the most subject to it. Such men feel themselves seated on an eminence. Looking down from their height upon the follies of mankind, they behold contending tenets wasting their idle strength upon one another, with common distain of the absurdity of them all. This habit of thought, however comfortable to the mind which entertains it, or however natural to great parts, is extremely dangerous; and more apt than almost any other disposition, to produce hasty and contemptuous, and by consequence, erroneous judgment, both of persons and opinions.

How true it is, that vanity and pride are often predominant in great minds who "feel themselves seated on an eminence," as Dr. Paley justly states.

This most true and reasonable answer is just as applicable to most who reject the Catholic miracles, as to those who reject the miracles recorded in Scripture. As to the amount of contempt with which Protestant writers, in general, speak of Catholic miracles, anyone can easily judge by the harsh terms they use, and by the general drift, tone , temper, and spirit of their arguments.

It is seldom that you can find a Protestant writer who will calmly, and in a gentle and courteous spirit, examine this subject. Whenever they approach it, they seem to repose, not upon "a bed of violets," but upon a bed of thorns. Even the dignified and distinguished Dr. Paley was forced to take most extraordinary ground to exclude what he calls "Popish miracles."

23. The Catholic theory

In reference to the Catholic theory of miracles, I shall quote the language of Dr. Milner: [16]

> Methinks I hear some of your society thus asking me: Do you then pretend that your church possesses the miraculous power at the present day? I answer that the Church never possessed miraculous powers, in the sense of most Protestant writers, so as to be able to effect cures or other supernatural events at her own pleasure; for even the apostles could not do this, as we learn from the history of the lunatic child.(Matt 17:16.) But this I say, that the Catholic Church, being always the beloved spouse of Christ,(Rev 21:9.) and continuing at all times to bring forth children of heroical sanctity, God fails not in this, any more than in past ages, to illustrate her and them by unquestionable miracles.

In reference to the case of the lunatic child, when the apostles inquired why they could not cast out the evil spirit, Christ told them, "because of your unbelief." But he also told them that "this kind goeth not out but by prayer and fasting."

Nothing, perhaps, could show more fully the efficiency of prayer and fasting than this case. No doubt, this saying of our Lord, as well as the practice of the apostles in so often praying and fasting, gave rise to the practice in the churches, of praying and fasting when they asked the special interposition of heaven. The case of Peter is an example.[17]

Dr. Paley, in treating his second proposition, and in laying out the case excluded by his first, mentions those miracles that he calls tentative, "that is" as he says, "where, out of a great number of trials, some succeeded." In support of this exclusion he says, "Christ never pronounced the word but the effect followed." Certainly, he is right as to Christ, for it would have been wholly inconsistent with his character as God to have failed in a single instance. But it was different with the apostles. They were only agents. The miracle was the act of the Principal, and performed only when He pleased. I confess I cannot understand the justice or good sense of his exclusion of all tentative miracles. I am compelled, with all due deference, to put a demurrer to his allegation.

The learned Divine admits that we can, at least in many cases, determine whether events be miraculous or simply natural. The whole of his argument for Christianity based on miracles, proceeds upon this ground. He first assumes, very correctly, that God could not make a revelation except by miracle. If we cannot *know* a miracle from any ordinary event in *any* case, then miracles can form no proof *for us*. They would simply be idle and fail to accomplish the very end intended.

If then, we can judge as to the miraculous character of an event, why should we reject a tentative miracle simply because the subordinate agent of Christ failed in some instances? For illustration, suppose a saint to have made many efforts to raise the dead, and to have failed; and then, upon further trial to succeed. Shall we reject this clear case because we cannot understand the hidden reasons of God for not answering the prayers of His children in the other case? I apprehend not. If there be one hundred failures, and one single clear case of a miracle, what right have we to reject it upon the ground that it is tentative?

True it is, there may be a case of doubtful character in itself, which may properly come under another class of exclusion mentioned by Dr. Paley. But his confessed ground of exclusion in this case is this, and this only – the miracles are *tentative*. It matters not how clear the case may be – raising the dead – healing the leper – opening the eyes of the blind, or any other clear case, still, as the miracle is tentative it must be rejected for that reason only.

The objection to tentative miracles gives rise to some important reflections regarding miracles. I suppose that every Christian will concede that man is a little more capable of some things than of others. He certainly can judge better of facts cognizant by his senses, than he can of the designs of God. He certainly can judge better as to the weight and credibility of the testimony of his own species, with whom he is familiar all his life, and in daily intercourse, than he can of the deep reasons of

God. If, therefore, he sees an event, or it is clearly proven, which he knows is miraculous, if he knows anything, by what sort of reason can he reject his positive knowledge, for his mere conjectures? If a miracle were performed, – the manner – the time – the agent – are all immaterial. It does not matter by whom, when, or where, here, or there. If the event were established by satisfactory proof, it is still a miracle. It is matter of fact, and can be proved. If, therefore, a miracle be performed in answer to prayer and fasting, or at the tomb of a saint, or by his relics, is it not equally a miracle?

What right has anyone to say that God must perform His miracles in a particular manner? True, the Jews sought a sign from Christ, but He gave them none. The Devil challenged Him to cast Himself from the pinnacle of the temple, but He refused. The Jews said, "if thou be the Son of God, come down from the cross, and we will believe you." But Christ heeded not their challenges.

Was it not reasonable that He should have thus acted? Could an infinite being be expected to consult a mere creature? Certainly not. It is true, Christ was bound to give proper and sufficient evidence; but the kind, the time, and the manner, and the amount, were for Him to decide – not for the party governed. It is enough that He has done right, whether men think so or not.

In reading the Gospel history, we cannot but be struck with the fact that Christ generally, if not always, performed His cures upon worthy persons, requiring them to have faith, and in many instances granting the request of the applicant, because of his faith. "Thy faith hath made thee whole." "Be it unto thee according to thy faith." And we are told by Mark that "he could there do no mighty work, save that He laid his hands upon a few sick folk, and healed them." Matthew says in reference to the same matter: "And he did not many mighty works there, because of their unbelief." And it was also true of the Apostles. Their miracles were usually performed upon worthy objects, except in some cases to inflict punishment, as in the case of Ananias and Sapphira, and Elymas the sorcerer.[18]

When I was a Deist, this conduct of Christ, in praising and rewarding every confiding display of faith, was with me a serious objection. I said: "This conduct is precisely such as we must expect of an impostor, as faith is the very element of his success." But reflection satisfied me that there was nothing in this plausible objection. And in arriving at this latter conclusion, I adopted a rule that I have uniformly followed, and one that I conceive is just and true in itself. It is this: I first inquire if the proposition to be proved is possible. If possible, then I take the proposition as true for the sake of the argument only, and inquire if such conduct be compatible with the truth of the proposition, and consistent with it, under the existing circumstances. This rule forced me to admit, that if Christ were a Divine teacher, He would naturally require faith in the truths he taught; and that such conduct was as natural in a true, as in a false teacher; and of itself, therefore, proved nothing, for or against the truth of Christianity.

Another reflection is, that the gift of miracles was only promised by Christ to *true faith*. The promise is conditional. And it must also be conceded that a man may have faith at one time, and not at another. The apostles could not heal the lunatic child for want of faith, and Peter sank in the waves because of doubt, and this doubt was produced by momentary causes. It must also be admitted, that the frequency of miracles must, in the nature of the case, depend upon the object for which they are performed. Therefore, the simple fact that they are not so frequent at one time as another, is no objection. They may not be as necessary at one time and place as at another.

Certainly Christ performed few miracles among his own kindred because of their unbelief. We are not competent to judge as to when, how, or where, or upon whom, or by whom, God will perform a miracle. No man knows the mind of the Lord as Saint Paul affirms.

Another reflection is, that the apostles were chosen witnesses of God, as well as teachers. To prove their competency as inspired witnesses, frequent miracles were required. In the beginning, when the only question was the truth of Christianity, and not which is the true church, no miracles could be required to prove this latter fact. We have no instance mentioned in the New Testament, where miracles were wrought by the relics of departed saints; but we are told miracles were wrought by aprons and handkerchiefs taken from Paul and by the Shadow of Peter, as also by the touch of Christ's garment. True, these appertained to living persons; but even upon abstract reasoning, were that to govern us, it is difficult to say that relics could not produce the same result, as the saint to whom they belonged is only gone home, and still lives, but in a perfect state. But in the case of the dead man brought to life by the touch of the prophet Elisha's bones, we have a positive example.[19]

If, then, the object were to point out and illustrate the true church, a miracle wrought by the relics, or at the tomb, of a particular saint, would accomplish that purpose as efficiently as if performed by the saint while living. Upon abstract principles there can be no objection, it would seem. As to the manner, or the agent by which a supernatural event is produced, there can be no difference. The alleged miracles performed at the tombs, or by the relics of saints, are just as easy of detection, as if performed in other modes. It is no more an objection to such miracles than it would be to the miracle of Christ in opening the eyes of the blind man with the spittle and clay, or opening the ears of the deaf by putting his fingers into them, The modes used by Christ were various. When he wished a piece of money to pay tribute, instead of creating it at once, he sent Peter to catch a fish, in the mouth of which he found it.

Doubtless the Jews thought the ceremony of anointing the eyes of the blind man with spittle and clay, exceedingly foolish and vulgar. But I apprehend such objections are not entitled to much consideration. The satisfactory proof of one single miracle will answer them all. Miracles afford a fund of amusement and ridicule to the unbelieving, the volatile, and the unfeeling. But to the sober, sincere, and patient inquirer, they will wear another aspect. The Scriptures are full of all sorts of miracles, great and small, sublime and ridiculous, as judged by some. Many were performed apparently for very trifling purposes. But we know not God's purposes.

In reference to Catholic miracles, Dr. Paley says: "It has long been observed that Popish miracles happen in Popish countries; that they make no converts."[20] I have often observed that when some writers wish to state a matter, for which they cannot vouch, and yet wish to get the benefit of it, they introduce it in this way: "It is said or observed."

That it has been so said is no doubt true; but the saying itself is untrue. The statement is general and simply says: "Popish miracles happen in Popish countries;" which means they never happen elsewhere.

It will be easily seen upon examination, whether this statement is true, in reference to either particular. And in reference to the specifications and historical proofs of the Catholic miracles, I must refer to Dr. Milner's *End of Controversy, Butler's Lives of the Saints*, Dr. Hay on Miracles, and the Works of Bishop England having already given to this subject all the space I can spare. In the work of Dr. Milner which is easily obtained, the reader will find a condensed but very able enumeration of Catholic miracles, and the proofs in support of them, as well as a most masterly exposure of the false theories, and misstatements of different Protestant writers, upon the subject of miracles. The work of

Dr. Hay is a full and clear discussion of the whole subject. In *Butlers Lives of the Saints*, the miracles performed by particular persons are stated. In Bishop England's works, a statement of recent miracles, and the proofs to sustain them, will be found.

---

[1] Thomas Starkie, A practical treatise of the law of evidence. Vol. 1.

[2] Cited by George Hay, The Scripture doctrine of miracles displayed, p. 196.

[3] John Douglass DD, Lord Bishop of Salisbury, *The Criterion or rules by which the true miracles of the New Testament are distinguished from the spurious miracles of Pagans and Papists.*

[4] *Cf.* Dr. William Paley, *A View of the Evidences of Christianity.*

[5] *Cf.* Acts 3, Acts 4.

[6] Cf. 1Kings 18, 20; 2Kings 1, 23.

[7] Estopple: in law any impediment to a party asserting a fact or claim inconsistent with a position he has already taken. Editor

[8] Cited in Milner's *The End of Religious Controversy.* Letter xxiii.

[9] John Hughes, *Hughes-Breckenridge Controversy* . p. 332.

[10] *Cf.* in the fifteenth chapter of his *Decline and Fall.*

[11] *Ibid.*

[12] Dr. William Paley, *op. cit.*

[13] John Milner, *op. cit.*

[14] Dr. William Paley, *op. cit.*

[15] *Ibid.*

[16] John Milner, *op.cit.* Let. xxiii.

[17] *Cf.* Acts 12.

[18] *Cf. Acts 5.*

[19] *Cf.* 2 Kings 13:20.

[20] Dr. William Paley, *op. cit.*

CHAPTER VIII

WHICH IS THE TRUE CHURCH?

1. Can the Protestant churches be the true church?

The question, can the Protestant churches, singly or combined, be the true church? has already been considered in part. A few additional considerations will be submitted.

While Protestants deny that the true visible church is infallible, they generally concede that she is so protected by Divine power, that she remains always the true visible church, always teaching the true faith. What difference can there be between such certain and unfailing protection and infallibility it is most difficult to see.

Nor can it be well seen how the theory of a true visible church, always reaching the truth, can be reconciled with the right of private interpretation in the last resort. It would seem that such a church should be implicitly heard when she speaks, as she always, in the contemplation of this theory, speaks the truth.

We have already given the admissions of Dr. Spring, Mr. Breckenridge, and Mr. Rice. We will also give those of the early Reformers.

The principle is distinctly admitted that when the Church should teach error, the gates of hell would prevail against her, and the promises of Christ would necessarily fail. From this admission two conclusions necessarily follow:

1. That the true Church could never teach error.

2. That she must remain visible and teaching from her birth to her final consummation.

It would then seem to be a very plain proposition, that whatever existing party of professed Christians claims to be the true church, must show a continued line of ancestors to the age of the apostles. Under the admissions of all parties, the title to the true church has always resided in someone. As we cannot conceive of the continued fulfillment of the promises of Christ, without the continued existence of the same church, always teaching the same faith, and united under one government, as was the case in the days of the apostles; so, it follows, that the party who claims this identify, must trace the title back through the same continued and existing association. We cannot conceive how, consistently with the nature and purposes of the institution and promises of Christ, the Church could die, and be buried, and afterwards arise from the dead, in another age, and commence her interrupted career again. The Church in the days of the apostles was unquestionably a visible, teaching, governing, united association of living men. She possesses all the vital elements of continued existence, and in the contemplation of the theory of our Lord is a glorious institution which:

"Spreads undivided – operates unspent"

The parties have conceded certain things upon the record, and among them are these:

1. That Christ did organize a perpetual, visible, and united association of men, called "The Church."

2. That He gave to this Church a law for its government, communicated in human language.

3. That he promised His unfailing protection to this Church, in fulfilling all the duties prescribed by the law.

4. That the protection has always been given, and such an institution has already existed.

The concession of these facts is, in truth, a substantial settlement of the whole question, as to the Protestant claims.

As each party claims the right to the same thing, and to be now in possession of it; the weight, or onus of proof, will lie equally upon each, in the first instance. But as the Catholic Church is admitted to be older than any now existing party, she has made out a *prima facie* case, liable, it is true, to be disproved; but until disproved, must be held good, as against them. Therefore, she has nothing to do until the title can be shown, *prime facie,* to be in some other party, extending back beyond the period of her admitted existence. As the title can only exist in one party exclusively, when title is shown to be in one, it, of necessity, excludes all others, until the proof is overcome by other testimony.

The Protestant sects are met at the threshold by a very great difficulty. They must appear in some definite and certain form. Their claim must be based upon something tangible and consistent with itself. They can assume any form and shape they please, if it is not multifarious and contradictory. But when they do assume a certain shape, they must sustain it by competent proof. Their allegations and their proofs must correspond. They cannot allege one thing, and prove another. They can make their alleged true Church consist of any consistent requisites they please; but their proofs must correspond and show the continued existence of a church possessing these requisites.

The question then arises, what requisites shall they claim, as making up the true church? If each Protestant sect claims to be the exclusive true church, it necessarily rejects all the others. If, on the contrary, two or more combine, the alleged true Church is composed of multifarious contradictory and independent creeds; and their allegations are confused and inconsistent. In what shape then, shall they appear? And if the Protestant Church, thus composed, is still claimed to be the one true Church, what differences and discords could constitute separate and antagonistic churches? And if they conclude to combine two or more different creeds in making up the Church, then what creeds shall be combined?

If we suppose that the first Protestant party is composed of those sects, called by some orthodox or Evangelical, such as Lutherans, Presbyterians, Moravians, Methodists, Baptists, Episcopalians and others, what a strange and singular true Church this would be, as compared with the confessions of all parties! Different and contradictory doctrines – separate, independent, and distinct organizations, with no common governmental head, composing the one united visible Church of the apostolic day!!! It might well be said of such an artificial being, that it "was without form and void."

But the greatest difficulty would be this: as they say the true Church is at *present* composed of these materials, so it must have been originally, and at all times, from the days of the apostles till the present era. Having assumed this distinctive shape, made up and composed of certain contradictory doctrines, and of many independent and distinct church governments, all acting separately, each for itself alone, with no visible union or dependence one upon another, or of each upon the whole, they must find ancestors composed of like heterogeneous materials. They must find a church, existing at all times, composed of parties separately governed, professing the *same* contradictory creeds. Where, then, can they find such a church? No such conglomeration of sects existed at the dawn of the Reformation, or before that period.

If, on the contrary, in opposition to the provisions of the creeds themselves, we hold all their differences as only about immaterial matters; and that, in reference to such points, Christ made no revelation at all, then we reduce the articles of faith to a very small and insignificant number. We crowd the system into very narrow limits, with the moral certainty of having soon to remodel it again. And after they have done this, then they must still find ancestors who held, at all times, the same doctrines that this new-modeled Church is now assumed to hold, and composed of the same independent fragments, separated from each other upon mere *immaterial* questions. Where, then, could they be found? No such church existed at the dawn of the Reformation, or before that period.

If we take each Protestant party, as claiming to be the exclusive true church, still the ancestors must be found. And where can they be found? The Vaudois held several fundamental tenets, that no Protestant sect could stand; and, as we shall see, the few that remained, when they joined the Calvinists, had to renounce certain errors. So of the Bohemian Brethren. And these two sects only extended back a small portion of the way. About nine centuries remain to be filled up. And how can this be done? Only by filling up the chasm according to Mr. Breckenridge's *new* method of supplying the defective records of history, by individual construction of the Scriptures.

If there was any true Church in the world, at the time of the Reformation, other than the Catholic Church, it was the unquestioned duty of Luther and all Protestants to join that Church, and not reform it. Could they not find it? If they could not, how could others find it? And if no one could find it, what sort of a true, visible universal Church was it?

They found the Vaudois, but they could not endure their admitted errors. What right had they, under the admissions of all parties, to organize another true Church, when one already existed? If the errors of the Vaudois were trifling, why were they required to recant? And when men tell us, in one breath, that the true Church must be visible and perpetual, and that at the date of the Reformation, there did exist such a church somewhere, and that such was the Vaudois; and then, in the next breath, tell us they hold doctrines never taught by the law of Christ, and that their true Church needed reform itself; what can we believe? How can we put these two contradictory theories together? If they had assured us that there was a *true false Church*, we could have understood them just as well. 'The man was a good honest fellow. True, he did steal six calves.'

Truly did Luther say: "I stood alone." And if the Catholic Church is not the true Church, then truly did the Book of Homilies of the Church of England, say:

> So that clergy and laity, learned and unlearned, all ages, sects, and degrees of men, women, and children, of *whole Christendom,* (a horrible and dreadful thing to think,) *have at once drowned in abominable idolatry,* of all other vices most detested of God, and most damnable to man, and that by the space of eight hundred years and more—*to the destruction and subversion of all good religion universally.*[1]

Really this is candid and manly language. It is full, definite, and certain. There is no studied ambiguity—no cowardly evasion. It does not "palter in a doable sense." It comes up to the *precise* point. It does not attempt to mock and degrade your understanding, by pretending the existence of true ancestors, that never could be found. It admits there were none. It speaks boldly, and tells a plain story. There is no concealment—no prevarication. And truly, it was "a horrible and dreadful thing to think" that Christ had forgotten His promises. And truly, if Protestantism be true, it is based upon "a horrible and dreadful" state of case.

The idea that there was a visible teaching Church, and yet that such a church could fail, would seem entirely inconsistent with the purposes of its organization, with the character of Christ as a Divine Lawmaker, and with His actual promises. Such a supposition is based upon incorrect ideas. It supposes that it was necessary for Christ to make a law and organize a Church – and that having exhausted His powers in the effort, or become otherwise employed, or for some other reason, He cast the Church upon the earth, as a vessel in the middle of the ocean without a pilot. And having retired to His apartments He said, "Let her travel."

The idea that the true Church could teach any single error and remain the true Church – that she could be reformed in matters of faith – or that she could be composed of contradictory creeds, distinct, separate, independent antagonistic organizations, would seem entirely illogical, and untrue in every particular. And we could just as readily believe that mere chance was the originator and projector as that any union could continue to exist in any association of men, under the Protestant principle of individual interpretation in the last resort. As chance may undo tomorrow what it has done to-day, such unity, if it should by the merest possible accident exist at any one time, could never be fixed and secure.

Taking the admissions of the parties as I find them, I am forced to conclude, that the Protestant sects, taken separately or all combined, or in different combined parties, have, each and all wholly failed in showing any title to be called the true church. And before they can make any consistent case, they must go back and amend their allegations. They must begin again at the beginning – withdraw their admissions – deny that Christ was any lawgiver – that any visible, universal, teaching Church was ever intended – and insist that Christ promulgated no law, and organized no church. They must insist that He merely discovered preexisting truths before undiscovered, and that, like any other philosopher, He left the truths He discovered, to be taught by those who pleased, and in the manner they pleased. This theory would at least be consistent with itself.

Well may Mr. Campbell say: "Protestants have all conceded too much in every age and period of this controversy."[2] This is true in one sense, and may not be true, in another. They have certainly conceded too much for their cause, and may have conceded too little for the truth. And while Mr. Campbell endeavored to correct this error, and himself conceded less, and disputed more, than other Protestants, he too, so far as I am competent to judge, "conceded too much." I apprehend that future controversialists will say the same of him that he said of his predecessors. When I first read the debate between him and Bishop Purcell, this passage struck me with great force. In my investigations afterwards, I could well see how true it was in the sense I have indicated.

2. Have the promises of Christ failed?

From the reasons and proofs heretofore given, the question was reduced, in my judgment, to this – have the promises of Christ failed? Is there any true Church now in the world? And if it cannot now be found in the only Church that can show a continued and uninterrupted existence, extending back to the days of the apostles, then it can surely be found nowhere on earth. It is an institution that was, and is not.

WHICH IS THE TRUE CHURCH

It was a matter of the first importance, as I conceived, to know what powers and prerogatives the Catholic Church had always claimed; for to my mind it was clear that the true Church must always know herself – her duty – know her faith – know her rights – and knowing them, must always claim and assert them. I could not conceive how the true Church could lie against herself, or against her Divine Founder, by denying the truth in reference either to herself or to Christ.

When I hear a Church admit that her creed has been reformed, I cannot understand how she can be the true church. If it were in regard to a matter of faith, it is quite clear that she concedes that she cannot be such. Either she was right at first, or wrong at last, or vice versa; and in either case she was not the true church at one period of her existence, and must fail in her connection with the apostles. And when I hear a church not only admit that her creed has been reformed, but that it may still need reforming, and under her theory may be so reformed, I cannot understand how she can be the true church. If she claim not infallibility, but only the promised protection of Christ in another assumed form, making a distinction between the two; yet she ought to know when she is the true Church, and when she has such protection. What sort of a true Church is it that cannot vouch for her faith – that admits she may be wrong, because she does not know the true faith – does not know herself. What sort of Church is it that cannot affirm that *she* has the promised protection of Christ? What sort of church is it that can only give you the assurance of her *present*, as opposed, certainly to her *past*, and will almost as certainly be opposed to her *future* opinion, that she is *now* in a state of fixed repose – that she has at last, as she *thinks*, arrived at truth, though the question is still unsettled?

The Church having left the hands of the apostles, in possession of the true faith, and united in one government, it seemed clear that the same church, in all ages, must claim, not only a continued succession from the apostles, but also to teach the same doctrines at all times. If, then, I could find a church extending back to the apostolic days, always visible, always teaching, and always claiming to teach the doctrines once delivered to the saints, this fact, of itself, would constitute a very powerful argument in proving that such church was the true Church.

It being conceded that the Church left the hands of the apostles, claiming only the faith delivered, and that teaching was the end of its institution, the law of reason would hold that, *prima facie,* the Church had always done her duty. For it is a plain principle of law, as well as of common sense, that an officer is always presumed to do his duty; and he who alleges the contrary, must prove it. The fact that the officers do their duty, as a general rule, throws the burden of proof upon him who alleges the contrary.

But in the case of the true Church, under the Christian theory, the fact that the true Church must always teach, and claim to teach, the true faith, is not a matter of simple presumption, but of irrevocable promise, and must be so, if there be truth in the promise itself. When, therefore, I find a church thus existing and claiming always thus to teach, I find a case made out presumptively correct. It is a *prima facie* case; and, unless rebutted and overcome by opposing proof, must stand good.

That the Catholic Church has always claimed to be the true Church, and to teach only the doctrines she received, in succession, from the apostles, is not denied by Protestants, during the period of her *admitted* existence. So long as they admit her to have existed, so long do they admit her to have claimed thus to act. As to the alleged period when the Catholic Church took its rise, Protestants are as much divided among themselves, as they are about other important questions. In his debate with Bishop Purcell, Mr. Campbell at first fixed this period at A.D. 1054, but subsequently fixed the time of the commencement of the degeneracy of the Roman diocese, and the separation of the true from the "grievously contaminated" Church about the year two hundred and fifty. But in his debate with Mr. Rice, some few years afterwards, Mr. Campbell further extended the existence of the Church of Rome to the second century. "Taylor and others," he says, "have shown that all the abominations of Popery were hatched in the second century."[3]

Mr. Rice says: "During the first five centuries of the Christian era, the church, though becoming gradually corrupt, did not become Papist."[4] Mr. Rice, I believe, gives the Catholic Church about as late a beginning as any other Protestant. By the admissions of all, she is at least a thousand years older than any of the existing Protestant sects. She has, then, an admitted visible existence for the period of thirteen, out of the eighteen hundred years of the Christian era.

The celebrated Dr. Middleton, in his *Free Inquiry*, as the extracts I have already given will show, at first contends that the chief corruptions of Popery as he calls them, were introduced in the third, fourth, and fifth centuries.[5] He says that those Protestant authors, as Tillotson, Marshall, Dodwell, Dr. Waterland, Dr. Berriman, and others who admit that miracles continued during the first three centuries unwarily betrayed the Protestant cause. After stating that:

> every one must see what a resemblance the principle and practice of the fourth century, as they are described by the most eminent fathers of that age, bear to the present rites of the Popish Church,

he says:

> By granting the Romanists but a single age of miracles, after the time of the apostles, we shall be entangled in a series of difficulties whence we can never fairly extricate ourselves, till we allow the same powers also to the present age. [6]

This, I must say again, is candid and manly language. The renowned Dr. Middleton was a man of clear head, and too bold not to say what was necessary to sustain his case, and make it at least apparently consistent with itself. The admission is very clearly made that it would not do to admit that miracles continued after the apostles, for the reason that it would be betraying the Protestant cause to the Romanists. He insists that the Romanists must not be granted "a single age of miracles after the time of the apostles."

While Protestants admit that the Church of Rome has an existence from between the second and the sixth century to this time, they deny it extends back to the very days of the apostles. They have all admitted the continued existence of *a* Church visible and teaching, claiming to teach only the doctrines received from the apostles, and to be the true church. Thus the Church from which the Novatians separated in 250, and the Donatists in 311, was that Church, and then contained the overwhelming majority of all Christians.

The existence then of a Church, at so early a day after the apostles, claiming thus to have received and thus to teach, and to be the true Church, will make out a *prima facie* case, until disproved. Those who deny that such a Church was the true Church, and did so teach, must then show some other Church that was this true Church. Since its existence is admitted by all, and one party shows a Church existing at that early day – widely extended, claiming so to be – it throws the weight of proof upon the party that disputes its claims.

When, therefore, we are referred to the Novatians and Donatists who not only separated without good cause, but perished and disappeared in a few centuries (as if the true Church could die), we cannot say the claim is at all disturbed, but we must say, it is strengthened, from the failure of proof against it. The attempt thus to defeat the claims of the Church, having the great mass of Christians in her communion, by such testimony, is a substantiation of her claim, as it shows no better can be brought against it.

If, then, the Catholic Church could not bring any testimony to prove her continued existence, back to the days of the apostles, except the admissions of her opponents, she would still make out her case from them, and from their entire failure to show where the true Church was before her admitted existence, and afterwards. For under the admission of all parties, whatever true church did exist at the death of the last apostle must continue to exist. Those, therefore, who say the Catholic Church was not the true Church, must show some Church existing continually, both before and after the alleged birth of that Church. When, therefore, they attempt to do this, by referring us to two sects that soon disappeared, they certainly fail. The advocates of the Catholic Church, bring in all the Christian writers of the first five centuries, from Saint Ignatius, the disciple of Saint John, to Saint Gelasius in A.D. 492, and from these they bring a mass of testimony that seems entirely conclusive.

3. Has the Catholic Church been uniform in her faith?

The next and most important question that arose in this inquiry, was whether the Catholic Church had always been uniform in her faith. That she had always so claimed, there could be no doubt. That the presumption, under the promises of Christ, as well as under the principles applicable to all governmental institutions, that they all accomplish the end intended, and in the manner prescribed, would throw upon her adversaries the burden of proof to the contrary, was to my mind equally clear. This position I understood to be substantially conceded by Protestant controversialists. They, therefore, acting upon this ground, make certain charges of alleged contradictions in the creed of the Church, at different periods of her existence.

To examine impartially, and estimate justly, the force of these objections, it becomes necessary to understand distinctly what the Church herself holds to be faith, and what not. I found, upon examination, that the Church herself makes these several divisions:

1. There are articles of faith, which include those positive truths, facts and doctrines, which she holds Christ revealed to the apostles, and commanded them and their successors to teach to all nations, in all days,

even to the end of the world. She holds that the system of Christianity is made up of certain truths, facts, and doctrines, that must be believed by all, in all places, and at all times – that they are of such a character as to be applicable to all persons, times, and places – are unvarying, certain, and fixed, and must ever so remain. She holds that under the law of Christ, there are certain things that must be believed – that faith is required by the system, and that as required, it must exist. As regards faith, she claims infallibility.

2. Besides articles of faith, there is discipline, which is entirely different from doctrine, and in regard to which no infallibility is claimed, and no faith required, but only obedience in act. Discipline consists in those minor practical regulations or rules, which may vary with changing circumstances, and may be adapted to different times. They consist of such regulations as are deemed expedient to facilitate and carry out the practical administration of the fundamental laws of the institution. They are similar to the rules adopted by courts, and liable to be amended or changed at their pleasure, and which merely regard the mode, time, and manner in which parties must proceed at their bar.

3. Besides articles of faith and discipline, there are opinions. These opinions regard questions concerning which Christ made no positive revelation, and the apostles made no certain declaration. The members of the Church are allowed to hold either side, in reference to these questions, for the very reason that they are not matters of faith. This distinction is not new. The celebrated and beautiful saying of Saint Augustine, so often quoted by statesmen, as well as Catholics, alludes to it: "In essentials, let there be unity – in non-essentials liberty – and in all things charity."

4. There are besides these, local customs peculiar to different countries and ages. These regard not faith.

These distinctions seemed to me to be based upon the nature and reason of things. I could not conceive of any system of truth, where *faith* was required, without these distinctions. Faith must exist—but must also have its limits. The *practical success* of every system, where faith is required at all, must require certain truths to be held as articles of faith, at all times, and yet permit the existence of disciplinary regulations, suitable to different times and circumstances. As to opinions, we have seen that Saint Paul in his epistles clearly allows them to exist in reference to matters held indifferent, such as keeping certain days, eating meats, or living on vegetables alone. All he requires, in reference to such matters, is, that each person shall be sincere, and not, therefore, act against his own conscience, and in that way commit a sin.

So far as I could ascertain, these distinctions are substantially recognized by Protestants. Thus Mr. Campbell says, speaking of the controversy of the Novatians in A.D. 250: "It was, indeed, a controversy about the purity of communion, and discipline, rather than about articles of doctrine."[7] And in reference to the same subject, Mr. Rice says: "Every system of truth has its fundamental principles, which are essential to it, and minor points, in regard to which those holding the same system, may differ."[8]

The charges of Protestants against the uniformity of the Catholic Church, may be classed as follows:

1. Those which relate to alleged divisions always existing in the Church.

2. Those which relate to the alleged introduction of articles, never held before, being alleged *additions to the faith.*

3. Those which relate to alleged contradictory decisions of the Church in reference to the *same* articles of faith.

4. Alleged divisions in the Catholic faith

The first objection coming under the first class, as divided above, is that Catholics are not agreed as to where infallibility is lodged. While they all agree that it resides in the Church, there exists a difference of opinion as to what particular department of the Church it was committed. Some hold it as a matter of opinion, that it resides with the Pope, and others that it is found with the Pope and a general council acting together; or, what is the same thing in substance, with the Pope and a majority of the Bishops, when united in the same judgment. This objection is considered of great importance by Protestants, while Catholics esteem it of very little force.

The objection, it will be at once seen, regards not the *existence* of infallibility in the Church, but simply its *distribution.* It is a faculty or attribute admitted by all Catholics to belong to the Church, and the only question is as to where it is placed. So far as the decision of the Church has gone, this is left simply as matter of opinion. The point of faith is the admission of its existence in the Church, and not as to its distribution. In tolerating these different *opinions* relating to a matter of *opinion*, (as considered *by the Church,*) she is not chargeable with any contradiction to her own theory. She is only charged with *not* defining a question that Protestants think of practical importance. They insist that infallibility, if given to the Church, must have been given for practical exercise; and, therefore, it becomes important to know through what organ it speaks, that its voice may be obeyed when heard. The objection is more practical than theoretical. It is one that, in its nature, regards practice more than faith. If there be no practical difficulty in tolerating these opinions as to the mere location of infallibility, there can be no necessity for such a definition. If all the practical ends contemplated by the system can be accomplished without it, good sense does not require it.

It is a well-settled rule with courts of justice, founded upon the obvious principles of good sense, never to decide cases not before them. If a judge, in delivering the opinion of the Court, upon a case then before it, gives his opinion upon a principle of law outside the case, this opinion is called a mere *dictum*, and is not regarded as of any authority. It is the mere *ex parte* opinion of the judge as an individual, and binds no one, not even his own future action. It is so with the Church. She only decides cases when they arise, and in reference to practical matters, when a decision becomes of practical utility.

To make my meaning clear, I will give an illustration which occurred to me in my reflections upon this subject. We will suppose that A wishes to purchase a certain tract of land. He finds it exclusively claimed by B, C, and D. He finds he can purchase all their separated and adverse claims for a price, not exceeding the value of the land, and he does so, taking a conveyance from each claimant. We will suppose that he takes possession, and afterwards sells to E, taking E's note, upon time, for the purchase money, and delivers E. his bond for a warranty deed, when the note is paid. E fails to pay the note when due, and A sues him; and E sets up, as a defense, and says in his plea or answer, that A derived his title by separate deeds from B, C, and D; that he, the defendant, admits that title was in some one of these persons at the time of the deeds to A, but insists that A has not shown in which *one* of these three persons the title resided; and, therefore, A could not make him a good title. Such a defense would not be heard, and the Court would not inquire into the question of title, so long as it was *admitted* that it resided in some *one* of the three persons named, and that A had good deeds *from all*.

So, in the Catholic Church. Every definition of doctrine and morals by a General Council, is conclusive, but no Council is General without the Pope's concurrence. Therefore, in the decrees of every General

Council, there is the concurrence of all. He who thinks that infallibility resides in the Pope, must submit, and so of all the others. So far, therefore, as these act together, there can be no difficulty. What practical difficulty can there be, in such a state of things? Until the Church herself shall find the difficulty to exist, to such an extent, as to call for such a definition, is there any force in such an objection? She must judge of such a necessity; and if her administration can be practically carried on, and all Catholics united in all she decides to be matter of faith, it cannot be said that Catholics differ as to faith.

Questions of this character, as to the mere *distribution* of powers, are often discussed in governments having different departments. They have occurred in England, and in the United States. So long as the departments act together, the questions are never determined. In the Treaty of Washington, as I have stated, the question came up, whether the President and Senate could make a treaty affecting the boundary of a State, without her consent, and the consent of Maine was had, as being more safe, and the question left where they found it. Perhaps in all coming time, such an occasion may not occur again; and should a similar occasion occur in the future, the difficulty may be again avoided, by the like *consent of all*. To deny, therefore, either that the power did reside in the government, or that it could not be practically exerted, because there was some difference of opinion among *individuals*, as to its precise location, it occurs to me, is to deny the positive practical results of experience, and the evident dictates of reason.

Mr. Campbell says: "It is a serious question. Why is the Roman church infallible in faith, and not in discipline?"[9] I must confess I cannot perceive the force of the objection. Why did Christ *reveal matters of faith*, and not matters of *discipline*? One must, for that reason, be *believed*, and the other, for that reason, need not. And for that reason, in reference to faith, infallibility should reside in the church; but as to discipline, it need not, as obedience *in act*, is all that is required. As discipline depends upon circumstances, and is liable, therefore, to be changed, I cannot see any reason for infallibility in reference to it, or how Christ could have well made any revelation regarding it. The promises of Christ made in the Commission, had reference to the truths revealed by Christ to His apostles. The Church would not properly claim infallibility, *without a promise.*

The fact that the Church claims infallibility in reference to *revealed* truths, and not as to discipline, is, to my mind, no objection; but on the contrary, is an argument in her favor. It shows that her claim is founded in reason and good sense, and makes a distinction that she *must* make, if her claim to infallibility be true. In my reflections and inquiries upon this subject, I have found a greater portion of the arguments used by Protestants against the Church, to be strongly for her, so far as I was capable of estimating their legitimate force. The error generally consists in drawing the wrong conclusion

5. Alleged additions to the faith of the Catholic Church

Let us refer to the second class of charges made by Protestants against the uniformity of the Church, as regards faith; and which relate to supposed additions to her articles. These charges are alleged by Catholics to have arisen from confounding the *definition* of the existing faith of the Church, with the *creation* of new tenets not flowing from the legitimate extension and application of admitted principles. Protestants suppose such definition to be the introduction of entirely novel and unheard of principles. In other words, that "they mistake the language of definition, for the words of creation."

In his late very able work, Dr. Ives says:

> This reminds me of an error which, in the course of my examination, showed itself continually in Protestant statements, viz.: to date the commencement of a doctrine or practice at the time, when from some denial or neglect, such a doctrine or practice was made binding by an explicit written decree, although it had always existed in the Church.[10]

The importance of these charges, especially the principles involved, led me to make a careful examination of the matter, so far as my opportunities would allow. Given any association of men, governed by a law promulgated in human language, and in which there resided any judicial power at all, I first inquired whether, these definitions would not, in the very nature and reason of the case itself, most certainly occur. Must definitions occur in the practical application of the law, to different cases as they should arise, in the course of ages? That is, I enquired whether these definitions, decrees, or decisions, are not inseparable from all practical government over such intelligences as men; and whether, from the nature of the judicial power, such definitions could be avoided.

The people of the United States have, as their fundamental law, a Constitution. By this instrument, there is one Supreme Court, whose duty it is to construe and apply the laws, constitutional and statutory, to cases that come before it. Much discussion arose at an early period, as to the proper construction of certain articles of the Constitution. In the nature of things, these questions still arise, and must arise in all future time. Events unforeseen will bring up new questions from age to age, so long as the government shall last. A very important amendment to our constitution was made in 1804; and was occasioned by a very unexpected question that arose in the House of Representatives, in the election of President in 1801. "The Election of 1801," says Chancellor Kent:

> threatened the tranquility of the Union; and the difficulty that occurred in that case, in producing a constitutional choice, led to the amendment of the constitution on this very subject; but whether the amendment be for the better or for the worse, may well be doubted, and remains yet to be settled by the lights of experience.[11]

A concurrence of circumstances may occur at the next Presidential election, that will fully test, by "the lights of experience," the wisdom of this amendment to the Constitution, and such a concurrence may not happen in ten centuries, and may then arise. When, however, it does occur, it must give rise to new definitions, or new amendments, or both.

Consider the questions of constitutional construction that must hereafter arise in our courts, as well as in our Congress. Suppose, then, a new case should come up before the Supreme Court, a thousand years hence, involving the construction of an article of the Constitution. If that Court, by its solemn decision, should settle the construction of that instrument, could any sensible man say that the Court, in the contemplation of our system, had created a new part of the fundamental law, simply by declaring what that law meant? And could any man of fair mind and logical head, say that the constitution had not always been what the Court declared it to mean? In other words, in the contemplation of our theory, would the Constitution itself be abrogated, or changed in any particular, because that august Court had given it a construction never given before, but necessary to decide a new case, involving the point in controversy? I apprehend not. On the contrary, it would be admitted that the Constitution had always meant what it is declared to mean; and that such had always been the law. The power to *declare* what is the law – the existing law, is very different from the power to *make* a law. One is judicial and the other legislative – one is the power to create, and the other the power to construe that which is *already made*.

If, then, there be any government at all in the Church, the judicial power must reside in the institution – and if it does exist therein, must not these definitions occur, from time to time, from the very nature of the power itself? Can anyone form a conception of an association of men kept in unity, and governed by a law communicated in human language, through a long course of centuries, and yet without any necessity for such definitions? I confess I cannot form such a conception. I cannot possibly, imagine what sort of association, unity, or government it could be.

Law, properly so called, is a rule of conduct (and in the Christian system, of faith also) prescribed to free intelligent agents; and as the parties governed possess these characteristics, the law will be violated; and not only so, but in a multitude of instances of the most complex character. This free agency of the governed will enable them to violate the law, and their intelligence will allow them to do so, in every variety of form, and under every plausible pretense. Hence continued definitions become inevitable, under any government of law.

Did not such instances occur in the days of the Apostles? And have they not occurred at intervals ever since? And must they not occur in the future?

A good while before the Council of Jerusalem was held, Peter had admitted the Gentile Cornelius and his household into the Church. The true faith had been preached over a great portion of the world, and churches formed at different places. Not during all this time had the question making circumcision essential to salvation been raised. Had it been postponed a few years longer, it would have come up for decision, after the death of the apostles. It was never decided, however, until it did arise. When, however, it did come up it was finally decided and the Council issued its decree, settling that case. This decree, as I have already said in another place, was, in my view, only the judicial construction and application of the law to a particular case.

We see like circumstances in reference to the dissensions among the Corinthians. These which were so unexpected, that they were not known to the inspired Paul, until informed by those of the house of Chloe. The case of Hymeneus and Philetus, mentioned by Paul in his second Epistle to Timothy is also similar. These men believed in the resurrection of the dead, but believed it was already past. In the latter particular they erred. This was also a *new case*.

After the days of the apostles, but at an early day, the question was first raised, whether it was necessary to re-baptize those who had apostatized, and then returned to the church. This question could not have arisen until some case brought it up. The persecutions of the early Christians long, bloody, and relentless as they were, gave rise to this question. Those Christians who had yielded under the terrors and pains of torture, denied the faith and sacrificed to idols, and afterwards repented and wished to return. Must they be re-baptized? The question was raised for the first time, and for the first time it had to be decided.

Suppose this persecution had not arisen for five hundred years afterwards, and then have come up. Those opposed to re-baptizing could have said, "We have never re-baptized any one in the Church." While others could have answered, "True; but you never had such a case before. This is a new case now first occurring in the Church. And under the legitimate intention of the law regarding the sacrament of baptism, must they not be re-baptized?" It is true, that the apostles never re-baptized anyone; but it is equally true, that they never refused to re-baptize any one. No one apostatized in their day, and afterwards offered to return to the Church. The case never arose in their day that could bring up this question.

Now the question in such a case regards the application of admitted principles to new cases – cases different in their circumstances. All conceded that Baptism was a sacrament. The only question was could it be twice administered to the same person under the circumstances stated? And it was decided by the Church that re-baptizing was not required.

In regard to the Divinity of Christ a similar situation arose. Until it was denied, and the question raised, no express decision was made by a Council. The moral and gifted Dr. Priestly, to whom Pope ascribes

"Every virtue under heaven,"

in his *History of Early Opinions*, argues that the Divinity of Christ, never held, as he insisted, in the days of the apostles, "crept in" as an "opinion" a short time afterwards, spread silently, became strong, until at last it was enacted into an article of faith, in the Council of Nice 325 A.D.

In reference to Priestly's way of thinking Saint Augustine says:

> The dogma of the Trinity was not perfectly brought out till the Arians declared against it; nor was penance until attacked by the Novatians, nor the efficacy of Baptism, till questioned by re-baptizers. Nay,

> what regarded the unity of the body of Jesus Christ was not discussed with minute exactness until the weak being exposed the danger... compelled the teachers of truth to examine those truths to the bottom.... Thus the errors of heresy, instead of injuring the Catholic Church, have really fortified it; and those who thought wrong were the occasion of ascertaining those who thought right. What has been but piously believed, became afterwards fully understood. [12]

Saint Paul had expressed the same consequences flowing from heresy as did Saint Augustine. "For there must be also heresies among you, that they which are approved may be made manifest among you."[13]

In addition, I confess I could not see how it could be otherwise. As I have insisted in a preceding page, law, from its very nature, only lays down general principles in general terms. It cannot, in advance, state all the facts and circumstances that go to make up each individual case. The general principles must then of necessity, be applied to these new cases *as they arise*. They cannot, with any practical propriety, be applied before the cases arise. The cases may never occur, and the definition would then simply be idle.

It must be evident to everyone who has any practical knowledge of the application and extension of the principles of law to new cases: that the number and character of the discussions and decisions in reference to the principle involved will be in proportion to the number and varied character of these new cases. Also the application of the principle will be the better understood in proportion to the number of new cases.

For the sake of illustration, I will take the proposition mentioned by Dr. Balguy, that "Christ is the author of eternal salvation." So long as the members of the Church believed this proposition in its natural sense – that Christ was the author of eternal salvation, because He bore our sins, in His own body, upon the cross – it would be wholly unnecessary to make any definition. There could be no good sense in calling a council to define that which had never been disputed, had always been believed and taught, and which might never be disputed. But suppose, in the course of time, certain persons raise the question whether Christ saves us by the atonement, or simply by His example. The Church would then call upon the parties and ask, "Do you believe that Christ is the author of eternal salvation? They would all answer "Yes." The Church would then ask, "In what sense?" They would answer, "By His example." Here is a *new* sense given to the proposition; and the Church must then determine, whether the general proposition itself can tolerate *such* an extension and application of its principles.

Protestants, while they make the objection that Catholics create new additions; they seem sensible of its entire unreasonableness. In their own practice, they act upon the judicial principles themselves, though contrary to their fundamental rule. The late divisions in the Methodist body in the United States, into North and South, in consequence of the different views regarding slavery, may be mentioned as an illustration. I apprehend, that if no Methodist had ever been a slave owner, the question would not have been determined as to whether slavery was a sin or not. They would have said: "Sufficient unto the day is the evil thereof; we will determine that question when it comes up."

Mr. Campbell seems also to act upon the principle of deciding new cases in reference to "a roll some five feet long, charged 75 cents extra franking privilege," and received from "one of his *once* much esteemed friends and fellow laborers," containing the views of the writer upon certain points, and asking the liberty of discussing them in the pages of *The Harbinger.* Mr. Campbell after other remarks, says:

> May we not hence conclude, that there is yet need of further investigation on these subjects, or of yet more clearly ascertaining what may or may not be discussed, in Christian communities, under the plea of Christian liberty, and freedom of debate?[14]

This *new* case seems to have brought up very forcibly the necessity "of yet more clearly ascertaining *what* may or may not be *discussed* in *Christian communities.*" It satisfied Mr. Campbell that a further *definition* was necessary.

When I first read this objection of alleged additions made by Mr. Campbell in his debate with Bishop Purcell, and so much relied upon by him, as well as by all Protestant controversialists whose works I have read, I could not but regard it as of very great importance, either *against* or *for* the Catholic Church. The objection had substance in it, in one-way or the other. If in the nature and reason of the Christian system, such new definitions were not required, but prohibited, then the objection was legitimate against the Church. But on the contrary, if such new definitions must occur from the nature of the system, and the parties governed, then it was a most powerful argument for the Church, as it would then show that she had, *in fact*, throughout the long course of her history, *always acted as the true Church must have acted,* under the same circumstances.

In my reflections upon this subject, I could not understand how the mere fact of a definition being made by the Church at *any* time, of *any* article of faith, could be the slightest proof, that such article was not always believed in the church, until the occasion arose for its definition. On the contrary, every presumption of reason and law would hold it as evidence, *prima facie* at least, that such a doctrine had so always existed. Like the decisions of the Supreme Court, all these decrees of the Church assumed, upon their face, to be only *declaratory* of not only the then existing belief of the Church, but of that which, at *all times*, had been such. Therefore, to say that the express written definition of an article of faith by the Church, was an evidence that such faith was *new* in the Church, because for the *first time defined*, was to my mind erroneous. It was as erroneous as to say, that every new construction of definition of an article of our Constitution by our Supreme Court, is the subversion of that instrument, in the contemplation of our Federal theory of government.

But to say that such definition was at least *prima facie* evidence that the doctrine defined was *not new*, was to my mind equivalent to saying, that the true Church had always been vigilant, decisive, and prompt in the discharge of her duties, and in the exercise of her legitimate powers. For I could not form a conception of a visible Church, without the necessity for the exercise of such a power; nor could I esteem a Church of any value at all, that had no such power, or that had not the moral nerve to use it when required. The irresistible conclusion in my mind was this: that whether the Catholic Church is the true Church or not, she did, in *fact, act consistently as if she were*; and as she claimed to be such, her acts had been in perfect unison with her professions in this respect.

When I came to look into the history of these definitions I found most ample historical proofs to show their reason and necessity. The statement made by the great Saint Augustine, in reference to certain questions defined before or in his day, was true of the definitions made by the Church afterwards. These definitions were made as often as cases arose requiring them, and were only declaratory of the existing faith of the Church. From the express declaration of the decrees, in unison with the rule of the church, expressly recognized at all periods of her existence, it was shown that she only taught the doctrine which came down to her without interruption from the apostles. But not only was this shown from the declarations it was affirmatively shown by the express testimonies of the Fathers, and historians of the Church, written at various times, in countries widely separated from each other.

The statement made by Mr. Campbell that "in the ninth century the doctrine of transubstantiation began to be talked of commonly, but was made infallible by Pope Innocent III, Fourth Lateran Council," I found was not sustained by the facts of history. It was true that the Fourth Lateran Council in 1215 first made the definition, and first used the word "transubstantiation," as best and most concisely expressing the faith of the Church. But it was equally true that this definition was brought about by the denial of the doctrine by Berengarius, and that it had been believed in all ages of the Church, as the testimonies of the Fathers abundantly show.

So long as the words, "This is my body" and "This is my blood" were understood in their plain literal sense, it was wholly unnecessary to define the faith of the Church. When Christ says, "This is my body," it is obvious that these words, if taken literally in their plain sense, express the entire change of substance. And when these words, in the opinion of the Church, are misconstrued, other words must then be used to express the idea the Church decides is conveyed by the language of Christ.

There are some words that can only be taken in one sense, and that sense is fixed and determinate, while other expressions may admit of different senses. If the Church finds her doctrines impugned by those who misconstrue the Scriptures, she is compelled, of necessity, to use other than the Scripture language (already misconstrued), otherwise her decrees would settle nothing. Those who had misconstrued the same language in the Scriptures, would again misconstrue the same language in the decrees, and insist that the Church had defined nothing, or that she had, in fact, confirmed their views. No single term, perhaps, could be found, so definite and certain as the word "transubstantiation." The words "This is my body" express the same idea, if taken literally. For when one says "this is a certain thing," naming it, he does not mean to say, it also contains another and a different thing. By this form of expression he speaks of a single thing, and not of two or more things existing together. This single thing may be composed of separate parts, but cannot consist of two separate and distinct things, like bread and Christ's body.

The fact that a new name is given to a thing, under new circumstances, is not at all surprising, but is very common. It is very natural for men to seek a single word to express several ideas, when a frequent repetition is required, either in spoken or written language. This tendency of common sense towards common convenience was very fully shown in California, in 1848, the year the gold mines were discovered. At first, when a man went out to search for new gold mines, they said he had gone "to hunt for new gold diggings;" but as the same answer, from the new circumstances existing, had to be made so often, some one called the whole operation "prospecting" and the term at once passed into general use, and so continues.

So, in theological controversy, it is matter of convenience, to use one term as expressive of several ideas. It is also proper in such cases, to use a term that is alone applicable to the particular case, as it is more certain. The use of these new terms is not the slightest evidence, that the thing itself has changed, any more than the fact, that the disciples were first called Christians at Antioch, was evidence that they were different from what they had been.

For these reasons, I considered the argument of Mr. Campbell and other Protestants, founded on the name *Roman Catholic* as entirely erroneous. For the same reason, I consider the arguments of some Catholic writers based on the term *Protestant*, as signifying only something negative, and nothing affirmative, as equally erroneous. We must look to the circumstances under which the name is given to know what it means.

The word Trinity nowhere occurs in the New Testament and shall we hence conclude that the doctrine expressed by the term is not found therein? All such arguments are based upon a remarkably shallow foundation, though they are very often used. It must be conceded that names are not given to things, before the things have either a real or an imaginary existence. When a new doctrine is put forth, there can seldom be found a short known term to express it. The lawmaker to make himself understood, must, of necessity, do one of two things:

1. He must coin a new term, or take an old one, and in either case, he must define the sense in which he used the term.

2. Or he must do the same thing in substance, by stating in full the particulars that make up the doctrine, leaving others to give it a short name.

To convey to the mind the doctrine of the Trinity, before that term was defined, a number of words was indispensable. After the doctrine is understood, convenience will force parties, even the cavilers themselves, to adopt a short term, expressive of all the ideas entering into and composing the thing understood.

In reference to other alleged innovations in the faith of the Church, I found the same thing to be true; to wit: that the Church was compelled to define them because they were assailed, and they had always existed in the Church from the beginning.

6. Alleged contradictions in doctrine in the Catholic Church

In reference to those charges against the uniformity of the Church, coming under the third division, being alleged contradictions in doctrine, Mr. Campbell gives several instances. In the first place he gives several alleged contradictions in the decrees of the Popes. But as the Church does not hold the infallibility of the Pope as an article of faith, therefore, whether those alleged contradictions be true or untrue, does not touch the question.[15]

In the second place, he alleges certain contradictions in the decrees of different general councils, in reference to the same matter. The first allegation is that "the Council of Constance says the Church in old times allowed the laity to partake of both kinds – the bread and the wine – in celebrating the Eucharist. The Council of Trent says the laity and un-officiating priests may commune in one kind only. Here then we have Council against Council. In the time of Pope Gelasius it was pronounced to be sacrilege to deny the cup to the laity; but now it is uncanonical to allow it."[16]

In regard to allowing both kinds to the laity, or only one, the first question that arises, is it held by the Church as a matter of faith or a matter of discipline? As Mr. Campbell states the challenge, it will be seen there is no contradiction between the two councils. The Council of Constance says the laity were anciently *allowed* both kinds and the Council of Trent says they *may* commune in only one. But the idea intended to be conveyed by Mr. Campbell, as I understand it, was: that anciently it was the *practice* to receive both kinds and now it is the *practice* to receive only one.

The Church regards receiving in one or both kinds by the laity, as only matter of discipline and not *essential* to the administration of the sacrament. The command "drink ye all of it" was given to the apostles as consecrating priests and that Christ is equally present, whole and entire, in both species, and therefore equally received under both kinds.

The whole question resolves itself, as I understand it, into the doctrine of the Real Presence. If that doctrine be true, then it is clear that Christ is equally present and received under both species alike; since His blood can no more be shed, and separated from His body. In the early ages of the Church, it was most generally administered under both kinds; but even then it was frequently administered under only one kind. Tertullian, Saint Dionysius of Alexandria, Saint Cyprian, Saint Basil, Saint Chrysostom, and others, prove this to have been true. It has always, therefore, been regarded as only a matter of changeable discipline.

Many Protestants as Bishop Forbes, White and Montague, of the English Church, not only admit the fact as to the ancient practice of the church, but also acknowledge that the authority for giving under both kinds is rather from tradition then from Scripture. So also Cassander and Grotius. In the Calvinistic Synod of Poitiers, in France, held in 1550, it was declared that: "the bread of the Lord's supper ought to be administered to those who cannot drink wine." The Acts of Parliament, which established communion under both kinds, made it lawful to administer in one kind only, when required. [17]

Communion under both kinds was not introduced by Luther, but by Carlostadius, while Luther was concealed. This was in 1521. Luther, in a letter he wrote on the reformation of Carlostadius, reproaches him "with having placed Christianity in things of no account – communicating under both kinds, taking the sacrament into the hand, abolishing confession, and burning images." [18]

That the whole question, whether receiving under both kinds by the laity, be matter of faith or discipline, depends upon the truth of the doctrine of the Real Presence, seems to be clear. Thus Mr. Breckenridge says:

> We come next to consider your defense of the Roman church *for taking the cup* from the people in the Eucharist. Your first reason is that Christ is present, whole and entire, under *each* of the species of the sacrament. But the force of this depends, as you are aware, on the truth of Transubstantiation.[19]

In reference to this type of argument Bossuet remarks:

> And, indeed, if there was reason to maintain baptism without immersion, because, in rejecting it, it would follow there had been no such thing as Baptism for many ages, consequently no such thing as a church, it being impossible for the church to subsist without the substance of the Sacraments: no less impossible was it, without the substance of the Sacraments: no less impossible was it, without the substance of the Supper. The same reason, then, subsisted for maintaining communion under one kind, as for maintaining baptism by infusion; and the church, in maintaining these two practices which tradition showed equally indifferent, did nothing else but, according to custom, maintain against contentious spirits that authority, whereon the faith of the people reposed.[20]

Receiving under one or both kinds, being a matter of changeable discipline dependent upon circumstances, in the days of Saint Leo, the Manicheans were discovered by him, by their refraining from receiving the cup. As they mixed with the Catholics, and had the liberty, as all had, to receive under one or both kinds as they preferred, it was exceedingly difficult to detect them. It was for the purpose of rendering them wholly distinguishable to the people, that an express requisition was made for all to receive in both kinds. By this means the Manicheans stood manifest. To show that this discipline was not founded upon the necessity of always receiving under both kinds, Saint Gelasius grounds it in formal terms on this basis, that those who refused the wine did it through a certain superstition.[21]

The statement of Mr. Campbell that "in the time of Pope Gelasius it was pronounced to be sacrilege to deny the cup to the laity" was founded upon the state of case above stated, and is not a fair and just statement of the matter of fact. For the Manicheans to deny that the wine was the blood of Christ, was to contradict the words of Christ, "This is my blood," as always understood by the Church, and was a denial of the whole doctrine of the Real Presence. If they could deny that the wine was the blood, they could deny that the bread was the body of Christ. It was, therefore, heresy in them to refuse the wine for heretical reasons.

As to the alleged contradictions in the Councils of the Church, in reference to communion under one or both kinds, I could see none, unless Mr. Campbell had shown that *one* Council held it a matter of *faith* to receive in *both kinds*. But I could find no such proof. The Church had always held it as matter of discipline. It depends upon the doctrine of the Real Presence. If that doctrine be untrue, there would be an *error of doctrine*, but not a *contradiction*, in the Church.

Exclude the authority of the Church and of Tradition, and it would seem difficult to sustain keeping the first for the seventh day of the week, or for not enforcing the washing of feet. But it is still more difficult to find any Scriptural authority for setting aside the decree of the Council of Jerusalem. The Council commanded the Gentile brethren to "abstain from meats offered to idols, and from blood, and from things strangled…" saying "it seemed good to the Holy Ghost and to us, to lay *upon you* no greater burthen than these *necessary things*." I confess it requires more discernment than I possess to find any authority in the Scriptures for holding these explicit commands *temporary*. They are not given in that *form* – they are, in their nature, such as might well be permanent – they were put forth without limitation as to time, and they are too explicit to be misconstrued. How any Protestant can avoid them under his theory, I am wholly unable to determine.

In regard to the alleged change in the doctrine of the Church, in reference to Transubstantiation, Mr. Campbell says:

> The fourth Council of Lateran, A.D. 1215, says, with the concurrence of Pope Innocent III. that the bread and wine in the act of consecration suffer a physical change. Then we begin to read of Transubstantiation.[22] "Did the Church always maintain this doctrine?" Nay, verily, for a host of fathers, nay the whole Church, for the first four centuries, say "the change is only moral" – a sanctification, a separation to a special use. Here we might read a host of fathers, if we thought their testimony necessary.[23]

When I first read this statement, I was under the impression that Mr. Campbell had made out a plain case of contradiction, as I did not believe that he would make assertions so confidently, without being able to sustain them. In his reply, Bishop Purcell said:

> No father of the Church, however, said, that the consecration of the Eucharistic, is a mere 'separation,' or the change only a 'moral change.' I defy him to the proof.[24]

The issue was fairly joined. There was a direct affirmation on one side, and a direct denial on the other. But I never could find the proofs to which Mr. Campbell referred, either in the debate in question, or in any other work. It did seem to me that Mr. Campbell had made the strength of his assertion support the absence of his proof.

The last alleged contradiction in the faith of the Church, made by Mr. Campbell was in regard to the marriage of the clergy. He says:

> Again the second Council of Lateran, the tenth ecumenical council, forbade the marriage of clergy. For 800 years the clergy were allowed to marry. For the first 600 years one-half the canons of councils were regulating the clergy as to the affairs of matrimony and celibacy. The ancient Church had not yet learned to forbid marriage to the clergy; for Saint Paul, the clergy yet believed, "marriage was honorable in all.[25]

In reference to the celibacy of the clergy, I found that the Church never held it as a matter of faith – that she had always regarded it as a matter of discipline, resting in her discretion and dependent upon circumstances. That she held celibacy to be a more honorable state, which anyone might, or might not voluntarily enter into, at his own will and pleasure. As I understand the views of the Church, upon this subject, she holds these distinct positions:

1. That marriage was a matter under the control of each individual.

2. That it was no sin to marry, and no sin to refrain from marriage.

3. That it was more honorable to refrain from marriage, when the motive was the greater service of God.

4. That individuals, male and female, had the clear right by a vow, voluntarily made, to dedicate themselves to the entire service of God.

5. That having made this deliberate engagement, they could not afterwards violate it without committing a grievous offense, by lying unto God, and His Church.

6. That the Church has the undoubted right to select her own ministers, and to judge of their qualifications.

7. That a body of clergy, who embrace celibacy, are more able to give their entire time and thoughts to their duties, and for that reason, are more devoted, more efficient, in proportion to numbers and having no families to support, are more economical, and a less burden to the Church.[26]

8. That for these reasons, the Church prefers those who pledge themselves to celibacy; and so long as she can find a number of such, sufficient for her ministry, she has the right to accept their services, in preference to those who are married.

9. That when she does so select an individual, with the pledge and distinct understanding, that he shall remain unmarried, that he is bound,

by all the rules of Christianity, to perform his promises faithfully; and when he does not do so, she of right excludes him from her communion.

In selecting His apostles, did Christ interfere with their free agency? Did He force them to become His apostles, against their consent? Surely not. But *after* they had voluntarily and deliberately undertaken the task assigned them, and after having received our Lord's instructions personally, for more than three years, could they, or anyone or more of them, have withdrawn, without good cause, from the duties attached to the position, and not have committed a grievous sin? They could not, it would seem, violate their solemn engagement. Was it not voluntary? Was it not lawful? And was it not binding? Christ fulfilled His part faithfully. Were they not obliged, by His law, to do the same? Saint Paul was not forced to be a preacher of the gospel, but he voluntarily undertook to be one, and he said: "Woe is unto me, if I preach not the gospel."[27] There was "a necessity laid upon him."

The very same principle applies to a person who voluntarily and deliberately engages to perform the duties of a priest. The Church instructs him for years to qualify him, as Christ did His apostles, for the work. These laborious instructions are given upon the distinct engagement to enter her ministry when qualified, if still mutually satisfactory to both parties. The candidate has ample time allowed him to make a deliberate choice, and may retract, at any time, before his ordination; of all which he is fully informed. Then, after the Church has done all on her part, in good faith, shall the minister, without her consent, violate his deliberate and lawful engagement, and still retain the position? Is there any common honesty in such an act? The Church must be a very poor and contemptible institution, altogether inferior to any civil government, if she be incompetent to make a binding engagement, or when made, impotent to enforce it.

If a man voluntarily, of his own free will, enlist in the army, he is bound to serve out his time. Is not this right? If the true Church has not the right to select her own ministers, what power and privilege has she? Is she not a very weak and feeble institution, when she is compelled to submit to the opinions of outsiders who wish to force themselves into her ministry upon their own terms? The power and the right to select its own officers must belong to the true Church.

Whatever opinion may be entertained in reference to this discipline of the church, it is clear that there is no contradiction in her faith, and no violation of her infallibility. I could not find any proof that she had ever held, at any period of her existence, either the marriage or celibacy of the clergy, as a matter of faith. Nor could I find anything in the teaching of Christ, or of His apostles, that made celibacy a sin, or that made marriage obligatory upon individuals.

These several charges of a want of uniformity in the doctrines and teachings of the Catholic Church, wholly failed to satisfy my mind that they were based upon any satisfactory foundation. The great and striking fact, that the church had existed for so many centuries – had passed through so many, vicissitudes – and yet, after all, had been so uniform in teaching all that she herself ever held as essential faith, was calculated to make the most serious impression upon the mind of the patient and fair inquirer. For to my mind it did show, that she was the most successful counterfeit of the genuine coin that ever did exist, if she were not the true coin itself. It is so difficult always to wear a mask – so difficult to wear it consistently – and for so many ages. How could this be? Her history was wonderful – her success most unaccountable. In the absence of infallibility, who can account for it? What reasonable hypothesis can be given ?

I found that at present her faith was taught in every land, among every people. I found that she had the same creed for the rude Indian, the imaginative Asiatic, the dark African, the enlightened European, and the practical American. I found that between the frigid zones of the North and South, and around the whole world, she had only the same sacraments – the same priesthood – and the same liturgical services – and the same creed of faith. In short, I found her ministers in every nook and corner of the accessible earth, and her missionaries in every sea. Here in California, where the varied races of the earth do congregate, where more languages are spoken, than were found in Jerusalem on the day of Pentecost, we find men of all classes, kindreds, nations, and tongues, meet around the same altar. They partake of the same sacraments, and though unknown to each other, save by the golden chain of faith, are each and all perfectly at home, in the same house of the Lord. Is not this as it should be? Is not this union? Apostolic Union? If not, where, Oh! where can it be found?

---

[1] Book of Homilies pronounced, in the 35th of the 39 articles, "to contain goodly and wholesome doctrine, and necessary for these times." 8, p. 261, ed. *Of So for Propagating Christian Knowledge.*

[2] A. Campbell and J. Purcell, A *debate on the Roman Catholic religion. p.* 49.

[3]A. Campbell and N. Rice, *Campbell Rice Debate on the Holy Spirit*. p. 423.

[4] *Ibid.* p. 298.

[5] Conyers Middleton, A *free enquiry into the miraculous powers, which are supposed to have subsisted in the Christian Church, from the earliest ages through successive centuries, upon the authority of the primitive fathers.* (1749)

[6] Cited Milner's *End of Religious Controversy*, Let. xxii.

[7] A. Campbell and J. Purcell, *op. cit.* p. 66.

[8] *Ibid.* p. 885.

[9] *Ibid. p.* 162.

[10] Silliman Ives *Trials of a Mind in its progress to Catholicism. p. 124* Note.

[11] James Kent, *Commentaries on American Law* I, p. 280.

[12] Saint Augustine cited in *Trials of the Mind*, p. 124

[13] 1Cor 11:19

[14] Harbinger Extra, Dec. 1844, p. 616, 617.

[15] [The Vatican Council defined papal infallibility in 1869-70. Editor]

[16] A. Campbell and J. Purcell, *op. cit.* p. 179.

[17] John Hughes, *Hughes - Breckenridge controversy*. 1885 p. 351.

[18] Jacques-Benigne Bousset, *Variations of the Protestant Churches* B. ii. Sec. 8-10.

[19] John Hughes, *op. cit.* p. 402.

[20] Jacques-Benigne Bousset, *op. cit.* Bk. xv., sec. 140

[21] *Ibid.* Book xi. Sec. 12.

[22] Coun. Lat. Iv., Can. 1.

[23] A. Campbell and J. Purcell, *op. cit. p.* 179. Mr. Campbell seemed to me to make assertions without due reflection. In this extract he says: "Then (1215) we begin to read of transubstantiation." In another place he says: "In the 9th century, the doctrine of transubstantiation began to be talked of commonly," &c. (Debate C. & P., 277.) But I found this amended statement equally untrue.

[24] A. Campbell and J. Purcell, *A debate on the Roman Catholic religion. p.* 186.

[25] *Ibid.* p.179

[26] According to the statistics published in a number of the *Civilta Cattolica*, the expense of the ministry of the Established Church in England amounts to a tax of about eight shillings to each person, per annum. While in France, the

maintenance of the Catholic clergy amounts to one shilling to each inhabitant peer annum.

[27] I Cor. Ix. 16.

PART I

INDEX

THE TRUE CHURCH

The Path which Led a Protestant Lawyer to the Catholic Church

PART 2 DOCTRINE AND DISCIPLINE

LONG CONTENTS

PART 2 DOCTRINE AND DISCIPLINE

CHAPTER IV RESULTS OF THE PROTESTANT THEORY 105

CHAPTER V TRANSUBSTANTIATION . . 201

CHAPTER I

CERTAIN OBJECTIONS ANSWERED

1. Objections by Protestant controversialists

Protestant controversialists have made assertions on the grounds of logic and common sense that the Catholic Church cannot be the true church. The sincere reader will sec that these objections fail when the logic is examined closely and when the common sense is placed in a broader context. We will examine nine of these leading objections:

1. Since private interpretation in the last resort is used to select the true church it must be right for members of the Church.

2. The Roman Catholic rule cannot be put into practice.

3. As an infallible judge, the Church cannot be as lucid as the Bible.

4. Catholic theory rests on a logical vicious circle.

5. The Church cannot be a judge in her own case.

6, The Roman Church has altered, amended, and mistranslated the Bible.

7, The Roman Church is incapable of reformation.

8, Wicked persons are found in the Catholic Church.

9. Apostolic succession cannot reside in fallible bishops.

2. Private interpretation for members of the true church

The first objection I shall examine is one that is considered by Protestants to be of great importance. In the language of Mr. Breckenridge:

> If private interpretation is sufficient to explain the whole word of God, in order to find out the true church, why is it not sufficient for the rest?[1]

The same objection is made by Mr. Campbell and by all Protestant controversialists whose works I have read.[2] The objection, upon its face, appears to possess great plausibility, and much force. It has already been substantially answered in preceding pages; but as those who urge it esteem it so much, some additional considerations will be submitted.

It will be readily seen, upon reflection, that the essence of the objection is founded upon these positions:

1. That the Scriptures contain the *only* evidence of the true Church.

2. That all portions of them are equally easy of interpretation; or that those portions relating to the Church, are as difficult as any other is.

3. That an individual bears the same relation to the Church, so far as the right of private interpretation in the last resort is concerned, *before* he joins the Church, as he does *afterwards*.

Each and all of these positions must be true, or else the objection is not good. For if there is other testimony to point out the true Church, then the original inquirer does not rely solely upon his private interpretation of the Scriptures, but, in part, upon other evidence. Also, if it is true, that there are some things in Scripture hard to understand, and many things easily understood, and these hard things relate not to the Church, then it is clear, that the inquirer may well be able to construe the plain portions of the written Word. He may be competent to find the true Church – his guide – in the same way that a man of good sense can be competent to choose a lawyer, although he is not himself acquainted with all the law. Also, when a man once becomes a subject of this visible kingdom – the Church – his relation towards it may be very different; and while his privileges may be increased, his responsibilities may be also increased in a corresponding degree.

To illustrate my meaning, I will suppose an inhabitant of another country to become convinced that he is not living under a good government, and that he at once looks around the world for a government that secures the greatest amount of individual freedom, consistent with order and protection. In this search he fixes his attention upon our country. How is he to know the leading features of our government? He may take the practical operation of the government, as now existing, claiming to possess certain powers, and to act under a constitution; or he may examine the instrument itself, with or without the aid of the commentaries of our great constitutional writers and jurists and the decisions of our highest courts; or he may take all these together. But whether he use one or more of these means, is a matter entirely for his individual consideration! The government will not interfere with him. If he errs, he remains an alien, and must bear the incidents belonging to that state. The government has no jurisdiction over him. His misconstruction of the laws, leads to no breach of the peace, to no crime, and to no treason.

But suppose he becomes a citizen. His relation is entirely changed. He enjoys the privileges. But also takes upon himself the obligations incident to this new state. He can now hold office and vote at elections; but he must also fight the battles of the country, and submit implicitly to the decisions of her courts. *He no longer construes any part of the law for himself in the last resort.* He now owes a paramount duty to his voluntarily adopted country. Next to his duty to God, his highest duty is to her. He must sacrifice his life, not his soul, for his adopted country, if necessary.

Are not these plain principles applicable to the Church, and to all associations of men? All outside the Church are but aliens from that kingdom, and must suffer whatever incidents belong to that state. This kingdom is open to the oppressed of every land.

How shall the honest inquirer find out the true Church? He *must* make a choice. And there are various means, by the use of which, he may know which is the true Church:

1. He may take the testimony of history.

2. He may take the words of our Lord and the apostles.

3. He may take the doctrines of the Catholic Church and compare them with scripture.

4. He may take all these together.

History he will find in the Bible in part, and in part in the writings of other historians. He will find the Bible, especially the New Testament, to differ from most other works, and to be composed of two parts, *historical* and *doctrinal;* and he will find the former much more easily understood than the latter. Persons of the most ordinary capacity, even children, can relate *facts* most correctly, and also understand such relations. The most intelligent and the most clear witness I ever heard testify in court, was a poor girl, of the age of fourteen, who could neither read nor write. Her statements were just as clear, logical, and consistent as the simple *facts* themselves, and no cross-examination could entangle her in the least. It was the remark of Mr. Van Buren, while Attorney-General of New York, that the most competent witness he ever heard examined in court, was a colored man of very ordinary mind, who was a witness in some great criminal case in that State, in which Mr. Van Buren appeared on the part of the prosecution.

If he take the simple historical narrative of the New Testament, he will find these matters of positive fact clearly established:

1. That about eighteen hundred years ago, Christ organized a visible association of men called "The Church."

2. That all who were regarded as His subjects, became members of this Church.

3. That this institution was but one in both faith and government, though spread over most of the habitable globe in the days of the apostles.

4. That "the Lord added daily to this Church such as should be saved."

5. That there was government exercised over this Church, and a law practically administered by officers in the Church.

6. That the apostles themselves most zealously opposed all discords, schisms, and divisions, in this association.

7. That this Church was the pillar and ground of the truth.

8. That she received members, rejected heretics, and ordained ministers.

9. That, in a word, she exercised all the powers of government necessary to keep in union and existence such a kingdom.

He will find that there is not the slightest intimation given anywhere in the narrative, that this Church was temporary, or that there would be any but the one. And that while there were heretics in those days they were rejected, and that the great and overwhelming majority of all those who ever claimed to be Christians, were members of this Church.

If he will follow down the stream of history, from the days of the apostles, he will find it historically true, that this same Church continued, having the same faith, the same government, always claiming the same, always saying we teach only that which came down to us – we teach nothing new. He will find the world full of her history. The medal, the coin, the sepulchral monument, "the stone in the wall," the written history, the tradition – all cry out and attest a Church united in faith and government. These also attest a Church spread over the world – so comprising in her communion the overwhelming majority of all, in every age, who named the name of Jesus. As in the days of the apostles, so also in all subsequent periods of her history, she has expelled heretics, and when expelled regarded them as heathens and publicans. And at all periods she has continually and consistently *claimed* to be the sole true Church – one and indivisible.

If the inquirer goes beyond the simple history, and take the simplest commands, he will hear our Lord say "hear the Church," and "the gates of hell shall not prevail against her." He will hear Saint Paul telling his brethren, in the most explicit terms, that they were under government to the rulers of the Church.

If he will then take the admissions of the different rival Churches, he will find them generally agreeing that the true Church must be, as she was in the days of the apostles, visible, perpetual, always teaching, Catholic and united. True, he will find a few, who insist that there was an invisible Church; but he will see that such a Church had no powers of government, and was, in fact, a modern invention, to escape a difficulty.

Taking these admissions and the historical proofs together, and he will at once see, that the Catholic Church is the only one now existing, that can possibly fill the promises of Christ. He will see that all the Protestant sects taken together, or any smaller number of them, or each one separately, cannot find any ancestors of their own faith or government, extending back to the apostles. That is if they, or any one or more of them, did exist before the sixteenth century, then history has wholly wronged them, and neglected to record the fact. If he takes their assumed chain of succession, he will find it so minute, so obscure, so discordant, so mixed and deformed, that he is forced to come to the conclusion, that either Christianity has been a failure, or the true Church is found elsewhere.

He may take the doctrines and act of the Catholic Church, and compare them together, and with Scriptures, reason, history, and experience, and he will see their consistency, one with the other. He will see how they are intimately connected as the parts of one whole must always be in every true system. He will see how taking away one article of faith, like taking out one stone from a beautiful building, destroys the harmony, and endangers the safety, of the whole. He may examine her acts, and see if they are not consistent with the character of a true Church – her invincible firmness – her never-tiring industry – her vigilance – her fruitfulness, and her wonderful tenacity of life under the most trying circumstances.

But whether he use one or more of these means we have enumerated, is a matter for his individual consideration. He is an alien and has not yet come within the jurisdiction of the Church. He has made no engagement with her, has taken upon himself no obligations as a subject of this kingdom. If he errs in using the means placed within his reach by the Founder of the Church, he will still remain an alien. He will be the principal sufferer. His misconstructions of the law – his disregard of history – his rejection of the evidence arising from her unity and consistency – cannot injure the Church to any great extent. He is openly an alien enemy. His true character is known. He speaks only in that character. What he may say cannot so well produce divisions in the kingdom. His acts tend more to unite, than sever and divide the members of the Church.

Whether he uses one, or all of the many means at his command, to become a member of the true Church, it does not matter. Saint Clement of Alexandria says: "The way of truth is one; but other streams run into it from various quarters, as into a perennial river."[3] This is beautifully expressed. So, the truth of Christianity may be proved by a thousand converging rays of testimony: and so, the true Church can be found in many ways, all leading at last into the *one stream.*

Whenever he becomes a subject of this Kingdom, his *state*, in the contemplation of the Christian theory, is entirely changed. He now enjoys the *privileges*, but also incurs the *obligations*, incident to this new state. He can hope for, and aspire to, that peaceful heaven promised by the Founder of this Kingdom; but he must also fight the battles of the King.

When he was an alien, he was exhorted to believe, repent, and be baptized; but now he is commanded to "hear the Church," and to "obey them that have the rule over him." Whatever may be his abilities to construe the law, he cannot do it independent of the Church. She is greater than he is, great as he may be. It is not now a question of *ability* alone, but a question of *peace* – a question of *union* - a question of *success* – a question of *right.* Now that he is in the Church, were he allowed to err and remain a member, he would be like a traitor in the camp, and would be tenfold more dangerous than if he had never joined the Church. And if he has this right of private interpretation in the last resort, he cannot be expelled from the Church but in mere *form*; for, in the contemplation of such a theory, it is not an expulsion of an inferior, but a mere separation of equals.

Suppose first that it was just as easy to construe the whole law of Christ, as that portion which relates to the Church, and that an individual is just as competent to do so in the one case as in the other. Then suppose that there is no other evidence to point out the true Church but the Bible alone. Still this right of private interpretation in the last resort, could not exist in each member in the very nature of the institution itself, nor under the explicit words of Christ and His apostles.

For when a man becomes a subject of Christ's Kingdom, his obligations regard not himself *alone*. His first and highest duty is to Christ and His Church. As the *success* of this Kingdom depends essentially upon the *unity of its subjects***,** he is bound to regard that object with the greatest solicitude. For it was dearest to his Master's heart, who died, not only to save him, but also to save others, and who wishes, and has the right, to use him as an instrument to save his fellow-beings. The whole world is entitled to salvation as well as himself. He lives not for himself alone; but his highest and holiest interest, if he only knew it, consists in his faithfulness to this Church.

He is the subject of a King, who seeks universal empire over men; and success lies alone through unity of faith and effort. His Lord prayed for such unity, for the very purpose "that the world might believe." When, therefore, he is guilty of heresy, he not only commits a grievous wrong against himself, but a still more grievous wrong against the Church of Christ, and against Christ Himself. As was said before, it is not a question alone regarding *ability* of individuals to construe the code in the last resort!

If every citizen of the United States possessed the legal ability, the justice, and impartiality of Chief Justice Marshall, they never could be allowed that privilege. This right rests in the government, from the necessity and reason of the thing. And so if every member of the Church possessed the same qualifications as the ablest theologian, this right must still exist in the Church, and not in him. It has well been said: "With the talents of an angel, a man may yet be a fool."

3. The Catholic rule is impracticable

The next objection is the alleged impracticability of the Catholic rule. This objection I find made by Mr. Campbell, Mr. Breckenridge, and by all Protestants whose works I have read.

The Council of Trent, at its fourth session, decreed:

> That no one relying on his own skill, shall – in matters of faith or morals, pertaining to the edification of Christian doctrine – wresting the sacred Scriptures to his own senses, presume to interpret the said sacred Scriptures contrary to the sense which Holy Mother Church, – whose it is to judge of the true sense and interpretation of the Holy Scriptures, – hath held and doth hold; or even contrary to the unanimous consent of the Fathers.

The substance of this decree is given by Mr. Campbell, with the exception that he uses the word *manners* instead of *morals*.[4] Dr. Spring, after quoting it says:

> The scarcely less celebrated creed of Pope Pius IV, embraces the same thought, and with almost the same precision of language.[5]

In various places Mr. Campbell says:

> Our rule is the Bible alone. The Roman Catholic rule contains one hundred and thirty-five large folio volumes super-added to the Bible, and the Apocrypha.... consists of Fathers, 35 Vols.; Decretals, 8; Bulls of the Popes, 10; Decrees of Councils, 31 ; Acts of Saints, 51 – in all 135.[6]

> But the priesthood are sworn 'to interpret the Scriptures according to the unanimous consent of the Fathers'... But how can they unless they examine all these Fathers? And what living man has read these 135 folios with or without much care?... Here is a task which I say never was, or can be performed by man...[7]

> The Roman Catholic rule is exceedingly unwieldy. It requires a whole council to move it, and apply it to a simple opinion. Ours is at least portable.[8]

The first matter that arrested my attention was a misconstruction of the decree. It will be seen that the decree is negative – that no one, relying upon his own skill, shall presume to construe the Scripture contrary to the Church, or to the unanimous consent of the Fathers. If then, a member of the Church construe contrary to the Church, or to this unanimous consent, then he violates the decree, and only then. But Protestant controversialists have taken the ground, that under it, no article of faith can be defined, unless there be a unanimous consent of the Fathers in support of it. If, therefore, they say, one single Father, is found dissenting from all the others, the Church cannot define that an article of faith, without a violation of this decree.

But I must confess in all candor, I could not see whereunto this would grow. "If ninety-nine Fathers state one thing to have been the faith of the Church, and one state the contrary, and that in relation to a matter not expressly defined by the Church, and a member construe with the ninety-nine, and against the one, he is clearly not guilty of any violation of the decree. In case the Church has defined at all, then he must not contradict her decree. This is the first negative. In case she has not defined then the member must not contradict the unanimous consent of the Fathers. Both these negatives are confined to faith and morals.

If we take the decree in its strict grammatical sense, as Protestants assume to take it, it is only by a misconstruction, that they can deduce the consequences they claim to flow from it. The decree does not say, that the Church shall not define an article of faith, because a few Fathers may dissent from the overwhelming majority of all, if such a case should exist. Nor does the decree say that individuals shall not construe contrary to the sense of the few, and with the sense of the majority, of the Fathers. The decree in its terms, relates to individuals, and not to the Church.

If, on the contrary, we give the decree a more liberal construction, and say that the word "unanimous" must be controlled by the general scope and context, and is equivalent to the expression "general consent," then no such consequence would follow, as contended. In either case, nothing but a misconstruction can lead to the consequences mentioned.

In reference, then, to the 135 volumes enumerated by Mr. Campbell, and the duty of the Priesthood to interpret the Scriptures, as well as tradition, according to these, Mr. Campbell thinks there is very great difficulty, and insists that no man ever did or can read these volumes, "with or without much care." It did not seem to me to be an impossible task. Most lawyers, in the course of their practice, read more volumes than these 135. There are very few law libraries that do not contain more than this number. And why a carefully educated priest could not, in the course of a few years, read these volumes, I could not see.

It may be necessary to the Church controversialist to have read all contained in the 35 volumes of the Fathers in reference to disputed points, and also all that refers to the same matters in the Decretals, and the other volumes. However, it is not necessary for every priest to have read them all, in order to know the faith of his church, so that he may know what to teach.

It must be obvious to any man of good sense, that the larger portions of these volumes, from the nature of the case, must relate to matters once discussed, but long since defined by the Church. The decrees of the Council of Trent, for instance, embrace much the larger portion of the questions discussed in the Fathers. These decrees, with the reasons for them, make a volume about as large as the New Testament. With the aid of proper indexes, it is just as easy to find the portions applicable to any particular point, as it is for a lawyer to consult his library, often consisting of several hundred volumes. Besides, there are compilations of the principal matters contained in the Fathers. For example, there is the one of Messrs. Berrington and Kirk of three volumes, so well arranged and indexed, that in a few minutes search, all of importance relating to any particular point, now in question, can be found. These 135 volumes are intended for reference, like the numerous volumes of reports in a law library. If a student of law could be alarmed at the number of volumes in any respectable law library, he would at once conclude that to be a lawyer, was a task "which never was, or can be performed."

But to say any one who has any knowledge of method and system, and how much labor of search can be abridged by them, such an argument seems like one addressed to ignorance, and ought not to be found in the mouth of an educated man. By the aid of a beautiful arrangement, we can turn to Webster's large dictionary, and out of some thirty-five thousand words, we can select any one we wish, and find its definition, in a single moment of time.

But one reflection arises in reference to Mr. Campbell himself. In his debates and other productions, he has referred to, and quoted from, a much greater number of volumes than 135, and no one can tell from the manner in which the quotations were made, whether he has read these works or not. It would at first seem that he had. But we have a right to suppose that he has relied upon the labor of others. Now why Mr. Campbell will not allow the Catholic clergy to avail themselves of the labors of each other, when they are all authorized teachers in the same Church, and all equally responsible, it is difficult to tell.

A lawyer, with a library containing a thousand volumes, will be able, by the aid of his alphabetically arranged Digests and Indexes, to give you the authorities upon a certain point of law, in a very short time. All professional men avail themselves of the labors of each other.

When I looked into the Protestant rule, I found the case, as regarded myself, as still worse. That theory told me to trust nobody; and yet necessity, stronger than this rule, told me I must. Under the Catholic rule I was allowed to take the true construction of the entire law, written and unwritten, from the authorized teachers of the Church. The labor was thrown upon the clergy, a carefully and thoroughly educated class of men. I was allowed to have confidence in some one.

But under the Protestant theory, I was not allowed to do so, without a palpable violation of the fundamental rule itself. If I took anything upon trust, I gave up, so far, my right and duty. God had made my mind the only tribunal for the construction of His word, according to this theory. This word was originally written in a few different languages. It was my duty not to trust the judgment of any other person as to the meaning of this Word. If I took the translations of others, I departed from the theory. I knew translation must come before my private construction. It seemed that the translator had to construe both languages. And as I found so great a discrepancy in the translation, showing great ignorance or unfairness in the translator, or imperfection in the languages, or all together (and of which I was not competent to judge), I could not trust them, or any of them. Still I found that "without faith it was impossible to please God." In the Catholic version I had found, "Hail Mary full of grace," and in the Protestant, "Hail thou that art highly favored," conveying to the mind very different ideas. This is only one of many instances. Who was right? There was great error somewhere.

Mr. Campbell declared that the "faults and imperfections of the common version, were neither few nor small."[9] True, I was assured by most Protestants, that the different translations were substantially the same, in reference to all material matters. But in all the discussions I read between Catholics and Protestants, and between Protestants themselves, I found much disagreement as to the fidelity of translations, and much discussion about these differences. These parties considered them material. I could not determine whether they were correct or not, from any knowledge I had of the original languages. All I could certainly say was, that they were very different. And if I took the statements made on other occasions, that they were substantially similar, contrary to my own judgment, that they were substantially very different, I would be taking the matter on trust, just like a Catholic.

If I admitted I could find a translation that I knew was correct, it had to be construed. This, at first, would seem to be an easy task. Mr.

Campbell, Mr. Rice, Mr. Breckenridge, Dr. Spring, and others say so. Still, after all that they could say and had said, in regard to the Bible being a plain book and easily understood, I found that they were not men of plain good sense since they have differed so widely from each other. Or maybe it was the case there was more difficulty in the construction of this wonderful volume than they seemed to understand themselves.

I found Mr. Campbell (whatever might be his abstract declarations) "eternally" acting as if he did not think the Bible so plain. For he was well satisfied that he could make it plainer; and in his efforts to do this, he had written, spoken, and published matter enough to make many large volumes; not as many, however, as the 135, but certainly approaching somewhat towards the thirty-five volumes of the Fathers. All of which he thought useful to be read. As for other Protestant writers they were equally convinced, that they could improve upon the plainness of the Bible. So certain were they of that fact, that the different sects had actually drawn up written creeds, much plainer than the Bible. Mr. Rice himself stated it as a matter of fact that:

> it is impossible to know anything of a man's faith, from the mere fact of his saying that he takes the Bible alone as his infallible guide.[10]

In my reflections upon this subject, I could not but reason in this way: "This is a singular state of case; a very anomalous state of things. Christ was the most important lawgiver, and promulgated the most extensive code in the world, for it embraces more matter, and more people, than any other. Yet it is solemnly alleged by one party, that this Infinite Lawgiver made no provision for any certain and authorized translations and construction of His law. He left all in perfect chaos, if chaos can be perfect! He made each one dependent upon himself (for a supreme cannot be dependent,) and yet He placed him in such a position, that inexorable necessity would force each man to rely upon the equally uncertain and contradictory translations of different parties, or choose between them, without any guide or qualification. The sense of the most important passage might depend entirely upon the proper translation of a single word.

Was there ever so strange a system? Did a lawgiver ever promulgate a code, and organize no association to be governed by it? If he did so, did he not do a very idle thing? And if he did thus organize any association, was there ever a case where he left no tribunal to construe his law? Was there, in short, such a strange anomaly as a lawgiver ever promulgating a code of law that had no system in it? No consistency?

No efficiency? And does not this theory make Christ the weakest, the most confused and incompetent of all lawgivers? What beauty, system, harmony, unity or certainty, is there in a theory, founded and based in suspicion and distrust of everybody but yourself?

It does seem to me that the Catholic theory honors Christ as a lawgiver. The Protestant theory degrades Him, as such, below the standard of mere human legislators.

Is it true, that our Lord did organize a visible Church, and yet leave not government in it? If so, what sort of a Church then is it? A Church so poor, so little entitled to respect, that the *whole united association* is absolutely inferior to each separate individual member; so that no one is bound to obey or believe her decision just, (in the contemplation of the theory itself,) unless he, in his supreme judgment shall *first sanction it.* A theory that places the individual above the association, and yet assumes to call it a Church. Where shall we go for any parallel, or for any *imagined* practical institution, that could be a parallel to this most anomalous and contradictory theory?"

But Mr. Campbell says:

> It requires a whole council to move it (the Catholic rule) and apply it to a single opinion.... Ought there not to be a general council eternally in session?[11]

This objection, I found, upon investigation, to be based upon an erroneous conception of the practical operation of the Catholic system.

Every Catholic Priest is a subordinate organ of the Church. They are carefully educated and instructed in her doctrine. They undergo a rigid examination before they are ordained. They are immediately responsible, each to His Bishop, and each bishop to the Pope. From the decision of the parish priest, an appeal lies to the bishop, and from the bishop to the Pope. These are the ordinary organs of the Church.

In the nature of all governments over men, under any system of law practically administered, difficulties must arise, as I have elsewhere stated, in the application of its principles to new cases; and these new cases will arise, at intervals, so long as the government exists, but with diminished frequency. This must be the general rule, to which there may be exceptions, caused by particular circumstances. It may happen indeed that a great number of new questions may be raised at the same time, and that at a remote period from the origin of the government. This was the case at the Reformation.

It is obvious that when a question is once determined by the Church, that it is not necessary to call a general Council to reaffirm it. It may be advisable, in reference to particular cases, when the Council is assembled for other purposes, for the Council to do so, in terms still more explicit.

But under the Catholic theory, a general council can only be required for the purpose of applying the principles of the law to new cases which come up, and about which there may exist some doubt in the minds of some members of the college of teachers. In regard to the question determined in the Council of Jerusalem, the difference of opinion arose among the teachers – hence the necessity of that Council. The result was harmony of sentiment, and unity of effort. The object of calling general Councils is still the same.

For these reasons general councils are not called except some great question or questions require them to be convened. After the commencement of the Reformation, the Council of Trent was convoked. This Council went extensively into the various questions raised by the reformers; and the result of its labors has been to settle, so far as Catholics are concerned, all the material points involved in the controversy. Since that period no occasion has arisen that called for the convoking of a general Council, in the judgment of the Church.

As all Catholics admit that the decrees of all general Councils, with the Pope's concurrence, and also the doctrinal decrees of the Pope, approved by the Church at large, through the consent of the great majority of the bishops, are infallible, it is not necessary to call a general Council for the definition of every article of faith. It is the solemn act of the Pope, with the concurrence of the Church, that all admit to be infallible; and whether this concurrence is given in a General Council, or through the bishops dispersed, it is not *material*, as the concurrence is still given. There is still the same mind and judgment.

The reasons given by Mr. Campbell why, under the Catholic theory, a general Council should be "eternally in session," was that "every age has its errors and divisions, and every individual has his doubts."[12]

Unless these errors and divisions arise in the Church, as a matter of course she would take no cognizance of them. If they arise among Protestants, they are outside of her jurisdiction. Until her own communion is disturbed, she has no reason to act. And as to the asserted fact that "every individual has his doubts," it may be very true as regards Protestants, and may not be true as applied to Catholics. They live under precisely opposite theories. If a Catholic has any doubts, he may apply to his pastor; and from his decision he may appeal to his bishop and from him to the Pope. With the Catholic, there is a very simple and conclusive method of solving doubts, while the Protestant begins with inquiring, and ends still inquiring. I could see no more necessity for a general Council to be "eternally in session," than for the Council of Jerusalem to have been continually in session during the lives of the apostles.

An objection occurred to me as to the authority for Cardinals, Archbishops, and Metropolitans. Upon examination, I found these were bishops or priests; and that the *additional* powers conferred upon them were part and parcel of the powers belonging to the Pope.

In the Constitution of the United States it is first provided that the "executive power shall be vested in a President;" and yet, in the second section of the same article, the President "may require the opinion, in writing, of the principal officer in each of the executive departments." These "executive departments" are but part and parcel of the executive power, which is all placed in "a President." So it is in the Catholic Church. The Pope has the right to control all bishops, priests, and deacons, and he has the right, therefore, to employ the aid of particular agents for that purpose. When the duties of an executive become too arduous for him to perform alone, he has the right to employ assistants, who only act as his immediate subordinates.

The Pope, therefore, employs the aid of an Archbishop or Metropolitan, to supervise the Bishops within certain limits; and Cardinals are employed to aid him by their counsel and advice. As our President has the right to take the opinion of the heads of departments, so the Pope has the right to take the advice of all bishops, Archbishops, Metropolitans and Cardinals. The College of Cardinals is the most accessible advisory body, because many of the members reside at Rome, and are easily assembled. This right of the Pope is an incident inseparable from all executive power. No executive power over any considerable body of men could be practically exercised without it. Almost every officer under any system has the right to appoint deputies.

Mr. Campbell speaking of the Protestant rule of faith, says: "Ours is at least portable." If by this he means it is easily carried about, he is correct. But I apprehend, from the connotation in which the term is found, that he does not use it in the ordinary sense. As I understand him, he means to say that it is much easier to read and understand the Bible alone, than to understand it with the aid of these 135 volumes. In other words I understand Mr. Campbell to take the ground that other Protestants take, that it is easier to get at the correct construction of the Bible without, than with, any external exposition, aid or assistance.

If that is the meaning, then there is no real or apparent force in the argument. If we go beyond the book in any particular case, it may be advisable to read and study all the principal works of every Protestant controversy among themselves. For if the point of difference between them are of such importance as each party thinks they are, the inquirer ought to look into all with due diligence. On the other hand, if the book alone is sufficient, one cannot quite understand the utility of discussion as to the different constructions.

It must be conceded that a code of law may be too concise, or it may be too prolix. This also may be true of a discourse, or a dissertation. The true medium is difficult to attain. He who expresses the greatest number of relevant thoughts, upon a given subject, with precision and certainty, and in the fewest words, has attained the medium. Some men are beautifully brief for want of thought. Others are brief because they extract the substance, and leave out the proofs and reasons.

In regard to laws, every judge and lawyer knows that the most difficult statutes to construe are those that are the most concise, and, therefore, expressed in most general terms. Broad principles are often laid down, embracing such a wide and varied number of cases, that it becomes a very difficult matter to apply these general principles to such a multitude of individual cases. Had the statute been more full and explicit, its construction would have been easier. In short, whoever reflects upon this subject carefully and impartially I think will arrive at these conclusions, that every system of law must embrace all cases that need practical regulation, or it must be defective in permitting injustice to exist without a remedy – that this regulation can be effected in one of three ways:

1. By the adoption of a very concise code, expressed in general terms, and embracing only general principles.

2. By the adoption of a very full and minute code, dealing more in details.

3. By the adoption of a mixed code, containing general principles and also minute regulations.

In all these cases it is assumed that the codes are consistent in their principles one with another.

The mixed system is ours, both with reference to the Federal and with reference to State governments. The Constitution of the United States is a very short instrument, and can be read in half an hour. One would suppose that its construction would be very easy, if there is anything in brevity to make it so. Yet how many great men have exhausted their powers of construction upon the concise fundamental law. Has there been no difficulty in this case? Is the proper construction of that instrument most certainly attained by reading it alone? Or by taking the decisions of our Courts, the opinions of our jurists, and statesmen, together with the instrument itself?[13]

The whole question as I conceive, resolves itself into this, and this only: was Christ a lawgiver, and is there any Church? For if there be a church, there must be government in it. And if there be Government in the Church, there must, of necessity exist the executive and judicial powers. And if these powers exist in the Church, they must be supreme, and her decisions are, and of right ought to be, final and conclusive. And if her jurisdiction extend to any part of the law, it must embrace all questions arising under it that require to be determined in this mode of existence. And if these positions be true, then it is important to know what the Church has decided.

And it must be obvious that the number and character of the decisions of any tribunal must be increased by certain circumstances:

1. By the concise character of the code.

2. By the extent and variety of the subjects embraced in it.

3. By the length of its duration.

The conciseness of the New Testament has been one of the main causes of the difference among Protestants. But this conciseness occasions no difficulty under the Catholic rule. The decisions of the Church extend the general principles to all new cases as they arise. And whereas the Protestant rule leaves every difficulty without any certain remedy, the Catholic rule provides an efficient remedy for every difficulty. The most defective governments in the world are those that provide no sufficient remedy for wrongs – no corrective for errors. And in proportion as proposed remedies are inefficient, so in proportion does the government approach the most unhappy of all conditions – anarchy.

THE TRUE CHURCH

When we go from the officers of the Church to the laity, the Catholic system is far more simple, certain and practical, than the Protestant rule. The inquirer, under both rules, must first be satisfied that Christianity is true. Having reached that conclusion, under the Catholic rule, the inquirer has only two points to determine; namely:

1. Which is the true Church?

2. Is he bound to hear her?

When he has decided these, all others follow as logical consequences.

Not so with the Protestant! He must, under his rule, arrive by his individual examination at all the truths of the Scripture necessary to be believed. If it is true that the simplest historical proof will point out the true Church then a great difference between Catholic and Protestant is manifest. The Protestant travels the whole journey alone while the Catholic finds his guide, and follows her.

Every true fundamental rule must, when *once admitted*, lead to the certain solution of all difficulties. If it do not possess this efficient and operative principle, it cannot be true. Upon its face, it is defective; and, therefore, untrue. In every system of truth there are certain leading *original* principles, from which all others legitimately flow, as logical extensions. In every system of faith, the mind must *first* be omitted to the original principles; and *afterwards*, to their *legitimate extensions.*

The process of admitting persons into the Church in the days of the apostles, was based upon the Catholic rule. On the day of Pentecost, Saint Peter addressed the Jews, who themselves knew of the miracles of Christ, as he states in verse twenty-two. As to the *evidence* of Christ's divine character, he addressed a *prepared* audience. And not only so, but the stupendous miracle of the cloven tongues was visible and palpable to all.

The *quickness* of conviction, regarding any truth, depends upon both the weight and directness of the testimony. In courts of justice we see this verified continually. In some cases, the witnesses are few, and testify directly to the point. In other cases, they are numerous, and their testimony is not direct, but circumstantial, and much more *diffuse*. But by putting all the circumstantial facts together, the result is certain, and even more certain than in many cases of direct evidence; for a few witnesses may be perjured, but a number testifying to a great variety of circumstances, and all substantially consistent with each other, cannot be mistaken or false. And the facts themselves cannot lie.

It is, then not at all astonishing that on the day of Pentecost, with the precedent evidence in their minds, and the stupendous miracles then before their eyes, that multitudes should have believed in a single day, after hearing a single discourse. The testimony was not only direct, (addressed to the senses,) but of a *conclusive* character. And from what they thus saw and heard, they were compelled to arrive at these conclusions:

1. That Peter was a true witness.

2. That Christ had risen from the dead.

3. That the apostles were His agents, as they alleged.

From these conclusions, it resulted inevitably that they were bound to believe whatever the apostles taught. The miracles attested the veracity of the apostles and of Christ. Whatever they stated, as witnesses, was true. This is the reason why they at once cried out, "what shall we do?" They only asked to know their duty, as pointed out by the Lawmaker, through His agents. They were prepared to believe anything, simply upon His authority. They did not stop to inquire about the nature of baptism, and how sins were remitted in it, or about other matters, but they took all this upon the word of the Divine Legislator.

In the case of the eunuch it was the same. He inquired for a guide. Philip acted as such. The eunuch believed that Jesus was the Christ, and then submitted himself to Philip, as His authorized agent.

In these cases, the mind stood committed to two radical principles, from which everything else followed. Whatever might be taught *afterwards*. they must believe, or unsay what they had previously admitted. They were only taught those truths that *must* be believed *before* baptism; and these truths were of such a character, that all others afterwards propounded by the teaching authority must also be believed.

It is possible that Peter and Philip may have taught all the doctrines required to be believed at any time, as *all* they said is not stated. But it is far more probable, from all the circumstances related, that they did not. In that portion of Peter's discourse that is recorded, he said nothing about the resurrection from the dead, and many other doctrines. As to Philip's discourse, we know not what it contained, except that baptism, and that Jesus was the Son of God, were mentioned. But the converts, having committed themselves to the authority of the Church, were bound afterwards to receive her teaching. Consequently, Hymenius and Philetus, after being admitted into the Church, by rejecting her teaching, made shipwreck of the faith. As the cardinal principles of the system were extended to new cases by the apostles, the members of the Church were bound to believe these extensions, as well as the original principles themselves.

The real difference in the fundamental rule is this: when the inquirer receives the Catholic rule as true, his labor is at an end. He has only to follow his guide. But when he receives the Protestant rule as true, his labor is but fairly begun.

While all who admit the Catholic rule must come into the unity of the faith and the bond of peace, it is precisely different with the Protestant. The practical result has been that the Catholic rule has kept in unity the overwhelming majority of professed Christians, while the Protestant rule has severed and divided those who held it into many discordant sects. One rule must lead to unity, the other to division. It is the great beauty of the Catholic fundamental rule, that unity must follow a concession of its truth, and that division cannot exist, until this fundamental truth is denied.

4. The Church cannot be as lucid as the Bible

Another objection that I found made by all Protestant controversialists was this – to use the confident language of Mr. Breckenridge:

> But when you have got the decrees, confessions, bulls, etc., of this infallible judge, are they better or more clear than our Bible? Can your judge be more lucid than our Lord and Saviour, Jesus Christ? And after you have got these infallible judgments, do they not also need an interpreter as much as the Bible? [14]

I have already given my reasons why a lawgiver, however competent, could not make a law, in advance, as plain in each particular case, as could a judicial tribunal, possessing the same capacity, after the particular case had arisen. Were a lawyer to use such an objection in reference to the decisions of the Supreme Court of the United States upon the construction of the Constitution he would be considered as quite green; and so evident would be his verdancy, that he would be set down as knowing very little of common sense, and less of his profession.

What is very remarkable, is the fact that Mr. Breckenridge belonged to a Church that had a creed considered by her as more plain than the Bible, or else there was no sense in making it. If the creed could not give a more definite and certain exposition of the faith of Presbyterians than the Bible, surely better not refine upon that which is already as plain as possible. Conceding the plainness of the Bible, it is exceedingly difficult to put the two positions together, except upon the ground that the creed and the Bible, though both equally plain, expressed very different things.

"But men have misconstrued the language of the Bible to such an extent," Mr. Breckenridge might well reply, (and as Mr. Rice assumed in substance,) "that it becomes indispensable to use *other* language to make ourselves understood." True. And this reason applies as well to the Catholic Church as to any other; and therefore, makes her definitions not only *necessary*, but practically *efficient*, in giving a clear idea of her faith. From this I conclude, that however plain we may take the Bible to be, it still can be misconstrued; and when so misconstrued, a judicial decision upon this misconstruction can make the Bible *still plainer*, in reference to that particular case. And if the Catholic idea be correct, that the Bible contains many things easy and some things hard to be understood, then there is still more reason and necessity for these definitions.

The fact is palpable that all parties understand that the Catholic Church puts a very different construction upon the Scriptures from that of Protestants. Protestants also understand the differences between themselves, while they do not find the Bible so clear as their creeds. Somehow or other, all parties have managed to make themselves understood, in most cases at least; while they have wholly disagreed as to the meaning of the Bible. Luther had no difficulty in understanding the Pope, when the latter condemned his propositions.

It is true that decrees and bulls need construction; but, being decisions upon particular points after they arise, and made with a single eye to them, they are, as a general thing, as easily understood as the decrees of the Council of Jerusalem. And when there is any difficulty in any case, there is always a living, speaking, and accessible tribunal to explain these decrees, until they are understood. Decisions of courts are sometimes misconstrued. In such cases the court can set the matter right. The Church is always as able to construe her decrees as she is to make them. Her living organs have always this right. In the very few cases where any difficulty occurs among Catholics, it is easily adjusted.

5. The vicious circle

I come now to examine an objection made originally, as Dr. Milner says, by Dr. Stillingfleet, and repeated in all the Protestant works I have read. It is so much esteemed by Protestant writers, that Dr. Watts, in his treatise on logic, thus states it:

> A vicious circle is when two propositions, equally uncertain, are used to prove each other. Thus Papists prove the authority of the Scriptures by the infallibility of their church, and then prove the infallibility of their church from the authority of the Scriptures.

Some illustrate this definition by saying, "this is like John giving a character to Thomas, and Thomas a character to John." When I first read this position, it seemed to strike me as expressed with the smoothness and sententious brevity of a mere catch. My subsequent reflections satisfied me that it was so. As the objection is so much relied upon, it will require more examination.

The essence of this objection regards the competency of witnesses, and not propositions of logic! Conceding for the sake of argument only, the facts are, that Christ did create an infallible Church, and did commit His Word to her keeping, then this objection distinctly takes the ground that she cannot prove by her testimony the authenticity and inspiration of the Scriptures. Although she is made the special depositary and guardian of the Word she may not testify to either of the facts. On the other hand, if she were to do this then she excludes herself from all evidence contained in the Word in favor of her claims to infallibility. This position certainly places the Church in a predicament. The proposition, if true, at once sweeps her from existence.

If she should refuse to give her testimony, she would be at once told that she could not be the true Church. "The reason why you refuse to testify is evident. You do not *know* the facts. You did not exist when they occurred. You are too young. You cannot possibly be the true Church. You are a contumacious witness, and the true Church cannot be such. Even according to your own theory, you knew the truth, and have not the courage to do your duty. Therefore you cannot be the true Church."

She did know the facts, because she lived when they took place. Christ Himself was the Founder of the true Church, and committed His law to her keeping for the very reason, He would not commit it to aliens and strangers. As He committed it to her, He endorsed her credibility, and imposed upon her the duty of testifying, because she *alone* knew the facts, and could testify as to them.

But if the Church testify, then she is in no better position, because she is at once met in this way: "You cannot use this Word to prove that you are the true Church, because *you* have proven its authenticity and inspiration. Therefore, as you cannot use the Word to sustain *your* claims, and as we reject all *other* testimony, it rather occurs to us that we *have you* silenced."

Certainly this arbitrary rule for the exclusion of testimony does overwhelm the true Church, wherever that Church may be found. She cannot use the Scriptures *without proof*; and when *she* proves them, *she* is not allowed to use them. And to find adequate proof outside the Church of Scriptures *committed alone to her*, is a difficulty equally great. Turn any way she will, she is met by one or the other horn of this dilemma.

The essence of the objection consists in the rejection of testimony however credible and numerous the witnesses, *simply* upon the ground that it is mutual. Therefore, if John give Thomas, and he give John, a good character, their testimony must be rejected, though they both, being good men, did swear the truth. And if John the Baptist gave testimony of Christ, and Christ of him, their testimony must be excluded, because they both gave each other good characters. If I have two good honest neighbors, who give each other good characters, because they could not do otherwise and tell the truth, I must discard their statements as false, simply because two good men happen to know each other, and tell the truth accordingly.

Had Mr. Starkie or Mr. Greenleaf, in their profound treatises upon the law of evidence, or if our courts of justice had laid down a rule so arbitrary and sweeping, regarding the competency of witnesses, the consequences of such a rule would be very speedily tested.

Under it two good men never could testify for each other, although the knowledge of the facts rested alone with them. The *mere fact* that two good men give each other good reputations is not the slightest evidence to show that the testimony is false. And the fact that two men testify for each other, in different cases, in reference to different matters, is no evidence that the witnesses are unworthy of credit. To discredit the witnesses, you must show a fraudulent combination to testify for each other. The proof of this when made out from the admissions, conduct, and character of the witnesses, will destroy their testimony. But if the witnesses be otherwise worthy of belief, the circumstances of their mutually testifying for each other will not destroy their testimony.

When the apostles, by their own testimony, proved the miracles and resurrection of Christ, and then, by His declarations, proved the truth of the religion they preached, did this destroy their testimony? Surely not. All depended upon the credibility of the witnesses.

Weak as this objection appeared to me, when applied to single witnesses, it was still weaker when applied to associated bodies of men. Who keeps the records of a nation but the government of that nation? To whom will you apply for correct copies of our Constitution, but to our own government?[15] Would you seek them among the enemies of the country?

When you want authentic copies of the decisions of the Supreme Court, will you apply to strangers, or to the clerk who keeps the records of the Court? If you wish to get at the true decision of a Court, will you not go to its own records, kept by itself? And why can we trust Courts, not only to keep their own records, but to certify that they are true, and have been faithfully kept?

The reason why all associated bodies of men, as well as all courts and legislative bodies, must be trusted, is because they have the knowledge of the facts – have no interest to distort them, for they are presumed to act conscientiously, and are composed of so many different individuals cognizant of the same facts, and belonging to the same body, that there is a security against mistake and fraud not always found in the case of single persons. Until all the members of such an association (knowing the facts) can be either corrupted or deceived a falsehood cannot be put upon the record and kept there. We are compelled to place confidence somewhere; and if we cannot trust associated bodies of men, public tribunals, and legislative bodies, to keep their own records, and prove their genuineness, whom can we trust? If there be any better security or testimony, I cannot conceive where it can be found among men. Until some wise person shall suggest better evidence, we must follow that sensible rule of law, and take the best the case allows.

So it is with the Church. Christ committed His law to her. He would hardly have committed it to His enemies, to aliens, and strangers. This would have been a very idle act. The law, then, being committed to the Church, to whom can we apply for correct copies of the law but to her?

She has the custody, she knows the facts. Shall we go to enemies of the Church for authentic copies of a law they always hated and opposed? Shall we ask them to prove facts of which they know nothing, and whose existence they deny? Who can be a credible and able witness of the facts but the party who knows them?

If we can trust civil governments, legislative bodies, and judicial tribunals, why can we not trust the institution of Christ? Did He do His work so badly that His Church is the poorest, and most unreliable of all institutions? Surely, if Christ committed His word to the Church, by that very act, He did endorse her veracity, and we are bound to believe her. It was one of the weightiest reasons for organizing a visible and infallible Church, that our Lord might commit His law to her keeping.

Is there the slightest reason for invalidating her testimony, because in the Written Word we find a portion of the proofs that she is the infallible Church? Where should we find those proofs, but in part, in this Word? Suppose the proposition to be true, for the sake of the argument only, that Christ did organize an infallible Church, and that He did commit His law to her keeping, to whom can we apply but to her? She alone had the custody – she alone knows the facts. If we must get the Scriptures from the true Church (and where else in God's name, can we expect to find them?) shall we reject all the testimony of these Scriptures as to the true Church? The moment we concede that an infallible Church is possible, we cannot, by an arbitrary rule of false logic, reject proper testimony to prove the fact. How then can true copies of the Scriptures be proven, and the true Church ascertained, but by the very method adopted by the Catholic Church? Whether she be the true Church or not, must not the true Church act as she does? Could the true Church do otherwise? And until some wise wit will show us a more able and reliable witness than the true Church of Christ, as to facts peculiarly within her own knowledge, we must, with all due deference, believe her.

I could not see how the Protestant theory avoided the supposed difficulty of the vicious circle, when they wished to prove the authenticity of the Scriptures, and which was the true Church, or any other fact relating to the Church. Though Dr. Spring used this vicious circle as an argument against the Catholic Church, he very unwittingly made admissions that completely neutralized his argument. He first tells us, in speaking of the New Testament Scriptures that copies of them were circulated and compared with the originals, until the evidence was satisfactory to the churches that they were both authentic and genuine."[16]

All these acts were done in the churches, the sufficiency of the evidence was decided by them, and by whom then can we prove the authenticity and genuineness of those copies but by the Church? In reference to the origin of the Scriptures he says:

> "The divine origin of the sacred books is not proved simply, nor principally, from historical testimony. Historical testimony has its place, and it is no unimportant place in the argument."[17]

The learned divine having referred us to the Church for proof of the divine origin of the sacred books, so far as the important part of historical testimony is concerned, how does he propose to ascertain this Church, *his witness* to prove the authenticity and genuineness of these Scriptures? He insists it must be proved by the Scriptures alone.

It will be readily seen that this arbitrary rule is based essentially upon the same ground as those of David Hume and Dr. Paley, for the exclusion of the *only* witnesses who could, *from their position, know the facts.* The Infidel and Protestant positions are in substance precisely the same, all having in view the very same end; namely, the suppression of testimony. They have both sought most diligently for some arbitrary and proscriptive rule, by which they could effectually close the mouths of all witnesses who testify to facts against their particular views.

6. Can the Catholic Church decide her own cases?

Another objection is made, based essentially upon a gross misapplication of a principle only applicable to individuals, and not to associations of men. I will state it in the language of Mr. Campbell, my learned opponent, says:

> In all monarchies, save that of Rome and Mahomet, a judge is not constitutionally a judge of his own case. But the Roman judge of controversy is the whole church, and her councils affirm with him. The whole church judging them between what parties? Herself and the heretics!! What a righteous, and infallible, and republican judge, is the supreme judge of controversy in the Catholic Church! The controversy is between two parties – the Church or the clergy on one side, and the heretics or the reformers on the other, as they may happen to be called; say the church and heretics. And who is umpire and who is supreme judge of both? One of the parties, indeed, the church herself! This is the archetype – the beau ideal of civil liberty, and republican government in the Supreme Roman hierarchy.[18]

This objection was originally made by the early reformers, and also by the Remonstrants at the Synod of Dort. It was made by Mr. Breckenridge.[19] I find it also in most Protestant controversialists.

From the very emphatic and pointed language of Mr. Campbell, and the extreme emphasis he puts upon the case, he must have considered it a most unheard of usurpation for a state, sovereignty, or church, to judge in her own case.

It is true, that the laws of all civilized countries lay down the principles, that a *man* cannot be a judge in his own case. But from all my reading, and from all my intercourse with intelligent men, I never knew that this principle, intended only for individuals, could be applied to states, or churches, or to any other associated bodies of men, until I read Mr. Campbell. A father, by the laws of all countries, is allowed to decide between himself and his child, as to any disobedience of his commands. And a State, Church, or association, bears the same relation to those under its jurisdiction. The right to decide its own cases, I had always supposed, was an attribute of supremacy, inherent in the very nature of every society. Every criminal offence is committed against the peace and dignity of the State – is prosecuted in her name – is determined by courts of her own creation, and composed by judges appointed and paid by herself, and who act only as her agents. And yet is this tyranny?

Because an individual, when he has an adverse interest against another, is not allowed to decide in his own case, is there the semblance of reason to say, that the State is not an impartial judge in her own cases? What interest has the State in convicting an innocent man? Is she not the equal protector of all? Can she ask anything but what is just? Is it not derogatory to her dignity, and to the people whom she governs for her to oppress the poorest or meanest of her citizens? It certainly is, in the contemplation of the theory whereon all government is based. As a father is compelled in justice to his family, to inflict punishment, so, the State is compelled to execute justice upon individuals.

Is it not so with the Church? And is it not so in all associations of men? What interest has the Church in unjustly expelling a member?

She does expel members for just cause, but even then, *with great reluctance*. If there be any sincerity in the church, (and how can she exist without it?) she must desire to increase her fold. Nothing but a sacred regard to principle can induce her to expel members. She is bound by every sacred obligation to keep the faith pure. The spread of impure principles is no object with her. The preservation of peace within her own flock is her duty. She would be recreant to her mighty trust if she did not do it. That duty is to do equal and exact justice to the faith, and to each member. She stands impartial. While it is her wish to save the faith from contamination, it is equally her wish to save souls.

What interest had Saint Paul in delivering Hymeneus and Alexander over to Satan, that made him a partial judge? And when Titus was commanded by him to reject heretics, was Titus a partial judge? As heretics *must be expelled*, I should really like to know where we are to go for a tribunal. Shall the Church call in strangers and aliens, to try *her own children*? Was such a thing ever done? Shall she call in *her* enemies? If not, whom shall she call in? Would not such a system of church government be unheard of and impracticable? It would certainly be very troublesome to the *outside* world, who would be called on to try cases very often.

And what sort of a true Church would that be, that was so more defective than the constitution of any civil state. A church that possessed so little dignity and impartiality – was entitled to so little respect – was so feeble that there were “none so poor to do her reverence” – so that she must depend upon aliens, strangers, and heretics to determine her own faith – to decide for her own children? I cannot, I must confess, form a conception of such a Church, any more than I could of a sovereignty, calling in the citizens or subjects of other States to judge her own people.

I could find no Protestant sect that did not, at least in form, act upon this same condemned principle. The Synod of Dort took the responsibility to try to excommunicate the Remonstrants, against their protest. So, the Methodists, Presbyterians, Baptists, and all others, so far as they pretend to exercise governmental power at all, even in mere form, assume and act upon this principle, and never call for outside help.

Even in Mr. Campbell's church, it was so. For each individual church, “with its bishops and deacons, is the highest tribunal on earth to which an individual Christian can appeal; that whosoever will not hear it, has no other tribunal to which he can look for redress." "We know whom to exclude.” “Such a one has denied the faith, and we reject him.”[20] This looks very much I must say, exactly like trying its own cases by each individual church.

I cannot conceive of a true Church, or even one *claiming* to be such, that would consider itself so poor, weak and ignorant, as to call in outsiders, to ascertain *its own faith*. It would be a most exquisite true Church! And in considering these last two objections, I was often reminded of William Law's answer to Bishop Hoadly's sermon: "Your Lordship tells Dr. Snape, that he sayeth and unsayeth, to the great diversion of the Roman Catholics."

7. Has the Catholic Church mutilated the Scriptures?

Among the charges made by Dr. Spring is one, which, if true, destroys her character as a trustworthy guardian of Scripture, and as a credible witness. He says:

> The Romanists have altered and amended, and so mistranslated the Bible, as to render it confirmable to their own standard.[21]

This charge I was wholly incompetent to determine myself. It was of a character so serious, that a fair-minded man would not lightly make it; and it alleged the existence of a crime, that required an overwhelming amount of turpitude to commit.

The learned divine made certain remarks afterwards, that left, in my mind, no doubt of his mistake. These considerations are aside from the wholesale enormity of the alleged crime, the extreme difficulty of committing it with any success, dispersed as copies of the Scriptures were over the world, and based as such a charge was upon the supposition of an entire apostasy in faith, honor, and integrity on the part of the Church. After making the above charge, he asserted that Catholics refused to disseminate their own version, and then goes on to ask:

> If they are willing that their *own copy* of the scriptures should be fully circulated among their own population, will they tell us so? We ask them if they will throw no obstacle in the way of disseminating their own version, without note or comment?[22]

I must confess, I could not well put these different positions together. I could not well understand why the learned Divine should wish to circulate, even among Catholics, a spurious version of the Scriptures. A version he alleged to be, "*altered and amended, and so mistranslated as to render it conformable to their own standards.*" He had spoken of the Roman Church in such strong terms of condemnation, calling her doctrines of "Transubstantiation, the Mass, Penance, Extreme Unction, Matrimony, Invocation of Saints, use of images," &c., "disgusting" and without "foundation in Scripture." Then having charged that Church with "*altering and amending and so mistranslated*" the Bible as to render it conformable to their own standard;" and yet after all of this, to desire the privilege of circulating this version, among deluded Catholics still more establishing them in their belief of those disgusting and unfounded tenets of their Church, is what I could not so well comprehend. There seemed to be a 'mighty screw loose' somewhere, in the several discordant and contradictory charges of the learned Divine.[23]

But in the course of my investigations I found, that before the art of printing was discovered, all copies of every book had to be the labor of the pen; and that in transcribing, it was alleged, some errors had been committed in some of the copies, by the transcribers. These errors Catholics insisted were not generally of importance, and the means of their correction existed in other manuscripts found in possession of the Church itself. As the labor of copying the Bible was so great, as to take an expert penman about one whole year's time, occasional errors could not be avoided. But to charge the Church with a deliberate and abandoned design of changing the sacred volume for the purpose, and with the intent of sustaining her own doctrines, was certainly a very harsh accusation. Such a charge ought to be sustained by the most ample proof, before it should be believed; and if not so proven must react upon those who recklessly make it.

8. The Church is incapable of reformation

I found it also objected to the Catholic Church, that she was incapable of reformation. In the language of Mr. Breckenridge:

> The very assumption of infallibility, while persisted in, renders all essential reform inconsistent and absurd; unnecessary and impossible. Hence the corruptions of the church of Rome in doctrine, morals and essential worship, have been perpetuated from age to age.[24]

This objection is also made by Mr. Campbell, and by most Protestant writers. It seems to be considered by them generally, as a very strong argument.

It is very natural that Protestants and Catholics should differ about the character of the true church. Their fundamental rules lead to very different results. While the Catholic rule makes the Church always the same, as Mr. Breckenridge declares. "unreformed and unreformable both now and forever," The Protestant rule, on the contrary, makes her the precise opposite, 'reformed and reformable,' "both now and forever."

One begins and ends with a fixedness and certainty – the other begins and ends with inquiry and doubt.

I must confess that I love permanency and stability in all institutions. I never found truth to waver. I found change marked upon the face of error, but I never found it labeled upon the brow of truth. Before I became a Catholic, and before I had made any investigation into the truth of that system I remember to have been told, in substance, by an eminent Protestant, that he thought the stability of the Roman Catholic Church, was her most admirable feature. It struck me, at the time, as one of the most sensible positions I had heard. It was evidently based upon sound sense, and pure philosophy.

In my after investigations, among the truths I thought I could find in the New Testament was the explicit fact that the true Church was not to change. I could not conceive of a changeable Church, and have any confidence in the promises of Christ. Besides, it did seem to me as just to mankind, that the same true Church, "unreformed and unreformable both now and forever," should exist in every age, that all might enjoy the same opportunities for heaven. I could not see any object in the organization of a reformable church. It could guide no one.

"It leads to bewilder, and dazzles the blind"

We often hear men speak of making a virtue of necessity. And it did seem to me that this objection against the stability of the Catholic Church, and, by consequence, holding *reformability* in the true Church, *as a virtue*, was based upon that ground. The Protestant principle had led to so many alleged reforms, and there were still so many in prospect; and as often as one alleged reformation was made, another was needed, that this inevitable necessity, under the rule, was at least esteemed as a virtue in the theory of a Christian Church – a Church alleged to have been organized by Christ. It seemed to me there ought to be, at least, one immutable institution in the world—some stable system by which men could be guided,

"Hence forward and forever."

While all human systems, from the limited capacity of their founders, and the changing circumstances of the world, would necessarily be defective, and, therefore, perishable, it would seem that a system founded by Christ should be *stable* for the very opposite reason.

But while I could well understand the entire truth of the position, that all reforms, under the Catholic theory, become impossible in reference to faith and morals, there was a difficulty arose in my mind, as to how these alleged errors and corruptions, in faith and morals, got into the Church *originally*. If they did get into the Church in violation of her established rule, they could certainly get out again in the same way. The fact that these alleged errors "have been perpetuated from age to age," of itself speaks volumes in her favor. It proves the inflexibility and integrity of the Church. It shows her vigilance – her perseverance – and her invincible firmness. And the very principle that makes her perpetuate these alleged errors, would have make her reject them at the beginning.

Whatever system Christ did establish He intended it to last through all coming time. It was not designed to meet the whims of men – the prevailing temper of the times – or to excuse the errors of heretics. Christ being infinite, the map of the future lay before Him, as evident as that of the past; and He adopted a system applicable to all times, all places, and all persons, and yet inflexible and unchangeable. His system when extended through all future ages, and legitimately carried out, would save more men in the end, than an uncertain, flexible, and changeable theory, which, upon its very face, was suspicious, from the fact, that it claimed nothing, and asked for no respect. If Christ organized any Church, no man has any right to set up another. If he does so, his act is void!

When we reflect upon the fact, expressly declared by our Lord, and shown in all the Epistles, and admitted by Protestants and proved by common sense, that the *success* of His system depends upon the unity of His followers. Furthermore, all Christians did join this one Church in the days of the apostles, so that we can then see the great *end* Christ had in view in organizing *one visible church*. If the success of His system had not required the united faith and efforts of His followers, there would have been no reason for the existence of this one Kingdom. The Christian army is like any other army. Its success upon the field of battle depends upon its unity. It must act like one man, ready, able and willing to face a foe from any quarter, at any moment.

Take then the two theories, and extend them through all time, and by the legitimate and practical operation of which, will you save most men in the end? If one loses more than the other in the aggregate, it does not matter to the Lawgiver, when or where, or here or there. It is the theory of error still. Because Christ knew that the success of His system depended upon the unity of His followers, He organized His Church, and gave it most magnificent promises of protection; and imposed upon men the corresponding duty to hear this Church, and of becoming members of this one fold. And having this glorious end in view was it not just as reasonable that He should require all men to hear this Church, and believe in this Church, as to believe any other truth He proposed?

Is it not as easy, if men are properly disposed, to join the true, as a false Church? And is it not one of the greatest obligations imposed upon men by Christ, that they should regard the success of His kingdom, as they regard the King Himself? Christ has promised great rewards for our limited services. But limited as they are, they must be performed. We must labor for Him and in the *way* He has appointed. The salvation of others must be as dear to us as it is dear to Him.

"He sees with equal eye as God of all."

So far as in us lies, we should imitate Him in His expanded views. We should take in all times, all races, and all countries. Local and temporary views are not found in world-wide Christianity. The poorest Indian wanderer, houseless and homeless, ignorant and rude, has a soul immortal, and as bright and beautiful, in the impartial eye of heaven, as the crowned and jeweled monarch on his throne.

I must say that I love a Church that claims to be the sole true Church. She acts like the true Church. It is the kind of Church we read of. She, at least, makes a consistent, rational, and Scriptural case, in her declaration. Upon the face of the papers, she makes out a good showing; not a wild and incoherent, mixed and multifarious claim, that contains so many inconsistencies, that new ones start up in every line. But when a Church comes to me and says: "I glory in having reformed my creed, and in being always reformable;" I cannot but say: "You will, perhaps, always need it."

Constitutional infirmities are never cured. They 'lead but to the grave.' I can well understand how the members of the true church could reform themselves in their own conduct. But how the work of our Lord – the Church herself – could be reformed, I cannot conceive. And I must ask, Who are you? When did you take your rise? When and where did you find the theory of a *reformable true Church?* You claim no infallibility, for, manifestly, you have none. You claim no certain competency to guide any one to glory, for your skill consists in making alleged reformations in the work of Christ. You claim no rest, for a reformable Church is never at rest, but always inquiring after new reformations. You claim no respect, either because you are entitled to none, or because you are too modest to claim that which is your right. This excessive modesty may be tolerable in individuals, but certainly is intolerable in the true Church.

"Will you not always need reforming, until you cease to be reformable? And can that ever be, under your theory? And if so, when will that period arrive? Can I possibly live that long? And if I could, what am I to do in the mean time? Must I be still inquiring? Must I be still left in painful uncertainty,

'And hungry hopes regale the while,
On the spare diet of a smile?'

"I know you are liberal. You admit salvation can be found in a great variety of Churches. But is it, in fact and truth, salvation? Is it that priceless jewel? Are you sure of it? From the very fact that you are so willing to compromise, and admit that salvation can be found even in the alleged Church of Anti-Christ, I fear your principles are too liberal to be true.

"I believe in truth. I am content to find it. I think it the best mercy – the best humanity – the best sense – the best logic – and it is certainly the safest. I have known many men set up false claims to property, and I never knew one yet, who was conscious of the fact, but was willing to *compromise*. He could lose nothing, and was certain to gain something. The terms were not very material. He was always liberal. Like the woman that falsely claimed the child before King Solomon, he was always ready, able and willing to 'divide it.' But not so with the true owner – the man conscious of his rights. It was matter of principle with him. He always said 'all or none' – 'My God and my right.'

"It seems it ought to be so with the true Church. She ought to listen to no one but her Master. Let her be as inflexible, stubborn, and intolerant as fact and truth always are. Is she not the more beautiful? – the more lovely? the more merciful? Is there any mercy but in the truth? any charity but in the fact?

"You may possibly be in the right, but my mind is so constituted as not to perceive it. Your theory is certainly very flattering. It raises my individual mind above yourself. But I am after salvation – not flattery. If I were not to be judged hereafter by a severe judge, who knows his own rights -- has the ability to protect them – and does not deal in flattery, that

'Medium of a knavish trade'

then I would like your system well. But I have my fears that it will not do. I can have no confidence in a Church that has none in herself – that cannot assure me of anything, because, *confessedly, she does not know.*

"It does not seem to have been so with the old Church. She possessed not that infirmity, but lifted her mighty head above the shifting storms below. Like a cloud-capped mountain peak, she aspired to the skies. Her claims were as manifest as the snow-clad Sierras. And like the eternal hills, she stood firm and high. And while she held up truth to the world, she never stooped to flatter. I would like to find that Church that has actually 'seen the Lord,' and for that reason has not been reformed, and cannot be reformed; *because she was so constituted in the beginning as never to need it."*

If we were to admit that salvation may be found in many different churches, under the reformable-true-church theory, where shall we fix the limits? Faith must have some determinate limits. If you adopt the theory of more than one Church, where will you stop? And wherever you do stop, are your limits more intelligible – more plain – more just – more certain than the limits of the one-unreformable-Church theory? Are they more charitable or more consistent? You must lay down some sensible rule, some fixed limits, or your theory will not have even the shadow of system in it. It will depend upon the sliding scale of the times. And would that be Christianity? Would such a theory save souls?

This difficulty has been great with Protestants – whatever limits they adopted in one age needed extension in the next. In the days of Luther, he and the Lutherans held the Sacramentarians as heretics. The Calvinists, at the Synod of Dort, as also those of France, held the Remonstrants as heretics. But in process of time these limits were extended. The Socinians, so much abhorred at the beginning, have grown into favor. The Arminians have also ceased, with the Calvinists, to be considered outside the pale of salvation. The tendency is now to take in every sect of every kind. The limits will then extend, as they have extended, with the increase of sects. Matters of faith become of no importance. Indifference inevitably succeeds. The certain result of such a theory is, that men cease to regard religion as of supreme importance, until at last they have no faith

"For which they bear to live or dare to die."

9. Wicked persons are found in the Catholic Church

One of the charges made by Mr. Campbell against the Catholic Church was, that wicked persons were sometimes members of her communion. He quotes this sentence from Bellarmine:

> Wicked men, infidels, and reprobates, remaining in the public profession of the Roman Church, are true members of the body of Christ.

He then quotes from the notes of the Rheimish Testament:

> Every branch in me.... Christ hath branches in his body mystical that be fruitless; therefore, ill livers also may be members of Christ's church.

This charge does not allege that the Church neglects to teach the faith, and to urge it continually upon all its members. It charges that she is too lax in her discipline, and does not excommunicate persons as readily as Protestants do for alleged errors on practice.

It must be manifest that no Church can certainly know who are at heart good, and who are evil. No being but God, "whose eye is on the heart," can determine this, question. In a visible Church, there must and will be members who are unworthy, and the Church cannot be held responsible for their individual vices. If we make the true visible Church responsible for the acts of wicked members, we place her safety and existence entirely at the mercy of her enemies, who have only to join and then to ruin her. Every member of the Church, from the most elevated and upright down to the most unworthy is a sinner, to a greater or less extent. We are all sinners.

> If we say we have no sin, we deceive ourselves, and the truth is not in us. If we say we have not sinned, we make him a liar, and his word is not in us. If we confess our sins, he is faithful and just to forgive us our sins, and to cleanse us from all unrighteousness.[25]

Saint Paul says of himself:

> But I keep under my body, and bring it into subjection, lest that by any means, when I have preached unto others, I myself should be a castaway.[26]

As all members are sinners, and only differ in degree, the question only regards the *degree* of misconduct that shall cut of a man from the Church, and what time shall be allowed him for repentance.

When Peter asked his Master how often he should forgive his brother, Jesus said to him, "I do not say to you seven times, but seventy times seven."[27] And again our Blessed Lord declares:

> Take heed to yourselves; if your brother sins, rebuke him, and if he repents, forgive him; and if he sins against you seven times in the day, and turns to you seven times, and says, 'I repent,' you must forgive him. [28]

This merciful rule was laid down by our Lord, Who knew full well the infirmity of human nature, and the frailty of man. And we find in His own blessed apostles, the full proof of how great this infirmity is. We hear the fervent and devoted Paul say of himself, "I am carnal, sold under sin.... For the good that I would do, I do not; but the evil which I would not, that I do." If then my brother trespass against me seven times in a day, and seven times in a day return and say, "I repent," I must forgive him. And I must do this upon his saying "I repent." I cannot judge his heart – I can know what he says. What then can the true Church do, but follow the merciful commands of her Master? She cannot make a new law. She must forgive as she has been commanded. If then a member returns and says, "I repent," the Church can only forgive him.

When I came to examine into this subject, I found that by the discipline of the Church, every member was required to confess his sins, and receive the sacrament of the Eucharist at least once a year. If he neglects this duty, when it is within his power, he commits a grave sin. If then he complies with this duty, how can the Church refuse him her fellowship? She allows him a certain period for repentance and confession. If he obeys, she must forgive. If he disobeys, he is not excluded from the privilege of repentance. Nor is he excluded from assisting in the celebration of her festivals, nor from attending her worship. All persons have this privilege. She knows, that many a wanderer has been called home by kindness. And while she urges all to the strictest obedience, and reproves all for their sins without distinction of condition, and holds up before their eyes the fatal consequences of every sin, she at the same time remembers, that she is bound by the command of her Master to forgive seventy times seven, if her children return and repent. How many by this merciful rule of our Lord, have been finally saved!

There is a marked distinction between the body and soul of the Church. All who are baptized, profess the true faith, assist at the same religious services, and comply with the rules of the Church, belong to the body of the Church, and are numbered among her children. But to faith and exterior communion, must be added hope and charity and the grace of God that we may belong to the soul of the Church. These two classes God alone can separate. The Church can determine as to what is faith, what is heresy, and while it is her duty to teach all the truth, she cannot judge the inward man. As Bishop Purcell beautifully expresses it:

> When Christ empowered the Church to throw her nets into the sea of human life, as the apostles did into the lake, she gathered into it fishes both good and bad, when the nets are hauled ashore, the good fish will be selected and the bad thrown back into the sea. So will it be at the end of the world. The angels of God will come forth and select the elect from the reprobate – they will gather the wheat into the garner, but the tares they will burn with unquenchable fire…. Hence as long as one of her members disqualifies not himself for the communion of the faithful by flagrant impiety, notorious depravity, or scandalous excess, she rejects him not. But like that charity of which Saint Paul speaks, "is patient, is kind, thinketh no evil, rejoiceth not in iniquity, but rejoiceth with truth, believeth all things, hopeth all things, endureth all things, with modesty admonishing men, if peradventure God may give them repentance."[29]

There is such a thing as being too strict. We see it exhibited in the conduct of the Pharisees. Christ was blamed because he ate with publicans and sinners, and because he was their friend. His disciples were blamed for eating as they went through the fields on the Sabbath day.

In the history of the Church subsequent to the days of the apostles, we find the same excessive strictness generally among heretics. The Novatians were condemned for their excessive severity. They would admit of no repentance – of no return to the Church. The Manicheans also claimed the most extraordinary piety, while teaching the most ruinous doctrines. The Vaudois also required their members to be poor and illiterate, making poverty a requisite instead of a perfection, as Christ had done. And if we look into the history of the different sects of condemned heretics, we shall find the greater portion of them always claiming the most rigid virtue, and placing the *essentials* of religion in the *counsels of perfection.*

It is very natural that Protestants should regard excommunication among them, if it can be so called, with much less caution than it is regarded by Catholics. This grows out of their theory. It springs necessarily from their rule. With them it is not an expulsion, but a mere separation. It affects not the party. It decides nothing. It does not show that he is a heretic. It is not the slightest evidence that he is so. It simply shows the mere opinion of those who differ with him. In the contemplation of the theory itself, their opinion is no better than his. They are each independent equals. They then can declare a separation without much danger of doing any injury to thc party, even if they are wrong. He can easily join some other church, in which his chances for heaven will be, perhaps, greater than they were in the Church he left.

But it is not so in the Catholic Church. In her theory excommunication still means something. It still has the effect it did of old. For this reason the Council of Trent at its twenty-fifth session, third chapter, required that excommunication should be "used with sobriety and great circumspection."

10. The successors of the Apostles must be successors in full

In his debate with Bishop Purcell, Mr. Campbell insisted that the apostles, if they had successors at all must have successors in full. He refers to the office of President, and says truly, that each succeeding President has the same powers as the first.

Protestant controversialists generally make this same objection. The essence of the objection is that the infallible assistance of the Holy Ghost was given to each apostle individually, while it is conceded that each Catholic Bishop is not personally infallible, except the Bishop of Rome.

But this infallible assistance is claimed to have been given to the college of teachers, as the organs of the entire corporation, the Church. This college, in its collective capacity, claims the same powers and qualifications to teach, as did the apostles. It will be observed, that the question does not regard the quantum of power, or the extent of the divine assistance, but solely the mode in which this assistance is given. The power and ability to do the same things, that is, to teach the same truths, are now claimed by the organs of the Church, as were claimed and exercised by the apostles themselves.

The apostles, being the first teachers, had necessarily in the beginning to travel into different countries, and remain for several years separated from each other; and this personal infallibility was required by the extraordinary circumstances in which they were placed. But it is still clear, from the history of the council of Jerusalem that the same infallible assistance was also granted to the college of teachers, including others besides the apostles. This infallible assistance came down in the latter form, to the successors of the apostles.

Besides this, the apostles were chosen witnesses as well as teachers. The powers they exercised being but delegated, they could act in two or more different capacities. The apostles were to bear witness of Christ; and one of the offices of the Holy Ghost was to bring to their recollection all things that Christ had said to them.[30]

Under the commission "Go teach," the infallible assistance was promised to the college through all coming time. Under the special promise that the Holy Ghost should bring all things to their recollection, this assistance was given to the apostles individually, because they had more capacities to fill them than their successors under the commission.

Witnesses can only act individually. Each can only state what he finds written upon his own memory. He is only called upon to state what he knows himself. Recollection is an individual act, and the promise that the Holy Ghost should bring all things to their recollection, in its nature, was confined to the apostles. The fulfillment of this promise necessarily made them individually infallible.

---

[1] John Hughes, Hughes - Breckenridge Controversy. p.151.

[2] A. Campbell and J. Purcell, A debate on the Roman Catholic religion., 181.

[3] Stromateis. 1. i.

[4] A. Campbell and J. Purcell, op. cit. p. 279.

[5] Gardiner Spring A Dissertation on the Rule of Faith. p.5.

[6] A. Campbell and J. Purcell, op. cit. p. 168

[7] Ibid. p. 181.

[8] Ibid. p. 168.

[9] A. Campbell and N. Rice, Campbell Rice Debate on the Holy Spirit. p. 160.

[10] Ibid. p 774.

[11] A. Campbell and J. Purcell, op. cit. p. 168.

[12] Ibid. 181.

[13] Suppose a lawyer, in addressing the Supreme Court, should use this language – "May it please the Court. In this case there is involved a very great Constitutional question, upon which the whole case will turn. In preparing myself to argue this point, and in giving advice to my client, I have only read and studied the Constitution itself. I preferred to go to the law itself to know what were the rights of my client. I preferred to go to the pure fountain head, and from that uncorrupted source, to drink in the clear waters of constitutional construction. I have not consulted at any time, either the voluminous decisions of this court, or of the State courts, nor have I ever read one word of what Story, Kent, Seargent, and other voluminous writers have said upon this subject. I preferred the shorter course, to look alone to the Constitution itself. I have read it over a number of times in a day. To read Story on the Constitution only once would have taken me several days. And to read the decisions of this Court, would have taken a much longer nine."

By the Court. – "The Court dislikes to interrupt any Gentleman, but we hope you will proceed to the point at once. How you prepared yourself, or how you obtained your views of the Constitution, is not important. Lawyers prepare themselves as they please."

Lawyer. – "If the Court please, I will then come to the point at once. There are several Acts of Congress, the first passed as early as July 31, I789, and others at different periods as late as 1799, giving to the United States priority of payment over private creditors in cases of insolvency, and in the distribution of the estates of deceased debtors. Now I hold that all these acts are unconstitutional."

By the Court. – "This Court cannot hear argument upon that question. It has been settled by repeated adjudications. The Court regrets to be compelled to stop an able argument, but the question has already been argued by able men, and decided. Had you examined these arguments and decisions, you would have saved both yourself and your client. If there was no difficulty in the construction of the Constitution, or if there was but one distinguished man, and this court had made no decisions, it might be well for this distinguished man to confine his attention alone to the Constitution. But the case is different. Besides, the Court cannot see any necessity of hearing argument, if your position be correct; for this court would scarcely learn anything from you if it be true that you could learn nothing from others."

And is not this reasoning applicable to the Church?

[14] John Hughes, op. cit. p. 13.

[15] I find apprehended to Hickey's copy of the Constitution of the United States, a facsimile of the certificate of the Secretary of State, in these words:

DEPARTMENT OF STATE, July 20th, I845.

This edition of the Constitution and amendments has been critically compared with the original in this department, and found to be correct in text, letter, and punctuation. It may, therefore, be relied upon as a standard edition. (The small figures designating the clauses are not in the original, and are added merely for convenience of reference.)

Secretary of State.

James Buchanan,

By the Secretary,

N. P. Trist, Chief Clerk.

The government itself was made the depositary of the Constitution, and through its own officers, gives its own testimony as to the existence of the original, and the correctness of the copy; and then, by the instrument itself, proves the extent and character of its own powers. Here we have the vicious circle complete; though I suppose the distinguished Secretary of State did not perceive the very singular fact, that in following the universal practice of all governmental institutions, he was violating a rule of logic, solemnly laid down as such, by the acute Dr. Watts. What would the argument drawn from this imaginary vicious circle be worth, in the estimation of an enlightened Court?

[16] Gardiner Spring. op. cit. p. 27.

[17] Ibid. p 28.

[18] A. Campbell and J. Purcell, op. cit. p. 280.

[19] John Hughes, op. cit.. p.133.

[20] Christianity Restored, I22, 123. –Cited in A. Campbell and J. Purcell, A debate on the Roman Catholic religion. p 804.

[21] Gardiner Spring op. cit .p. 74.

[22] Ibid. p. 76.

[23] Ibid. p. 52.

[24] John Hughes, op. cit. p 224.

[25] 1 John. 1:8-10.

[26] 1 Cor. 9:27.

[27] Matt. I8:21,22.

[28] Luke 17:3-4.

[29] A. Campbell and J. Purcell, op. cit. p 7I.

[30] Cf. Jn 14:26.

CHAPTER II

CHARGES OF CATHOLIC MISCONDUCT

1. Charges against the Jesuits

Among other charges made against the Catholics, by Mr. Campbell, I found certain allegations against the Jesuits. Although the cause of the Catholic Church is not identical with this order – though she can stand alone without it – and though at one time it had many enemies among Catholics, yet, as it is an influential order in the church, I examined these charges, to the best of my opportunity. The charges of Mr. Campbell were based mainly upon "The Secreta Monita of the Order of Jesuits." He states he was informed by the lady from whom he obtained it, that it had been brought to the United States by the Secretary of Lafayette. As Bishop Purcell stated, this Secretary was an Infidel and a Jacobin.

Mr. Campbell says:

> The "Secreta Monita" then, is just as accurate and fair a view of the spirit, design, and policies of that order, as can be given. Such is our faith; and on no mean testimony either. We shall give some account of the discovery of this said book:
>
> "We are indebted for this terrible book of Jesuits' secrets, to the Parliament of Paris. They passed the act to abolish the Jesuits' society; and the execution came on the Jesuit college like a thunder stroke. Their palace was surrounded by troops, and their papers and books, and these 'Secret Instructions' were seized before they had heard that the parliament had taken up their cause!"
>
> The reasons which the Parliament of France, in 1762, gave for extirpating this order, which has been thirty-nine times proscribed, speak volumes:
>
> "The consequences of their doctrine destroy the laws of nature: break all the bonds of civil society: authorizing lying, theft, perjury, the utmost uncleanness, murder, and all sins! Their doctrines root out all sentiments of humanity: excite rebellion: root out all religion: and substitute all sorts of superstition, blasphemy, irreligion, idolatry."
>
> Other reasons for the suppression of this order will be found in the following extract from their oath:

> "In the presence of Almighty God and of all the saints, to you, my Ghostly Father, I do declare that his holiness, the Pope is Christ's vicar-general, and the only head of the universal church throughout the earth; and that by virtue of the keys given him by my Saviour, Jesus Christ, he hath power to depose heretical Kings, princes, states, commonwealths, and governments, all being illegal without his sacred confirmation; and that they may safely be destroyed. Therefore, I to the utmost of my power, shall and will defend his doctrine, and his holiness' rights and customs against all usurper, etc.
>
> "I do renounce and disown any allegiance as due to any heretical king, prince, state, named Protestants or obedience to any of their inferior magistrates or officers.
>
> "I do further promise and declare, that notwithstanding I am dispensed with, to assume any religion heretical for the propagation of the mother church's interest to keep secret and private all her agents, counsel, etc.
>
> "All of which, I, A B, do swear by the blessed Trinity, and the Blessed Sacrament, which I am now to receive. And I call all the heavenly and glorious hosts above, to witness these my real intentions, to keep this my oath. In testimony, hereof. I take this most blessed Sacrament of the Eucharist, and set my hand and seal."[1]

The "Secreta Monita" having been denied by Bishop Purcell as genuine, and alleged to be a forgery, Mr. Campbell in reply says:

> Knowing, my fellow-citizens, how much depends in such a discussion as that now in progress, on having authentic documents, I determined, from the beginning, to rely on none which could, on proper evidence, or with justice, be repudiated. I know that in all debates so far back as the very era of the Reformation, this party have been accustomed to deny authorities, to dispute versions, translations, etc., even of their own writers who were so candid as to give a tolerably fair representation of themselves.

After some further remarks of the same tenor, and in reference to the Jesuits, Mr. Campbell continues:

> Here is another document, not from the ashes of a monastery, I do not know the writer of this article but it is from an encyclopaedia. [2]

One would naturally suppose from this avowal of Mr. Campbell that he was determined to quote from some authority that could not be questioned. But the *Encyclopaedia of Religious Knowledge,* from which he quoted, was a very recent Protestant work, published by Fessenden &

Co. I afterwards consulted the work myself. It seemed to be generally fair enough to the Protestant sects, usually giving their tenets in the words of some leading member of the particular church. But in all that related to Catholics, it was prejudiced and partial, as could readily be seen by anyone having any tolerable idea of the Catholic faith. Its articles in reference to that Church bear upon their face, to my mind, the impress of one sided and partial statements.

I will give so much of the extracted article as gives the essence of the charges against the order:

> The essential principles of this institution, namely, that their order is to be maintained at the expense of society at large, and that the end sanctifies thc means, are utterly incompatible with the welfare of any community of men. Their system of lax and pliant morality, justifying every vice, and authorizing every atrocity, has left deep and lasting ravages on the face of the moral world. Their zeal to extend the jurisdiction of the Court of Rome over every civil Government, gave currency to tenets respecting the duty of opposing princes who were hostile to the Catholic faith, which shook the basis of all political allegiance, and loosened the obligations of every human law. Their indefatigable industry, and countless artifices in resisting the progress of the Reformed religion, perpetuated the most pernicious errors of Popery, and postponed the triumph of tolerant and Christian principles.
>
> The evils of Jesuitism arise not from the violation of the principles of the order; on the contrary, they are the natural and necessary, fruits of the system; they are confined to no age, place, or person.[3]

This indictment was certainly the most formidable I had ever read. All the forms in the Criminal Precedents could not equal it. It did not charge this abandoned order of men with certain specified crimes only, but with every crime under heaven; and not only so, but with everything unclean, low, vile, and idolatrous. There was no crime, no degrading practice, of which they were not alleged to be guilty. They were alleged human monsters. So unlimited were their alleged deformities, that they had but one single virtue left, and that was indispensably necessary to complete their alleged system of villainy. They were conceded to have *consciences*, upon which you could predicate the obligation of an oath.

These charges certainly contained enough to satisfy any enemy. If the order had a bitter and slanderous enemy in the world, he certainly could find food enough in this indictment upon which to feast his enmity.

He could well say: "This is full, final, and complete. They are charged with everything. Nothing could be better because nothing can be added."

How shall such unfortunate men be tried? With such charges impending over them, can they hope for justice in this world? They come into court crushed with a mass of such a wild multiplicity of charges, that the court and jury instinctively turn from these miserable beings, either guilty of, or unfortunate enough to be charged with, such a total abandonment of all and every moral principle. The very reading of such an indictment is enough to overwhelm them, and to half convict them of its most horrible charges. Ought men so unfortunate as to be charged with such unlimited depravity, even though innocent, to get justice in this world? Why should they? Are they not like the alleged leper, though clean, still dreaded and shunned everywhere? Is it not better humanity to sacrifice such an order of men, than to face such a calumny? Is it not better to let the melancholy victims of slander go to their graves in shame and ignominy, than to vindicate human nature itself from such a libel? Had we better not hang the principle on high, that the bare making of such charges is conclusive evidence of their truth, and thus put the reputations of all men at the mercy of their enemies?

But are not these Jesuits men? Are they not our brethren? Are they not entitled to the rights of human nature? Ought we not to judge them as we would other men? And not believe them guilty of all the crimes possible against God and humanity, without evidence full and satisfactory, and strong and conclusive, in proportion as the crimes alleged are monstrous and incredible? In other words shall we not judge them by the same rules of charity by which we would be judged ourselves and under which alone human virtue can claim a home upon this earth?

Shall we permit the mere fact that these men have been so frequently accused, by their enemies, of wrong and injury against society itself, and especially of those vague and general charges, behind which slander is wont to hide itself, to weigh with us? For is it not too true, that as the last refuge of discomfited slander, society contents herself with accusing her victim of some general meanness – of some universal depravity – of a suspicion of being suspected?

Shall we take the mere clamor and vehemence of their enemies as evidence in such a case? If we do so, we place the cause of truth in the power of its enemies, for they can always raise a clamor; and the less proof they have, the more clamor they need, and, therefore, the more naturally resort to it; and if we reason upon that basis, and take clamor as evidence, we shall reject Christianity itself; for we must remember that millions of Jews, by clamor, brought Christ to the Cross. Were they right? Was He guilty? And when Paul met his Jewish brethren at Rome, they had naught to say against the disciples of the Lord Jesus, but that the "sect was everywhere spoken against."

We ought to remember that for centuries the Christians were overwhelmed with a mighty mass of accusations, imputing to them crimes the most enormous, improbable, and unreasonable themselves; and in almost all cases, alleged to have been committed in secret. As the mighty sum total of all their alleged iniquities, they were charged with being "enemies of mankind." And so general was the belief of their guilt, that when the tyrant Nero burned the city of Rome, his first thought was to charge it upon the Christians; a charge like all other wholesale charges, requiring nothing but malice to make, and nothing but prejudice to believe. Had we lived in that age, and had taken the clamor and vehemence of the millions as evidence of the truth of their charges, we could not have been Christians at all. We ought further to remember that Christ expressly foretold that his sincere followers should be "hated of all nations for his name's sake." It is one of the most beautiful truths of Christianity, that this prediction made so long ago, has been so literally fulfilled in all after ages.

Were an intelligent and observant stranger just arrived from a distant land, called upon, with revelation and reason as his sole guide, to select the true followers of Christ, he would unhesitatingly fix upon that body of men most distinguished for their energy, zeal, and devotion; and who especially were most violently abused and opposed by Infidels and discordant sects.

2. These charges examined

This charge of universal depravity is expressly made against the entire order. It is not limited to individuals. It includes each and every member. They are all expressly alleged to take the oath. They all concur in everything. They all have the secret instructions. The sum total of this unlimited system of vice is alleged to be comprised in this short sentence "The end sanctifies the means."

I must say, that ingenious malice, with the whole world for its range, and all time for its duration could not possibly have invented a charge more extended in meaning, and more concise in words. This short sentence of only five omnipotent words, embodies a charge of every crime under heaven; and is so short that it can be repeated oft and oft again; and is yet so extensive in meaning, that as often as it is repeated, it leaves the prejudiced and disordered imagination, in selecting the food it feeds upon, to revel, untrammeled, in all the wide fields of human iniquity. Like the charge against the early Christians of being "enemies of mankind," or like that often made by malicious persons "he is a mean man," it has no limits; and everything may be included under it that may suit the appetite of each individual.

There are certain instincts in envy, malice, and prejudice that seem to have been provided by God himself, on purpose to defeat the ends aimed at by these base passions. Envy always depreciates superior merit; and when the act itself is too good to be denied, never fails to impute an improper motive to him who performed it. While malice in its bitterness, is never satisfied with imputing to its victim anything short of the most enormous and improbable crimes. The more innocent the victim, the more cordially it hates him, because the more unlike itself. Prejudice could not claim its peculiar merit, if it believed reasonable charges, upon sufficient testimony, but must out-suspect and out-guess everything else.

One of the difficulties that occurred to me, in my reflections upon this alleged oath was the extreme folly of attempting to bind men, by an oath, who had no conscience. To swear men by "the blessed Trinity," and the blessed sacrament while they called "all the heavenly and glorious hosts above to witness" that they would commit all the crimes possible, if necessary, did seem to me the most futile and the most idle. What ideas of the obligation of an oath could such men have? They are alleged to have had no virtue upon which conscience could rest. Men who could deliberately go into such an association, and then undertake to obey these secret instructions, could no more be trusted than rogues and murderers.

When, for my own satisfaction, I was inquiring into the truth of Christianity, I was struck with the peculiar force of one argument. It was insisted that we could not account for the conduct of the apostles, upon the supposition that they had combined to assert a system of falsehood, and to palm it upon the world. It was impossible to combine twelve men, and send them out into all the world, to preach the same falsehoods and that all of them should remain faithful, on all occasions, however painful the test, and not betray the secret. I could well understand how such a union could be formed and kept together, upon the basis of truth – but never upon that of falsehood, when the whole party knew the same. I knew there were moments when the truth will come;

"For e'en the rogue by fits is fair and wise" –

that all men had an inward conviction and dread of future punishment, and in the honest hour of death, when the

"Scathing thoughts of execrated years,"

brought up before the dying vision of the guilty culprit the blurred and blotted page of the ignominious past – that then murder would out. Some of them would tell it – some would let it out.

How then will this argument apply to the Jesuits as an order of men, governed by certain rules applicable to the whole class? It is alleged in substance by their accusers, that they had one set of rules for the public, which were good enough, and another set of rules to be kept a profound secret, from all persons but members of the order. These secret rules contained the horrible sentiments charged, and were all alleged to be printed in a book called "The Secreta Monita," and kept for the use of the members.

This order was intended to be perpetual, and its members were expected to become numerous, and to be scattered all over the wide earth. And so they were. They numbered some ten thousand members, at the date of their suppression. It was a most extraordinary combination. The mind that originated it must have been at one and the same time a giant and a pigmy – must have possessed grand and sublime ideas – systematic powers, and yet not a particle of principle, and not the slightest knowledge of human nature. All the members of this body must have had strange and singular views. Like other men, they knew they must die – that their ranks must be supplied with new members – that these would be induced to apply for admission upon the basis of the published rules, which were honest. But that after they became members, they were to be changed from pious, honest, and sincere men, to monsters of crime. And that so perfect was the logic of the order that it never failed to make this conversion from honesty to villainy, so that there was not one left to tell the story, that such infamous principles and oaths had been proposed to him, and by him rejected with scorn and indignation. In other words, they must have thought that the most effectual way to organize a band of abandoned reprobates, was to put forth a platform in public, that would only invite the pious and good, but when once in the order, that each new member, though deceived and defrauded, would at once, by some extraordinary magic, abandon all his previous views, and submit willingly, kindly, to this infamous deception, and work faithfully, and continuously, in upholding this same stupendous fraud.

Not only so, but they must have thought that the book containing their secret rules, could never come to light by any of the ten thousand accidents of life – that although in the hands of all Jesuits, scattered all over the world, that still when one died his book would not be left behind him, to fall into the hands of some one who might betray the mighty secret – that when one of their members committed murder by poison or assassination, that no chemical test could be found to show the existence of the deadly drug in the stomach of the deceased, and the spilled blood of the assassinated would leave no stain – and when they went upon their midnight excursions of crime, they would leave no trace, nor track, but flit through the air, like wicked spirits, unseen, but felt. These men seem never to have understood the one plain simple fact, that the introduction of every new conspirator, only increased the danger of detection; but like some foolish people who tell their secrets to everybody, that they may have good help to keep them, these men, while utterly destitute of principle, still had unlimited confidence in each other, and never once suspected, that men, capable of, and pledged to commit, every possible crime, must certainly sooner or later, fall out among themselves, and betray the whole conspiracy.

If these monstrous charges were true these men were extraordinary monsters, destitute alike of all principle and of all common sense. If I could believe such charges, then I should not only consider the Jesuits as the greatest mass of conglomerated vice that ever disgraced humanity, but the greatest collection of fools that ever degraded human intellect.

I am willing to say, in the face of all men, that I am one of those charitable, credulous creatures (fools if you please) who believe that the great mass of all churches, and of all the different orders of those churches, are honest in their convictions. In the very nature and reason of things, it could not be otherwise. I believe that honest conviction, though erroneous, is the only basis upon which any society of men can be held together from age to age – and that no man, or set of men, having the least claim to intellect, ever did dream, or ever will dream of organizing a permanent order of men, upon any other basis. Could it be assumed that a resident and fixed community could all be rogues, who would wear out the very property itself in stealing it continually one from the other, and yet that competition would not ruin the trade, and destroy the union and peace of their society. As well might it be assumed, that a numerous, widely-dispersed, and gifted body of religious men, could be held together when even a majority are hypocrites and villains – much less when all are so.

But the history of the Jesuits, as well as the admissions of candid men not of their religion, show that they are a most distinguished order of men – distinguished for their profound and varied erudition – their indefatigable industry – their zeal – their heroic devotion – their untiring energy, and their unfaltering and steady perseverance. These are noble traits are fit companions of integrity.

When I see the fervid and intrepid Paul leave his own country, and go through strange lands, suffering persecution and shame at every step, and wearing out his very existence in preaching the mild gospel of the despised Nazarene, I am compelled in the innermost recesses of my heart, to admit his motives were good – his integrity unquestioned. I cannot find any other adequate motive, upon any principle of reason or charity, by which to account for such voluntary sacrifices. And when I see the labors and sacrifices of the Jesuit Fathers in every land, among all nations – how they composed the noblest orations, the finest histories, the sublimest poems, and wrote the ablest treatises on every branch of science, (even that of gunnery) – when I see these devoted missionaries go

"Through foaming waves to distant shores,"

visiting every people in the world, and like the sainted Xavier,

"Whose lips were love, whose touch was power,
Whose thoughts were vivid flame,"

leaving their worn-out or slaughtered bodies in every savage clime, and enduring toils and dangers, sufferings and privations, second only to those of the apostles and earlier saints, I cannot deny to these men holy and lofty motives. For it seems not more natural for the oak to grow from the acorn, than for noble and virtuous deeds and heroic sacrifices, to spring from corresponding motives. As certain acids are the sure tests of certain metals, so great and voluntary sacrifices, without temporal reward, are the never failing criteria of sincerity. I see the perseverance, and patient and continued duration of this body of men through calumny, hatred, and contempt, in a cause in which they can have no greater personal interest than others do. When I witness this, I cannot see any other adequate motive than those high and holy purposes that spring from a fixed conviction of being in the right, in the noblest of causes.

I am compelled to this conviction, notwithstanding all the clamor against these men: and why? If it were true, as nearly all Catholics think, and many others admit, that this order of men are the most eminent for their knowledge, virtue, zeal, and devotion, of all the orders in the Roman church or in the world, then from the very reason and nature of things, this state of misrepresentation must follow. For if there were any envy in rival orders of their own church, it would fix itself upon them, for envy always seeks "higher game." And if there were any fear, malice, or prejudice in the ranks of opponents, they would be mainly directed against them. For fear has an unerring instinct in apprehending the most formidable danger, while malice is fertile in inventing, and interested prejudice most ready in believing, charges against the most distinguished men in the ranks of opponents.

When we hear the writer in the encyclopaedia say, as I have quoted above, that "their indefatigable industry, and countless artifices in resisting the progress of the reformed religion, perpetuated the most pernicious errors of popery," we have the key to the motive that keeps alive this denunciation. When we hear Mr. Campbell say:

> The Jesuits that standing army of the Pope, are revived and inundating our country. Other fraternities are but the Militia; but these are the trained band lifeguards of the papacy…[4]

We can readily see where the shoe pinches. When you go into an orchard, even months after the fruit is all gone, and you see there a noble looking tree, whose wide-spreading top is filled with sticks, so that you know everybody has been "pitching into it," you may know, with unerring certainty that this tree produces the best fruit in the orchard.

The circumstances connected with the alleged discovery of this "Secreta Monita" upon their face, proved to my satisfaction that it was a forgery. This event happened in the Infidel times preceding the horrors that followed the French Revolution. It was the age of Voltaire and other distinguished Infidels. Voltaire was accustomed to say that:

> He was tired of hearing it said, that twelve men had been able to convert the world from Paganism to Christianity, for that he would let it be seen that one man was able to unchristianize it.

At the head of his letters to his infidel conspirators against revelation, he was accustomed to say, "Let us crush the wretch" meaning Jesus Christ and His religion. In the private correspondence of Voltaire and D'Alembert, it is acknowledged there was no hope of success in destroying Christianity, unless the Jesuits were first put down. This order of men, by their talents, industry and zeal, were able to keep in check the attempts of the Infidels by refuting and exposing their sophistry. The Parliament of France in 1762, notwithstanding all they say about religion, etc., was composed mostly of the disciples of Voltaire.

A parliament thus constituted could be imposed upon readily. It required only a few conspirators to accomplish this. It is a fact well shown by the testimony of history, that a legislative assembly, from its constitution, is as readily deceived in times of prejudice and excitement, as the same number of individuals taken promiscuously. Such assemblies are peculiarly sensitive to outside clamor. They readily believe almost anything that they think is popular.

These facts are shown by the history of the English Parliament. This body was deceived to such an extent as to believe the repeated perjuries of Titus Oates and others, and many innocent persons were sent to the block in consequence. In 1666 the city of London was burned, and the conflagration charged upon the Catholics. It was believed, and a monument erected and inscribed, commemorating the supposed dark deed, of which Pope has this expressive couplet:

"Where London's column, pointing to the skies,
Like a tall bully, lifts its head, and lies."

A few years ago, the corporation of London had the magnanimity to have this inscription chipped off.

The Infidels knew the suppression of the Jesuits in France could not be done by any outward attack of theirs. They stood as declared enemies of religion! The plan was to operate upon the Parliament. They knew from the examples in the English Parliament how easy this could be effected, when the prejudices of the members were appealed to. It was easy to reproduce this forged "Secreta Monita" originated by some anonymous calumniator in 1616. All they had to do was palm it upon the Parliament as the work of the Jesuits. That was easily done. Ever since Joseph had the silver cup concealed in the sack of Benjamin, this expedient was well known. Joseph used it from a good motive, but malicious persons have resorted it to in every age. No artifice is more frequently practiced, or is more easily accomplished. Cases of the kind have often occurred in every country.

Two men were once partners, and had some difficulty in their settlement. One became the violent enemy of the other, and persecuted him on every occasion. The persecuted determined he would leave the Kingdom and emigrate to America to avoid his implacable enemy. In preparing to make his departure he went to London and took a room at a public house. His old enemy met him in the streets, and watched him go into his room. The next morning his enemy watched the room until he saw him leave and go into the street. His enemy then went to another room on the same floor, and stole a watch, and secreted it in his victim's room. The owner of the watch missed it, and gave the alarm. This man went by, and informed the police that a very suspicious character lodged in a certain room. Of course, they searched the room and found the watch. The victim was arrested, protested his ignorance of the whole matter, was tried, convicted, and executed. Years afterwards, his murderer was brought up to receive sentence for some criminal offence, and before the court, admitted that he had caused this man's execution.

The circumstances stated, show clearly, that such an artifice was used upon the occasion of the alleged discovery of this "Secreta Monita." The very haste with which the Parliament acted in reference to so important a measure, shows they had been informed that such a work would be found. Intimations had been no doubt given out that if such a hasty measure was adopted the insidious Jesuits would be caught. Having succeeded in procuring the passage of such an act, it was easy for a single individual to carry with him the book concealed under his dress, and when the apartments of the college were searched, to place this book among the others found there. It required but the act of a single individual – one of the police, or any other individual who was permitted to go there.

How easy it is, if we depend upon such testimony, to ruin any man's reputation, or the character of any body of men. Such a system of reasoning places all good men at the mercy of conspirators. And when the charge upon its face, is so utterly absurd and impracticable, and beyond all reason, such a circumstance ought not to weigh as a feather against a body of men so numerous – so distinguished – so much in the way of its opponents – and for whose suppression there existed so many manifest motives. To ruin such a body of men, if sensible and just men can believe such mighty charges upon such testimony, requires nothing but a want of principle, – small amount of cunning – and the adroitness of an ordinary rogue, in a single individual.

Having succeeded in obtaining the suppression of the order in France, the next step was to secure its suppression in other states, and finally by the Pope himself. If we examine into the character and motives of the principal men who took the leading part in these violent measures against the order, we shall see that they were just the men to urge them onward. They were generally either avowed or secret enemies of religion, and especially of the Catholic system. As a very candid Protestant writer, speaking of the persecution of the Jesuits by the Portuguese government, and the destruction of their college at Pernambuco, says:

> Reader, throw a veil over thy recollection for a little while, and forget the cruel, unjust, and unmerited censures thou hast heard against an unoffending order. This place was once the Jesuits' College, and originally built by those charitable fathers. Ask the aged and respectable inhabitants of Pernambuco, and they will tell thee, that the destruction of the society of the Jesuits was a terrible disaster to the public, and its consequences severely felt to the present day.
>
> When Pombal took the reins of government into his hand, virtue and learning beamed within the college walls. Public catechism to the children, and religious instruction to all, flowed daily from the mouths of its venerable priests. They were loved, revered, and respected throughout the whole town. The illuminating philosophers of the day had sworn to exterminate Christian knowledge, and the College of Pernambuco was doomed to founder in the general storm. To the long-lasting sorrow and disgrace of Portugal, the philosophers blinded her King, and flattered his prime minister. Pombal was exactly the tool these sappers of every public and private virtue wanted. He had the naked sword of power in his own hand, and his heart was as hard as flint. He struck a mortal blow and the society of Jesuits, throughout the Portuguese dominions, was no more.[5]

The Pope was induced to suppress the order in 1773. In the Brief of Clement XIV. he is careful not to say that he believed the charges to be true, but on the contrary, bases the suppression upon the grounds of expediency, and for the sake of peace. The parliament of Paris restored the order. In 1801 it was restored in Russia, and in 1814 in Sardinia, and in 1814 by Pope Pius VII. The King of Prussia, though Protestant did not suppress the order in his dominions, but fostered it. He did not believe the charges.

It has been the misfortune of this order to incur the hostility, of Infidels, and especially those of Europe. We see that an Infidel brought the "Secreta Monita" to the United States. The distinguished novelist, the Infidel Eugene Sue, in his late work, *The Wandering Jew*, has imputed to the Jesuits all the dark and horrible traits of his own vitiated imagination. This order is evidently a foe worthy of their steel, and *in* their way. Unable to meet their arguments and exertions by fair means, they resorted to forgery and base imposition to suppress the order. They succeeded for a time under a state of clamor and excitement. But justice, though slow, is certain, and the order has been restored. It had once many enemies among Catholics, but these have dwindled to a very few.

That these charges against the entire order are absurd and barefaced fabrications I have no doubt. That individuals of the order, as individuals of any and every body, have sometimes erred, I have as little doubt. They would be more than men if they had not. That the suppression of the order by Clement XIV. was mainly produced by the exertions of Infidels in that Infidel age, I have no doubt. And that the clamor is still attempted to be kept up by persons whose interests or prejudices render them capable of believing any charge, supported by even the semblance of testimony, against their opponents in religion, I have no doubt.

The charges, if made against individuals of the order, would not affect the order itself, in the minds of just men; and when made against the entire order, assume a shape so monstrous, unreasonable, and absurd, that I do not think any impartial and well-informed man could be deceived into a belief of them. When I first read them, I was a Protestant, and all my sympathies were with Protestantism; but this charge of universal and unmitigated depravity against so numerous a body of men, was rather too heavy a draft upon my credulity.

It seems to me that every good man should be very careful to be just to others. The rule of sweet charity is the only one under which human virtue can live. It is better to allow too much merit to men than too little. Men are frail enough, and their virtues are sufficiently scant; but when we detract from that little, and accuse them of monstrous crimes they never committed, we certainly commit a most grievous sin against them, and especially against ourselves. If we err in imputing too few sins to our fellow-creatures, we may be called weak, but not criminal. We at least lean to the side of charity. But if we impute to them crimes they never committed, we commit ourselves, a grievous fault; for we are commanded to "judge not, that ye be not judged: for with what judgment ye judge, ye shall be judged." It is a fearful thing for us to judge harshly and unjustly, as we must expect to be judged by the same rule.

These considerations satisfied me that the Jesuits were an eminent, devoted, and yet misrepresented body of men. When I find what I take to be slandered merit, I hesitate not to avow myself its friend. For I do not know what other rule a good man can follow, than to do that which is strictly right in itself, and trust in God and his country. Too many well-disposed men are apt to flinch from a good, but unpopular victim; but

"tis not so above."

Innocence is purer when persecuted,

"And love is loveliest when embalmed in tears"

and virtue is never so beautiful as when calumniated and despised. It was so in the beginning. It must always be so. It could be that a good and impartial man has taken up an impression that such wholesale charges are true. If any such man will reexamine the question calmly and dispassionately, he will enjoy that sweet and generous pleasure which a just man feels when he finds he has been mistaken in supposing that his brother had been guilty of a crime.

3. Charges against certain Popes

Among other charges made by Protestant controversialists against the Catholic Church, is the wicked character of some of the Popes. The instances can be seen in the debate of Campbell and Purcell, and in the controversy of Hughes and Breckenridge.

The most general and sweeping charges I found in the Dissertation of Dr. Spring, on page 71, where the learned Divine says:

> But it is a fact that no Romanist will deny, that the Popes of Rome, as a body of men, have been a disgrace to the human race.

This statement must have been made at random, for I found it contradicted by every Catholic writer whose works I read at the time and since, who spoke upon the subject at all. I have not been able to find a Catholic writer who did not deny it, when the subject he treated made it proper for him to notice the charge. All those that I have read very cheerfully admitted that the conduct of some individual Popes had been scandalous and wicked. However, they insisted that the great majority were worthy of the station they filled, and many of them martyrs and saints of the first character; and that these wicked Popes did not bear a greater proportion to the whole number, than Judas did to the twelve.

These charges related to some of the Popes of the Middle Ages. Those of the first ages of the Church are admitted to have been saints: while those of the later ages are admitted, by Catholic and Protestant writers, to have been unexceptional in their moral deportment: as by the Protestant writer Ranke, in his history of the popes. [6]

In making these and other charges against the Catholic Church, both Mr. Campbell and Mr. Breckenridge quoted Du Pin as an authentic Catholic historian. But his character as such was denied by both Bishops Hughes and Purcell.

It appeared that Du Pin had a secret correspondence with Archbishop Wake, with a view to the union of the English and Catholic churches. His secret papers were examined on the 10th of February, 1719, at the Palais Royal in Paris, and it was found as Lafitau testifies, that in his letter to Archbishop Wake he proposed to give up Auricular Confession, Transubstantiation, Religious vows, the fast of Lent and abstinence, the Supremacy of the Pope, and the celibacy of the clergy. He was also secretly married, and after his death, his widow came publicly forward to assert her right to his property.

To support Du Pin's authority, Mr. Campbell read the certificates printed with the work, and purporting to be the approbation of the doctors of the Sorbonne. Two of these certificates purport to be signed by "Blampton, Rector of Saint Merris; and Hideux, curate of Saint Innocents," and one by the former only. They approve the work as containing "nothing contrary to the Catholic faith or to good manners," but do not approve of disapprove the work as authentic history.

The king appointed the Doctors of the Sorbonne. The authority is not of the highest grade, though respectable. Du Pin at the time he wrote his history was not suspected of any hypocrisy. He was a very distinguished writer, and stood high with his associates. His work was voluminous and the hasty reading of an author of his standing, in all historical work so extended, would not enable anyone to judge properly of its historical character. A work upon doctrine or morals can be judged very soon by any competent divine, but a work on history, so extensive, would be far more difficult. It would require time and patient investigation to detect its errors. Such approbations are too often given hurriedly, the judge relying too much upon the standing and character of the author. Besides,

Du Pin was a Jansenist, and was censured by Pope Clement XI even during his lifetime; and Louis XIV removed him from the Sorbonne, which was approved by the Pope.[7]

It may be possible that Du Pin was an authentic historian; but certainly he appears under circumstances most suspicious. An honest man may be a member of a certain church, and may write its history, and that work may be good authority after he has changed his faith, and left the Church. But when man remains a traitor in a church, and seeks to betray it, and lives a hypocrite while in it, there is no trusting him for anything. A man of distinguished ability, and yet a hypocrite, would naturally seek in the most insidious manner possible, to injure the Church of which he was a member. He could not but hate a church whose faith he could not believe; and he could not but have some fell purpose when he believed one thing and told another. Who can trust such a man?

Mr. Campbell did indeed state that he relied upon him only insofar as he is sustained by other historians. But as he continued to quote from him after objection was made by Bishop Purcell, and after Mr. Campbell had read the objections of Bishop Hughes, as he states himself, I could not well understand his reasons.[8] If, as he asserted, Du Pin was sustained by other historians, it certainly would have been more satisfactory to have read entirely from them.

Herein I remarked a great and palpable difference between the course of Catholic and Protestant controversialists. I found the Catholics generally quoting from the most eminent and reliable Protestant writers and historians, men of the most unblemished character, private and public, while on the contrary, I found Protestants generally quoting from the most unworthy and suspicious Catholics, such as Du Pin, Father Paul Thuanus, and others. The debate between Elder Campbell and Bishop Purcell is a proof of this. So is the controversy between Hughes and Breckenridge. And if any man of fair mind will calmly watch both parties, he will soon see which most relies upon unworthy authority.

Mr. Breckenridge quotes Thuanus Book 37, p. 776 as a Catholic historian, to prove alleged corruptions at Rome. In reference to whom, Bishop Hughes says:

> The history of Thuanas has been condemned at Rome, by two public decrees; the one of November 9, 1609, the other of May 10 1757, from which fact the reader may see, with how little propriety he assumes to be called a "Roman Catholic historian." He was, says a modern author

> (Paquot), "an audacious writer, the implacable enemy of the Jesuits; the calumniator of the Guises; the copyist, flatterer, friend of the Protestants; and was far from being even just to the Holy See, the Council of Trent or anything Catholic.[9]

But aside from these disputed and not trustworthy historians, from the testimony of Baronius and other authentic Catholic historians quoted by Mr. Campbell and Mr. Breckenridge, there can be no doubt of the scandalous lives of certain Popes, such as Stephen VII, Vigilius, Alexander, and others.

The whole number of Popes has been nearly two hundred and sixty. "Of these," says Bishop Purcell,

> the first forty were saints, or martyrs; a small number only, not more than twenty can be called bad men; the rest were remarkable for eminent virtue, charity, zeal, and learning, and patronage of letters.[10]

Mr. Breckenridge and Mr. Campbell asserted that the number of bad Popes was greater than twenty. Mr. Campbell quotes Genebrard, who says, under the year 904,

> For nearly one hundred and fifty years, about fifty Popes deserted wholly the virtue of their predecessors, being apostate rather than apostolical

But Bishop Purcell denies the accuracy of this statement as to the number. And, indeed, the statement seems very loose and general. Such statements are not often accurate.

As to the exact number of Popes who disgraced their position, it is difficult at this time, to determine. That injustice has been done to some of them, there can be but little doubt. It must seem obvious to sensible men that the character of a prominent man depends greatly upon the temper of the age in which he lived. There are often many causes, and a peculiar concurrence of circumstances, that involve a man's reputation in doubt in some cases, and in ignominy in others, when his motives were good, and when his measures, under the existing circumstances, were the best that could have been adopted. The bitter prejudice, or inveterate enmity, of a single able and influential individual, in an age when books were few, (for the reason that the art of printing was then unknown,) might do the greatest injustice to the person whose history is sought. Nothing but a patient and careful examination of the contemporary manuscript documents on file in the various extensive libraries of Europe can enable us to do anything like justice to the Popes of the Middle Ages.

CHARGES OF CATHOLIC MISCONDUCT

When I have been induced to examine charges against individuals, I always go to them for their side of the question; for I never could get all the truth from their enemies. Most cases of the kind are overdone. Men are prone to have victims of some kind. We see it often in communities, in reference to particular persons. The public must blame some one, and from some cause or other, it matters not what it is, censure starts in a particular direction, and when once under way, it is as difficult to stop as a mountain torrent. It must run its course. Even good men are often swept along with it. It is even so in business. All hands rush into great excesses at intervals. Human nature is prone to varied and unsteady courses.

Most of these scandalous excesses of the Popes occurred in a certain period, and about the tenth century. As several bad Popes lived near each other, it is very natural for historians, as well as the people of that age, to confound both good and bad, and place them in the same class. Poor Tray suffered for being in bad company, and some of the Popes who lived in the Middle Ages, may have suffered from the misfortune of having governed the Church at that period of time.[11] Even the most pious and candid writers, from their very detestation of vice, may, in their melancholy moments, do great injustice to those who, though guilty of some faults, are not guilty to the extent supposed.

It has become a habit to censure everything done in those ages; and doubtless there was much to be blamed. But this habit, like all other habits, may have misled even just men. Those ages were not distinguished for great learning, and the people of those times were encompassed with difficulties of the most oppressive character. They have, therefore, few friends to do them justice, and many disgusted and interested enemies to reproach their memory. The natural tendency of human opinion is to elevate some favorite ages to the skies, and to depreciate even the real merits of those that are despised and neglected.

But justice should be done. The genuine truth ought to be known. And it appears that of late, a better spirit begins to show itself. "Within the last ten years" says Dr. Wiseman,

> a succession of works have been appearing on the continent, in which the character of the Popes of the Middle Ages has been not only vindicated, but placed in the most beautiful and magnificent point of view And I thank God that they are, as I just said from a quarter that cannot be suspected– every one of the works to which I allude being from a Protestant.

> We had within these few years, several lives, or vindications of the Pontiff who has been considered the embodying type of that thirst for aggrandizement which is attributed to Popes of the Middle Ages. I speak of Gregory VII, commonly known as Hildebrand. In a large voluminous work, published a few years ago by Voight, and approved by the most eminent historians of modern Germany, we have the life of that Pontiff drawn up from contemporaneous documents, from his own correspondence, and the evidence of both his friends and enemies. The result is, and I wish I could give you the words of the author, that if the historian abstract himself from mere petty prejudices and national feelings, and look on the character of the Pontiff from a higher ground, he must pronounce him a man of most upright mind, of a most perfect disinterestedness, and of the purest zeal; one who acted in every instance just as his position called upon him to act, and made use of no means, save what he was authorized to use.
>
> In this, he is followed by others who speak of him with an enthusiasm which a Catholic could not have exceeded; and of one, it has been observed, that he cannot speak of that Pontiff without rapture.[12]

Of these other Protestant writers Dr. Wiseman gives in a note the names of Eichhorn, Luden, Loo and and Muller. Dr. Wiseman also says:

> We have had, too, within the last two years, another most interesting work, a Life of Innocent III. one of the most abused in the line of Papal succession, written by Hurter a clergyman of the Protestant church of Germany. He again has coolly examined all the allegations which have been brought against him; and has based his studies entirely on the monuments of the age; and the conclusion to which he comes is that not only is his character beyond reproach, but that it is an object of unqualified admiration. And to give you some idea of the feelings of this work, I will read you two extracts applicable to my subject in general. Thus writes our author: "Such an immediate instrument in the hands of God, for securing the highest weal of the community, must the Christian of these times, the ecclesiastic, and still more, he who stood nearest to the center of the church, have considered him who was its head. Every worldly dignity, works only for the good of an earthly life, for a passing object; the Church alone for the salvation of all men, for an object of endless duration. If worldly power is from God, it is not so in the sense, and in the measure, and in the definitiveness in which the highest spiritual power of these ages was; whose origin, development, extent, and influence, (independently of all dogmatical formulas) form the most remarkable appearance in the world's history."

> In another passage he thus speaks: "Let us look forward and backward from any period upon the times, and see how the institution of the Papacy has out-lasted all the other institutions of Europe; how it has seen all other states rise and perish; how, in the endless changes of human power, it alone invariably has preserved and maintained the same spirit; can we be surprised, if many look upon it as the rock which raises itself unshaken above the stormy waves of time?"

I am satisfied myself, that the vices of those ages have been much exaggerated. I admit most cheerfully that I am but partially acquainted with the history of those times. My pursuits have led me into other fields of inquiry. But my opinion is formed upon general principles – upon my ideas of the nature of men and things.

If the literature of an age happens to be inferior, the scholar turns from it with indifference, if not with disgust. In such cases, few, if any, will feel any interest in doing justice even to the solid virtues and common sense of that age. Their faults are narrated in harsh and severe terms, while their virtues are not recorded in the glowing pages of polished eulogy. I like to read the correspondence of men – public and private – when I wish to understand their characters. In all my experience – in all my travels in different modes – in cities – at taverns – and in all other positions, the most just and certain mode I could ever adopt to find out the true character of people, was to let them tell their own story – to state their own principles, and then to watch, calmly and impartially, the general drift and spirit of the narrative. Men will generally talk of that which they love most. I never met an unprincipled man that I know of, except in one solitary instance, that did not unduly elevate talent above integrity. Such men invariably put forth some vicious principle, or applaud some smart, but dishonest trick, in someone else. An unprincipled man, one who is so habitually, will never fail to show it in his own statements. There will be a vein of vicious principle found somewhere in his discourse. A man must be supremely adept at hypocrisy that can wear the mask always. He must be remarkable for his patience and perseverance.

In estimating the character and conduct of the Popes of the middle ages, we must place ourselves back in the circumstances that then existed, we must enter into the spirit of those times, and take things as we find them. We must remember that men, nations, and ages must be judged with reference to their opportunities and positions.

THE TRUE CHURCH

The Middle Ages succeeded the fall of the Roman Empire in the West, and the terrible scourge of the Saracens in the East and South. Literature, science and arts had suffered extensively by these devastations. It was emphatically the period of misfortune. The very fact that nearly all of the bad Popes existed at one period in this long line of succession, is, of itself, almost conclusive proof, that the circumstances of the times mainly produced these sad delinquencies.

Making then, every fair allowance, there seems to be no doubt that some twenty out of near two hundred and sixty Popes have been wicked men. And Catholics, whose histories record these vices, have freely condemned their excesses. These Popes followed each other by succession. That in a long course of ages, instances of personal misconduct would occur even among the Popes, must be expected.

What then is the legitimate effect of these scandals upon the Catholic system? Are they abuses, or are they, the natural result of the system? Do they prove that the Papacy never existed? that it could be thus forfeited or that the misconduct of a few individuals, at intervals in the long line of her history, has destroyed the true Church?

In considering this matter, we must distinguish between personal and official misconduct. In personal matters, men act for themselves – in official matters – for others. In one case they exercise personal and inherent natural rights – in the other they are clothed with delegated powers. To confound these, is to confound the most manifest distinctions – distinctions which must exist where government exists.

As I have elsewhere stated, I never understood that Christ had guaranteed the personal virtue of His apostles. He left the personal free agency of all men untouched. But when they act as His agents, and for Him, then I understand that He did guarantee their official acts. Thus, Peter could personally sin, and so could Paul, but they never could give false testimony. A true prophet cannot lie. He is not permitted to do so. It is conceded as a plain principle of law that the agent, from the nature of the relation, is not free in reference to the business of his principal, except when discretion is given. Christ did not leave the apostles any discretion. They were bound to testify and teach the whole truth, and only the truth. Therefore, if Christ guaranteed the integrity of the Church, then her official acts must be right, as to all matters within the guaranty.[13]

CHARGES OF CATHOLIC MISCONDUCT

The Popes, like all men at the heads of great institutions, were placed in a position where they had every incentive to do good, and yet were exposed to very trying temptations. Many persons who held the High Priesthood under the Jewish dispensation disgraced the position, from Heli to Caiaphas, who was a wicked man and a good high priest. As Mr. Campbell says, Aaron made the golden calf. But all these sad instances of human infirmity did not destroy the office, nor forfeit the existence of the institution. Is the church then responsible for the personal vices of these Popes? Could the Church take away their free agency, and prevent their sins?

When we come to take a view of the general official conduct of these Popes, we find one of the most beautiful proofs of the invincible stability of the Church. It is indisputable, and now conceded by many, if not by most Protestant writers, that the alleged errors of the Roman Church were introduced long before the main portions of these disorders occurred, if they were not in the Church at the beginning. It is true, some attempts are still made by particular controversialists to prove that at least a portion of them originated after these scandals commenced. But any one can easily see that this is untrue, by a very slight examination of the proofs. It is also true, that in the Pontificates of some of these Popes, Christianity was extended by their exertions into several savage countries. In fact, some of the greatest conquests made to religion occurred at those periods. There were no new heresies introduced – there was no cardinal doctrine of faith lost. This showed unity – this showed diligence - this showed integrity as to faith.

How then can we account for these great and illustrious results, but upon the hypothesis that Christ protected the faith of the Church, as He had promised? Looking to that age – the times – the circumstances when these scandals existed, and what other Church could have ridden out the terrible storm? Could Protestantism (which has only existed for about three centuries, and that in the most fortunate and enlightened period of the world, and has yet severed and divided into so many fragments,) have withstood this trial?

When we look into the matter carefully, there is something wonderful in this history. For the Catholic says to himself: "As the old Church withstood all this, what can she not withstand? Is she not invincible under circumstances that have crushed all existing institutions? They died out like falling stars – she shone on. They were – she was, and is, and is to be. It was the glory of our Lord to stand alone. So it is with His church."

The more the opposers of the Church urge these disorders, the more they, strengthen the conviction in the mind of the Catholic, that it is impossible for the Old Church to have sustained herself under such untoward circumstances, without the help of Christ. What Christ has instituted, men cannot destroy. They have power over the works of their own hands, but here their power ends. Despite the desolation of the Goth and Vandal the ravages of the invincible Saracen – the trials and evils of the age – and above all, the personal wickedness of some of her own Chief Pastors, the Old Church faltered not, but kept the faith, preached the Gospel to the world, and actually extended the Master's Kingdom. She, of all the institutions of the world, has lived unscathed through that day. Amidst all the ruin, she alone held up her head.

"As some tall cliff, that lifts its awful form,
Swells from the vale, and midway leaves the storm,
Though round its breast the rolling clouds are spread,
Eternal sunshine settles on its head."

In my reflections upon this subject, I could not but consider the triumph of the Church, under such circumstances, as one of the most forcible and beautiful proofs of the truth of Christianity. It did show that the Lord Jesus was to be trusted. That even the personal misconduct of her own children – of her own chief officer, could not ruin the work of Christ. He had said it should be so, and it was so.

I could not but wish to put these questions to those who exaggerate these personal sins of the Popes: "My friends, the more you overdo these allegations, the more difficult, I apprehend, you make your own case. You say in substance, that there was no virtue in the Papacy. Where, then, was that wonderful virtue that saved the Church? Under your supposed state of case, give us some good reason for that wonderful preservation of the Church. There was evidently great vitality and virtue somewhere. Your alleged true church had to change its faith and features very often to live at all; and in those trying times was not on the field of battle. Or if so, did nothing. Was it 'buried beneath the darkness of those ages,' as Waddington says? If so, why did not that darkness overwhelm the Catholic Church? Was the Protestant true Church alone unable to hold up her head in the stern hour of trial, while the alleged false church did all the good that was done? And what Church did save Europe from Barbarism? What Church saved Christianity, if not the

Catholic? You have certainly much fault to find with her. But who won the victory over the savage and the Saracen, but the Catholic Church? In short, who else did anything for learning virtue, civilization, and religion in those most perilous times? Her children had many vices, no doubt, but their trials were such as you have never witnessed."

Speaking of those times Mr. Wheaton says:

> The influence of the Papal authority, though sometimes abused, was then felt as a blessing to mankind: it rescued Europe from total barbarism; it afforded the only asylum and shelter from feudal oppression.[14]

And the Rev. John Lord, in his introductory essay to the *Chronicles of Sir John Froissart*, says:

> Moreover, the Papacy was a great central power, needed to control the princes of Europe, and settle the difficulties which arose between them. The Popes, whatever may have been their personal character, were conservators of the peace. They preserved unity amid anarchy, and restrained the impulses of passionate kings. Again, the Papacy in the best ages, is thought by many profound historians to have been democratic in its sympathies. It guarded the interests of the people: it preserved them from the violence of their oppressors: it furnished a retreat, in monasteries, for the contemplative, the suffering, the afflicted, and the poor. The monks and nuns were taught, by their quiet and industrious life that:
>
> *"There exists*
> *An higher than the warrior's excellence;*
> *That vast and sudden deeds of violence.*
> *Adventures wild, and wonders of the moment,*
> *These are not they that generate*
> *The calm, and blissful, and enduring mighty"*

There are many brave men who have much theoretic, but very little actual blood to shed upon the battlefield, who nevertheless complain loudly of the alleged errors of those who won the victory. Had they but been there, the difficulties might have been much greater than they appear in the distance. Men are generally brave at a safe distance, and generally virtuous, in the absence of temptation. It is easy to find fault. The less we know of a matter, the more fault we can find in many cases. You have lived in the most favored age of the world, after the great art of printing was invented in 1444, and America discovered in 1492, and the consequent revival of literature, and the arts, and the extension of commerce; and you have still committed many grievous errors. True, you can boast of the number of your small and diversified Churches, as the fox did of her numerous progeny, while the Catholic theory can only boast of one; but that is a lion.

4. The disorders of the Papacy cannot destroy the Papal office

In reference to the effect of these disorders of the Popes, Mr. Campbell has a summary position as follows:

> 3. That Christ gave no law of succession.
>
> 4. That if He had, that succession has been destroyed by a long continuance of the greatest monsters of crime that ever lived, and by cabals, intrigues, violence, envy, lust, and schisms so that no man can believe that one drop of apostolic grace is either in the person or office of Gregory XVI. the present nominal incumbent of Peter's chair.[15]

It will be seen that this language is sufficiently confident and strong, to sustain any *sustainable* position. But with deference to the logic and opinion of the learned debater, there are some reasons that seem to render doubtful the entire conclusiveness of his position. As to the position marked 3, I have already spoken of it. It was only given to make clear the other position designated as 4.

The essence of this bold assumption is that an individual officer could not only forfeit his right to the office, by his own misconduct, but he could go farther, and destroy the office itself. In other words, the office created by Christ – His own work – could be destroyed by the acts of individuals. This is a startling proposition, and leaves all future generations at the mercy of those who precede it. Under this theory, I cannot understand how Christ could be a Divine Lawgiver, when He created so poor an institution as to be within the power of men.

I had supposed that the continued existence of the Church, with all the offices created by Christ, was dependent upon His will, and not upon the personal virtues or vices of individuals. It may be, that though Our Lord did promise to protect the Church against the gates of Hell, He did not mean to bind Himself to protect her against the gates of men. I had thought that both the creation of the office of Pope, and the consequent continuance of same, depended upon the will of the Founder of the institution, and not upon the will of men.

I am aware that inferior corporations, which are but the creatures of statutory enactments, may forfeit their charters by nonuser or misuser; because such is a part of the law of their creation. The misuser is the act of the controlling majority of the stockholders, and is, therefore, the act of all.

But this doctrine cannot apply to governments. Political governments may be changed at the pleasure of the founders; but the act of making such change is the act of the sovereign power. If it should happen that the President should commit treason, this would only forfeit his right to fill the office, but the office itself would remain unimpaired. The office was not created by him – was not his work – was made by the nation, and the Nation alone can unmake or destroy. If twenty Presidents in succession were to commit all the crimes possible, the office would still remain. The People might be induced to change the form of the government, but such change would be their act, not the act of those Presidents.

Is this not so with the Church? The Church is not an inferior corporation, but a supreme government. Christ is the head and founder of this kingdom, with subordinate officers under him. These officers were created by His act, and cannot be destroyed by the vices of subordinates. The office of Pope, if established at all, was created for some great and beneficial purpose. The Christians of all ages are equally entitled to these benefits, as subjects of the kingdom. They cannot be deprived of them by the personal vices of preceding Popes. It would be unjust that they should. If Christ had been a mere fallible lawgiver, and had made a mistake in creating the office, He might be induced to abolish it; but having had an eye, as Mr. Campbell justly says, to all the future in all He did, such a supposition cannot be indulged.

The idea that a perpetual office, created by Christ himself, in His own Church, against which the gates of Hell shall never prevail, could be abolished by the vices of individual incumbents, is a supposition too hard for me to understand. If that office could be abolished by the vices of incumbents, every other office in the church could be destroyed in the same way, and unless re-established by Christ, the Church itself must fail, as no institution can exist without offices. If the Church is to be considered as an inferior corporation, and the office of Pope could be destroyed, then the whole corporation must fall. For such inferior corporations do not forfeit the right to a particular office by nonuser or misuser, but they forfeit their entire existence. The law would hardly mutilate and cripple the corporation, and still expect it, after thus being maimed, to perform the functions it failed to do, when whole and entire.

In every view where this summary position may be considered, it certainly is an extreme assumption. That Christ should organize an institution and create offices so perfectly defective that they may be entirely abrogated by individuals is a position I apprehend, too sophistical to be entertained.

The whole force of the argument against the existence of the Papacy, upon the ground of the personal delinquencies of individual Popes, at intervals in the long line of succession, is based upon the essential error of confounding individual acts with official duties. It is true, that a man may be a good officer, and a bad man. It is conceded that a bad man is not so apt to be a good officer as a good man would be.

This distinction between personal and official conduct, I find admitted by most Protestant writers on some occasions, and then practically denied by them on others. We have seen the admissions of Mr. Campbell and Mr. Rice, when arguing against each other. But when Mr. Campbell was debating with Bishop Purcell, he had not then discovered that Caiphas could be a very good high priest, though a bad man. Time improved his views.

This confusion of personal with official capacity, is supported by plausible cases, that are put forth with apparent earnestness, and seemed to be believed by those who use them. The case *usually* made I find used by Mr. Breckenridge. He seems to have been in earnest since it was written, not spoken, by him. He says:

> The moral of 'bad man good pope' reminds us of the Archbishop (he was also a prince) who swore profanely in the presence of a peasant; the peasant exclaimed, with surprise, "Archbishop, do you swear." "No," he replied, "I swear as a prince." "Then," said the peasant, "when Satan comes for the prince, what will become of the Archbishop."[16]

This supposititious case is an instance of mere play on words. By artful arrangement, the most clear and manifest distinctions are confounded. The swearing was the act of an individual. However often Satan might come for the person called Archbishop, he would never get him until he died. Then I apprehend, he would leave the office behind him, and being no longer Archbishop, Satan would only get the individual after all.

CHARGES OF CATHOLIC MISCONDUCT

When an officer fails to use his legitimate powers in proper cases, or when he abuses or perverts them, or usurps powers not belonging to the office, then he is a bad officer. His personal sins may injure his official usefulness indirectly, by reason of the destruction of confidence in his official conduct. But in the contemplation of the theory they are distinct, and are so, in point of fact, in many cases.

Official delinquency does not necessarily follow from personal vices. The reason of this is plain. Men have different views of things, and there is a difference in criminality in different acts. A man may commit one class and not the other. All men commit some sins; and yet there are sins that few will commit. A man may be guilty of many personal sins, and yet regard his official obligations as sacred, because he considers that his personal vices affect himself mostly, while his official misconduct would affect others. When we assume that the official acts of a wicked clergyman are void, we certainly go beyond the truth.

I knew a most eminent preacher who baptized many persons in Mr. Campbell's church, who has fallen away in California, giving pretty conclusive evidence that he never was sincere. Was the baptism administered by him void, in the contemplation of Mr. Campbell's theory? Or was the truth proclaimed by him, void, because falling from his lips? Is the true coin vitiated simply because it has passed through the hands of a rogue?

The supposititious case is as irrelevant as the case by which the slave discomfited his master. The slave was a Baptist and the master a Methodist.

"Massa, do you read the Scripture?"

"Yes Jim I do."

"Then you read of John the Baptist?"

"Yes I do"

"But do you read of John the Methodist?"

The master was silent.

I found in Protestant works many arguments of a similar irrelevant character. They were in character with the reply of a man who was mildly reproved by a sincere Baptist minister for profane swearing; "My dear Sir, there is no difference between us. I swear, and mean no harm by it; and you pray and mean no good by it." Of course, the minister had no reply to make to such a false assumption of fact.

---

[1] A. Campbell and J. Purcell, *A debate on the Roman Catholic religion.* p. 293

[2] *Ibid.* p 301.

[3] *Encyclopaedia of Religious Knowledge*, p. 685, as given by Mr. Campbell.

[4] A. Campbell and J. Purcell. *op. cit.* p. 301.

[5] Charles Waterton Esq., *Wanderings in South America.* p. 82. Cited by John Hughes, *Hughes-Breckenridge Controversy.* p. 461.

[6] Leopold von Ranke, German Lutheran historian quoted in Wiseman's *Moorfield Lectures*. Lec. VIII.

[7] *Cf.* A. Campbell and J. Purcell, *op. cit.* p 32, 37. And John Hughes, *Hughes-Breckenridge Controversy.* p. 372.

[8] A. Campbell and J. Purcell, *op. cit. p.* 28.

[9] John Hughes, *Hughes-Breckenridge Controversy.* p. 372.

[10] A. Campbell and J. Purcell, *op. cit. p.* 146.

[11] Stephen Foster's song *Old Dog Tray.—E*ditor.

[12] Nicholas Wiseman, *Moorfield Lectures*, L viii.

[13] It so happened that Our Lord and Saint Paul were placed in almost the same situation. Paul had the advantage of his Master's previous example before him; and it is interesting to see how differently they acted. When Our Lord was before Ananias, one of the officers struck him with the palm of his hand, saying "Answerest thou the High Priest so?" Jesus answered him, "If I have spoken evil, bear witness of the evil: but if well, why smitest thou me?" This was the forgiving answer of a God.

But Paul was smitten by the order of the same High priest, he indignantly exclaimed: "God shall smite thee, thou whited wall." This was the language of an indignant man.

Is not the difference a most beautiful of the truth of Christianity? Could this difference in the conduct of Our Lord and Saint Paul, under circumstances so similar, have been the result of a forged narrative? Would such circumstances have been thought of?

[14] Henry Wheaton, *History of the Law of Nations in Europe and America.* p. 33.

[15] A. Campbell and J. Purcell, *op. cit.* p. 139.

[16] John Hughes, *op. cit.* p. 65.

CHAPTER III

EFFECTS OF THE CATHOLIC SYSTEM

1. Saints of the Catholic Church

In estimating the effects of any system of religion, the only fair and just method would seem to be, to look to those who humbly receive, and faithfully reduce to practice, its faith and morals, in their true spirit, as taught by the church herself. It is surely true, that individuals, under all systems, will err and come short of their duty. But after making a fair allowance for these cases, which no system can prevent, then take the best members of each communion, and see which has produced the greater number of saints, those noble and heroic souls, whose piety most resembles the spirits and acts of the early Church. What was Christianity in the beginning? What works—what sacrifices were then required of Christians? How did they bear themselves to the Church, to each other, and to the world?

Was not Christianity intended as an unchangeable system? As it was in the beginning, should it be now, henceforward and forever? Is man the same – still an inhabitant of the same world – still bound to die – and still aspiring to the same heaven? If so, Christianity must be still the same – requiring the same humility – the same devotion – the same patience – the same charity.

In considering this subject, there is this very remarkable fact. That all the saints who are recorded as such in the Calendar of the Church of England, with one exception, and in whose name their churches are dedicated, lived and died strict members of the Catholic Church, and were earnestly attached to her doctrines and discipline. "For example," says Dr. Milner,

> In this calendar we meet with a Pope Gregory, March 12th, the zealous assertor of the Papal Supremacy, and other Catholic doctrines; a Saint Benedict, March 21, the Patriarch of the Western Monks and Nuns; a St. Dunstan, May 19, the vindicator of clerical celibacy; a Saint Augustine, of Canterbury, May 26, the introducer of the whole system of Catholicity in England; and a venerable Bede, May 27, the witness of this important fact.

It is sufficient to mention the names of other Catholic saints, for example, David, Chad, Edward, Richard, Elphege, Remigius, and Edmund; all of which are inserted in the Calendar, and give names to some of the other churches of the establishment. Besides these, there are many of our other saints whom all learned and candid Protestants unequivocally admit to have been such, for the extraordinary purity and sanctity of their lives. Even Luther acknowledges St. Anthony, Saint Bernard, Saint Dominic, Saint Francis, Saint Bonaventure, &c., to have been saints though avowed Catholics, and defenders of the Catholic Church against the heretics and schismatics of their times.

But independently of this and of every other testimony, it is certain that the supernatural virtues and heroic sanctity of a countless number of holy personages of different countries, ranks, professions, and sexes, have illustrated the Catholic Church, in every age, with an effulgence which cannot be disputed or withstood. Your friends, I dare say, are not much acquainted with the histories of these brightest ornaments of Christianity. Let me then invite them to peruse them, not in the legends of obsolete writers, but in a work which, for its various learning and luminous criticism, was commended even by the infidel Gibbon; I mean *The Lives of Saints*, in twelve octavo volumes, written by the late Rev. Alban Butler, President of Saint Omer's College.

Protestants are accustomed to paint, in the most frightful colors, the alleged depravity of the Church when Luther erected his standard, in order to justify him and their followers, in their defection from it. But to form a right judgment in this case, let them read the works of the contemporary writers, an a Kempis, a Grisan, and Antonius,

Or let them peruse the lives of Saint Vincent Ferrer, Saint Lawrence Justinian, Saint Francis Paula, Saint Philip Neri, Saint Cajetan, Saint Teresa, Saint Francis Xaverius, and of those other saints who illuminated the Church about the period in question.

Or let them, from the very accounts of Protestant historians, compare as to religion and morality, Archbishop Cranmer with his rival Bishop Fisher; Protector Seymour with Chancellor More Anne Boleyn with Catharine of Aragon; Martin Luther and Calvin with Francis Xaverius and Cardinal Pole; Beza with Saint Francis of Sales; Queen Elizabeth with Mary Queen of Scots; these contrasted characters having more or less relation with each other.[1] From such a comparison, I have no sort of doubt what the decision of your friends will be concerning them, in point of their respective holiness."[2]

2. Catholic clergy adopt celibacy for the greater glory of God

I did not confine my attention alone to the conduct of both parties during the progress of the Reformation, in estimating the effects of the two systems. I looked also to general causes. I found, upon examination, that the Catholic clergy made far greater personal and worldly sacrifices than the Protestant. They dedicate themselves to the ministry exclusively – they give up all temporal hopes – they debar themselves from marriage – they come under the commands of superiors – they go to the uttermost bounds of the earth when required-and they devote their whole lives to the single performance of their duties.

The Catholic clergy look upon celibacy, when voluntary and for the greater glory of God, as a higher state than matrimony, and that it is revealed in Scripture. For Christ did say:

> Whosoever shall put away his wife, except it be for fornication, and shall marry another, committeth adultery; and whoso marrieth her that is put away, doth commit adultery. His disciples say unto him, If the case of the man be so with his wife, it is not good to marry. But he said unto them, All men cannot receive this saying save they to whom it is given. For there are some eunuchs, which were so born from their mother's womb; and there are some eunuchs, which were made eunuchs of men; and there be eunuchs, which have made themselves eunuchs for the Kingdom of Heaven's sake. He that is able to receive it let him receive it.[3]

The Catholic translation has it "all men do not." And Catholic writers insist that the Protestant is a plain mistranslation. But it does not seem to me that the sense is at all affected. It remains the same with either translation.

From this extract there would seem to follow certain plain conclusions:

1. That there were *two* classes of persons mentioned by our Lord.

2. That the saying prohibiting a man from putting away his wife, *except* for the cause stated, did not apply to one of these classes.

3. That this excepted class was the class mentioned in the second instance; and that such persons were allowed to put away their wives without any such misconduct on their part as that mentioned.

The Christian, like other systems of law, has provisions, both mandatory and prohibitory. Whatever, therefore, is not prohibited, may be done under any code. This provision of the law is prohibitory, not mandatory. It says you *must not* do a specified act, except for the cause mentioned. This provision then only applies to the class to whom it was given; and, therefore, leaves out the *excepted* class, who do not come within the prohibition. The excepted class, not being prohibited from doing the act specified, are not controlled by this provision, and we must look to other portions of the law that apply, either *specially* to this excepted class, or to *all classes*, which of course would include this. We must give all the provisions their full, but harmonious force. They must stand and operate together, as the intention of the Divine Lawmaker could not have been confused.

It is clear that eunuchs, being the excepted class, could put away their wives without the misconduct mentioned. And if the first two classes of eunuchs could do so, the third class could also. If, then, a man makes himself chaste for the kingdom of heaven's sake, and puts away his wife with her free consent, when given under proper circumstances, does he not fill the character spoken of by Christ? Does he violate that saying of our Lord, given in the ninth verse? And does he, by this act, violate any other prohibitory provision of the law? If so, why did Christ make him one of the *excepted class?*

But this question arises: If the man who makes himself chaste for the kingdom of heaven's sake, may put away his wife without the general cause mentioned, may he not also marry another, as no part of the prohibition applies to him? I apprehend not. He belongs to the *excepted class*, because he makes himself chaste from the motive stated; and by marrying another wife, he ceases to be chaste, at once forfeits his claim to be one of the *excepted class*, and thus comes properly within the prohibition. But it may be asked: If a man in the case supposed, can put away his wife with her consent, why cannot he do so without her consent, if it be true that this prohibition does not apply to him? Because to put her away *without* her consent, would be a violation of those *general* principles of the law which apply to *all classes*, including this excepted class. For whether we regard marriage as a contract, or both as a sacrament and a contract, its duties cannot be avoided in the case mentioned, without the mutual consent of both parties. Their first engagement is to each other; and the law of Christ does not require or permit us to violate our honest and lawful engagements, to fill a mere *counsel of perfection*. And the same general principle would prevent the separation of husband and wife, even when they had given their mutual consent from motives of piety, if it would materially interfere with the discharge of their duties to their children or other dependents.

Unless the passage has this meaning, I cannot understand it to mean any thing. That Christ does lay down the general rule in the ninth verse is not only clear from the general language used, but also from the nature of the subject matter itself. That He intends an *exception* to that rule in the twelfth verse would seem to be plain. For He says expressly, "all men cannot receive this saying, save they to whom it is given." It could not, then, have been given to *all*; and those to whom it was *not* given, were certainly *excepted.*

Now were those who made themselves eunuchs [chaste] for the kingdom of heaven's sake, to blame for doing so, or were they worthy of commendation, in the eye of Christ? It would seem clear, that they were either blamable or commendable for the act, and that it could not be merely indifferent. That this act was commendable seems clear, not only from the fact that Christ mentions it without censure, but because the *privilege* of putting away the wife, without the cause mentioned, was extended to them, as well as the other kind of eunuchs spoken of. The language of our Lord in the twenty-seventh verse, that those who forsake wives shall receive certain rewards, makes His meaning still more clear. By putting these considerations together, the intent of our Lord to place celibacy above marriage, as a more holy state, would seem to be undoubted.

When we take the language of Saint Paul in connection with that of Christ, the intention would seem to be plain. For the apostle, in the fifteenth chapter of his first Epistle to the Corinthians, certainly does place celibacy above marriage, as a more holy state. The only doubt as to the sentiments of Saint Paul regards the question whether his recommendation was *temporary or continuing.* Whatever Christ intended could not have been temporary, but continuing; for it is given in a form as permanent as the general rule itself, that a man shall not put away his wife, save for the cause stated. So, if the general rule be permanent, the exception is also permanent, for no distinction is made between them in *this* respect.

If the language of our Lord, and that of Saint Paul, relate to the *same* matter, they both must be of the same import, and, therefore, are either both temporary, or both continuing. It is true, the apostle says in the twenty-sixth verse:

> I suppose therefore that this is good for the present distress. I say that it is good for a man so to be.

Now did this verse apply to *all* the preceding matters in this chapter? If not, to what portion did it apply? Many things are staged in preceding verses, and to which of them did the apostle refer? My own impression is, that he intended it as a limitation to the wish expressed in the seventh verse: "I would that all men were even as I myself."

However, after the statement made in the twenty-sixth verse, and when he seems to speak of the two states *generally* without regard to *time*, he says:

> He that is unmarried careth for the things that belong to the Lord, how he may please the Lord: but he that is married careth for the things of the world, how he may please his wife. There is a difference also between a wife and a virgin. The unmarried woman careth for the things of the Lord, that she may be holy in both body and spirit; but she that is married careth for the things of the world, how she may please her husband.

If the apostle intended his recommendation as only temporary, and not continuing beyond the then "present distress," he gave, it would seem, some most illogical reasons for it – reasons that apply to *all time*, in support of a mere temporary matter. But these reasons are of such a character, that it seems impossible that they could be intended to apply to a mere temporary recommendation, arising *solely* from the then present circumstances. For the apostle speaks of virgins being "holy *both in body and spirit*;" and holiness in both these respects, could not be possessed by the married woman. And is it not clear, that holiness in both body and spirit, must be superior to holiness in spirit only? The apostle does say most distinctly, "there is a difference between a wife and a virgin," and he does make this difference consist in the virgin being "holy both in body and spirit," while the married woman was not holy in both these respects, but only in one. And as there was an express difference, it was in favor of the virgin. And if this be so, was there not good reason why this superior holiness should be recommended by Saint Paul for all coming time? Or did the apostle mean to say, that the virgin was holy both in body and spirit *only during* the then present distress?

I must confess, I cannot understand him as giving *permanent* reasons for a *temporary* matter; for permanent reasons cannot, with any sort of truth or consistency, be given in such cases. *Temporary matters must arise from temporary causes.* That permanent causes could produce mere temporary effects would seem clearly erroneous. If a temporary practice is intended to be inculcated, there can be no force in permanent reasons, when applied to such a case. There is no connection between the cause and the assumed effect. The answer of a witness must be responsive to the question propounded; and the effect must legitimately flow from the cause, and be as consistent with it as the stream is to its fountain.

The following beautiful testimony to celibacy is from the late work of Dr. Schaff, a distinguished Protestant divine, not less remarkable for his learning than for his love of antiquity, and for his temperate sentiments respecting the Reformation:

> To Paul, who spent his life in missionary travel, and who was exposed to all privations, hardships, and persecutions, the married state, with its temporal cares, and all sorts of personal matters of attention, must have seemed rather a hindrance to the fulfillment of his apostolic calling, and the single state more favorable to his activity in the service of his Redeemer. With him celibacy was actually an elevation above all earthly cares, an entire devotion to the purest love and the holiest interests, in anticipation of the *vita Angelica.*
>
> And who will deny that such cases repeatedly occur? Who does not know that the voluntary celibacy of so many self-denying missionaries, especially in times of wild barbarism and dissolution, as at the entrance of the Middle Ages, was, in the hand of God, a great blessing, in mightily promoting the spread of the Gospel among the rude nations, and under numberless privations? Here Christianity deviated from the old Jewish view, in which celibacy was a disgrace and a curse; it can transform this state into a charm, and use it for its own ends. Without the knowledge of the peculiar value and manifold benefits of this virginity, which grew out of unreserved enthusiasm for Christ and his Gospel, it is impossible properly to understand the history of the Church, especially before the Reformation.

3. Duties of Catholic Clergy

The Catholic clergy not only do they make greater sacrifices than the Protestant, in giving up so many privileges dear to human nature, and so highly esteemed by Protestant clergymen generally; but they take upon themselves a ministry far more laborious, painful, and hazardous. They have the preaching of the gospel to do as well as the Protestant: and besides this, they have, in addition, other duties to perform, still more arduous. The discipline of the church to which they belong is far more rigid and strict than that of the Protestant, and far more rigidly executed and enforced. For the Catholic clergyman is not only under the strict supervision of his superior, but he is bound by his vows to perform his duty regularly.

As Christ enjoins constant prayer, the church requires all her clergy, from the sub-deacon to the Pope, daily to say the Seven Canonical Hours. These consist chiefly of scriptural Psalms and Lessons, which take up in the recital near an hour and a half in addition to their other devotions.

In reference to fasting, the Church of England in her Homily iv. uses this language: "That we ought to fast is a truth too manifest to stand in need of any proof." In pursuance of this sentiment, that church enjoins in her Common Prayer Book the same days of fasting and abstinence with the Catholic Church; that is to say, the forty days of Lent, the Ember days, all the Fridays in the year, etc. But who observes these rules? Who keeps these days? Where is the Protestant to be found who imitates the example of old Paul and the early Church, in their frequent fasting? After all the ridicule which has been, or can be, thrown upon the practice of fasting, is it not founded in apostolic practice, in reason, truth, and right? Is it not beneficial, in and of itself? Is not man a creature that needs discipline at every step of his existence? Does he not need a trial – a test – a sacrifice – at all times? If he never could forget his duty – his dependence – his end – in other words, if he was perfect without the use of discipline, it might not be so. And if the practice was not eminently beneficial, why did the early church observe it so much? There must have been some good reason for such a practice, in that day of light, certainty, and devotion.

Among the regular and painful duties of the Catholic clergyman, may be mentioned that of hearing confessions. This duty requires much time, labor, patience, study, and attention, as well as the qualities of clear discrimination and mild firmness. Those outside the Church hardly can know how great the labor of the confessional is, and the amount of true patience required to discharge well its delicate and important duties. The Confessor must not only hear the narration of the vices and sins of each individual – those painful errors so humiliating to human nature – but he must suggest a remedy for the ten thousand diseases of distressed souls, who tell their sins, their mistakes, and their shortcomings to him. He has to deal with every variety of character and disposition – the selfish – the obstinate – the reckless – the passionate – the wayward – the idle – the over scrupulous – the imaginative – and the timid. In short, he has to deal with every variety of character, from the repentant criminal to the humble saint. That such duties are onerous and painful, as well as laborious and responsible, would seem to require no proof with the sensible and reflective mind.

But the most painful and arduous duty, because it is the most irregular, the most sudden and dangerous of the duties of the Catholic clergy, is the sick call. However poor, destitute, and unworthy the sick person may be, it is the imperative duty of the priest to go and see him. There can be no excuse short of the most insurmountable obstacle. The poor dying soul has a right to the last sacraments of the church. And the priest must go. It does not matter what may be the personal danger or inconvenience to himself, he must go. Through the darkness of midnight, beneath the withering summer's sun, or facing the scathing blasts of winter, through storm and calm, he must go. And when the pestilence and famine rage,

"When nature sickens, and each gale is death,"

he must still go. He has undertaken a sacred duty and has pledged his life to it. It must be discharged. He professed himself a true under-shepherd of the flock, not a hireling, and he must lay down his life for the sheep, and not desert his flock in the hour of danger. His rigid Church permits no recreancy in the discharge of such a trust. He cannot flee. He must stand and die in the deadly breach. Did he not deliberately and voluntarily undertake to drink this cup, and must he not drink it? In this ministry he meets with tears, and groans and agonies. He has no smile to greet him, but the sweet smile upon the lips of the departing saint.

Besides these sacrifices and labors, the whole spirit of the Catholic system tends to merge the importance of individuals in that of the church. She is everything – individual fame and importance, comparatively, nothing. The Catholic clergyman knows that the important functions performed by him, are equally performed by others. He knows that the very vestments he wears, while performing his official duties, belong not to him, but to the church. The only advantage he can gain over others is in the more faithful discharge of his duties; and this can only be obtained by increased labor and devotion.

Before he becomes a minister in the Catholic Church, if he is proud and vain of his own personal qualities and appearance, he had better not enter her ministry, if he expects to indulge these passions; for he will find himself checked and mortified at every step. If he has not the faith and moral nerve to face death deliberately in the discharge of his duty, at every step, when required, he had better desist. If he is self-willed, headstrong, obstinate, and fond of flattery, he had better not go there. If he is like Demosthenes, whose brilliant orations elicited only one response from the Athenians, "Let us rise and march against Philip;" but who, when Philip and his armies appeared, was among the first to flee, he had better not undertake the daily sacrifices to be found in this laborious and devoted ministry.

These sacrifices, labors and dangers, are more conclusive evidences of deep and abiding faith and devotion, than all the eloquent discourses ever delivered. These are the decisive tests that cannot be disputed. They are simple, practical, and certain. In vain may the motives of such men be assailed. Such grapes do not grow upon thorns. Men do not voluntarily live poor, work hard, and die willingly, from improper motives.

I see the Catholic clergy always at their posts, ready to die with the members of their suffering flocks, and so many of them thus falling martyrs to their duty. While so many Protestant clergymen (with some noble exceptions), so promptly act upon that saying, "A wise man foreseeth the evil, and fleeth therefrom." When I see this I cannot but draw the conclusion that there is, and must be, some great radical difference in the two systems. One seems studiously adapted to keep alive and perpetuate the apostolic spirit of self-abnegation, while the other is as studiously adapted to suppress it.

If an aspirant to the Protestant ministry be self-willed, and fond of his own opinions, among the five hundred sects in Protestant Christendom, he will be very apt to find one to suit him; but if not, he can organize a new sect to suit himself, and the older Protestant sects cannot consistently assail him upon the ground of innovation. If they do, he has ample materials for refutation and triumph. Let him join with one if he will, he is free to settle where he pleases, and to stipulate for his salary. If he is a man of talents, and a popular speaker, he can obtain a much larger salary. The matter rests with him and the particular congregation. The church does not interfere. If he is ambitious, and fond of public meetings, the offices of the country are open to him, and hence we find them in our legislative halls, both State and Federal.

In short, the Protestant clergyman preaches as long he pleases – to whom he pleases – and if the ministerial duties do not please him, and anything preferable should offer, he is at liberty to lay aside the clerical profession at his own election. He lives as well, dresses as well, has all the comforts of home, wife, children, and friends: for the Protestant clergy, taken as a class, enjoy as many of the comforts of life as lawyers, physicians, and other professional men, while their labors are not more arduous, if so much so. In short, they have all the privileges of their lay brethren, and are required to make no more sacrifices. Such are the general facts with reference to the general Protestant ministerial system. There are some exceptions in reference to a portion of these particulars, in some of the Protestant churches. The Methodist clergy are under a more rigid discipline than those of other Protestant sects. There may be other exceptions as to some other parties.

These characteristics of the Protestant ministry have made it a mere profession, sought as a means of making a living, like other professions, in too many cases. It is a profession lucrative to some, and comfortable to the great majority. It is true, that the great majority of Protestant ministers cannot hope, if they wished, to make a fortune; but it is equally true that the great majority of every calling and profession cannot expect to grow rich; and that most men are well satisfied if they enjoy the ordinary comforts of life, without being rich. And it is very natural that a system of Christian ministry which requires very few, if any, sacrifices, affords comfortable livings, and imposes only moderate labor, must necessarily contain a greater number of venial and unworthy ministers.

Is it, then, at all surprising, that in the hour of extreme danger, when the rigid test of acts, and not of words, is applied, so many Protestant ministers flee from their flocks, and leave them to take care of themselves? that when the sickly season approaches in New Orleans, the eloquent Mr.— ,the powerful Mr. —, and the declamatory Mr. —, should leave their flocks for a pleasure trip to the North, and return with the returning frosts in the Fall? or that so many should have left Norfolk during the prevalence of the Yellow Fever there?

4. The piety of the different orders of the Church

In addition to the sacrifices made by regular clergy of the Catholic Church, those made by numerous orders in her communion constitute the most conclusive test of faith and humility. After all the ridicule and contempt that has been poured out upon these orders; after all the calumnies and aspersions that have been heaped upon them; after all the occasional vices of individual members; and despite all the envy and misrepresentation of their enemies; a sublime, simple, and inflexible fact will stand apparent. The fact is that they do make sacrifices, and exhibit devotion that their enemies cannot reach.

There is something beautiful and holy in the example of a humble follower of a meek Savior in voluntarily giving up all earthly pursuits and enjoyments and dedicating his whole life entirely to the service of the crucified Redeemer. Like the poor widow commended by our Lord for casting all her money into the treasury, the act of giving up all for Christ is the most conclusive test of abiding faith in the truth of His sublime system. One such example is worth more than the example of a thousand frigid Christians. Such a dedication is but the legitimate and logical result of a full, firm, and implicit faith.

That a life of holy poverty and entire devotion to Christ was a more holy state, would seem to be most distinctly and clearly stated by Christ. We are told in Saint Matthews's gospel, that a young man came to our Lord and asked, "What good thing should I do to have eternal life?" And he said to him. "...If thou will enter into life, keep the commandments." When Jesus enumerated the commandments the young man said, "All these things have I kept from my youth up; what lack I yet?" Our Lord made him this plain and explicit reply: "If thou wilt be perfect, go and sell what thou hast, and give to the poor, and thou wilt have treasure in heaven; come and follow me"

The young man would not do this, but "went away sorrowing, for he had great possessions." He unquestionably understood our Lord as recommending voluntary poverty, incurred for His sake, as a more holy state. Other wise there would be no cause for his sorrow.

The language of our Lord is so plain and explicit that it would seem to need no additional explanation. If it did, it could be found in His language to His disciples on the same matter in succeeding verses. For when Peter said, "Behold, we have forsaken all and followed thee," Our Lord answered,

> And everyone that hath forsaken houses, or brethren, or sisters, or father, or mother, or wife, or children, or lands, for my name's sake, shall receive a hundred fold, and shall inherit everlasting life.

To illustrate my meaning, even at the risk of an apparent solecism, I will suppose this young man to have pursued two different courses:

1. He went away, kept his money, married a wife, raised a virtuous family and became an exemplary member of the Church of Christ.

2. He went away, sold his property, distributed the proceeds to the poor, took up his cross, and followed Christ, dedicating his whole being to his Master's Kingdom, and became holy in "Both body and spirit."

Now let the honest and sincere, the meek and humble, put this question in their hearts – Under the law of Christ which of these two states was more holy? Can there be a doubt as to what the answer must be?

It is true, that those who oppose celibacy (and as a matter of course holy poverty, for the second cannot well be recommended without the first) have advanced many abstract general reasons that are true; and yet they do not touch the real question. If I remember correctly, among many beautiful things said by Jeremy Taylor in favor of marriage, he said in substance, "Marriage peoples heaven with angels." This is true, but it equally true that Saint Paul filled heaven with angels though he was never married. It is equally true that he saved more souls in that holy state of celibacy than he could have done with a family on his hands. The reason being that he was thus enabled to perform more labor for his Master. Suppose we take one hundred ministers, of equal qualifications and sincerity, fifty of whom shall be married, and fifty shall remain unmarried—will not the fifty unmarried be able to perform much more labor for the Church, at much less cost? The superior efficiency and economy of an unmarried clergy must be apparent.

If it was insisted that Christ had laid it down, as an inflexible law, that celibacy and poverty were incumbent upon *all*, then these *general* objections cannot apply. Marriage and property is the *general* rule—celibacy and poverty, the exception.

Our Lord put forth a permanent system, adapted to all time, taken as one whole. He knew (and so declared) that the great majority of men would never be good and worthy members of his Church, for many should be called, and few chosen. These, of course, would not embrace his counsel. He also knew that the great and overwhelming majority of Christians would never embrace His perfect state. For them His saying was not intended. The recommendation was then only intended, and only calculated, in its nature, for the *few*—those noble and heroic souls who could and would voluntarily embrace such a state.

It must be obvious to good sense, that while no state could exist in peace and prosperity without marriage, no country can contain beyond a given number of inhabitants; and that the earth itself has its limits, as to its capacity to sustain population. It is equally obvious that when a population attains a proper point of density, that all excess beyond this becomes a burthen to the state, and to the starving peoples themselves. And it must be equally clear, that the marriage of almost all persons in a thinly populated country will so increase the population, that in a century or two, at most, the population will reach the proper point of density. Then it is equally clear that after it attains this point, under the same cause, the population will become redundant, and, therefore, suffering and dependent. With a redundant population, when commercial disasters, or short crops, then members must perish. Of all the physical evils that waylay and beset the thorny path of life, none is so great as that of starvation. It is not a sudden and desperate onset upon the physical and mental process; but it is a desperate and continued assault, that undermines both body and mind; and destroys both, inch by inch.

From these considerations, it would seem evident to the political economist, that while marriage is the general rule, celibacy is a useful exception, under proper circumstances. And while the great majority of persons in every community should marry, there are persons who should not. By not entering the marriage state, they select wisely for themselves, and also for the state. So far, then, as general and abstract considerations go, they are not against the counsel of celibacy and holy poverty in the *few*; but would seem manifestly to support it.

It is true, it is said by some that celibacy is an unnatural state, and, therefore, cannot be supported with fidelity. But this is true in general, and untrue in particulars. Saint Paul seems to have had a very different opinion; for he most clearly distinguishes between those who can remain chaste, and those who cannot. Both Saint Paul and Saint John were able to remain in that state of holiness, in both body and spirit. So, the great majority of respectable single persons of both sexes, that either never marry, or marry at a late period of life, remain chaste. These persons, without any religious vows, maintain their chastity; and why persons cannot do so who take a vow, and dedicate themselves to the sole service of God, it is difficult to understand. Certainly, they had additional and more powerful motives, and are surrounded with additional checks.

The "necessity" of marriage was maintained by Luther. However, as he himself only married at age forty-five, his case proved one of two things:.

1. Either he had remained chaste through wild youth, and therefore was mistaken about the *necessity*, or

2. He had himself been guilty of scandalous excesses.[4]

From the passages it is plain, that our Lord did recommend the young man to sell all his property and *give to the poor*, and for *thus doing*, he should have *treasure in heaven.* And it is equally clear, that Christ did offer rewards to those who forsook either the property or the persons mentioned. If then the more devoted Christians in all ages should follow the example recommended by Christ to the young man, do they thereby sin? On the contrary, do they not do *precisely* that which the meek Savior recommended, and to the performance of which He did promise "*treasure in heaven*"? Can all the eloquent and polished sophistry in the world avoid the plain intent of Christ? Can all the whisperings of immediate self-interest, (powerful as they are,) and all the deductions of sensual pride, explain away this plain language? And if we have not sufficient faith and virtue of our own – or if our circumstances will not permit us – to do as our Lord recommended, should we envy and asperse those who do? On the contrary, ought we not to have the noble and manly candor to admire and love those heroic souls who can and do attain superior virtue?

The most difficult of all virtues to acquire and practice, is that of sweet humility. It is the truest test of practical piety. How hard it is to overcome the spirit of revenge, that natural impulse of the human heart! How difficult to withstand the finger of scorn—the withering sarcasm – the sallies of villainous wit – and above all,

"The Godless look of earth!"

But this most difficult of all the practical virtues has been attained in the greatest perfection by the great majority of those who belong to these orders:

> those courageous souls, who form the most absolute and efficacious purpose to pursue the right road, in spite of every obstacle, and without examining whether they have to experience relief or disgust, pleasure or pain, consolation or desolation… Who go straight to God, by an unconditional surrender and complete denial of

themselves, in the spirit of a profound humility, of a sweetness of heart, and an equality of mind.

Among the most notable examples may be mentioned that of Saint Jane Francis de Chantal, who was descended from a noble and wealthy family, and who was the widow of a wealthy nobleman, but who gave up all for Christ. This eminently holy person was the foundress of the order of The Visitation. The misfortunes, the trials, the calumnies, contradictions, and insults to which this devoted woman was subjected were certainly most grievous, long continued, and oft repeated. She had to endure every sort of test, short of that of actual personal violence. And under all these trials, she was never known to return reproach for insult, nor a railing accusation to calumny. For her noble and beautiful sentiment was, that:

> without solid humility there can exist only shadows and phantoms of virtue. Blessed is the soul that humbles herself before God, and unfeignedly accuses herself before creatures: she will recover what she has lost by her own fault. Humility of heart, and submission of will and judgment, must ever be deemed the ground of all perfection.

5. Contemplative religion

In reference to contemplative religion, an eminent divine of the Church of England has said:

> In England, I could almost say, we are too little acquainted with contemplative religion. The monk, painted by Sterne, may give us a more favorable idea of it than our prejudices generally suggest. I once traveled with a Recolet, and conversed with a Minim at his convent; and they both had that kind of character which Sterne gives to his monk; that refinement of body and mind, that pure glow of meliorated passion, that polished piety and humanity....[5]

These are certainly most beautiful traits of the saint. Are they offensive to heaven? And if we find them so common among the inmates of the cloister, is it not an evidence that there is the nursery of these superlative virtues?

"A poor monk of the order of Saint Francis," says Sterne,

> came into the room to beg something for his convent. The moment I cast my eyes upon him, I was pre-determined not to give him a single sous.

After having refused the boon asked by the monk, the writer continues:

> "But we distinguish," said I, laying my hand upon the sleeve of his tunic in return for his appeal, "we distinguish, my good father, between those who wish to eat only the bread of their own labor, and those who wish to eat the bread of other people, and have no other plan of life but to get through it, in sloth and ignorance, *for the love of God"*

There was bitter sarcasm in all that. We can well imagine the contemptuous expression of Sterne's countenance, when he said it. The reply itself imputed to the poor monk the most despicable motives, as well as the most consummate hypocrisy. Sterne was a great wit—not always very chaste, and had no particular humility to restrain him. The feelings of the poor recluse were, therefore, in his power. So far as insult was concerned, the monk was his prisoner.

To this bitter accusation Sterne says:

> The poor Franciscan made no reply: a hectic (frown), for a moment, passed across his cheek, but could not tarry. Nature seemed to have done with her resentments in him; he showed none, but letting his staff fall within his arm, he pressed both hands with resignation upon his breast, and retired.

But to the honor of Sterne he repented for what he had done, and candidly states it. "My heart smote me," he says,

> the moment he shut the door. 'Pshaw!' said I, with an air of carelessness, three, several times – but it would not do: every ungracious syllable I had uttered crowded back into my imagination; I reflected I had no right over the poor Franciscan but to deny him; and that the punishment of that was enough to the disappointed without the addition of unkind language. I considered his gray hairs; his courteous figure seemed to re-enter, and gently ask me what injury he had done to me? And why I could use him thus?

I do not know that this monk was the one to whom Dr. Hay refers, as I have not now access to Sterne's works, and have taken these extracts from another book. But this incident is a beautiful illustration of the influence of holy poverty upon the Christian character. Here two very opposite characters were contrasted, face-to-face. They were both members of different Churches. One was a poor Catholic monk, the other a distinguished Protestant preacher. One could give an insult – the other could bear it in Christian silence and submission. "Nature seemed to have done with her resentments" in the monk – "he showed none" – made no reply – crossed his hands with resignation, and retired. This poor insulted and despised monk possessed "that refinement of body and mind, that pure glow of meliorated passion, that polished piety and humanity" so befitting the character of the perfect Christian.

We must admire Sterne's candor in stating the facts of this incident, so much to the advantage of the gray-haired and courteous monk. We know not who he was. His name is not given. It has been doubtless forgotten. But this incident will live, and warm the hearts of the pious and the good. Who would not prefer to be the poor monk, in preference to the witty and scornful Sterne? Is not pure piety – that "holiness both of body and spirit," as Saint Paul has it – more estimable and lovely, than all the wit and sarcasm in the world? And will it not pass better in heaven? Wit ends with earth; but virtue lives on. One passes current with men – the other with God.

It seems to have been the opinion of Sterne, that the contemplative orders had nothing to do, and lived in idleness and ignorance. But this opinion resulted from an ignorance in Sterne himself, of the discipline and devotions of these orders. No doubt, the courteous monk was as learned as Sterne himself, perhaps even more so. But many men like to take a view of things at a distance, and to form their conclusions from some general and sweeping assumption. We always blame that which we do not understand; and we never understand that which we do not investigate with care and impartiality.

It seemed also to be the opinion of Sterne, that these contemplative orders were of not practical use to religion. But with all due deference to his opinion, I must say, he seems to have overlooked the practical value of example. The single touching incident of the poor Franciscan has done more for Christianity – pure, genuine, holy and gentle Christianity – a thousand-fold, than all that Sterne – the wit, the scholar, and the wag – every wrote, said or did. That poor monk gained a greater and more difficult victory than that of the orator, statesman, or warrior. *He conquered himself.* The witty writings of Sterne may excite the admiration of men; but the noble example of that poor monk excites the deep and intense love of pure and holy hearts. And what tribute of praise can equal the free, unbribed gushings of pure love? And whatever may be the opinion of others, I unhesitatingly say for myself, that I would rather be like that poor monk, than to attain all the glory of all the wits who have ever left, or ever will leave, their names to undying fame. O! that I could gain such a victory over myself.

But these holy contemplative orders have done more than by their example. Who copied the Scriptures before the art of printing was discovered? Who preserved the learned works of the Greek and Roman historians, statesmen, orators and poets? Did they not do it? And who have composed the noblest works of piety ever written, except the Divine Scriptures? Who composed those inimitable works, "The Imitation of Christ" and "The Spiritual Combat" not to mention others, but members of the monastic orders? The authors of those works were men who had also gained the great victory. They had that "refinement of body and mind." The author of the "Imitation of Christ" was severely slandered; but he submitted in patience, and asked, "What are words but words? They fly through the air, and hurt not a stone."[6]

What works have been composed by men mixing with the world, that can equal these in deep Christian learning and sweet humility? The nearest approach to them by any Protestant writer, so far as my knowledge extends, is the work of John Bunyan, "The Pilgrim's Progress;" and if I remember well, this was written in prison, while the author's mind and soul were abstracted from the cares of earth. Who does not feel the advantages, and even necessity, of such abstraction from temporal cares, when writing upon such holy subjects?

In these abodes of poverty and peace, the pious and contemplative spirit can indulge her emotions undisturbed by the warring elements of the outside world. The great Dr. Johnson had some beautiful conceptions of the peace of such a state. "Many," says Dr. Johnson,

> are weary of their conflicts with adversity, and are willing to eject those passions which have long busied them in vain; and many are dismissed by age and diseases from the more laborious duties of society. In monasteries the weak and timorous may be happily sheltered, the weary may repose, and the penitent may meditate. These retreats of prayer and contemplation have something so congenial to the mind of man, that perhaps there is scarcely one that does not propose to close his life in pious abstraction, with a few associates, serious as himself....
>
> Whatever is done by the monks, is incited by an adequate motive. Their time is regularly distributed; one duty succeeds another, so that they are not left open to the distraction of unguided choice, nor lost in the shades of listless inactivity. There is a certain task to be performed at an appropriate hour; and their toils are cheerful, because they consider them as acts of piety, by which they are always advancing towards endless felicity.[7]

It must be conceded by persons of experience and observant disposition, that it often occurs that the spirits of individuals are totally broken by a concurrence of misfortunes, until they are unfit for the active duties of life, and become tired of the world. In such a case there is only one of two retreats offered—a monastery, or the modern remedy of suicide. The emotions with which the victim of disappointment would retire from the world, were feelingly expressed by Wolsey:

> O father abbot, an old man, broken by the storms of state, is come to lay his weary bones among you; give him a little earth for charity.

"A good society," says a French author, "provides for everything, even for the wants of those who detach themselves from it by choice or by necessity."

A great French philosopher has also said:

> Let us grant to virtue that right of asylum which crime had formerly. There are always upon earth men who are fatigued with life's journey, and no one can be sure that some day or other he will not be of their number.[8]

Mabillon, as cited by the eloquent Digby, in his great work, *Ages of Faith,* has these beautiful remarks:

> For who is there that has a just sense of Christian piety, and who examines the thing before God, but must esteem those men very useful to the Church who endeavor to conform assiduously to the life of Christ; who cultivate the worship of God with all the devotion of which they are capable, offering their body and soul as a constant sacrifice of praise; who retain the ancient vestiges and specimen of Christian penitence in the Church; who opened public schools of virtue; who, by their labor, transmitted the monuments of ancient writing to posterity; who gave example to clerks to institute laudable societies; who erected as many hospitals for the poor as monasteries, in which diseases of the soul were cured, in which baptismal innocence was preserved inviolate, or restored when lost, and in which the wants of all the needy are supplied? Monasteries are hostels, in which not alone the cloistral flock, but, as Leodegavius testifies, the whole world is delivered from the corruptions of the age. Finally, who can say that they were useless to the civil and Christian republic, who covered with towns and villages so many provinces before uninhabited and desert, adorned them with edifices, enriched them with letters, and, by giving Episcopal and pastoral institutions, brought so many millions of pagans to the faith?[9]

6. The active orders of the Church

The contemplative orders are not the only orders of the Church. There are many active and laborious orders, who give their whole lives for the benefit of others, without any regard to the religion, name, or class of the sufferers. These active orders, since the discovery of the art of printing, are greater in proportion than they were formerly. Among the active orders, I may mention the Jesuits, the Monks of Saint Bernard, and the Monks of La Trappe. Also the sisters of Notre-Dame, the Sisters of the Sacred Heart, the Sisters of Mercy, and the Sisters of Charity. They have different disciplinary rules; and while some confine their attention mostly to teaching, others are found in the hospital, by the side of the sick and dying.

The sublime and simple example of these orders, especially those of the Sisters of Mercy and the Sisters of Charity, is "far more touching than the outpourings of eloquence, however lofty." And it is not only so, because their duties are the most laborious and humiliating, the most gloomy and melancholy, and the most dangerous, but because they are performed so silently and unostentatiously. Silently they pray – silently they smooth the brow of death, and sweetly they point the dying vision to the upper sky. They ask no meed of praise. They seek no approving eye, but that of Him "whose eye is on the heart."

> They are more exposed to the world than members of a religious order, having, in most instances, not other monastery that the houses of the sick or school-room. No other cell than a rented apartment, no other chapel than the parish church, no cloister but the public street or hospital, no enclosure but obedience, no grate but the fear of God, no veil but that of holy modesty.

These devoted Sisters know no race, no color, no creed, and no condition in the objects of their labors. They know no geographical lines but those of suffering humanity. Wherever distress and suffering appear, there they are found. When the craven minister flies from his afflicted flock – when the brother deserts his dying sister, and the father his plague stricken child, in their flight they meet the Sisters making their hasty way to the abandoned scenes of death and sorrow. They seek those melancholy scenes from which other flee. Their joy is to die in the discharge of their duty. They heed not the aspersions cast upon their faith. As they blush at fame, and shrink from praise, like the "man of sorrows" they are silent under imputations and calumnies. The praise they receive is voluntarily bestowed upon the order by others.

Their individual names, as their individual deeds, are unknown. Each Sister wears out her life in labors of charity – lives at all times prepared to die, and when death does come,

"Steals from the world, and not a stone
Tells where she lies."

Her name, her virtues, and her deeds are forgotten. And because no monument and no chronicle perpetuates her individual deeds, we are not to suppose from this, that she possessed no individual merits of the highest order; for in this world, monuments are "often raised without merit, and lost without a crime." The unknown and unchronicled Sister, who sleeps in a humble grave, possessed an intrepid soul, and

"A heart once pregnant with celestial fire."

Her virtues, though inflexible, were yet as gentle and beautiful

"As the ling'ring beam, that eve's decline
Will paint on the vanishing day."

But are not the devoted members of all these orders wild enthusiasts? They are enthusiasts, but not *wild* enthusiasts. It is the intense, yet calm, persevering enthusiasm of Christianity. For it is one of the most beautiful and rational traits of the Catholic Church, that the enthusiasm of her children is *a regulated enthusiasm.* It is not that ungovernable mountain torrent that overflows the cultivated plain below; but it is that unfailing steady stream, which does not rise too high with freshets, nor descend too low from droughts, but in its gentle course, fertilizes, without deluging, the country through which it passes.

There is every motive in the Catholic Church to excite the zeal of her children, and everything to keep down fanaticism. The most zealous souls in her communion are taught discipline and humility. The great and voluntary sacrifices made by the members of these orders are the legitimate results of the abiding conviction they have of the truth of Christianity. For as certain as Christianity is true, so certain is it that the saints in glory will differ from each other as the stars of heaven, and that this difference will be in proportion to the difference of their course on earth. The perfect Christian must then inherit an increased glory; and this increase is surely worth every possible sacrifice that we can make on earth. Those holy souls who give all their lives, not to the practice of display, but to the practice of "solid virtues," as Saint Jane Francis de Chantal has it, without the intention of gaining personal fame or distinction, must surely legitimately fill the counsels of perfection, if any such were given.

In the Catholic Church, all her children are under her discipline. Whatever enthusiasm they may possess cannot go beyond the limits fixed by the Church. Their enthusiasm cannot degenerate into fanaticism. But it cannot be so under the Protestant rule of private interpretation. There are no limits to the fanaticism of the Protestant enthusiast, but the mind of the enthusiast himself. In vain will you prescribe limits, when you have no *right* to prescribe. The enthusiast defeats you upon your own principle. It is mainly owing to this erroneous fundamental principle that Protestants cannot organize and sustain any religious orders. Their charitable efforts are undisciplined, unsteady, and limited for that reason! Under such a principle there could not exist such an order as the Sisters of Charity, without a violation of the fundamental rule. There could be no continued unity of effort, because there could exist no obedience to one superior.

7. Charges against these orders considered

In reference to the general charges of delinquency, so often made by their enemies against these orders of the Catholic Church, I could not believe them, after examination and reflection, for these reasons:

1. Assuming, for the sake of the argument only, that these orders are as devoted and faithful as they are generally believed to be by Catholics, then such calumnies would naturally follow such superior virtue. It is in the nature of Christian perfection, that it should be envied, calumniated, and despised, by those who cannot or will not attain it.

2. The sacrifices these orders are *known* to make, are so much greater than those their enemies *do make*, that the only possible plan of putting them upon anything like an equality, is to accuse the members of these orders of *secret sins.* Whenever that most just and salutary principle of law, that a man must be presumed innocent until he is proved guilty, is set aside, then human virtue cannot be known to exist in this world; for no man can prove a negative, and show that he never did commit any crime. He may sometimes do so, by proving an alibi in reference to a particular charge of an act alleged to have been committed at a specified time and place. But as to general charges, no one can prove a negative. If, therefore, the mind can be induced to believe charges of secret sins without proof, there is no limit to such belief but the prejudices, interests, and passions of men; and these have few limits, if any.

3. These charges were too wholesale and therefore upon their face the more incredible. And unless they were of this wholesale character, they could not have any force, if true, against the entire orders themselves. It became apparent to me, that such gross and continued wickedness could not exist in so large bodies of persons, without all knowing it who live together in the same convent. And if all knew it, and it was general in all the convents, it certainly constituted a wonderful example of the combination of the most degraded vices with the most devoted and self-sacrificing virtues, in the same persons. And what was most astonishing was this: that their published rules and public practices, showing the labors and sacrifices the members must endure, would certainly only attract the most pious and heroic; and how they could become so soon converted from saints to vile prostitutes and debauchees, is what I could not quite understand. In all my reading and observation, I had never heard of prostitutes and debauchees loving poverty and hard work, humility and danger. From Benedict Arnold down to the meanest rogue, without scarcely an exception, all unprincipled persons are fond of wallowing in luxury and dissipation. And it may be said of all persons who look to this world alone for their enjoyments, that they are devoted to the good things of life. As the Infidel Mirabeau, on his death-bed, said, in substance:

> Cover me with flowers – smother me with sweet perfumes – and let me die amidst the strains of delicious music.

The almost, if not the only exception, is the senseless miser, who hoards with an object, and lives without an aim. That base sensuality, that would make the Sisters prostitutes, and the monks debauchees, would forever unfit them for the exercise of those sublime virtues, and the exhibition of that noble courage for the relief of others, that we do *know* them to possess. Can these opposite traits be put together, and kept there?

4. The ranks of these orders are continually filled, as is well known, by great numbers of persons from the very best ranks of society—persons possessed of wealth, education, and of every worldly advantage. These persons voluntarily forsake all for the kingdom of heaven's sake. And can such be insincere? Can such be vile? If so, where can superior virtue be found? And what can be its evidence?

5. The most candid and reliable, impartial and just Protestant historians and theologians do not believe these wholesale charges. For instance,

Waddington the Protestant, quoted with so much approbation by Mr. Campbell, says, among other things:

> Of the more modern orders, there is also one which may seem to require our notice – that of the Ursulines. Its origin is ascribed to Angela de Brescia, about the year 1537, though the saint from whom it received its name, Ursula Benincasa, a native of Naples, was born ten years afterwards. Its character was peculiar, and recalls our attention to the primitive form of ascetic devotion. The duties of these holy Sisters were the purest within the circle of human benevolence – to minister to the sick, to relieve the poor, to console the miserable, to pray with the penitent. These charitable offices they undertook to execute without the bond of any community, without the obligation of any monastic vow, without any separation from society, any renouncement of their domestic duties and virtues. And so admirable were those offices, in millions of instances, performed, that had all other female orders been really as useless and vicious as they are sometimes falsely described to be, the virtues of the Ursulines had alone been sufficient to redeem the monastic name.
>
> But it is very far from true, that these other orders were either commonly dissolute or generally useless. Occasional scandals have engendered universal calumnies."[10]

How concisely and beautifully Waddington states a great truth. "*Occasional scandals have engendered universal calumnies.*"

How true it is, that the prejudiced, the ignorant, and the idle, are prone to draw *wholesale* conclusions, from *single* instances. If one man is dishonest, all men must be so. If one man may be bribed, all men may be bought. If one man cannot or will not control his passions, of course all others must be like him. If one will lie, all must lie.

But in reference to the Mendicant orders, the same historian, among other things, said:

> It is not without reason that the Roman Catholic writers vaunt the disinterestedness of the early Mendicants – how assiduous they were in supplying the spiritual wants of the poor, how frequent in prisons and in hospitals, how forward to encounter the fire or the pestilence; how instant on all these occasions where the peril was imminent, and the reward not in this world. They were equally distinguished in other, and not less righteous, duty, the propagation of Christianity among remote and savage nations.

After alluding to different missions, the historian says:

> It is certain that the number of Christians was not inconsiderable, both among the Chinese and Moguls, as late as the year 1370, and they were still increasing, when they were suddenly swept away and almost wholly exterminated by the Mahometan arms. Howbeit, the disastrous overthrow of their establishment detracts nothing from the merit of those who constructed it; and it must not be forgotten, that the instruments in this work were Mendicants, and, for the most part, Franciscans.[11]

There is a beautiful testimony to the devotion and courage of the Catholic clergy, in Lieutenant Gibson's "Report of his tour through Peru." "There is no part of Peru," he says,

> which is more densely populated than the valley of Juaga. There, close under the mountains, on the east side, stands the town of Ocopa, with its convents and schools. From that place missionaries have branched off in different directions to the forests in the east, at great risk of life, and loss of all its comforts, to teach the savage red man how to change his manners, customs, and belief. Some have succeeded, others have failed, and were murdered or driven back by the battle-axe; their settlements destroyed by fire, and years of labor lost; yet some never tire.

The eloquent senator from Virginia, Hon. R. M. T. Hunter, in a speech made in 1855, in Virginia, uses this chaste and touching language: "Deprive," said he,

> the Catholics of all the offices, bar them out from every avenue to political distinction, deny to them the opportunities which you have accorded to Infidels and Atheists; and when you have done it all, when you have placed their honest ambition to enjoy the honors and emoluments of political preferment under the ban of a ruthless prescription, your work is not yet finished. There will still remain offices for them. Yes, my friends, the sweet offices of Christian love – will still be left, and in the midst of your persecutions, their bishops and priests, as in the recent pestilence in your Southern cities, will throng the hospitals and pest-houses, bringing succor and consolation to the poor victims of the plague. Aye, and their sisters of Charity will still brave the terrors of loathsome and infectious disease, will still wipe the death damp front the suffering brow, will still venture in where the courage of men shrinks back appalled, and will point the dying gaze through the mysterious gloom of the Valley of the Shadow of Death, to the Cross and the Crucified.

I will also quote from a late able and manly letter, written by Judge Longstreet, a distinguished and worthy member of the Methodist Church. Speaking to the Methodist preachers of the Catholics, the judge says:

> To hate their religion is to hate your own religion, which they adorn just at this time, much more than you do. "No man that warreth," says Paul, "encumbereth himself with the affairs of this life." The Catholic priest obeys this precept strictly. But where are you – some of you at least? Candidates for this, that, and the other office – going from beat to beat, and county to county, stumping it for votes – haranguing the multitude amidst thumps, and screams, and yelis – firing at opposition, and almost coming to blows – telling vulgar anecdotes – suppressing truth – encouraging, if not spreading falsehood. These things are not done in a corner; and yet if any bishop, any Elder, any Deacon, any brother, any press of our church, has raised a warning voice against them, except my poor solitary self, and one old brother more, I have yet to learn who, when, or where. From the holiest chamber of my soul, I lift a prayer to God to have mercy upon us, and save our church from degradation and ruin. Brethren, I am not near done with you but I must stop. My powers of calm discussion are suspended. My heart and my eyes take up the cause of my periled church, in utterances which you might appreciate, but which I cannot expose to the ridicule of an unfeeling world.

There is a melancholy vein of truth and sincerity running through this extract that cannot be mistaken. But the state of things, so feelingly deplored by the judge, must inevitably flow from the theory of Protestantism, sooner or later. It is one of the legitimate results. Let anyone read the history of the Protestant churches from the days of Luther down to this time, and he will find the same decline of the apostolic spirit. New Reformations will be constantly required. What Wesley did for the Church of England someone else will have, sooner or later, to do for the Methodists.

In reference to the great mass of Protestants, and Catholics, the difference between their observable conduct as Christians may not be great and may be very similar. I bear a most cheerful testimony to the personal piety of great numbers of Protestants with whom I have associated. So far as practical morality is concerned – that which regulates our conduct as citizens and neighbors – I have not found much difference among men of any denomination. I have found the qualities of kindness, sobriety, and integrity among many unbelievers, in a great degree of perfection. So far as the practice of that morality is concerned which renders men happy in a state of society, and prosperous as a community in this world, I apprehend there is no very marked difference among professed Christians of different denominations.

But the system of Christianity has a design beyond this. It looks not alone to man's happiness here. Virtues that alone produce an improved state of society are not the principal objects of the system. Dr. Paley admits, "that the teaching of morality was not the primary design of the mission" of Christ. In another place he says:

> For however the care of reputation, the authority of public opinion, or even of the opinion of good men, the satisfaction of being well received, and well thought of, the benefit of being known and distinguished, are topics to which we are fain to have recourse in our exhortations; the true virtue is that which discards these considerations absolutely and which retires from them all to the single internal purpose of pleasing God.[12]

This is certainly a beautiful Christian sentiment, as beautifully and forcibly expressed. The temporal considerations alluded to are certainly such as may be urged upon men in society, with equal force, whether Christianity be true or false. They are worldly and temporal motives, addressed to present interest and aspirations; and are not calculated to inculcate the true spirit of Christianity. Did Christ, or Paul, or Peter, ever urge such motives? In vain may we look in the New Testament for any such reasons in support of the Gospel. And the great truth stated by the learned divine, that Protestants are "faint, have recourse in their exhortations" to such topics, is, to my mind, a very great and serious objection to their theory, and does show the inevitable worldly tendency of their fundamental rule. And if we look into Protestant works – their sermons, addresses, and especially their arguments in support of their theory – we shall find the general drift and spirit of the great majority of them conformable with these temporal considerations. In a system like Christianity, where both faith and works – good motives as well as good actions – are required; to urge such reasons upon men, and especially upon Christians, is to lower and debase the system itself, and to ruin and destroy the souls of men. "*The single internal purpose of pleasing God*," and thus meriting the *future* rewards, and escaping the *future* punishments, promised and denounced in the Gospel, should constitute the true motive that actuates the humble Christian.

The blessed Paul said that without charity he was nothing; and the same apostle also said, that without faith it was impossible to please God. In the contemplation of Christianity a man must not only do justice to his neighbor, but he must also have faith and humility. Practical morality alone will never, therefore, constitute the whole Christian character. There must be deep humility; and this virtue is much more rare among Protestants than Catholics, so far as my means of information have enabled me to judge.

The Samaritans who adored in the mountain, where they had their schismatic temple, were distinguished for their hospitality. So great was their character for hospitality, that a Roman Emperor erected a statue in their city to the hospitable Jupiter, in conformity, says an ancient historian, to the genius of the nation. And so remarkable were they for their charity, that when our Savior wished to illustrate this great virtue, he gave the parable of the Good Samaritan. But still, with all their virtues, they were not good and complete models of the true worshipper of God. For Christ did not hesitate to tell the Samaritan woman at the well: "Ye worship ye know not what: we know what we worship: for salvation is of the Jews."[13]

No doubt these virtues of hospitality and charity were even more prevalent among the Samaritans than among the Jews. But with all their amiable characteristics, they never could produce such examples of holiness as Simeon, the prophetess Anna, and others among the Jews. I suppose that if all the virtues of the Samaritans had been concentrated in a single person, that such individual could not have compared with the holy Simeon.

---

[1] In reference to the great Sir Thomas More, Thompson has these beautiful and just lines:

"Like Cato firm, like Aristides just,
Like rigid Cincinnatus, nobly poor,
A dauntless soul, erect, who smiled on death."

[2] John Milner, *The End of Religious Controversy.* Let. xxi.

Note. The only one of the Reformers recorded as a saint in the calendar of the Church of England, is King Charles I, in reference to whom Dr. Milner says:

"I must except King Charles I., who is rubricated as a martyr on January 30: nevertheless, it is confessed that he was far from possessing either the purity of a saint, or the constancy of a martyr; for he actually gave up Episcopacy and other essentials of the established religion, by his last treaty in the Isle of Wight." (note to Let. xxi.)

His name, I believe, has, by a late command of the Queen, been stricken from the calendar

[3] Matt. 19:9-12.

[4] The same sentiment I heard expressed by an unmarried man not long since. He was about age thirty, and I knew him well. He insisted that all men possessed the like passions, and therefore, did, and must, indulge them in the same degree. From this he concluded there could be no chaste persons. I was forced to reply to him, in substance, "That admitting all men did possess the same passions, they did not possess them in same degree, and they controlled them in a different manner. And that he had the most evident motive for his conclusion, as it excused and sustained his own conduct, for there was one certain truth in his theory, that he himself was not chaste."

I was once told by a man that he did not believe there was an honest man in the world. I concluded, that while I did not agree with him in whole, I did in part; for it was clear that he was not honest himself.

[5] Dr. Hay's *Lectures on Divinity*, vol. I. 364. Cited in Milner's *End of Controversy*, Letter xxii.

[6] Charles Butler, in his account of the life and writings of the Rev. Alban Butler, who was esteemed the most learned man in Europe, and yet one of the most humble and pious, says:

"Our author was not so warm on any subject as the calumnies against the religious of the Middle Age: he considered the civilization of Europe to be owing to them. When they were charged with idleness, he used to remark the immense tracts of land which, from the rudest state of nature, they converted to a high state of husbandry in the Hercynisn wood, the forests of Champagne and Burgundy, the morasses of Holland, and the fens of Lincolnshire and Cambridgeshire. When ignorance was imputed to them, he used to ask, what author of antiquity had reached us for whose works we were not indebted to the monks. He could less endure that they should be considered as instruments of absolute power to enslave the people: when this was intimated, he observed that during the period which immediately followed the extinction of the Carlovingian dynasty, when the feudal law absolutely triumphed over monarchy, the people were wholly left to themselves, and must have sunk into a state of absolute barbarism if it had not been for the religious establishments. These, he said, softened the manners of the conquerors, afforded refuge to the vanquished, preserved an intercourse between nations, and, when the feudal chiefs rose to the rank of monarchs, stood as a rampart between them and the people. He thought Saint Thomas of Canterbury a much injured character. He often pointed out that rich tract of country, which extends from Saint Omer's to Liege, as a standing refutation of those who asserted that convents and monasteries were inimical to the populousness of a country. He observed that the whole income of the smaller houses, and two-thirds of the revenues of the greater houses, were constantly spent within twenty miles round their precincts; that their lands were universally let at low rents; that every abbey had a school for the instruction of its tenants, and that no human institution was so well calculated to promote the arts of painting, architecture, and sculpture, works in iron and bronze, and every other species of workmanship, as abbeys or monasteries, and their appendages. "Thus,' he used to say, "though the country in view was originally a marsh, and has for more than a century wholly survived its commerce, it is the most populous country in Europe; and presents on the face of it as great display of public and private strength, wealth, and affluence, as can be found in any other part of the world."

The libraries attached to these institutions were extensive. Thus Digby says: "The library of the Abbey of Cluny, before the Protestants pillaged and burnt it in the sixteenth century, was deemed one of the wonders of the world; and, in fact, it equaled that of the emperors at Constantinople." (Digby, *Ages of Faith*, Book x., chap. ix.)

[7] Samual Johnson, *Rasselas, Prince of Abyssinia.*

[8] Cited Kenelm Digby *Ages of Faith*, Book x., c. iii.

[9] Kenelm Digby *Ages of Faith* Book x., c. iii.

[10] George Waddington, *A History of the Church from the Earliest ages to the Reformation.* p. 325; N. Y. Ed., 1835.

[11] *Ibid.* p. 547.

[12] William Paley, *Evidences of Christianity*

[13] John 4:22.

CHAPTER IV

RESULTS OF THE PROTESTANT THEORY

1. Character of the Reformers

It is not my purpose to enter into a minute investigation of the character of the principal agents who brought about what is called the Reformation. The limits of my work would not allow me a full investigation in point of that holiness, humility, and gentleness required by Christianity. I can only refer to the works of Dr. Milner and others, who have treated this subject at large. I gave the question the best examination I could do under the circumstances, and I must say, that the result was the conviction in my own mind, that the reformers were not the best models of Christian virtue. It seemed to me as an eminently just sentiment, that the men who assumed to *reform* the entire Church should have been the best models of piety. The apostles were so.

I could not find in the lives, conduct, or language of the early reformers, any prominent and continued displays of that humility and disregard of self, which surely do constitute the most conclusive tests of personal piety, of the first order. I was much struck, upon my first examination, with the remark of Dr. Milner, that we had not the same reason to expect the same amount of personal virtue in those officers who follow one another by succession as we had in reformers.

The account given by the Duchess of York, of her own conversion, is one of the most beautiful and simple statements I have anywhere met, and made a deep impression upon my mind when I first read it. It bears upon its face the sure marks of sincerity. It is found entire in the Duke of Brunswick's *Fifty Reasons*. This eminent lady says among other things:

> And first I do protest in the presence of Almighty God, that no person, man or woman, directly or indirectly, ever said anything to me, (since I came out of England,) or used the least endeavor to make me change my religion. It is a blessing I wholly owe to Almighty God; and, I hope, the hearing of a prayer I daily made Him, ever since I was in France and Flanders. Where, seeing much of the devotion of Catholics, (though I had very little myself,) I made it my continual request to Almighty God, that if I was not, I might, before I died, be in the TRUE religion. I did not in the least doubt but that I was so,

> and never had any manner of scruple until November last, when I read a book called *The History of the Reformation*, by Dr. Hoylen, which I had heard very much commended, and had been told if ever I had any doubt in my religion, that would settle me. Instead of which I found it the description of the most horrid sacrileges in the world; and could find no reason why he left the Church, but for these, the most abominable ones that were ever heard of among Christians: First, Henry VIII, renounces the Pope's authority because he would not give him leave to part with his wife, and marry another in her lifetime. Secondly, Edward VI was a child, and was governed by his uncle, who made his estate out of church lands. And thirdly, Queen Elizabeth, who, not being lawful heiress to the Crown, could have no way to keep it but by renouncing a church that could never suffer so unlawful a thing to be done by one of her children. I confess that I cannot think that the Holy Ghost could ever be in such counsels; and it is very strange that if the bishops had no design (as they say) but restoring to us the doctrine of the primitive church they should never think upon it till Henry VIII made the breach, upon so unlawful a pretense.

This lady afterwards says in another place:

> After this I spoke severally to two of the best bishops we have in England, both of whom told me there were many things in the Roman Church which it were much to be wished we had kept, as confession which was no doubt commanded by God. That praying for the dead was one of the ancient things in Christianity; that, for their parts, they did it daily, though they would not own it; and, afterwards, pressing one of them very much upon the other points, he told me that if he had been a Catholic, he would not change his religion; but being of another church, wherein he was sure were all things necessary to salvation, he thought it very ill to give scandal by leaving that church wherein he received his baptism….

The prelates referred to were Sheldon, Archbishop of Canterbury, and Blandford, Bishop of Worcester.

In my examination of the history of the Reformation, I became satisfied that if we exclude from our consideration the opinions and conclusions of the most candid Protestant historians of the Reformation, and confine our attention to the main and undeniable facts they themselves record, and from these facts and our knowledge of men and things – their motives, passions and actions – we will be forced to draw these conclusions.

1.That ambition, love of wealth, and thirst for distinction had more to do with that event than religion itself.

2. That the bishops and clergy who joined the Reformation generally followed the lead of others, and very seldom went before.

If we look to England, for instance, we shall find, that of all the English bishops in the time of Henry VIII the venerable Fisher was the only one who loved his religion well enough to die for it. We shall find that even when the clergy, either during his reign or afterwards, remonstrated against and opposed the proposed changes their scruples were almost always overcome, and they seldom resisted unto death.

If we look to the continent, the same general result will follow. Luther, Melancthon, Bucer and others, granted the Landgrave of Hesse a dispensation to marry another wife, while he did not even put away the first. But when Henry VIII, who had been a zealous defender of the Pope, solicited a dispensation to put away his wife and marry another, the Pope refused. The success of the Reformation in England is mainly to be attributed to the firmness of the Pontiff in resisting such a demand. In this connection if we also take the Catholic historians of that day, and put them also, side by side with the Protestant historians, and take the great leading facts recorded by both, or sufficiently proved by one, when either omitted or denied by the other, it occurs to me there can be but little doubt, as to the conclusion that must follow.

2. The Alleged right of appeal to the Day of Judgment

While inquiring for the true Church, I found the different Protestant sects, each acting for itself, under separate and independent organizations, and each assuming, at least in form, to exercise certain powers of government over its members. They generally recognized the principle, that both faith and works were required by the law of Christ. In so far as they assumed to exercise any powers of government, they assumed to do so, in virtue of this law. They, therefore, professed to enforce all the those provisions of this code, in reference to both faith and works, intended to be reduced to practice in *this* world.

In all cases where an individual is charged with any violation of law there are necessarily two questions involved:

1. Did the accused commit the act, or hold the opinion, alleged? This is a simple question of *fact.*

2. Is the act or opinion a violation of the law? And this is a question of law.

Every conceivable case, arising under any system of law, must embrace these two questions. As to the first question, the fact being peculiarly within the knowledge of the party, he may concede it, and thus waive the necessity of proof. When the charge involves the crime of heresy, the fact is generally, if not always, conceded. The concession of the fact only waives the necessity of proof to establish it. But the question of fact is still involved, whether the fact be admitted or denied. As to the question of law, the admission of error by the accused will not, of course, control the action of the tribunal. A criminal court would not inflict the punishment of death upon a criminal, contrary to law, simply because he preferred this punishment to that of life imprisonment.

When a member is brought before a Protestant Church, the tribunal which assumes to try him must, of necessity, ascertain the fact, if denied, and construe the law for him; otherwise, it could not be a trial, even in mere from. If the accused were allowed to settle the fact and the law, or either of them, he could readily escape by his own act. He would certainly get himself out of difficulty. The whole end and purpose of the trial would be defeated, the moment the party is permitted either to settle the fact or the law.

The result is that the Protestant tribunal, which ascertains the fact, and construes the law for the individual member, does most clearly violate the right of private interpretation, in so far as the punishment inflicted. To mitigate this palpable violation of the fundamental rule, they are compelled to concede two points, which in practical and logical effect defeat the entire end and purpose of the formal decision:

1. That the tribunal that determines the case is fallible and may err; and therefore, its decision, in contemplation of the theory itself, is no evidence of the truth, does not settle the question, and is entitled to no respect or obedience. Consequently the party condemned is not bound to abide the decision, unless his supreme judgment concurs in it.

2. That the punishment inflicted amounts to nothing; as expulsion from the church, under the decision of a merely fallible tribunal, does not affect the Christian standing of the party in anyway; and his chances of salvation must be conceded, by the theory itself, to be as good out of, as in the Church.

As a matter of course, the party expelled could not be expected to yield up his private opinion for the mere farcical decision of such a tribunal. In doing so his chances of safety would not be *increased*, and he would be violating the fundamental rule itself, which constitutes his own mind the tribunal of last resort on earth. Were he to surrender his views to such a decision it would be as an appellate court giving up its judgment to an inferior tribunal.

The legitimate result is this, that since in the days of the apostles the Church did expel heretics, and exercise all the powers of government necessary to execute that portion of the law obligatory upon individuals in this world, the Protestant Churches are compelled to go through the solemn farce of a trial in form. In this way they make a *formal* compliance with the law, but to save their fundamental rule at the same time. They are compelled to allow the right of appeal from their decision to the supreme individual judgment of the accused himself. They say to him in substance: "We must try you, and if you are found guilty, in *our* opinion, we must expel you. But we concede, while doing this, that we are just as apt to be wrong as yourself, and our decision amounts to nothing but *expulsion*, and this in our theory is just as apt to be wrong as right." The *form* of a trial and decision is necessary to conform, in *appearance*, with the *actual* practice of the Apostolic Church. The futility of the decision made is conceded to save the fundamental rule.

The government exercised by these Protestant churches is but a mere shadow, without substance, of supremacy – the form, without the power. Of course, it is entitled to no respect or obedience, because the contradictory theory itself claims none. It cannot possess that which it does not claim.

However, it may be said that the Protestant theory is consistent and true, if we hold that the decisions of the Church are subordinate to that of Christ in the Day of Judgment. Consequently the right of appeal from the decisions of the inferior court below would lie to the Supreme Court above. But can this be true?

The Church, being a visible continuing corporation, intended to exist and exercise all her functions of government in this world; the law given for the government of her members must be practically administered *here*. All the acts of obedience, in respect of faith and works, must be performed by the parties governed while *they are in this mode of being*. All that they are required to do must be done here. The future state is simply and solely one of rewards or punishments – of enjoyment or suffering. All ends with death so far as obedience is concerned.

If then, the right of appeal exists from the decisions of the Church to the General Judgment, this right would be wholly nugatory, unless the appeal, when taken, *suspended* the execution of the judgment until the case could be heard above. The right of appeal, without the effect of suspension, would be equivalent to allowing the appeal *after* the prisoner was executed.

On the other hand, if this right of suspensive appeal exists on the part of the individual condemned by the Church, then the power to decide is wholly idle, for the plain reason, that the decision remains suspended, and therefore, for the time defeated until the Day of Judgment. And then it is too late to inform the inferior tribunal of its duty, or to benefit the defendant himself.

Each individual condemned takes his appeal at once, and the question then stands adjourned from the date of the decision to the Day of Judgment. As cases arise continually, and each one is appealed, the calendar of causes must increase form age to age, without a decision in a single case to correct a single error, until the end of time. The result is, that the inferior tribunals labor and grope on in the dark, throughout all time, still compelled to render farcical decisions, that no one is bound to respect or obey. But after the institution itself has run its entire course on Earth, where alone the law could be practically administered and obeyed, then comes a decision of the Supreme Tribunal, correcting errors, when such correction is idle for all beneficial purposes, so far as regards either the Church or the appellant himself. This would be about as wise and efficient as if the Constitution had organized a Supreme Court, with the right of suspensive appeal from all inferior Federal tribunals; and yet only permitted the Supreme Court to sit once, at the end of the existence of the government itself.

It may be said, that there certainly will be a future Day of Judgment. And this being true, for what purpose was that day set apart if not to hear appeals from the Church on Earth? A little calm attention to the law of Christ, as He promulgated it, and a due consideration of the ends and purposes of the system, will show the true theory upon this subject. As Our Lord appeared on earth a living, visible lawgiver, and as His system requires both faith and works, and as He ascended into heaven and will not again visibly appear until the end of the world, He left His law with his agents. These agents He infallibly guides in their administration of this law on earth.

The result of this theory is, that *portion* of the code that was required to be obeyed by individuals in this state, is committed to the Church for *final decision.* The decision of this infallible Church is but the decision of Christ Himself, acting by and through His own institution. This is the reason why our Lord said to His apostles, 'Whatsoever ye shall bind or loose on earth, shall be bound or loosed in heaven.'

This power of binding and loosing was given for some great and beneficial purpose, because the exercise of it was confirmed in heaven. It was given by the Founder of the Institution, as a part of its permanent constitution. On the day of Judgment there will be no question to decide what has been decided by the Church. The questions to be then determined will be: firstly questions of *fact*, regarding the "secrets of all hearts" which have not been confessed and repented of in this world, as the law required; and secondly apportioning the rewards and punishments due to individuals.

The rewards and punishments promised and denounced by the system could not, from their very nature, be enjoyed or suffered in this mode of existence. For that reason, the administration of this portion of the law was not committed to the Church, but reserved to the future Judgment. Individuals who hypocritically conceal their sins injure no one but themselves. The infallible knowledge of these individual facts was never given to the Church, because they are not at all necessary to enable her to execute the law.

3. Private interpretation is unjust to the Divine lawgiver

But the theory of private interpretation in the last resort on earth, is a disastrous theory, when carefully and calmly considered. It is extremely unjust to the Divine Lawgiver, because it depreciates the character of His work; and, therefore, impugns His justice and capacity.

You may praise an architect in words to any extent you please, while you depreciate his work, and he never will appreciate this left-handed compliment. It is also unjust to our Lord, because it defeats the beneficent purposes of His system. It leaves the difficulties inevitably arising in the practical administration and application of this perfect and extended system of law, to accumulate and remain uncorrected from age to age, throughout the entire course of the Church on earth, and only proposes to settle them *after* the institution has closed its earthly existence, and after that portion of the code intended for practical administration in this state of being, has ceased to operate. It proposes to close the door, after the steed is stolen.

4. Private interpretation is unjust to individuals

But it is equally unjust, harsh, and ruinous to the parties governed. The theory concedes that without faith it is *impossible* to please God; and therefore, each person must believe the truth, and the whole truth required by Christ to be believed. It must, then, concede the right of ultimate construction of the law, to reside in the Divine Lawmaker; and, therefore, that the construction of the individual will not save him, unless it happens to be right. Whether this individual construction is right or wrong, the individual has not certain means of knowing. He finds his individual construction opposed to the views of the overwhelming majority of all professed Christians, in all ages. Yet he must adhere to his private construction at his eternal peril, or give up the theory.

As often as new and difficult questions arise, he must either pay no attention to them, or form some judgment of his own, right or wrong. If wrong, he is lost. If right he does not know it. All he can say, under his theory, is that *he thinks* he is right. The questions accumulating from generation to generation remain undetermined, except by his own opinions. The previous construction of the Church cannot be his guide, and can afford him no relief, because, under the Protestant theory, "the act of contravention," as Professor Greenleaf justly says, "remains a sin in the last transgressor as well as the first."[1]

He cannot rely upon authority – upon anything but his own confessedly fallible construction of the law. He is, therefore, placed in a position of terrible individual responsibility, without any certain guide. He must know and obey the will of the Great Lawgiver in all material respects, or be lost. But at the same time that he must arrive at a just solution of all difficulties, he is left in the most painful state of destitution. He knows there are things hard to be understood that must still be understood. Yet questions that perplex his judgment must remain postponed until the last day. True, when that day arrives, he will know whether his construction of the law has been right or wrong. If wrong, he is condemned, and his knowledge comes entirely too late. If he had only known the true construction of the law on earth, he would have been saved. But there were no means afforded him to attain this certain knowledge, and all that he could do was to be "darkly wise" as to his Master's will.

5. Private interpretation is ruinous of unity and government

Julius Caesar said, "he would rather be the *first* man in a village than the second man in Rome" So long as the sentiment of Julius Caesar shall find an echo in human ambition; then under any theory of private interpretation in the last resort; so long will "leaders rather than creeds make parties and keep them," as Mr. Campbell very justly says. Even if there were no great difficulties in the construction and application of Scripture, as of every other code, and conceding all men unprejudiced; still, as so few can be qualified and have the time to investigate and decide the entire law for themselves, leaders, from motives of ambition, revenge, or a zeal *not according to knowledge*, would always make parties and keep them, under such a theory.

If a law were given to only twenty men, all independent equals, and each, therefore, bound to decide alone for himself, it would be remarkable if even that limited number could agree. If they disagreed, one could not, consistently with the rule, say to the other, you are wrong. If every one of the twenty differed from all the others, they might deplore the differences with all the fervor and zeal possible; but still this lamentation would not begin to settle the difficulty. Each must still abide in his own judgment. To say to men, under such a rule, "be united," would be about as efficient to produce the end desired, as to say to the naked and hungry, "be ye clothed and fed." The necessity of unity could not produce unity in fact.

The necessity of unity in *action,* may induce men to yield up their judgments to others in temporal matters; but when a matter of faith and conscience is concerned, how can a man, acting upon the rule of private interpretation in the last resort, give up his faith for that of any other mere fallible man? He can only yield when convinced, and to yield without this conviction, would be sinful hypocrisy. This the honest and sincere mind cannot do. The only possible plan for unity under this rule is the *accidental* agreement of so many different minds, in reference to so many different and difficult points. However sincere, however meek, and however void of ambition and prejudice, men might be, they would have all to possess the same mental organization, the same mental training, and be surrounded, substantially, by the same circumstances, before they could ever arrive at the same judgment, in reference to so many different matters.

When we go from theory to facts, we shall find the truth of this position most fully and conclusively shown. How has the theory worked out in practice? What has been the effect among those who have confessedly acted upon the rule? Have they kept the unity of the faith? Into how many parties are they divided? Who can tell? And which of these various parties are in the right, as judged by the theory itself? Who knows? Why do they not agree? Is it because of too much light? Have they too much knowledge? And is it the inevitable result of knowledge, that men are more and more incapable of arriving at truth? And, therefore, the better men are qualified to judge, the less apt they are to judge correctly? And the more they are prone to differ?

Nothing can be more demonstrable of this impracticable theory, when applied to law intended for the government of associated men, then a candid and fair study of the main features of Protestant Christianity. It is not within the compass of my design to speak of the varied divisions among Protestants, or of the many fruitless, yet persevering, efforts to heal them. They have divided and subdivided so often, that the most condensed statement of these separations, would occupy more space than the limits of this work could spare.

The human mind, when rightly disposed, must ever love consistency, because truth is always consistent in every particular; and truth is lovely and worthy of admiration. Every system of truth must be harmonious, united and practical. If the fundamental principle of a theory be erroneous, the superstructure, if consistent with it, must of course be defective. But if inconsistent with the fundamental principle, the superstructure cannot be secure, and there can be no harmony in the theory. If the leading principle be practically nullified, there must exist a continual war between profession and practice, and men must sooner or later discover the discrepancy. When the mind is placed in the painful position of self-contradiction, it can never rest in peace.

The history of these ever-varying and distressing changes is one full of instruction and interest. It is the history of the most gigantic and persevering struggles of the human mind, to erect a firm and consistent structure upon a false foundation – to make a theory logical and well proportioned, that has for its fundamental rule, an impracticable basis. It has been one continued and never-ceasing attempt to reconcile two irreconcilable elements – the right of private interpretation in the last resort, and the right of government in the Church. These two principles, in their very nature, are radically and fundamentally opposed, and never can coexist. Like any two precise opposites, they never can be put together. Union and peace, the legitimate results of rightful government alone, can never be found where the right of private interpretation, in the last resort, exists in each party governed.

But the reader must be referred to the works of others, who have treated this subject at large. After a careful examination, the dispassionate observer will not fail to see how far Protestants have departed from the faith of the early Reformers, who were held, especially Luther, as instruments of God, raised up by Him for that special purpose. Now can the candid and impartial inquirer fail to mark the incidents of this progress; "how as Bossuet says,

> they first separated themselves from the Catholic Church, and afterwards from one another; by how many subtleties, evasions, and equivocations, they labored to repair their divisions, and to reunite the scattered members of their disjointed reformation.[2]

By taking the opinions and views of Protestants of the present day, and comparing them with the doctrines of the first Reformers and their immediate followers, he will be enabled to see how completely, in the space of little more than three hundred years, they have veered around to the opposite extremes, upon the most important points.

6. Luther was forced to adopt private interpretation

When Luther contemplated the Reformation, he found himself placed in certain circumstances. No intellect, or zeal, however great, can lift their possessor above the controlling influence of circumstances.

The law of Christianity itself was complete, and the legislative power of the kingdom had been all exercised as to all the *permanent* features of the code, and the executive and judicial powers only remained. It was, therefore, obvious, that the first and most important matter must be the construction of the law governing the Church. This law was positive, expressed in human language, and must, of necessity, be construed by some one. This article designating the tribunal to construe this law in the last resort, was, for that reason, the first and paramount rule to be made. This would necessarily hold the first place. It would constitute the principal basis, upon which the whole theory must rest.

But from the invincible nature and reason of things, this right to construe the law in the last resort, could only be placed in one of two tribunals, namely: a tribunal deciding *for others,* or each one deciding *for himself.* There was no other possible theory but these. It was, in its essence, a question between government and no government in the Church. Traced out, and carried to its plain, logical results, it could possibly lead to no other conclusion.

The Old Church was in possession of the governing principle. She assumed the exercise of the executive and judicial powers. If Luther admitted the rightful existence of these powers in the Church, he would be himself condemned, and could only make such a reformation as the governing power of the Church would sanction.[3]

He was, therefore, forced to assume the common ground held by the various sects of heretics that preceded him. So far, necessity compelled him to build upon another man's foundation. But he could not adopt the *entire* theory of any one of these sects, for these reasons:

1. Their theories had been tried and failed.

2. He would be building *entirely* upon the foundation of another.

3. He could not conscientiously sanction their condemned errors.

Now whether all these reasons, or only a portion of them, and which portion, induced him to discard all and each of these condemned theories, must be left with each person to determine for himself. My own impression is, they all had their influence.

The principle of private interpretation in the last resort was, therefore, forced upon Luther. It was either that or no Reformation. There was no possible middle course. Either the right to construe the law in the last resort resided in the Church, or with each individual. It could not be divided between them. Two supreme tribunals to execute the *same* law over the *same* persons could not exist under the *same* system of government. We could just as readily conceive of two Supreme Deities, creating and governing the same universe.

The authority of the Church was the last restraint that Luther cast aside. It cost him much pain, as he himself relates. "After," says he,

> I had gotten the better of all the arguments which were opposed to me, one remained still, which, with extreme difficulty and great

> anguish, I could scarce conquer, even with the assistance of Jesus Christ; namely, that we ought to hear the Church.

But it must be conceded that Luther may have been mistaken in the supposed assistance of Jesus Christ. He may have mistaken Christ's abandonment of him for His assistance. Whether this be true or not, there was a very remarkable circumstance connected with his rejection of the authority of the Church.

After having prevailed over his scruples, and in his last struggle to shake off the authority of the Church, "he cries out," says Bossuet,

> like one set free from some irksome bondage, "Let us break their bands asunder, and cast their yoke from us."[4]

This quotation, made by Luther, is from the third verse of the second chapter of Psalms, where it stands in this connection:

> 2. The kings of the earth set themselves, and the rulers take counsel together against the Lord, and against his anointed, *saying,* 3. Let us break their bands asunder, and cast their yoke from us.
> *4. He that sitteth in the Heavens shall laugh: the Lord shall have them in derision.*

The Catholic thinks that Luther made a quotation precisely suited to his position and the effort he was making.

7. Doctrines produced by dissent

When Luther commenced his reformation, he assumed a most grievous responsibility. He who sets himself up to reform the entire Christian Church, in matters of fundamental faith, ought to be very certain that he is in the right. No motives of human pride or passion can excuse such a revolution. The causes to justify such an extraordinary attempt ought to have been primary, important, and certain, and palpable to the world.

To assume to have made any new discovery in science, the domains of which are admitted by all to be yet imperfectly explored, is not extravagant or inconsistent with the recognized basis upon which it assumes to rest. But to assume to reform an institution like the Church of Christ, whose integrity is admitted to have been guaranteed by the immutable promises of the Founder Himself, and which Church is conceded to be governed by a perfect, positive and unchangeable law, fully understood and reduced to practice at the beginning, is certainly assuming the most lofty pretensions. At the same time it lays to the charge of preceding ages, the most grievous and criminal delinquencies. In short, such a reformer must begin by condemning all others, and end by elevating himself, by contrast with them, to the most perilous height. He ought, by all means, to be very certain he is in the right. No mere probabilities could justify such a position.

It may seem remarkable, that reformers are themselves generally the most impatient of contradiction. While assuming to reform all others, they receive propositions to reform their own theories with the utmost dislike. They never can see the wit of such a joke. They are like those merciless wits, who rejoice when they can inflict pain upon others, but who, themselves bear a keen cut with a remarkably ill grace. Yet nothing is more natural than this conduct in a reformer. He assumes to place himself in a very elevated and sublime position,

"like a star,
That from its incommunicable height,
Looks coldly on the feverish world below."

If, then, he cannot sustain these lofty pretensions, his position becomes truly painful. When a proposition is made to reform his own reformed doctrine, the *new* reformer says to him, substantially:

> You have been plying around your all-destroying scythe, cutting and mangling all you met in your way; and yet you are yourself incompetent to reform what you attacked. You have sense enough to see there is error, but not enough to see where, or what it is, or how to cure it. I admit that reform was needed, but *you* did not know how to accomplish it. You did your work so badly, it must be done *over again.* You who assumed to know so much, yet know so little, that *you* also need reformation.

If the reformer have any pride or ambition in his heart, he must feel keenly under such circumstances. The proposition to reform Luther's doctrine, who claimed a special and extraordinary mission, was certainly a very strong and direct imputation of error in an assumed special agent of God.

John Wesley, in his old age and years after he commenced his course, and in a public conference before his leading associates, admitted his Calvinistic and Antinomian errors. It is one of the conclusive proofs of his sincerity and humility. It is one (if not the only one) of the noblest instances of humility ever displayed by one claiming to be a reformer.

RESULTS OF THE PROTESTANT THEORY

Luther seems to have had many fears of the principle of private interpretation in the last resort, although it was the only possible ground upon which he could consistently base his own conduct. For this reason, we find he hedged it around with many restrictions, inconsistent with the principle itself, and yet necessary to prevent its weakness from destroying the whole project. Hence, he held that the Church was visible, and that ministers could not preach without vocation, either ordinary or extraordinary. Therefore, he placed his own right and authority upon the ground of an extraordinary mission attested by miracles. He assumed the position that all teachers must derive their authority to teach Christianity from one of two sources:

1. From the regularly constituted authorities of the Church, who had the right to confer the power by regular ordination; or

2. From the special call of God, attested by miracles.

For he insisted, with reason, that when God departed from the regular law of succession, as established by Him in the Church, He would only do so for some special reason; and would, therefore, prove the authority of His special agent, by the special attestation of miracles.

This ground was logical, considered in itself. For Luther knew, that to trace *his* right through the Catholic Church from which he had been expelled, when by his excommunication the Church had revoked his right to exercise the powers that she had bestowed, would be a solecism in the science of government.

But in escaping one difficulty, he ran upon another. Whenever God had, under the old dispensation, (which was but preparatory to the new,) raised up a prophet, or lawgiver, or teacher, as His special agent, He never failed to attest the fact by miracles, as Luther assumed. He also *inspired and qualified* the person so chosen. In the very nature of a special mission, this special qualification is required; otherwise, the special agent could not know how to perform the special duty enjoined upon him. The permanent law of Christianity having been completed during the life of Christ could not be improved. The only inspiration, then, that Luther could claim, was that of *interpreter of the existing law.*

This being true, wherefore did this necessity for reformation arise? Christ had surely promised that He would be with His visible Church until the end of the world. If the promises of Christ had not failed, there was no necessity for such a mission. If they had failed, why should Christ have raised up Luther? As he could only live for a few years, and as after his death other questions must still arise, requiring still further constructions of the law, the same error would occur again, and it would be again necessary to raise up other inspired expounders of the law from time to time. Why not hold that the promises of Christ were immutable and unfailing? Luther conceded the Church to be a visible and continuing association of men, and to be the pillar and ground of the truth; and if so, for what purpose was his special mission required? If the promises of Christ had failed, who could have any confidence in the mission of Luther? It was clear, that if the promises of Christ had once failed, that he could not be trusted. But if His promises had not failed, who could see the necessity of such a mission?

But the necessity of such a mission would have been admitted, had the assumed miracles referred to by him been apparent and conclusive in their character. They were, however, not like the miracles by which God was usually wont to attest the extraordinary missions of His special servants. They were not cognizant by the senses. They could readily be explained upon natural grounds, and in accordance with the Scriptures, in another way. He cured no diseases – he raised no one from the dead. His alleged miracles consisted only in visions – in the extraordinary success of his preaching, and in his own boldness. All of which could be readily accounted for, upon other grounds than that they were miracles. [5]

In conformity with this claim to an extraordinary mission, he did teach and decide as one having such authority. Being the great leader of the alleged Reformation, that circumstance alone would have given him great influence over his followers. Besides these claims, his indomitable will and iron nerve – even his obstinacy – were in character with his claims to an extraordinary mission. If God had raised him up for a certain purpose, of course He would have given him the necessary authority to accomplish the end intended. Hence we find Luther generally firm, and nearly always adhering to his first positions; and even when he did change, never admitting it, except in one instance, and that in reference to his first books, wherein he admitted there were some remnants of Popery, in regard to Indulgences.[6]

The Catholic theory that Luther attacked possessed in itself all the elements of *certainty and consistency.* The mind that *once* adopted that theory, *as true,* relied with the same certainty upon the infallible attestation and construction of the code, as upon the perfection of the law itself. In other words in the contemplation of that theory, the mind which believed it, had equal certainty as to the inspiration of both the Lawgiver and the Law-interpreter.

As Luther was forced, from necessity, to adopt the principle of private interpretation in the last resort, it followed very logically, that he should also adopt the doctrine of justification by faith alone, and reject free will, and to assume as he did, "that God works the evil in us as well as the good," "that free will was a vain title," and in his declamatory style, that "God thunder-strikes and breaks to pieces all free will."[7]

In lieu of the old system, it was necessary to propose some other, which, when *once* adopted by the mind *as true,* promised *certainty.* Therefore, there was a more deep philosophy in his theory than would at first view appear. So there was in Calvin's, which was but a legitimate extension of Luther's leading principles. As every member must construe for himself, there could be no *certainty* in the contemplation of such a theory, unless other elements were mingled with it. But by assuming that man's will was overruled by God, each one who believed this, could rest content that he was as sure of being in the right, as any one else holding the same principle, whatever might be his want of capacity to construe the Scriptures for himself.

The theory that denies free will is certainly calculated, when once implicitly believed to produce repose and confidence. So too, the idea that we are among the few favored and predestinated is certainly flattering to the mind that entertains it. And that by the sovereign act of God alone for His own glory! If firmly believed it must produce confidence and consolation. It being a *partial* theory, the favored ones would necessarily esteem it the more. It is natural that they should.[8]

Luther could not have well adopted any doctrines better calculated, in their nature, to enable him to succeed, than those of justification by faith alone, and the rejection of the free will. They are not so well suited to the calm reasoner, as to the declamatory zealot. They suited the impetuous temperament and the vehement eloquence of Luther. In times of excitement, when positions are not examined with care, these tenets would be well received. They are themes upon which an eloquent declaimer can dilate with eminent success. These doctrines made the way of salvation easy, simple and certain. A man had only to believe, and he was safe.

The denial of free will in man is a necessary weapon to enable a party to tear down an existing institution holding free will. It was this element in the theory of Mahomet that mainly produced that fanatical zeal and invincible valor displayed by his followers on so many trying occasions.[9] Nothing but time can wear out the effects of such a principle. Derogatory as it is to God's character as a lawgiver, it is yet so flattering to the mind, that in seasons of intense excitement, it is the principle always adopted with success. Conquerors and other military heroes generally inculcate it as always tending to make men more fearless of death, and more cool in positions of extreme danger.

But as Luther insisted that free will appertained to God alone, it was extremely difficult to understand upon what ground, and for what reason, God should give a *positive* law, expressed in human language, "commanding what is right, and prohibiting what is wrong," to a being who could neither obey nor disobey it. We can well understand why any lawgiver should make such a law for the government of intelligent agents, who could *know,* and free agents, who could either obey or disobey the law, as they willed. But we cannot conceive of any reason for giving a law for the government of the *predestinated,* or of him who can have no will.

Where some other irresistible force overpowers the will, outside and independent of the law itself, then the law must be entirely idle, because it can accomplish nothing. When the promulgation of such a law cannot change the final result, in any way, it can only be inconsistent with the object of all law. And it was well said by one of the Vaudois leaders, speaking of the work of Luther against free will:

> But should all come to pass of necessity, as Luther says, and the predestinated not have it in their power to turn reprobate, nor contrariwise, to what end so much preaching and so much writing, since, everything happening by necessity, matters never will be better or worse?[10]

But these doctrines of predestination and justification by faith alone, led to such excesses of theory and practice, as to force the larger portion of the Protestant world to reject them; although they thereby gave an example of versatility and change, entirely inconsistent with the claim of Luther to an extraordinary mission. The doctrines were not only indefensible upon the grounds of reason, tradition, and Scripture, but they operated badly in practice, when legitimately carried out.

8. Using the same doctrines to tear down and build

The followers of Luther, especially while they were all immediately engaged in the process of destruction, more than in building up, believed in his pretensions to an extraordinary mission. However, they soon began to doubt as to the fact, at least so far as regarded any special qualification he assumed to have. The fundamental rule being common to every member, Stork, the founder of the Anabaptists, soon disputed infant baptism, and insisted that children would be saved out of the Church without baptism. In like manner Calvin, extended Luther's doctrine of the certainty of justification to the certainty of salvation, and denied that grace could be lost after justification. Soon after that, Carlostadius and Zuinglius denied the doctrine of the Real Presence, and in a very short time Calvin followed with his extensions of Luther's main principle of justification by faith alone.

The celebrated German Protestant writer, Henke, in speaking of these divisions, remarks:

> Discord and schism among the Protestants were inevitable. We can fancy to ourselves two periods in the formation of their religious opinions: the first, their common struggle with Catholicity, the protest and separation of all these new religious parties from the Catholic Church; the second, their own internal process of reconstruction. In the first, all was pulling down; in the second, building up; the first was revolution – the second, constitution or organization. But it also followed that, in the one case, there was unity of purpose and community of exertion, and, therefore, union; in the other, diversity of purpose, and, therefore, discord and separation….
>
> As soon as they seriously set about reconstructing the sole true edifice of Christian faith – as the architects were not of one mind, and were self-opinioned and obstinate enough to wish each for his own plans, models, and designs, in the erection and ornamenting of the edifice, although often they did not understand each other's language – confusion and strife at one became unavoidable: oftentimes, before any considerable part of the work was done, they separated, each building a hut for himself, or taking up some temporary lodging, until he ultimately returned to the original dwelling.
>
> The expositions of Scripture, and the conclusions from it, which one party adopted, were rejected by another; and that, notwithstanding the claims of human authority, which they determined not to allow. But, meanwhile, although authority was driven out at one door, it was let in at another, although in a new and more friendly shape. Before, it

> had dictated as an arbitrary and infallible lawgiver; now, it spake merely as an unerring interpreter of the law. Instead of the dogma prescribed without proof or warrant of Scripture, proven and Scriptural tenets were now proposed; but, unfortunately, many now considered the proofs as worthless, and of as little power as, before, all had deemed the authority of the church from which they had seceded.[11]

There is certainly much truth, with some error, contained in this extract; and one must admire the candor of the courteous author. He very properly describes the Church under the figure of an edifice. The process of pulling down the Church is properly called revolution, and the process of "reconstructing the sole true edifice of Christian faith," is very properly called "constitution or organization." In reference to the first, he says there was "unity of purpose and community of exertion, and, therefore, union;" but in reference to the second, there was "diversity of purpose, and, therefore, separation."

Now, I am compelled to say, that it seems difficult to understand this "diversity of purpose" in the reconstruction of but one "sole edifice." The purpose was, as he states, first, to pull down, and second to reconstruct. There was then unity of purpose in both cases. They were perfectly agreed as to the necessity of pulling down and reconstructing this sole edifice; and they set about to accomplish both purposes, but each in its natural order. Therefore, there was unity of purpose as to both – but as to the *manner* and not the purpose of this reconstruction. There was a diversity of views among the architects. There was no diversity as to the *end* to be attained, but only as to the *manner* in which this should be reached.

The lion and other beasts of prey, in the fable of the partnership hunt, were well agreed as to two purposes; first, to take the game, and second, to dispose of it. In the pursuit, each beast was left to run upon his own legs, and utter his own cry, in his own way, there was no disagreement. But when they came to dispose of the game, adverse interests and views came up, and rival plans arose for the disposition of the prey. So it was here. In pulling down, each one acted in the attack as he pleased, and consequently, there was no discord, for no motive to disunion could arise. But when they come to build up again, *one* certain manner and form must, of necessity, be adopted, for the *one* sole true edifice; and they must all agree as to this plan, or separate.

The figure selected by the learned author to represent the Church, is the same used by our Lord, and by Saint Paul, for the same purpose. No illustration could have been selected more forcibly showing the radical defects of the fundamental principle, upon which all Protestantism is ultimately based. The architects were all *master builders* – all independent equals. There were no superiors – no subordinates. There was no admitted head and no subordination among these men; and how, therefore, could there be unity of views?

Under the fundamental principle that each was to decide for himself, how, could each one be otherwise than "self-opinioned and obstinate," in regard to his own plans and models? Each architect was required, by the rule, to decide conscientiously for himself, and to rely upon his *own* convictions, as matter of *conscience.* Consequently, an honest man could not give up his views, when he was not convinced, without admitting an authority in others that could not exist under the rule. If he pretended to be convinced, when he was not, then he was a hypocrite. In no view of the case could these architects yield to each other their own conscientious convictions. It would have been a palpable violation of the rule itself. The only ground upon which they could yield up their different plans, was that of being convinced by argument; and among so many independent equals, this could never happen. Well may the author say, "confusion and strife became unavoidable.... discord and schism among the Protestants were inevitable."

The learned author says authority was driven out at one door, in one shape, and let in at another door, in a different shape. In one shape it spoke, he states, as an infallible *lawgiver*, in the other as an *unerring interpreter.* In the first case, he alludes to the Catholic Church; in the second, to the Protestant Churches. Now I cannot understand upon what ground the author assumes that the Catholic Church spoke as an infallible *lawgiver.* She does speak as an infallible interpreter. She assumes to make no law, but simply to explain and execute that which is already made. Her functions are simply judicial as to matters of faith, not legislative. The *forms* of her decrees, it is true, are as positive expositions. This is in unison with her character as an infallible tribunal. In all courts of justice, the judgment, which is the final and binding act of the court, is always in form positive. So was the decree of the Council of Jerusalem. The *opinion* giving the reasons for the judgment is in a different form, but the determination itself is always positive, and must, in the nature of a judgment, be so.

The fact stated by the author, (and so fully proven by the events succeeding the advent of the alleged Reformation,) that authority was driven out at one door, and was let in at another, is but another proof of the incessant exertions made by Protestants, to reconcile two precisely opposite principles. It is true, this authority assumed to come in at the other door, in a new and friendlier shape but it was still the *thing itself.* It wore another dress, as was supposed, or the same dress, turned the other side out. It only assumed to be an *unerring interpreter.* But this claim, to be the unerring interpreter of Scripture, was wholly incompatible with the recognized right of private interpretation. Private interpretation in the last resort could not exist under the authority of an unerring interpreter. It was, of course, the duty of all to hear this "unerring interpreter," and to follow this unerring interpretation; otherwise, for what purpose was the power assumed?

If the unerring interpretation of this interpreter were to be subject to the fallible revision of each individual member, then it would make the *certain* yield to the *doubtful.* This would be reversing all the rules of logic and right reason. On the other hand, to admit this authority, was admitting the infallibility of the visible Church. This once conceded, the only inquiry would be, in which Church can it be found? And if conceded, it must be in virtue of the promises of Christ; and must, therefore, have always existed in the Church. This would be at once giving up the fundamental principle upon which the whole alleged Reformation was itself based. Hence this assumed authority of unerring interpretation could not be sustained, and, as the author says, "many now considered the proofs as worthless and of as little power as, before, all had deemed the authority of the Church from which they had seceded."

The leading principle of Wesley's system has in it a deep philosophy. It is better expressed in the words of Mr. Topham in his letter to Dr. Milner. "Is it possible," asks he,

> to go against conviction and facts? Namely, the experience that very many serious Christians feel, in *this day of God's power*, that they are made partakers of Christ and of the Holy Ghost, and who hear him saying to the melting heart, with his still, small, yet penetrating and renovating voice: *Thy sins are forgiven thee: Be thou clean; Thy faith hath made thee whole?* If an exterior proof were wanting to show the certainty of this interior conviction, I might refer to the conversion and holy life of those who have experienced it.[12]

Now, whether the *conviction* that this voice has been heard, arises from a certain excited state of the *imagination*, and a certain *warmth* of sentiment, or from reality, the *effect* upon the mind and conduct of him who entertains it, is still the same. He must, so long as he entertains this conviction without doubt, be *certain*, in his opinion, of the correctness of his faith, and of his acceptance with God. His construction of the law *at the time* he had this conviction, must, under this theory, have been right, as his faith could not make him whole, unless it were, in his view, the true faith. And the intemperate zeal and boisterous joy of the Methodist convert are but the legitimate effects of this conviction.

So, too, the calm, confident, and abiding faith of the Catholic is the legitimate result of the leading principle of his system, *the infallibility of the Church*. So long as the mind entertains firmly this conviction, there must be continued confidence and peace.

It cannot escape the attention of the patient inquirer, how many efforts have been made, by the projectors of different theories, to substitute something for the Catholic *certainty*. It has ever been one continued struggle to find some principle that would afford to the mind the same consolatory grounds of certainty, while at the same time the fundamental principle of private construction in the last resort, could be sustained. Some place it, as we have seen done by Luther, or as by Calvin, or by Wesley, and others, in holding so *few doctrines essential*, that almost every one may be sure, under such a theory, that he believes all that is required.

But how hard it is to keep counterfeit coin always in circulation. The different parties are each equally certain their different and contradictory substitutes are true. This cannot be. And, therefore, all are left in doubt, sooner or later. Those who hold to private inspiration have given such contradictory, yet positive testimony as to this private spirit, that no one can tell who is right. There is no test – no tribunal to determine.

This restless and continued struggle to attain, not only infallible certainty in the making of the law itself, but also in its construction and application to particular cases, as they arise from time to time, is a proof of its invincible necessity, in the very nature of the human soul, and of every supernatural system intended for men. There must be infallible certainty in the construction of the law, as well as in its creation, or there can be no fixed faith, and no consistence in the system. That there should be an *infallible* tribunal to construe a *perfect* law, requiring perfect faith of an imperfect creature, is a conclusion so logical, simple, and consolatory, and so much needed by our wants and frailties, that every man's heart and common sense tell him it must be true; and when it is rejected, there must be at least some plausible *substitute for it.*

Well may the Protestant Professor Kohler say:

> In truth, the Catholic supernaturalism is the only consistent scheme.[13]

And also the German Protestant writer Reinhold:

> If a religion contains mysteries – if its path towards faith lie over prodigies, the *system of infallibility is the only possible one.* It is the *only system* recorded in history, which, in the natural dependence and harmony of its parts, *can be said to deserve the name.*[14]

Quoting Gforer:

> The Catholic faith, if we concede its first axiom, which neither the Lutherans, nor the Reformed, nor even the followers of Socinus denied, *is as consistent and as consecutive as the books of Euclid.*[15]

Quoting Marheinecke

> We, Protestants as we are, when we take in at one view this wondrous edifice, from its base to its summit, must acknowledge that we have never beheld a system which, the foundation once laid, is raised upon such certain and sure principles; whose structure displays, in its minutest details, so much art, penetration, and consistency; and whose plan is so proof against the severest criticism of the most profound science.[16]

The Calvinists were called "The Reformed," on the continent. The art, penetration, and consistency, mentioned by the learned author, would necessarily be found in the work of Christ.

9. Protestant theories of the Church

But in no respect have the changes among Protestants been more marked and palpable, than those in reference to the constitution and powers of the Church. The question of powers of the Church, in its nature, was of the greatest importance. Recognizing the existence of any Church at all, some clear and definite idea of her form, functions, mission, and duration, was indispensable to unity of design and success in any system.

It was palpable to common sense, that in organizing the Church, our Lord must have designed the accomplishment of some great practical end; and that He would so frame His system that this end should not be defeated. If He organized a visible Church, composed of living, associated men, He would necessarily give a law for its government, and bestow upon it certain powers of government, to preserve unity in the association. As great practical results were designed to flow from the existence of the Church, it could not but be of the utmost importance to understand her powers and duties, and the relation the faithful bear to her.

It was also manifest, that as the law was promulgated in human language, and committed to the Church, she must be visible and continuing. Her visible existence must be commensurate with that of the visible law intended for her government, and committed to her keeping. She must be capable of knowing and construing the law, made known by signs addressed to the senses, and must, therefore, exist as a visible corporation. If great practical results were to follow from the organization of a Church at all, that Church must, in the nature of things, be visible and continuing. Whatever practical powers or functions were bestowed upon such an institution could only be given to the visible Church. Such a Church could only speak – she could only be heard and obeyed. Men could only *certainly* join themselves to a visible Church. They could not know, except by special inspiration, when they were joined to an invisible Church, if they could join such an impalpable thing at all. It was only the visible true Church that could answer the prayer of our Lord, that His followers should be united, that the world might believe. An invisible Church could never give evidence to the world of any thing.

The reason for this view is fully confirmed by Scripture. All the powers bestowed upon the apostles were visibly exercised by them in the visible Church. The Council of Jerusalem made the decision of the visible Church. Every act of teaching – every act of government – was always found in the visible Church. "*The Church*" is often spoken of in the Scriptures. In all places where the phrase "The Church" is used without being confined to the Church at a particular place, as the Church at Ephesus, at Corinth, &c., (which were only *parts* of the Church, located at particular places, and subject, as branches of the Church, to its government, in the same way that the Church at Antioch, and all other branches, were subject, to the decision of the Council of Jerusalem,) the attributes assigned to the Church show plainly that it could be heard, seen, and obeyed. The general expression, *the Church*, must have had a different meaning from the expression, for example, of *the Church at Corinth*; and this being so, it could only mean the entire Church, as composed of all the branches.

When converts were baptized, they were baptized by officers of the visible Church, and added unto her. The expression "the Church" can only mean but one. The definite article only points to but one Church. To that one Church are attributed all the powers and privileges bestowed upon her. When, therefore, Saint Paul says: "And he hath set some in the church," he not only alludes to the one Church, including all branches, but he evidently alluded to the visible Church, and to that only. These apostles, prophets, teachers, and evangelists, set in the Church, for certain purposes, could only perform their functions in the visible Church. Hence Luther, Calvin, and Zuinglius, and their respective followers, for the first hundred years succeeding the date of the Reformation, held the Church to be visible.

Charles V., Emperor of Germany, called the Diet of Augsburg in the month of June 1530. Each party appeared. The Lutherans presented their Confession of Faith, drawn up by Melanchthon, in concert with Luther. The four towns of the empire, Strasburg, Meiningen, Seidau, and Constance, who opposed the literal sense, gave in their Confession, drawn up by Bucer. Zuinglius, though not of the body of the empire, also sent to the emperor his Confession of Faith. Melanchthon drew up an Apology for the Augsburg Confession, which was also received by the whole part, and presented to the emperor. The Confession and Apology were both equally important and authentic.[17] In the Augsburg Confession, the Church is spoken of in this way:

> We teach that there is a holy Church which must eternally subsist....
>
> The Church is the assembly of saints, wherein the Gospel is rightly taught, and the sacraments rightly administered.
>
> And in the Apology: "We have never dreamed that the Church was a Platonic city not to be found on earth: we say that the Church exists; that in it there are true believers and men truly just, spread over all the universe. We add to this its marks, the pure Gospel, and the Sacraments, and it is such a church that is properly the pillar of the truth....
>
> The Catholic Church is not an exterior of certain nations, but is men dispersed over the universe, who have the same sentiments with regard to the Gospel, who have the same Christ, the same Holy Ghost, and the same sacraments.

Here the Church was admitted to be visible and perpetual, and the pillar of the truth, having the Gospel rightly taught, and the same sacraments rightly administered, all the members having the "same sentiments with regard to the Gospel."

In the articles of Smalkald [Schmalkalden], the same view is taken. So also in the Saxonic Confession, that of Wittenberg, that of Strasburg in 1530, that of Basil in 1536, and of the same in 1532, the same character of the true Church is substantially admitted.

The great and solemn Helvetic Confession of 1566, defines the Church as that:

> which has been always, which is, and which shall ever be, the assembly of the faithful, and of the saints who know God, and serve him by the Word and the Holy Ghost;" "that lawful and true preaching is her chief mark, to which must be added the sacraments, as God has instituted them.

This definition contemplates the Church as visible, perpetual, and composed of pastors and people, with true preaching and the right administration of the sacraments.

But it is remarkable that in this Confession we have the first idea of an invisible Church to be found in any authentic creeds of the Reformation. They subjoin:

> that God has had his friends out of the people of Israel; that, during the captivity of Babylon, the people were deprived sixty years of the sacrifice; that, through a just judgment of God, the truth of his Word and worship, and the Catholic Faith, are sometimes so obscured, that it seems almost as if they were extinct, and no Church at all subsisting, as happened in the time of Eli, and at other times; so that the Church may be called invisible; not that the men she is composed of are so, but because she is often hidden to our eyes, and, being known to God alone, escapes from the sight of men.

The celebrated French Calvinist minister, M. Jurieu, states the cause of this invention as follows:

> That which moved some reformed doctors, in their Confessions of Faith, to cast themselves into the perplexity they were entangled in upon their denying the perpetual visibility of the Church, was because they believed, by owning the Church always visible, they should find it difficult to answer the question which the Church of Rome so often asks us: Where was our Church a hundred years ago? If the Church

> be always visible, your Calvinist and Lutheran Church is not the true Church, for that was not visible.

The minister ought to have said, whole churches of the Reformation, instead of "some reformed doctors."

The Church of England speaks ambiguously. "The visible Church," says she,

> is a congregation of faithful men, in which the pure Word of God is preached, and the sacraments are duly ministered, according to Christ's ordinance.

Nothing is said as to whether she is always visible, or whether she is perpetual.

In the Confession of Scotland, the Catholic Church is defined the Society of all the Elect: "She is," they say,

> invisible, and known to God only, who alone knows his elect.... that the true Church hath for its mark, preaching and the sacraments.... which is understood not of the universal Church just spoken of, but of the particular Church of Ephesus, of Corinth, and so forth, wherein the ministry had been planted by Saint Paul.

In the Catechism of the French Calvinists, composed by Calvin, they teach that the name "Holy Catholic Church," in the Apostle's Creed, was given to her

> to signify there is but one head of the faithful, so all are to be united in one body; so that there are not many churches, but one only, which is diffused all the world over....
>
> There is indeed a visible Church of God, conformable to the signs he hath given us to know her by; but in this place, (the Creed,) properly speaking, is meant the society of those whom God hath elected for salvation, which cannot be discovered fully to the eye... that no man obtains pardon of his sins, unless he be first incorporated with God's people, and persevere in unity and communion with the body of Christ, and so be a member of the Church....
>
> out of the Church there is nothing but death and damnation; and that all those who separate themselves from the company of the faithful, to make a sect apart, ought not, whilst divided, to hope salvation.

It will be seen that in this Catechism the unity and universality of the Church are admitted, and that she has a twofold union, *interior* and *exterior*, and both of them are necessary to salvation. Making "a sect apart," is undoubtedly breaking the exterior union of the Church; so that this Church is visible in her exterior, and known by the marks they speak of, and out of which there is no salvation; for which reasons they cannot say we cannot see or hear her, but only that we could not see her *fully*.

In the French Calvinist's Confession of Faith, presented to Charles IX in 1561, at Poissy, by the whole party, the Church is only spoken of as visible, and no intimation is given of an invisible Church. They there teach as a fundamental point, that

> the Church cannot subsist, unless there be pastors in her that have the charge of teaching....
>
> That no man ought to withdraw apart, nor rest on self-sufficiency, but should join himself to some Church, and this in whatsoever place God shall have established a true form of a Church.

They speak of the alleged errors of the Church of Rome, and conclude:

> We hold that all those who join in such deeds, and communicate in them, do separate and cut themselves off from the body of Jesus Christ.

Nothing could decide more clearly, that there is no salvation in the Catholic Church. And this was conformable to Calvin's sentiments, "that the essential doctrine of Christianity was entirely forgotten by us."

In reference to the vocation of ministers, they say:

> We believe, then, that no man may intrude himself, of his own proper authority, into the government of the Church, but that this ought to be done by election.

But they add an exception, "which exception," they say

> we add expressly, because it hath been necessary sometimes, nay, in our days, when the state of the Church was interrupted, that God should raise men in an extraordinary manner, to set up the Church anew, which was fallen into rain and desolation.

"They could not denote," says Bossuet,

> in more clear and more general terms, the interruption of the ordinary ministry established by God, nor carry it farther than to be obliged to have recourse to an extraordinary mission which God himself dispatches, and accordingly furnishes with the particular proofs of his immediate will.

The entire omission of all allusion to an invisible Church in this authentic Confession of Faith, created great difficulty among the French Calvinists, and accordingly the Synod of Gap was held in 1603, to consider the propriety of changing the twenty-fifth article; "so much the more," say they,

> as our belief, regarding the Church, whereof mention is made in the creed, being to be expressed, there is nothing in the said Confession that can be understood of any other than the Church militant and visible.

A general command was given by this Synod, "that all come prepared on questions concerning the Church." The National Synod of Rochelle, held in 1607, after all the provinces had thoroughly examined the question, decided "not to add to or diminish any thing from the twenty-fifth and twenty-ninth articles" – the very same in which the visibility of the Church was expressed most fully – "nor to meddle anew with the subject of the Church."

In reference to the vocation of the ministers, the Synod of Gap, as in the Confession, referred it *only* to the "extraordinary vocation whereby God interiorly stirred them up to this ministry, and not to the small remains amongst them of that corrupted ordinary vocation;" but the Synod of Rochelle, four years afterwards, not satisfied with the Confession and the decision of the Synod of Gap, modified it by saying, they must *principally* have recourse to this extraordinary vocation.

This change, made by the Synod of Rochelle, was carried farther by the two celebrated French Calvinist ministers, M. Claude and M. Jurieu, who abandoned the extraordinary mission entirely, and put forth some new views in regard to the true Church. M. Claude admits the visibility of the Church, as in the Confession, and the promises of Christ to her; and in expounding the commission "Go teach," he approves this comment thereon, "with you teaching, with you baptizing," and concludes: "I acknowledge that Jesus Christ promises the Church to be with her, and to teach with her, *without interruption*, to the end of the world."

As M. Claude had abandoned the ground of an extraordinary vocation claimed by Luther and Calvin, and their followers generally, and relied upon ordinary vocation, he was compelled to own that "this body in which the true faithful are nourished, and this ministry whereby they received sufficient food without subtraction of any part, was the body of the Church of Rome, and the ministry of her prelates." This was expressly contrary to the Confession, to the Synods of Gap and Rochelle, and to Calvin, when he says, speaking of the Catholic Church, "that the doctrine essential to Christianity was there buried, and she was nothing but a school of idolatry and impiety."

The minister M Jurieu is still more explicit. He holds "that all Christian societies which agree in some tenets, inasmuch as they agree, are united to the body of the Christian Church, though they be in schism one against another, *even to daggers drawing*. And he compounds "the body of the Church of all that great heap of sects which make profession of Christianity in all provinces of the world put together," so that they believe "the fundamental articles." After mentioning the Greeks, the Armenians, the Copts, the Abyssinians, the Russians, the Papists, and Protestants, he says, "all those societies have composed the church, and therein does God preserve his fundamental truths."

In speaking of the two marks of the true Church, which are found in all the Protestant Confessions of Faith; to wit: "The pure preaching of God's Word, and the administration of the sacraments conformably to the institution of Jesus Christ," he says: "We lay them down: we, that is to say, we Protestants; but, for my part, I would give the thing another turn, and would say, that to know the body of the Christian and universal Church in general, there is but one mark requisite; viz., the confession of the name of Jesus Christ, the true Messiah and Redeemer of mankind."

These ministers made a distinction between addition and subtraction. If a church subtracted from the fundamental articles, she could not be the true Church. But if she only added false tenets, even as matters of positive faith, she did not cease to be the true Church, as "God applies to His elect what good there is, hindering whatsoever of human institution from turning to their prejudice and destruction."

From which it would seem to follow that Saint Paul was mistaken, in pronouncing a curse upon those who add to or take away from the Gospel. So, too, the Council of Jerusalem was mistaken, in condemning the heresy requiring the *addition* of circumcision to the requirements of Christ's law, in order to salvation.

The minister Jurieu attributes the origin of the doctrine of the unity of the Church to the third century; and ascribes it to Firmilian and his bishops, from whom, he says, it passed into Africa, where the great martyr, Saint Cyprian, he says, embraced it. And the minister gives this singular explanation:

> that the false idea of the unity of the Church was formed on the history of the two first ages, down to the middle or end of the third.

"We must not wonder," says he,

> that the Church accounted all the sects which existed during these times, as entirely separated from the body of the Church, for that was true....
>
> it was at that time, namely, in the two first ages, down to the middle of the third, that they got a habit of believing that heretics did not in any manner appertain to the Church.

It was, therefore, confessed, that from the beginning of Christianity down to the middle or end of the third century, all the heretics that were then expelled from the Church, "were entirely separated from" her – that this was the practice of the Church; but as it suited the theory of this minister, he insists that those heretics denied what he calls the fundamentals of Christianity, and for *that* reason, and not for the reason that all heretics were considered as cut off from the Church when excommunicated, the ancient Church looked upon them as out of the true fold.

Certainly, in the days of Saint Paul, *all condemned heretics* were held as not in any manner appertaining to the Church. If heretics at all, they were criminals in the eye of the law of Christ, in the same way as murderers, fornicators, and others, mentioned by the apostle. Heresy of every kind excluded from the kingdom of heaven.

These views of the ministers were generally received by the Calvinists of France, and introduced into the Lutheran Churches in Germany by Calixtus, one of the most learned men among them, where they also prevail to a great extent. M. Jurieu defines the Church to be "the body of those who make profession of believing Jesus Christ the true Messiah; a body divided into a great number of sects."

10. Potential Protestant ancestors

In the Confession of Augsburg, and in the Apology, as late as 1530, Luther and his followers insisted that they contended for nothing contrary to the Church of Rome – that they only opposed certain abuses which had crept into the Church, as they alleged, without any certain authority. Luther, speaking of this Church as late as 1534, stated, that "she is the true Church, the pillar and ground of the truth, and the most holy place."

But when the separation from the Catholic Church became incurable, and as the true Church was admitted to be perpetual and visible, and that the promises of Christ were given to her, it became necessary to seek a succession up to the days of the apostles through some body of professed Christians, other that the Church of Rome. To do this, however, constituted the greatest difficulty.

There had been heretics existing in every age, in some part of the world. Sect after sect, to the number of about four hundred, had arisen, and most of them had vanished before the time of Luther. Some continued longer than others. As one went down, another rose; and so they had succeeded each other, from Simon Magus down to the alleged Reformation. Among so great a number and variety, it would seem, there ought to have been no difficulty in finding good and worthy predecessors.

"We have," says Bossuet,

> in the councils held in the communion of the Roman Church, anathemas pronounced against an infinity of different sects; we have the catalogues of heresies drawn by Saint Epiphanius, by Saint Austin, and several other church authors. The most obscure and the least followed sects - those which appeared in a corner of the world, as that of certain women called Collyridians, who were to be met with in some part of Arabia; that of the Tertullianists or Ahelians, who were only in Carthage, or in some villages near Hippo, and many others equally obscure – did not escape their knowledge. The zeal of the pastors that labored to bring back the strayed sheep, discovered all to save all: none but those separatists on account of ecclesiastical revenues were unknown to everybody.[18]

But these sects were as different in their doctrines and practices, as they were different in the terms of their duration. Their errors were both great and various, as admitted by Protestants themselves. They not only differed so much from each other, but they equally differed from all the Protestant parties. And what increased the difficulty to an insurmountable degree, was the fact, that those various sects, while they differed from the Catholic Church upon certain points, still held the doctrines generally denied by Protestants, and imputed by them to her as errors. And not only so, but no one sect could be found, that had existed during the whole period from the apostles to Luther. To trace succession through several different and discordant heretical sects, with no single one of which any one of the Protestant parties could agree, even in fundamental and material respects, would seem to have been a very illogical attempt.

But the attempt was made. To say, in uncertain and general terms, that they traced their succession through those sects who had renounced the authority of the Catholic church, would have been unbecoming sensible and candid men, and would have admitted a fraternity with all. It therefore became necessary to specify the particular sects through which this alleged succession was to be traced.

11. The Vaudois as Protestant ancestors

Among the sects selected as ancestors, especially by the Calvinists, was that of the Vaudois, or poor men of Lyons, who took their rise under Peter Waldo, in 1160. Waldo was a merchant of that city, and was so much affected by the sudden death of one of his brother merchants, that he at once sold all his property, distributed the proceeds to the poor, and afterwards led a life of poverty himself.

Their peculiar tenets have an affinity with the historical circumstances connected with their origin. Their leading tenets were:

1. That it was unlawful for the clergy to own any property.

2. That neither lands nor people ought to be divided.

3. That every oath is a mortal sin.

4. That all princes and judges are damned, because they condemn malefactors contrary to these words: "Vengeance is mine, saith the Lord;" and "Let both grow together until the harvest."

5. That every layperson, even a woman, ought to preach.

6. That the functions of ministers, and the validity of their acts, depend upon their personal virtue.

7. They held the seven sacraments, with the exception of Orders.

8. They held Transubstantiation.

They knew nothing about the doctrine of justification by faith alone, nor of the impossibility of falling from grace, nor the doctrine of Luther and Calvin denying free will. As they made the ministry depend upon personal merit, and required extreme poverty to constitute that merit, they repudiated the authority of the Pope and bishops, and held the See of Rome as the harlot of the Revelations. They held that a holy layman could administer the sacraments as well as a holy priest. They rejected the Mass, Purgatory, and the Invocation of Saints.[19]

But the difficulty of tracing succession for more than three centuries, through this singular people, became very great when they held so many doctrines condemned by both Protestants and Catholics; such as forbidding the clergy to hold any property, thus making poverty an essential of religion, when it was only a counsel of perfection; that property ought to be held in common by the laity; that oaths were sinful; that the punishment of death could not be inflicted, by the state, upon the vilest offenders; that all lay persons, even women, ought to preach; and that the validity of the sacraments did not depend upon the virtue Christ had given them, but upon the personal merits of the administrator. But, besides these errors, (condemned by both parties,) these people held Transubstantiation, and six out of the seven sacraments held by Catholics. It would seem to have been difficult to find any affinity between the Calvinists and the Vaudois. Besides, the Vaudois knew nothing of justification by faith alone, predestination, and final perseverance. In claiming them as predecessors, the Calvinists were compelled to overlook the grossest alleged errors, and also to suppress their own cardinal doctrines. They claimed to be the successors of a sect that needed more reformation than the Catholics, (from whom they separated,) according to their own theory.

But the greatest difficulty lay in the undeniable fact, that Peter Waldo, and all his followers, were mere laymen, who preached without a vocation, either regular or extraordinary. They had never claimed any extraordinary ministry. They performed no miracles, nor claimed that any were performed, to prove such an extraordinary mission. They claimed no regular mission, for they denied its necessity.

The Vaudois, then, obtained their authority to preach in neither of the ways admitted and required by the Lutherans and Calvinists. In claiming the Vaudois as predecessors, the Calvinists, in violation of their own theory, claimed to be engrafted upon a branch that did not connect with the trunk itself.

Besides, this sect only extended back to the year 1160. How were they to get beyond that period? Efforts were made to trace the origin of the Vaudois back to the time of Constantine the Great, but these efforts failed. It was claimed that in the days of Sylvester I., when that Christian emperor endowed the Church with temporal revenues for ecclesiastical purposes, that one of the Pope's companions, called Leo, withdrew from his communion with his followers, and abided in their poverty and simplicity of faith. Leger, one of the Vaudois Barbes, (as they called their pastors,) who was the most celebrated historian, though a very bold and ignorant man, had embraced this error. But, unfortunately, the Calvinists could, not approve the ground upon which the alleged withdrawal of Leo and his followers was based. What was still more against the whole assumption, was the fact that no historical proof could be found among the writings of the ancient Fathers, nor in the proceedings of any of the councils.

12. The Bohemian Brethren as Protestant ancestors

Among the obscure sects existing at the beginning of the Reformation, was that of the Bohemian Brethren. The Real Presence had been impugned by the Manichean Heretics of Orleans in 1017, and by Beringarius in 1030. , Beringarius recanted his errors, and died in the Catholic Church. In the fourteenth century, Wickliffe impugned this, as well as other doctrines of the Catholic Church. Wickliffe also renounced his doctrine, and died in the Catholic Church. Among the disciples of Wickliffe was John Huss, who, however, disagreed with Wickliffe about the Real Presence. The only two points of Catholic doctrine disputed by Huss were, communion under one kind, and the Pope. In other respects, he was a Catholic.

After Huss' death two sects arose under his name, the Calixtins and the Taborites. The Taborites were so cruel and seditious, that they have been alike condemned by Catholics and Protestants. The Calixtins on the other hand, only objected that the cup was withheld from the laity, and were willing to recognize the authority of the Pope if this privilege were granted to them. These Calixtins, it was said, "romanized in everything but the cup." To reform them, the tradesmen placed at their head, one Kelesiski, a master shoemaker who drew up for them a body of doctrine, called the Forms of Kelesiski. Afterwards they chose themselves a pastor named Matthias Conraldi, and openly separated from the Calixtins in 1467.

In their Apology of 1532, the Bohemian Brethren admit they were made up "of the meaner sort, and some Bohemian priests in small numbers, all put together but a handful of men, a small remnant, and the despicable refuse left in the world by John Huss."[20] Their leading and distinctive tenets were:

1. The necessity of re-baptizing all those who joined them from other churches.

2. That the efficacy of sacraments depends upon the merit of the administrator.

3. They rejected the Mass.

4 They rejected the authority of the Pope.

5. They rejected Transubstantiation.

They agreed with the Catholics in the seven sacraments, in observing days of fast, in the celibacy of the clergy, and the perpetual virginity of the Blessed Virgin.

Luther reproached them for knowing nothing of the common foundation of the Reformation, justification by faith, for they "placed it," he said, "in faith and works together, as many fathers had done; and John Huss was wedded to this opinion."[21] As for the doctrine of the Real Presence, it was matter of some doubt whether they held it or not. Their language was confused and uncertain upon this point. They were claimed both by the Lutherans and Sacramentarians. It seems, however, that they held the doctrine, as they afterwards joined the Lutherans. The Lutherans, in the Preface they placed before the Brethren's Apology, and printed at Wittenberg in Luther's time, say that in this small and ignorant body of men, "the Church of God was preserved when she was thought entirely lost."[22]

In reference to these Bohemian Brethren, Bossuet remarks:

> These are the men whom Protestants admire. Does the question turn on condemning the Church of Rome? They never cease to upbraid us with the ignorance of her priests and monks. Is the question regarding the ignorant individuals of these latter ages, who have set up for reforming the Church by schism? They are fishermen turned apostles, although their ignorance stands eternally on record, from the first step they took.[23]

It was in this small sect, in one corner of Bohemia, that the Church was preserved, as the Lutherans insisted, and through this body they were willing to trace their succession. But there were many difficulties in the way. The Bohemian Brethren were only a small party, who had separated from another small remnant of Hussites the Calixtins, the only Hussites in existence at the time. They knew nothing of the cardinal doctrine of Justification. They believed in Works. Besides that, they had no vocation ordinary of extraordinary. They were mere laymen, who made their own minister. They went, according to Luther, without being sent. They held the seven sacraments – celibacy of the clergy – days of fast, and other Catholic views so much opposed by the Lutherans.

In addition, they held the tenet borrowed from the Manicheans, that the validity of the sacraments depended upon the virtue of the administrator, as if the virtue given them by Christ, could depend upon such a circumstance. They also held invalid all baptism conferred by any other church. This was assuming to be the only true church. But the greatest difficulty in the matter was that these Brethren were about as modern as the Lutherans. They had only existed some fifty years when the reformation began. It would then be indispensable to find the True Church in some other body of professed Christians, before the days of Kelesiski, the founder of the Brethren.

13. Albigense as Protestant ancestors

Among the other sects claimed by the Protestants, at least by the Calvinists, as their predecessors, were the Albigenses. As Beringarius and Wickliffe organized no churches, and recanted their errors and died in the Catholic Church, they could not be claimed as ancestors. Berengarius impugned but one article, and Wickliffe advocated many confessed and manifest errors, that all parties of the Reformation condemned no less than the Catholics. However much, therefore, some of the principles advocated and recanted by these men, especially Wickliffe, were approved by the Calvinists, as well as others of the Reformation, when taken as a whole they could not but be rejected.

But in claiming the Albigenses as ancestors, the Calvinists admitted a fraternity with a sect that only extended back to the eleventh age, and was far more objectionable in doctrine than the Vaudois. The Albigenses, as proven by Bossuet in the eleventh Book of his Variations, was but a branch of the Manicheans, and held their principal errors, with some superadded tenets of their own.

The fundamental principles of Manicheism may be found in Plato, and sprung from Paganism. Manes, a Persian, towards the close of the third century, endeavored to engraft these principles upon Christianity. The theory turned upon the origin of good and evil. These being so precisely opposite in their nature, must of course spring from different sources. In conformity with this idea, they held the existence of two Creators, one the source of good, the other the source of evil. These two Creators were enemies by consequence, and in their strife one filled the world with good, the other with evil. All the peculiar views of the Manicheans may be traced as logical consequences drawn from these principles.

These heretics drew consequences from these principles no less absurd than infamous. They held the creation of the world, of men, of all animals, and of all things visible, as the work of the evil principle, and Heaven, the human soul, and all things invisible, as the work of God, the infinitely good principle. Upon these grounds they rejected the Old Testament, holding it as the product of the evil principle. As Christ was the son of God, they denied the incarnation, and held his body to have been but a phantom, a body in appearance only. Our bodies being the creation of the bad principle, and our souls of the good, it was not lawful to unite the good with the evil; and therefore it was wicked to beget children, and marriage was for that reason prohibited. Every thing proceeding from generation proceeded from the wicked principle, and was impure by nature, and therefore the use of all meats, as well as wine, was criminal.

These people made extraordinary pretensions to virtue, and were exceedingly seductive in their discourses, in which they covertly concealed the most glaring absurdities of the theory. They adopted a system of secrecy, consisting of several different degrees. Those who were called auditors were not let into the whole mystery, which was kept close from the probationers. The elect only, after passing through several gradations, were admitted to the whole secret. This secrecy was one of the principal causes, not only of the widespread and long continued success of the sect, but also of the artifices and dissimulation practiced by the Manicheans.

Acting upon this principle, the Manicheans mixed with the Catholics, attended their churches, acknowledged their doctrines, and dissembled their own, propagating them by degrees, and as a secret, in secret corners and places. They assumed the appearance of extraordinary piety and poverty. Faustus, the Manichean, thus speaks to Catholics, as stated by Saint Austin:

> You ask me whether I receive the gospel? You see I do, inasmuch as I observe what the gospel prescribes: of you I ought to ask whether you

> receive it, since I see no mark of it in your lives. For my part, I have forsaken father, mother, wife and children, gold, silver, meat, drink, delights, pleasures; content with what is sufficient for life from day to day. I am poor, I am peaceable, I weep, I suffer from hunger and thirst, I am persecuted for justice" sake, and do you question whether I receive the gospel?

As this sect denied the existence of Christ's body, they of course denied the Real Presence; and as they refused the use of wine, when they communed with Catholics they only received the bread. They were detected by Saint Leo from this circumstance, and that they might be distinguished, all were required to receive in both kinds.

The sect grew strong in Armenia, a province bordering on Persia, in the seventh century. They were there settled, or confirmed by one named Paul, and hence took the name of Paulicians. These Paulicians held a great aversion to the Images of Christ crucified, as they denied his crucifixion; to the Virgin Mary, as they held her not to have been the mother of Christ; and to the Eucharist. From Armenia they sent preachers to Bulgaria, where the heresy took deep root, and they were hence called Bulgarians.

About the year 1000, they first made their appearance in the Latin Church. An Italian woman brought it into France, where it took root as Orleans. In Italy they were called Cathari, that is to say, *pure*. It was introduced into Italy from Bulgaria. It spread into Languedoc, Toulouse, and especially into Gascony, where they were called Albigenses, in token of the place they came from, namely Bulgaria. They also spread into Germany and England. Those in England were from Gascony, and were called Poplicans or Publicans. It was stated by Renier, who wrote about the year 1254, that in his time, when the sect was weakened, "the perfect Cathari did not exceed four thousand in all Christendom," but that "the believers were innumerable, a computation which several times had been made amongst them." The perfect Cathari were those admitted to the highest secrets, while the believers were made up of all sorts of people.

These various branches of these heretics, though often changing some of the doctrines of the sect, and often differing from each other in many particulars, were yet always distinguished by the great leading principle of their origin. They all rejected marriage, the Old Testament, and the use of meats. They generally held oaths unlawful, opposed all ordination of the clergy, held that the efficacy of the sacraments depended upon the personal virtue of the administrator, and that all good persons could administer the sacraments. They generally rejected baptism, the invocation of saints, oblations for the dead, and the resurrection.

This very condensed statement of the leading features of these heretics, is made up from Bossuet, to whom I must refer for more full and accurate information. The distinguished author, in the close of his account, remarks:

> Such were the Albigenses, by the testimony of all their contemporary authors, not one excepted. The Protestants blush for them; and all they can answer is, that these excesses, these errors, and all these disorders of the Albigenses, are the calumnies of their enemies. But have they so much as one proof for what they advance, or even one author of those times, and for more than four hundred years after, to support them in it? For our part, we produce as many witnesses as have been authors in the whole universe who have treated of this sect. Those that were educated in their principles have revealed to us their abominable secrets after their conversion. We trace up the damnable sect even to its source; we show whence it came, which way it steered its course, all its characteristics, and its whole pedigree, branching from the Manichean root.

One cannot but be astonished at the errors of this sect; and yet there is no cause for surprise. It is but another proof of the truth of Christianity, as this sect was explicitly foretold by Saint Paul, in the fourth chapter of his first Epistle to Timothy:

> Now the Spirit speaketh expressly, that in the latter times some shall depart from the faith, giving heed to seducing spirits, and doctrines of devils; speaking lies in hypocrisy, having their conscience seared with a hot iron; forbidding to marry, and commanding to abstain from meats, which God hath created to be received with thanksgiving of them which believe and know the truth. For every creature of God is good, and nothing to be refused, if it be received with thanksgiving; for it is sanctified with the work of God and prayer.

The Fathers are unanimously agreed that this prediction had reference to the Manicheans, whose tenets, and the reasons they gave for them, taken in connection with their acts and history, so completely fill up the picture drawn by Saint Paul. The apostle not only points out specifically the two *false doctrines* to be taught, but with wonderful brevity and accuracy gives us the *character* of the teachers, the source of their doctrines, and the manner of their teaching. The teachers were "seducing spirits" who taught the "doctrines of devils" by "speaking lies in hypocrisy" with "seared consciences." The *mode* of teaching adopted by these heretics – their hypocrisy – their secrecy – their enchantments – their extraordinary pretensions to superior piety – every part of their conduct, pointed them out as "seducing spirits, speaking lies in hypocrisy." And well might Saint Paul say they would teach the "doctrines of devils," since they taught that God did not create the world and the things therein, thus robbing Him of the honor due to the Sovereign Creator of the universe, but giving it to the evil principle; thereby flattering the pride of the evil spirits, and pampering their jealousy against God and blaspheming the Creator by imputing impurities to His works.

But the apostle not only points out the two doctrines that distinguished these heretics, and at the same time gives us the character of the teachers, the source of their errors, and their manner of teaching; but he is careful to defeat the very *grounds* upon which they predicated these doctrines. For whereas they attributed the creation of the bodies of men and of animals to the evil principle, and from thence deduced the conclusion that the propagation of the human race, and the use of meats, were criminal, Saint Paul expressly alleged that "God *created meats* to be *received* with thanksgiving;" and not only so, but that "every *creature of God* is *good*, and *nothing* to be refused, if received with thanksgiving: for it is sanctified with the word of God and prayer."

Nothing could be more clear and explicit in pointing out the teachers, their character, their manner of teaching, the doctrines taught, the source from which they sprang, but the "doctrines of devils;" but also in anticipating and confuting the *false grounds* upon which these doctrines of devils were based, than those brief and accurate passages of the apostle. That this sect filled up fully the entire picture of the apostle, there would seem to be no possible doubt. Each and every portion of the prediction, is completely fulfilled in their character, doctrines, manner of teaching, and the grounds upon which their tenets were based.

14. Reflections on the ancestral claims

Consider the peculiar doctrines of the Vaudois, the Bohemian Brethren, and the Albigenses, claimed as ancestors of the early Protestant Churches, and especially by the Calvinists. While it is evident they differed in many great and leading respects from each other, from the Catholic Church, and from each and all the Protestant parties themselves, it must be conceded that these sects did hold certain tenets in common. With many of the sects of old, and with Wickliffe, they held that the validity of the sacraments was lost if administered by wicked men, although such wickedness was hidden in the heart, and could only be known to God. This seems to have been a common ground occupied by many sects of heretics, before the Reformation, and was based upon some great reason and necessity.

In all ages those who rejected the authority of the Church, were compelled, like Luther, to adopt some theory having at least the appearance of logical consistency in its fundamental principles. The Church being in the *prior* possession of the governing principle of authority, those who denied her power, were compelled to adopt the scriptures as the entire code, and the right of private interpretation in the last resort, or renounce their opinions.

The principle that the virtue of the sacraments depended upon the personal character of the administrator, and not upon his official powers, when legitimately extended, would necessarily set aside all authority in the Church as a united and visible body of men; and would make the authority of teachers depend upon their personal merits alone. If the sacraments necessarily lost their validity when administered by a wicked, but regularly ordained minister, then the only logical test required under this rule, must be the personal virtue of the individual. This virtue was the efficient test of the right to administer. And as this personal virtue did not depend upon the Church in any way, and yet constituted the only qualification required, of course the authority of the Church could not exist in the contemplation of such a theory. Hence these sects held that any good person could preach and administer the sacraments.

In contemplating the character, tenets, and history of these sects, one cannot but be struck with the great and perplexing necessity that compelled the Reformers to admit a fraternity with them. The Lutherans, Calvinists, and Zuinglians, had all admitted, as fundamental truths, that the true Church was visible, Catholic, and perpetual, and that the promises of Christ appertained to her. As a part of this idea of the Church, they insisted that ministers must have a vocation, either ordinary of extraordinary. Having assumed these grounds, they were then compelled to find a visible church always existing from the days of the apostles down to the days of Luther. In attempting to do this, they displayed extraordinary industry, talent, and research. One cannot but admire their intense perseverance and assiduity, as well as the great ability they exhibited.

But all the abilities in the world cannot annihilate the inflexible facts of history. Nor can any amount of ability reconcile irreconcilable principles. Misguided abilities may mistake and conceal, for a time, the facts of history, and, for the moment, may render inconsistent theories as apparently consistent. But time is certain, sooner or later, to expose the true state of the case. The truth must and will stand revealed at some period. Intrepid and right-minded men will, sooner or later, carry out the main principles of a theory, in all their ramifications, to their logical and legitimate results.

In searching for the true visible Church before the Reformation, they were placed in a painful predicament. They denied it to be the Church of Rome. If she had been the true Church, they ought to have heard her. If she had been the true Church, then there was no necessity or justification for destroying her, and reconstructing the alleged true Church upon her ruins. When, therefore, they turned from her to seek for another, where was it to be found? The Vaudois extended only back to 1160 and the Bohemian Brethren only to 1467. The Albigenses were only a branch of the Manicheans, in the main, holding their essential and fundamental errors.

If the Albigenses were not Manicheans, (and all the histories attesting that fact were false,) still they only extended back to about the year 1000. If, on the contrary, they were Manicheans, and therefore could be traced back to Marcian, in the second century, who taught the existence of two principles, the first one good and the other evil, and prohibited marriage, but not the use of meats, then the line of succession would be almost long enough. But the abominable errors of these people were too great. They could not be claimed as the true Church. The only ground upon which the Albigenses were claimed was, that the excesses charged against them were calumnies. But to accuse so many authors, exhibiting every evidence of sincerity, of such excessive calumny was to accuse them of indulging a most captious and suspicious spirit.

The Manichean sect's beginning could be traced clearly to the second century, if not to Simon Magnus, in the first century, and continued without interruption near, if not quite, to the fifteenth century, and extended over the world so far, and contained such numbers. If it could not be claimed as the true Church on account of its manifest errors, then it was clear that the true Church must be made up of various short-lived, independent, and discordant sects, each differing from all the others, as well as from the Protestants, and never even claiming any affinity with each other.

This would compose the chain of Christian succession of many dissimilar links, some deformed in some respects, and some in others. But not only would the links be deformed, and so dissimilar even in deformity, but the chain itself, while dominative, would be extremely small. Having rejected the great sects of the Manicheans, Arians, and others, containing almost the entire mass of dissenters from the Church of Rome, this theory reduced the true visible Church to a few scattered fragments of different sects, dispersed up and down the course of centuries, confined to a very small portion of the earth at a time, and containing scarcely any members, with a large mass of error. The members of the alleged true Church were exceedingly few, while their errors were grievous, many, and discordant.

This theory made Christianity a practical failure – a system of splendid promises and of meager results – the Church a "city of magnificent distances:" and few inhabitants. The Church, the pillar and ground of the truth, according to this theory, had held and taught the most discordant and fatal errors; and this Church universal was confined to one corner of the world. Not only was the Church a failure at particular periods, but this theory also made it a failure almost throughout its entire course.

The Church of Rome had held in her communion, throughout her entire history, the great and overwhelming majority of all professed Christians; but she was not the true Church. Nor was the true Church found in the great sects that separated from the Church of Rome. She was only found in the most diminutive and obscure sects, each differing from all the others, and, as Calvin said, "not seen fully." The kingdom of Christ had dwindled so as scarcely to be seen. It was not quite, but almost, invisible.

If the visible Church came from the hands of the apostles united, and with a regular ministry; and if, according to the theory of the Reformers, all ministers must have a vocation, either ordinary or extraordinary; and if the expulsion from the visible Church, according to the same theory, destroyed or withdrew the ordinary vocation of the minister excommunicated; and the true Church could only exist with authorized preaching and the right administration of the sacraments, as they admitted – how then did these sects get their authority to be the true Church? They claimed no extraordinary authority, for they did not claim that any miracles attested it. If, then, they had any authority, it must have been ordinary. But they were mere laymen, claimed no ordinary vocation, and therefore denied its existence. Their common principle, making the validity of the sacraments dependent upon the personal virtue of the administrator, rendered every kind of vocation unnecessary. How, then, could the Reformers claim these sects, or any one of them, to be the true Church, according to their theory?

These sects were not united to each other either in the succession of ministers or doctrine. With the exception of the Albigenses who could rightfully claim as their ancestors the Manicheans these sects, not anyone or more of them, have any just claim to have succeeded others in succession of doctrine or ministers.

15. Mr. Campbell's theory of Protestant succession

In his debate with Bishop Purcell, the first proposition of Mr. Campbell was this:

> That the Roman Catholic institution, sometimes called the Holy Apostolic, Catholic Church, is not now, nor was she ever, catholic, apostolic, or holy; but is a sect, in the fair import of that word, older than any other sect now existing, not the 'Mother and Mistress of all churches,' but an apostasy from the only true, holy, apostolic Church of Christ.

In his argument to sustain this proposition, Mr. Campbell fixed upon the day when the Church of Rome became a sect, and separated from the true Church. He says:

> We have not time for this, as we are now, before we sit down, to give you and day and date of the separation of the Roman Church from the Greek Church, which must be regarded as the day of her separate existence, when she became what she now is, a *schism,* a *sect.*
>
> The Catholic body was not yet divided into two great masses.

Mr. Campbell here speaks of the period of the contests between Pope Nicholas, in the ninth century, and Photius, Patriarch of Constantinople. He then goes on to quote from Du Pin, to show that Pope Leo IX., through his legates, excommunicated Michael Cerularius, Patriarch of Constantinople, by a bull, published in the church of Saint Sophia, on the 16th of July, 1054. Mr. Campbell then says:

> If, then, there be any truth in history, from that day the present sect of the Church of Rome began its existence.

RESULTS OF THE PROTESTANT THEORY

In his reply, Bishop Purcell said:

> The gentleman told us that he would put his finger upon the precise day and date, as recorded in history, when the Roman Church separated from the holy and ancient apostolic Church, but he has not kept his word. I warrant that that pledge will never be redeemed.

Mr. Campbell here explained that he had fixed it at the 16th of July, 1054.[24]

This was certainly very explicit, and did avoid the objection so often made, that no date had been fixed upon when the Roman separated from the *alleged* true Church. But in avoiding one difficulty, Mr. Campbell very evidently ran upon others. Several questions necessarily arise from this position:

1. If the Church *before* the separation was the Catholic Church, as admitted, then, which was the true Church after the separation, the Greek or Roman?

2. If the Church before the separation was not the true Church, then how did the Church of Rome become a *schism,* a *sect*, for the first time in July, 1054.

3. If the Church, when composed of the Greek and Roman churches united, was not the true Church, where was she?

In answer to the new difficulties involved in this position, Mr. Campbell says:

> The question was asked me yesterday evening, "Where was the true Church before the time of the Greek schism?" I observed, this morning, that my having shown the Greek Church to be the senior, as the original of the Roman, did not necessarily involve the idea, that the Greek church was, at the time of the separation, the true Catholic Church.[25]

But I must confess that I could not perceive how this answer avoided the difficulty. It is true that Mr. Campbell's position, that the Greek was the senior of the Roman Church, did not, *of itself*, prove that the Greek was the true Church; but taken in connection with his first proposition, it did prove one of three things:

1. That the Greek was the true Church before the separation; or,

2. Or that Mr. Campbell contradicted his first proposition wherein he assumed that the Roman Church is a sect "older than any other sect now existing.

3. Or that the Greek Church does not *now exist.*

Mr. Campbell had evidently involved himself in "perplexities," as the Minister Jurieu might say.

Before the separation, there was not distinction between the Greek and Roman churches, except *as parts of one united whole.* Which of these two parts was first established, could be of no moment as to jurisdiction, when both were *united.* If they were both parts of one united Church, as Mr. Campbell admitted, then this Church must have been the true Church before the separation, or Mr. Campbell had failed to do what he promised, and assumed that he had done, namely: to show when the Church of Rome separated from the true Church. If this united Church before the separation, was *not the true Church*, then *she* was but a sect and a schism, and Mr. Campbell ought to have gone farther back than the year 1054, to fix the date. If on the contrary, this united Church was the true Church up to the separation in 1054, then one party or the other must have continued the true Church afterwards, unless we assume that the separation destroyed both. And if the separation destroyed both, what then became of the true Church? And what became of the promises of Christ?

Mr. Campbell had fixed the date of the Papacy. "Thus in the year 606," he says, "two years after the death of the saint, the first Pope was placed in the chair of the Galilean fisherman, if indeed Peter had ever sat in a chair at Rome."[26]

From that year up to the Greek Schism in 1054, Mr. Campbell admitted that the churches of the West and East were united under the Pope of Rome. If this Church, thus united with the Pope, was not the true Church, it was clear that Mr. Campbell's date or 1054 amounted to no more than this; it showed when a sect or schism had divided into two sects or schisms; and it yet remained to show where was the true Church, and what was the origin of the Church of Rome. It was also clear, that Mr. Campbell's position, that the "*Catholic* body was not yet divided into two great masses" in the ninth century, was inconsistent with the supposition that the Church, before the separation, was not the true Church. Mr. Campbell expressly admits the truths of the Apostles' Creed, while he does not concede that it was composed by them, and says: "All the Protestant world believes this 'apostles' creed,' as it is called, and are as uniform in this faith as the Mother Church herself.[27] When, therefore, Mr. Campbell said the "Catholic body was not yet divided," I understand him to mean that the Catholic Church was the Catholic body to which he alluded and that he intended to maintain the position, that the Church in communion with the Pope, before the Greek Schism, was the Church.

But the position admitting the Church, before the Greek Schism, to have been the Catholic Church, involved too many consequences. The Catholic doctrines held at the present day, were held in the Church at that day. Hence Mr. Campbell as I must think, abandoned that position, and sought the true Church elsewhere. All that he had before said in reference to that position seemed to me set aside by other ground taken afterwards. On page 65 as he continues:

> We can, however, show that, from the earliest times, there has existed a people whom no man can remember, [number?] that have earnestly and consistently contended for the faith *once* delivered to the saints. If he requires me to put my finger on the page of history on which is described the commencement of the degeneracy of the Roman diocese from the true faith, I will turn back to about the year of our Lord 250. Then the controversy between Cornelius and Novatian, about the bishopric of Rome, embraced the points at issue, which separated the true Church from that which was grievously contaminated with error and immorality. It was, indeed, a controversy about the purity of communion and discipline, rather than about articles of doctrine.

"I hold in my hand," he continues,

> one of the latest and best historians – Waddington… The account he gives of these reformers is sustained by Jones, and other ecclesiastical historians. I prefer Waddington for his brevity and perspicuity. He [Waddington] says:
>
> "We may conclude with some notice of the sect of the Novatians, who were stigmatized at the time both as schismatics and heretics, but who may perhaps be more properly considered as the earliest body of ecclesiastical reformers. They arose at Rome about the year 250 A.D. and subsisted, until the fifth century, throughout every part of Christendom. Novatian, a proselyte of Rome, was a man of great talents and learning, and of a character so austere that he was unwilling, under any circumstances of contrition, to readmit those who had once separated from the communion of the Church. And

> this severity he would have extended not only to those who had fallen by deliberate transgression, but even to such as had made a forced compromise of their faith under the terrors of persecution. He considered the Christian Church as a society, where virtue and innocence reigned universally, and refused any longer to acknowledge as members of it those who had once degenerated into unrighteousness. This endeavor to revive the spotless purity of the primitive faith, was found inconsistent with the corruptions even of that early age; it was regarded with suspicion by the leading prelates, as a vain and visionary scheme; and those rigid principles, which had characterized and sanctified the Church in the first century, were abandoned to the profession of schismatic sectaries in the third."
>
> This sounds a little like Protestantism.

Truly it seems so. But what is gained by the paternity? If Protestantism and ancient heresy are alike, is that any advantage to the former? But I confess I could not see how Mr. Campbell had improved his case. He proposed to show "the commencement of the degeneracy of the Roman diocese from the *true faith,"* and then speaks of the contest which "embraced the points at issue which separated the *true* Church from that which was grievously contaminated with *error* and immorality." After making these promises regarding *faith* and the *true* Church, which he takes to be the Novatians, he suddenly lowers his standard, and tells us, "it was indeed a controversy about the purity of communion and *discipline*, rather than about articles of doctrine." Mr. Campbell also says:

> I have here before me, Eusebius, the oldest of ecclesiastical historians, who informs us that Novatus and his party were called Cathari or Puritans. And although he appears greatly incensed against Novatus and his party, he can record no evil against them, except their '*uncharitableness;* in refusing to commune with those of immoral and doubtful character.[28]

The *only* ground, then of separation, as insisted upon by Mr. Campbell in his reference to Eusebius, is the sole one given by Waddington, namely: "He (Novatian) was unwilling, under *any circumstances of contrition,* to readmit those *once separated* from the communion of the Church;" even in cases where they "had made a *forced compromise* of their faith under the *terrors of persecution.*"

Was Novatian right? Was his doctrine true? Who is now prepared to sustain the *same* ground? And when Mr. Waddington says, so doubtingly, that the Novatians "may perhaps, be more properly considered as the earliest body of ecclesiastical reformers," does he mean to take the clear and distinct position that they were *right* in the *only* ground alleged by them, and given by *him* as the cause of separation? And when he speaks of "this attempt to revive the spotless moral purity of the primitive faith" does he mean to say that the *faith* of the primitive Church was similar to that of Novatian in *this* respect? And when he speaks of "those rigid *principles*" of the Church of the first century, does he mean to say that a person "*once separated*" from the Church at that early day, would not have been readmitted "*under any circumstances of contrition?*" And when he speaks of "the corruptions even of that early age," does he mean by this the doctrine and practice condemned by Novatian? Namely: readmitting into the Church, after due repentance, those who had fallen. And was this merciful doctrine and practice, heresy and corruption?

If Mr. Waddington did not intend to indorse the *only* ground given by him as the one *taken by Novatian*, then what did he mean? Did he mean to condemn the *treason,* and yet praise the *traitor*? Did he mean to say to Novatian in substance: "Sir, you are *wrong* in the only ground assumed by you, and yet it is the *true faith* of the primitive Church"? In a word, did he mean to condemn the *principles* of Novatian, and, at the same time, hold him to be a *true reformer*? Or was the truth this, and this only: that the learned historian could not sanction the ground taken by Novatian; and yet such was the inexorable necessity to find reformers, "*even at that early age,*" that he must needs hold the Novatians such, when they were unequivocally in the wrong? And was he compelled, as a *historian,* to give the matter of *fact* truly, and yet, as a *Protestant*, to give his *opinion*, indorsing *admitted error*? Or did he mean to hold every *attempt* at reformation, whether right or wrong, as still commendable? Or did he mean to take the ground, that when there are alleged errors in a church, that he who *assumes* to reform her, but who, *in fact*, only adds other admitted errors to those *already existing,,* is still entitled to the appellation of a reformer?

It is true, the historian, in the *beginning* of the extract, speaks *doubtingly*, as he says "*perhaps*" the Novatians may be properly called reformers; but in the close he says expressly that "those rigid *principles* which had *characterized* and *sanctified* the Church in the *first* century, were *abandoned* to the profession of schismatic sectaries in the third." The *principles* of the Church of the *first* century were *abandoned* to the

Novatians! Then was not Novatian right, according to this explicit statement?

If it were a doctrine or principle of the first century, then it ought to be sustained. But I never could find any satisfactory evidence that such was the doctrine of Christ. When the chosen disciples all became offended and fled, and this after being specially warned by Christ, and after having made the most solemn pledges of fidelity; and when Peter had denied his Master, in His immediate presence, and under His own eye, and affirmed his denial with an oath, they were not so treated by our Lord. Peter went out and wept bitterly, and was restored.

The incestuous Corinthian was not so dealt with by Saint Paul. In the letters of the churches of Lyons and Vienne, giving an account of the martyrdom of many Christians at these places, in the second century, (as recorded by Eusebius, and published in the first volume of the Oxford Tracts,) it is stated, that many Christians, under the terrors and pains of torture, at first denied the faith; but they subsequently repented, and died glorious martyrs for the faith. "But," they say,

> the mean time was not fruitless to them, but through their patience the infinite mercy of Christ appeared. For the dead members were enlivened through the living, and the martyrs showed favor to those who were not martyrs, and there was great joy to the Virgin Mother, the Church, in receiving again, living, whom she had cast away as dead and abortive. For by these good men, the greater number of those who had denied Christ were renewed, and reconceived and rekindles, and learned to confess, and now, living and full of nerve, were brought before the tribunal.... But Christ was greatly glorified in those who had denied before, but then confessed, contrary to the expectation of the heathen. For these were even separately examined, as on the idea that they were to be dismissed; but, confessing, were added to the number of they martyrs.

Now had Novatian been right in his "*uncharitableness*," Christ would not have been glorified, and the Church rejoiced by the return of these stray sheep, who so willingly and gloriously, like Old Peter, *at last* laid down their lives for the faith. *One* error of poor, weak human nature, was enough, with this "austere man," to exclude from the Church forever. And we of this distant day, who have never shed one drop of blood for the faith, like raw recruits, who never smelt "villainous saltpeter," or witnessed the battle's "magnificently stern array," are over-confident that none of us would ever flinch, should the invincible trial come. But like young eaglets, whose newly fledged pinions have only born them in short gyrations around the parent eyry, and which fix their confident gaze upon the sun, and complacently conclude that they will soon be able to soar to that luminary; so we, at distance safe from harm, may console ourselves with the self-complimentary reflection, that had we lived in the day of trial, *we* should never have fallen.

I supposed when Mr. Campbell asserted that the Novatians were the true Church and "earnestly and consistently contended for the faith *once* delivered to the saints," and had, as he alleged, separated from that Church "which was then grievously contaminated with error and immorality," that he was surely prepared to sustain the ground assumed by Novatian, as the cause of the separation. I was, however, mistaken, for Mr. Campbell afterwards says:

> They (the Novatians) had one fault, which we both allow – they were too severe in one branch of discipline – they could never receive those who had grievously fallen – no repentance would obtain re-admission, if the penitent had flagrantly sinned.[29]

In this language Mr. Campbell puts in conditions not mentioned by Waddington, but contrary – "very flagrantly sinned" – "grievously fallen." Waddington says in *no case* were they readmitted, even when they had compromised their faith under the terrors of persecution. And I could not but observe how Mr. Campbell had receded from his first position. He first assumes to show "a people" who "have earnestly and consistently contended for the *faith* once delivered to the saints" – he next spoke of degeneracy from the "*true faith*" in A.D. 250 – then of the separation of the "*true*" from the "grievously contaminated" Church – then he makes the separation take place only upon the grounds of "purity of *communion* and discipline," and not faith – then he disapproves of the very ground upon which this "*true* church" did separate from the "grievously contaminated" – and, finally, winds up by saying: "They had other objections besides this against the opposing party; but this was sufficient for a division."[30]

But what those *other* grounds were, neither Mr. Campbell nor Waddington informed us. And Mr. Campbell had taken good care to preclude himself from any such a retreat. For he said in the beginning that the "controversy" which "separated the true church from that which was grievously contaminated… was about the purity of communion and discipline, rather than about articles of doctrine." As Mr. Campbell had it, whatever points were involved regarded "purity of communion and discipline," and not doctrine. And when Waddington assumes to give the *cause* of the separation, he gives only *one*. And Mr. Campbell when praising Novatian and his party, says Eusebius could "record no evil against them, except their 'uncharitableness.'" Now, as Mr. Campbell says, Eusebius "appears greatly incensed against then," and, of course, agreed with the opposite party in their views; had there been other grounds alleged as existing, surely Eusebius could have recorded them.

That there were other grounds, in the opinion of Mr. Campbell there can be no doubt; but Novatian did not think so. And if he did think so, Mr. Campbell places him in a very awkward position; for while there were several causes alleged by Mr. Campbell to have existed, he makes Novatian so perverse as to discard all those that were *true*, and rely solely upon that one which was *false*, and which Mr. Campbell himself is compelled to condemn *at last*. Whatever other causes might *possibly* have existed, Novatian thought so little of them that they were not even assumed as a *part* of the grounds of separation. True, Cornelius, on his part, argued against Novatian himself, certain personal faults, independent of his heresy; but these did not constitute the cause that Novatian assigned as the ground of separation.

Now I could not see in what *possible* respect Novatian had reformed the Church. After all that had been so confidently said,

"The whole amount of this stupendous fame"

was this, and this only: Novatian took with him *all the doctrines* of the other party, as Mr. Campbell calls the Church, except that one which he condemned, and in this Novatian was *confessedly* in the *wrong*. .So far, then, from improving, he had only *added error*. He had, upon a false ground, separated from the Church, set up for himself, excommunicated those who did not agree with him in this false ground, and assumed a system of severity, extreme, unscriptural, and cruel. But to my mind this case, as well as that of the Vaudois, Manicheans, and others, proved the truth of the assertion, that ancient heresy generally based its pretensions upon the claim of extreme virtue. *Some* members of the Church did not come up to their standard of personal piety, and they, to improve individual members in virtue, assumed to reform the entire Church in matters of faith. But their zeal was not according to knowledge.

"These Puritans, or reformers," Mr. Campbell continues,

> spread all over the world, and continued to oppose the pretensions of those who, from being the major party, claimed to be the Catholic or only church. They continued under the name of Novatians for more

than two centuries; but finally were merged in the Donatists, who, indeed, are the same people under another name. These Donatists were a very large and prosperous community. We read of 279 Donatist bishops in one African council. Of these Donatists the same historian deposes:

"The Donatists have never been charged, with the slightest show of truth, with any error of doctrine, or any defect in church government or discipline, or any depravity of moral practice; they agreed in every respect with their adversaries, except one—they did not acknowledge as legitimate the ministry of the African church, but considered their own body to be the true, uncorrupted, universal church.

"It is quite clear that they pushed their schism to very great extremities, even to that of rejecting the communion of all who were in communion with the church which they called false; but this was the extent of their spiritual offence, even from the assertion of their enemies."(George Waddington. *History of the Church from the earliest ages to the Reformation.*, p.154)

The Donatists, in some two centuries, were amalgamated with the Paulicians. They, too, were called Puritans. Jones, who has been at the greatest pains to give their history, gives the following account of them:

"About the year 660, a new sect arose in the east, under the name of Paulicians which is justly entitled to our attention.

"In Mananalis, an obscure town in the vicinity of Samosata, a person of the name of Constantine entertained at his house a deacon, who, having been a prisoner among the Mahometans, was returning from Syria, whither he had been carried away captive. From this passing stranger Constantine received the precious gift of the New Testament in its original language, which, even at this early period, was concealed from the vulgar—that Peter Siculus, to whom we owe most of our information of the history of the Paulicians, tells us the first scruples of a Catholic, when he was advised to read the Bible was, 'it is not lawful for us profane persons to read these sacred writings, but on the priests only."

Indeed, the gross ignorance that pervaded Europe at this time rendered the generality of the people incapable of reading that or any other book. But even those of the laity who could read were dissuaded by their religious guides from meddling with the Bible. Constantine, however, made the best use of the deacon's present – he studied the New Testament with unwearied assiduity – and more particularly the writings of the apostle Paul, from which he at length endeavored to deduce a system of doctrine and worship. "He investigated the creed of primitive Christianity," says Gibbon, "and whatever might be the success, a Protestant reader will applaud the spirit of inquiry."

The knowledge to which Constantine himself was, under the divine blessing, enable to attain, he gladly communicated to others around him, and a Christian church was collected. In a little several individuals arose among them, qualified for the work of the ministry, and several other churches were collected throughout Armenia and Cappadocia. It appears, from the whole of their history, to have been a leading object with Constantine and his brethren to restore, as far as possible, the profession of Christianity to all its primitive simplicity."(William Jones, *The History of the Christian church, from the birth of Christ to the eighteenth century.* p.239)

"The Paulician teachers," says Gibbon, "were distinguished only by their Scriptural names, by the modest title of their fellow pilgrims, by the austerity of their lives, their zeal and knowledge, and the credit of some extraordinary gift of the Holy Spirit. But they were incapable of desiring, or at least, of obtaining the wealth and honors of the Catholic prelacy. Such anti-Christian pride they strongly censured."(*Ibid.,* p.240)

I might read almost to the same effect from Waddington and Du Pin. True, they are called heretics by those who call themselves Catholics and us heretics; but what does that prove?

Until the appearance of the Waldenses [Vaudois] and Albigenses, these Protestants continued to oppose the church of nations in the east and in the west, until at one time they claimed the title of catholic. We read of hundreds of bishops attending the different councils in which they met to oppose the violent assaults of their enemies.[31]

The first point that I considered, was the statement of Mr. Campbell that the Novatians, after more than two centuries, were merged in the Donatists. The Donatists arose in Africa, in A.D. 311. Donatus and his supporters disputed the election of Cecilian to the Episcopal see of Carthage, upon the death of Mensurius. In 313 a council held at Rome, before which Cecilian and Donatus both appeared, each accompanied by ten bishops of his party, decided in favor of the regularity of the ordination of Cecilian. Again, in 314, a ynod at Arles decided in the same way.

At the time of the separation from the same church from which the Novatians had, sixty-one years before, separated, the only ground alleged was this one regarding the legitimacy of the ministry of Cecilian. In every other respect, according to Waddington, they agreed with their adversaries. Whatever doctrines were held by the Church, were held by them. Donatists arose in Africa, and were confined to that continent, and the Novatians arose at Rome. If, then, the Novatians ultimately joined the Donatists, it was only by giving up all that was peculiar to them, and recanting the only ground upon which they separated from the Church originally. In joining the Donatists, they lost all identity of organization and doctrine. They in fact became members of another and a distinct sect. There was not the slightest identity between these two parties, except that they both stood opposed to the Church, but upon different and antagonistic grounds. One merely died out, and the other lived on a while longer. The former members of the deceased Church may have joined, and become identified with, another sect, holding the very doctrine that caused these Novatians to sever the Church in 250. It was surrender, not a compromise.

But I could find no evidence of any merger whatever, independent of Mr. Campbell's statement. The language of Waddington does not convey any such idea. That the Novatians continued until after the Donatist schism, was true. But this, of itself, did not prove any merger. And from the fact that their doctrine was different from that of the Donatists, and that they claimed to be exclusively the true Church, while the Donatists did the same, there could have been no merger.

I could not see any thing in the Donatists that entitled them to the claim of being the true Church. They divided the Church upon a question simply regarding the legitimacy of a single bishop. "They pushed their schism to very great extremities," says Waddington. Was this any merit? If the Church was "grievously contaminated with error," as Mr. Campbell contends, these Donatists did not propose to remedy these evils. What, then, was their *peculiar* merit? Was it simply dividing the Church? Was the act of simply protesting upon right or wrong grounds, still a merit? I could not see any merit in mere schism. "No heretic," says Waddington,

> was as likely as the Donatist to lay claims to the name Catholic; yet even the Donatist, while he maintained that the true spirit and purity were alone perpetuated in his own communion, would scarcely have affirmed that that was *bona fide* the universal church, *which did not extend beyond the shores of Africa,* and which had not the majority even there.[32]

Mr. Campbell says: "The Donatists, in some two centuries, were amalgamated with the Paulicians." But I could find no evidence of this alleged fact, other than the statement of Mr. Campbell. And several questions arise in regard to Mr. Campbell's merger and amalgamation:

1. He says the Novatians merged in the Donatists. Waddington says the Donatists were confined to Africa. The Novatians arose at Rome. Now how did those Novatians out of Africa merge in the Donatists?

2. He says the Donatists, in some two centuries, amalgamated with the Paulicians. Jones says that the deacon left the New Testament with Constantine in 660, and this was in Armenia in the East. Then how did the Donatists, who were confined to Africa, amalgamate with the Paulicians, who were never on that continent? And how did this amalgamation take place before the Paulicians existed?

But as respects the Paulicians, Jones, the Protestant historian, gives us the circumstances of their origin, and *his opinion* of the intention of Constantine to restore the primitive worship of Christianity in all its simplicity, which is always the object avowed by all separatists of every age. He does not, in the extract, give us their peculiar doctrines – the tenets that distinguished them from others. Jones himself speaks rather doubtingly. True, he says Constantine "studied the New Testament with unwearied assiduity.... from which at length he *endeavored* to deduce a system of doctrine and worship." The language of Gibbon is still more equivocal: "*whatever might be the success.*" All that Gibbon could say was that the Protestant would "applaud the spirit of inquiry." In the extract from Gibbon, their peculiar tenets are not given, but he speaks of their demeanor and practice of poverty, and their claim to "*some* extraordinary gift of the Holy Spirit," without saying what it was.

But the question arose in my mind, whether "studying the Scripture with unwearied assiduity," with the intent to restore primitive Christianity, and arriving at the *wrong conclusion* and the wrong *faith*, could constitute the *true* Church. In other words, whether *any* faith was required by the Christian law; and if so, whether it must not be the *true* faith. If mere *sincerity* was required, the law laying down what was to be believed and done, must be simply idle. I must confess I could not understand what sort of *true* Church it could be with a *false* faith.

When I examined to see what the peculiar doctrines of this sect were, I found them to be Manicheans in their leading principles, as fully shown by Bossuet in his History, as already stated. It is true, as stated by Mr.

Campbell that they continued to "oppose the Church of *nations* in the *East* and in the *West*," until the times of the Waldenses and Albigenses. But these Albigenses were also a branch of the same Manichean root. In addition to the testimony of the historians quoted by Bossuet, Waddington says, in speaking of the sects of Dauphine and other errorists condemned at Arras in 1025:

> It is proper to mention what these opinions really were, which were condemned at Arras, lest it should be supposed that they were at variance only with the Roman Catholic Church, and strictly in accordance with apostolic truth....
>
> It was asserted that the Sacrament of baptism was useless, and of no efficacy to salvation – that the Sacrament of the Lord's Supper was equally unnecessary. It appears that the objections of the heretics on this point went beyond the mere denial of the change of substance – that the sacred orders of the ministry were not of divine institution – that penance was altogether inefficacious – that marriage in general was contrary to the evangelical and apostolical laws-that saint worship is to be confined to the apostles and martyrs, &c., &c., so mixed and various is the substance of these opinions to which learned writers on this subject appeal with so much satisfaction...
>
> They were all tainted more or less deeply by the poison of Manicheism; and since it is our object to establish a connection with the primitive church, we shall scarcely attain it through those whose fundamental principle was unequivocally rejected by that Church, as irrational and impious.[33]

Mosheim, the Lutheran Church historian, says:

> Among the sects that troubled the Latin church this century, (the 12th.) the principal place is due to the Cathari, or Catharists, whom we have had already occasion to mention. This numerous faction, leaving their first residence, which was in Bulgaria, spread themselves throughout almost all the European provinces, where they occasioned much tumult and disorder. Their religion resembled the doctrine of the Manicheans and Gnostics, on which account they commonly received the denomination of the former, though they differed in many respects from the genuine primitive Manicheans. They all agreed, indeed, in the following points of doctrine, viz., that matter was the source of all evil; that the creator of this world was a being distinct from the Supreme Deity; that Christ was neither clothed with a real body, nor could he be properly said to have been born, or to have seen death; that human bodies were the production of the evil principle, and were extinguished without the prospect of a new life.

> They treated with the utmost contempt all the books of the Old Testament, but expressed a high degree of veneration for the New.[34]

Speaking of the Waldenses, Mosheim says:

> They committed the government of the church to bishops, presbyters, and deacons, but they deemed it absolutely necessary that all these orders should resemble exactly the apostles of the divine Saviour, and be, like them, *illiterate,* &c., &c. The laity were divided into two classes, one of which contained the *perfect* and the other the *imperfect* Christians.[35]

Of the Pasaginians, Mosheim says:

> They circumcised their followers, and held that the law of Moses, in everything but sacrifice, was obligatory upon Christians.[36]

The same historian says of the brethren of the free spirit,

> they maintained that the believer could not sin, let his conduct be ever so horrible and atrocious.[37]

He also says:

> A sect of fanatics called Caputiati, infested Moravia and Burgundy, the diocese of Auxerre, and several other parts of France, in all which places they excited much disturbance among the people. They declared publicly that their purpose was to level all distinctions, to abrogate magistracy, to remove all subordination among mankind, and to restore that primitive liberty, that natural equality, which were the inestimable privileges of the first mortals.[38]

That the Cathari mentioned by Mosheim were the same people called Paulicians, is certain. Mr. Campbell says the Paulicians "were called Puritans," which is the English of Cathari; and he says, "these Protestants (Paulicians) continued to oppose the church of nations in the *east* and in the *west*, until..."

Such were the doctrines to which Constantine and his followers attained by the unwearied study of the New Testament, and the "divine blessing," as Jones has it. That the Catholics called them heretics is true. So they are by Waddington and Mosheim. And conceding the truth of that article of the Apostles' Creed, "I believe in the Catholic Church," and that the promises of Christ were given to this visible Church, I could not see any beauty or truth in this chain of succession. It was strangely and singularly irregular, diminutive, deformed, isolated, and broken.

RESULTS OF THE PROTESTANT THEORY

First, the Novatians separated from the Catholic Church in A.D. 250, upon a *specific* but *false ground*; and although that distinctive characteristic which made them Novatians was *conceded* to be wrong, still the *true* Church was most inconsistently said to be with them. Then came the Donatists, who separated upon another and a mere local ground, still retaining all the *errors* of that "grievously contaminated" church they left, and who, therefore, repudiated the very error that constituted the Novatians – and then the true Church is alleged to have passed into the Donatists, while the only *additional* merit which *they* could claim over and above that "grievously contaminated" church, was, that "they pushed their schism to very great extremities," as Waddington says. But the Donatists, *now* the alleged true Church, were destined soon to perish, and the alleged true Church passed from the dead body of this sect into that "new sect," as Jones called the Paulicians. But this alleged new true Church, (full of Manichean errors of the grossest character,) like its predecessors, was only to continue *until* other sects, the Albigenses and Waldenses arose. With them, as with the others, this alleged true Church was to have another temporary "local habitation and a name" until the days of Luther. According to this theory, the true visible Catholic Church had made several transmigrations, in every case passing from one perishable sect into another, each one differing from all its predecessors; as if the true, the Catholic Church, the pillar and ground of the truth, was really in pursuit of obscurity, variety, and endless change.

Well might Waddington say:

> So mixed and various is the substance of these opinions to which learned writers on this subject appeal with so much satisfaction.... and since it is our object to establish a connection with the primitive church, we shall scarcely attain it through those whose fundamental principle was unequivocally rejected by that church, as irrational and impious.

Nor could I see how Mr. Campbell could be so fond of those errorists, who rejected baptism and the Lord's Supper as useless, when Mr. Campbell always held that baptism was for the remission of past sins.

I confess I could not possibly understand how the following extract, made by Mr. Campbell from Waddington, in immediate connection with the first extract from that author regarding the Novatians, could help his case any;

> "From a review of what has been written on this subject, some truths may be derived of considerable historical importance; the following are among them:
>
> "1. In the midst of perpetual dissent and occasional controversy, a steady and distinguishing line, both in doctrine and practice, was maintained by the early church, and its efforts against those whom it called heretics were zealous and persevering, and for the most part consistent. Its contests were fought with the 'sword of the spirit,' with the arms of reason and eloquence; and as they were always unattended by personal oppression, so were they most effectually successful – successful, not in establishing a nominal unity, nor silencing the expression of private opinion, but in maintaining the purity of the faith, in preserving the attachment of the great majority of the believers, and in consigning, either to immediate disrepute, or early neglect, all the unscriptural doctrines which were successively arrayed against it."[39]

From this I understand Waddington to say, substantially, that the early Church was known by a "*steady and distinguishing line of doctrine and practice*" – that this early Church was not the Navatians nor the Donatists, as Mr. Campbell contended, for Waddington expressly held the latter as not composing the true Church; as we have seen. While he seems to speak doubtingly of the Novatians in the beginning of the first extract, he clearly, *in this*, places them among the heretics whose doctrines were consigned by the Church to "disrepute or neglect," for he speaks of the early Church as "preserving the attachment of the great *majority of the believers,"* which could not be true of the Novatians, who constituted a very small party, nothing like so numerous as the Donatists, who *themselves* were confined *alone* to Africa, and had not even a majority there (as Waddington notes.)

If the early Church was thus known by this "steady and distinguishing line, both in *doctrine* and *practice,"* and was: "*successful in maintaining the purity of the faith,"* as this Protestant historian says, how did these alleged errors get into the Church, of which Mr. Campbell speaks? And how and when did this *steady* Church, which preserved the "purity of the faith," lose "those *rigid principles* that characterized and sanctified her before the days of Novatian? I confess my inability to put the positions, either of Waddington or Mr. Campbell, together, and make them consistent with themselves. In one place, this historian makes the early Church abandon her principles to others, and, in another, he makes her preserve them; and Mr. Campbell quotes both passages to show that she did abandon them.

Mr. Campbell placed much emphasis upon the fact that the Donatists and the Greeks each claimed to be the sole true Church. The Novatians also claimed the same for themselves. Mr. Campbell says: "Mark it. The Donatists considered *their own body to be the true, uncorrupted, universal church.*"[40] In reference to the Greeks, he says: "The Greek church, be it noted with all distinctness, did stand upon this point, that *she* was the only true Church; and *that no ordinance, baptism or the Eucharist, was at all valid, unless administered by her authority.*"[41]

The fact that each of these sects claimed to be the sole true Church, as did most, if not all, the sects before the Reformation, as well as did the Catholic church from which they separated, went to prove this point, as I understand it; namely: that by consent of all parties – heretics, schismatics, and Catholics – from the first to the sixteenth century, the doctrine that there was but *one sole* true visible Church, in whose communion salvation must be found, *was universally believed and held to be true;* and that the doctrine that the true visible Church could be composed of a conglomeration of separate and distinct antagonistic organizations, differing in faith and discipline, and excommunicating each other, is an *after-thought,* invented since the Reformation. And the only possible *other* result I could see was this, that these conflicting claims would only compel us to choose between them, without, in the slightest degree, weakening the claim of the rightful proprietor. If twenty men each claims to be the *sole* owner of an estate, by the admission of all, there is but *one* exclusive owner, while the nineteen false, but adverse claims, will never defeat him in whom the true title is vested. A million counterfeits will never disparage one dime of this genuine coin.

When I considered this most strange and deformed chain of alleged succession, I could not but wish to ask these plain and pointed questions: "Is this really the best you can do? Is there no possible chance for the better showing? If not, had you not better

'Go and 'contend 'your family is young;
Nor own your fathers have been fools so long?'

Would it not be better to concede, at once, that you have no ancestors? Why not take a bold, neat, clean ground? Why halt between two false opinions? Had you not better take that one which is, at least, consistent with itself?"

16. The new ground of Mr. Breckenridge

In reference to that most important and difficult point, where was the true Church before the Reformation, if it was not the Church of Rome? Mr. Breckenridge, in his controversy with Bishop Hughes, takes a new position.

Bishop Hughes had made this distinct proposition:

> Either the Protestant religion is a religion *differing* from the religion of Christ, or else the religion of Christ was *not professed by any society of Christians previous to the time of Luther.* To which of these alternatives will you cling? One of them is inevitable.[42]

In his first answer, Mr. Breckenridge claims the Waldenses, the Greek church, the ancient Arminian church, the Jacobites, Syrians, the Egyptian and Abyssinian Christians as Protestant ancestors, and says:

> How plain it is, then, from these testimonies, that the Protestant religion was professed, not only before the days of Luther, but existed from the beginning, and descended for centuries, even in your own church, until she corrupted it, and made it an anti-Christian Papacy.[43]

To this very confident answer Bishop Hughes replied showing the tenets of the Waldenses, such as we have seen, differing so widely from Protestants, and holding so many of the alleged errors of the Catholics.[44]

Mr. Breckenridge having again called the attention of the Bishop to the Syrian Christians,(page 405) the latter replied, on page 416:

> About the year 1500, the Portuguese having doubled the Cape of Good Hope, penetrated into India, and, to their amazement, those Christians of Saint Thomas were found on the coast of Malabar. This was reported in Europe, and gave rise to much speculation; but, unfortunately, it was made known that their faith had been corrupted by the errors of Protestantism. They were heretics, and the Reformers, who had just separated from the faith of the church, and of the world, took it into their heads that, of course, they were Protestants. La Croze, a Protestant, wrote a treatise to maintain this supposition, under the title of 'History of Christianity in India.' But Assemani refuted La Croze's book, and convicted him, as usual in such cases, of twelve or thirteen gross misrepresentations. (Joseph Assemani, *Bibliotheca Orentalis* Tom. 4, c. 7, & 13.)

> Their errors were condemned by the Catholic Archbishop of Goa, but the *denial of the real presence* was not among them. In their Liturgy, to which Mr. Breckenridge refers, are found the following words: "With hearts full of respect and fear, let us approach the *Mystery of the precious body and blood of our Saviour*....
>
> And now, O Lord, that thou hast called me to thy holy and pure *altar*, to offer unto thee this living *and holy sacrifice,* make me worthy to receive this gift with purity and holiness." At the communion, the Priest says: "O Lord, my God! I am not worthy, neither is it becoming that I should partake of the *body and blood of propitiation,* or even so much as touch them. But may thy word sanctify my soul, and heal my body." In thanksgiving, after communion, he says: "Strengthen my hands which are stretched out to receive the holy one... Repair, by a new life, the bodies which have *just been feeding on thy living body*....
>
> God has loaded us with blessings by his living Son, who, for our salvation, descended from the highest heavens, clothed himself with our flesh, and mixed his venerable blood with our blood, a Mystery of propitiation." (Renaudot's Latin translation)

These extracts conclusively proved that they held the doctrines of the Mass and the Real Presence.

In reference to these Syrian Christians, Bishop Hughes further observes on page 418:

> But besides that, they venerated the crucifix, made the sign of the cross, *fasted from food on certain days, and abstained from meat on others,* celebrated festivals in honor of the blessed Virgin, and prayed for the dead.... (Le Brun, Tom. iii., Dis. xi., Art. 15.)
>
> They believed in the remission of sins by the Priest's absolution, held three sacraments, Baptism, Holy Order, and the Eucharist, and taught that in Christ there were two persons, the divine and human; that the divinity dwelt in Jesus, as in a temple.[45]

On page 418 the Bishop shows the doctrines of the Arminians, Jacobites, Egyptians, and Abssinians to be very different from that of Protestants.

In reference to the Greek church the Bishop says:

> The Greeks believe in seven sacraments, in the real presence, in transubstantiation, the sacrifice of the mass, prayers for the departed, and even the invocation of the saints....

> When the Patriarch Cyril Lupor, was detected holding correspondence with the leaders of the Reformation in Germany and Holland, and it was ascertained that he had imbibed a *partiality for their novelties*, the consequence was, that for this he was *deposed and disgraced.* His successor summoned a council of twenty-three bishops, including the patriarchs of Jerusalem and Alexandria, in which Cyril and his *Protestant doctrines* were condemned in language as vigorous as that of Leo X. The same took place in a subsequent council of twenty-five bishops, including the metropolitan of Russia. Again, in 1672, Dositheus, patriarch of Jerusalem, held a third council at Bethlehem, which expressly condemned the doctrine of Cyril Lupor and the Protestants. (See Prepet, de la Far, vol. 4, liv. 8)

Mr. Breckenridge says, on page 405:

> It is also notorious that the Christian churches in England and Ireland held the Protestant doctrines in their essential purity, *before* and *when* the first emissaries of the Church of Rome invaded them, and began to proselyte them to the Roman Hierarchy.

Blackstone, in his *Commentaries on the Laws of England*, asserts the same position, in substance, that

> the ancient British church, by whomsoever *planted*, was a stranger to the Bishop of Rome and his pretended authority.[46]

As these churches are acknowledged to have been in communion with the See of Rome many ages before the days of Luther, it is not a matter of so much importance as to what was their early faith. But as to the matter of fact regarding the ancient British Church, Dr. Ives in his able work, *Trials of a Mind,"* had demonstrated that the learned divine and the distinguished commentator are both mistaken in their positions. This he has done by a careful examination of contemporary testimony.[47]

This brings me to the new position of Mr. Breckenridge. "The inquiry," he says,

> as to the existence of Protestantism *before* Luther, and *when* and *where,* (besides my previous replies,) may thus be finally settled. You admit that the doctrines taught by the apostles, and recorded in the Bible, are true Christianity – so do I. We both also allow that these doctrines have been, according to Christ's promise to his Church, held and taught by the true Church ever since. Thus, if *your* present doctrines contradict the Bible at every step, and if *ours harmonize* with it, it follows that we are the true Church, and that our

> doctrines have been taught and held in every age. But I have proved this at large, as to both faith and morals, and worship.[48]

I must say that this position, whether true or false, is more frank, bold, open and manly, that the attempt to prove, from historical testimony, that the Protestant doctrines ever were held and taught by any party, great or small, before the alleged Reformation. It does not seek to delude you with the confident profession of ability to sustain such an *historical fact*, and then utterly fail to do it.

The essence of this new ground is this: it makes the solution of every question, as well historical as doctrinal, depend upon the construction put upon the Scriptures by each individual. If true, this position renders wholly unnecessary all the grounds previously taken by Mr. Breckenridge. It wholly excludes the necessity of historical inquiry, so far as the Church is concerned. The settlement of the question, what Church did exist during certain ages before the alleged Reformation, is settled simply by deciding, from individual construction, what Church *ought* to have existed during those times. This position is one of those short, pithy, but comprehensive grounds that go directly to the point. Like the theory of an invisible Church, it avoids many old difficulties, though it may have some new ones of its own.

It always occurred to me, that if we wish to prove the fulfillment of an admitted promise, then the simplest and most satisfactory mode was to show the historical fact, that it had been so fulfilled. It also seemed to me, that if we wish to show the continued identity and existence of a *visible* and *universal* Church for and during the long period of fifteen centuries, then the most logical and certain mode of doing so was to produce the direct historical proof of the simple *matter of fact*. As such a Church is admitted to have been promised by Christ, its existence during that period could be proved, if true, from the simple records of history.

But Mr. Breckenridge proposes a different mode. He proposes to look into Scripture, and from his own construction, to arrive at the conclusion what doctrines, in *theory*, the true, *visible Catholic Church* ought to teach, and from this verbal construction, to assume the historical *fact* that these doctrines have been taught in every age. He proposes to supply the defective records of history by *construction*; and, in the *same* way, to refresh the memory of past ages.

He who holds the doctrine of an *invisible* Church, when asked what historical testimony he can produce to prove its existence, may very consistently reply that *history* could not attest the existence of that which was *invisible.* But Mr. Breckenridge assumes to prove by verbal construction, the actual and positive existence of a great *visible* Church, that no one ever saw – a *teaching* Church that no one ever heard – a *universal* or Catholic Church that was never known to spread anywhere – or if this Church was *seen, heard,* and did *extend over the earth,* then the negligent and ungenerous past *forget to record the fact* – that while they recorded the existence of some four hundred different, schismatical, contaminated, and apostate Churches, they only forgot the true Church, visible and Catholic. Where were the divines and writers of this alleged true Church, that they never spoke of her, and have given her no place upon the page of history? Where were her *enemies*, that *they* were silent? Or did the *true* Church have neither enemies nor friends? Was she a blank? Was she neither good nor bad, and, therefore, unworthy of any notice whatever? What sort of a *true* Church was it, of which no one cared to speak? Where were her glorious martyrs? Did they too pass away?

"Unswept, unhonored, and unsung?"

In short, what sort of a visible universal Church was it that existed for so long a time, of whose existence history saith not? Is it not much more rational to suppose, that Mr. Breckenridge may be mistaken in his construction of the Bible, about which *so many* men, equally learned, have so widely differed, than to suppose all history at fault? We have, as Bossuet says, the most full and minute lists of the ancient heretics, and the peculiar tenets of each party, and yet no mention is made of this assumed true visible Catholic Church.

How the assumed facts of history will multiply, under this most flexible position! As Mr. Breckenridge by his construction, can prove the historical existence of a Calvinistic Church, extending from the days of the apostles to the present time, so each of the five hundred existing sects in Protestant Christendom can do the same, in the same way, and make themselves worthy ancestors, of the same faith with themselves. How the imaginary ancient sects will rise from the dead, at the bidding of each individual! Like the fabled men of Roderick Dhu, they rise and fall as mystic shadows.

To form a new party under such a theory, all that need be shown is, that in the opinion of individuals, the scriptures have been misconstrued. It is not necessary to show from history, that such opinions were ever held in point of fact – that there ever was such a Church as the *new one* proposed; nor will the entire absence of any and all historical testimony, defeat the claims of such an institution, under such a theory. The originator has only to say that it existed in the days of the apostles, and whether it died out so suddenly and silently, and, like the closing furrow of the ship as she glides through the waves, disappeared so completely as to leave no historical trace behind, he may still consistently contend that it visibly existed at one time, and must have existed ever since, though "buried," as Waddington says, "in the darkness of those ages," and still remained buried at the alleged Reformation.

Is it not a curious and distressing state of *necessity*, that compels learned men to stultify themselves by denouncing certain tenets of the Catholic church, as alleged monstrous errors; and yet, when they are called upon to select their ancestors, they choose, as their alleged true Church, those sects holding in part, these *same alleged errors?* In a word, they condemn those tenets as heresies, and then insist that the true Church can still teach them. And they compose their true Church of sects, not only holding and teaching so many of the very alleged errors they denounce, but also holding *others*, equally objectionable to both Catholics and Protestants.

17. The theory of Bishop Hoadley and Dr. Balguy

The theory concerning the Church, as devised by Bishop Hoadley, and more clearly and fully developed by his distinguished disciple, Dr. Balguy, is still more latitudinarian than that of the French Calvinist ministers, Claude and Jurieu. As the bishop did not agree with the views of his own Church, whose creed he had subscribed and publicly acknowledged, in reference to the Church question, as well as all other questions connected therewith, it became necessary to give a definition of his own. He accordingly defines a Church to be,

> The number of persons, whether great or small, whether dispersed or united, who are sincerely and willingly subject to Christ alone, as to a lawgiver and judge, in matters relating to the favor of God and eternal salvation.

According to this definition, neither the purity of doctrine, nor the right administration of the sacraments, nor the unity of its members, nor the succession of ministers, is at all requisite to constitute the true Church. All that is required is, that the members shall be "sincerely and willingly subject to Christ alone, as to a lawgiver and judge..." From his definition, and from his language in other places, it appears to be clear, that the Bishop only required integrity of purpose to constitute a Christian; "as God's favor," he says, "cannot depend upon his actual being or continuing in any particular method, (of religion,) but upon his real sincerity in the conduct of his conscience."

The reason that induced this distinguished Bishop to adopt this theory, was his struggle to free the Protestant fundamental rule from the charge of cruelty and contradiction, and to substitute something for the Catholic certainty. To say that each individual must construe the entire Code of Christ for himself alone, and yet to hold that he must construe correctly, or be finally lost, was to lay down a cruel and contradictory theory. To avoid this plain logical result, the Bishop placed the safety of the Christian "in his real sincerity in the conduct of his conscience." If he failed to arrive at the true faith, in the exercise of this *sincerity*, it was not his fault, and he would be saved as well without, as with true faith. The Protestant fundamental rule had placed a burthen upon the individual, too grievous to be borne. It imposed upon him an individual responsibility, evidently disproportioned to his capacity.

But this definition still contained some *restrictions*. The believer had great latitude left him, it is true, but he was still required to be subject to "Christ *as a lawgiver and judge*." The Bishop made the Church universal, and then composed it only of those persons who are "sincerely and willingly subject to Christ alone." The tests of willingness and sincerity were impracticable. These qualities being known to God only, the Church could not determine the question, whether they did or did not exist in each individual member.

The clear-headed Dr. Balguy saw that a visible Church must contain members not *willing* and *sincere*; and yet these members must ostensibly enjoy, in her communion, all the privileges enjoyed by others. He also saw that a visible Church was the only one that could be defined with any practical utility, and with which we could make ourselves acquainted. Therefore, the tests of willingness and sincerity, as applied to a visible Church, which must expel heretics, were simply idle. No one could practically apply them.

"The good must merit God's peculiar care,
But who but God can tell us who they are?"

Besides this, Dr. Balguy could not see the consistency between the Bishop's definition of the Church, and his leading principle of integrity alone. As God's favor to each individual depended upon his "real sincerity in the conduct of his conscience" it was difficult to see how, or why, he should be subject to "Christ alone *as a lawgiver.*" In such a case, our Lord must have been a most anomalous Legislator. To say that He was a lawgiver, and had made and promulgated His Code in a *positive* form expressed in human language, commanding and prohibiting what He pleased, requiring this truth to be believed, and that error to be avoided, and this or that to be done or omitted, and promising, *in advance,* certain rewards for obedience, and denouncing certain punishments for disobedience; and, then, after all this labor, and all these pledges of His *veracity*, that certain results should follow certain states of faith and obedience or of disbelief and disobedience, to make our Lord's favor to depend, not upon the *actual* doing or omitting that which was *actually* commanded and prohibited, but simply upon the "real sincerity in the conduct of each one's conscience," was certainly making Christ do a very idle and useless thing. It is just as easy to understand the logic and good sense of a positive law for the *predestinated*, commanding them to do or not to do certain specified things, which they *must* do, or not do, as well without the law as with it, as to understand the position of Bishop Hoadley.

It, therefore, became necessary for Dr. Balguy to improve upon the definition of Bishop Hoadley. Unless a definition includes all that is required, and no more, it lacks completeness and certainty – two requisites necessary to constitute a good definition. Dr. Balguy, therefore, defined a Church very briefly and comprehensively, as follows:

> A Church is a number of persons agreeing to unite in public assemblies, for the performance of religious duties.

This definition cannot be exceeded in some respects. It is as brief, comprehensive, and latitudinarian *as possible.* It cannot be made shorter in *words*, or wider in *meaning*. It includes all of every religion—Christian, Jewish, Mahometan, and Pagan. It would seem that the learned divine was predetermined that no improvement should ever be made upon his definition, by any Protestant of the latitudinarian school. In that line he at once attained the summit of excellence and stands without any rival, even among those of his own school. And it certainly is an improvement upon the Bishop's definition, in the way of consistency. It is like some bills in Chancery, framed with a double aspect, so as to meet every *possible* state of case. It is wide enough to embrace every worshipper of every kind.

But this definition is *too wide* for any man professing to be a Christian. The only truly consistent Protestant creed, is the fundamental rule itself. All being independent equals, every one should have the right to preach who pleased, and to preach what he pleased, and to baptize in any mode he pleased, and to administer any sacrament he pleased. The right in all to preach and baptize should be equal, and the *actual exercise* of that right should depend upon the will of each one, and his power to secure hearers. If he did not preach to suit others, they, being equally free to hear or not to hear, to contribute or not to his support, might leave him to preach to the forests and hills, or be silent. There would be no necessity for any form of Church government, no expulsion for heresy, as there would be a "sovereign antidote against" it, as Mr. Campbell says. The theory and practice would be consistent. All the privileges guaranteed by the fundamental rule itself, would be *practically* secured. Each one would be left to construe for himself, and to hold any doctrine he pleased, so he referred it to the Bible alone.

That Protestantism has been regularly approaching this consistent creed, step by step, may be readily seen by any patient inquirer, who will examine into its history. The plan of holding matters of difference as not material must, sooner or later, end in holding all immaterial, except the fundamental rule itself. As all can agree as to that, this would form a basis of practical union. To Zuinglius is to be ascribed the first step in this consistent, but latitudinarian path. In the Conference of Marpurg, after he found he could not convince Luther in regard to the doctrine of the Real Presence, he then asked Luther to tolerate the difference. The next step was taken by the Calvinists in holding this doctrine immaterial. Then in England, under Elizabeth, it was so held. Then came the Hoadley School, which would tolerate almost, if not quite, everything. The Lutherans on the Continent degenerated into a veiled Deism, if not downright infidelity. The Calvinists of Geneva have also done the same. Without a professed change upon the face of their creeds, they have, like the members of the Church of England, departed from them in practice. And the theory of Mr. Campbell is a decided and consistent step in that direction, in reference to many tenets, though not in reference to all.

Among some Indian tribes it is a practice, when two or more of their warriors or chiefs have a dispute about a piece of property, and the dispute is likely to result in serious consequences, to destroy the property itself. If, for example, the dispute were about a horse, they kill the animal. The *cause* of dispute being removed, though injustice is done, peace is thereby restored. This same result must follow when former articles of faith are subsequently held immaterial. If once held immaterial, of course, they can constitute no matters of serious difference among sensible men.

18. Reflections on these theories of succession

In reference to Mr. Campbell's claims to be a reformer, Mr. Rice remarks:

> I do not remember to have seen a man who pretended to religion of any kind, who did not consider himself rather more orthodox than others. This is a common weakness of human nature. It displays itself everywhere, and especially in men who imagine themselves to be great reformers, and believe all but themselves in serious error. If it be true, as my friend evidently thinks, that of all the world, he only, and those who agree with him, are in the light, whilst all Christendom grope in midnight darkness; it follows, as a necessary consequence, that he is one of the most orthodox men. There can be no doubt about it.[49]

There is certainly great force and truth in this statement. But while it applies to Mr. Campbell, does it not equally apply to Mr. Rice? How stands the case with him? Did not Luther, his predecessor and head, make even greater pretensions that Mr. Campbell? Luther not only claimed that all "Christendom groped in midnight darkness," but he claimed the right to reform it, not only because he understood the Scriptures better than any other man who then lived, or had lived during the preceding thousand years, but also in virtue of an *extraordinary mission, attested by miracles.*

But how natural is it for men to lay down one rule for themselves, and another rule for others. Even the rogue who steals from others, complains bitterly if another steals from him. When Luther claimed the right to reform the Church of Rome, he denied the right to Zuinglius and others to reform his Church. Calvin, who resisted Luther's pretensions to the entire right of reformation, and claimed an equal right for himself, nevertheless was instrumental in having Servetus burned for assuming the same right. And in all cases, the older Protestant sects declaim loudly against all newcomers into the common domain of Reformation. But in condemning others, they inevitably condemn themselves.

Mr. Rice says in another place:

THE TRUE CHURCH

Reform is the watchword of every demagogue and of every fanatic.[50]

This is surely a great truth – a notable fact, and gives rise to some very important and useful reflections.

All the bad and immoral men in Christendom are, at heart, infidels. They *all* belong to that class. The natural instincts of their conduct lead them there. There is something so utterly inconsistent between the belief of Christianity and the practice of gross immorality, that the two cannot be found together. Many men, however, who do not believe in Christianity, are yet practically good men as citizens and neighbors. But it is a great and gratifying fact, and a most powerful argument in favor of Christianity, that *all* the bad and wicked men are on *one* side, and at heart *opposed* to it, whatever may be their professions.

So all the demagogues and fanatics in religion are Reformers, as Mr. Rice justly says. They are one and all the incessant advocates of the principle of private interpretation in the last resort. Demagoguism and fanaticism in religion cannot, in the very nature of things, be found in the Catholic system. They cannot live there. There is no demagogical or fanatical oxygen in that atmosphere. There is nothing there for them to feed upon. Their necessary and indispensable food is found outside. There being nothing in the creed of that Church to reform, and nothing changeable in her infallible theory, such a watch ward is not permitted to be used with reference to her articles of faith. It would be as logical to speak of reforming the original law of Christ, as to speak of reforming a creed assumed to be infallible. Whoever, therefore, embraces that creed, cannot say reform in reference to the creed itself. It is a word unknown to a stable religious system of faith. And it is a gratifying fact, and a strong argument in favor of the Catholic system, that all the demagogues and fanatics in religion are opposed to it. They are invariable found *all* on *one* side and *against* it.

While I cheerfully admit that all reformers were not demagogues or fanatics, truth compels me to say that I think most of them have been so. Admitting that I may be mistaken as to the proportion, yet it is clear that the Protestant principle produces the *very* and *only* food upon which they can live. And while it produces this food in superabundance, it provides no sufficient and consistent check to its use. Under the fundamental and supreme rule of individual and independent interpretation, what was allowed to Luther must be allowed to the Lutherans; and what was allowed to Calvin and his colleagues, must be allowed, under the same rule, to others. Mr. Campbell had, therefore, the common right existing under, and guaranteed by, the rule, itself. What check, then, is there upon demagogism and fanaticism in the Protestant theory? Nothing but the opinion and judgment of each individual! And in the war of contending demagogues and fanatics, how shall they decide? How *have they decided in the past? Let facts and history answer.*

19. Mr. Campbell's theory of Protestant union

In reference to the differences among Protestants, Mr. Campbell says:

> There are one or two Protestant sects who differ in some important matters, and are as repugnant to each other as are Jansenists and Jesuits in the Roman church; but all Protestant sects unite in several acts of religious worship, in acknowledgment of the same code of morals, and in the positive institutions of Christianity, such as the Lord's day, the Lord's supper, baptism, prayer, praise, &c. Sects and differences exist which ought not: but still they harmonize as much in their general and special bonds of union, as do the Romanists themselves. What are the Augustinians, Dominicans, Franciscans, Jansenists, Jesuits, &c., but orders *(or sects) called after the different saints?"*[51]

The essence of this statement, if true, is based upon the principle of compromise or compensation. Mr. Campbell says, in substance, if we are divided, so are you. If this were true, it might well be asked, what, then, has your alleged Reformation accomplished? Has it produced any greater union?

But are the assumed facts here stated, *true?* What does a calm, fair, and dispassionate detailed examination of the differences existing among Protestants, show? Mr. Campbell says they agree in "several" particulars. That is true; but does this agreement in *several* things constitute that unity in speaking the *same* things, and in being perfectly joined together in the *same* mind and in the *same* judgment, as Saint Paul has it? All Christians, as well as Jews and Mohammedans, agree in several matters, but is this unity?

What, then, constitutes the unity contemplated by the law of Christ? Certainly, the *same* agreement that existed in the Apostolic Church! That Church was united in the *same judgment* in reference to *all things* held material by the *church herself,* and in the same *church government.* And it must be obvious, that if there be a true visible Church, that she must know herself, and must also know what requisites make up her faith; and that, consequently, when she decides that certain specified articles are necessary to her creed, and condemns others as untrue, that she must be right. On the contrary, if a Church determines certain articles *as essential* to faith, and certain other articles as not essential, if there be error in *either* case, that Church cannot be in the right, and cannot, for that reason, be the true Church. If then, two or more Churches decide differently upon the same matter, held by them to be essential to faith, it is clear, that they cannot all be the true Church, or *parts* of the true Church.

For example, when Mr. Campbell and his Church hold that immersion alone is baptism, and that infant baptism, in *any* mode, is null and void, how can such a Church be a part or a branch of a Church, which holds precisely the contrary? And when Mr. Campbell (as well as Mr. Breckenridge and other Calvinists) come to speak of Transubstantiation, Confession, and Absolution, as grievous errors of the Catholic Church, and make these tenets a most material portion of the reasons assigned to justify the alleged Reformation, how can they call the Lutherans, who hold Consubstantiation, Confession, and Absolution, a part of the true Church? For every sensible man must see, that all their objections against Transubstantiation apply to Consubstantiation; and that the latter, as the Sacramentarians insisted in the days of Luther, is more inconsistent with the Scripture than the former, conceding them both to be untrue.

How can they claim the Church of England as part of this great, but discordant, *alleged* true Church? She holds Confession and Absolution. And when the great Synod of Dort, representing the entire Calvinistic world, laid down these stern Calvinistic doctrines, and expelled the Remonstrants from their communion, did *both* these parties belong to the same Church? If so, how did the Remonstrants bear the relation of "heathens and publicans" to the Calvinists? One part maintained predestination, election, and final perseverance, and the other the reverse; and the Synod held the Calvinistic doctrines as fundamental articles of faith, and the opposite tenets as heresy.

The Methodists, and all the other five hundred sects, differ from each other in so many points deemed by them, and each of them, so far material, that they cannot be induced to unite under *one system* of church government, having *one* acknowledged head; and how can they form parts of *one* Church? The Lutheran excommunicates the Calvinist – the Calvinist the Arminian – the Baptist the Paedo-Baptists – the Trinitarian the Anti-Trinitarian – the Episcopalian the Independent – the believer in the Atonement the Unitarian – the Methodist the Antinomian.

Yet. under this confused theory, these different parties, while they are thus excommunicating each other, are held to be but parts of the true Church, as were the Churches of Jerusalem, Antioch, Ephesus, and other places but branches of the Apostolic Church. A Church that does not know herself – does not know her faith – does not know the members of her own body, is still the true Church, under this most latitudinarian theory. What assistance does Christ, the alleged head of this confused Church, give to her, when she remains in this state of *profound ignorance of her own faith?* Is confused and contradictory ignorance an attribute of the one true Church of Christ? If, on the contrary, it be assumed that this mongrel Church does know herself and her faith, then why is she continually excommunicating her own children for *immaterial errors of mere opinion?*

But the Church of Christ is a Kingdom, and a visible Kingdom – a united Kingdom. It has but *one* law for its government. This law requires uniform faith in certain fixed truths. How, then, can this visible Kingdom have different governments, antagonistic to and independent of each other, and requiring faith in precisely opposite tenets, so that there is one faith for one part, and a different faith for another part? Did two or more communities, having entirely separate and independent governments, each acting for itself alone, ever constitute one government, because their citizens or subjects accidentally agreed in race, language, customs, laws, and manners, and in the forms of government? How can any associated body of men exist, without having *one* government? Do all the sovereign independent states of the civilized constitute but one government, simply because they are all sovereign, and agree, substantially, in a great number of particulars? Unity of faith and unity of government must exist to constitute the one Church of Christ. Separate organizations, each acting exclusively for itself, and teaching its creed as its own, and for itself alone, never can form "*The Church*" spoken of so often by Saint Paul.

But Mr. Campbell says that Protestants harmonize as much as Romanists themselves. He asks, "What are the Augustinians, Dominicans, Franciscans, Jansenists, Jesuits, &c., but orders (or sects) called after different saints?"

When I first read this statement, I was under the impression that these alleged differences among Catholics would compensate or balance the undeniable discords among Protestants. But there was one reflection which forced itself upon my mind with great power: that if this assumed state of case was in fact true, then it was clear that the true Church, if it existed at all, was in the most wretched and disorganized state, very much like a clean neat apostasy from the true original faith. For my common sense assured me that this faith was an *entire* – an indestructible whole, consisting of *united parts* – and that the moment one of these parts was lost, the identity of the Church was at once destroyed, and the promises of our Lord had clearly failed.

I could just as easily conceive of a house with nothing but the foundation, or of a steam engine consisting of nothing but the boiler, as of a true, visible, catholic, and apostolic Church, which had either denied a single true article of faith, or added a single false tenet to the true. If the Church could err in one essential particular, and still be the true Church, she could err in two or more; and the limit once passed, which was set by the inflexible, whole, and entire law of Christ, there could be no bounds fixed beyond which she could not go. Such an idea was utterly destructive of the whole theory, that Christ was a Divine Lawgiver. I could not understand how our Lord could ever have contemplated a mutilated Church. I could not think that He ever intended that one bone of her should be broken; but that while she might be wounded by her enemies for the moment, she would soon rise, like her Master, still sound, though scarred, and as triumphant and beautiful as ever.

But I inquired, is it true, as Mr. Campbell states? What are the genuine facts? In reference to the Jansenists and Jesuits, I found that they had discussed a theological question, taking different sides; and that the Church condemned the Jansenists, and that ended the matter with Catholics.

In reference to the Augustinians and other orders in the Church, I found that they were not *sects* in the just import of that word, but were only *subordinate* communities, organized for different purposes, and having different disciplinary rules for their own direction, in reference to matters *peculiar* to each. I found that all the members of these different orders were required to believe every article of the creed, in the same way precisely that every member of the Church was required to do. They had then the *same faith,* and were united in the *same judgment,* as were all members of the Church. And not only so, but I found that not one of these orders could exist, without the express act and consent of the

Church – that the Church reserved the power to suppress them at any time, and had exercised it in particular cases – that the matters *peculiar* to each order did not relate to faith at all, (which was a matter they could not touch,) and that they were in everything *subordinate* to the Church. I found also that the questions they were allowed to discuss, being questions outside the creed – questions of expedience or of discipline, or questions which the Church had not settled by any decision; and that so soon as a decision was made on any question, the matter was ended.

I must confess, that in these orders I could see no divisions in the Church, any more than I could see divisions in the State, because subordinate municipal, and other corporations, were allowed to exist by express acts of the Legislature, *prescribing* and *limiting* their powers to such matters *only as do not interfere or clash with the exercise of the legitimate powers of the State herself.* These corporations are the mere creatures or agents of the State deriving all their powers from her, existing by her will and pleasure, and are not, therefore, divisions producing discord in the government. And so it was with reference to these orders. They derived their existence from the express act of the Church, exercised all their powers subordinate to her, and held their existence at her pleasure. These powers had no relation to faith, were expressly limited to matters indifferent, and were not allowed, in any way, to interfere with the powers of the Church. They are merely subordinate limited orders, organized for special purposes, and governed by disciplinary rules, first *approved by the Church herself.* I could see no discord in these orders, nothing antagonistic to the Church, unless I could see discord between a subordinate and his superior.

But in reference to Protestant divisions, I found the case far different in two great and essential particulars:

1.They differed as to matters of faith, holding precisely opposite views in reference to the same matter.

2. They each had entire separate and independent Church organizations, acting each alone for itself, and acknowledging no *common superior.*

In other words, they were independent associations, having no visible connection. The Methodists, for instance, *formally* decide all questions of faith and practice for themselves, and from this decision there is no appeal to any other power on earth. So of all the others! They are no more connected in government (if such a thing exists among them at all) than independent States. Whatever similarity of views, in reference to some points, may exist among them arises not from their theories of organization. Each association being separate and independent, there can be no subordination among them, and no union.

From Mr. Campbell's language in his debate with Bishop Purcell, one would be compelled to infer, that these divisions were very slight, except as to the "one, or two Protestant sects" not specified; and even as to these, they were not greater than the alleged divisions among Catholics. Among other things they *all* united in, as stated by him was *baptism.* But when we look to his debate with Mr. Rice, and see the grounds he there took, and the language there used, we begin to see the mighty chasms that lie between the professed views of different Protestant sects. Even in Mr. Campbell's view, there are some things so different from most other Protestants, that they constitute a mighty wall of separation. In the debate with Mr. Rice, two of the propositions maintained by Mr. Campbell were: "Baptism is for the remission of past sins," and immersion of a proper subject "is the only apostolic or Christian baptism." Putting these two propositions together, and drawing there from the inevitable conclusion, the Church that practices sprinkling and infant baptism, has no baptism, according to Mr. Campbell, and her members who have been thus sprinkled, no remission of past sins. How such could be saved, or how, consistent with his view, he could call such a Church either the true Church, or even a part of it, I am not able to perceive. And as the overwhelming majority of Protestant sects were in this condition, those left as parts of the true Church were certainly few, comparatively. Although Mr. Campbell did permit Dr. Fishback to hold the negative of the proposition that "baptism is for the remission of past sins," as matter of opinion, he never, so far as I am advised, tolerated the difference in the mode. What sort of Christians were they, in Mr. Campbell's view, who had never been baptized? And whose past sins were never remitted? And what sort of a Church was it that was entirely composed of the unbaptized? the unwashed? the unregenerate? Where was Mr. Campbell's true Church – baptizing by immersion – before the Reformation? Did all those he claimed as the true Church, baptize by immersion? If they did not, then they had no baptism, under his theory. And the Paulicians, who denied baptism, were they the true Church?

20. Dr. Spring's theory of Protestant union

In reference to the views of Protestants, Dr. Spring insists:

that there is a remarkable uniformity in the views of Protestants on the great and fundamental doctrines of Christianity. The thirty-nine articles of the Church of England – the confession of faith of the Assembly of Divines at Westminster – the Savoy confession, and the symbols of the Reformed churches in Holland and France, as well as the published works of the continental, English, Scotch, and Dutch Reformers, and their followers, in this and other countries, where the reformed religion obtains, present a coincidence of views, with which, for its extent and importance, the boasted uniformity of Rome furnishes no comparison....

The unity of the Papal Church is a unity of the most jarring materials.[52]

In the Westminster Confession referred to by Dr. Spring, and drawn up by the Assembly of Divines at Westminster, in 1647, I find the following articles:

To these (church officers) the keys of the kingdom of heaven are committed, by virtue whereof they have power to retain and remit sins, to shut the kingdom against the impenitent, both by the word and censure; and to open it unto penitent sinners by the ministry of the Gospel, and absolutions from censures, as occasion shall require.[53]

He (the civil magistrate) hath authority, and it is his duty, to take order, that unity and peace be preserved in the Church, that the truth of God be kept pure and entire, that all blasphemies and heresies be suppressed, all corruptions and abuses in worship and discipline prevented or reformed, and all the ordinances of god duly settled, administered, and observed. For the better effecting whereof, he hath power to call Synods, to be present at them, and to provide that whatever is transacted in them, be according to the mind of God.[54]

These extracts are given, not for the purpose of showing that the Presbyterians in the United States hold these tenets, (for they, in a General Assembly, held about the year 1783, rejected these articles,) but to show what that "remarkable uniformity" was which was spoken of by Dr. Spring.

In reference, then, to the symbols of the Reformed Churches, to which the Doctor refers, it will be seen that they were made by the Lutherans and Calvinists. As to the Calvinism of the thirty-nine articles, there could be no doubt.[55] It has long been said truly, that the Church of England had a Calvinistic creed and an Arminian clergy.[56] It will also be seen, that these confessions were generally made in the first fifty years after the dawn of the alleged Reformation, and before the Protestants were divided and subdivided into so many parties. Besides, it will be seen that the differences between Lutherans and Calvinists were either most material, or they themselves were mistaken in considering them so. So, it will be seen that the Westminster divines thought it so important "that the truth of God be kept *pure and entire,*" that they held that the *civil magistrate* had power to: call synods, to be present at them, and to *provide* that whatever is transacted in them, be *according to the mind of God.*" In their theory they placed the civil magistrate above the Synod in reference to the *mind of God.*

But as to the materiality of these differences among Protestants, and as to the statement of Dr. Spring in substance, that there is more uniformity among Protestants than among Catholics, the learned divine himself has saved me the labor of any further examination, by his own clear and distinct admissions. The learned divine conducted himself like Calvinistic ministers, who in the doctrinal portion of their sermon will often insist upon the stern tenets of predestination, election, and final perseverance; and yet, in the close of their discourse, when they come to the last exhortation, will generally urge their brethren to do their duty, and persevere in well-doing, as if they did not believe in the doctrines just taught. So Dr. Spring after having insisted, in one portion of his Dissertation, that Protestants were more united than Catholics, towards its close says:

> Nothing has given Rome so much the advantage as the disunion of Protestants. And nothing, under the favor of Almighty God, would be so ominous of her overthrow as their cordial union in the great truths of the Gospel, and the love of the Spirit.[57]

I confess I could not put the different positions of the learned author together. I could not understand how "Rome" could have "*so much the advantage*" in consequence of the "*disunion of Protestants*" in regard to "*the great truths of the Gospel,*" if it were true, as he alleged, that Rome was *still more divided* – that her "unity is a unity of the most jarring materials." There appeared to me to be something quite "*jarring*" in these different positions.

21. Reflections on theories of Protestant union

In connection with this subject, Dr. Spring assumed that

> the man who implicitly receives the Scriptures as the infallible rule of faith, cannot doubt whether any of his religious opinions are true.[58]

After all the confusion that has been thrown over this subject by loose and uncertain language, arising from confused thought, or from a desire to avoid a difficulty, nothing can, it occurs to me, be plainer than this; that the Protestant inquirer, under his rule, must be certain of *two* points before he can be certain that he is right:

1. He must be certain as to the *identity* of the code – he must know that the Bible is the written, and only, Word of God.

2. He must know that *he* has correctly construed it.

If he does not know *both* these points with certainty, he does not know his faith with certainty. How then can it be true, as asserted by Dr. Spring, "the man who implicitly receives the Scriptures as the infallible rule of faith, *cannot doubt whether any of his religious opinions are true?"* Does the learned divine mean to assert the proposition, that he who so implicitly receives the Scriptures cannot misconstrue them? Or does he mean to say, that while he does so misconstrue them, that the simple fact of his so receiving the Bible, will make him *certain* even while he is in the wrong? Or does he mean to take the clean, neat position, that, while all Protestants *profess* to receive implicitly the Scriptures as their infallible rule of faith, *they only so receive them who properly construe them?* And if so, does he mean then to say, that all Protestant sects but one, do not so receive them? Or does he mean to admit, that while numbers, or even the majority of each sect, so receive the Bible, and yet give it such discordant constructions, they cannot still doubt whether any of their religious opinions are true? In other words, that the simple *fact* of so receiving the Scriptures is, *in and of itself,* efficient to remove all doubt from the minds of all those holders of opinions so contradictory? As if the *fact* that twenty different lawyers all agreed as to the *identity* of the statutes, would make each one certain that his own construction of them was right, when different from that of each of the other nineteen.

But if the position were true, that such a reception of the Bible is efficient to produce such certain conviction, is it not clear that it does so without reason and against the truth? What sort of a rule is that which produces this fatal repose, while believing the most contradictory tenets and holding the most opposite opinions? "There is a way which seemeth to a man right, but the end thereof is death."

I cannot understand the proposition in any other sense. The language is plain, clear, and certain. If a man implicitly receives the Scriptures, he cannot doubt whether any of his religious opinions are true, whatever those opinions may be. This is but another struggle to find a substitute for the Catholic certainty. As the same learned divine had before said, "The human mind reluctantly rests short of certainty. Indeed, without this it does not rest at all," he was bound to propose some rule which would produce this certainty, or leave his readers in the dark.

When I first read the Dissertation of Dr. Spring upon the Rule of Faith, I was a Protestant. His statement that the human mind does not rest at all without certainty, I could not but admit as unequivocally true. But the rule he gave me to attain it gave rise to the most serious reflections. After examination and consideration, I became satisfied that his position was fatally erroneous in one of two particulars; namely: either it could not produce that certainty; or if it did, then this certainty was not founded upon reason or truth, but was a more temporary certainty, that might do to live upon, but would never do to die by.

While engaged in this examination, and during its progress, my reflections ran substantially in this way: "All Protestants profess to receive the Bible implicitly, as Dr. Spring. requires: and yet I have no doubt it is true, as he states, that "Great multitudes, who have been religiously educated, and more who have not been so, while they have a prevailing belief that the Scriptures are a divine revelation, have by no means the *conviction of certainty* on this great subject."

But while I must believe this, I am also compelled to believe that a large portion of the members of the various Protestant parties are sincere, and do implicitly receive the Scriptures, as the rule of Dr. Spring requires. And yet, while they do so receive it, they unequivocally disagree in its interpretation, and hold the most opposite doctrines.

Although Dr. Spring speaks of a remarkable uniformity in their views, where can this *remarkable* uniformity be found? He had, indeed, referred me to the early creeds, drawn up mostly within the first fifty years of the alleged Reformation, by *only two parties* of Protestants, Lutherans and Calvinists, and before they had divided into so great a number of sects as now exist; and even in these creeds the discrepancies were great and manifest, and were held *material* by the parties themselves, at the time the creeds were made. The Lutherans held the Sacramentarians as heretics, heathens, and publicans, and not as brethren of the same Church. And the Calvinists so held the Lutherans for many years, and then only permitted them to communion about the time the theory of an invisible Church was invented. And when I look into their creeds, these discordant views are held *as doctrines of Scripture;* and there is no marked distinction in each creed to show where the fundamental doctrines end, and the indifferent opinions begin.

If I consider all the points of difference between Protestants, or between the principal sects, as matters indifferent, and this contrary to their own creeds, how much will there be left of fundamental Christianity? For instance, can I say a man has free will, or that he has it not – or that he will certainly persevere because predestinated, or that he may fall – that Christ is really present in the Eucharist, or that He is not – that immersion alone is baptism, or that it is not – that infant baptism is valid, or that it is void – and so of every other difference, and yet all these views be held as *matters indifferent?* Can I say that Christ has made no revelation upon these points of difference? And if I say He has, by what sort of logic can I say His revelation is unimportant? *Why revealed, if not to be believed?* And how can a mere fallible interpreter mark the line that separates the revealed fundamental, from revealed, but immaterial, doctrines?

If, then, these various sects differ in fundamental doctrines, it is clear they cannot all be right. It is equally plain they cannot form parts of the true visible Church. She ever must be a unit, with the same faith, and the same government. And if, on the contrary, these sects agree in fundamentals as asserted, then why do they not unite? What excuse can be given for ruinous divisions, so much deplored by Dr. Spring himself, as well as other Protestants, when they only differ about *trifles?* Or is it in the wise and irrevocable purpose of the Great Redeemer, that division and discord should be written, in letters of living light, upon the front of every sect that has ever separated from that Church which holds the governing principle of authority, from the beginning of Christianity even to the present time?

Despite the statement of Dr. Spring, is it not palpable that, while Protestants have had great difficulty in implicitly receiving the Scriptures, they have had still greater difficulty in their construction, as the five hundred sects in Protestant Christendom do most abundantly show? Then under the Protestant fundamental rule, I must construe the bible for myself. God, according to the rule, has made my mind the only tribunal. If I trust to the opinions of others, and believe upon their authority, while my own mind does not itself understand the proof, then I violate the will of God, and become *subordinate* to an independent equal. I can, therefore, take nothing upon authority. I must examine., and be myself convinced in reference to each particular point, And who am I? I am a mere fallible man. My judgment and my opinion I cannot rely upon, any more than upon the judgment and opinion of any other man of the same sincerity, diligence, opportunity, and capacity. It is true, the *rule* itself compels me to rely upon myself; but so far as correctness and certainty of construction are concerned, my chance to be right would be just as great in following the judgment of another person. The fact that it is *my* opinion, ought not to give me any more assurance of its truth, than the fact that it is the opinion of another individual. Unless I deceive myself by self-love and personal vanity, this must be true. And if I should so deceive myself, would that deceive the great and just Judge? What have I to gain by self-delusion but my own ruin?

But I am not only thrown upon my own judgment by the Protestant *rule* itself, but by another overwhelming consideration. For if I adopt the creed of any one Protestant sect, (and I cannot adopt any two or more of them,) I find the overwhelming majority, even of Protestants, against me. And if I consult all the sects that have separated from the Church of Rome, from the days of Simon Magus to those of Luther, I find each and every one, without one solitary exception, against me. And when I go to the Catholic Church, I find the overwhelming majority of all professed Christians, saints, and martyrs, of every age in her exclusive communion – and they too are all against me.

I am, then, invincibly thrown back upon my own individual fallible judgment; for if I rely upon authority at all, under the Protestant rule, which admits of no infallibility, then I must take the voice of the majority, and I cannot, upon any principle of common sense, prefer the authority of one, to that of ten persons, all equals. I must stand unsupported, "solitary and alone." When I heretofore looked into the Bible, my construction satisfied me that Mr. Campbell was right. I was always told it was a plain book, easily understood. But after all I often thought I could see some things hard to be understood, and yet that must be understood. And whether other Protestants find these hard things to understand or not, the fact is palpable, that they are always explaining and re-explaining this plain Bible; and what is still more surprising, they can never explain it alike. They seem to explain the meaning quite away. And the more loudly and the more unanimously all Protestants continue to assert that the Bible is a very plain book, and easily understood, the more utterly at a loss I am to understand why it is they differ so much about so plain a matter as the construction of so plain a book. There must be some deep, fundamental, and efficient reason for this. There is a great and radical wrong somewhere. Is it because Protestants are too learned? Or is it because they study the Bible too much?

It is indeed true, that all Protestant writers I have ever read, charge the Catholic Church with holding a very erroneous maxim upon this subject – Dr. Spring, Mr. Campbell, and others. The former of whom says: "Never was there a more palpable error than the maxim of the Roman Church, that 'ignorance is the mother of devotion.'"[59] But if I understand the language of Dr. Spring he does attempt to show that the maxim is, in fact, true, as regards Protestants; for he says:

> Men of common honesty and common discernment cannot fail to understand the great and fundamental truths God has revealed. They do understand them, and quite as well as the more learned and philosophizing.

By this I understand the Dr. to put the two classes upon an equality. But when he comes to speak of the trial of the faith of men, in which so many are wrecked for eternity, he says:

> Most men, at one period of life or another and especially educated men, pass through this fiery ordeal, &c. …
>
> A trial in which the faith and hopes of so many are consumed…."[60]

And by this is I understand him to mean distinctly, that *educated men, especially,* are more exposed to this severe trial, and more of them are lost, in proportion to numbers than among those of "common honesty and discernment." And is not this giving the advantage, in point of *fact*, to the uneducated, and saying, in substance, "ignorance is the mother of devotion" among Protestants?

Also Mr. Campbell, speaking of that passage, "there are some things hard to be understood," says:

> Philosophers, as they love to be called, are generally the most unteachable, and the greatest wresters and perverters of the Scripture. Peter had those too wise to learn in his eye, when he speaks of wresting the Scriptures; and not the simple, honest, and unassuming laity."[61]

Now if I understand Mr. Campbell he does say that, in point of *fact*, there is more religious error among the learned than among the "simple, honest, and unassuming laity." And is not this making "ignorance the mother of devotion" among Protestants?[62]

But I find this charge denied by Catholic writers. And, indeed, I cannot see how it can be found in the Catholic theory. That system assumes to put them all upon an equality. It has the same tribunal to construe for all; and it equally requires implicit submission from all. The poor and the rich, the high and the low, the learned and the unlearned, are each and all *elevated* to the same sublime faith – the same exact construction of the law. There is *practical* justice, beauty, reason, and logic in this theory:

"All states can reach it, and all heads conceive."

I am but a man. I am no wiser or better than others. I cannot reasonably have any more confidence in my individual judgment and construction of the Scriptures, than I can in those of any other man of equal capacity, sincerity, and means of information. Certainly I must have, or I cannot rest. Where then can I find it?

"Plant of celestial seed—if dropt below,
Say in what 'blessed' soil then deign'st to grow."

Shall I be compelled to seek elsewhere than in any Protestant communion for that consistency, system, and unity, that did unquestionably dwell in the Church of Old? Must I be driven, at last, into the alleged "Man of Sin" – the "Great Apostasy – the *best-abused* Church in the world? That Church against which charges enough, and grievous, are made, if true, to sink a universe? The alleged false – the base – the corrupt – the venal – the cruel – the apostate Church? The oldest, and yet the most unpopular – the most hated – the most suspected – the most despised – of all the Churches of Christendom? Is it possible that I must go there to find that faith, and that certainty, that will satisfy a hungry, but honest soul? How can I endure the thought of confessing my sins to a mere man? My pride says I cannot, but grace whispers, "you *can*, if truth requires you." And so I will, if it is right. I resolve to follow truth, wherever it may lead me. There's reason and sense in truth. There's logic and honesty in it. There is certainty, and there is consistency in it. Let me only know it. If it can be found in the Old Church, I go there. The consequences I will take. If such a step subjects me to censure, I will bear it. I would rather suffer in this world than in the next. It may subject me to many evils for a long time,

"if long in life can be."

But what of that? Unlimited space is wider than the world, and eternity longer than life. Heaven, and all that Heaven means, are worth a struggle – a sublime and manly struggle. Was Christianity ever designed to be popular with the mass of evil in this world? Does it indulge men's passions? Does it pamper pride? Does it flatter men in any way? He who wins Heaven, must struggle. He must be prepared to resist the onset of earth. He must expect its dire opposition. *He must fight.*

But are those manifold charges against the Old Church true? If so, she has been a hoary-headed sinner for many a long and weary century. Who can then estimate the evil she has done? False and apostate from her early faith – recreant to the heavenly trust of her Lord – she has filled the world with error and misery. If this be true, she ought to be despised.

But it may be that these charges are untrue. Her faith, after all this mighty mass of acrimonious and passionate accusation, may be the pure and holy faith once delivered to the saints. She has always, and at all times, and in all places, for more than fifteen hundred years, as conceded by many of her enemies *claimed* it to be true. It may be that her very firmness in resisting all ambitious novelties, has brought upon her the unceasing opposition of all sectaries, in every age and clime, of whatever tenets and character. Her very consistency, her beauty, and invincible courage, may have brought against her all the malice and ridicule of all infidels, past or present. Who knows? If we concede that she is the true Church, for the sake of the argument only, (and she may be such, as the thing is *possible*,) then would not the bitter and relentless opposition of all the proud, the vain, the ambitious, be leveled against her? Would not every demagogue in religion – every wild enthusiast – every man of a cold, suspicious disposition – every self-willed individual, be against her? Did not our Lord say, Woe unto you when all men speak well of you: for so did their fathers of the false prophets?

There is something remarkable in the history of this venerable Old Church, even as stated by her enemies. Mr. Campbell says she "is older than any other sect now existing." *She is older!* Her continued existence for so long a period, under this alleged accumulation of errors, is one of the most remarkable circumstances in the world's history. And the more errors are charged upon her, and the more bitterness there is displayed in attempting to sustain these allegations, the more difficult it is to account for this most remarkable moral phenomenon. If, indeed, she be the true Church, then her unfailing existence is easily accounted for; because the promises of that poor, despised Nazarene never yet did fail. And slander never did make a modest charge—malice always lays it on thicker and thicker—and hatred forever overshoots the mark. And it seems as if

God, in His infinite wisdom and mercy, has given the true Church this protection.

I will, then, look into these charges calmly and dispassionately. I will endeavor to make a fair and just allowance for individual human frailty. I will judge the past by the circumstances existing in the past. I will try to place myself back in the olden time. I will interrogate the distant ages gone by. I will commune with the venerable departed. I will judge them by that charity wherewith I wish to be judged. At least, so far as my poor abilities will allow. I will then make up my mind, and upon that conviction I will act. I will not halt between two opinions. My face is set for the truth, and when I find it, I mean to follow it.

---

[1] Simon Greenleaf, Examination of the Testimony of the four Evangelists by the rules of Evidence as Administered in the Courts of Justice, with an Account of the Trial of Jesus. p. 517

[2] In considering this question, I was referred by Dr. Spring to the works of Bossuet, speaking of which the Doctor says: "The celebrated Bossuet, in his history of the variations of the Protestant churches, (speaking of which, Hallam, in his History of Literature, says 'there is nothing perhaps in polemical eloquence so splendid,') undertakes, with great research, to show, that the difference in religious opinions in Protestant churches, is a natural and necessary result of abjuring the supremacy of Rome." (Gardiner Spring A Dissertation on the Rule of Faith. p. 58.)

In a note to page 14, the learned divine says: "For the best argument I have seen in favor of the views of Romanists, the reader may be referred to the controversial writings of that very learned and eloquent writer, Bossuet"

As I read the Dissertation of Dr. Spring, among other Protestant works, when I was inquiring into the truth of the Catholic rule, and being referred to the works of Bossuet, I read them in the course of my examination, and they certainly merited all the encomiums bestowed upon them. They are distinguished alike for candor and fairness.

[3] The Hon. Alex. H. Stephens of Georgia, in a speech delivered in the House of Representatives, February 12, 1859, in reference to the admission of Oregon into the Union, said:

"When I was going to address the people at a particular place, meeting a gentleman on the way, I asked him if he was going to the court-house? He said, 'No; that I was going to speak, and that he only wanted to know what side I was upon to be against it.' I said, 'That is the reason you are always in the minority; you give me choice of sides upon all questions, and of course I take the best.'"

So it was with the Old Church. She had choice of sides, and of course took the true one, leaving Luther the false.

[4] Jacques-Benigne Bousset, Variations of the Protestant Churches. B. 1, n. 26.

[5] It seems never to have occurred to Luther and his disciples, that his success and the number of his followers, could constitute no proof of his being sent of God, for the reason, that Saint Paul had expressly foretold the same result should follow the heretics and seducers mentioned by him. "And their word will eat as doth a canker." (2 Tim. 51:13.) "But they shall proceed no farther, for their folly shall be manifest unto all men." (2 Tim. 3:9.)

[6] Jacques-Benigne Bousset, op. cit. App. To Book xiv., sec. 2.

[7] Jacques-Benigne Bousset, op. cit. B. i., sec. 8,9,18. B. ii., sec. 17

[8] The question regarding the merit of good works under the law of Christ, has been, perhaps, perplexed by not observing the true character of the question, and not keeping it distinctly in view.

The rewards and punishments bestowed and inflicted upon free agents must always depend upon the law by which these free agents are governed. As judged by one system of law, a particular act may be a crime, while, as judged by another code, the same act may be innocent. When we judge an act, we must always keep in view the particular law by which we would estimate its merits or demerits. The law, in its finished state, and just as it is, must always decide the question. Whatever may have been the motives or reasons which prompted the lawgiver to enact the law, whether in the view of abstract reason they may be thought sufficient or not, it is still the law, if passed by competent authority, and must decide the question, whether a particular act, or class of acts, be either commanded or prohibited. The motives and reasons leading to the enactment of the law, may be well inquired into, when questions of construction are considered; but the intention of the lawmaker, being once ascertained, must govern.

When we consider the disproportion that exists between the reward of heaven and the little we can do, we must at once admit, that we could never merit so much, so long as we are judged by the law of abstract justice; which law results from the relation we bear to God and the universe the natural relation and fitness of things. But when we are judged by that system of mercy established by Christ, we can merit.

The free grace of our Lord was shown in the adoption of a system, by which acts are considered as meritorious, that would not be so when judged by the system of abstract justice. This merciful system, which considers that as merit which, in itself, could not be such in the contemplation of any other system, was the result of the voluntary action of Christ. The origin and completion of the system, rest entirely with Him. It cost Him humiliation and death. We had no right to ask it.

We did nothing to advance it. But voluntary as the system was, and unmerited on our part, when it was once established, it became a matter of covenant, and a matter of law. More correctly speaking, it was a voluntary, but irrevocable, promise. It was a promise actually made, without any consideration moving from us. But as a sealed instrument in the law, from the solemn nature of the act, imports a consideration, and, therefore, the question of consideration cannot be inquired into; so, the voluntary promise of Christ is irrevocable, having been sealed with His own blood. This voluntary promise, owing to the character of Him who made it, has all the stability and binding force of an irrevocable covenant.

Making the promise was, therefore, all free grace; fulfilling it, only carrying out a pre-existing engagement. The free grace was displayed in perfecting the system. Whence it follows that everyone owes our Lord gratitude -- whether he avail himself of the rewards of the system or not. Christ has still died for him—has still paid his debt, and has promised to reward him according to his faith and works.

It is clear, that man has no cause to glory in what he does, although it is considered merit, when judged by a system founded on free grace. For when a man glories in the merits of his own acts, he can only properly do so, when they are meritorious, as judged by the law of abstract justice. In the eye of this code, he can do no act to merit heaven, or the forgiveness of his sins. All he can say is, that Christ has so loved him that He has pledged himself, in advance, to call that merit which is not meritorious of itself. So that the original source of all what we can merit, is the blood of Christ. And in the eye of abstract justice, when Christ rewards us for our acts, He but crown His own gifts; for the very merit He rewards is His own, though the act, to which the merit is attached by Him, is ours. Therefore, in the contemplation of this abstract justice, the act is voluntarily ours -- the merit is voluntarily Christ's. But in the contemplation of the system purchased with His blood, both the act and merit are ours.

[9] Ockley's History of the Saracens.

[10] Cited in Jacques-Benigne Bousset, Variations of the Protestant Churches. B. xi., n. 119

[11] Heinrich Henke, Allgemeine Geschichte, der christlichen Kirchenach der Zeitfolge. Th. Iii. 276-9. Cited in Bible Question Fairly Stated.

[12] Cited Milner's End of Controversy. L. vii.

[13] Schrieben an Prof. Hohn, s. 54.

[14] Karl Rienhold, Uber die Kantische Philosophie, s.197.

[15] August Friedrich Gforer, Kristische Geschichte des Urchristenthums, Bd. I. Prf. P. 15-17.

[16] Philipp Marheineke, Institutiones Symbolica. p. 705-6.

[17] Jacques-Benigne Bousset, op. cit. B. iii., s, 1-6,

[18] Ibid. .B.x., n. r. The authority of Waddington, the Protestant historian sustains this statement of Bossuet.

"In our journey back towards the apostolic times," says Waddington, "these separatists conduct us as far as the beginning of the twelfth century; but when we would advance farther, we are interrupted by a broad region of darkness and uncertainty. A spark of hope is indeed suggested by the history of the Vaudois. Their origin is not ascertained by any authentic record, and being immemorial, it may have been coeval with the introduction of Christianity.

But since there is not one direct proof of their existence during that long space; since they have never been certainly discovered by the curiosity of any writer, nor detected by the inquisitorial eye of any orthodox bishop, nor named by any Pope, or council, or any church record, chronicle, or memorial we are not justified in attaching any historical credit to their more unsupported tradition. It is sufficient to prove that they had an earlier existence than the twelfth century; but that they had been perpetuated through eight of nine centuries, un-commemorated abroad, and without any national monument to attest their existence, is much more than we can venture, on such evidence, to assert. Here, then, the golden chain of our apostolic descent disappears; and though it may exist, buried in the darkness of those previous ages, and though some writers have seemed to discern a few detached links which they diligently exhibited, there is still much wanting to complete the continuity." (Page 554 of the History of the Church, from the earliest ages, by Rev. Geo. Waddington, A. M., Fellow of Trinity College, Cambridge, and Prebendary of Ferring, in the Cathedral Church of Chichester: New York edition, 1835. Cited by Bishop Purcell, in Campbell and Purcell's Debate, at Cincinnati, 1837, p. 24, 25.)

From this extract it appears that the most that Protestants can say in reference to the links necessary to complete their alleged chain of succession is, that they "may exist buried in the darkness of those previous ages." When we have so many Christian writers from the third to the sixth age, and yet no mention is made of this sect, all we can certainly say is, that there is a bare possibility of the continued existence of such a sect.

[19] Ibid. B. xi., where the subject is very fully treated.

[20] Jacques-Benigne Bousset, op. cit. xi. 170-4.

[21] Ibid. 179.

[22] Ibid. 176.

[23] Ibid. B. xi. 176.

[24] A. Campbell and J. Purcell, A debate on the Roman Catholic religion. 38, 39, 40, 41.

[25] Ibid. p. 65.

[26] Ibid. p. 30.

[27] Ibid. p. 77.

[28] Ibid. p. 66.

[29] Ibid. p. 75.

[30] Ibid. p. 76.)

[31] A. Campbell and J. Purcell, op. cit. 30 67.68.

[32] George Waddington, op. cit. p. 154.

[33] p. 554, 555. Cited A. Campbell and J. Purcell, A debate on the Roman Catholic religion. 80.

[34] Johann Mosheim, Instutiones Historiae. Vol. I., p. 328.

[35] Ibid p. 332.

[36] Ibid. p. 333.

[37] Ibid p.428.

[38] p. 333. Cited A. Campbell and J. Purcell, A debate on the Roman Catholic religion. 80, 81.

[39] A. Campbell and J. Purcell, A debate on the Roman Catholic religion. p. 66.

[40] Ibid. p. 67.

[41] Ibid. p. 40.

[42] John Hughes, Hughes - Breckenridge controversy. p. 254.

[43] Ibid p. 278.

[44] Ibid. p. 288.

[45] P. 417.

[46] William Blackstone B. 4, c. 8, p. 105.

[47] p. 215-25.

[48] John Hughes. op cit. 446..

[49] A. Campbell and N Rice, Campbell Rice Debate on the Holy Spirit p. 761.

[50] Ibid.p. 842.

[51] A. Campbell and J. Purcell, A debate on the Roman Catholic religion. 175. Note. The Jansenists were not an order in the Church, but the teachers of certain errors of doctrine.

[52] Gardiner Spring A Dissertation on the Rule of Faith p. 60, 63.

[53] Chap. xxx., art. ii.

[54] Chap. xx., sec. 3.

[55] Boswell states that he himself asserted that the Presbyterian "Confession of Faith and the thirty-nine articles contained the same points, even the doctrine of predestination." To which Dr. Johnson replied: "Why, yes, sir; predestination was a part of the clamor of the times, so it is mentioned in our articles, but with as little positiveness as could be." (Boswell's Life of Johnson.)

[56] See Milner's End of Controversy., Let. ix.

[57] Gardiner Spring. op cit. p. 100.

[58] Ibid. p. 59.

[59] Ibid. p. 66.

[60] Ibid. p. 37, 57.

[61] A. Campbell and J. Purcell. op. cit. p. 266.

[62] That I was right in my construction of Mr. Campbell's language appears clear from a passage in his debate with Mr. Rice, page 905.

"This land is full of infidelity. Your schools, your colleges, are full of skepticism. The great majority of your educated men are infidels."

Now Mr. Campbell does distinctly state, as a matter of fact, that Skepticism and Infidelity are mostly found in the institutions of learning, and among educated men, while Christianity is best understood by the "simple, honest, and unassuming laity."

CHAPTER V

TRANSUBSTANTIATION

1.The discourse of our Lord concerning the Eucharist

The Catholic doctrine of the Real Presence and the Protestant doctrine of the real *absence* of the body of Christ in the Lord's Supper are as much opposed to each other as any two precise opposites can possibly be imagined. There can be no medium between the two – no possible middle ground. Christ is either present or absent. If present, the Catholic is right – if absent, then the Protestant is right.

If the Catholic doctrine is true, it is a tender, sublime, and awful dogma – if false, a monstrous invention – a pure fabrication. If not in the Church originally, and not among the doctrines once delivered, it must have been introduced as a whole, and not in piecemeal. There could from the very nature and reason of the thing, have been no middle doctrine – no shades of opinion, gradually preparing the minds of Christians for the reception of this great perversion of the true faith. It was one bold leap from the well-understood and generally received doctrine of the *real absence*, to that opposite, so hard to flesh and blood, the *Real Presence*.

The first portion of Scripture relied upon by the Catholic, is found in that wonderful chapter, the sixth of Saint John. The first twenty-five verses are taken up in giving a history of the stupendous miracle of Christ in feeding the multitude, and His subsequent occupations until the next day. On the second day, the crowd again came around Him, and His discourse to them commences at the twenty-sixth verse, and extends to the close of this long chapter.

It was the practice with our Lord and his apostles to suit their discourses to the circumstances in which they were placed.[1] The Jews had witnessed the miracle of feeding the five thousand; and if our Lord ever intended to promise to give His body and blood to His followers, there is no time mentioned in the history of His labors more appropriate than the one mentioned in this chapter.

In reference to the sense of this chapter, most Protestants insist that it relates to faith in Christ. Several distinguished writers though, as

Calixtus, Hackspan, and Groenenburg, not of England, and Dr. Jeremy Taylor and Dr. Sherlock, of England, concede that the larger portion relates to the Eucharist, though they deny the literal sense.

Catholic writers contend that about the forty eight verse the Savior passes to another topic, by a very easy and natural transition. Dr. Wiseman has given very conclusive reasons to prove that the transition commences at the forty eight verse. For myself, it seems to be true, that the transition not only takes place at that verse, but that both the main subjects of the discourse are clearly alluded to in verse twenty-seven.

The multitude who had been fed, declared, "this is of a truth the prophet that is to come into the world;" and such was their admiration of our Lord, that they would have taken Him by force, and made Him a King.[2] They seem to have believed in him as one eminently competent to be a temporal sovereign. Since the kingdom of the second Moses, the Messiah, was to be a temporal kingdom, it would be one of the vocations of Christ to furnish them with food. They sought Him not because they saw the miracles but to furnish them with food.[3] The Jews had a tradition among them that the Messiah, among other points of resemblance to Moses, would like him, bring down manna from heaven. The Mildrasch Coheleth, or exposition of Ecclesiastes, thus expresses it:

> Rabbi Berechiah said, in the name of Rabbi Isaac, as the first *Goel* (deliverer), so shall the second be. The first *Goel* brought down manna, as it is written, "I will cause bread to reign upon you from the heaven." So, likewise, will the later *Goel* cause manna to descend.[4]

The existence of this tradition and its belief among the Jews is shown from the facts historically stated in this chapter of Saint John's gospel. They first followed Him into the desert, "because they saw the miracles which he did on them that were diseased." Secondly although they had witnessed these miracles on them that were diseased, they never once thought of making Christ a King until after the miracles of the loaves and fishes. Upon witnessing this peculiar miracle, they seem at once to have considered Him as sent of God as a temporal Sovereign, a part of whose vocation would be to supply His people with food, as God had done through the ministry of Moses in the wilderness. All the circumstances taken in connection with the miracle they saw, were doubtless the reasons that induced them to seek to make him a king, and to take shipping and to follow him to Capernaum. It was not the expectation of obtaining another meal, as some Protestant writers have supposed. Such a motive would seem wholly inadequate to produce such a result, and such a position is inconsistent with the fact that they so ardently desired to make Him a king.

Tradition is the reason why the Jews referred to the manna in the thirty first verse. They ask Christ for a proof of His commission, and then, without the slightest seeming reason, they refer to the manna in the desert. What connection this matter could have with the question they asked could not well be seen without a knowledge of the existence of this tradition. The Jews under the influence of this opinion, and, no doubt, still desiring to make Christ a King, that they might be fed by His power and bounty, pursued Him the next day. Adapting His discourse to the state of their opinions it seemed that our Lord had two main points to propound:

1. That He was the Son of God in whom they must believe.[5]

2. That it was no part of His mission to give them perishable food but the imperishable food of his own body and blood.

Both these points are stated in one verse and in one sentence.[6]

It was natural and appropriate that our Lord should first inform the Jews that He understood their views and motives, and that these were erroneous, before propounding His own doctrines. After telling them that they sought him, not because they had witnessed the miracles, but because they had eaten of the loaves and fishes, He very naturally, at this place, warns them not to labor for that meat which they so much regarded, but for that imperishable meat that He would give them. He then confirms His power to fulfill His promise with that emphatic expression, "for him hath God the Father sealed."

The first point to be discussed (though secondly stated) was the proposition that He was the Son of God, and commissioned by Him; and that, as such, they were to believe in him. When He gave them sufficient evidence of His true character, they were bound by the plainest principles of right reason to believe Him upon His authority alone. They were bound to receive every doctrine propounded by him, however hard the saying might be. The only proper inquiry the Jews could make was that which they made in verse thirty. That being answered and proved by what they had seen and heard before and at that time, they were bound to believe, without doubt, all that he might require them to believe. If He was the Christ, then He was legitimately entitled to unlimited confidence. And when He performed the miracles before their eyes, He conclusively established His character and veracity, and, therefore, His account of Himself they must receive as infallibly true.

Our Lord, in verse twenty-seven, does not define what he meant by meat that should endure to eternal life, except simply to state its quality in contrast with perishable food.[7] He does not state it in terms calculated to arouse prejudice in the beginning of His discourse, and thus close the ears of his hearers against His doctrines. He does not then say in what it shall consist. He merely states the heads of His discourse in such a way as to create no prejudice, and yet shows what two main points would come under discussion. The reader will observe that in verse twenty-seven, our Lord promised that He will give this imperishable meat, and that in verses fifty-one and fifty-five, He says He will give His flesh, and that His flesh is meat indeed. In both cases He speaks of a future gift, which He Himself will give, showing that the same thing is alluded to in all these verses.

It must be conceded that the doctrine of the Real Presence is a hard and revolting doctrine to flesh and blood, and especially so to the Jews, as we shall see. It was then proper in itself that Christ should select an occasion when some miracle, or other great event, would form the proper introduction to this unpleasant topic. And not only so, but on an occasion when the Jews were well disposed towards him. On this occasion all these circumstances concurred. The Jews, in multitudes, had fed upon the miraculous food created by the Son of Man. They had hailed Him the day before as a Prophet. In their enthusiasm they had sought to make Him a King by force; and they followed Him beyond the sea, and sought Him until they found Him. The respectful manner in which they addressed Him, shows the state of their feelings towards Him. It is true, they entertained erroneous views and opinions in reference to the object of their admiration, but that was the very time to correct these errors of opinion. In justice to them, it was the opportune moment. If they could not hear that hard saying at this time, they never could hear it. No wonder then that those disciples who could not hear that doctrine on this occasion "walked no more" with their deserted Lord.

As I take it, our Lord proceeds from the twenty-ninth to the forty-seventh verses inclusive, to teach the great doctrine that He is the Son of the Father, and the general necessity of faith in Him, as such. In answer to the allusion made by the Jews to the manna, and after having previously told them, in verse twenty-nine, that the work of God was to believe on Him whom he hath sent, He tells them that His Father giveth them the true bread from Heaven. He then proceeds to define the meaning in which He there used the word bread, by saying, "For the bread of God is He which cometh down from heaven… I am the bread of Life."[8] The Jews understood Him correctly, for they did not inquire "how can this man be bread?" but they, did say, "How is it, then, that he saith, I come down from heaven?"[9] They disbelieved the assumed fact that He came down from heaven, but they did not misunderstand the sense of His words.

It will be seen that there are several marked differences in the language of that part of Our Lord's discourse, from the twenty-ninth to the forty-seventh verses inclusive, and that from verses forty-eight to fifty-eight inclusive. These peculiarities are such as to show a change of topic.

Our Savior, after having explicitly defined the word bread as figurative of Himself, proceeds to speak exclusively of faith in the next fourteen verses; and it is very remarkable that in this part of His discourse, he carefully avoids the use of the phrase eating Him, and does not even use the expression to eat the bread of life. This care in avoiding any reference to eating Him shows how clearly our Lord kept within the limits of the first topic. From the moment that He begins to use literal terms He proceeds to speak of His doctrine under the phrases "cometh to me," "believeth in me," (which mean the name thing,) until verse forty-seven, which is a complete summing up of that part of His discourse.

But His language after this is very different, for He not only speaks of eating this bread, but of eating His flesh. It was not unusual with our Lord to repeat the same thing a number of times in succession, and after each repetition, to introduce new matter.[10]

In the chapter under consideration, He says, "I am the bread of life," in verse thirty-five and then proceeds to speak of faith in Him as the Son of God. Having summed up in verse forty-seven, He says again, "I am the bread of life" in verse forty-eight. He then proceeds to state the want of a living principle in manna in verse forty-nine, and then puts in strong contrast with it the bread of life in verse fifty.[11] And He repeats again in verse fifty-one, in language more emphatic "I am the living bread," and proceeds to introduce new matter in these words: "And the bread that I will give is my flesh, which I will give for the life of the world."

Our Lord, previous to verse fifty-one, had asserted that He was the bread of Life – that He came down from Heaven – that a man may eat of that bread and not die. All these propositions are repeated in verse fifty-one, preparatory to the definition He was about to give of the new sense in which He used the word bread, as figurative of His real flesh. In verse thirty-two He speaks of the quality of the bread, calling it the "true bread," and then defines what it is by saying: "For the bread of God is He which cometh down from Heaven." So here he speaks of the quality of the bread in verses fifty and fifty-one, and then defines what it is in language of very similar form,

1. "For the bread of God is he which cometh down from heaven."

2. "And the bread that I will give is my flesh."

Now the word bread, in both these extracts, is used in a figurative sense, but not in the same figurative sense. There are two separate and distinct definitions given – the first, of Christ as a Lawgiver or teacher, and the second, of His real flesh. These two definitions would be idle, if they meant the same thing. And if these definitions give us different meanings, it is clear that when the second one was given, there was a change of topic.

It will also be observed, that in the first definition, the pronoun "he," the nominative after the verb "to be," is not a figurative, but a literal expression; so, the nominative *flesh*, in the second, is not figurative but literal. Our Lord could not be supposed to use the same figurative word to represent Himself literally in one portion of His discourse, and in another part of the same discourse, to represent His flesh figuratively – thus not only using the same word under similarly constructed sentences in a different sense, but using a figurative expression to represent a figurative substance. It would seem perfectly clear, that the word flesh was used by our Lord literally.

If a speaker use words in any known sense, he is not bound to define the sense in which he uses them, unless there be some special circumstances requiring it. If, on the contrary, he uses known terms in unknown senses, he is compelled, by every consideration of justice to himself and his hearers, to define the new sense in which he uses the same. Our Lord seems to have acted upon this just rule. Although it was common among the Jews to use the words bread or food for wisdom or doctrines, it was not so common to use these words for a lawgiver or a teacher of doctrines. Our Savior was, therefore, careful to show the exact sense in which He used the word, in the two different figurative senses stated.

2 The literal and metaphorical meanings considered

It will also be observed that in the first portion of our Lord's discourse, while speaking of Himself under the image of bread, he represents this as given by the Father; but after verse forty-seven, He speaks of the food now described, as being given by Himself. This marked difference in the giver, shows a difference in the gift. There could be no ground for this difference, if faith only is intended; but if there be a transition to a real eating, the whole is clear. While we contemplate Christ as the object of our faith, and as the Sent of God to redeem the world, he is justly said to be given by His Father. "God so loved the world…" But when we view Him as giving us His own flesh to eat, it is more correctly said to be by His own love for us.

There is another difference between the language of the two portions, of our Lord's discourse, still more marked and explicit. That the same words, by usage, may have both a literal and figurative meaning, must be conceded. That the meaning of a speaker must be determined by the usage existing at the time, and not by that existing afterwards, must also be clear. It must also be conceded that it is the duty of every honest speaker who uses words or phrases having a known signification in a new and unknown sense, to define this new sense,

If, therefore, the phrase, to "eat the flesh" of any one, had any fixed figurative as well as literal meaning, at the time it was used by Christ, then the Jews and disciples could only understand this expression in one or the other of those established meanings. They could have no right to understand them in a new or unknown sense, unless Christ had given an express definition, as He did of the word bread, or unless the context was so clear as to leave no doubt. What right had they to put an unknown sense upon a known phrase, with fixed meanings? If hearers could put such a construction upon the language of a speaker, there would be no bounds to this licentious privilege. Once beyond the control of the only rules governing the sense of words and phrases, they are at sea without chart or compass.

If the phrase, to "eat the flesh" of anyone, had an established metaphorical sense besides its literal sense, then how must the Jews have understood it? If it had more than one metaphorical meaning, how must they have understood it? In the first case, they could only understand it either in its literal sense, or in the only metaphorical sense known to the language. In the second, they could only understand it in its literal sense, or in one of its metaphorical senses.

Now what was the metaphorical meaning of the expression? In all cases when used metaphorically, it meant to do a person some grievous injury, principally, by slander or false accusation. The following are examples of its figurative meaning in Scripture:

1. “When the wicked, even mine enemies and my foes, came upon me to eat up my flesh.”[12]

2. "Why do you like God, pursue me? Why are you not satisfied. with (eating) my flesh?”[13]

3. “who eat the flesh of my people”[14] '

4. “The fool folds his hands, and eats his own flesh.” [15]

I am not aware of any other passages in the Old Testament where this expression is used in a figurative sense. In all the above cases, the idea of inflicting upon the person a grievous injury is clearly conveyed.

The following examples are found in the New Testament:

1. “and will eat your flesh like fire.” [16]

2. “But if you bite and devour one another.” [17]

Regarding the meaning of this phrase among the Arabs, and in the language that our Lord spoke, Dr. Wiseman, in his lectures on the Eucharist has shown conclusively, that it has only the same figurative meaning.[18]

The differences between the language of the two portions of our Lord's discourse, are marked and clear. We are forced to concede, not only a change of topic, but we are forced to take the expression, “eat the flesh of the Son of Man” in its literal sense, or we must take it in the metaphorical sense of calumniating our Lord.

The reason upon which this usage among so many nations is founded, would seem to be plain. The metaphorical sense of a term always comes after the literal; and, for that reason, will participate of its character. If the literal sense conveys a harsh meaning, the figurative will do the same. If one knows the literal meaning of a term, he can almost at once fix upon its metaphorical sense. To literally eat the flesh of a person is naturally a revolting idea. Therefore, when such an expression is used metaphorically, it conveys the same harsh meaning. For this reason, we find no examples, even among classical writers, where a person is figuratively said to eat the flesh of another, except those which convey the harsh idea of the literal sense.[19]

If we take the expression, to eat the flesh of Christ, in the only figurative sense known at the time, and say that such was His meaning, His words reduced to literal language would stand about thus: "Except ye do some grievous injury to the Son of Man, ye have no life in you." This interpretation must at once be rejected; and this being true, we are forced to take the expression in its literal sense, or in some new and unknown, and undefined figurative sense. And what right have we to do the latter?

But there is another consideration of very great importance. Our Lord certainly intended to be understood, otherwise he would have been making an idle display of words. He was putting forth an important doctrine, which He could not mitigate or soften, however repugnant to human pride or prejudice. He could not but state the truth and whether the truth was accepted or not, His practice was always to state it. "If I shall say I know him not, I shall be like you, a liar."[20]

While therefore, our Lord would never soften His doctrines, he would hardly resort to repulsive figures of speech to inculcate pleasing doctrines. Faith in the death of Christ is one of the most cheering doctrines of Christianity; and to inculcate this doctrine would our Lord say, "Except ye eat the flesh of the Son of Man and drink His blood, ye have no life in you," thus resorting to a revolting figure of speech without the slightest necessity?

There are certainly some mutual rights existing between a speaker and his hearers. The object of every just speaker is to elucidate, not to confuse his subject – to enlighten, not to insult his audience. He will necessarily be led by this consideration, to adapt his mode of instruction to the capacity and feelings of his hearers. This was the uniform practice of Saint Paul, who was "all things to all men" and of Saint Peter when he said, "I know, brethren, that you did it through ignorance, as did also your rulers." This was also the course of our Lord Himself.

The question then arises, were the ideas of eating human flesh and drinking blood revolting to the Jews? If they were so, then we cannot suppose our Savior to resort to them as images of cheering doctrines; nor can we suppose He used these expressions at all, unless the doctrine He inculcated necessarily compelled Him to use them for the purpose of propounding the exact truth itself. If the literal sense given by the Jews was correct, then the use of these expressions was clearly necessary. And to show that these expression were revolting to the Jews, I need only to refer to the texts cited below.[21]

It was doubtless this revolting idea that the Jews had of eating human flesh and drinking blood that induced many of the disciples to "walk no more" with our Lord, and to disbelieve the doctrine he taught. They considered it not only impossible, but contrary to the law of Moses. The law of Moses having been given by God, and they not understanding its temporary character, and looking upon the literal doctrine of our Lord as conflicting with the law of Moses, they at once rejected it.

It may be said that our Lord did, on other occasions, clothe His ideas in images almost, if not quite, as offensive to his hearers. For example, he represents the necessity of patient suffering under the harsh image of carrying the cross. But this case is not in point for two reasons:

1. The death of the cross, though disgraceful, was often inflicted upon the innocent; while eating flesh and drinking blood was wicked in itself; and to select such an example to inculcate a doctrine was very different from referring to an example simply disgraceful.

2. The doctrine of mortification is necessarily harsh in itself, requiring a harsh figure to represent it truly.

The figure of carrying the cross selected by our Lord was fit and appropriate, and had the advantage of His own example. But the figure of eating flesh and drinking blood to illustrate a pleasing doctrine has no parallel anywhere in Scripture.

3. How did the hearers of our Lord understand Him?

The preceding remarks relate to the sense in which the hearers of our Lord must have understood Him, according to the then existing usage. It is now proper to inquire in what sense they did, in fact, understand Him.

The construction put upon the language of a speaker by those who hear him is at least *prima facie* evidence of his true meaning. This presumption becomes almost conclusive, when the speaker is aware of the construction placed upon his language, and does not object to it; and it becomes entirely conclusive, when the speaker by his acts or words, confirms the interpretation of his hearers.

It is true, that in regard to a point of no importance, a speaker may well let his audience remain in error, as that error would, in no material respect, influence their determination. But if the error be material, it is the clear duty of the speaker to explain except in special cases, as where a future event will give the hearers the true interpretation. In the case under consideration, the error was most material.

That the hearers of Christ understood Him in the literal sense is scarcely denied by any writer. When our Lord said, "And the bread that I will give is my flesh" the Jews "strove among themselves saying, 'How can this man give us His flesh to eat?'" That they understood Him in the literal sense is apparent from these considerations:

1. First that the Jews considered the expression just used as totally *different* from those in the first portion of the discourse. For if they had understood by *eating His flesh*, the same *as having Him, the bread of life* – this having been already explained by himself of believing on him – they could not ask in what manner this manducation was to take place.

2. Secondly we must conclude that the Jews understood the transition to be the doctrine, literally expressed, of feeding upon Christ; for their objection supposes Him to be teaching a doctrine impossible to be practiced; "How *can* this man give us his flesh to eat?" Now no other but the literal signification could possibly give rise to this objection.[22]

3. Thirdly. If nothing *new* was asserted by Christ, (as they understood Him,) then there could have been no apparent cause for the *increased excitement*. Nothing but understanding our Lord in the literal sense can be consistent with the intense excitement that followed our Lord's declaration.

4. Did they understand Him correctly?

To arrive at a true answer to the question, 'did they understand him correctly?' we must inquire, in addition to that which has already been advanced, whether Christ, by word or act, confirmed the interpretation put upon His words by those who heard Him. To understand the meaning of His conduct on this occasion, we must examine it on other occasions, and ascertain what was His usual mode of action under similar circumstances.

Let us examine when He used words in a figurative sense, and His hearers understood Him literally, and made objections. What was His usual course in these circumstances?

When Christ said to Nicodemus, "unless a man be born again he cannot enter into the Kingdom of God," Nicodemus understood Him literally, and our Lord at once corrected the error. So, when He said to His disciples, "Beware of the leaven of the Pharisees and Sadducees," they understood Him literally, and He at once explained His true meaning. So, when He said, "I have food to eat that ye know not of," and they misunderstood Him, He corrected the error. So, when He said, "Lazarus our friend sleepeth," they understood Him in the literal sense, and He at once explained. In this case the explanation was not so important, as no doctrine was propounded.

When He said, "Whither I go you cannot come," the Jews understood Him in a gross material sense, and asked, "Will he kill himself?" Our Lord at once removed this absurd construction by saying, "You are from below, I am from above; you are of this world, I am not of this world."[23]

When He said, "It is easier for a camel…" His disciples understood Him that a rich man could not be saved, and he at once corrected their mistake.[24] When He spoke to the Jews of spiritual slavery, they understood Him literally, and He at once corrected their misconstruction.[25]

When our Lord told the Jews that if they were the children of Abraham they would do the works of Abraham, and they understood Him to mean literally that they were not Abraham's descendants, He explains by saying, "You are of your father, the devil, and your will is to do your father's desires." showing that He meant their spiritual, not natural descent.[26] And when His disciples said one to another, "What is this that he saith, 'a little while'? We know not what he speaketh." Our Lord in succeeding verses explains His meaning until He was properly understood.[27]

From these examples it appears that our Lord acted upon the just and generous rule that requires every speaker to explain his meaning when misunderstood. And that He was so much in this habit that He not only explained to His disciples, but even to His most perverse and obstinate enemies.

Let us examine when, on the contrary, He used words in their literal sense, and his hearers understood Him correctly, and made objections, what was then His usual course? The following examples will form an answer to this question.

When our Lord said to the sick of the palsy, “Take heart, my son; your sins are forgiven.” His hearers understood him correctly, made objections, and our Savior stood to His words.[28] So, when He said to the Jews "Your father Abraham rejoiced that he was to see my day; he saw it, and was glad.” Those who heard Him understood Him literally, as saying that He was coeval with Abraham, and our Lord at once stood to his position, notwithstanding that He foresaw that personal violence would be the result of His course.[29] This eighth chapter of John affords us marked examples of our Lord's method of acting in both cases.

In the very chapter under consideration we have an instance. Christ having asserted that He came down from Heaven, and His hearers understanding Him literally, and making objections, He stands to His position, and repeats the same assertion in other parts of the chapter.[30]

From these numerous examples we are forced to adopt these two rules:

1. When His hearers misunderstood Him, and objected, He explained His true meaning.

2. When they understood Him correctly and objected, He repeated His proposition.

This course was in perfect accordance with reason, justice, and truth. Where a speaker uses words susceptible of different meanings, and he is aware, as our Lord was, of the construction placed upon His words, and he then repeats them without explanation, he adopts, expressly, the construction of his hearers. He makes it his own by his own most explicit act, and the construction becomes conclusive. We can imagine a case where a human speaker, under the influence of fear, or some other extraordinary motive, might thus act, and his conduct not to be conclusive; but we are at a loss to imagine a case where a Divine Lawgiver could thus act, without fixing the meaning put upon his words, by those who heard him. We will endeavor to apply these rules to the case in hand.

After our Lord had explicitly stated that the bread he would give was His flesh, and the Jews had asked the question, “How can this man give us his flesh to eat? our Lord makes no explanation, but repeats the proposition in terms, still more emphatic, reaffirming the truth of the proposition he had just before advanced.

> Verily, verily, I say unto you, except ye eat the flesh of the Son of Man, and drink His blood, ye have no life in you. Whoso eateth my flesh and drinketh my blood hath eternal life; and I will raise him up at the last day. For my flesh is meat indeed, and my blood is drink indeed.

The case under consideration then falls plainly under the latter rule. His words being correctly understood, in their literal sense, and His proposition itself being disputed, our Savior makes no explanation, but stands to His words, and repeats them in six different forms, still more emphatic than before.

5. Alleged exceptions to the rules deduced

Let us now examine certain alleged exceptions to the two rules we have deduced from our Lord's conduct. If we find exceptions to either rule, let us carefully examine and see how far, and how far only, such exception will limit the application of the rule. In other words, let us see whether the exceptions, if any such exist, establish or destroy the rule, or simply limit it. There are only two cases found in the history of our Lord's conduct, relied upon as conflicting with these rules.

The first case is that found in the fourth chapter of Saint John, in our Lord's conference with the Samaritan woman. This case is only an apparent exception to the first rule. I say apparent only, for, as I take it, the woman not only should have understood Him correctly, but did so understand Him; and that the whole circumstances and language, taken and considered together, very clearly show it; and that so far from constituting an exception to the first rule, it is a case in support of it.

Our Savior in the tenth verse, in answer to her question as to why He, being a Jew, would ask of her to drink, replies: "If thou didst know the gift of God, and who is he that saith to thee, give me to drink, thou perhaps wouldst have asked of him, and he would have given thee living water." She evidently understood Him in a literal sense, and shows this by her answer. The language of Christ was simply "living water;" a phrase that might well be taken literally. Our Savior, in the thirteenth and fourteenth verses, gives her an explanatory answer, defining the qualities of the water He would give, and concluded by saying, "But the water that I will give him, shall become in him a fountain of water, springing up into life everlasting."

This language is plainly metaphorical, and is so plainly so, that no one reader, to my knowledge, ever understood it otherwise. But the Samaritan woman still understood Him literally, for the reason, that at this part of our Savior's discourse, she did not yet know who it was that spoke to her. A knowledge of His character would at once give her the key to the true meaning. Christ knew that she had correct conceptions of the character of His mission. She tells him, in the twenty-fifth verse, that she knew that the Messiah cometh, and when he is come "he will" (not create a world, or wells, or streams of water, but) "tell us all things" or, in other words, teach us all truth. Our Savior, therefore, instead of giving her any further verbal explanations, breaks off abruptly, and says, "Go call thy husband, and come hither." This was evidently done to give Him the opportunity to show her that He possessed divine power; and in the end, to tell her plainly, he was the Christ. The effect of this information upon her mind is shown by the twenty-eight and twenty-ninth verses. She left her water pot, (a circumstance showing her haste and her excitement,) and went into the City and said unto the men there, "Come, and see a man who has told me all things whatsoever I have done. Is not he the Christ?" This, taken in connection with the language of the men to her in the forty-second verse, shows plainly, that she believed He was the Christ, and that she understood Him.

But our Savior had other objects in view, as well as the instruction of a single person, and those objects were of paramount importance. "Upon perusing this interesting chapter," says Dr. Wiseman,

> it has often struck me as one of the most beautiful instances on record of His (our Savior's) amiable ingenuity in doing good. He desired to make an opening for his religion among the Samaritans. But had He presented Himself among them uncalled, had He commenced His preaching of His own accord, he could have only expected to be rejected, to be ill treated as a Jew, and punished as a religious innovator. He wishes therefore, to be invited by the Samaritans themselves, and he selects the most favorable moment and means for effecting his purpose. He dismisses all His disciples to the city of Sichem, and seats Himself at the well, where he was sure to find some of the inhabitants, and where the rules of hospitality in the East would give him a right to enter into conversation. A female accordingly comes, and he uses this right by asking her for water.

The conversation, which follows, was all adapted to excite her curiosity; and the replies of our Lord and the ingenious manner in which He introduced the subjects, all go to show the great leading object he had in view. After leading her from one topic to another, and exciting her curiosity to its highest pitch, and after showing that He knew her most intimate domestic relations, (a matter best calculated to excite the attention of a woman in her condition,) He tells her plainly, that He is the Christ. The woman at once goes into the city, as Jesus designed, and tells the men of the wonderful person she had met, and invites them, in the most exciting and urgent manner, to come and see Him, giving them the most extraordinary reasons for the request she made. Our Savior accordingly did not go into the City, until they came to Him and invited Him in, and desired Him to tarry with them. After He was invited He remained with them two days, making many proselytes.

An examination of the whole narrative, and a consideration of the relation the Samaritans bore to the Jews and their religion, must convince any one that the principal object Christ had in view, in His conference with this woman, was, at first, more to excite than to gratify curiosity. For this reason, (although He gives her an explanation of His meaning in verses thirteen and fourteen sufficiently clear to her when she was afterwards informed of His true character,) He so manages His discourse as to accomplish the great end had in view by him. If she had not finally understood Him to speak of spiritual waters, instead of natural, she would naturally have said, after "who has told me all things whatsoever I have done," and has promised to give us a fountain of water, more excellent than the well of Jacob.

But putting the most extreme construction upon this incident, and thence concluding that the Samaritan woman never did understand our Savior otherwise than in the literal sense, still the case is most clearly distinguishable from the one under consideration, in these most important particulars:

1. He was not speaking of a doctrine that must be believed upon pain of eternal death.

2. The woman still believed in Him, and was not lost for want of an explanation.

3. She was not His disciple, who already believed on Him, and was still permitted to go away forever, simply for want of an explanation of one hard saying.

4. Christ did not tell her, when she simply misunderstood, that she did not believe

The second case often relied upon is found in the second chapter of Saint John's Gospel. When our Lord had driven out the moneychangers from the temple, and the Jews had asked for a sign of His authority, He answered:

> Destroy this temple, and in three days I will raise it up. The Jews then said, six and forty years was this temple in building, and wilt thou raise it up in three days? But He spake of the temple of His body. When, therefore, He was risen again from the dead, his disciples remembered that He had said this, and they believed the Scriptures and the word that Jesus had said.

Our Lord, in this case, had used language susceptible of two meaning, and the Jews took the word temple in the wrong sense, and He suffered them to remain in their erroneous construction, without any explanation.[31]

Many commentators think that the Jews did understand Christ correctly. To quote Cardinal Wiseman:

> Jews did understand Christ correctly, and it was only malignity which made them raise objections to His words. They suppose that the apostles fully *understood* them, as Saint John tells us, that they did not believe them 'till after the resurrection.[32]

With all due deference for the opinions of those commentators, I must say, that I am forced to believe that neither the Jews nor the apostles understood our Savior correctly at the time He made the prediction. Nor do I believe it was His intention that they should then understand Him correctly. Nor can I see any necessity that they should so understand Him at that time. It does appear to me that there were the best of reasons why the meaning should be left in doubt, to be settled by the event of His resurrection.

That the Jews put the most natural construction upon His words, would appear from these reflections. He had driven out the moneychangers from the temple, and told them not to make the house of His Father a house of traffic. So far He spoke of the temple. The Jews asked for a sign of His authority for driving out those men from the temple, and our Lord, without explanation, answered: "Destroy this temple...." The only temple that had been spoken of was the Jewish temple, and the Jews inquired for His authority in what He did in that temple, and our Lord said, in reply, *this* temple. Suppose we strike out verses twenty-one and twenty-two, that contain the special explanation, (the advantages of which the Jews had not at that time,) and exclude from our consideration the resurrection of Christ – in other words, place ourselves precisely in the same position of the Jews, and what construction would we place upon the language of our Lord? Surely, the construction they did.

That this case constitutes an exception to the first rule, must be conceded. Our Lord though misunderstood, gave no explanation. It is true, He did not repeat His statement, thereby making their construction His own, but simply left them without explanation. This is not, therefore, an exception to the second rule.

In this case our Lord was only making a prediction, and not putting forth a doctrine, which He required then to be believed: and this distinction is most material. The only object our Lord had in making this prediction was to constitute it, when fulfilled, evidence of His Divinity. This is shown by verse twenty-two. To accomplish all he intended, He had simply to make the prediction. The act of making it did not constitute any proof, but it was both the making and fulfillment, taken together, that did. His words showed two things:

1. That a miraculous event was foretold.

2. That it could be known when it happened.

Now was there any necessity for any explanation? Christ could not be expected to do an idle thing. Suppose He had explained His true meaning; would have that removed the unbelief of the Jews? It was just as great a miracle to raise His own body from the grave as to raise the temple. The event fulfilling the prophecy would make all clear. Our Lord did not wish to interfere with the personal free agency of the Jews, and it was not His purpose to make His prophecy plain. The event, predicted, in fact, constituted a part of the prediction itself, for the purpose of explanation. It is so in reference to prophecies generally. They are purposely left obscure, for the best of reasons, until their fulfillment makes them clear.

This being a conceded exception to the first rule, how far does it affect that rule? Does it not establish and sustain it, rather than destroy it? It being a special exception, for special reasons, and the fact of its being an exception being expressly marked, does, indeed, strengthen the rule; and why? Because the same apostle who records the words and conduct of our Lord in this special case, also records His words and conduct in the sixth chapter; and in reference to this special case, he puts in himself an express explanation of our Lord's meaning and does not do so in the other. Why does he do this in one case, and not in the other? The reason is palpable. Our Lord was misunderstood in the one case, and as it was not proper for Him then to give the explanation, Saint John gives it afterwards.

However, as to eating His flesh, He was correctly understood; and therefore Saint John purposely fails to give any explanation. When a writer takes pains to point out certain exceptions expressly, he, by this very act, negatives all idea of other exceptions not so stated.[33]

So it is with respect to a statute. If the lawmaker himself assumes to state exceptions to his own general rule, he must be presumed to intend to finish his work, and not leave it unfinished, like a man who attempts to build a house, and fails. Saint John was in the habit of making these explanations in cases of obscurity; and, had our Lord failed to make an explanation when misunderstood as to eating His flesh, the apostle would no doubt have given it. Two explanations occur in this very chapter, verses six and seventy-one. There is also one in the last chapter. We are nowhere told that the Jews misunderstood Christ. No subsequent event explains His meaning. On the contrary, as we shall see, subsequent events confirm the construction of the Jews.

6. Our Lord confirmed the construction put upon His words

I have endeavored to show that the case under consideration comes under the second rule; namely, that our Lord was correctly understood, and His proposition itself being disputed, He repeated it again with increased emphasis. Is there a single instance to be found, where His hearers misunderstood Him, and, in reply to them, He repeated His words without explanation? Can any such a case be shown, either in the conduct of Christ or in that of any other just speaker?

The Jews had made the objection that Christ could not literally give them His flesh to eat; and in *reply to this objection*, "Jesus said unto them, Verily, verily, I say unto you, Except ye eat the flesh of the Son of Man, and drink His blood, ye have no life in you..." All that Christ said in verses fifty-three to fifty-eight inclusive, was said in the form of a reply to the objection of the Jews. The language of the reply of our Lord is most emphatic. If, therefore, the Jews simply misunderstood Him, what possible purpose could He have had in making such a reply? Or was his reply without a purpose, and simply idle? Was it meaningless?

Can we impute such a weakness to Christ, the Son of God? We dare not do that.

Then what could He mean by this most emphatic reassertion of His proposition itself, when that proposition had not been, in fact, disputed by the Jews, in making their objection? A proposition cannot be believed, unless it is first understood; nor can it be disbelieved, unless first understood. We can believe or disbelieve a proposition without *comprehending* it, but we can do neither, without understanding the proposition. If the Jews simply misunderstood Christ, their objection was not aimed at the real proposition itself, but at an imaginary proposition, never made. Therefore, for our Lord to repeat to them the same proposition, in substantially the same language, and without explanation, would have been about as idle and senseless an act as can well be imagined. What possible end could the repetition, without explanation, of a misunderstood proposition, accomplish? Would such repetition secure the reception of the real proposition? On the contrary, would not the repetition, without explanation, of a misunderstood proposition, but defeat the very purpose the speaker had in view, by expressly confirming His hearers in their mistake? When Christ put forth His proposition, did He wish to be understood? Did He wish His proposition to be believed? If He did not, for what purpose did He put it forth? He was not simply making a prediction. He was propounding a doctrine. Did He propound this doctrine without a purpose? If He propounded a doctrine, it must have been true; and if true, He must have intended it to be believed; and if so, He must have *then* intended to be understood.

If we say, the metaphorical sense is the true one, then we make our Lord's conduct, on this occasion, the strangest anomaly, at war with His own uniform practice upon all similar occasions, and that of every sincere speaker. And we do this without any authority or example to sustain us. In all my reading, observation, and experience, I have never met with an instance where a speaker, having put forth a proposition that He wished to be understood, and where his hearers misunderstood his proposition, simply repeated it in language still more emphatic, but without explanation.

When the proposition is understood and disputed, it is very natural and proper, that the speaker should repeat it, and reaffirm it with increased emphasis. It was so with our Lord on this occasion and upon other occasions. The Jews disputed the truth of the understood proposition itself and our Lord at once replies, in substance, believe or perish! When Peter said to his Master, "Thou shall never wash my feet," our Lord replied at once, "If I wash thee not, thou hast no part with me." In substance, He replied as he did to the Jews. In both case the language is strictly confirmatory of the words used before.

Is this language at all consistent with any but the literal sense? Peter understood our Lord in the literal sense, and objected. Our Savior at once held up before him the penalty of the law. This was perfectly consistent with his claim to the character of a Divine Lawgiver. Was not this line of conduct proper toward the Jews? Peter as little understood the reason why his Master should wash his feet, as the Jews understood why He should give them His flesh to eat and his blood to drink. Our Lord having given then conclusive proofs of his divine character had the unquestioned right to demand implicit obedience. While it is the clear duty of the a Divine, as well as a human lawgiver, to make His law understood that it may be obeyed, it is not his duty to make its reasons comprehensible. It is enough that Christ did right, whether we comprehend His reasons for His law or not.

For the reasons given, this conclusion seems to follow, that the acts and language, of our Lord are wholly irreconcilable with the metaphorical sense, and cannot be explained, except upon the hypothesis that the Jews did understand Him correctly in the literal sense.

7. His disciples understood him in the literal sense

The verses from fifty-nine to sixty-five inclusive, are taken up mainly in relating what the murmuring disciples said, and in our Lord's reply to them. The words, "these things," in verse fifty-nine, refer to the entire discourse; while the words "this" and "it" in verses sixty and sixty-one, refer to only one thing; namely, that hard saying. What was that hard saying? It could be nothing but the statement of our Lord that He would give them His flesh to eat. In other words the disciples murmured at the same thing that caused the Jews to strive among themselves and ask: "How can this man give us His flesh to eat?"

The audience of Christ, on this occasion, consisted of the admiring multitude that had followed Him into the wilderness, among which He had many disciples, "many believed in his name."[34] There were no proud Pharisees or cunning Sadducees there. They (the multitude) accounted Him as a prophet.[35]

We are told that "the people took shipping and came to Capernaum, seeking for Jesus."[36] From verse twenty-five to thirty-five inclusive, the historian used the pronoun "they" to designate the persons who had asked Christ the questions, and to whom He gave the answers recorded. The inquiries made were such, up to this point, that the whole multitude could join in asking, as the questions themselves were not improper. But in verses forty-one and forty-two, we are told that the Jews murmured, and asked the question, "How then saith He, 'I came down from heaven?'" Now it is clear, that the disciples who "believed on His name," did not join with the Jews in denying that Jesus came down from heaven. They believed that proposition, and did not murmur at it, as did the Jews. The first and only thing they murmured at was that "hard saying," which caused the Jews to strive among themselves. The word *strive* is a very expressive term, and shows a more intense degree of excitement than is expressed by the word *murmur*. When our Lord said He came down from heaven, the Jews murmured, while the disciples believed. But when He put forth another proposition, more difficult for them to believe, the Jews, "strove among themselves" and the disciples murmured. It is clear that the term *Jews* is used by the historian to distinguish those who did not, from those who did, believe on Christ.

If then, it is true, that Christ only continued to teach the same doctrine He had taught in the first part of His discourse, and which His disciples believed, and they still understood Him correctly in the metaphorical sense, how could they have murmured at it, and called it a hard saying? Would they now murmur at what they had before believed? If so, why? Such a course as these murmuring disciples pursued is utterly inconsistent with any other hypothesis than the one, that, like the Jews, they understood Christ in the literal sense. The whole narrative is full and clear to this point. The historian states that the murmuring disciples heard this hard saying, and asked, "Who can hear it?" Saint John unquestionably refers to the saying that gave so much offense to the Jews; and, as he speaks of these murmuring disciples asking a question substantially the same with that asked by the Jews, he must mean that they (the murmuring disciples) understood our Lord in the same literal sense.

It being a proven position, that these murmuring disciples understood our Lord in the literal sense, the question arises, did they understand Him correctly? Let us, then, examine the language of our Lord, used by Him in His reply to these murmuring disciples: "He said unto them, Doth this offend you?" Is not this unaccountable language in the mouth of a Speaker, whose hearers have simply misunderstood, but have not, in fact, disputed His real proposition? Did Christ mean to ask, "Does the imaginary proposition, which I did not make, offend you?" That they were offended is certain; and if they simply misunderstood our Lord's language, then they were only offended at an imaginary proposition. They had simply misunderstood Him, and there was, therefore, in their minds, no real cause of offense.

But such a question could alone be predicated upon the fact, that the cause of offense was a real subsisting, and not a mere imaginary doctrine. And the efforts of Christ are, therefore, not directed to an explanation of His meaning, but to a proof of the truth of His proposition.

In further sustaining His proposition, in His reply to these murmuring disciples, who had heard His answers to the Jews, our Lord adapted His arguments to the state of their minds and predicated them upon the state of their previous belief. They had believed and readily embraced His doctrine – they had not disputed the fact that He came down from heaven, and that He was there before; but like those disciples represented by the good seed falling into stony ground, they now met a real, not an imaginary difficulty.[37] Christ, therefore, said to them,

> What and if ye shall see the son of man ascend up where he was before. It is the spirit that quickeneth; the flesh profiteth nothing; the words that I speak unto you, they are spirit and they are life. But there are some of you that believe not. Therefore said I unto you that no man can come, unto me, except it were given unto him of my Father.

The meaning of Christ in these extracts would seem to be clear, and perfectly consistent with the literal sense, and wholly irreconcilable with the metaphorical. The substance was this: "You consider it impossible that I should give you my flesh to eat; you question my power; you did believe that I came down from heaven; if you see me ascend up where I was before, will that be more difficult than for me to have come down? And are not both as difficult as for me to give you my flesh to eat? The proposition is hard to the natural man. It is the spirit that quickeneth the mind to believe – the flesh profiteth nothing to this result. You must not rely upon yourselves alone, but upon God, for I have told you already that no man can come to me unless it be given him of my Father, and this you did not dispute: my words are spirit and life, but there are some of you that believe not the proposition I have propounded."

We may give the words of our Lord, in reply to the objection of these murmuring disciples, any construction we please; and still, one thing is clear; they were solely directed to sustain an understood and disputed proposition. If not, why did our Lord say, "My words are spirit and life," when they had simply been misunderstood? To say that words are true, when their true meaning has not been disputed, would be idle.

Besides this, our Lord makes a statement of a matter of simple fact that could not possibly be true, unless these murmuring disciples did understand Him correctly. He tells them, "But there are some of you that believe not." They had said, "This is a hard saying, who can bear it?" which means, who can believe it?[38] And Christ tells them that they do not believe. They could not disbelieve a proposition they never understood. The only thing they had disputed was the hard saying that He would give them His flesh to eat: and it was in reference to this proposition, and to this only that our Lord told them they "believed not."

If these murmuring disciples simply misunderstood our Lord's meaning how could He tell them, "You believe not?" If the Protestant view be right, these disciples refused to believe a proposition never advanced, and one that was not true. How can you class men, who simply misunderstood a proposition, with unbelievers of the proposition itself? What sort of logic or truth is there in saying to a man, who simply, misunderstands you and has a mere imaginary proposition in his mind, "Sir, you believe not?" Christ certainly intended to let these disciples know that their error consisted in not believing. This could not be true, if they simply misunderstood. There could be no wrong in disbelieving a supposed untrue proposition. And Christ not only tells these disciples that they did not believe; but the apostle himself classes them among genuine unbelievers.[39]

But it may be said, that at the precise time when these murmuring disciples said, "who can bear it," they did misunderstand our Lord; but that His subsequent words, found in verses sixty-two and sixty-three, so explained His meaning as that they did correctly understand Him at the time He said, "you believe not." This would be assuming facts outside the record, not only without the slightest evidence, but contrary to the simple narrative of the facts as stated in it. We are informed that Jesus knew in Himself that the disciples murmured but there is not the slightest intimation anywhere, either by Saint John, who puts in several explanations of his own in this same chapter, or by the words or acts of Christ, that He was misunderstood by any one.[40] On the contrary, we are expressly informed that these disciples did dispute one proposition and we are not informed that they did dispute any other; and, therefore Christ could only refer to that one – the hard saying as they at first understood it.

8. How the apostles understood our Lord

Let us now ascertain how the twelve understood our Lord. We are told that many of His disciples left Him, and walked no more with Him. It was then that our Lord put this mournful and solemn question to the twelve: "Will ye also go away?" And then the intrepid and ardent soul of Peter answered, "Lord, to whom shall we go? Thou hast the words of eternal life. And we believe and are sure that thou art that Christ, the Son of the living God."

It is apparent that Christ's question to the twelve was predicated upon the same state of facts as His question to the murmuring disciples, "Doth this offend you?" and upon the ground that the twelve had the same inducements to disbelieve, as these murmuring disciples who had left Him. If the twelve understood Him in a different sense from the Jews and disbelieving disciples, there could be no reason for asking such a question. The fervent and confiding answer of Peter shows conclusively that the twelve also understood their Lord as the others had understood Him; that is, literally. The minds of the twelve had to overcome the same difficulty that had wrecked the faith of the many who abandoned their Lord. The reason given by Peter was the most simple, logical and rational. We are sure you are that Christ, and have the words of eternal life. This was enough, and they were compelled to believe anything that Christ propounded, whether they comprehended it or not.

The twelve then understood Him in a literal sense, and believed that which the others disbelieved. And if they at that time believed the doctrine that Christ would literally give them His flesh to eat, when and where did they ever change their opinion, and where is that important fact recorded?

We find a part of the disciples at one time disbelieving a certain doctrine, and the chosen twelve believing the same thing at the same time; and if we can find no evidence of any change in the minds of the twelve, what right have we to say, either that there was such a change, or that they did not correctly understand the meaning of our Lord's words?

At a given time we find, in the minds of the apostles, a certain construction of our Lord's words; we find this construction was not objected to by Him, but was confirmed by word and act, that could not be reconciled with any other construction; and we find afterwards not the slightest evidence to correct such an error, if error it was, and upon what ground can we assume that these apostles were then mistaken?

It is true, there are several cases where it is stated that the chosen apostles misunderstood our Lord's meaning at the time His words were spoken; but in these cases we are expressly, informed of the fact, and of the further fact, that they afterwards understood Him correctly, and we are also informed what Christ did in fact mean. Now, in these instances, our doubts are wholly removed by explicit explanations. Yet, in this important case, where a great doctrine was taught, upon which hung eternal life and death, and where the misconstruction of our Lord's words was in reference to a most vitally essential matter, and gave them a meaning precisely opposite to the one intended; and yet we have no explanation, – not one of those so often put in by Saint John to make the meaning clear.

9. The objection that the doctrine was unclear

Some object that the Eucharist was not instituted at the time of the discourse in the sixth chapter of Saint John, and for that reason, neither the Jews nor the disciples could correctly understand what our Savior meant. This is one of those abstract objections, founded upon our preconceived views of things, which should be very carefully considered, before we allow it any force against the obvious and natural construction of words and phrases. Not only so, but as I take it, the abstract position itself is wrong.

Was it improper that our Savior should promise a sacrament, and teach the doctrine of the same, before its institution? I think not. Our savior taught for more than three years before His death, and preparatory to setting up His kingdom. In the nature and reason of things, it was proper first to teach His doctrines, and then to put them in force. And we find this was His course. For instance, in His conversation with Nicodemus, which was before the institution of baptism, the necessity of it is *taught*. And I must say that there is a wide difference between teaching the simple fact that baptism is essential to salvation, and the mere *manner* of its administration—a wide difference between teaching the simple fact of giving us His flesh to eat, and the *manner* in which it was to be given. The *first* thing to be taught in both cases, is the necessity and effects of the sacrament; and as to the *manner*, this would be better shown by its institution and practical administration. I say *better* shown. As to the *spiritual effects* of a sacrament, they must be explained in words sooner or later, and, therefore, the proper time to explain these effects is when the *promise* is given, and before the actual institution. But as to the *manner* of administering the sacrament, no description in words could be as satisfactory as the act of administering it.

Our Lord only explained so far to Nicodemus as to show him that He did not speak of a natural birth; and that He could not understand the spiritual birth; but gave him no explanation at all as to the manner of the birth by baptism. So, in the sixth chapter of John, our Lord gives no explanation of the mere *manner*. Also, when He washed the feet of Peter, He would give no explanation. In all these cases He required submission upon His word and character, *as Christ*. The first thing Nicodemus said to Him, was to acknowledge He was a teacher sent from God; and upon this acknowledgment our Savior at once announces to him the difficult doctrine of the new birth, and only explains enough to make His words understood, and then very properly required implicit belief. A mere fallible teacher ought to be believed, when he proves the truth of his proposition by facts, or reasons, or both; but an *infallible* teacher has only to prove that he is *such*, and then his propositions are to be believed upon his *assertion*. "This discourse in the sixth chapter of John stands in the same relation to the institution of the Eucharist, as the conference with Nicodemus does to the institution of baptism."[41]

But if there be any thing in this objection, it applies with as much force to the metaphorical view. The Jews and disciples could *comprehend* it as little when applied to feeding on Christ by faith, as when applied to the Eucharist.

> For to call bare believing in Christ, eating his flesh, and drinking his blood, is so remote from all propriety of speaking, and so unknown in all languages, that to this day those who understand nothing more by it but believing in Christ, are able to give no tolerable account of the reason of the expression.[42]

10. The objection that the literal construction proves too much

There is an objection that the literal construction proves too much. For if we give the language of verses fifty-three to fifty-seven a literal construction, we must say that those who do not eat the flesh shall *all* die, those who do shall *all* live, and all abide in Christ. In other words, we must put in some restrictions, such as *worthy* and *so far*. Now an interpretation clogged with restrictions is not to be preferred (other things being equal) to one having no restrictions.

This argument is much relied upon by many Protestant writers. When a general principle is asserted in one place, and the qualifications or exceptions stated in another, this does not form the slightest ground for opposing the construction. Our Savior says, "he that believeth and is baptized shall be saved." There is no restriction here, and yet, unless the act is performed with the proper dispositions, there is no salvation. "Ask and yet shall receive." No limitation here. But Saint James says, "ye do not receive, because ye ask amiss." In all cases where certain effects are attributed to certain acts or sacraments, the implied condition is always understood, that it must be well performed. But in reference to the Catholic construction, there is not the slightest difficulty, for Saint Paul tells us explicitly that "whosoever shall eat this bread and (or) drink this cup of the Lord unworthily, shall be guilty of the body and blood of the Lord."[43]

This must be taken and construed with the language of our Lord in the sixth chapter of John, according to the fourth and fifth rules of construction we have laid down. Everything said in Scripture upon the same subject must be considered as part of the same discourse. If the Catholic construction is correct, there is nothing inconsistent with it in this objection. Another reflection that ought to have at once satisfied these objectors, is this: that the question as to the *effects* that Christ attributes to His doctrine, is not the matter in dispute at all; but we are inquiring, not as to what *effects* are given to the doctrine, but as to what *doctrine* was propounded. It is manifest that the *effects* Christ attributes to His doctrine, would apply as well to the metaphorical as the literal sense; and that in either case there must be restrictions, if they can be properly called such.

11. The objection that language is spiritual

A third objection urged generally by ordinary controversialists, but entirely given up by the best Protestant writers, is founded upon the language of verse sixty three. "It is the spirit that quickeneth; the flesh profiteth nothing: the words that I speak unto you, they are spirit, and they are life." Our Lord is supposed by these words to intimate that His language was to be taken spiritually, and so to have intended this as a key to the preceding part of the discourse.

It would seem at once that this language could not refer to the mode of *construing words*, but to the *difficulty* of *belief*, and the *aids to it.* I have already given what I considered the fair interpretation of this language, taken in connection with what immediately follows and precedes it.

Let us then examine the usage of Scripture, to see in what sense the word "flesh" is used, when standing alone, and not used to designate the flesh of a particular person or thing, and especially when used with the article "the" before it, as in the text. When it is used as in the text, there is no instance in the Old or New Testament where it is used literally. Yet it must have been used in the text in the literal sense, for us to understand by the word *spirit* the figurative or spiritual sense. If by *the flesh* we are to understand the material flesh of Christ, then by *the spirit* we must understand *His* spirit. This can in no way show us that His words are to be taken *spiritually*, for it could not relate to *construction* of words at all. The asserted fact that His spirit gives us life, would not relate to the manner of construing His words.

The terms *flesh* and *spirit* are contrasted with or opposed to each other in the text. The examples in Scripture of this usage are very numerous, and in *all* the cases, these words have one definite and unvarying meaning. A full explanation of these terms may be found in the eighth chapter of Romans. "For the wisdom of the flesh is death, but the wisdom of the spirit is life and peace. "[44]

Now, in all these cases, there is not the slightest intimation given that the ideas conveyed by these phrases have any reference to the construction of language, but they show that two different powers or states are meant. By the flesh we understand the natural dispositions and corrupted thoughts of human nature, and by the spirit, the opposite effect of grace upon man. The qualities attributed to these powers or states are the same as in the sixth of John. "The wisdom of the flesh is death." "The flesh profiteth nothing." "The wisdom of the spirit is life." "It is the spirit that quickeneth."

The Protestant writers, Kuinoel, Kappe, Sartorious, Stow, Schmid, Bloomfield, Schleusner, and Horne, agree with the Catholic interpretation. Bloomfield says, "This translation (the popular one) cannot be proved from the *usus loquendi* of Scripture." Mr. Horne says:

> The Holy Spirit is put for his effects.... (2 Cor 3:6) Here, by the word *letter*, we are to understand the law, written in letters on stone.... By the *spirit* is meant the saving doctrine of the gospel, which derives its origin from the Holy Spirit. In the same sense Jesus Christ says, "The words that I speak, they are spirit and life," that is, they are from the Spirit of God, and if received with true faith, will lead to eternal life.

Now this view is manifestly a support to the literal sense. Our Lord had propounded a very difficult doctrine, to which stern objections were made; and how natural and appropriate the sentiments expressed in this verse. It is as if He had said: "It is the spirit (or effect of grace) that quickens the mind to believe; the natural disposition and corrupted thoughts of men are not profitable towards this result – my words are from the Spirit of God, and if believed with true faith, will lead to eternal life." Thus, He reaffirmed the truth of the proposition already made, and without explaining the meaning of His words.

This long chapter is one of the most wonderful to be found in Scripture. It is, in my view, the most clear and unequivocal statement of the sublime doctrine of the Real Presence. It would seem that a calm and attentive examination of its language, taken in connection with the simple facts stated, could leave no doubt. The Protestant construction gives rise to the most distressing and palpable contradictions. For example, if it is conceded that the murmuring disciples understood Christ in the literal sense, then, to avoid the Catholic view, we must hold that Christ was mistaken when He told those disciples that they "*believed not*." And if we say that the twelve understood Christ in the figurative sense, then we can see no possible reason for our Lord asking them if they would also go away. If He had proposed nothing *new*, and nothing hard to flesh and blood, there was nothing to constitute a *new* and severe trial of their faith.

In any and every view, it is a wonderful chapter, full of high and holy truths. Like any other sincere speaker, our Lord was never disposed to gain followers at the expense of truth. He taught His doctrines boldly, and sustained them with an energy and power proportioned to the intensity of the opposition. His language, especially in reply to the Jews, is one of the noblest specimens of Divine eloquence, and of unflinching assertion of the truth, to be found in the history of His life. There is, perhaps, no portion of His discourses, more energetic and emphatic.

12. The words of institution

As the Catholic understands it, the Blessed Eucharist was promised in the sixth chapter of Saint John's Gospel, leaving the mere manner in which it was to be given to be explained by the institution of the Sacrament. The history of this institution is given in the first three Gospels, and in the epistles of Saint Paul. The narrations are substantially, the same, though differing in some slight particulars. In all, the words are given "This is my body.... This is my blood." Saint John, in his Gospel, says nothing about the institution of the Sacrament.

Our Lord says: "This is my body;" and the Catholic responds: "Lord, I believe it to be thy body;" while the Protestant replies: "Lord, I believe it to be a figure of thy body." Who replies, yea, yea, to our Lord's assertion? Is it the Catholic or Protestant?

The Catholic maintains that the verb to be, in the passage, is to be taken in its ordinary literal sense, and the Protestant contends that it ought to be taken in a figurative sense, equivalent to the word represent. In the Old and New Testament this verb is used many thousands of times in its literal sense. These examples are too numerous to require any specifications. The literal sense of the term is then the general rule. Those who oppose the literal and simple construction are compelled to show two things:

1. That there are exceptions to the general rule.

2. That the verb to be in this case, comes properly within the exception.

Dr. Paley draws an argument in favor of the truth of Christianity, from the *difficulty* of arriving at the metaphorical sense, from the words of institution. He says:

> I think also that the difficulty arising from the conciseness of Christ's expression, "This is my body," would have been avoided in a made-up story. I allow that the explanation of these words, given by Protestants, is satisfactory; but it is deduced from a diligent comparison of the words in question, with forms of expression used in Scripture, and especially by Christ on other occasions. No writer would have arbitrarily and unnecessarily cast in his reader's way a difficulty, which, to say the least, it required research and erudition to clear up.

It would seem that the learned author might have made his argument much stronger had he taken the literal sense to be correct. He might then well have insisted that the invention of such a doctrine was a task of superhuman difficulty. Nothing but the Divine Mind could have framed it, and no mere imposter would ever have "arbitrarily and unnecessarily cast" in the way of his followers a doctrine so much at war with the pride of the human heart, and so difficult to be believed by the proud human intellect – a doctrine requiring so much *greater faith.*

It would seem upon reflection, to be difficult to understand the force of the argument as stated by the learned divine. It must be conceded that the maker-up of a fictitious story would not have *arbitrarily* thrown this "difficulty in his reader's way." At the same time, it is exceedingly difficult to understand why Christ should have done so. Whether Christ was an imposter or not He must have equally desired the success of his system. For that reason He would not have "arbitrarily and unnecessarily cast a difficulty" in the way of His followers. If He was the true Messiah it would have been *as much* against his policy, and *more* against His justice to have done this than it would have been against the policy of an imposter. It is improbable in both cases, but more so under the hypothesis that He was the true Messiah.

The honest and sensible infidel can well understand why Christ should sometimes be misunderstood when speaking of high and supernatural truths. In their nature, they are difficult, even when minutely stated. But he could never understand why Christ, in his last Testament, and instituting a most important sacrament, would use language in its plain literal form, which He designed to be understood in a *new* and *unknown* figurative sense. He could never understand why Christ would do this without any explanation when an explanation would be so easy, and with a perfect foreknowledge of all the consequences of such "arbitrary and unnecessary difficulty." The mere substitution of one word for another would have avoided all difficulty. I apprehend that the honest inquirer could see nothing in this argument to prove that Christ was a Divine Lawgiver, who, in a plain matter is alleged to have "arbitrarily and unnecessarily cast in his reader's way a difficulty, requiring research and erudition to clear up."

In this extract from Dr. Paley the author admits there is one "difficulty requiring research and erudition to clear up." Consequently he admits that the New Testament is not 'plain and easily understood' as generally alleged by Protestant writers when arguing with Catholics. But this ground must be abandoned when they come to argue with Infidels.

From the admission of the author, as well as from respective positions of the two parties, the Catholic mode of interpretation is the most simple and natural, and must be overcome by research and erudition of the Protestant. While, according to a well-known rule of evidence, we may take Dr. Paley's admissions as evidence against himself, we are not bound to believe his conclusions.

The first thing the Protestant must show, is, that there are exceptions. To do this they bring forward a number of passages which may be arranged in three classes as follows:

Class 1: Genesis chapter 41 verses 26, 27, "The seven good cows are seven years." Daniel chapter 7 verse 24, "The ten horns are ten kings." Matthew chapter 13 verses 38, 3. "The field is the world…." First Corinthians chapter 10 verse 4. "And that rock was Christ." Revelations chapter 1 verse 20. "The seven stars are the angels of the seven churches." Galatians chapter 4 verse 24. "These are the two covenants." John chapter 10 verse 7. "I am the door."

Class 2: John chapter 15 verse 1, "I am the true vine."

Class 3: Genesis chapter 17 verse 10: "this is my covenant." Exodus chapter 12 verse 11: "This is the Lord's Passover."

Some of these cases clearly establish the first point, that there are exceptions to the general rule. The next and most important point to prove, is, that the words "This is my body," come within the exceptions. To do this the same passages are relied upon.

In considering these texts, let us see how they are marked so as to be known as exceptions. There must be some mark or distinction to point out exceptions; otherwise, we could not know them to be such. The usages, habits, and practice of the writer, considered in connection with the usages of language will enable us to determine the exceptions. If we find that in relation to a certain class or classes of cases, the verb to be is used in a metaphorical sense, when it is generally used in its literal sense, then all cases that come within such class or classes, constitute exceptions. But the existence of such exceptions, thus marked and distinguished, is no evidence that other exceptions exist, which are not thus marked and distinguished. So far from it, the existence of such exceptions, thus marked and distinguished is a clear proof that other cases, not thus designated, are not exceptions, but are intentionally left to be governed by the general rule.

It is perfectly, clear that exceptions do exist – that they are so marked as to be distinguished from the general rule – and that we must distinguish between them. Before the words of institution can be considered as an exception, it must be shown that they belong to one or the other of the classes stated. In other words, it must be shown that these passages are parallel to the words of institution, otherwise they prove nothing.

Now what constitutes parallelism? Clearly two things, namely:

1. A similarity of *word,* and

2. A similarity of *things.*

This is substantially the definition of the Protestant writer Mr. Horne, and others. Mr. Horne says:

> Whenever the mind is struck with any resemblance, in the first place consider whether it was a true resemblance, and whether the passages are sufficiently similar; that is, not only whether the same word, but also the same thing answers together, in order to form a safe judgment concerning it. It often happens that one word has several distinct meanings, one of which obtains in one place, and one in another. When, therefore words of such various meanings present themselves, all those passages where they occur are not to be immediately considered parallel, unless they have a similar power.

To illustrate briefly this sensible rule, suppose I wish to show the meaning of the phrase, "It is the spirit that quickeneth: the flesh profiteth nothing;" I would refer to the cases already given, wherein not only the same words are used, but where they were put in contrast, and where they refer to the same thing. So if I wish to illustrate the passage, "the seven good kine are seven years," I would refer to that of, "the field is the world," and both these by, "these are the two covenants," for they all have the same words and relate to the same thing; namely: the explanation of symbolical instruction.

13. The first class of alleged exceptions considered

How do we know that the passages in the first class stated do constitute exceptions? In the first two cases we are expressly told that Joseph and Daniel were interpreting dreams, and in the third, that our Lord was interpreting a parable. In the fourth case, Saint Paul first says: "And did all drink the same spiritual drink, for they drank of that spiritual Rock; and then tells us, "And that Rock was Christ." The apostle, for the purpose of explanation, first transforms the real rock of Horeb into a spiritual or fictitious rock, and then says that spiritual rock was Christ. The language of Saint Paul, taken in connection with the historical relation of the Israelites, drinking the water flowing from the rock of Horeb, leaves his meaning so clear, that no one has ever misunderstood him.

The case from the Apocalypse is equally clear. "Write the things which thou hast seen.... The mystery of the seven stars.... The seven stars are the seven angels." Here the apostle John was explaining a mystery.

The case from Galatians is similar. Saint Paul is careful to inform us that he is explaining an allegory. "Which things are an allegory, for these are the two covenants."

In reference to the last case, "I am the door," our Lord was interpreting a parable. We are first informed that Christ opened the eyes of a man blind from his birth – that Jesus had found the man after the Jews had cast him out, and some of the Pharisees being present, and making objections, our Lord commences the discourse in which these words occur.[45] In the tenth chapter he continues the same discourse, and in the first five verses gives in part the parable of the sheepfold. In verses six and seven we are told, "This parable spoke Jesus unto them, but they understood not what things they were which He spoke unto them. Then said Jesus unto them again, Verily, verily, I say unto you, I am the door of the sheep." Our Lord goes on in succeeding verses, still speaking of the same thing, and in verse 26 He tells the Jews that they "believe not because ye are not of my sheep, as I said unto you."

In all these cases we are clearly told that these passages are explanations of symbolical instruction. Some are dreams, some parables, some allegories, and some mysteries. They all have the same character, and belong to the same class. The reason for this is plain. In symbolical instruction, the symbolical characters are fictitious, and the characters represented are real. Hence, when we are first told that the symbolical characters are fictitious, and the represented characters are real, the usages of language allow the use of the verb to be between two nominatives, (one fictitious and the other real,) in a figurative sense.

There is no greater chance for a mistake in the explanation of a dream, parable, or allegory, because the form of the expression is in the positive, than there is in the narration of the same when the language used is in the *same* positive form. We are first told that it is symbolical in all the cases and this constitutes a key to the meaning. When we are once so informed, the statement proceeds as if the facts are real. "Behold a sower went forth to sow…."

Now these cases constitute a class of exceptions, for the simple reason, that they were all cases of symbolical instruction, in which the characters representing others were expressly stated to be fictitious, not real. How can such cases apply to the words, "This is my body?" Are we informed that there had been any dream here? any parable? any allegory? any mystery? or any explanation of any such things? Not at all.

We find the exceptions of the first class so plainly marked and distinguished, that no one ever yet had any difficulty in understanding them as such. But in reference to the words of institution, we find no such distinction. And is this want of such a character any reason why we should put them into the same class with parables, dreams, allegories and mysteries? The very fact that they are different requires us to put them in different classes. If the writer intended that the words in this case should be taken metaphorically, why did He not follow His usual course, and mark them as exceptions? Having marked all the cases that we know to be exceptions, why are we not given here the same marks to aid us, as in the other cases? For this reason, that the words of institution constitute no exception, and are purposely left to come under the general rule of literal interpretation!

The imaginative French writer Rousseau, objected to the practice of stating in fables that dumb beasts had a conversation with each other, for fear that children, seeing the positive form of the relation, would thence conclude that animals had the power of speech. Cowper, in one of his fables, takes off this writer very handsomely. He says, in substance, that a boy that could be led into error in this way "must have a most uncommon skull."

Despite the witticism of Cowper, and the fact that no child was ever deceived, there is a bare possibility that children may hereafter be deceived. Maybe there is something in Rousseau's objection? If grown and learned men can believe that the sense of words used in the explanation of a dream, parable, or allegory, can be at all applicable to texts where no such thing exists, then why not children be deceived by the positive *form* of words in a fable?

14. The second class of alleged exceptions considered

The case given under this class is simply one of comparison and constitutes no exception to the general rule. The words, "I am the vine," occur in a long discourse of our Lord with the eleven. Our Lord instituted a comparison between Himself and the vine. His meaning is, "I am as the vine, ye are as the branches." This is clearly shown in verses four and six.

In comparing two known and similar things together, it is very common to omit explanatory terms, such as resembles, like, as, similar. The reason is, because the known resemblance of the two things compared together, renders the use of these terms unnecessary. The tendency of all usage is toward brevity. Every composition is full of elliptical sentences.

There is not the slightest parallelism in the expressions, "I am the vine," and "This is my body." The first sentence is simply elliptical, and you only have to fill up the ellipsis to make the sentence complete. In the case of, "This is my body," if the Protestant construction is correct, you must first expunge the verb to be; and then substitute in its place a verb that represents a word having a different meaning.

The words of institution cannot be put into the second class for the reason that no comparison was intended by Christ between bread and His body. No one, so far as I am advised, has ever contended that any comparison was meant.

15. The third class of alleged exceptions

The two cases stated in this third class constitute no exceptions to the general rule, but come strictly within it. The verb is used in its literal sense.

The first passage, "This is my covenant between me and thee," has been made by a misconstruction to apparently support the metaphorical sense. I must say that I am at a loss to understand how so plain a mistake could be made. Had the question come up before a court of justice, this misconstruction, I think, could never have arisen. In this chapter we are told that God appeared to Abraham, and entered into a covenant with him and his posterity. From second verse to eight inclusive, the chapter is taken up with the conditions *on the part of God.* In verse nine, God tells Abraham expressly that the covenant embraces him and his seed. In verse ten, God gives Abraham the part of the covenant to be kept by him and his posterity, on their part. "This is my covenant, which ye shall keep, between me and you, and thy seed after thee. Every male child among you shall be circumcised."

The phrase, "This is my covenant," refers to the condition mentioned in the same sentence to be kept by Abraham; to wit: "Every male child among you shall be circumcised." The whole covenant is called God's covenant; but when God comes to speak of the part to be performed by Abraham He designates it by, "this is My covenant *which ye shall keep.*" He then gives the part of the covenant to be kept by Abraham.

This form of expression is common and proper among men. I may first state the conditions constituting the agreement and then say, "this is my agreement." Or I may say "this is my agreement," and then give the conditions. The sense is the same in both cases.[46]

It is true that God tells Abraham, in verse eleven: "And ye shall circumcise the flesh of your foreskin; and it shall be a token of the covenant betwixt me and thee." Now what is it that constitutes the *token*? Is it that part of the covenant that requires circumcision? Surely not. The covenant was one thing and the execution of it another thing. The covenant could exist without the execution of it. It was the *execution* of this part that constituted the token of the entire covenant. We can well understand how the executed act could constitute a token of the whole covenant, but we cannot well understand how part of the conditions could form a token of the covenant itself. God did not mean to say, "This my covenant is a token of my covenant."

The second passage in the third class, "It is the Lord's Passover," is simply the name of the feast. Before inflicting the tenth and final plague upon Egypt, the Lord instituted the Passover. God promised Moses and Aaron that He would pass over the houses of the Israelites harmless, if they would keep the feast. The twelfth chapters of Exodus from the third to the eleventh verses, is taken up in prescribing the manner in which the paschal lamb should be prepared and eaten with bitter herbs. After giving these particulars, the eleventh verse ends with the words: "Ye shall eat in haste (the lamb prepared as directed:) it (the same thing) is the Lord's Passover." Then language is very clear and simple. The word Passover, in this place, refers to the feast itself and not to the Lord's passage over the houses.

In the close of the eleventh verse, God intended to give the new feast a name, and to state that it was sacred to Him. The name is used for the first time in verse eleven, and afterwards in verses twenty-one and forty-three. It is so used in the New Testament: "Now the feast of unleavened bread drew nigh, called the Passover."[47]

God often gave names to things. In Genesis we are told he named the heavens and the earth. He sanctified the *seventh* day, and in Exodus in chapter twenty he calls it the *Sabbath*. In the New Testament Saint John calls it "The Lord's day."[48] It is clear from many examples in Scripture that whatever is sacred to the Lord is properly called "the Lord's." That the Passover was sacred to the Lord is shown in Exodus and is properly called the Lord's Passover.[49]

16. The three classes of objections in fact reveal the literal sense

We have now finished the consideration of some of those alleged cases of exception to the general rule; and we have seen that the only cases wherein the verb to be is used in the figurative sense, are those cases where an explanation of symbolical instruction is given.

I have endeavored to show that none of these passages has any application to the words of institution. They are not cases in point – they are plainly marked and distinguished, in most of the cases in express words, and in all by the clear context as special cases not coming under the general rule, but as clear exceptions to it – and that the words of institution cannot be brought into this class of exceptions, for the reason there was no dream – no parable – no allegory – and no explanation of any such thing in these words, nor in the circumstances attending their utterance. They were used in making our Lord's last Testament – in the solemn institution of the Sacrament and at a time, and in reference to a subject where the use of words in a new and unheard of symbolical sense would have been certainly as much out of place as we can possibly imagine.

I must think that if the question of construction regarded the language of a human lawgiver or writer, and such examples, taken from the mere interpretation of dreams, parables, and allegories, were brought forward by any party for the purpose of interpreting language used in its plain form, and not in application to dreams, parables, and allegories, that such party would be considered as governed by some strange and most singular delusion. In reference to the interpretation of Scripture, I must think that such a resort arises from the extreme destitution of materials in the shape of parallel passages. Nothing but the dry distress of writers could induce them to bring forward such examples.

With all due deference, I submit to the candor of my readers, whether these cases of exception, being thus so clearly marked and designated, as such, do not the more clearly show the literal sense of the words of institution. He who seeks to show an exception to the general rule of the plain ordinary literal sense, ought to make his case clear, by showing that the passage is strictly within a particular class of exceptions. The very fact that all conceded exceptions range themselves under one class – namely, the explanation of symbolical instruction, and that they are thus clearly marked as such does strengthen the general rule, by showing that no other exceptions are intended. Is there, in the Bible, one solitary case, where, in the solemn institution of a Sacrament, or in making of a last testament, language is used in a new and unexplained symbolical sense?

17. An objection from naming the figure with the thing represented

This is one of the most popular objections against the literal sense of the words, "This is my body." It is relied upon by Protestant writers generally. The examples cited are, a picture, a map, or bust. If we point to a portrait or bust, and say, "this is" such a person, naming him, or if we point to a map, and say "this is Europe," we are at once understood.

Portraits, busts, and maps are representations by resemblances. They are but images of the things they represent. Symbol is the very essence of their existence. They can only exist as symbols. This fact is known to all. Common usage is always founded upon common sense, and never requires the doing of an idle thing. Therefore, when we point to a picture, we are not required to inform the person whom we address, that it is a picture. His own senses assure him of the fact. But as he does not know the person or thing represented, we must inform him of this fact.

The case under consideration is wholly different. According to the Protestant view, Christ was for the first time constituting bread the symbol of His body. There being not the slightest natural resemblance between the figure and the object, and the bread having an independent existence as a real object in itself, and not as a figure, it was just as necessary to inform us of the fact that it was then made a figure as to inform us of the thing it represented. When an arbitrary figure is first constituted such, no one can know that it is a figure at all, unless so informed.

If a speaker should use a known term in a new figurative sense for the first time, he should give us a definition of this new sense. Thus when our Lord instituted the Sacrament of the Last Supper, and, for the first time, made it commemorated, He was careful to inform us of that fact "Do this in remembrance of me." If, then, the bread was used for the first time on that occasion to be a figure of the body of Christ, why did he not inform us? Why inform us in one case, and not in the other? Is not the fact that upon that occasion He did so inform us in one case, and not in the other, a very strong proof that the two cases are not alike?

This objection is founded upon the same basis as that drawn from symbolical instruction. It is but an attempt to apply the language used in the explanation of pictures, to the interpretation of positive forms of expression, not relating to any such thing. The symbolical characters in mysteries, parables, allegories, and dreams are all stated to be fictitious, and a picture is known to be but an image because it can be nothing else; and when we come to point out the thing represented, which has a real, or assumed real, existence, usage allows us to use the verb to be in a figurative sense because we are speaking of things first admitted to be figurative. But in reference to the bread, we are not told that it was figurative – there was no resemblance, such as a picture has to the thing represented --how, then, could we know it was a figure?

18. The objection that Christ spoke of the "fruit of the vine"

Another objection that is sometimes made is that no change could be admitted, because our Savior called the contents of the cup, "the fruit of the vine." This difficulty is entirely avoided by the explanation of Saint Luke, as referring to the cup before the institution of the Eucharist. It refers to the paschal cup, and not the sacramental.

This is shown by the simple narrative itself. Christ ate the Passover to close the sacrifice of the old law, and then, after supper, instituted the Eucharist.

19. The words of Saint Paul

Saint Paul in his first epistle to the Corinthians, speaks in two places of the Eucharist. As the King James and the Douay translations differ in one material point, I shall give both.

> The cup of blessing which we bless, is it not the communion of the blood of Christ? The bread which we break, is it not the communion of the body of Christ?

> The chalice of benediction which we bless, is it not the communion of the blood of Christ? And the bread which we break, is it not the partaking of the body of the Lord.[50]
>
> Wherefore, whosoever shall eat this bread, and drink this cup unworthily, shall be guilty of the body and blood of the Lord… .For he that eateth and drinketh unworthily eateth and drinketh damnation to himself, not discerning the body of the Lord.
>
> Therefore, whoever shall eat this bread, or drink the chalice of the Lord unworthily, shall be guilty of the body and blood of the Lord… For he that eateath and drinketh unworthily, eateth and drinketh judgment to himself, not discerning the body of the Lord.[51]

"The communion of the body of Christ." The word "communion" is here used in the sense of partaking, as shown by the two succeeding verses. There is then a real partaking here, and not a figurative eating. In the sixth of John the words "eat the flesh of the Son of Man," the Protestant says, mean a figurative eating, and in this extract they mean an actual partaking of the bread, and not of the body. In the sixth of John the real flesh was meant, but not the real eating. Here the real eating is meant but not the real body. The Catholic understands that it was a real eating, and a real flesh and body, in both cases; and certainly this construction is the most simple, natural, and consistent.

If the words "body and blood" are used in the first extract from Saint Paul in their literal sense, the Catholic is right. So, if the sixth of John refers to the Eucharist, the word "flesh" being used in its literal sense in verse fifty-two the equivalent word "body" in the extract from Saint Paul, should be used in the same literal sense. For if the Scripture in these different places refers to the same thing, then the words should be taken in their literal sense in both places.

Our Lord having instituted the Eucharist before Saint Paul wrote, there is nothing inconsistent with the Catholic view, in the language of the apostle, as to "eating the bread and drinking the cup," because the practice of still calling a thing after its change, by its former name, is very common in Scripture. This would be particularly so, when the appearances were still the same.

When the sense is once settled, the term will afterwards be used in that sense. Joseph was repeatedly called the father of our Lord.[52] And yet no one was misled by this, because we are informed in preceding places that Joseph was only His foster father. So, when the water was changed into wine, it was still called water after the change. So, when the eyes of the blind man had been opened, he was afterwards still called the "blind man."[53] So, when Aaron's rod had been changed into a serpent, it was still called a rod.[54] So, the angels that came to Lot were called men in some places, and angels in another. They were called men after they were stated to be angels.[55] Things in Scripture are often represented according to their appearance. Joshua is represented as commanding the sun to stand still, and the sun as obeying him. So the Catholic continues to call the elements bread and wine after consecration, and yet he believes in the change.

What will we do with the word "body" in the first extract from Saint Paul? If we construe it literally, and say that it was a literal partaking of a real body, then the sense is entirely consistent with the Catholic view. In the first extract the apostle says "communion of the body," and in the second "guilty of the body," not discerning the body." Now if the word "body" were used figuratively in one of these places, must it not be used in the same sense in the other passages? Is it not used in all the three cases to designate the real body?

"Guilty of the body and blood of the Lord." What is the meaning of this phrase, as shown by Scripture usage? "He deserves death;" referring to the punishment.[56] "For whoever keeps the whole law but fails in one point has become guilty of all of it."[57] This case from Saint James is the only parallel case in the New Testament. Here the phrase is applied to the object against which the offense was committed. In like manner the offense of an unworthy communion is against the body of our Lord. So, if the body and blood of Christ be present in the Eucharist, we can well see how Saint Paul could use the expression "guilty of the body and blood."

"Not discerning the Lord's body." We are first told by Saint Paul, that the party is guilty of the body; and then afterwards we are told that he drinks judgment to himself, not discerning the body. If the body were not present, how could it be discerned? But if the body were present, and was received as profane food, then we can well understand how the unworthy communicant would not discern the body.

It would seem that the passages from Saint Paul are not only consistent with the Catholic view, but that the literal sense can alone give them their legitimate force and effect. When the language of Saint Paul is taken in connection with that of Christ in the sixth chapter of John, and in the subsequent words of institution, the unity, simplicity, and force of the Catholic view, can be seen at once.

We have one united and consistent view, running through a number of passages, and harmonizing with the whole and forming one plain and simple system of interpretation. The arguments in support of Christianity, when taken and considered separately, are not so strong and conclusive as when united. Like the ten thousand small streams, that, separately considered, are insignificant, yet when united, form the mighty river, rolling its resistless volume to the ocean: so, the arguments of Christianity, when taken separately may fail to convince, yet when united and considered as a whole, they pour their combined proof in one overpowering stream upon the mind.

In like manner, the proofs of that wonderful doctrine the Real Presence, when taken separately, do not seem so conclusive as when combined and viewed in their concentrated force. It is then that the harmonious and beautiful features of that tender and sublime faith appear in their united consistency. So strong are the proofs from the most simple and unequivocal construction of the language of the Scriptures, that if the doctrine was not so hard to flesh and blood, it would seem that there never could have existed any doubt upon the subject.

20. The objection that it is a contradiction of our senses

Objections concerning the impossibility of contradicting our senses are much relied upon by most Protestant writers, such as Mr. Hallam, Dr. Clark, Mr. Horne, Dr. Tomline, and others. Mr. Faber objects to this mode of treating the subject and says: "Contradictions we can easily fancy, when in truth there are none." Again, he says, "The contradiction may not be in the matter itself, but in our mode of conceiving it."[58]

This is very candid and manly language, and becoming every humble and firm believer in the truth of Christianity. But notwithstanding this acknowledgement of the learned and courteous author, it must be conceded that he has given up the most effective argument against the literal sense. In saying *effective*, I do not mean an argument that should be effective but only practically so. It is giving up an argument based on the all-sufficiency of human reason to judge everything. The all-sufficiency of human reason addresses the pride of the human heart, in which it finds an every-ready echo. The fact of it being addressed to pride should cause it to be watched with the greatest care by the sincere and humble.

TRANSUBSTANTIATION

Mr. Horne tells us that "whatever is repugnant to natural reason cannot be the true meaning of the Scriptures." In what essential particular does this assumption differ from the very basis upon which the Infidel stands? They are both founded upon the supposed sufficiency of human reason to determine the essential laws of matter, and the rules by which God should govern the world, and the limits of His power. The Infidel takes the Scriptures, and gives them what he thinks a natural and proper construction, and he finds therein stated, facts and doctrines at war with his reason and his experience; and he, therefore, rejects the entire system.

Mr. Horne is less clear, and not so consistent. He first admits that the Scriptures are true – that they reveal stupendous mysteries, proven by stupendous miracles; and after these admissions, whatever construction, however plain, simple, and natural, which evolves a doctrine "repugnant to natural reason." or what he may consider such, he rejects. In other words, he prunes off all absurd shoots from the tree of Christianity, until he brings it to that form of abstract ideal beauty, existing in his own mind. The Infidel, upon the basis of the sufficiency of his reason to determine what is possible with God, and what sort of government God ought to give to man, rejects the entire system. Not so with Mr. Horne. He admits the system, but tears it into fragments, and then selects only such as may suit his "natural reason."

There are certainly some things more properly within the sphere of human reason. The weight and force of human testimony is a matter coming peculiarly within the province of man's intellect. He ought to know the habits, feelings, and character of his own species, with whom he is identified in all his natural powers. He may have a perfect knowledge of some of the laws of nature. Aided by his knowledge of the more obvious and well-known laws of nature, he is competent to determine that a certain event is miraculous, and that the person who performed it is gifted with supernatural power. But when misled by the "meteor ray" of reason, he quits his own sphere. He rushes "into the skies," assumes to set limits to the power of God, and he deserves the severe language of Pope:

"Go, wond'rous creature, mount where science guides;
Go, measure earth, weigh air, and state the tides.
Go, teach Eternal Wisdom how to rule,
Then drop into thyself, and be a fool."

We shall proceed to examine these arguments at one view, for they are all essentially based upon the same principle; that is, the ground of physical impossibility. We have already spoken of known miracles, as being violations or suspensions of the known laws of nature. We find, as a part of the known laws of nature, that two substances cannot occupy the same space at the same time and that the same body cannot occupy different spaces at the same time. If we should see a single body occupy different spaces, or two bodies the same space, at the same time, we are competent to say that it is a miracle. But while we could well say that such an event was a miracle, could we undertake to say that such an event is impossible? There is immeasurable distance between the two! In one we undertake only to determine what is consistent with the present known laws of nature; but in the other, we assume to put limits to the Eternal. What ideas have mere finite beings of Infinite power? Just in the same proportion as finite to infinite – as time to eternity.

The Protestant philosopher admits that God spoke the world into existence from nothing – that miracles are not only possible, but have occurred – yet when told that the same Infinite Creator can suspend, modify, overcome, or change any of the laws of nature, and can give to a body some of the properties of the spirit, he objects, upon the ground of impossibility. He concedes that some of the laws of matter are within the power of God, but insists that others are not. And such objection is simply based upon the results of his limited experience of an existing system; when he knows absolutely nothing of mere possible systems; and could not, therefore, pretend to form any accurate conception concerning them.

The properties of matter were given it by the Creator, when He formed the universe from nothing. He who made, surely can destroy, suspend, or change. If God can take from matter one property, or overcome or suspend, for the time, its effect, upon what principle of reason can we say that He cannot do so in reference to another or to several? We believe that God created spirits. These we consider not subject to the laws of matter. The Atheist rejects the belief in the existence of the soul, because the eye and knife of the surgeon cannot detect its seat in the human brain. He does this notwithstanding he knows we have no accurate conceptions of the magnitude or minuteness of organized bodies. He knows that minute insects exist, with perfect organizations, hundreds of which can sport in a single drop of water; and that the flea, when examined by a microscope, appears a horrid monster of enormous size.

The Protestant believes that Satan is a created but fallen spirit; but he tempts men in Europe, Asia, America, and Africa, at the same time. Now, upon what principle of reason or philosophy can we say that God has power over some of the properties of matter, and not over all? If God can create a spirit, could He not impress a portion or the whole of its properties upon a body, and overcome or suspend some or all of the properties of matter, at the same time? In other words, could not God, by His infinite power take from a body, or overcome, for the time, that property which prevents it from occupying two or more places at the same time? Who is that philosopher who would venture to say that Christ, who raised his own body from the grave, could not give that body the property in question? Can any man with all his pride of intellect have sufficient confidence in his imaginary knowledge of mere possible systems, as to put it against the assertion of God?

There are metaphysical but no physical, impossibilities with God. The former result from the unchangeable character of His attributes. When the Infidel alleges truly that God could not make two hills without a valley between, the impossibility is metaphysical, not physical. The valley is a part of the two hills, and it is metaphysically impossible for God to do and not to do, the same thing at the same time. But all material things were created by God, and He has, for that reason, perfect and unlimited physical dominion over them to do anything He pleases that is not, in its effects, contrary to His own nature. The presence of Christ's body in the Eucharist cannot be against the character of God, and cannot be physically impossible. In Scripture, we are assured of metaphysical impossibilities with God, but it would be difficult to find any intimation that there could be any physical impossibility with Him. On the contrary, our Lord, when speaking of a supposed physical impossibility, declares that "all things are possible with God." There is no limit to this general declaration, and no qualification of it, as applicable to the class of possibility our Lord had in His mind when using these broad words.

If our knowledge of the existing laws of matter ought to have any effect upon our ideas of physical possibility or impossibility with God, then I must say, that the position of the Atheist is more consistent than that of those who first concede that God can control some of the laws of matter and then deny His power over others. The Atheist lays down a consistent rule, when he will admit of no interference to the laws of matter. But the Protestant philosopher admits the power of God over the subject matter, and then presumes to set limits to the power itself.

That the Real Presence of Christ in the Eucharist is a most incomprehensible mystery, and a most stupendous miracle, must be conceded. It is like any other mystery. Human reason cannot fathom mysteries. If it could, it could fathom everything. There could then be no limits to its power. We should be as wise as our Creator. No man can comprehend the mysterious union of the human and Divine in Christ. Had I waited until I could comprehend that mystery, I should never have been a Christian.

There are many of the most familiar facts that we cannot comprehend. How is it that a single spark will set on fire and consume a whole city? How does the fire increase? How is it that the simple will of a man will put into instant motion all his muscular powers, and at once overcome some of the cardinal laws of matter? How is it that the heart, from our birth to our death, never ceases its pulsations day or night? What power keeps it going? How is it that the moment the mysterious principle of life is extinguished, our bodies become like any other inert mass of matter? I suppose if an individual was brought up on a solitary island, with no opportunity to see or hear of a single instance of death, that at the age of thirty, he would have no conception of death, and would think it impossible if suggested to him. Even with our conclusive knowledge of the fact, people in health never feel like dying, and most of them act as if they never expected to die. The idea of death is not intuitive, but acquired.

How to explain the mystery of the Trinity I cannot tell. But on the other hand, I cannot see how I can reject the belief of this great mystery, without holding Christ to be a mere impostor. Nor can I understand how He could be either a Mediator or Redeemer, unless the doctrine of the Trinity be true. The doctrine of original sin presents many difficulties; but reject it, and then I cannot understand how Christ could be a Redeemer at all or what He had to redeem us from. Take away any of these doctrines, and we have but the shadow of Christianity left. The confident Socinian thinks that the absurdity of the doctrine of the Trinity is mathematically demonstrable. But all this, against the clear revelation of Jesus Christ, does not amount to anything. We find ourselves too often mistaken in reference to abstract matters to rely with any confidence upon our weak ideas of such things.

The evidence of some of our senses in receiving the Eucharist ought not, any more than our abstract ideas of possibility, to influence us to doubt a revealed truth, especially a mystery. It may be a theme for ignorant ridicule or senseless declamation, but will hardly stand the test of theological or scientific truth. Philosophy and experience teach us that some of our senses at times deceive us.

We are told that the Holy Spirit descended upon our Lord in the form of a dove. To the eye it was a dove, and had every appearance of a dove; and yet we believe it was not a dove. So, the Jews rejected Christ upon the evidence of some of their senses. They said, "Is not this Jesus, the son of Joseph, whose father and mother we know? How is it, then, that he saith, "I came down from heaven?" "In like manner Joshua thought he saw a man,[59] and Jacob that he touched one,[60] and Abraham, that he ate with three men,[61] when in all these instances there were no real men but embodied spirits present, the different senses of those patriarchs misleading them. Again: were not the eyes of the disciples going to Emmaus held so that they should not know Jesus?[62] Did not the same thing happen to Mary Magdalene and the apostles?[63]

After the resurrection of Christ, we are told that He appeared twice to His disciples when the doors were shut for fear of the Jews.[64] The circumstance of the doors being shut is mentioned to let us know that His sudden appearance was miraculous. How did His body pass through the wall or door? It might be that He made an opening, and closed it again after His entrance; but this does not seem to be consistent with other circumstances. After traveling with the two disciples to Emmaus, while their eyes were holden, He opened them in the breaking of bread, and after their eyes were opened and they knew Him, "he *vanished* out of their sight."[65] He again appeared to many disciples, and from the simple narrative, it would seem plain that the first they saw of Christ, He was standing in their midst. "And as they thus spake, Jesus stood in the midst of them."[66] Not only this language, but the circumstance of their terror, goes to show that He was not seen until He was standing in their midst. Now when He vanished out of the sight of the two disciples at Emmaus, it is clear that they had their senses, and that Christ rendered His body invisible. So when He appeared in their midst.

It is true, that in the Eucharist, there are more senses than one deceived; and that in some of the cases mentioned, it was equally so. The dove was only subjected to the test of sight. But in the case of the angel that spoke and wrestled with Jacob, and those that spoke and eat before Abraham, more than one sense was deceived. This is the case also of the Jews regarding Christ. And in regard to the two angels that appeared to Lot,[67] and spoke with him, and eat before him, and caught hold of his hands, there were three senses deceived. They looked like men, spoke like men, and felt like men; so that sight, hearing, and feeling were all deceived, as well as in the case of the angel that wrestled with Jacob. What, then, is the essential difference in the cases? Why should the *Christian* say one is possible, the other not?

I would not dare to assert that it was impossible for God to make known to us His will, even against the evidence of all our senses. But in the Eucharist all the senses are not deceived. If, therefore, God, as in the cases mentioned, deceived a portion of our senses, and yet conveyed to us the truth through the sense of hearing, why cannot this be true of the Eucharist? I most readily admit that I cannot perceive any difference in the two cases. Such an objection is consistent in the mouth of an Atheist, but out of place in the mouth of him who professes to believe in the Scriptures.

Should I think that such an objection had any reason in it, when applied to Christianity, (that wonderful system, founded and based upon, and proved by, miracles of almost every kind and form,) I should then be placed in a painful position. I would be placed between two difficulties; for if I take the Protestant view, I am thrown upon a difficulty, still more inconsistent with all my conceptions of possibility and impossibility. In such a case, I am forced to attribute to our Lord a course of conduct and teaching not only at war with all my ideas of what is just and proper in a lawgiver, not only to himself, but to his subjects; but especially inconsistent with all my conceptions of Christ as a Divine Legislator. We are assured in Scripture that there are *moral* impossibilities with God, for He cannot lie; and I am forced to choose between that which I cannot justify, upon any conceivable ground of moral right, and that mere abstract objection to the literal sense, founded upon our uncertain knowledge of what is or is not a physical impossibility with God. Which difficulty shall I choose? If I take the Catholic view, and should be mistaken, I only give to Christ more power and love than are due to Him. But if I take the other view, and should be mistaken, I not only rob Him of the power and love due to Him, but I place Him in a position as a teacher of truth, wholly at war with all our conceptions of moral right.

If I am to err at all, O! let me err on the side of faith and love. I would rather give Christ too much than too little power. I would rather believe too much than too little. If I am to err, let my errors "lean to virtue's side." If I take the Catholic view, I find a great physical mystery, which I can believe, but which is incomprehensible. If I take the Protestant view, I find a moral mystery that my reason cannot justify or explain.

Were I to indulge my reason as to what a religion should be, I would ask, what would religion be worth without mysteries? What heavenly principle is there in that proud faith that refuses to believe in mysteries, because incomprehensible to fallible reason? What reason is there in the supposition that a fallible mind can comprehend the nature of mysteries? Were a being to appear to me for the purpose of teaching me a religion, the first thing my reason tells me I have a right to ask, is a sufficient proof of his character. As I am competent to judge of testimony, and to determine from my knowledge of some of the laws of nature, whether a particular event be a miracle or not, I could form a conclusion as to the fact whether the messenger was sent of God, or whether he was an impostor.

When satisfied that he was divinely commissioned, I should be prepared to believe him upon his *word alone*. Knowing my own limited powers, I should expect him to reveal to me many plain and simple facts and doctrines, regulating my conduct towards my fellow men on earth. But in reference to the heavenly world, and the nature of the blessed spirits who inhabit it, and the nature of God and His institutions, I should expect Him to reveal to me some incomprehensible mysteries, which He would rightfully require me to believe implicitly upon His word alone. If He revealed to me no truth or mystery above my finite comprehension, I should be tempted to doubt whether he knew any thing supernatural, and whether he had come from that heaven which even the learned, eloquent, and inspired Paul would not attempt to describe.

21. Reflections on the mystery of the Sacrament

While I readily and cheerfully admit that there is a mystery and a miracle in the Real Presence, and that I cannot comprehend the mere manner of this mystery, I can see in the institution itself the utmost reason, beauty, and love. In other words, I can see the best reasons for its institution, the greatest beauty in its doctrine, and the utmost display of love in its administration.

Whoever has read the Bible, and has any tolerable knowledge of God's dealings with His servants, must have been struck with the fact, that He often tested their faith in the most severe and conclusive form. These tests were not designed for the information of God, but for the benefit of His servants. It is right and beneficent, in the nature of the relation of servant and master, that the fidelity of the servant should be submitted to a conclusive test. It is good for the servant himself, especially when his eternal welfare depends upon his strict fidelity.

Under the Old dispensation, when the Almighty appeared to His prophets, at intervals, as occasion demanded, we find different tests of faith adopted. Some of these were designed to try the faith of only one person, while others were designed to try the faith of a whole people. In the twenty second chapter of Genesis, we have the simple and affecting narrative of the severe test of faith to which God subjected His servant Abraham, when He commanded him to sacrifice his own son Isaac – the son that had been born to him in his old age, by a miracle. And we are informed with what fidelity the old patriarch complied with the command of his Master, until prevented by an angel from destroying his young son, while in the very act of taking his knife to shed his blood. Here was an example of pure and holy faith, worthy of all imitation.

In the sixteenth chapter of Exodus, we are informed that the Israelites murmured in the wilderness of Sinai, because they had no bread, and that God sent them manna to prove them.

> And then said the Lord unto Moses, Behold, I will rain bread from heaven for you; and the people shall go out and gather a certain rate every day, that I may prove them, whether they will walk in my law or no.

These are only two out of the many instances contained in the Old Testament.

In the New Testament we find many instances in which our Lord tested the faith of His disciples while He was with them, among which it will only be necessary to mention a few. In the sixth chapter of Saint John, our Lord tried Philip by asking him, "Whence shall we buy bread that these may eat?" A very affecting instance is given where Christ subjected the faith of Martha to a severe test, when He says to her: "He that believeth in me, though he were dead, yet shall he live; and whosoever liveth and believeth in me, shall never die. Believest thou this?"[68]

But perhaps the most affecting instance mentioned in any of the four gospels, is the case of the woman of Canaan, found in the fifteenth chapter of Matthew.

> And behold, a woman of Canaan came out of the same coasts, and cried unto him, saying, Have mercy on me, O Lord, thou son of David; my daughter is grievously vexed with a devil. But he answered her not a word. And his disciples came and besought him, saying, Send her away; for she crieth after us. But he answered and said, I am not sent but unto the lost sheep of the house of Israel. Then she came and worshipped him, saying, Lord, help me. But he answered and said, It is not meet to take the children's bread and to cast it to dogs. And she said, Truth, Lord; yet the dogs eat of the crumbs which fall from their master's table. Then Jesus answered and said unto her, O woman, great is thy faith; be it unto thee even as thou wilt.[69]

What a beautiful instance of pure and humble faith! I can scarcely ever read this simple narrative without the tribute of a tear, and a hearty wish that my heart had as little pride in it as the heart of that poor woman.

The examples we find in the Old and New Testaments show the utility of tests of faith. These tests all passed away with the old dispensation. As Christ left us a finished and universal system, which is to endure unto the end of the world, and applicable to all nations, in all subsequent time, it would seem to have been reasonable and just, in itself, that He should establish a permanent test of faith, as enduring and uniform as faith itself. And if any test of faith was to remain, what could be more conclusive than the doctrine of the Real Presence?

That Christianity is a system founded on miracles, must be conceded. He who believes it must believe in wonderful displays of supernatural power. He must believe all the miracles of the Old and New Testament, and must do so without regard to the occasion of the nature of the miracle itself. He must believe all, from the crossing of the Red Sea to the widow's cruse of oil. However great or small the miracle, he must regard it as equally easy with God, and equally worthy of his power. This belief in the mind of the Christian must be a living and continued faith, not to be banished by the "Godless look of earth," or the sneer of the proud and vain.

Now it must be manifest that it requires a much greater degree of humble faith to believe in the Real Presence of Christ in the Eucharist, than in a mere symbolical presence. This is conclusively shown by the fact that most of those who believe in the metaphorical sense, rely upon the testimony of their senses, and upon their abstract ideas of possibility. When Dr. Tomlin, Bishop Porteus, Dr. Clark, Mr. Horne, Mr, Hallam, and others tell me that they believe it *impossible* for the body of Christ to be present in the Eucharist, they tell me that if they were satisfied that such a doctrine was revealed in Scripture, they would reject the entire system of Christianity. For it is clear, that a man cannot believe that which he considers impossible.

The man that sincerely believes in the doctrine of the Real Presence has no seeds of infidelity in his mind. Such a man relies with implicit and unfaltering faith upon the Word of God. It is much easier, and requires a much less degree of faith, to believe in the miracles of the dim, distant past, than in those that are alleged to occur in our own presence, and in contradiction to some of our senses. We may believe, upon the Word of God, that the sense of Abraham and Lot, and others, were deceived; but when, upon the same Word of God, we are required to believe that our own senses are deceived in part, then comes the genuine and living test of faith in the Word of God, and the truth of the whole system.

In looking over the chapters of the New Testament, especially the Gospels, one cannot but be forcibly struck with the great and paramount importance of faith. Our Savior never failed to reward this cardinal virtue. In some cases He went out of the usual course of His ministry to reward it, as in the case of the woman of Canaan. He never failed to express His warm approbation of every confiding display of it. We find Him often reproving His disciples for their want of faith. And while our Lord was so careful to inculcate the absolute necessity of this first fundamental principle, He was no less careful to condemn that vice in the human heart which is the most determined enemy of faith. If there be one human passion against which Christ and his apostles warred energetically than against any other, it

"Is pride, the never-failing vice of fools,"

as Pope has expressed it. The gospel narrative will show how often this evil principle was the mother of disobedience and unbelief, in the chosen twelve, even after they had heard the divine lessons of our Lord, and witnessed all his wonderful displays of power for more than three years. We see it exhibited in Peter when he refused to let his Master wash his feet.

TRANSUBSTANTIATION

There is no doctrine that so forcibly inculcates simple and unflinching faith as the doctrine of the Real Presence; and there is no doctrine that requires a greater disregard of the natural pride of the human mind. This is shown by the proud and contemptuous sneers of the majority of writers whom I have mentioned.

It was evidently the intention of Christ to keep the faith pure and entire. In the nature of the system it could not accommodate its truths to the views of men. It was, and ever must be, one and inflexible. While our Lord and His apostles, as to the mere manner of inculcating truth, were as kind and gentle as could have been desired, they never softened the doctrines themselves, for the purpose of gaining converts.

Every attempt to extend the principles of the system, either by latitudinarian construction, or by any other means, so as to bring it down to the comprehension of natural reason, or the loose opinions of men, is only so much injury to the purity of the system itself. Like the idle attempt to increase the value of the circulating medium by debasing the coin, every attempt to shake this unchangeable system to suit the humors and versatilities of men, must necessarily render the system less lovely and beautiful, and, therefore, in the end, less attractive to the really pious and virtuous. In this way the progress of the system itself would be retarded. But by requiring a firm and implicit belief in continued displays of omnipotent power and this upon the once-delivered and unqualified Word of God, and in opposition to some of our own senses, our Lord has given us, not only one of the most practical and severe tests of faith, but has given us a golden tie that binds us still more powerfully to the cause of virtue.

For what can more powerfully impress the human soul than this awfully sublime and tender faith? What can more fully display, and continue to display, that invincible love wherewith Christ has loved us? When we look back over His mortal career, and see how much He suffered, how many most grievous insults He endured, and then reflect that all this was purely voluntary, we cannot think that this great display of His love, is unbecoming His unbounded mercy towards those who love Him.

The legitimate and natural effect upon the mind of the humble and sincere believer in the Catholic view cannot be well described in words. It would seem manifest that such a belief must fill the mind and soul with the most tender and fervent impulses. Well might the Infidel Voltaire say:

> Behold the man, who, amidst the awful ceremonies of the Mass receives the holy communion. His whole soul is seized and strongly affected. Hardly does he breathe. He is detached from every earthly thing – he is united to his God. God is incorporated with his flesh and blood. Who will dare --who possibly can, after such an action, be guilty of any future relapses into sin? Is it possible to imagine a mystery that could bind a man more forcibly to virtue?

The following extract from a very recent work Hilliard's *Six Months in Italy* describes the services at Christmas, at Saint Peter's, in Rome:

> High Mass was said by the Pope in person, and the responses were sung by the choir. He performed the service with an air and manner expressive of true devotion, and though I felt that there was a chasm between me and the rite which I witnessed, I followed his movements in the spirit of respect, and not of criticism. But one impressive and overpowering moment will never be forgotten. When the tinkling of the bell announced the elevation of the Host, the whole of the vast assemblage knelt or bowed their faces. The pavement was suddenly strewn with prostrate forms. A silence like that of death fell upon the church, as if some celestial vision had passed before the living eyes, and hushed into stillness every pulse of human feeling. After a pause of a few seconds, during which every man could have heard the beating of his own heart, a band of wind instruments, near the entrance, of whose presence I had not been aware, poured forth a few sweet and solemn strains, which floated up the nave and overflowed the whole interior. The effect of this invisible music was beyond anything I have ever heard or expect to hear. The air seemed stirred with the trembling of angelic wings, or as if the gates of heaven had been opened, and a "wandering breath" from the songs of seraphs had been borne to the earth. How fearfully and wonderfully are we made! A few sounds, which, under ordinary circumstances, would have been merely a passing luxury to the ear, heard at this moment, and beneath this dome, were like a purifying wave, which, for an instant, swept over the soul, bearing away with it all the soil and stains of earth, and leaving it pure as in infancy. There was, it is true, a refluent tide; and the world, displaced by the solemn strain, came back with the echo; but though we "cannot keep the heights we are competent to gain," we are the better for the too brief exaltation.

The eloquent Protestant has beautifully described his own feelings; but who shall adequately describe those of the humble Catholic? I cannot. Language is poor. There are some holy things beyond its power.

22. Discipline of the Secret

In order to understand the meaning of the Fathers, and to explain certain passages or their writings, it is necessary to understand the practice of the early suffering Church, in reference to the mysteries. For several centuries it was the general practice to hide, as far as practicable, the leading mysteries of the Christian Religion from Pagans, and even from the catechumens. A knowledge of these mysteries was generally communicated to the *baptized*, or to the *initiated*, as they were called. This practice was called the Discipline of the Secret.

Saint Clement, of Alexandria, is the first writer who mentions this Discipline. He speaks of it without hesitation, doubt, or apology, as a practice in the Church, and grounds it upon these words of Christ: "Cast not your pearls before swine...." He says:

> And since not this tradition alone is made manifest to him who has felt the greatness of the Word, the wisdom spoken in a mystery, which the Son of God taught, is to be concealed.... He (Christ) has permitted us to impart the divine mysteries, and that holy light, to those who are able to receive them.... We have performed our task in such a manner as to render the discovery of the holy traditions no easy task for any of the uninitiated."[70]

Tertullian, speaking of heretics, says:

> In the first place it is doubtful who is a catechumen, who a believer: they have all access alike; they hear alike; they pray alike; even if heathens come in upon them, they will cast that which is holy unto dogs; and pearls, false though they be, before swine.

Origen says:

> Celsus frequently calls our doctrine hidden, though the gospel of the Christians is, almost throughout the whole world, better known than the opinions of philosophers....
>
> But there being, besides the exoteric doctrines, some things which are not manifested to the crowd, is not peculiar to the doctrines of Christians only, but was also amongst the philosophers, amongst whom some discourses were exoteric, and some also esoteric."[71]

Saint Hypolitus says:

> But see that you do not confide these things to unbelieving and blasphemous tongues, for the danger is not slight, but entrust them to faithful men.

"And we are also ordered," says Saint Cyprian,

> to keep what is holy within our own knowledge, and not expose it to be trodden on by swine and dogs.[72]

"These mysteries," says Archelaus,

> the Church now unfolds to those who are passed from the class of catechumens; to the Gentiles it is not the custom to manifest them.[73]

Lactantius says:

> Beyond the mere words, he cannot please those who are ignorant of the sacrament, inasmuch as the things that he has written are mystical, and purposely designed to be understood by the faithful only.

This is said in reference to Saint Cyprian's writings.[74]

One of the chapters of Eusebius is headed thus:

> That it beseems not to make known to all, the more venerable doctrines of truth.[75]

And Saint Athanasius says:

> As to the mystic cup, what was, or when was it broken by Macarius?…
>
> Nor are they (the Arians) ashamed to display publicly the mysteries before the catechumens; and what is worse still, before the heathens.…
>
> For the mysteries ought not to be publicly exhibited to the uninitiated, lest the Gentiles, who understand them not, scoff; and the catechumens, becoming curious, be scandalized.[76]

I might add the testimony of Saint Gregory of Myssa, Saint Basil, Saint Philastrius, Saint Epiphanius, Saint Ambrose, Saint J. Chrysostom, and many others. But it is unnecessary, as the fact is not disputed.

It has sometimes been denied that the Eucharist was had among the mysteries. But the extracts from Saint Athanasius and Lactantius are clear that it was. So the testimony of Saint Gregory of Nyssa is full to that point. If a mystery, it came under the general discipline which included all mysteries. And Saint Ambrose says: "The time admonishes us to treat of the mysteries, and to proclaim the meaning of the sacraments." And Saint Augustine says: "If we say to a catechumen, 'Dost thou believe in Christ?' he will answer, 'I do believe,' and sign himself: he already carries on his forehead the cross of Christ, and is not ashamed of the cross of his Lord. So he has believed in his name. Let us ask him: 'Durst thou eat the flesh of the Son of man. and drink the blood of the Son of man?' he knows not what to say, because Jesus has not trusted himself to him."[77]

And Saint Paladius says:

> And the evil stopped not here, but the Soldiers, of whom some, as we have learned, were even uninitiated, entering into where the holy things were deposited, saw every thing that was within, and the most holy blood of Christ, so great was the tumult, was spilt upon their dress.[78]

Saint Cyril, of Alexandria, says:

> When he (the catechumen) has joined his praise to that of the perfect (initiated), he withdraws from the more secret mysteries, and is excluded from Christ's sacrifice.[79]

Theodoret also places the Eucharist among the mysteries. And Tertullian, in his Apology, says: "It is the common law of all mysteries to keep them secret."

If, then, we wish to correctly understand what were the sentiments of the early Church, we must look mainly to those instructions given to the *initiated*, and not so much to those intended for the multitude without, in which the language used is often obscure, in pursuance of the Secret Discipline.

23. Testimony of Saint Ignatius.

The first Father who speaks of this doctrine, is Ignatius, Bishop of the great Eastern city of Antioch for forty years, and a holy martyr under the Emperor Trajan. This holy and distinguished person was the disciple and friend of the apostles; particularly of Saint Peter and Saint John. In A.D. 106, in his old age, and about six years after the death of Saint John, the persecuting Roman Emperor came to Antioch, and had the holy man brought before him. Ignatius "confessed and denied not," and the Emperor "commanded that he be carried by soldiers in chains unto the great city of Rome, there to be devoured by wild beasts for the public gratification." "When the holy martyr," says the account of his martyrdom, "heard this announcement, he cried out with joy: 'I thank Thee, O my Master, for that thou has permitted me to show forth in the penalty I am to suffer, the perfect love I have toward Thee; and has associated me with thine Apostle Paul in these iron bands.'" "From

Syria," he says in his Epistle to the Romans, "unto Rome I carry forward my sufferings, by land and sea, night and day; enchained of ten leopards, which are the soldiers ranked around me; who by kindness are made harsher."

On his journey to Rome, he visited the Holy Polycarp, Bishop of Smyrna, the "Angel" of Smyrna mentioned in Revelation 2:8-11. During his journey he wrote several Epistles to different churches, and one to Polycarp. We owe it to Polycarp that these important Epistles were preserved to after ages. While at Smyrna he wrote several of them, especially that to the Romans; and after leaving them at Troas, he wrote his epistles to Polycarp, and the Church at Smyrna. His Epistles are seven in number, and were separately addressed to the Ephesians, the Magnesians, the Trallians, the Church at Smyrna, the Romans, the Philadelphians, and Polycarp.

In his Epistle to the Romans, he besought his brethren not to interfere for his safety, in terms the most simple, touching, and beautiful. "You can give me no better gift," says he,

> than my immolation to God, while yet the altar is ready... I long for the wild beasts that are prepared for me... Fire and the cross, the assaults of beasts, the rending of my bones, the laceration of my limbs, the crushing of my whole frame, dire tortures of Satan, let them come upon me, so that I but go to Christ....
>
> Have pity on me my brethren... Suffer me to imitate the sufferings of my God...
>
> If, when I come among you, I claim of you to interfere for my preservation, yet listen not to me. Keep faith rather with the terms in which I now write to you. I live, but while I am writing to you, I long to die. My affections are crucified... This is no time for holding peace; when Christianity is hated of the world, it calls for high exertion... I have written to you in few words. Place confidence in me. Surely Jesus Christ shall make this manifest to you, that I have spoken truly... Remember in your prayers the Church that is in Syria, which hath God for its shepherd instead of me. Its only Bishop now will be Jesus Christ, and your love. I feel unworthy to bear the name of my flock. I am the last among them.

Before he arrived at Rome, and after landing at a place called Portius, a short distance from the city:

> He was met by certain brethren, whose minds were in a mingled state of fear and joy... To some of them he expressed a wish that they

should hold back from interference; as in the ardor of their feelings, they declared their intention of inducing the populace to ask that this good man might not be killed. Knowing this, he implored all, after saluting them, to show him a true love; expressing himself more largely on the point than in his Epistle; and entreating them not to injure the prospects of one who was hastening to his Lord. And so, with all the brethren on their bended knees, he besought the Son of God for the churches, that he would remove from them this persecution, and confirm the brotherhood in all mutual love...

He was thrown to the wild beasts close to the temple. We personally witnessed everything," say the writers of this account, "and passed the following night within doors, in tears; and often knelt we down and addressed to the Lord a prayer, that He would strengthen that reliance in Him, which the event of the day had tended to disturb.

In his Epistle to the Ephesians, he says:

Obeying the bishop and the presbytery with an entire mind; breaking one bread, which is the medicine of immortality; an antidote that we should not die, but live forever in Jesus Christ.

In his Epistle to the church at Smyrna, he speaks of the Doceta, who denied that Christ had a real body. He says:

He (Christ) suffered all these things for us, and for our salvation; and he verily suffered, as He in verity also raised himself again; and not, as some unbelievers say, that He suffered in appearance only, being themselves only in appearance; and according to their belief, so shall it be unto them, seeing that they are Phantastics and Demoniacs.

He further speaks of these heretics, and says:

But I forewarn you against beasts in human shape; these you must not only not admit to your society, but, if possible, not even come in their way. Only pray for them, that if by an means they may repent.... They (the heretics) abstain from the Eucharist and prayer, because they confess not that the Eucharist is the flesh of our Savior Jesus Christ, the flesh which suffered for our sins, which the Father in his mercy raised again. They, therefore, who deny the gift of God, perish in their disputing. Well had it been for them to make much of it, that they also might rise again.

The same sentiments are expressed in his Epistle to the Romans, and in that to the Philadelphians.

This language of Ignatius is so plain, and the intention so manifest, that I am not aware of any attempt to explain them away by any

Protestant writer. For he does state most explicitly, that the "*Eucharist is the flesh of our Savior Jesus Christ*;" and then to make it still more clear and certain as to what flesh he did mean, he says: "*the* flesh which suffered for our sins, *which* the Father, in his mercy, raised again." And he calls those heretics who denied this doctrine; and ascribes an efficacy to the Eucharist, which could only belong to it in the view of one who held the Real Presence of Christ in this Sacrament. He says: "Well had it been for them to make much of it, that they also might rise again; "clearly alluding to the words of our Lord: "Whoso eateth my flesh, and drinketh my blood, hath eternal life; and I will raise him up at the last day."[80]

But, Old Martyr, what right had you to say so? What right had you to put forth that as a doctrine of the Church? You speak of it, in your Epistle to the church, over which the sainted Polycarp then, and for many years afterward presided as bishop, as a doctrine of the Church. For you introduce it "without hesitation, doubt, or apology," as our Dr. Paley has it. And where did you find this wonderful and visionary doctrine? Were you the inventor? Did your acute and metaphysical mind originate it? You were the disciple of the apostles – were instructed and appointed by them – and claimed to have learned all you knew of Christianity from them.

Did you learn this doctrine from the author of Saint John's Gospel? If not, you were in great haste to introduce heresy. This was certainly very inconsistent in you. Did you not warn your Magnesian brethren not to "be led astray by strange doctrine, or by old fables, which are unprofitable?" Did you not urge the Trallians "to use only the Christian nourishment, and to abstain from that strange herb, which is heresy?" And did you not urge upon all the necessity of unity, and to "concur in professing the name of one faith, and one Jesus Christ?" And did you not urge holy Polycarp to "be in all things 'wise as the serpent and harmless as the dove?'" Did you not warn him to "stand firm as the anvil under the stroke?" How then, in the face of all these expressions, could you introduce this strange doctrine? And how could you, on your very way to martyrdom, after using the glowing, yet simple language, so befitting the valiant martyr for the cause of Christ, put forth such a doctrine? Was all your firmness, all your devotion, all your tenderness, but assumed, only to give force to your statement of this alleged false and absurd doctrine? Did you die with a falsehood in your mouth? It would seem impossible, old Christian hero, that you did.

But were you not deceived yourself? And how could this be? You were a leading man, eminent for talents, zeal, and fidelity, and for many years bishop of the great city of Antioch; and your memory has ever been sweet to your brethren. Your reputation for all the qualities that meet and mingle in the character of the eminent saint, was widely diffused. Your praise was in all the churches. Your Epistles have been transmitted to us of this distant day, and will doubtless go down to later generations. They are full or words of sweet humility and holy confidence, of resignation and hope. Who can read them with a tearless eye? Who can believe that you were either an impostor or a dupe? And if you were a dupe, who made you so? How did you so soon forget the instructions of the apostles, who converted and appointed you? Was not this doctrine of such an extraordinary character, as to arrest, at once, your attention, and arouse your determined opposition, *if untrue*? Your "*integrity* was insured by the insults you suffered;" and your *ability* by the opportunities you enjoyed. How then could you deceive, or be deceived?

If this doctrine be untrue, how did you succeed in deceiving the Ephesians, the Romans, the Philadelphians, and the church at Smyrna, and its holy bishop and martyr, Polycarp? This holy man knew what was in your Epistles, for *he* preserved them all. Why should he transmit to posterity, *uncontradicted,* Epistles containing so gross an alleged error? Was he a faithful servant of his Master to do this? Was he wise as the serpent and harmless as the dove, and as firm as the anvil under the stroke? And is it not clear that he, and the churches to which your Epistles were addressed, agreed with you in sentiment? If any, or all of them, disagreed with you, why did they not dissent? And if they did dissent, why did they not preserve and transmit that dissent with your erroneous Epistles to after times? Why send down the poison without the antidote?

But, valiant and intrepid Old Martyr! Had you anticipated what wise men would say of your doctrine in modern times, would *you* have made the statement you did? They speak of it in very harsh, indignant, and contemptuous terms. Keen is their ridicule, bitter their sarcasm, and stern their denunciation. Could *you* have withstood all that?

You did not live in an age of printing, steamboats, railroads, and telegraphs. The world is now endowed with a sensibility it never felt before. Had you lived in these bright days, you could have been able to decide upon the truth or falsity of an alleged *Christian mystery,* simply from its supposed absurdity, or scientific reasonableness, as apparent to improved human intelligence.

But you seem to have acted upon a different principle. You trusted to the positive instructions of the apostles, for your faith in this great mystery. What they taught, you were content to believe. You did not dispute upon abstract grounds, as to such a *mystery*, but condemned those who did. And after all our progress in the arts and sciences, it is still somewhat doubtful whether our reasoning powers are much improved, and very doubtful whether our memories, or our Christian knowledge, have improved at all.

I must still think, that had you foreseen all the hard things substantially said against you by the wise and learned men of modern times, that you would, nevertheless, have written what you did. You evidently acted upon the example of the apostles, to tell the truth and take the consequences. For I am told, in the history of your martyrdom, that you withstood the mighty Roman Emperor to the face, and remained firm under all his frowns and ridicule. You neither feared his power nor heeded his sarcasm, when he pronounced against you this sentence:

> We command that Ignatius, who says that he carries about within him one who has been crucified, be carried by soldiers in chains to the great city of Rome, there to be devoured by wild beasts, for the public gratification.

What, then, shall we think of you and of your testimony? You said to your Roman brethren, "Place confidence in me." Old Soldier of the Cross, for one, I do. I respond to that request. I love your memory. I covet your company. I ask your prayers. I can see nothing to prove you either a knave or a fool – either an impostor or victim. I have read your Epistles. They are beautiful. They are full of ardent piety. They speak in the strain of candor and humility. I can see no vein of vice or deception peeping out at any point. If you intended to conceal any cheat or imposition, most successfully have you done it. I confess myself too weak to detect it. And I find nothing in your history to enable me to come to any other conclusion than that you were both honest and intelligent. As such I trust you, whatever wise wits may say, either of you or of the doctrine you held. They may call you a "mystic," a "visionary," and say you were fond of old wives' fables, (the very thing you wrote against). But it was by such mystics and visionaries as you that Christ's Kingdom was built up; and all these arbitrary and unsupported assertions are more than overcome by your exemplary life, your noble Epistles, and your glorious martyrdom.

24. Testimony of Justin the Martyr, Polycarp and Irenaeus

The next Father who speaks upon this subject is the holy Justin, the philosopher and martyr, and usually called Justin Martyr. He was born in Samaria of heathen parents, and he was ignorant of Christianity in growing up. He was vigilant in the pursuit of knowledge, and joined different sects of philosophers, and was yet dissatisfied. One day he was wandering by the seaside, when he met an old man, who preached unto him Jesus. This led to his conversion in A.D. 132, about thirty years after the death of Saint John. About eighteen years after this he fixed his residence at Rome. There he composed several writings in defense of the Gospel. He was also a distinguished preacher. Among the works he composed was his *Apology for the Christian Religion*, which was presented to the Roman Emperor, Antoninus Pius.

In A.D. 167 he suffered martyrdom at Rome. He and his companions were arrested, and brought before the Roman Prefect, Rusticus, who asked, "Art thou not, in short, a Christian?"

Justin answered, "Yes, I am a Christian." The other glorious martyrs also answered, each for himself, "I, too, am a Christian."

After attempting, in vain, by threats and arguments to induce them to sacrifice to the heathen gods, and after they had told the Prefect, "Do what thou wilt, for we are Christians, and do no sacrifice to idols," the Prefect pronounced the sentence. "Let such as refuse to do sacrifice to the gods, and to obey the decree of the Emperor, be scourged, and then led away to capital punishment, in pursuance of the laws." In accordance with this decree, they suffered.

Justin says:

> And this food is called amongst us Eucharist: of which no one is allowed to partake but he who believes what we teach is true, and has been washed in the laver (of baptism) which is for remission of sins, and unto regeneration, and who so lives as Christ has delivered. For we do not receive these things as common bread and common drink; but in the (same) manner as Jesus Christ, our Savior, being made flesh by the word of God, had both flesh and blood for our salvation; even so we have been taught, that the food over which thanksgiving has been made, (eucharistized,) by the prayer of the word which came

> from him,–by which (food) our blood and flesh are nourished by transmutation,–is both flesh and blood of that same incarnate Jesus. For the apostles, in the memoirs composed by them, which are called Gospels, have delivered, that Jesus gave them this injunction: that, having taken bread, and given thanks, he said, *Do this in remembrance of me; this is my body;* and that, in like manner, having taken the cup and given thanks, he said, This is my blood; and that he distributed (them) to these alone.[81]

The language of this extract is also so plain, and the meaning so clear, that I am not aware that there has ever been a serious doubt entertained of the true intention of the writer. He states explicitly that they did not receive these things *as common bread and common drink* – that Christ was made flesh by the *word* of God, and even so the food by the prayer of the word which came from Christ, is both flesh and blood of that same Jesus incarnate. Then to confirm this sense he quotes the words, *Do this in remembrance of me: This is my body; This is my blood.*

It will be seen that Justin departed from the usual practice, under the Discipline of the Secret, in revealing this mystery to one outside the church. The reason why he did so would seem to be this: in his apology he assumed to set out the leading tenets of his religion; and as it was a professed statement of these tenets, intended for the Emperor, the head and representative of the whole Empire, it was proper he should state the facts plainly.

There was a respect due to the head of the nation, and to officers, not due to individuals, as such. This can be seen in the letter from the Church at Smyrna to the Church at Philomelium, giving an account of the martyrdom of the holy Polycarp, which took place under the Roman Emperors Marcus Aurelius and Lucius Verrus,. There it is stated, that when the Proconsul had urged the holy man to "swear by the fortune of Cesar," he replied, "I am a Christian; and if you wish to hear the Christian doctrine, appoint me a time, and hear me."

The Proconsul answered, "Persuade the people."

Polycarp replied, "To you I thought it right to give account, for we have been taught to give to rulers and the powers ordained of God, such fitting honor as hurteth not our soul; but them I deem no worthy, that I should defend myself before them."

The third Father who mentions this subject is Irenaeus, Bishop of Lyons in France. He was born about forty years after the death of Saint

John, and was the disciple of Polycarp. He, and nineteen thousand of his flock, were martyred at Lyons by a mob, A.D. 202. Irenaeus says:

> But how shall they feel assured that that bread, over which thanksgiving has been made, is the body of their Lord, and the chalice of his blood, if they do not declare him the Son of the World's Creator…? But how again do they say that, that flesh which is nourished by the body of the Lord, and by his blood, passes into corruption, and partakes not of the life?[82]

> But if it (the flesh) is not saved, then neither did the Lord redeem us by his blood; nor is the chalice of the Eucharist the communication of his blood; nor is the bread which we break the communication of his body.… Since, therefore, both the mingled cup and the created bread receive the Word of God, and the Eucharist becomes Christ's body and blood, and out of these the substance of our flesh increases and subsists, how can they say that the flesh is not susceptible of the gift of God – which (gift) is life eternal – that flesh which is nourished by the body and blood of the Lord, and is his member?[83]

This language seems too plain to be misunderstood.

Between Irenaeus and Saint John, the apostle, there was only one link, the martyr Polycarp. As we have seen, Polycarp was the intimate friend of Ignatius, and alike distinguished in the church. He was then, doubtless, well acquainted with the faith of Ignatius. The historical facts and circumstances relating to these persons all show that Ignatius and Polycarp held the same faith. The fact that Irenaeus held this doctrine and he being the disciple of Polycarp, of whom and of whose faith he speaks so plainly and confidently, is very conclusive proof that Polycarp and the Church at Smyrna held this same faith. Irenaeus also expressly declares, as we have seen, that the church throughout the world held the *same faith*, and was united in the same government. The only exception was the heretics of those days, who did hold doctrines that no one now can endorse. *Their heresy consisted in opinions that Protestants will not maintain.* Those heretics who denied that Christ had a real body, of course were compelled to deny his Real Presence in the Eucharist.

25. The unity of belief

Ignatius was from Antioch, and wrote on his way to Rome. Justin resided and wrote at Rome. Irenaeus was Bishop of Lyons in France, and wrote there. These writers, and the churches to whom they wrote, and in which they lived, were widely separated, and yet they all agreed in this doctrine.

If, then, the fact be certain and sure, that the Catholic Church, in the days of Irenaeus, was united while still spread over the whole world, the church must have then held this doctrine. For it would seem impossible to reconcile any other state of case with the clearly proved facts of history.

First we have the explicit testimony of Ignatius. We then have the testimony of Polycarp, and of the Churches to which Ignatius addressed his Epistles; for while they have not, in so many words, expressly endorsed the sentiments expressed by Ignatius, they did so by their explicit *acts.* Then we have the testimony of Justin, who assumes to state, for the Roman Emperor, the faith of the Christian world. He must be presumed to have done what he expressly undertook to do; for he gave the most conclusive proofs that he was both *competent and honest.* Then comes Irenaeus, who also states the faith of the Catholic Church, which he affirms was then spread in unity throughout the whole world.

And against the array of testimony as to the historical fact, that the church, from the days of Ignatius in A.D. 106, down to the time of Irenaeus in A.D. 178, did hold this doctrine, what is there to oppose? Who disputed it? What divisions and controversies did arise? Who denounced it, except those heretics that all condemn? Where were those who held the true faith, if this was not? How, then, did this doctrine get into the church, if not originally in it? Why were other heresies denounced, and this was not noticed, if it was a heresy? Who can account for such a remarkable phenomenon under such a state of circumstances. What rational hypothesis can be assumed for such a supposed case?

26. Testimony of the Fathers subsequent to the days of Irenaeus

In reference to the faith of the church after the days of Irenaeus and down to the beginning of the sixth century, the testimony of the Fathers regarding this point is so full, that I can only quote a few passages from their numerous works. In my examination of the authority of the early church writers, I found Protestant controversialists, in many cases, claiming their authority against this tenet. Of course they were obliged, by every rule of right, reason, and justice, to specify the particular Fathers, and quote from their works the passages, at least in part, that were alleged to be opposed to this doctrine.

My course was to take the passage from a particular writer, and keeping in view the practice under the Discipline of the Secret, and making a due allowance for the circumstances under which the author wrote, and especially the precise point he was discussing, to compare it with other passages from the same author. No author speaks with the same certainty in all places; and it is only by comparing all he says upon the same point that we can hope to do him justice. In this way I found no serious difficulty. I found Protestant writers neglecting the Discipline of the Secret, and often quoting from those writings of the Fathers, expressly intended for strangers; and, therefore, purposely general, and not explicit as to the mysteries.

In reference to Saint Clement, of Alexandria A.D. 190, certain Protestant writers have insisted that this Father never interpreted the language of the Sixth of John, in a literal sense. To prove it, they quote from his allegorical interpretation of that chapter. The fact was, that this Father had interpreted this chapter in both a literal and figurative sense, and after giving the literal sense, then professedly declares the other interpretations allegorical. Saint Clement of Alexandria says:

> *Eat my flesh,* he saith, *and drink my blood.* The Lord supplies us with these befitting aliments, and gives flesh and pours forth blood; and nothing is wanting for the children's growth. Oh the incredible mystery.[84]

A.D. 216, Origen:

> You who have been accustomed to be present at the divine mysteries, know that when you receive the body of the Lord, you take care, with all caution and veneration, lest any part thereof, however small, should fall, lest any portion of the consecrated gift should be lost. For if any part of it should fall, through your negligence, you think yourselves guilty; and you think rightly.[85]

A.D. 248, Saint Cyprian:

> The mouths sanctified with heavenly food, after the body and blood of the Lord rejected the profane contaminations and the leavings of idols.
>
> The fallen against the upright, and the wounded against the sound, utters threats; and because he does not at once receive with defiled hands the Lord's body, or drink with polluted mouth the Lord's blood, the sacrilegious is wrathful against the priests.[86]

> Since, therefore, he says, that whosoever shall eat of his bread shall live forever; and as it is manifest that those *live* who touch his body, and receive the Eucharist by right of communication, so, on the other hand, it is to be feared, and is matter for prayer, lest any of us, who while cut off is separated from the body of Christ, remain far from salvation. According to his threat and word: *Unless* you eat the flesh of the Son of Man, and drink his blood, you shall not have life in you.[87]

A.D. 252, Saint Cornelius, Pope:

> When he (Novatian) has made the oblations, and is distributing a portion to each, at the time that he gives it, instead of the blessing, he, seizing with both his hands the hands of the communicant, leaves not hold until each pronounces this oath (for I will give his own words) : 'Swear to me, by the body and blood of our Lord Jesus Christ, never to desert me, or to return to Cornelius.[88]

Saint Dionysius, of Alexandria, A.D. 258: An individual who had been baptized by heretics, and seeing baptism administered in the Catholic Church, was struck with the difference, and applied to Saint Dionysius to be rebaptized. He, in his turn, writes for advice to Pope Xystus:

> For I did not dare to renew from the beginning one who had heard the Eucharists, and joined in the amen, and stood by the table, and stretched forth his hands for the reception of the holy food, and had received it, and who had partaken, for a considerable time, of the blood of our Lord Jesus Christ. But I had bade him to be of good courage, and with firm faith and a good conscience to come to the participation of the holy things. But he ceases not from his grief, and trembles to approach the holy table; and can scarcely bear, even when requested, to be present at the prayers.[89]

A.D. 325, Eusebius:

> And they, who were according to Moses, once in every year sacrificed the paschal lamb on the fourteenth of the first month, in the evening; but we, who are of the New Testament, on every Lord's Day celebrating our Passover, are unceasingly filled with the body of the Lord, we unceasingly partake of the blood of the lamb.[90]

A.D. 330, Saint Theodore,:

> And let the catechumens who are in the monasteries, and await the dread remission of their sins, and the grace of the spiritual mystery, learn from you that it behooves them to weep over and bewail their

former sins, and to prepare themselves for the sanctification of their souls and bodies, so as to be able to endure the blood and body of the Savior Lord, to think of which is even terrible.[91]

A.D. 340, Saint James Bishop of Nisibis:

But our Lord did this before he was apprehended, and leaving the place where he made the Passover, and gave his own body that they might eat, and his blood that they might drink, he went with his disciples to the place where he was seized. As, therefore, his body had been eaten, and his blood drank, *he was reputed to be among the dead.* For our Lord, with his own hands, gave his own body for food; and though he was not yet crucified, he gave his own blood for drink.[92]

Saint Liberius, Pope:

This is he, who with five loaves, and two fishes, fed four thousand of the people in the desert. He could have fed more, had there been more. In fine, he has called many to the nuptials, but now not bread from barley, but a body is served out from heaven.[93]

A.D. 356, Saint Hilary of Poitiers:

If, then, Christ truly assumed the flesh of our body, and the man that was born of Mary is truly Christ, and if we truly receive the flesh of his own body under the mystery, (and through this we shall be one, because the Father is in him, and he in us,) how is it that a unity of will is asserted whereas the natural possession (of flesh) through a sacrament, is a sacrament of perfect unity?

For what we say concerning the natural verity (very nature) of Christ in us, unless we have learned it from him, we say it foolishly and impiously. For himself says, *My flesh is truly meat, and my blood is truly drink. He that eateth my flesh and drinketh my blood abideth in me, and I in him. (*Saint John 6:56-7) Of the verity of the *flesh and blood*, there is no room left for doubting. For now, both by the declaration of the Lord himself, and by our faith, it is truly flesh and it is truly blood; and these being received and drunk effect this, that both we are in Christ, and Christ in us. Is not this the truth? Let not this be the truth for those who deny that Christ Jesus is true God. He is, therefore, himself in us by means of flesh, and we are in him; whilst with him, that which we are, is in God.[94]

A.D. 325, Council of Nice:

> Neither canon nor custom has handed down that they who have not authority to offer, should give the body of Christ to those who do offer.[95]

A.D. 362, Saint Athanasius,, Bishop of Alexandria, In his discourse to the *baptized*, this great saint speaks thus:

> Thou wilt see the Levites bearing bread and a chalice of wine, and arranging the table. As long as the supplications and prayers as yet take not place, there is simply the bread and the cup; but after that the great and marvelous prayers have been completed, then the bread is the body, and the cup the blood of our Lord Jesus Christ.
>
> Let us come to the perfection of the mysteries. This bread and this cup are simply such, as long as the prayers and supplications have not as yet taken place; but after that the great prayers and holy supplications have been sent on high, the Word descends into that bread, and that cup, and it is his body.[96]

A.D. 363, Saint Cyril of Jerusalem: Explaining to the newly baptized the abjuration, he says:

> I renounce the devil and all his pomps. Moreover things hung up at idol festivals, either meat, or bread, or other such things which are polluted by the invocation of the unclean spirits, are classed in the pomp of the devil. For as the bread and wine of the Eucharist, before the invocation of the adorable Trinity, was simple bread and wine, whereas, after the invocation, the bread becomes Christ's body and the wine Christ's blood. So in like manner such meats pertaining to the pomp of Satan, though in their own nature simple, become, by the invocation of the evil spirits, profane.[97]

In another catechetical instruction to the newly baptized, he says, among other things:

> He himself therefore having declared and said concerning the bread, *This is my body*, who shall dare to doubt henceforward? And, he himself having settled and said, This is my blood, who shall ever doubt, saying, This is not his blood?
>
> Wherefore do not contemplate the bread and the wine as bare (elements), for they are, according to the Lord's declaration, Christ's body and blood; for even though sense suggests this to thee, yet let faith establish thee. Judge not the thing from the taste, but from faith be fully assured without misgiving, that thou hast been vouchsafed Christ's body and blood.

> These things having learned, and being fully persuaded that what seems bread is not bread, even though sensible to the taste, but Christ's body; and what seems wine is not wine, even though the taste will have it so, but Christ's blood.[98]

A.D. 370, Saint Ephrem, Syrus,:

> "*The lion shall eat straw like the ox.*" (Is 11:7) Because the just as well as sinners eat the living body which is upon the altar.
>
> ...The reality was by our Lord exhibited, when on Mount Zion he broke his own body and distributed his blood, saying, "Do this in commemoration of me.[99]
>
> The Jewish maidens placed their glory in their veils: in a like veil also do we place our glory, Christ's blood, which is of inappreciable value. The assemblies of those who have abandoned the right path, have not in their veils the blood of Christ; they who believe that Jesus has no body, have a figure of his blood. For real blood will be found to be there, whence a real body is not absent.[100]
>
> Become a blameless believer. Partake also of the spotless body of the Lord with all faith, having a most full assurance that thou sincerely eatest the very Lamb himself.... But that which the only begotten Jesus Christ, our Savior, has done for us transcends everything, both apprehension and words.[101]

A.D. 370, Saint Gregory of Nyssa:

> For as a little leaven, according to the apostle, assimilates to itself the whole mass, so, when that body, which was by God smitten with death, is within our body, it changes and transfers the whole to itself... The question, therefore, was, how the body of Christ in each man gives life to the whole nature of those men in whom there is faith; is shared amongst all, and is itself not lessened?[102]
>
> Again, the bread is, at one time, common bread, but, when the mystery shall have made it sacred, Christ's body it is both called and is.[103]

A.D. 370, Saint Gregory of Nazianzum speaking of Athanasius, says:

> After being thus nurtured and tutored, as beseems men who are now about to be set over the people, and to handle the mighty body of Christ....[104]

Speaking of the manner in which the Jews eat the Paschal lamb, and his application of that type to our Passover, he says:

> But on this occasion the law prescribes to thee the *staff* that firmly supports. That thou mayest neither stagger in thy reason, when thou hearest of the blood of God, and of his passion and death; nor involve thyself in Atheism, in the attempt to play the defender of God, but, without shame or doubt, eat the body, drink the blood, if thou desirest life. Neither disbelieving what is said about flesh, nor affected rigorously by what is said of his passion.[105]

A.D. 370, Saint Basil the Great:

> With what fear, with what full conviction, with what disposition, should we partake of the body and blood of Christ? The *fear* is taught us by the apostle when he says, *He that eateth and drinketh unworthily, &c.* The faith of Christ's words produces full *conviction*, seeing that he says, This is my body, which is given for you. Do this for a commemoration of me....[106]

> *Rule the eighth* – That we ought not to draw distinctions, and to doubt of what is said by the Lord, but be fully persuaded that every word of God is true and possible, even though nature repugn. For therein is the struggle of faith.

As examples he adduces Matt. 14:25-31; John 6:53-4: The Jews strove among themselves, saying, how can this man give us his flesh to eat?[107]

A.D. 371, Saint Macarius of Egypt,:

> ...But the children whom he has begotten of his own seed, and whom he has made partakers of his grace, in whom the Lord has been formed, he nurtures with a peculiar aliment and food and drink, differing from that of the rest of men, and he gives himself to those who have their conversation with their Father, according to that saying of the Lord, *He that eateth my flesh and drinketh my blood, abideth, in me, and shall not see death.*[108]

A.D. 372, Saint Pacian of Barcelona:

> One guilty of (taking) human life could not be absolved: shall the violator of the body of the Lord escape?[109]

A.D. 385, B. Jerome:

> Many also of those who live in the world feel this energizing influence of the Holy Spirit; I mean those who assist at the altar, and those who approach to partake of the mysteries of Christ, for of a sudden they are filled with joy, and tears, and gladness. Wherefore the Christian is fully convinced that he partakes not of mere bread

and wine, but of the body in verity, and the blood of the Son of God, sanctified by the Holy Spirit.[110]

A.D. 386 Saint Siricius, Pope: –Speaking of apostates he says:

Such we order to be cut off from Christ's body and blood, with which, in times past, they were at the new birth redeemed.[111]

A.D. 387 Theophilus of Alexandria:

From this it is manifest that Christ could not have been crucified for demons, lest demons might be partakers of his body and blood.[112]

A.D. 385 Saint Epiphanius:

For the only begotten has come, and so holds our mother the church, that tranquil harbor of peace, our joy, she that breatheth of the cypress of the vine,[113]

...and she that beareth to us that grape cluster of the eulogy, and daily gladdens us with that care dispelling drink, Christ's blood, unmingled, true.[114]

A.D. 385, Saint Ambrose:

Perhaps thou wilt say, 'I see a different thing; how is it that you assert to me that I receive the body of Christ?' It yet remains for us to prove this also.

Now if human benediction availed so much to change nature, what shall we say concerning the divine consecration itself, where the very words of the Savior operate? For this sacrament which thou receivest is effected by the word of Christ. Now if the word of Elias so availed as to draw down fire from heaven, shall not the word of Christ be of avail to change the natures (species) of the elements? Concerning the works of the whole world, you have read He spake and they were made; He commanded and they were created; the word, therefore, of Christ, which could, out of nothing, make that which was not, cannot it change those things which are, into that which they were not?

Why seekest thou here the order of nature in the body of Christ, when the Lord Jesus himself was, contrary to nature, born of a virgin? Real, in truth, was Christ's flesh that was crucified, that was buried; therefore is this really the sacrament of that flesh.[115]

A.D. 390, Marius Victorinus:

...For if what we receive is the body of Christ, and Christ is life, we ask for supersubstantial bread, for riches dwell in Christ bodily.[116]

A.D. 395, Saint Paulinus: Describing the death of Saint Ambrose, he says:

> having come down, he (the priest) presented to the saint the body of the Lord, which, when he had received and swallowed, he gave up the ghost, taking with him a good viaticum, that his soul, being more refreshed by virtue of this food, might now be gladdened with the companionship of angels, whose life he led on earth.[117]

A.D. 390, Saint Jerome:

> But let us understand that the bread which the Lord broke, and gave to his disciples, is the body of the Lord, the Savior himself saying to them, Take, eat, this is my body; and that the chalice is that concerning which he again spoke: Drink ye all of this; for this is my blood of the New Testament which shall be shed for many.[118]
>
> No one can understand the sacraments of the passion of the Lord, and of his body and blood, according to the majesty of the things.[119]
>
> Besides, we already know that wine is consecrated into the blood of Christ.[120]

A.D. 387 Saint John Chrysostom:

> When you are about to approach to the dread and divine table, and the sacred mystery, do it with fear and trembling, with a pure conscience, with fasting and prayer….
>
> Reflect, O man, what a sacrifice thou art about to touch; what a table thou art going to approach; think that though dust and ashes, thou receivest Christ's body and blood.[121]
>
> For whilst they were eating and drinking, having taken bread, he brake, and said, *This is my body which is broken for you for the remission* of sins. The initiated understood what is said. And again the chalice, saying, *This is my blood which is shed for many for the remission of sins.* And Judas was present when Christ said this. This is that body which thou hast sold, oh Judas, for thirty pieces of silver: this is that blood for which, a little while since, thou hast made that shameful bargain with the impious Pharisees. Oh, the loving kindness of Christ! Oh, the folly, the madness of Judas! For Judas sold him for thirty pieces of silver; but Christ, even after this, refused not to give that very same blood that was sold, for the remission of his sins that sold it, had he but wished it. Judas was present, and was a sharer of that sacred table….

But it is at length time to approach to this awful table. Wherefore let us come unto it with becoming sobriety and watchfulness: and let no one be any longer a Judas; no one wicked; no one envenomed; no one bearing one thing on his lips and another in his mind. Christ is present, and now he that set forth that table, the same sets forth this now. For it is not man that makes the things that lie to open view become Christ's body and blood, but that same Christ that was crucified for us. The priest fulfilling his office, stands pronouncing these words: but the power and the grace is of God. *This is my body,* he says. This word transmutes the things that lie to open view. And as that word that said, *Increase and multiply and fill the earth*, was pronounced indeed but once, but through all time is actually operative on our nature for the procreation of children; so also, that word uttered but once, makes from that time to this, and till his own advent, the sacrifice perfect, at every table in the churches.[122]

Wherefore let us on every occasion obey God, and gainsay nothing, even though what is said seems contrary to our reasoning and sight; but let his word be more powerful than both, than reasoning and sight. Even so let us act in the matter of the mysteries; not looking on the things laid out, but holding fast his words. For his word is incapable of being deceived; but our senses are very easily deceived.[123]

A.D. 387, Saint Gaudentius of Brescia,:

Wherefore that same creator and Lord of nature, who, out of earth, produces bread, out of bread again (for he is both able, and has promised) makes his proper body; and he who, out of water, made wine, also out of wine made his own blood.

For when he was delivering the consecrated bread and wine to his disciples, he thus says: *This is my body; this is my blood.* Let us believe, I beseech you, him in whom we have believed. Truth cannot lie.[124]

Fourth Council of Carthage:

That a deacon, if ordered, may, in the presence of a priest, administer the eucharist of the body of Christ to the people, if necessity require it.[125]

A.D. 400, Saint Augustine:

The Jewish sacrifice was formerly, as you know, according to the order of Aaron, in victims of animals, and this in a mystery; as yet the sacrifice of the body and blood of the Lord was not, which the faithful, and they who have read the Gospel, understand, which sacrifice is now diffused throughout the whole world.

But whence did he entrust to us his body and blood? Out of his humility. For unless he were humble, he would neither be eaten nor drunk.

And he was borne in his own hands. Now, how this can be done by any man, who can understand? For who is carried in his own hands? By the hands of others a man may be carried, but by his own hands no one is carried. How it may be understood literally in David himself we find not, but we do find in Christ. For Christ was carried in his own hands; when committing to us his own very body, he says, This is my body. For he carried that body in his own hands.[126]

The bread which you see on the altar, after being sanctified by the word of God, is the body of Christ. That chalice—yea, rather that which the chalice contains—after being sanctified by the word of God, is the blood of Christ.[127]

A.D. 448, Saint Nilus:

Before, indeed, the prayer of the priest, and the descent of the Holy Ghost, the things that lie to open view are plain bread and common wine; but after these awful invocations, and the advent of the adorable, and vivifying, and good Spirit, the things that lie upon the holy table are no longer plain bread and common wine, but the precious and immaculate body and blood of Christ the God of all, which (body and blood) purify from every defilement those who partake thereof with much fear and eagerness.[128]

A.D. 428, Saint Cyril of Alexandria:

…The hypostatic wisdom of God the Father, that built for itself a temple not made with hands, distributes its body as bread, and bestows its life-giving blood as wine. Fearful mystery! Oh, ineffable dispensation! Oh, humility incomprehensible! Oh, goodness unsearchable! The Creator sets himself before the work of his hands to be partaken of; the Self-existent gives himself to mortals for food and drink.

But if Christ's body be food, and Christ's blood be drink, and he be, as they pretend, a mere man, why is he proclaimed as being unto everlasting life, to those who draw nigh to the sacred table? And how does he dwell both there and everywhere, and is not made less? A mere body is in no way the source of life to those who partake of it.[129]

I will close these extended extracts with the following beautiful passage from Eusebius of the Latin Church:

> A victim veritable one and perfect, not to be estimated by its appearance, but by faith; not to be valued by the eye of the outward man, but by inward affection. Hence does the authority of heaven assure us, *That my flesh is meat indeed, and my blood is drink indeed.* Away, then, with every doubt of unbelief. seeing that he who is the author of the gift, is himself the witness of the truth. For the invisible priest, by his secret power, converts, by his own word, the visible creatures into the substance of his own body and blood, saying thus, *Take and eat, for this is my body,* and after the sanctification has been repeated, *Take and drink, this is my blood.* Therefore, as at the nod of the commanding Lord, there at once sprang into existence out of nothing, the lofty heavens, the deep waves, the vast earth; with equal potency does the power of the word command, and the realized effect obeys.[130]

I have passed over the testimonies of a number of Fathers, and have given those of the more distinguished. It will be seen, upon inspection, to be very explicit. They not only speak of the literal view, "*without hesitation, doubt, or apology*," but they often expressly say that the *initiated* understand what they state – that it is the faith of the church.

They also, in many cases, treat the doctrine as admitted by their opponents, (the heretics,) and from it they make deductions in support of other doctrines, particularly those of the Trinity and resurrection of the dead. They also speak of the Eucharist as a great and awful mystery, and ascribe to it spiritual graces, wholly irreconcilable with any other than the literal view. And they urge the faithful to trust the *Word of God*, and not *their senses.* They also quote the words, This is my body, and give them an emphasis that could not belong to them, except when taken literally.

In short, the whole drift and spirit, as well as the express words of these holy and venerable Ancients, most clearly do prove to my mind, that the doctrine was universally held by the Church of their day; and not only by the Church itself, but by many of the heretics of that time. For, when any of these writers, in their controversies with heretics, assume this doctrine as admitted, they not only assume to state the faith of the Church, but also that of their opponents. When they treat it as *conceded* ground, it could only be reconcilable with the fact, that it was held by both parties. It was so held by the Novatians and Donatists. *In their catechetical instructions to the newly baptized, the Fathers are explicit in stating when and how the change occurs in the elements, and by whose word and power it is produced.*

It is true, that many of the Fathers, in imitation of Christ and His apostles, give the same passage different interpretations, but which are still compatible with each other. Examples occur in Scripture, where the passage or incident has two meanings. The Fathers often gave both a literal and figurative meaning to the same passage. This was the case with Saint Clement of Alexandria, and others.

Protestant writers, in quoting from the Fathers, have overlooked the Discipline of the Secret, and also the circumstance now mentioned, and have, therefore, produced passages seemingly confirmatory of the figurative sense, or at most equivocal. In this way they have often claimed the authority of certain Fathers, who most clearly maintain the literal sense, such as Saint Ambrose, Saint John Chrysostom, Saint Augustine, Theodoret, and others. In many cases the quotations are against the figurative view, but are made to support it by a misconstruction. But when these doubtful passages are collated with those that are clear and explicit, the intention becomes so evident, that it would seem to admit of no doubt whatever.

The *only* case that seemed to present any reasonable difficulty to my mind, was that of Tertullian, A.D. 195. He is claimed as an authority for both sides. In his works intended for the faithful, he seems clearly to speak of the literal sense.

> The flesh is fed with the body and blood of Christ, that the soul also may be fattened of God.[131]

But when he is arguing against Marcian, who denied the reality of Christ's body, and maintained that He had a body in appearance only, Tertullian uses language, which, taken by itself, would seem clearly to prove the figurative view. The passage quoted by Protestants is this:

> The bread received and distributed to the Disciples, he made it his own body, by saying, *This is my body*; that is, a figure of my body. But there would not have been a figure unless there were a body of veritable reality.[132]

In the context this Father assumes that bread was an ancient figure of the body of Christ, and quotes Jeremias to prove it. The point of his argument being to prove the reality of Christ's body, was as well maintained by holding the figurative as the literal view of the words,

This is my body. If either view be true, Marcian was wrong. As the object of Tertullian was to convince the Marcianites, while at the same time he did not expose this mystery to their contempt and ridicule, he may have assumed the figurative sense, under the influence of the Secret Discipline. The figurative sense would answer all the purposes intended, without incurring any danger of injury. Whether he assumed the figurative sense in obedience to the Discipline of the Secret, or whether his meaning is explained by the context, and shows him to have intended the literal sense, or purposely to leave it doubtful, are questions that may admit of reasonable controversy.

There are considerations and circumstances, independent of his language, which would seem to put the matter at rest. That he was very strict in his observance of the Discipline of the Secret, is shown by the extract already given from him, to prove its existence in the Ancient Church. He afterwards became a Montanist, and while his errors in that respect were condemned, I am not aware that he was ever accused of error in regard to the Real Presence. By the church historians his real sentiments were always held as those of the other Fathers, and as sustaining the literal sense. The fact that no discussions arose upon this point – that no excommunications were made – is, under the circumstances, a very strong proof that the Fathers all held the same doctrine.

Another circumstance of a very clear character is the fact that the ancient Christians, before and after the days of Tertullian, were charged with feasting upon the flesh of infants. Saint Justin Martyr says in his Apology, "We are so far from committing any injustice or impiety (as implied in the charge of devouring children), that we have learned that none but wicked expose infants when they were born." And Tertullian says: "Oh! How great the glory of that magistrate who should hunt out one who has already eaten an hundred infants."[133] "We are said to be the most accursed of men, as touching a sacrament of child murder, and thereon to feast…."[134]

This charge must have arisen from the doctrine of the Real Presence, and from an erroneous conception of the nature of that doctrine, and of the manner of Christ's presence, as understood by the Christians. And, the very fact that the Eucharist was considered a mystery, can only be accounted for upon the hypothesis that the doctrine of the Real Presence was held to be true. Unless this doctrine was in fact held to be true, there could have been, it would seem, no sufficient reason to place the

Eucharist among the mysteries at all, much less to conceal it from the Pagans, and even from the catechumens.

In conclusion I may say that the language of Luther in regard to the consent and authority of the Fathers in support of the literal sense, is very forcible. "That no one among the Fathers," says he,

> numerous as they are, should have spoken of the Eucharist, as these men do, is truly astonishing. Not one of them speaks thus. "There is only bread and wine, or, the body and blood of Christ are not present." And, when we reflect how often the subject is treated by them, it ceases to be credible, it is not even possible, that not so much as once, such words as these should have dropped from some of them. Surely it was of moment that men should not be drawn into error. Still, they all speak with such precision, evincing that they entertained no doubt of the presence of the body and blood! Had this not been their conviction, can it be imagined that, among so many, the negative opinion should not have been uttered on a single occasion? On other points this was not the case. But our Sacramentarians, on the other hand, can proclaim only the negative or contrary opinion. These men, then, to say all in one word, have drawn their notions neither from the Scriptures nor the Fathers.[135]

It certainly is most unaccountable that, while so many Fathers have, beyond all question, maintained the literal sense, in terms too plain to be misunderstood, that no one opposed to such a view could ever be found to say in plain, explicit, negative terms, "The body and blood of Christ are not present." Certainly, if those who did support the literal sense, did speak in plain terms, those who did oppose it, if any, ought to have spoken in terms equally explicit. An explicit and plain affirmative assertion of such a doctrine, would instantly produce as plain and explicit a negative, if such was intended. Direct negative must be the opposite of any direct proposition, and would naturally be expressed in opposite terms, and, therefore, be equally plain.

---

[1] Jn. 4:10,24; Jn. 9:39; Acts 3:6-16.

[2] Jn. 6:14, 15.

[3] Jn. 6:26.

[4] Cited by Nicholas Wiseman *Morefield Lectures*. p. 42.

[5] Note how Saint Peter adapted his discourse, when he told them to repent and be baptized, without mentioning faith, because they already believed.

[6] Jn. 6:27.

[7] Our Lord and his apostles were in the habit of putting opposites in contrast, see Jn. 6:63 and Rom. 8:1-14 .

[8] As the meaning of the words (literal and symbolic) depends on usage, the figurative application of the words, bread or food, to wisdom and doctrines, was common among the Jews. This figure is used in the following passages Is. 4:1,2; Jer. 15:16; Amos 8:11; Ecc. 15:3; Proverbs 9:5, 4:17; Ecc. 20:17,18.

[9] Jn. 6:42.

[10] In the tenth chapter of Saint John's Gospel He repeats the phrase "I am the door." In the fifteenth chapter He uses the expression, "I am the true vine," and then says His Father is the husbandman, again repeating, "I am the true vine." In the twenty third chapter of Matthew he repeats the withering phrase, "Woe unto you, Scribes and Pharisees," seven or eight times

[11] If the Catholic doctrine is true, how beautiful is the contrast between the qualities of manna and the flesh of our Lord. The Jews had a great reverence for manna, which was a miraculous and literal food. If Christ intended to give His flesh for food, to sustain spiritual life, how appropriate it was to contrast the two in the strongest manner. One is living, the other perishable; both were literal.

[12] Ps. 27:2(King James version.)

[13] Job 19:22.

[14] Mic 3:3

[15] Eccles. 4:5.

[16] Jas. 5:3.

[17] Gal. 5:15.

[18] *Cf.* Nicholas Wiseman, *Moorefield Lectures,* p. 73-81

[19]. *Ibid.* p. 85.

[20] Jn 8:55.

[21] *Cf.* Lev 3:17 and 7:26; Gen 9:4; Deut 12:16 and 15:23; Lev. 17:10; 1 Kings 14; Ezek 33:25; Jud 11:10-I2; Wis 11:7; Is 49:26; Jer 19:8, 9; Acts 15: 29.

[22] Nicholas Wiseman, *op. cit.* Euc. p. 102.

[23] Jn 8:23.

[24] .Matt. 19:24.

[25] *Cf.* Jn 8: 34, 35.

[26] *Ibid.* 44.

[27] Jn 16: 17, 18.

[28] Matt. 9: 2.

[29] Jn 8: 56.

[30] *Cf.* Jn 6:50, 51, 59.

[31] It was common practice to call the body a vessel, house, tabernacle, or temple among the Jews. Saint Paul calls it a vessel, house, tabernacle, and frequently a temple. Cf. 2 Cor 4:7, 5:1-4; 1Thess. 4:4; 1 Cor. 3:16, 6:19; 2 Cor 6:16. Also see Is 38:12.

[32] Wiseman *Op.cit.* p118.

[33] In the great case of *Gibons vs. Ogden*, Chief Justice Marshall says in his opinion, "It is a rule of construction, acknowledged by all, that the exceptions from a granted power mark its extent. For it would be absurd, as well as useless, to except from a granted power that which was not granted – that which the words of the grant could not comprehend." Wheaton *Elements of International Law* 9. p.191.

[34] Jn 2:23; 3, 22.

[35] Jn 6:14.

[36] Jn 6:24.

[37] *Cf.* Matt 13:20, 21.

[38] *Cf.* Jn 8: 43; 9: 27.

[39] Jn 6:64.

[40] Jn 6:61.

[41] Nicholas Wiseman, *op.cit.* p. 147.

[42] Dr. Sherlock, 364-367. cited Wiseman's *Moorfield Lectures*, E. I most cheerfully acknowledge the great assistance I have received from the Lectures of Dr. Wiseman on the Eucharist.

[43] I Cor. 11:27-29.

[44] See also Gal. 5:13-26; 1 Pet. 4:6; Matt. 26: 41; Jn. 3:6; Rom. 7:5, 5, 25.; 1 Cor. 5:5.; 2 Cor. 7:1.; Gal. 3:3.; 4:8 ; 1 Pet. 3:18. The origin of the phrase will be further explained by Jn. 8:15 ; Rom. 13:14 ; Gal. 2:20.; 2 Pet. 2:10.

[45] *Cf.* Jn 9:1-41.

[46] There are many instances in Scripture parallel to this. See Is 59:21; Jer 31:33; Exod 16:16-23; Levit 16:34, 17:7.

[47] Luke 22:1; see also Mat 26:17.

[48] Rev 1:10; see also Ex 32:5, 13:12.

[49] Ex 12:14,48.

[50] 1 Cor 10:16 (King James and Douay translations.)

[51] 1 Cor 11:27, 29 (King James and Douay translation.)

[52] *Cf.* Luke 2:41, 48.

[53] Jn 9:17.

[54] *Cf.* Ex 7 and 8.

[55] *Cf.* Gen 19.

[56] Matt 26: 66.

[57] Jas 2:10.

[58] George Stanley Faber, *Difficulties of Romanism.* p. 54.

[59] Joshua 5:13.

[60] Gen 32:24.

[61] Gen 18: 8.

[62] Luke 24:16.

[63] See Jn 20:15. Also Dr. Milner. *End of Controversy.* p. 234.

[64] Jn 20:19, 26.

[65] Luke 24:31.

[66] Luke 24: 36.

[67] Gen. 19.

[68] Jn. 11.

[69] Matt 15:22-28.

[70] *Stromateis*, L. i., n. 12, p. 348; *Ibid.*, L. i., n. 1, p. 323; *Ibid.*. L. v., n. 12, p. 886.

[71] T. i., L. 1, *Contra. Celsum.*, n. 7.

[72] Lebn. *Ad Demetrianum* 423.

[73] *Disp. Cum Manete.*

[74] *Institutionum Divinarum, De. Justit.*, 1. v., c. i.

[75] *Praep. Evang.*, 1. xii., c. 7.

[76] *Apol. Cont. Arian.*, n. xi., t. i., p. 105.

[77] T. iii. *Tractatus in Joh, Ev.*, n. e.

[78] *De Vita, S. J. Chrysostom.* Dia., c. 2.

[79] T. i., lib. xii., *De Ador. In Sp. et Vir.*, p. 445.

[80] Jn 6:54.

[81] *Apol.* i., n. 65, 66, p. 82, 83.

[82] *Adv. Haeres.*, l. iv., c. 18, n. 4, 5, p.251.

[83] *Ibid.*, l. v., c. 2, n. 2, 3, p. 293, 294.

[84] *Paedagogus.* l. i., c. vi.

[85] T. ii. Hom. xiii. *In Exod.* n. 3.

[86] *De Lapsis*, p. 372, 377, 380-382.

[87] *De Orat. Dom.*, p. 420-1.

[88] *Ep. Corne. Ad Fabium Episc.* Antioch. Ap. Euseb. H. E., l. vi., c. 43.

[89] *Ep. ad Xystum*, p. 163-5.

[90] *Ex. Tract. De Paschate*, t. i., p. 253-7.

[91] Ep. 12, t. iv.

[92] Serm. xiv. De Pash., n. 4-6.

[93] *Or. In Consecr. Marcell. Soror, S. Ambrosii.* n. i.

[94] *De Trinitate*, l. viii., n. 13-17.

[95] *Con.* xviii.

[96] *Maii Nov. Collect. Veter. Script.* T. ix., p. 625.

[97] *Catech. Mystag.* I. [xix.,] n. 7.

[98] .*Ibid.* V. [al. 23,] p. 331-2.

[99] T. ii. Part 2, *Syr. Comm. In Esai.*

[100] T. ii. Syr. Serm. xivii. *Adv. Haereses.*

[101] T. iii. *Gr. Adv. Scrutat.*

[102] T. iii. *Orat. Catech. Magn.*, c. 37.

[103] T. iii. In Bapt. Chr., p. 369-71.

[104] T;. i. *Or.* xxi.

[105] *Ibid. Or.* xlii.

[106] *Reg. Brev. Interrog.* Clxxii. T. ii. P. ii.

[107] Luke 1:13, 18:28; Rom. 4:19-22. T. ii. P. i. *Hom. Moralia.*

[108] *Hom.* xiv., n. 4.

[109] *Param. Ad Poenit.*, n. 7.

[110] *Comment. Util.*

[111] *Ep. ad Himn.*, n. 4.

[112] *Epis. Pash.*, n. xi.

[113] Cant. 1:14.

[114] T. i. *Adv. Haeres.* [Expos. Fid.] p. 1096-7.

[115] T. ii. *De Mysteries*, c. viii.-ix.

[116] L. ii. *Adv. Arian*, n. 8.

[117] *Vita S. Ambros.* [Int. ap. S. Ambr.] n. 47. T. ii. P. xii.

[118] T. i. Ep. exx. *Ad Hedebiam*, n. ii.

[119] T. v., l. xiii.

[120] *T. vii. Comm.* In Galat.

[121] T. ii. *In Divn. Nat. Jesu Christ*, n. 7.

[122] T. ii. Hom. i. *De Prodit. Judae*, n. 5, 6.

[123] T. vii. Hom, 82, in Matt. n. i. 4-6.

[124] *De Paschae Observ.* Tr. Ii. T. v. Bib. Maxim.

[125] *Con.* xxxviii.

[126] T. iv. Enarr. In Ps. Xxxiii. Serm. 1, n. 5, 6, 7, 8, 10.

[127] T. v. Serm. ccxxvii. *Ad Infantes, De Sacramentis, in Die. Pashae*, n. 1.

[128] L. Ep. xliv.

[129] T. v. Par. Ii. Hom. in *Mystic. Coenam.*

[130] *De Pash. Hom.* vii., t. vi.

[131] *De Resurrect. Carnis.,* n. 8.

[132] *Adv. Marcian*, l. v., n. 40-1.

[133] *Apol.* n. 2.

[134] Apol. l. c.

[135] *Defensio verborum; Coenae*, T. viii, P. 391 ; Edit. Wittemb. 1557, cited John Hughes, *Hughes-Breckenridge Controversy*, p 317.

CHAPTER VI

PENANCE

1. The general nature of the Sacrament of Penance

The great end and purpose of the mission of Christ, was to rescue fallen man from sin. That must be conceded by all who really believe in His divine character. That the blood of Christ was most ample to perfect the new law, and put it in a shape for practical administration, in this present mode of our existence, must also be conceded. As we have before insisted, the mercy of Christ was displayed in perfecting the system itself, but when it was once adopted it became a matter of irrevocable promise – a matter of law. As judged by this law (which law is the result of free grace), we can merit the forgiveness of sins. Our obedience to this law will entitle us to apply the merits of Christ to ourselves. He says, substantially: “If you will obey this law, you may call my merit your own, and receive the reward accordingly.”

We shall assume that man, under the law of Christ, does possess free agency – that he can commit sins before baptism – that he can commit them afterwards and that he can obtain forgiveness in both cases. That baptism is for the remission of past sins is clear from the simple and explicit statement of Saint Peter to the believing Jews on the day of Pentecost. They cried out: "What shall we do?" and Saint Peter promptly answered: “Repent and be baptized for the remission of sins.” He did not tell them to believe, because he saw that they did already believe; and he, therefore, did not do that which would have been idle. Now it is clear that either baptism and repentance are both required for the remission of sins, or that neither is. If we can take out baptism, we can take away repentance. They are both closely joined together by the copulative conjunction, and must form requisites to remission of sins. The language is clear and explicit.

When we look into the system of Christ, we see that He instituted a visible association of men, to which He gave a code of law for the government of each member, and of the whole – that He bestowed upon the officers of this visible continuing corporation, all the necessary powers to enforce the practical operation of His law in this world. We see that He used men as His agents, for the application of the law to particular cases. For this reason He instituted external visible ordinances or sacraments, as channels of grace and remission. The administration of these is committed to the officers of His own kingdom. It could not have been otherwise in the very nature of things.

If we once concede Christ to have been a lawgiver at all, then we must concede that a visible organization of those submitting to His government would follow – that visible Sacraments must exist in a visible Church; and that where those sacraments do exist, the only purpose they can exist for, must be as channels of grace and remission. If a lawgiver, Christ must administer His own law; either directly by Himself, or through His agents or officers.

If, then, the visible external sacrament of baptism was given for the remission of past sins, and this sacrament cannot be repeated, is it not necessary, in the very nature of Christ's beautiful and harmonious system, that another visible sacrament should exist for the remission of sins committed after baptism? Are not sins committed after baptism as great if not greater, than the same sins when committed before baptism, and equally as difficult to remit? Is not the Sacrament of the Lord's Supper intended for believers only?

With regard to the faith of the Catholic Church in reference to this Sacrament, we shall quote the language of Dr. Wiseman, as found in his *Moorfield Lectures:*

> We believe, therefore, that the sacrament of penance is composed of three parts – contrition, or sorrow – confession, or its outward manifestation – and satisfaction, which, in some respects is a guarantee of perseverance in that which we promise.[1]

By contrition the Catholic Church means all that any other Church means by repentance. The Catholic Church, therefore, not only requires all that any other church does, but also the additional requisites of confession and satisfaction. And all those must be performed worthily, in order to obtain the grace of the sacrament.

The practice and necessity of confession were required by the old dispensation. We are told that the Lord commanded Moses to:

> Speak unto the children of Israel, when a man or woman shall commit any sin that men commit to do a trespass against the Lord, and the person be guilty, they shall confess their sin which they have done.[2]

They were not only required to confess, but to make satisfaction.[3]

It is perfectly natural that the proud should consider confession as a burden, while it is equally natural that the humble should esteem it as a privilege. The truly humble penitent will naturally seek relief in confession. We see this proven by general experience. The most penitent criminals are always most willing to make a true confession of their crimes. The tribunal of confession is a kind retreat for the truly sorrowing. It was given by our Lord in compassion to those who take up their cross, and meekly follow Him, as He required.

2. The apostles' power to remit and retain sins

After our Lord had risen from the grave, and before He ascended into heaven, He said unto His disciples: "Receive ye the Holy Ghost: whose sins ye remit they are remitted unto them; and whose sins ye retain they are retained."[4]

The Douay Bible says *forgive.* The sense is the same in both translations, as to remit and to forgive sins mean the same thing. That an entire forgiveness was meant, cannot be doubted. The language is general, and not limited; and must be as extensive in meaning, as the same expressions used in other passages.[5]

From this plain and explicit passage, it is clear that our Lord conferred upon the apostles the power to forgive or remit sins. But there was also another power bestowed upon the apostles the power to *retain sins.* Not only were these powers bestowed upon the Apostles but our Lord expressly pledged Himself that the exercise of these powers should be ratified by Him, in the same way that He pledged Himself to ratify in heaven, what they should do under the power to bind and loose.[6]

In bestowing these important powers, did our Lord do an idle and useless thing? What did He intend by the very act of conferring them? Surely he intended nothing else but that they should be put into *practical operation.* They could not have been given without intending to accomplish some great end. The very act of conferring these powers was, in itself, a command to use them for the purpose intended. When the Constitution of the United States conferred certain powers upon the different departments of government, it was intended that they should be put into practical operation; and the officer who fails to do so is guilty of a dereliction of duty.

If then, these powers were given for practical application, it follows invincibly, that the right to use all the means necessary to carry them into full and complete operation, was also given, as inseparable incidents of the powers themselves. To give the powers, and, at the same time, to deny the use of all the means necessary to carry them into execution, would have been entirely idle; because it would have defeated the very purpose He had in view, when giving the powers themselves. It is a plain and fixed principle of the civil law, as well as of the law of common sense and of pure justice, to confer the use of the necessary means with the power itself. To give the power and withhold the means would be about as sensible and efficient, as the exhortation, "be ye clothed and fed." The incident must always follow the principle. Thus Chancellor Kent, speaking of a decision of the Supreme Court of the United States, says:

> The powers given to the government imply the ordinary means of execution; and the government in all sound reason and fair interpretation must have the choice of the means which it deems the most convenient and appropriate to the execution of the power.[7]

It would seem impossible for any fair and logical mind, after due consideration, to deny the truth of either of these two propositions:

1. That the power to forgive and the power to retain sins were conferred upon the apostles;

2. That with the main powers, were also given all the necessary incidents, to enable the apostles to carry the powers into practical effect.

These two positions being true, it follows that remission of sins committed after baptism, could only be had through the exercise of this power by the apostles. For it will be observed, that they had not only the power to remit, but also to retain sins. Both powers were given at the same time; and both were equally intended for practical application to individual cases.

If the transgressor could obtain remission, without the consent of the apostles, then their power to retain sins would have been idle, because it would be inefficient. Christ meant something effectual in giving the power to retain sins; and therefore, He could not have intended to confer a contradictory power upon others. He would not give the power to the apostles, and require them to exercise it, and promise Himself to ratify their acts, and at the same time give the party offending, the power to escape the exercise of this function. He said explicitly, "Whosesoever sins ye retain they are retained;" and He could not, therefore, violate this promise. If the party offending could obtain remission of sins, without applying to the apostles, who had the power to retain, as well as to remit; then, as a matter of course, he would not apply to them, for fear they would retain his sins. In practical effect, the exercise of these two most important powers would have been defeated, unless we concede that, when given, they were intended as exclusive and supreme.

The apostles, then, had the exclusive power to forgive and retain sins. What is sin? It is a violation of the law of God. One violation of this law constitutes one sin, and two or more violations constitute sins. Each transgression constitutes a separate and distinct offense. It is so in all laws defining crime. If a man steals two different pieces of property, at different times, he commits two separate and distinct offenses.

The power to remit and the power to retain sins were the powers to remit or retain each particular transgression of the law. How, then, could the apostles remit or retain sins unless they knew what they were? It was not intended that these great powers should be exercised blindly. It could not have been intended that they should have the powers to remit and retain sin in one undistinguished mass; because the authority was to remit sins, not sin. If they could remit and retain sin, not sins, without distinguishing between different violations of the law, then the whole end and purpose of these powers would have been substantially defeated. Such a view would confound all distinctions between different sins, and different individuals; and would, by this confusion of all just distinctions, render the exercise of these powers useless. How could the apostles tell what sins to remit or retain, unless they first knew what they were? That each separate and distinct offence was intended is shown by the command of Saint James: "Confess your faults (in the Douay Bible, *sins*) one to another."[8]

Now here the term sins (in the plural) must mean different transgressions. This is not only clear from the word itself, but from the purpose of the provision. This confession of sins was unquestionably a great duty; otherwise, it would not have been imposed. It was not put upon us for a mere idle purpose. It must have been intended to accomplish something important. If each individual were only required to confess the general fact that he had sinned, (and not his *sins* as the apostle commanded,) then the whole purpose of this command would be defeated. The plain reason for this is it would place the flagrant offender with the most circumspect upon the same footing. For a man simply to say that he is a sinner is simply to confess that he is as bad as the apostles, for they sinned also. It would be not the slightest humiliation to confess that which *all* must confess. Such a confession is no check upon transgression, as all must equally confess the *same thing*, and no more, whether they sin much or little. What possible reason could there be in requiring only such a confession as that? What good could it accomplish? What humility could it require? Each and every one would have plenty of company. Such could not have been the intention of Christ, or of the apostle.

The right to acquire this knowledge of the particular sins of each individual, must have been given with the delegation of the powers to remit and retain sins, because *needed* to give force and effect to the powers themselves. How, then, did the apostles attain this knowledge of the sins of individuals? Did they possess the power to see into the hearts of all men, so as to know their secret thoughts? If so, what proof is there of this fact? On the contrary, is it not clear that Saint Paul did not know of the divisions among the Corinthians until informed by them of the house of Chloe? So, a special vision was required to inform him that he could remain safely in a certain city. And is it not true, that many who "believed came and confessed, and *showed their deeds?*"[9]

The only way in which the apostles could know the secret sins or deeds of individuals, was by their confession. As the apostles had the right to remit or retain, they had the right to know the sins committed; and as the power, unless exclusive, would have been idle, it was the duty of all to apply to them. The facts being peculiarly within the knowledge of the party committing the sins, it was his duty to state them. The power given to the apostles to do certain things, imposed upon the parties governed, the corresponding duty to obey the apostles in respect to those things. As all sins are but transgressions of the law, the Church has the right to know them for two reasons:

1. Because her jurisdiction extends to all violations of the law she was left to execute; and her entire success and purity require this knowledge;

2. Because it is necessary for the safety of each individual member.

3. These powers descended to the successors of the Apostles

I have endeavored to show, in another place, that Christ did create a permanent system; and for that reason, the provisions of His code were generally permanent. In other words, the permanent provisions of any permanent code must constitute the general rule, while the temporary provisions would constitute the exceptions. All the provisions of such a code are, therefore, *prima facie* permanent; and the exceptions must be so marked, either by express words or by the nature of the power conferred or command given, as to show that they are temporary only.

He who alleges exceptions to a general rule, or to a *prima facie* case, must show them. This rule results from the plainest principles of right reason. For example, when we look into the Constitution of the United States (which organized a permanent system of government in the contemplation of the theory itself,) we find that there is not a single permanent provision expressly marked as such, while the temporary provisions are so marked. Where permanent powers are conferred, they are given without any limitation, as to time – as in this case the power to collect taxes, borrow and coin money, regulate commerce, declare war, etc. But the temporary provisions are expressly marked, so as to be readily distinguished from the permanent features of this instrument.[10]

It would seem clear that this rule is equally as applicable to the system of Christ as to that of any other lawgiver. That He did organize a permanent system is certain; and that the great and overwhelming mass of the provisions of His code is permanent and component parts of this system of law, is equally certain. These positions are true:

1. That the act of conferring these powers upon the apostles was a command to exercise them in proper cases.

2. That the powers are such, in their very nature, as may come down, through the Church, to the end of time.

In the commission, the apostles were expressly commanded to teach all nations to observe all things whatsoever they – the apostles – had been commanded to observe. As I have elsewhere endeavored to show, this wide commission, by its very express terms, carried forward to the successors of the apostles, in their proper capacities, all the powers, promises, and duties incumbent on, or given to, the apostles themselves, except those marked as temporary, either in express words, or by the peculiar nature of the act to be performed.

The apostles having been commanded to exercise these powers, and they, being permanent in their nature and nowhere marked as temporary, must still reside in the Church – the permanent institution created by Christ Himself. Those who once concede that these powers were originally conferred upon the apostles, will find it very difficult to escape this conclusion; for if they can defeat the present existence of these powers in this case, they can, upon the same basis of reasoning, defeat all the powers of the Church, and the entire system itself.

Bishop Porteus seems to have been aware of the decisive strength of this position. Therefore, he insisted that the word of Christ did not confer upon the apostles any real power to forgive sins, only "a power of declaring who were truly penitent, and of inflicting miraculous punishments on sinners, as likewise the preaching of the word of God."[11]

How such a misconstruction of so plain a passage could have been tolerated by any learned man, is surprising. The text is exceedingly explicit. The two main words *remit* and *sins*, upon which the sense depends are remarkably definite and certain in their meaning. It so happens that these terms can mean nothing else in that connection but the view I have taken. Lawmakers are not wont to indulge in the use of mere surplus words. Their aim is to be concise and certain. Now could Bishop Porteus, or any other man, select words more concise or certain than those of our Lord if he intended to confer the *real* power to forgive and retain sins. And if this be true that Christ did use the most concise and certain terms possible to confer real power, then what right have we to say He still did not intend to make such a delegation of power? It was our Lord's practice to use concise and certain terms.

Let us inquire into the purposes for which these powers were originally delegated. They were certainly bestowed by our Lord for great and beneficial ends. It was not an idle display of words only. Far from it! What, then, could these purposes be? It could not have been a mere personal privilege given to the apostles alone. We cannot conceive of any practical ends to be accomplished by it, as such.

Miracles were special gifts. This gift of miracles was given to the apostles individually, as proofs of their veracity as witnesses of the facts they saw, and of the discourses they heard. The words of Christ was the evidence of their commission as officers of the Church, in the same way that these same words will constitute the evidence of the authority of their successors to the end of time.

But the power to remit, and the power to retain sins, were not required as proofs of the veracity of the apostles as witnesses, or of their being agents of Christ. For what purposes were these powers given? As already stated in substance, they were given for the safety of the Church, and of each individual member. What other purpose could our Lord have intended to accomplish? The exercise of these powers could constitute no proofs of the truth of Christianity; for the truth of the system had first to be conceded, before the exercise of these powers could be invoked by the individual. If he did not first believe in the exercise of these powers, he could not ask for their exercise.

The very same reasons that induced our Lord to confer those powers upon the apostles at the beginning would have induced Him to continue them in the Church to the end of time. That the actual and practical exercise of these powers was merciful and beneficial to the members of the Church, in the days of the apostles, must be conceded; for after all the suggestions of pride, and the cavils of prejudice, every humble Christian must concede at last, that such an institution is beneficial.

It may then be well asked, are we living under a crippled and mutilated code of law, which has lost some of its most beautiful and consolatory features? If the powers to forgive and retain sins, and the corresponding duty of confession, were confined to the apostolic day, how do we enjoy any benefits from the same? What good does it do us to know that the apostles did forgive sins – that the happy and favored Christians of that day did enjoy the blessed consolation of this certain and not mere inferential forgiveness? Could that have been the intention of Christ? Did He design His system to be perfect at the beginning and imperfect afterwards? Did He intend to make this great difference among Christians? If so, why? Is there any reason for it – any Scripture? We are all living under the same dispensation.

What was necessary then is necessary now. As witnesses the apostles left their testimony with the Church, and we enjoy the benefit of it at this day, as much as our brethren did in their day. If these great and important powers to remit and retain sins be taken away, we are, indeed, left in a state of destitution. This cannot be true. Either Christ never gave these powers, or they yet remain in the Church, and will continue there, with the other permanent powers, to the end of time.

There are the best reasons for the practice of confession. Is not man a frail creature that needs discipline and aid at every step of his perilous journey through life? And yet can anything defiled enter heaven? The struggle for a seat in that happy abode is a great struggle. The rewards are unspeakable in degree, and endless in duration. They are worth a life of humility and labor. For these reasons man needs a test of his faith and practice at all times. His memory needs to be refreshed. He needs these tests while he has time to amend, if wrong. After death, it is too late. As the doctrine of the Real Presence is a great test of faith in the truth of

Christianity, so confession is a great test of virtuous practice. The proud cannot submit to it. Christ knew this, and He never intended to reward the proud. He pronounced a sweet blessing upon the poor in spirit; but He had no blessing for the proud. Confession strikes a fatal blow at pride. It humbles and corrects self-conceit. It is a great check upon self-delusion.

There are some things that we can know with certainty, and among them is the fact, that we did do a certain thing, and the motive with which we did it. These are facts within our own knowledge, and are of so plain a character, that we cannot be mistaken. There is no room for delusion. But when we come to make up our judgment as to the character of the act itself, then our self-love and our interest will be most apt to mislead us. If we confess to God alone, we have no one to instruct us as to the character of the particular act, or to cross-examine us as to the circumstances attending the act itself. The whole work we do ourselves, and we do not know whether we are certainly forgiven or not.

In confession it is different in some material respects. The penitent not only gives a statement of all the acts he has committed, that he himself esteems sinful, but he is subjected to cross-examination, that powerful test of truth. Did the most honest witness ever state all the material facts he knew, without cross-examination? Such instances are exceedingly rare; not because the witness does not desire to tell the truth, the whole truth, and nothing but the truth; but because he cannot correctly judge as to all that is material. He will almost certainly omit some circumstance of importance. When we are not only required to confess to God, but to man also, we have two checks instead of one. Besides this, there are many persons of the most pious dispositions that are often afflicted with groundless scruples; and these find a complete relief and correction in confession. As every one has the right to select his own confessor, he can have recourse to that one in whose discretion and judgment he has the greatest confidence.

That God should select human agents to administer His law among men is entirely consistent with the nature and purposes of His government. It was evidently the intent of our Lord to honor human nature. He died for it! He deemed it worthy to be trusted. His system, upon its face, shows the intimate union and mutual dependence that Christians should sustain to each other. His system is not based on universal suspicion.

The objection, based upon considerations of delicacy, is one that is without any real foundation in reason or Scripture. We are assured that one day our sins will be revealed to an assembled universe. It is only a small question of time, to say the least of it. The jurisdiction of the Church extends to all violations of law, or to none. If Christ, by His law, prohibits sins of every character, why should the church pass any of them over in silence? Can a man escape responsibility, simply because he takes care only to commit indelicate sins? The criminal law of the land defines and punishes a great variety of offences, some of them of a very indelicate character; and yet our courts of law are compelled to execute justice upon offenders openly by a public trial. No code of law could pass over these indelicate offences without an abdication of justice, and the consequent increase of these very crimes.

The rights of the church, and the salvation of her children, cannot be sacrificed to motives of mere delicacy. In the pure and impartial eye of God, sins are obnoxious in proportion to their turpitude. In a true legal, moral and philosophical view, the question of delicacy, does not affect that of jurisdiction, but only the mode of investigation.

It was to avoid the scandals of public confession, that secret sins are confessed as secret, and kept sacred by the proper officer. In this way, the Church and the individual members receive the benefits flowing from the sacrament while the injuries that might result from a public confession are avoided. And one of the most powerful arguments in favor of confession is the fact, that a priest was never known wrongfully to reveal anything confided to him in the tribunal of penance. It does not matter whether he has subsequently become an Atheist, or even a criminal; his lips are sealed in eternal silence.

If the Church has any jurisdiction over offences at all, she has the right to know of every violation of the law. The hypocrite to his own ruin may defraud her of this right, but still she has that right, though it may be evaded. It is difficult to understand that sort of morality that would hypocritically conceal a violation of the law the Church was charged to execute, and yet allow the party to enjoy all her privileges and protection, and still hope to get to heaven through her communion. If he is for the Church, he ought to be for her; if not, let him be for the world. Let him be squarely and decidedly for one or the other.

It is about as difficult to conceive a logical idea of a religious system, requiring both faith and holiness, and promising forgiveness of sins committed after baptism, without confession, as it is of a system of law without free agency in the party governed, and without any tribunal to construe the law in the last resort. If the powers to remit and retain sins, and the necessarily corresponding duty to confess them, do not reside in the Church, the system is defective, to the best of my judgment. It is simply a question of government, or no government in the Church; and this again is a question simply of Church or no Church. And the whole controversy, as I conceive, between Catholics and Protestants is ultimately resolvable into one single question. *Was Christ a lawgiver or not?* If he was, the Catholic is right. If not, then the Protestant is nearer right. This is the only point really at issue, and it must come to that, sooner or later. It is the only point that needs to be determined. All else follows invincibly.

4. The views of confession in some Protestant sects

In the confession of Augsburg, and the Apology, it is held:

1. That particular absolution ought to be retained in confession; that to reject it is an error of the Novatians, and a condemned error.

2. That this absolution is a true sacrament, and properly so called.

3. That the power of the keys remits sins, not only in the sight of the Church, but also in the sight of God.

In the little Catechism of Luther are these words:

> In the sight of God, we must hold ourselves guilty of our hidden sins; but with respect to the Minister, we must confess those only which are known to us, and which we feel within our hearts.

The absolution given by the confessor is in this form: "Do you not believe that my forgiveness is that of God?"

"Yes," answers the penitent.

"And I," replies the confessor, "by the orders of our Lord Jesus Christ, forgive you your sins, in the name of the Father, and of the Son, and of the Holy Ghost."[12]

In the Common Prayer Book of the Church of England, it is ordained that when any minister visits any sick person:

> The latter should be moved to make especial confession of his sins if he feels his conscience troubled with any weighty matter. After which confession, the Priest shall absolve him if he humbly and heartily desire it, after this sort: Our Lord Jesus Christ, who hath left

> power to his Church to absolve all sinners who truly repent and believe in him, of his great mercy, forgive thee thine offences; and by his authority committed to me, I absolve thee from all thy sins, in the name of the Father, and of the Son, and of the Holy Ghost, Amen.[13]

It will be observed that this duty is only imposed upon the minister in cases of *sickness*. But it would seem to be exceedingly difficult to understand the reason why a sick person needs forgiveness, while a person in health does not, and why our Lord could be held to have left power to absolve in the one case and not in the other. The person in health may die suddenly. It is an effort, on the part of the Church of England, to retain the power in *form*, but to dispense with its exercise, except in particular cases. Did Christ ever make such exceptions? Did He, in bestowing the power upon the apostles, limit it to cases of sickness?

It must be conceded that this practice of the Church of England wears the appearance of a mere practical evasion of the injunction of Christ. To concede that our Lord, in general terms, did leave the power to absolve from sins with His Church, and then to arbitrarily restrict it to sick persons, would seem to be a perversion of the very purpose intended by conferring the power itself. Thus to mutilate and cripple, limit and restrict, a power of such a general character, would seem to be an arbitrary act, unjustifiable by reason or Scripture.

In the discipline of the Methodist Church may be found the regulations of Band Societies.[14] The questions that must be put at every meeting are these:

1. "What known sins have you committed since our last meeting?"

2. "What particular temptations have you met with?"

3. "How were you delivered?"

4. "What have you thought, said, or done, of which you doubt whether it be sin or not?"

5. Testimony of the Fathers

In reference to the testimony of the Fathers, I find the most important passages collected by Dr. Wiseman in the tenth of his Moorfield lectures. I avail myself of his labors, and take the following from the passages he quoted.

Saint Irenaeus mentions some women who accused themselves of secret crimes. Of others he says: "Some, touched in conscience, publicly confessed their sins; while others, in despair, renounced their faith." "Look," says Dr. Wiseman, "at this alternative; some confessed and others renounced the faith. If there had been any other means of forgiveness, why should they have abandoned their faith."

Tertullian says, among other things:

> Of this penitential disposition the proof is more laborious, as the business is more pressing, in order that some public act, not the voice of conscience alone, may show it....
>
> If you still draw back, let your mind turn to that eternal fire, which confession will extinguish; and that you may not hesitate to adopt the remedy, weigh the greatness of future punishment. And as you are not ignorant that, against that fire, after the baptismal institution, the aid of confession has been appointed, why are you an enemy to your own salvation?

The aid of confession has been appointed after the baptismal institution; that is, for sins committed *after* baptism.

Saint Cyprian, speaking of those who had *thoughts of sacrificing* to idols, or of surrendering the Scriptures, says:

> This they confess, with grief and without disguise, before the Priests of God, unburdening the conscience, and seeking a salutary remedy, however small and pardonable their failing may have been....
>
> I entreat you, my brethren, let all confess their faults, while he that has offended enjoys life; while his confession can be received, and while the satisfaction and pardon imparted by the priests are acceptable before God.

Origen of the Greek Church says:

> There is yet a more severe and arduous pardon of sins by penance, when the sinner washes his couch with tears, and when he blushes not to disclose his sin to the priest of the Lord, and seek the remedy....
>
> They who have sinned, if they hide and retain their sin within their breast are grievously tormented; but if the sinner become his own accuser, while he does this he discharges the cause of all his malady.
>
> Only let him carefully consider to whom should he confess his sin, what is the character of the physician; if he be one who will be weak with the weak, who will weep with the sorrowful, and who

> understand the discipline of condolence and fellow-feeling – so that, when his skill shall be known and his pity felt, you may follow what he may advise. Should he think your disease to be such that it should be declared in the assembly of the faithful, whereby others may be edified, and yourself easily reformed – this must be done with much deliberation, and the skillful advice of the physician.

From this passage it is seen that the penitent had the right to select his confessor – that he should select a prudent and skillful one – that the confessor had a right to require a public confession if deemed advisable for the edification of others and the reformation of the penitent – and that this public confession *followed* the private confession, and presupposed its existence. This passage is a proof that both private and public confessions were practiced in the ancient Church, the latter depending upon the judgment of the confessor. Again, this Father says:

> They who are not holy die in their sins; the holy do penance; they feel their wounds; are sensible of their failings; look for the priest; implore health; and through him seek to be purified....
>
> If we discover *our sins*, not only to God, but to those who may apply a remedy to our wounds and iniquities, our sins will be effaced by Him who said: *I have blotted out thy iniquities as a cloud, and thy sins as a mist.* (Is 44:22)

This last passage shows the duty of confessing to *both God and His ministers.*

Saint Basil says:

> In the confession of sins, the same method must be observed, as in laying open the infirmities of the body. For, as these are not rashly communicated to every one, but to those only who understand by what method they may be cured, so the confession of sins must be made to such persons as have the power to apply a remedy.

He tells us who those persons are who can apply the remedy:

> Necessarily our sins must be confessed to those to whom has been committed the dispensation of the mysteries of God.... That woman, guilty of adultery, and who had confessed it, should not be made public, agreeable to what the Fathers had appointed.

Saint Gregory of Nyssa says:

> You whose soul is sick, why do you not run to a physician? Why do you not confess, and discover your malady to *him* by confession? .....

> Impart your trouble to the priest, as to your Father; he will be touched with a sense of your misery. Show to him what is concealed without blushing; open the secrets of your soul as if you were showing to a physician a hidden disorder; he will take care of your honor and of your cure....
>
> Whoever secretly steals another man's good, if he afterwards discover, by confession, his sin to the priest, his heart being changed, he shall cure the wound: but then he must give to the poor, and thereby clearly show that he is free from the sin of avarice.

Saint Ambrose, speaking of those who do not make a full disclosure of their sins, says:

> There are some who ask for penance that they may at once be restored to communion. These do not so much desire to be loosed, as to bind the priest; for they do not unburden their own consciences, but they burden his, who is commanded not to give holy things to dogs; that is, not easily to admit impure souls to the holy communion.

Saint Pacianus says:

> I address myself to you, who, having committed crimes, refuse to do penance; you, who are ashamed to confess, after you have sinned, without shame. The apostle says to the priest: *Impose not hands lightly on any one; neither be ye partakers of other men's sins.* (1 Tim 5:22) What then wilt thou do who deceivest the minister? Who either leavest him in ignorance, or confoundest his judgment by half communications?

Saint Jerome says:

> In like manner with us, the bishop or priest binds and looses; not those who are merely innocent or guilty, but having heard, as his duty requires, the various qualities of sins, he understands who should be bound and who loosed.

The priest must not be content simply to give absolution *without inquiring into the particular sins.*

Pope Leo the Great writes thus to the Bishops of Campania:

> Having lately understood that some of you, by an unlawful usurpation, have adopted a practice which tradition does not allow, I am determined, by all means, to suppress it. I speak of penance, when applied for by the faithful. There shall be no declaration of all kinds of sins, given in writing, and publicly read; for it is enough that the guilt of conscience be made known to the priest alone, by a private confession. That confidence, indeed, may be thought

> deserving of praise, which, on account of the fear of God, hesitates not to blush before men; there are sins, the public disclosure of which must excite fear; therefore let this improper practice be put an end to, lest many be kept from the remedies of penance, being ashamed, as dreading to make known to their enemies such actions as may expose them to legal punishment. That confession suffices that is first made to God, and then to the priest, who will offer up prayers for the sins of penitents. And there will more be induced to apply to this remedy, when the secrets of the confessing sinner shall not be divulged in the hearing of the people.

This sacrament is more often assailed by sarcasm and appeals to pride, than by earnest and respectful argument. It is often spoken of by professed Christians in very harsh and indignant terms. Thus Mr. Breckenridge says the "priest is like a common sewer, the depository of all the sins of his people." But Mr. Breckenridge would make the ear of God this "common sewer." Did the learned controversialist intend his sarcasm for the ordinance of God, which, in the old law, required confession to the priest, and satisfaction for sin? Was not the priest, in that case, made this "common sewer," as Mr. Breckenridge has it, by God Himself?

The learned controversialist also objects, in very strong terms, upon the ground of indelicacy, to the table of sins found in Catholic Prayer Books, and designed to aid the penitent in his examination of conscience. But, with all due deference, it would seem that this objection was not only captious, but very inconsistent, in the mouth of a Protestant.

The language used in these tables is as delicate as could well be, to be intelligible. It would seem to be one of the plainest dictates of reason, as it is certainly of all law, that the party governed should know what the law requires, and what he may or may not do under the law by which *he is governed.* The sole object in prescribing the law was to secure the obedience of the party governed. To be able to obey, he must know. If it was not wrong to prescribe the law itself, can it be wrong to administer it *as given?* There may be a choice of *modes* in which this should be done; but I apprehend that no better mode could be suggested than the one pursued by the Catholic Church.

Protestants seem to have taken up false ideas of true delicacy – that delicacy which is compatible with the law of Christ. They seem to think that the confessor must propound to *all* penitents *all* questions arising under the law. This is a mistake. The course of examination is governed by prudence; and Catholic priests are most carefully instructed as to this duty. The penitent *first* makes a statement of what he accuses himself as sinful. From this statement, the confessor can readily perceive the course pointed out to him. He will not inquire into every possible offence in every case. There must first be some ground laid by the confession of the penitent himself, before the confessor will proceed to inquire as to the circumstances under which the offence was committed.

It must be conceded by all fair and just minds, that delicacy may be carried to extremes. And it must also be admitted, that people often become indelicate by an over-sensitiveness upon this subject. Some patients, under the influence of false delicacy, would rather die than reveal to their physician the true character of their disease.

6. Satisfaction, the third part of the Sacrament

Satisfaction is the third part of the Sacrament of Penance. The Catholic Church holds that, while the guilt and eternal punishment due to sin are remitted in repentance, confession and absolution, there yet remains some duty to be performed by the penitent. In the accurate language of Dr. Wiseman:

> We believe that upon this forgiveness of sins – that is, after the remission of that eternal debt which God in His justice awards to transgression against His law – He has been pleased to reserve a certain degree of inferior or temporary punishment appropriate to the guilt which had been incurred; and it is on this part of the punishment alone that, according to the Catholic doctrine, satisfaction can be made to God.[15]

The Council of Trent declared:

> That it is wholly false, and foreign from the word of God, that the guilt of sin is never remitted by God without the whole punishment being also pardoned. For clear and illustrious examples are found in the sacred writings, whereby, besides divine tradition, this error is most manifestly evinced. And truly the nature of divine justice seems to demand that they who, through ignorance, have sinned before baptism, should be received into favor in a different manner from those who, having been once freed from the servitude of sin and of the devil; and having received the gift of the Holy Ghost, have not feared, knowingly, to violate the temple of God, and to grieve the Holy Spirit. And it befits the Divine clemency that sins be not pardoned without any satisfaction, so that, taking occasion from thence, thinking sin less grievous, and offering an affront to the Holy Ghost, we should fall into

> more grievous crimes, *treasuring up wrath against the day of wrath.* For doubtless these satisfactory punishments greatly recoil from sin, and check as it were with a bridle, and make penitents more vigilant and cautious for the future; and by acts of the opposite virtues, they remove evil habits acquired by living ill.

In reference to the true source of the merit of these penitential acts the Council declares:

> But the satisfaction which we make for our sins is not so ours, that it be not through Jesus Christ; for we, who can do nothing of our selves, as of ourselves, can do all things, He cooperating who strengthens us. Thus man has not wherein to glory; but all our glorying is in Christ; in whom we live; in whom we merit; in whom we satisfy; bring forth fruits worthy of penitence. Which fruits have efficacy from him; by him are offered to the Father; and through him are accepted by the Father.

In reference to the duty of confessors, it was declared, among other things:

> Let them keep before their eyes, that the satisfaction which they impose be not only for the preservation of a new life, and the medicine of infirmity, but also for avenging the punishment of past sins.[16]

The above extracts, if attentively considered will place before the mind of the reader a clear conception of the Catholic faith, and the main grounds upon which it rests.

If there be any free agency in man at all, so that he can obey or disobey the law of Christ at his own present election, then it follows necessarily, that he must voluntarily cooperate, to some extent at least, with the assisting grace of God, in the work of his own salvation. The only question is as to the amount and extent of this cooperation. The Catholic theory requires more, the Protestant theory less. This is the essence of the difference between the two theories, in reference to the remission of sins committed after baptism. If we can do anything at all in the great work of salvation, when aided by the grace of our Lord Jesus Christ (always freely, given to those who rightly seek it), there can be nothing more natural and reasonable in itself than that we should suffer some temporal punishment for our sins, not only as a partial atonement, but also as a useful correction of evil habits, and as evidence of a true repentance.

When we look into the Old Testament, and see the uniform course pursued by God towards His servants, when transgressing His law, we find abundant examples. When our first parents had fallen, and were restored by repentance through the merits of the future Messiah, the Almighty inflicted temporary punishments upon them, and all their posterity. Although the guilt of original transgression is remitted in baptism, we must all undergo the temporal punishments inflicted in the beginning. When God had put away the sin of David, Nathan said to him: "Because by this deed you have utterly scorned the Lord, the child that is born to you shall die."[17] So, when the same King had sinned in numbering the people, the Lord gave him, upon his repenting, choice of one of three grievous temporal punishments.[18] So the Lord forgave the children of Israel in answer to the prayer of Moses, but at the same time declared that they should not see the land of promise.[19]

This same temporal punishment was inflicted upon Moses and Aaron after they had been forgiven.[20] Holy Job, when he had exceeded in speech, repented in dust and ashes.[21] The men of Nineveh, when the prophet had proclaimed their destruction, observed a general fast for three days, saying: "Who knows, God may yet repent and turn from his fierce anger, so that we perish not?"[22]

It is true that this infliction of temporal punishment after sins were forgiven, occurred under the old dispensation; but it is equally true, that they relied upon the same source of pardon as we; namely: the blood of Christ. They looked forward and we look backward, to the same atonement for sin, both original and actual. There were many things in the old law, and especially those things which naturally flow from our relation to God, which are contained in the new. Those temporary enactments, which were but the result of positive legislation, and which were adapted to the then condition of things, are no doubt laid aside. But the infliction of temporal punishment for sin, flows from the permanent relation we bear to God under both systems; and was not, therefore, repealed by the new law.

This temporal punishment never had been prescribed by any positive law, but was uniformly inflicted by God. Unless we find in the new law some positive dispensation of this punishment, we must suppose it to have continued. It is only upon the ground that God does inflict punishment upon men in this world, that we can believe in the special interposition of Providence.

We not only find no intimation in the New Testament opposed to the practice of penitential works, but we find very clear evidence that they were continued. Our Lord expressly says that His followers shall fast.[23] And we find it was the constant practice of the apostles and others in their day. So, when our Lord reproached the then existing generation, He referred to the example of the men of Nineveh, not only without censure, but with evident approbation.[24]

The language of Saint Paul is still more explicit:

> I now rejoice in my sufferings for you, and fill up that which is behind of the afflictions of Christ in my flesh for His body's sake, which is the Church[25]

Upon this passage Dr. Wiseman remarks:

> What is wanting of Christ's sufferings! And this to supplied by man, and in his flesh! What sort of doctrine call we this? Or rather, does it not suppose that much is to be done by man, toward possessing himself of the treasures laid up in our Savior's redemption? And that suffering is the means whereby this application is made?

The distinguished author makes this clear summary of the Catholic faith:

> The doctrine that is thus collected from the Word of God is reducible to these heads:
>
> 1. That God, after the remission of sin, retains a lesser chastisement in His power, to be inflicted on the sinner.
>
> 2. That penitential works fasting, alms-deeds, contrite weeping, and fervent prayers, have the power of averting that punishment.
>
> 3. That this scheme of God's justice was not a part of the imperfect law, but the unvarying ordinance of His dispensation, anterior to the Mosaic ritual, and amply confirmed by Christ in the Gospel.
>
> 4. That it consequently becomes a part of all true repentance to try to satisfy this divine justice, by the voluntary assumption of such penitential works as His revealed truth assures us have efficacy before Him.

The satisfaction already mentioned may be properly called prospective, because it is intended to avert that temporal punishment which has been reserved for the sinner. But there is a retrospective satisfaction of the most important character, without which there can be no remission of sins in the sacrament of penance. This consists in repairing so far as in our power, the injury we may have done to others.

It is an essential act of justice towards an injured fellow being that must be performed; otherwise, the absolution granted will avail nothing. The stolen, or dishonestly obtained property, must be restored to its rightful owner; and amends must be made to the person whose character and feelings have been injured by slander or detraction.

That this doctrine and practice of satisfaction was the faith of the Church of the first four centuries is conclusively shown from the testimony of the ancient Fathers. The system called the penitential canons was founded on this basis.

The first extract is form Hermas, who wrote in the first century:

> I know that they do penitence with all their hearts. But dost thou, therefore, think that their offences, who do penance, are immediately blotted out? No: they are not presently; but it is necessary that he who does penitence afflict his soul, and show himself humble in spirit in all his affairs, and undergo many and divers vexations.

Tertullian in the second century, said:

> For, by the afflicting of the flesh and the spirit, we at the same time both satisfy for things past, and build up before hand a barrier against temptations to come.[26]

> What then, is the working of patience in the body? In the first place, the afflicting of the flesh, an offering propitiating the Lord by the sacrifice of humiliation...This patience of the body commends our prayers, strengthens our entreaties for mercy; this opens the ears of Christ our God, scatters abroad his severity, draws forth his mercy.[27]

Origen says:

> Wherefore if any one be conscious to himself that he has within him a mortal sin, and that he has not cast it off from himself, through a penitence of the fullest satisfaction, let him not hope that Christ will enter into his soul.[28]

Saint Cyprian says:

> Do entire penance; evince the contrition of a sorrowing and grieving mind. That penance which may satisfy remains alone to be done; but they shut the door to satisfaction who deny the necessity of penance.[29]

Saint Augustine says:

> It is not enough that the sinner change his ways, and depart from his evil works, unless, by penitential sorrow, by humble tears, by the

> sacrifice of a contrite heart, and by alms-deeds, he make the satisfaction to God for what he has committed.[30]

I have passed over the testimonies to the same effect of Lactantius, Saint Gregory of Nyssa, Saint Basil, Saint Pacian, Saint Ambrose, Saint Jerome, Saint John Chrysostom, and others.

7. Purgatory

The Council of Trent declared, as the faith of the Catholic Church, that:

> There is a purgatory, and that the souls there detained are helped by the suffrages of the faithful, but principally by the acceptable sacrifice of the altar.

This is all that is required to be believed. As to the kind, and measure of the purifying punishment, the Church defines nothing. This doctrine has been very much misrepresented, and has most generally been attacked by sarcasm and denunciation. But is this a satisfactory method to treat a grave matter of faith coming down to us from olden times

The doctrine of purgatory is most intimately connected with the doctrine of sacramental absolution and satisfaction, and legitimately springs from it. That there is a distinction in the guilt of different sins must be conceded. All our criminal laws, and those of all nations, are founded upon this idea. To say that the smallest transgression, the result of inadvertence, is equal in enormity to the greatest and most deliberate crime, is so utterly opposed to the nature of all law, and to the word of God, which assures us that men shall be punished or rewarded according to their works, as not to require any refutation.[31] Our Lord assures us that men must give an account in the Day of Judgment for any idle word they speak; and Saint John tells us that nothing defiled shall enter heaven.[32] Then Saint John says there is a sin unto death, and there is a sin which is not unto death; and he also tells us that "All wrongdoing is sin, but there is sin which is not mortal."[33] So we are told by the same apostle, that if we confess our sins, God is faithful and just to forgive us.[34]

We must put all these texts together, and give them their full harmonious, and consistent force. We must carry out the principles laid down to their fair and logical results. Suppose, then, a man speak an idle word, and die suddenly, before he has time to repent and confess his sin, will he be lost everlastingly? Must there not in the very nature of Christ's system be a middle state, wherein souls can be purged from their lesser sins? Was not the great Dr, Johnson right when he said, speaking of the Catholic faith in reference to purgatory?

> They are of opinion that the generality of mankind are neither so obstinately wicked as to deserve everlasting punishment, nor so good as to merit being admitted into the society of blessed spirits; and, therefore, that God is graciously pleased to allow of a middle state, where they may be purified by certain degrees of suffering. You see, sir, there is nothing unreasonable in this.[35]

In reference to prayers for the dead the Doctor also maintained, that

> if it be once established that there are souls in purgatory, it is as proper to pray for them, as for our brethren of mankind, who are yet in this life.

The Doctor was in the habit of praying for his deceased wife. He states that he spent March 22 1753, in prayers and tears in the morning; and in the evening he prayed for her conditionally.

> O Lord, so far as it may be lawful in me, I commend to thy fatherly goodness the soul of my departed wife; beseeching thee to grant her whatever is best in her present state, and finally to receive her to eternal happiness.

It is clear that the practice of praying for the dead must rest upon the basis, that there is a middle state. It would be useless to pray for those in heaven, who needed no relief; and equally idle to pray for them who were beyond the reach of help.

It is related in the twelfth chapter of Second Macabees, that the valiant Judas collected and sent 12,000 drachmas of silver to Jerusalem

> for sacrifices to be offered for the sins of the dead thinking well and religiously concerning the resurrection. And because he considered that they who have fallen asleep with godliness had great grace laid up for them. It is therefore a holy and wholesome thought to pray for the dead, that they may be loosed from their sins.

It has been settled by the Catholic Church that this book constitutes part of the canon of the Old Testament, while it is not admitted by Protestants. But all must concede that it is authentic history, and shows the faith of the Jewish Church, one hundred and fifty years before Christ. It is still the faith of the Jews. Our Lord, in his discourses to the Jews, knew what their belief was. This fact is of no inconsiderable importance, for the reason that He nowhere condemns this belief while He did condemn certain other practices of the Jews. Again, Saint Paul speaks of the practice of baptizing for the dead without censure.[36] That there is a distinction of sins and their punishments is clear from several texts besides those already referred to.[37]

Our Lord, in speaking of the sin against the Holy Ghost says: "It shall not be forgiven him, neither in this world, neither in the world to come." Now our Lord meant to convey some idea by saying "neither in this world, neither in the world to come." We cannot suppose He used it without design. Then what else could He mean, but to say that this sin was *peculiar*, and could not be forgiven in either state, while other sins might be forgiven in the one or the other? If no sin could be forgiven in the world to come, than for what purpose did He say this sin could not *there* be forgiven? Why distinguish it from other sins, in this respect, when no distinction, in fact, existed? Did our Lord do an idle thing? Those who deny that our Lord meant to say that *some* sins could be forgiven in the world to come, should do one of two things: either tell us what He did mean, or say at once that He meant nothing. To object to our interpretation, and then assume to give us nothing better, is certainly not magnanimous. If there be remission of sins in the world to come, it follows that there must be a middle state, as this forgiveness could not be in Heaven, or in the place of eternal punishment.

There is a passage in one of Saint Paul's Epistles that relates to a middle state of purgation. That this has always been held by the Church will be seen from the quotations that we will make from the Fathers. The passage is this:

> Now if anyone builds on the foundation with gold, silver, precious stones, wood, hay, stubble –each man's work will become manifest; for the Day will disclose it, because it will be revealed with fire, and the fire will test what sort of work each one has done. If the work which any man has built on the foundation survives, he will receive a reward. If any man's work is burned up, he will suffer loss, though he himself will be saved, but only as through fire.[38]

There is a great deal more expressed in this passage, than would at first appear. Suppose a man had built only gold, silver, or precious stones, or all together, then he would be entitled to a reward, without suffering any loss. But suppose he had built only wood, hay or stubble, or all these together, he would be entitled to no reward, and could not be saved. It is only in the case where the gold, silver, or precious stones have been intermixed with the wood, hay, or stubble, that the builder can be saved, while he suffers loss himself. The apostle does not say that the party escaping is himself tried by fire, but he escapes as if so tried – comparing the ordeal through which he himself must pass, to that of fire. If the apostle had not added the words: "but he himself shall be saved; yet so as by fire," we could only have concluded that he alluded to the test of the work alone. But these words show that he first alludes to the test of the work; and, afterwards, to the ordeal through which the builder himself must pass, because of his having built such materials upon the foundation – Christ Jesus. To have intermixed such gross materials with those that were suitable for a foundation so precious, is a sin, for which the party must suffer loss, by being, for the time, deprived of heaven, and undergoing the punishment of purgation.

In reference to the testimony of the Ancient Fathers, I find the passages from their works bearing upon this subject so well arranged by Dr. Wiseman, that I extract his quotations and remarks upon them entire.[39]

> Now nothing can be more simple than to establish the belief of the universal Church on this point. The only difficulty is to select such passages as appear the clearest.
>
> I will begin with the very oldest Father of the Latin Church, Tertullian, who advises a widow to pray for the soul of her departed husband, entreating repose to him, and participation in the first resurrection, and making ablations for him on the anniversary day of his death, which, if she neglect, it may be truly said that she has divorced her husband.(*De Monogamia*, c, 10.) To make an oblation on the anniversary day of his death; to pray that he may have rest, –is not this more like our language and practice than those of any other religion in England? And does not Tertullian suppose that good is done to the faithful departed by such prayer? And, moreover, does he not prescribe it as a solemn duty, rather than recommend it as a lawful practice?
>
> Saint Cyprian thus writes: "Our predecessors prudently advised that no heathen, departing this life, should nominate any churchman his executor. And should he do so, that no oblation should be made for him, nor sacrifice offered for his repose: of which we have had a late example, where no oblation was made, nor prayer, in his name, offered in the Church." It was considered, therefore, a severe punishment that prayers and sacrifices should not be offered up for those who had violated any of the ecclesiastical laws.
>
> There are many other passages in this Father; but I proceed to Origen, who wrote in the same century, and than whom no one can be clearer

regarding this doctrine: "When we depart this life, if we take with us virtues or vices, shall we receive reward for our virtues, and shall those trespasses be forgiven to us which we knowingly committed? or shall we be punished for our faults, and not receive the reward of our virtues?" That is, if there be in our account a mixture of good and evil, shall we be rewarded for the good without any account being taken of the evil, or punished for the evil, without the good being taken into consideration? This query he thus answers: "Neither is true; because we shall suffer for our sins, and receive the reward of our good actions. For if on the foundation of Christ you shall have built, not only gold, and silver, and precious stones, but also wood, and hay, and stubble, what do you expect when the soul shall be separated from the body? Would you enter into heaven with your wood and hay and stubble, to defile the kingdom of our God? or, on account of those encumbrances, remain without and receive no reward for your gold, and silver, and precious stones? Neither is this just. It remains, then, that you be committed to the fire, which shall consume the light materials. For our God, to those who can comprehend heavenly things, is called a consuming fire. But this fire consumes not that creature, but what the creature has himself built, – wood, and hay, and stubble. It is manifest, that, in the first place, the fire destroys the wood of our transgressions, and then returns to us the reward of our good works."(Homil. xvi. *Al xii in Jerem.*, T. iii, P. 23I, 232.)

Therefore, according to this learned Father, (two hundred years after Christ,) when the soul is separated from the body, if there be smaller transgressions, it is condemned to fire, which purges away those light materials, and thus prepares the soul for entering into heaven.

Saint Basil, or a contemporary author writing on the words of Isaiah, "Through the wrath of the Lord is burned," says that the things which are earthly shall be made the food of a punishing fire; to the end that the soul may, receive favor and be benefited. He then proceeds: "And the people shall be the fuel of the fire" this is not a threat of extermination; but it denotes expurgation according to the expression of the apostle: "If any man's work burn, he shall suffer loss; he himself shall be saved, yet so as by fire."(1 Cor 3:15.) Now mark well the word purgation here used. For it proves that our very term purgatory is not modern in the Church.

Saint Ephrem of Edessa writes thus in his testimony: "My brethren, come to me, and prepare me for my departure, for my strength is wholly gone. Go along with me in psalms and in your prayers and pleas constantly to make oblations for me. When the thirtieth day shall be completed, then remember me; for the dead are helped by the offerings of the living." The very day observed by the Catholic Church, with peculiar solemnity, in praying and in offering mass for the dead. "If also, the sons of Matthias (he alludes to the very passage I have quoted from Machabees,) who celebrated their feasts in figure only, could cleanse those [from guilt] by their offerings, who fell in battle, how much more shall the priests of Christ aid the dead by their oblations and prayer!" (*In Testament*, T. ii, p. 234.)

In the same century, Saint Cyril of Jerusalem thus expresses himself: "Thus (in the liturgy of the Church) we pray for the holy Fathers and the bishops that are dead, and, in short, for all those who departed this life in our communion. Believing that the souls of those for whom the prayers are offered, receive very great relief while this holy and tremendous victim lies upon the altar."(*Catech. Mystag*. v. n. ix. x., p. 328.)

Saint Gregory of Nyssa thus contrasts the course of God's providence in this world with that in the next. In the present life, "God allows man to remain subject to what he himself has chosen. That, having tasted of the evil which he desired, and learned by experience how bad an exchange has been made, he might again feel an ardent wish to lay down the load of those vices and inclinations which are contrary to reason. And thus, in this life, being renovated by prayers and the pursuit of wisdom, or, in the next, being expiated by the purging fire, he might recover the state of happiness which he had lost...

When he has quitted his body, and the difference between virtue and vice is known, he cannot be admitted to approach the Divinity, till the purging fire shall have expiated the stains with which his soul was infected. That same fire in others will cancel the corruption of matter and the propensity to evil."(*Orat. de Defunctis*, T. ii, 1066-S.)

Saint Ambrose, throughout his works has innumerable passages on this subject, and quotes Saint Paul's Epistle to the Corinthians, (3:15) which you have heard already cited by the other Fathers: "If any man's works burn, he shall suffer loss; but he himself shall be saved, yet so as by fire. I will quote one passage out of many: "But he shall be saved, yet so as by fire." He will be saved, the apostle said, because his substance shall remain, while his bad doctrine shall perish. Therefore, he said, yet so as by fire; in order that his salvation be not understood to be without pain. He shows that he shall be saved indeed but he shall undergo the pain of fire, and thus be purified; not like the unbelieving and wicked man, who shall be punished in everlasting fire."(*Comment. in 1 Ep. ad Cor.,* T. ii, in app., p.122.) And in his funeral oration on the Emperor Theodosius he thus speaks: "Give 0 Lord, rest to thy servant Theodosius, that rest which Thou hast prepared for Thy Saints. May his soul thither tend whence it came, where it cannot feel the sting of death, where it will learn that death is the termination, not of nature, but of sin. I loved him, therefore I will follow him to the land of the living; I will not leave him till, by my prayers and lamentations, he shall be admitted to the holy Mount of the Lord, to which his deserts call him."

Saint Epiphanius, in the same century: "There is nothing more opportune, nothing more to be admired, than the rite which directs the names of the dead to be mentioned. They are aided by the prayer which is offered for them, though it may not cancel all their faults. We mention both the just and sinners, in order that for the latter we may obtain mercy."(*Haer,* 1v. sive lxxv., T. i., p. 911)

Saint Jerome: "As we believe the torments of the devil, and of those wicked men who said in their hearts there is no God, to be eternal; so, in regard to those sinners who have not denied their faith, and whose works will be proved and purged by fire, we conclude that the sentence of the judge will be tempered by mercy."(*Comment. in c.* lxv. Isai., T. ii, P. 492.)

Not to be tedious I will quote one Father more, the great Saint Augustine: "The prayers of the Church," he writes, "or of good persons, are heard in favor of those Christians who departed this life, not so bad as to be deemed unworthy of mercy, nor so good as to be entitled to immediate happiness." (*De Civit. Dei,* Lib. xxi, c. xxiv, p.642) St Augustine's reasoning is here precisely the same as I have used, and as every Catholic man uses. In another passage he quotes the words of Saint Paul, as follows: "If they had built *gold and silver and precious stones,* they would be secure from both fires; not only from that in which the wicked will burn forever, but likewise from that fire which will purify those who shall be saved by fire. But because it is said, *he shall be saved* that fire is thought lightly of, though the suffering will be more grievous than anything man can undergo in this life."

These passages contain precisely the same doctrine as the Catholic Church teaches; and had I introduced them into my discourse without telling you from whom they are taken, no one would have supposed that I was swerving from the doctrine taught by our Church. It is impossible to imagine that the sentiments of these writers agreed, on this point, with that of any other religion.

I will only add one extract to those given by the distinguished lecturer. It is the language of Saint Monica, the mother of the great

Augustine, addressed to him by her while she was on her deathbed. "Lay," then she said,

> this body anywhere; let not the care of it in any way disturb you: this only I request of you, that you would remember me at the altar of the Lord, wherever you be.[40]

8. Indulgences

No doctrine of the Catholic Church has been more misunderstood, or more distorted, than the article concerning Indulgences. The best method of correcting these misapprehensions on the part of sincere persons is to give a clear statement of the doctrine itself. In the first place, an indulgence has not the slightest reference to future sin, and is not; therefore, any license to commit it in any form. Nor is it a remission of either the eternal guilt of sin, or of the eternal punishment due to it. It is simply a remission, in whole or in part, of the temporary punishment deserved for sins committed after baptism, or a commutation of that punishment.

In the Catholic theory, as we have seen, the interior or eternal guilt of sin, and the eternal punishment due to it, are both remitted by contrition, confession, and absolution, except in that class of cases wherein we have injured our neighbors and wherein a further act – an act of just reparation – must be performed before the remission of the eternal guilt and punishment becomes complete. After the eternal guilt and punishment of sin have been remitted in the sacrament of penance, God has reserved a certain degree of mere temporary punishment, proportioned to the offense. The object of this temporary punishment is to make a partial atonement for the sin committed, to correct the evil habit, and to give evidence of a true repentance. The power to relax this temporary punishment, or to substitute another for it, as after circumstances may justly require, is the power to grant an indulgence.

The power to grant indulgences is but a legitimate consequence resulting from the powers to bind and loose, to remit and retain sins, originally conferred by Christ upon the Church. These powers necessarily include the power and duty to determine the character of the particular sin committed after baptism, and the weight of the circumstances attending it, and to assess the amount, and designate the kind, of the temporary punishment named by the law of God. It is strictly a judicial power, applying the existing law to the facts and circumstances of each particular case. If this right and duty of the

Church be conceded, then the right to mitigate this punishment, or to substitute another for it, as subsequent circumstances may justly require, must belong to the power that originally imposed this temporary punishment. It will be seen at once by the calm and sensible reader, that, in the contemplation of the Catholic theory, the granting of an indulgence cannot affect, in any way, the eternal condition of the party to whom it is granted, but only his temporary condition.

This power of pardon or commutation after conviction and sentence, is retained by all civil governments. The exercise of it depends upon subsequent circumstances, unforeseen at the time the punishment was assessed. The object of criminal punishment is expiatory, preventive, and reformatory. The good conduct of the criminal during his imprisonment may constitute strong evidence of a real reformation. It often happens that the executive of a state will pardon the convict at such a time as to remit the punishment in part only. It is not uncommon for pardon to be granted upon conditions, or only a few days before the expiration of the term of imprisonment fixed by the sentence, so as to restore the prisoner to the rights of citizenship.

The case of the Corinthian who had his father's wife, is one in which the power of granting an indulgence was exercised in the Apostolical Church. In reference to this case the apostle says:

> For I verily, as absent in body, but present in spirit, have judged already, as though I was present, concerning him that hath so done this deed. In the name of our Lord Jesus Christ, when ye are gathered together, and my spirit, with the power of the Lord Jesus Christ, to deliver such an one unto Satan for the destruction of the flesh, that the spirit may be saved in the day of the Lord Jesus.

There are several important facts to be collected from this passage:

1. The apostle had judged the party guilty of this crime.

2. He *commanded* his brethren, in the name and with the power to the Lord Jesus, publicly to deliver the guilty party to Satan.

3. This punishment was *temporary*, as it was intended for the destruction of the flesh, and the ultimate safety of the spirit.

4. The punishment was inflicted by the authority of Christ.

The effect of this punishment was such as was anticipated. The culprit was plunged into the deepest affliction; and the apostle in his second Epistle thus refers to this case:

> Sufficient to such a man is this punishment, which was inflicted of many. So that contrariwise ye ought rather to forgive him, and comfort him, lest perhaps such a one should be swallowed up with overmuch sorrow. Wherefore I beseech you that you would confirm your love toward him. To whom ye forgive any thing, I forgive also: for if I forgave anything, to whom I forgave it, for your sakes forgave I it in the person of Christ.

It will be seen by examining the two chapters from which these extracts are taken, 1 Cor 5. and 2 Cor 2, that the punishment was prescribed by the apostle himself, and the party forgiven by him *in the person of Christ.* The Church at Corinth only acted under the command of the apostle. The apostle in his second Epistle refers to the severity of the punishment inflicted by the whole congregation under his command; and tells his brethren that they ought to forgive and comfort the member, "lest perhaps he should be swallowed up with over much sorrow." In the case of Hymenaeus and Alexander, the apostle says *he* delivered them to Satan; but is does not appear that it was done publicly.[41] By his sorrow, the offending member procured a mitigation of his sentence, and was forgiven and restored to the full privileges of membership. The temporary punishment for sins inflicted by the ancient Church, consisted in abstaining from all amusements, giving the time of the sinner to prayer and good works, rigorous fasting, other penitential exercises, for and during a period of time proportioned to the nature of the offence. Sometimes this penance only lasted a few days, sometimes for several years, and in very extreme cases during life.

During the continuance of several persecutions that occurred in the first three centuries of the Christian era, many believers denied the faith and sacrificed to idols. The Council of Nice in A.D. 325 decreed that:

> those who had fallen away without necessity, or without the taking away of their goods, or without being in danger, or something of this kind, as happened under the tyranny of Licinius, though they were unworthy of indulgence, they should nevertheless be dealt with mercifully. And as many, therefore, as truly repent, shall pass three years amongst the *hearers* as believers, and during seven years they shall be prostrators, and during two years they shall communicate with the people in the prayers with the oblation.[42]

In the next canon it was decreed, among other things, as follows:

> But in all these persons it is proper to examine the purpose and appearance of their penitence; for as many as, in fear, and tears, and patience, and good works, manifest their conversion indeed, and not

> in appearance (only,) these having completed the appointed time as *hearers*, may communicate in the prayers; together with authority to the bishop to determine something yet more indulgent respecting them. But as many as have borne (their sentence) indifferently, and think the form of entering into the Church sufficient for their conversion, must complete the whole time.

It will be remembered that the Novatians separated from the Church because she permitted the lapsed or fallen, as they were called, to return to the Church, after undergoing due penance. This penance was called canonical, because of the canons or rules adopted for its regulation.

The Council of Ancyra in A.D. 315, in its fifth canon, says, in reference to those who had fallen:

> But the bishops have the power, having considered the manner of their conversion, to deal indulgently with them, or to add a longer period. But, above all things, let their previous as well as their subsequent life be inquired into, and so let the *indulgence be measured out*.

One of the means of procuring this mitigation of the temporal punishment inflicted, was the recommendation of the holy martyrs, given on the eve of their martyrdom. This practice was but following the example of Saint Paul, who forgave the incestuous Corinthian for the sake of his brethren. In reference to this practice, Tertullian says, before he became a Montanist:

> Let not the devil so prosper in his own kingdom, as to set you at variance, but let him find you guarded and armed with concord, because your peace is war against him, which peace some not finding in the church, have been wont to entreat of the martyrs in prison.[43]

After he became a Montanist he inveighed against this practice; but his subsequent invectives could not destroy his testimony as to the practice of the Church, while he was one of her members.

Saint Cyprian, in the third century, speaking of the same practice, and addressing the martyrs, says:

> And, therefore, I entreat you to specify by name in your tickets, persons whom ye yourselves see and know, whose *penitence* you behold approaching very near to *satisfaction*.[44]

In his address to his clergy, speaking of the lapsed and fallen, he says:

> Since I find that it will not be in my power to come amongst you, I think that the cases of our brethren ought to be met, so that they who have received tickets from the martyrs, and who are helped by their privilege with God, if they are seized with any ailment, or danger of sickness, may, without waiting for my presence, make confession of their sin before any priest whatever... that they may go to the Lord with that peace which the martyrs, by their letters unto us, have desired might be granted.[45]

I will add only one other testimony, that from Saint Gregory of Nyssa, who wrote in A.D. 370:

> The canon law is this: that they who have defiled themselves by fornication, shall be utterly cast forth from prayer during three years: be allowed to be hearers only for three further years. But, in favor of those who, with special zeal, avail themselves of the (time of) conversion, and in their lives exhibit a return to what is good, it is in his power, who has the regulation of the dispensation of the church for a beneficial end, to shorten the period of hearing, and to introduce such men earlier to the (state) of conversion, and further to lessen this period also, and to bestow communion earlier, according as, from his own judgment, he comes to a decision respecting the state of the person *under cure*."[46]

I have passed over the testimonies of Saint Basil, and Saint Innocent, in support of this doctrine. I have also passed over the decrees of the Council of Orange in A.D. 441, and Fourth Council of Carthage, in A.D. 398,

I have included Penance, Purgatory, and Indulgences in one chapter, because they constitute, in fact, but portions of one subject. The limits of my work have not allowed me to notice more than the main points; and I must refer the reader, who desires more full and detailed information, to the *Moorfield Lectures* of Dr. Wiseman, who has treated these different heads with great fullness and the most masterly ability. I will conclude this chapter with his summary of the grounds upon which the doctrine of Indulgences rests:

> From all I have said, you will easily conclude that our indulgence, and that of the ancient Church, rest upon the following grounds:
>
> First, that satisfaction has to be made to God for sin remitted, under the authority and regulation of the Church.
>
> Second, that the Church has always, considered herself possessed of the authority to mitigate by diminution or commutation, the penance

which she enjoined; and that she has already reckoned such a mitigation valid before God, who sanctions and accepts it.

Third, that the sufferings of the saints, in union with, and by virtue of Christ's merits, are considered available towards the granting of this mitigation.

Fourth, that such mitigations, when prudently and justly granted, are conducive towards the spiritual weal and profit of Christians.

---

[1] Nicholas Wiseman, *Moorfield Lectures* vol.*2, p* 10.

[2] Num 5:6,7.

[3] Lev 5; Num 5.

[4] Jn 20:23.

[5] *Cf.* Luke 7:47,48 and Matt 9:2.

[6] *Cf.* Matt 18:18.

[7] James Kent *Commentaries on American Law* 1 p 252.

[8] James 5:16.

[9] Acts 19:18.

[10] For example, in clause 3, section 1, and in clause 1, section 9, and in clause 2, section 3, of article 1, and in article 5. It is much easier to expressly mark each of the few exceptions than to expressly mark each of the numerous cases coming under the general rule.

[11] Bishop Porteus, cited in Milner's *End of Controversy.*

[12] Cited Jacques-Benigne Bousset, *Variations of the Protestant Churches,* Book iii., sec. 46, 47.

[13] Order for the Visitation of the Sick.

[14] Edition of 1835, New York, p. 83, 84.

[15] Nicholas Wiseman, *Moorfield Lecture,* vol. 2, p 35.

[16] Sess. xiv. C. viii.

[17] 2 Sam. 12:I4.

[18] *Cf.* 2 Sam. 24:10-15.

[19] *Cf.* Num. 14.

[20] *Cf.* Num. 20:10, 29; Deut. 34:1-6.)

[21] Job 42:1-6.

[22] Jon 3:9.

[23] *Cf.* Matt 9:15.

[24] *Cf.* Matt 12:4I.

[25] Col. 1:24. In the Douay bible it says "those things that are wanting of the sufferings of Christ.

[26] Tertullian. *De Baptismo* n 20. This he said of those who were about to enter upon baptism.

[27] Tertullian. *De Patiencia.* n. 13.

[28] T. ii., Hom. xii. *In Levit.*, n. 3.

[29] *De Lapis,* 192.

[30] *Hom.* i., T. x., p. 208.

[31] *Cf.* Rom 2:6

[32] *Cf.* Matt 12:36; Rev 21:27.

[33] 1 Jn 5:17.

[34] *Cf.* 1 Jn 1:9.

[35] James Boswell. *Life of Johnson.*

[36] 1 Cor. 15:29.

[37] *Cf.* Matt 5:22; Luke 12:43-48; Matt 23:23; 16:27.

[38] 1 Cor 3:12-15.

[39] Nicholas Wiseman, *Moorfield Lectures*, vol. ii, p. 50, sec. xi.

[40] T. i., L. ix. *Confess.*, n. 27, col. 285.

[41] 1 Tim 1:20.

[42] Can. xi., col. 33, t. ii., *Lubbi.*.

[43] *Ad. Martyr.*, n. 1, p. 137.

[44] *Ep. x. ad Martyr. Et Confess.*, p. 51-54.

[45] *Ep. xii. Ad clerum*, p. 55.

[46] T. ii., *Ep. Con. ad S. Letoium*, p. 119.

CHAPTER VII

INVOCATION OF THE SAINTS

1 The invocation of saints

In reference to the doctrine of the Catholic Church concerning the Invocation of Saints, the Council of Trent declares:

> ...the saints who reigned with Christ, offer up to God their prayers for men, that it is good and profitable suppliantly to invoke them, and to fly to their prayers, help, and assistance, for the obtaining of benefits from God through His Son Jesus Christ, our Lord, who is alone our Redeemer and Savior.[1]

It will be seen that this language is very clear and distinct. That matters affirmed are simply these:

1. That the saints in glory offer up prayers for us.

2. That it is good and profitable to invoke them.

3. That this is done for the obtaining of benefits from God through His Son, who alone is our Redeemer and Savior.

By this decree it is not declared to be essential, but only good and profitable, to invoke the prayers of the saints in glory. It will also be observed, that the Giver of all the benefits asked for, is God Himself, who bestows them, in and through the merits of Christ; and that the saints who pray for us, are regarded simply as inferior petitioners, in behalf of their own brethren.

2. The Communion of Saints

The Apostles' Creed, conceded by most Protestants to contain true doctrine, it is said: "I believe in the communion of saints." What is meant by this *communion of saints*?

When we concede that our Lord was a Divine Lawgiver, and that He organized a visible Church, we concede that this Church must be a continuing corporation. It is an artificial person, composed of all the members belonging to it in every age and nation. In the contemplation of the theory these members or corporators, never die. They change their state; but they, in fact, die not. They quit earth, and reach heaven; but they still live on. As never-dying members of one great corporate body, they are each and all interested in the success of the corporation; and as the aggregate rightful success of the whole is made up of the rightful success of each member, they are all interested in the welfare of each, and are thus all constituted "members one of another," as St. Paul says.

The apostle, in different passages, speaks of all Christians as forming members of but one corporate body. When he speaks of those Christians who will be alive at the second coming of Christ, he says: "We that are alive…." So, when he speaks of the resurrection of Christians, he says: "We shall be changed." To show the intimate relationship existing among Christians, he tells his brethren that they come to the heavenly Jerusalem and to the spirits of just men made perfect.[2]

This apostle in the fourth chapter of Ephesians, and twelfth of first Corinthians, gives us the clearest statement. He therein calls the entire Church the body of Christ; and says that our Lord gave certain orders to the Church. And these different orders were given by Christ to the entire Church, not alone to the Church of the apostolic day. And as every member of the natural body must sympathize with every other; so, every member of this corporate body – the church – must equally sympathize with all the others. And as all the saints are immortal members of the same enduring corporation, and are each and all interested in the spiritual welfare of each and of the whole combined, they can assist each other, and this sweet relationship is fitly termed "the communion of saints."

That there is a connecting chain of sympathy and good offices between the suffering saints on earth and their own brethren in heaven would seem to follow from the very nature and purposes of the system of Christ. It not only follows from this, but from many facts expressly stated in the Scripture.

In the dealings of the Almighty with his chosen people, angels were often employed as instruments of God. The examples are too numerous to require any reference. We are told by Christ that we shall be "as the angels of God in heaven."[3] Our Lord also said, "Take heed that ye despise not one of these little ones; for I say unto you that in heaven their angels do always behold the face of my Father which is in heaven."[4] In the passage we are warned not to offend against those little ones because it will offend their guardian angels, and these being present with God, will use their influence with Him to bring down punishment. Saint Paul also tells us that angels are "all ministering spirits, sent forth to minister for them *who shall be heirs of salvation.*"[5] We are told by our Lord that there is joy in heaven over one sinner doing penance.[6] Saint John tells us:

> Another angel came and stood at the altar, having a golden censer; and there was given unto him much incense, that he should offer it with the prayers of all the saints upon the golden alter, which was before the throne. And the smoke of the incense, which came with the prayers of the saints, ascended up before God out of the angels hand.[7]

In reference to these texts, Dr. Wiseman has these clear and forcible remarks:

> From all this it is proved that the saints and angels know what passes on earth –that they are aware of what we do and suffer; otherwise they could not rejoice in any good that we do, nor resent any misfortune that befalls us. In the second place, we have it sufficiently proved that the saints do more than barely know and interest themselves about us, for they actually present our prayers to God and intercede in our behalf with Him. Here, then, is a basis, and a sufficient one, for the Catholic belief, – such a basis as surely should give rise to some doctrine or other in the true religion. Where is this doctrine to be found in those religious systems which reject and exclude all intercession of the saints, all intercourse between those on earth and their brethren in bliss? Assuredly these texts prove something. For if all contained in the Word of God is true and must form a rule of faith, such clear testimony as this regarding the connection between mankind and the blessed, must form the subject of a doctrine. Where, then, is this found? Nowhere but in the Catholic belief, – that prayers are offered for us by the saints, and that, therefore, we may apply to them for their supplications.[8]

The moment we concede the existence of God and His superintending care over us, that moment it becomes as natural for us to pray as to breathe. And it is just as natural to pray for those we love as it is to pray for ourselves. And by the law of Christ, it is our express duty to pray for even those who persecute us.[9]

In the last chapter of the Book of Job, the Lord directed Eliphaz to procure the prayers of his holy servant, saying: "My servant Job shall pray for you: for him will I accept." Moses often prayed for the chosen of Israel, and averted, by his prayers, the threatened wrath of God. In the New Testament it is shown to have been the universal practice for the saints to pray for one another, and that St. Paul constantly prayed for his brethren and often asked their prayers for himself. And St. James tells us that "The effectual fervent prayer of a righteous man availeth much."[10] This he says with reference to prayers *for others.* So plainly is this principle established, that all professed Christians pray for each other. It would seem that no man who admits the duty of prayer at all, could deny the necessity of this practice. It is our duty to do all the good we can; and therefore, we should aid others by our prayers, as well as other good offices.

This duty and utility of prayer must rest upon some great principle. As the practice is not an idle one, it must have its foundation in some great fundamental truth. It must rest upon the intimate connection between the seen and the unseen world –between the governing creator and the governed creature –upon the never-ceasing power and disposition of God to grant us favors, at all times, when we need and properly ask for them. And our duty to pray for each other arises from our natural relationship, and the duty we owe to our Lord, who desires alike the salvation of all men. Are we not all brethren? Are we not bound to extend our Master's Kingdom by every just means? Is not this right?

If, then, a saint, while on earth, can aid his brethren by his prayers, upon what principle can we say that his power for good ceases, when the same saint gets to heaven? Can he not still make known his wishes to God? And has not the Almighty still the same power and disposition to hear the devout and humble petitions of His servants? Did the ardent Paul and the intrepid old Peter cease to love their brethren the moment they reached heaven? Are we not assured that faith and hope are swallowed up in absolute certainty in that blissful abode, while charity, the ever beautiful, still lives on? And is not this sweet virtue called the greatest, because everlasting? Who can believe that the saints in glory forget to love their suffering brethren on earth? Is not such a theory one of the driest and most withering in the universe, and well suited, in its very nature, to the coldest heart and the most perverted understanding?

If the saints in glory love us, this love must be active and *effectual.* Of what value is a love that never does any good for the object beloved? Did our Creator implant in our hearts and souls the desire of immortality, without any intention to gratify so beautiful and so natural a wish? And will our Lord permit the saints in glory to love us, and of course ardently to desire our good, and yet not permit this holy love to do us any service? Why is this holy love and desire permitted to exist, if not for practical exercise? Are there no sweet prayers offered in heaven? Have the saints in glory no wishes to gratify, no favors to ask for their brethren in this tempting world? Who can believe that they love us not? And if they love us who can believe that they never pray for us? – that while they love us they are still indifferent as to our condition? – that if they do desire our good, they still dare not make these desires known? Who can believe that if they do make these desires known, that still God will not gratify them, in proper cases? If the saints in glory love us, and aid us, in what way can they help us more effectually than by praying for us, as they did while still on earth? What sort of a communion of saints is that which is limited alone to this poor earth? What would Christianity itself be worth if it did not look beyond the grave? How can immortal members of such a corporation as that of the Church ever cease to pray for their brethren, so long as there is one left to suffer?

If it be true that the saints in heaven love us, that this love is active and efficient, and not merely passive and idle; and, therefore, that they can and do pray for us. Surely, it can be no wrong in us to ask their prayers, to fly to their help and assistance. To ask of our own brethren – the copartners of our joys and sorrows – to grant us a favor that they love to grant, and that affords them pleasure to perform, cannot be justly held to be erroneous. It would be a strange philosophy, and a still more singular theology, that would make it a crime to ask of a brother that which he had the power and the disposition to give; and which, in itself, was "good and profitable" to us, and no loss to him.

In fact, the objection to the invocation of saints, when calmly and thoroughly considered, resolves itself, at last, into an objection against the duty and utility of all prayer. For it would seem to be clear, that if we can pray for ourselves we can pray for others – that if our prayers can be effectual in the one case, they can in the other – that if we can pray for our brethren while we are in this state of being, we can still do so in the next – that if we can, we *must* do so unless we cease to love our brethren. It is also clear that God must hear our prayers as well in one state as in the other, and that if we can ask the prayers of our brethren present with us, we can upon the same principle ask the prayers of those gone before us. The only consistent ground upon which the invocation of saints can be denied is, in substance and effect, to deny the duty and efficacy of all prayer.

3. Must the saints be omnipresent to hear our prayers?

It is insisted by most Protestant writers, as by the Bishop of Durham that:

> It is blasphemy to ascribe to angels and saints, by praying to them, the divine attribute of universal presence.[11]

But is it true that, because the saints can know that we invoke their prayers, they must possess the "divine attribute of universal presence?" How do the saints know that a sinner on earth does penance? Or do they rejoice without this knowledge? If they can and do know this fact, upon what semblance of reason can we say that they cannot know when their brethren invoke their prayers? Is not the one fact as easily known to them as the other? The fact is certain that there is joy in heaven over one sinner doing penance. The fact is also certain that the guardian angels spoken of by our Lord "always behold the face of the Father," and that those angels do know when we offend against those little ones placed under their charge.

God is able, instantaneously, to reveal to the saints in glory every fact that occurs on earth. Unless we deny the existence of this almighty power, we must concede the entire futility of this objection.

4. The objection that Christ is the sole mediator

It was objected by Bishop Porteus and by many Protestant writers (although the objection has been abandoned by others) that this doctrine is inconsistent with the sole mediatorial power of Christ. Saint Paul says: "There is one mediator between God and men, the man Christ Jesus."[12]

A mediator must always be the equal of both the parties between whom he interposes. One sovereign independent state can interpose as a mediator between other sovereign independent states; but individuals, as such, however distinguished, would never be permitted by sovereign states to mediate between them. When the chief executive officer of a nation interposed as a mediator, he only does so in his capacity as a representative of the sovereignty of the entire nation. He is but the organ through whom the nation speaks.

Whatever is said by a mediator is addressed by him to both the parties, and as the equal and friend of both. For this reason it was necessary that Christ should be both God and man, that He might be the mediator between two of His equals.

The position of the saint, who prays for his brethren, is totally different from that of a mediator. The saint is only the equal of one of the parties, and his prayer is solely addressed to the other. He assumes not the position of a mediator, but that of an inferior petitioner for favors for his own friend and equal.

The object of a mediator is not to ask favors, but to do exact justice to both parties. When Christ interposed between God and men, He did so as an equal and friend of both. Justice was done to God and mercy displayed toward man. He paid our debt to Divine Justice by His own sacrifices. He then gave us a law under which we may cancel the debt we owe Him as the friend who voluntarily paid our debt to God the Father. He thus restored us to a state of freedom from the old debt, provided we comply with the terms of the new law given by this Mediator.

Besides all this, I could not possibly perceive how such an objection could be valid. For this plain reason, that if the prayer of a saint in glory is inconsistent with the mediatorial power of Christ, the prayer of the same saint on earth must be equally so. The interposition was the same precisely, for the same purpose, and by the same inferior. Why then, the mere change of state of the petitioner himself should make this petition assume the form of a mediation it is most difficult to understand. Why precisely the same thing, done by the same saint, could be a virtue in one instance and a sin in another I could never perceive.

"It requires optics mighty keen, I ween,
To see a thing that never can be seen."

5. The charge of idolatry

The charge of idolatry which has often been recklessly made by some Protestant writers, but which has been abandoned by the more candid Protestant controversialists, is one requiring very little notice. The charge is certainly a very grave one. Those who make it, in view of the awful responsibility they assume, should make very certain they are right. It is an extreme charge that is at once confuted by a simple statement of the Catholic theory.

This charge is not modern. It was originally made by unbelieving and persecuted Jews in the second century, from whom it was borrowed. The

Epistle of the Church of Smyrna to the Church at Philomelium was written about the year 169 A.D. giving an account of the glorious martyrdom of the holy Polycarp. Polycarp was the disciple of Saint John and an intimate friend of Saint Ignatius the martyred Bishop of Antioch. In it, we find this statement:

> But the envious and wicked Adversary of the generation of the righteous – when he saw the mightiness of his testimony; and his blameless conversation from the first, and how he was now crowned with the crown of immortality, and had borne away a prize that could not be spoken against – contrived that his poor body might not be obtained by us. Through many much desired to secure it and communicate over his holy remains. For some suggested to Nicetus, the father of Herod and brother to Alce, that he should persuade the governor not to give up his body, "lest" he said, "they leave the Crucified and take to worshipping this fellow."
>
> And these things they said, as instigated and supported by the Jews, who ever watched us when some of us were about to take his body from the fire. For little they knew how impossible it was for us either to forsake the worship of Christ, who suffered for the salvation of the whole world of them that be saved, or to pay worship to any other.
>
> For to Him truly we pay adoration for as much as He was the Son of God. But the martyrs, as disciples and followers of the Lord, we revere as they deserve for their incomparable loyalty to their King and Master, praying that we may be made their patrons and their fellow-disciples[13]

It will be seen that this extract gives a very clear statement of that inferior respect the Catholic gives the saint for their "loyalty to their King and Master," while he gives supreme honor to Christ.

The same false charge was made by Faustus, as Saint Augustine states:

> That Faustus hence also slanders us, because we honor the places dedicated to the martyrs, saying that herein we have made an exchange of idols, does not so much move me to reply to this slander, as to show that this Faustus, in his eagerness to slander, has chosen to wander even out of the follies of Manichæus himself…[14]

The Catholic doctrine has been misunderstood, in some instances, by not observing that the word w*orship* has several different meanings. In King James' translation it is used in different senses. Thus in Luke chapter fourteen verse ten it is used to express the lowest degree of respect. When used by Catholic writers in reference to the honor due to the saints and their relics, it is used in its subordinate sense. Worship, like love, may be given to different objects, in different degrees. When the lawyer asked Christ which was the greatest commandment, He answered: "Thou shalt love the Lord thy God with all thy heart, and with all thy soul, and with all thy mind." By this our Lord did not mean to exclude all love of others, but only required for God our supreme love; for He immediately adds: "You shall love your neighbor as yourself."[15]

As God requires our supreme love, so He requires our supreme worship; and as He does not prohibit us from loving others, while we love Him supremely, so He does not inhibit that inferior respect we pay to His saints, while we give to Him and to Him only, the supreme homage of our souls. The two are entirely compatible with each other; and they no more conflict than do the powers of a subordinate with those of his superior. And those who confuse the two, and refuse to distinguish between them, and upon that false basis say, that God is injured by this subordinate respect paid to His holy servants, simply because they were such, are about as much mistaken as the man who abandoned his faithful wife, for the sole reason that she loved her mother. He could not see how his wife could love her mother and at the same time love him.

6. The Blessed Virgin Mary

"Virgin and mother of our dear Redeemer!
All hearts are touched and softened at her name;
Alike the bandit with the bloody hand,
The priest, the prince, the scholar and the peasant,
The man of deeds, the visionary dreamer,
Pay homage to her as one ever-present . . .
So mild, so merciful, so strong, so good,
So patient, peaceful, loyal, loving, pure,
This were enough to prove it higher and truer
Than all the creeds the world had known before."

Longfellow.

In the Letters Apostolic, issued by Pope Pius the Ninth, in December 1854, making a dogmatic definition of the doctrine of the Immaculate Conception of the Blessed Virgin Mary, and which has given so much satisfaction to the entire Catholic world, it is declared:

> That the doctrine which holds that the Blessed Virgin Mary, at the first instant of her conception, by a singular privilege and grace of the Omnipotent God, in virtue of the merits of Jesus Christ, the Savior of mankind, was preserved free from all stain of original sin, has been revealed by God, and therefore should firmly and constantly be believed by all the faithful.

The hasty objection that this doctrine did not exist in the Church until it was defined, is thus met by Dr. Bryant, in his late beautiful work upon the Immaculate Conception:

> There be some, who absurdly affirm of any given doctrine, that it did not exist before such and such a period, the date at which it was solemnly defined. The fallacy of such an assertion is sufficiently exposed by the following. The canon of the Sacred Scriptures was not defined until the time of the Council of Hippo in the fourth Century. Therefore, according to these men, the Sacred Scriptures did not exist until then. Apply this rule to the doctrine of the Immaculate Conception, and to every other, and words need not be multiplied or wasted in vindication of the Church in every case.[16]

I have already substantially noticed this and similar objections, and given reasons why, in the very nature of a system of law, there must be additions from time to time. This must be so or we must conclude that there is no judicial power in the Church. The Council of Jerusalem is a clear example. Gentiles had been admitted into the Church for some years without circumcision. The Council simply determined a judicial question, namely; whether the Old Law in this respect was obligatory.

It is true; the Council when in session went beyond this single question and adopted certain regulations in reference to other matters. But it will be observed, that these had nothing to do with the *necessity* of circumcision. The council first distinctly negated that proposition, and then made the regulations found in the decree. Now could anyone say that the doctrine that circumcision was not necessary did not exist in the Church until the Council authoritatively determined the question? Every one must see that the law was the same before as after the decision – only that it had not been so judicially declared.

To some it may seem erroneous that the Church should require all her children to believe a tenet when once defined, while they were permitted to deny it conditionally before the definition was made. This plausible objection will be found without any weight when fairly and justly considered. Saint Paul told Titus to reject a heretic after the first and second admonition. It is the *condemned* heretic who is outside the Church.

Those teachers who insisted upon the necessity of circumcision taught that which was in itself heresy. It was heresy because it assumed as essential to salvation that which the Divine Legislator Himself did not require. This improper extension of the principles of the code was a violation of the will of the Lawmaker. But those who did this at the same time submitted themselves to the lawful agents of Christ for correction. They thus conceded a supreme principle of government that must lead to a correct conclusion sooner or later.

When the question was raised in Antioch, the friends of circumcision were not at once expelled from the Church, for the reason that they submitted themselves to her decision. Their belief was conditional, not final. It was subordinate, not supreme. It only assumed that inferior form. Those who held it did not say, "We will hold this in defiance of the Church." Suppose one or more of them had died (and it is almost certain that some who believed with them did die) before the decision of the Council, does any one believe they would have been lost?

The doctrine of the Immaculate Conception is the result that necessarily flows from facts and principles plainly laid down in Scripture. It is but a true judicial extension of those principles.

When our first parents had fallen, the Lord declared that the seed of the woman should bruise the serpent's head. Eve, by whose act original sin was introduced, was created sinless. . John the Baptist was filled with the Holy Ghost, even from his mother's womb; and Jeremiah, the plaintive prophet, was sanctified before he was born.[17] It was fit, in the nature of God's system of redemption, that Mary, the second Eve, should also be created sinless.

It is difficult, if not impossible, for us to form any adequate conception of the greatness of the Incarnation of our Lord – that awful and mysterious union of the human and divine. Yet, if that doctrine not be true there is no Christianity. It does not fall within the scope of this work to discuss the great doctrine of the Trinity. However, I will say that the Scriptural Proofs when taken and considered together, and when the necessary logical results are drawn from them do conclusively establish it – in my view. The contrary doctrine is wholly incompatible with clearly stated facts. When the people wished to offer sacrifice to Paul and Barnabas, an act of supreme worship, Paul and Barnabas rent their clothes in order to express their extreme opposition. When Herod permitted himself to be regarded as God, he was signally punished for the impious act. But when Thomas cried out, in the full fervor of faith, "My Lord and my God," Christ did not rebuke him. This supreme homage was received without objection; it must have been deserved.

Whenever God created an agent to accomplish some great purpose, He always bestowed upon the person the necessary grace and power. And these were always duly proportioned to the magnitude of the end to be attained. When, therefore, Infinite Purity was about to be united with the human, and to choose for himself a mother, He would necessarily make a fit habitation for Himself. That He had the power, no one will question. "Who," asks St. Cyril, "hath ever heard of an architect building for himself a house, and yielding the occupancy and possession of it to his prime enemy?" And it has been well said by a learned writer:

> It is not permitted to other children to select a mother according to their good pleasure; but if this were ever granted to any one, who would choose a slave for his mother, when he might have a queen? Who a peasant, when he might have a noble? Who an enemy of God, when he might have a friend of God? If, then, the Son of God alone could select a mother, according to His pleasure, it must be considered as certain that He would choose one befitting a God.

St. Bernard expresses the same sentiment when he says: "The Creator of men, to be born of man, must choose such a mother for Himself as He knew to be most fit." And it was well said by an ancient Heathen writer: "Whenever you introduce a God, let Him act like a God."[18] And the eloquent Bryant very appropriately asks:

> Could it be otherwise, then, that a pure and holy God would choose other than a pure and holy mother? He knew not sin Himself, and in order to take of her flesh He must have created her without sin also.[19]

If the Blessed Virgin was not created without the stain of original sin, then during a portion of her existence she was the slave of sin. She was a subject of the Evil-Spirit, and unfit to be the mother of our Lord. As the learned author from whom I last quoted, forcibly remarks:

> To have united Himself to that which had been polluted, would have been a violation of His infinite sanctity. It would have been a union of Himself with that which He abhors – a body contaminated with sin; it would have been an abnegation of Himself.[20]

When the angel Gabriel appeared to Mary, he said: "Hail full of grace," according to the Douay Bible; and "Hail thou that art highly favored," as the translation of King James has it. There are many instances given in the Old and New Testaments, where angels appeared to men; but this is the only case in which one of those blessed spirits ever saluted a human being in this form. This is a deeply significant fact.

When Christ was arrayed in the purple robe, the soldiers said to Him in mockery: "Hail King of the Jews." After the resurrection of our Lord, He saluted the occasion by the expression "All hail." But there is no instance mentioned in Scripture where the form of salutation used by Gabriel was ever employed by a superior when addressing an inferior. When the same angel appeared to Zacharias, he simply called him by his name. The salutation "hail" was a form employed by an inferior when addressing a superior.

This is the reason why that lowly maid – the humblest of the humble – "was troubled at his saying, and cast in her mind what manner of salutation this should be." Observe that she was affected by the manner of the salutation. The angel had not then announced the object of his visit. Her perfect humility was shocked, because an angel from heaven had addressed her in that manner.

If, then, the Blessed Virgin was superior to the angel sent to her, is it not certain that she must have been sinless at every period of her existence? The objection that Mary could not have been sinless in her conception, because the apostle Paul says in Adam all die, is not applicable to her case, for the reason, that she was one of the instruments employed by God in his great plan of redemption – that she was the blessed among women – and her case was an exception to the general rule. It is conceded by all that Christ was perfect man, and by those who believe in the doctrine of the Trinity, that He was also perfect God; and yet it is admitted that He was free from original sin. He could be perfect man without bearing the taint of original transgression. So could Mary, through the grace of God.

7. The perpetual virginity of the Virgin Mary

It is manifest from the simple facts stated by Saint Luke that Mary was determined to preserve her virginity. When she asked the question, "How shall this be?" she did not doubt, but simply inquired as to the manner in which the promise should be fulfilled.

When Zacharias asks the question, "Whereby shall I know this?" he was punished for his unbelief. Saint Ambrose asks:

> How would it have happened that Zacharias should be struck dumb for his unbelief, and Mary, though not believing, should be honored by the infusion of the Holy Spirit? Her prerogative was greater, so must she have been endowed with greater faith. She did not doubt of the event, but only inquired into the manner of its accomplishment.

If we pause at the point where Mary asks the question, and consider what had been made known to her up to that precise point, we shall see that the event predicted by the angel was in the future. No definite time had then been fixed for its accomplishment, and nothing had then been stated by the heavenly messenger to show that her Son was to be divine. If we say that Mary was to be married to Joseph and not remain chaste how could she have asked such a question? If she was not to remain a virgin after her marriage then nothing was more natural than that she should have a son. What sense was there, under this theory, in her question? The only hypothesis upon which the Scripture narrative can be made consistent with itself is, that Mary and Joseph were to remain chaste – that as barrenness was a great reproach among the Jews, the humility of Mary induced her to make a vow of chastity – that Joseph being a just man consented to her views – that she was willing to marry him with this understanding in obedience to the wishes of her parents. This is the opinion of Saint Gregory of Nyssa and Saint Augustine.[21]

8. The objections based on Christ treating his mother harshly

It has also been said by some Protestant writers, and is a very common objection to be found in sermons, that our Lord treated His mother harshly, especially at the wedding in Cana of Galilee.[22] Before the truth of such a charge should be believed, it should very plainly appear.

It is true, that such an inference might be drawn from a hasty examination of the language of our Lord on that occasion. But when we observe His general mode of addressing His mother, we can see that it was usual with Him to call her simply, woman. This expression he used when hanging on the Cross. He said to Her, "Woman, behold thy son." Bloomfield, the distinguished Protestant Commentator, very justly says:

> This word was a form of address which implied nothing of disrespect, and was employed by our Lord on the most affecting of all occasions, and when He especially evinced His exquisite sympathy and tender

> regard for this very parent. This being the case it is scarcely necessary to advert to the classical authorities, which have been produced, from Homer to Dio Cassius, in proof of the above position.[23]

The great St. Augustine gives one of the true meanings:

> The mother demanded a miracle; but He, in divine operations, does not recognize maternal authority, and says, as it were, thou didst not bring forth my wonder-working power: thou art not the mother of *my* divinity.

When it is remembered that our Lord was subject to His parents, and that His time had not then arrived, we can see that He had two objects to accomplish by what He said:

1. By the question He asked, He intended to inform His mother that He could not be subject to her in divine things.

2. By the statement, "Mine hour is not yet come," He intended to let her know that He would perform the miracle, even before His time, at her request.

The purpose of our Lord was to place Himself right before His mother, so that she would know the true ground upon which He performed the miracle before His time had come. The very fact that she at once said to the servants, "Whatsoever He saith onto you, do it," shows conclusively that she understood Him to promise a compliance with her wish. So far from the conduct and language of Christ on this occasion, when taken and considered together, showing any harsh treatment of His mother, they show precisely the contrary. Indeed it would have been very strange that our Lord should have been harsh to His mother, even if his conduct to the humble Syrophonician woman might be tortured, by misconstruction, into unkindness.

It only remains to show what was the doctrine of the Ancient church upon this subject. I find the authorities so well stated in the work of Dr. Bryant, that I shall avail myself of his labors, and select such as my limits will justify.

But before doing so, it maybe useful to remark that all writers have the right to use words and phrases in other than the ordinary senses, when they clearly specify the sense in which they are to be used. It is also but just that a fair allowance must be made for the ardent language of poetry and devotion. We must, of course, refer to works that expressly speak of them as such.

The expression, "Mother of God," as applied to the Blessed Virgin by Catholic writers, and especially by the ancient Fathers, as will be seen, and as found in Catholic books of Devotion, does not mean what many Protestants may suppose. As we have just seen by the extract of St. Augustine, the Catholic Church does not hold that our Lord derived His divine nature, but only His flesh from His mother.

In the Christian theory, the soul of each human being is created by God from nothing, and is united to the body before birth; and yet the mother is said to be the mother of the compound being called man, although he derived but one part of his being from his parents. It is the Catholic faith, that while our Lord did not derive His divinity from his mother, the two natures, human and divine, were united in him before His birth. And this is all that is meant when we say that Mary was the mother of God. It is not intended to convey the idea, by this expression, that God did not exist prior to, and independent of her. He was her Creator – she, His creature. We find the language of the Scripture, when put together, about as strong as the expression referred to. For example, Saint John says the Word was God – that the Word was made flesh and dwelt among us – that Jesus Christ was the Word – and that Mary was his mother. It is very true, that this is explained in other passages, and so is the expression "Mother of God" as used by Catholics.

9. The faith of the early Church in regard to the Blessed Virgin

The ancient Liturgies, being public and established forms of divine worship, constitute satisfactory evidence of the faith of the early Church in regard to the Blessed Virgin.

1. The Liturgy of St. James the Apostle, as it is called, is certainly very ancient, if it was not composed by him. This Liturgy is quoted by St. Cyril, of Jerusalem, A. D. 347. It is the one in most common use among the Orientals. In this the Blessed Virgin is called "Most holy, most glorious, immaculate Mother of God, and ever Virgin." It also adds the very marked expression, "In every respect out of the range of sinful men."

2. In the Liturgy of St. Mark the Evangelist: "Most holy, immaculate, and blessed Mother of God, and ever Virgin Mary."

3. In that of St. John Chrysostom: "In every part wholly, altogether untainted."

4. In that of St. Basil: "Chiefly with the most holy, spotless, above all blessed, our glorious Lady, Mother of God, and ever Virgin Mary."

5. In the Alexandrian: "But chiefly of our most holy, most glorious, immaculate, most blessed Lady, Mother of God, and ever Virgin Mary."

6. In the Roman Liturgy of undoubted antiquity: "Most glorious, most holy, immaculate Mother of God, and ever Virgin Mary."

In reference to the duty of the following the traditions of the apostles, Saint Hippolytus wrote:

> These testimonies are sufficient for believers who study the truth. As to unbelievers, they believe no one. Let us, therefore, blessed brethren believe according to the traditions of the apostle.[24]

Dr. Bryant says:

> There is a letter extant known to the priests and deacons of Achia, which contains an account of the martyrdom of the illustrious Apostle Saint Andrew, and a discourse which he pronounced in the presence of the proconsul Egeus, just previous to his suffering. In the discourse the holy apostle speaks thus: "And moreover, as the first man was created from immaculate earth, it was necessary that from an Immaculate Virgin should be born a perfect man, namely, the Son of God." This antistrophy, or reciprocal conversion of the terms immaculate earth and Immaculate Virgin, exhibits the apostle as declaring Mary to be immaculate in her conception as was Adam when he issued perfect from the hand of his Maker. The most ardent friend of the Immaculate Conception could wish for no stronger testimony than this.
>
> St. Andrew suffered martyrdom in the year 96, and his discourse incontestably proves that the Immaculate Conception was believed in the apostolic Age.[25]

In the second century, St. Justin Martyr calls her the Mediatrix between God her Divine Son, and our fallen race; and St. Irenaeus, of the same age, says of her:

> If Eve disobeyed God, yet Mary was counseled to obey God; that the Virgin Mary might become the advocate of the Virgin Eve. And as the human race was bound to death through a virgin, it is saved

> through a virgin; the scales being equally balanced; virginal disobedience by virginal obedience.[26]

In the third century, St. Hippolytus calls her “Holy and Immaculate," and Origen says: "She has not been tainted with the breath of the venomous serpent.”[27]

Saint Anselm of the same age says of her, “God hath preserved the angels from sin, among the others sinning: hath He not been able to preserve the Mother pure from sins of others?”[28]

Saint Cyprian of the same age says, “Neither did justice suffer that the vessel of election to be open to the common inquires; for being far exalted above others, she was a partaker of their nature, but not of their sin.”[29]

In the fourth age St. Ephraim says: “Mary is immaculate and most remote from every taint of sin.”[30]

Saint Amphilochius says, “who created the virgin perfect; He Himself created the second without blemish and without sin.”[31]

Saint Ambrose calls her, “a virgin through grace, preserved from every stain of sin.”[32]

In the fifth age Saint Augustine in confuting the error of Pelagius, who says that the children of baptized persons were born free from original sin, says:

> Except the Holy Virgin Mary, concerning whom, for the honor of the Lord, I wish to entertain no question, when sin is the subject of discussion; since we know that more grace hath been given her to overcome sin in every respect who was worthy to conceive and bring forth Him whom it behooved to have no sin.[33]

10. Relics and Images

In reference to the relics of the saints, the Council of Trent declared:

> That the holy bodies of holy martyrs, and of others now living with Christ, which were the living members of Christ, and the temple of the Holy Ghost, by Him to be raised up, and glorified, unto everlasting life, are to be venerated by the faithful, through which many benefits are bestowed on men by God; so that they who affirm that veneration and honor are not due to the relics of the saints, or that such relics and other sacred monuments are uselessly honored by the faithful, and that the places dedicated to their memories are in vain

> visited for the sake of impetrating their aid – are absolutely to be condemned, as the Church has long since condemned, and now also condemns them.[34]

And in reference to the pictures and images of the saints, the same council decreed:

> That the images of Christ, of the Virgin Mother of God, and of other saints, are to be had and retained especially in Churches, and that due honor and veneration are to be shown them; not that it is believed that any divinity or virtue is inherent in them, on account of which they are to be worshipped, or that anything is to be asked of them, or that trust is to be placed in images, as of old was done by the Gentiles, who placed their hope in idols; but because the honor which is shown them is referred to the prototypes which they represent; so that through the images which we kiss, and before which we uncover our heads, and fall down, we may adore Christ, and venerate the saints, whose likeness they bear.[35]

It is just as natural for all good men to entertain a profound veneration:

"For those who greatly think, or bravely die,"

in a good and holy cause, as to love the beautiful cause itself. It is just as natural to respect the relics and images of those we love, as to love the objects themselves. In fact, the love of the relics and images of the great and good is but the inevitable result of the love we bear the objects to whom these appertain. If the sincere believer loves anything, it must be the sublime system of Christianity itself; and if he loves the cause, he must love those who have done most to advance it. If there be in the mind and heart of the true believer any human object most worthy of his love, it is the holy martyr for the cause of Christ. And after all the frivolous and unfeeling objections that have been, or may yet be urged against an impulse so natural and innocent, the human heart will still tell us that it is just and right in itself. The heart is as often right as the head. The heart of Daniel Webster, in opposition to the doubts of his head, assured him that the glowing sermon of Christ on the Mount was not the production of man; and happy would he have been had he followed this holy impulse of his heart, which was as true as instinct itself. It is useless and vain coldly to argue against the simplest and sweetest impulses of the soul, as if we wished to banish from the heart all sympathy for the good and great.

Is the love of the humble and true Christian for his brethren a sin or a virtue? In that last and most mournful discourse delivered by the meek Savior, just before His passion, He said to His disciples: "A new commandment I give unto you, That ye love one another; as I have loved You, that ye also love one another." And so important did our Lord consider this new commandment, that He repeated it several times, in the same discourse.[36]

Saint James , in reference to this command says:

> And this is His commandment, that we should believe on the name of his Son Jesus Christ, and love one another as he gave us commandment.[37]

Should our love cease the moment the holy brother dies? And is this love confined alone to those of our age – are we of this day not to love the apostles and other martyrs for Christ? The church is but one corporation and we are all members of it and one another. We must then love the saints of all ages and nations. Would it not be a narrow and pitiful theory that would confine our love alone to the saints of our own generation?

If we are bound to love the great and noble champions of the cross, are we not bound to keep this love ever "green in our souls?" And if so, are we not allowed to use the means best adapted to that end? Strange, if we are not! The honors paid to Saint Paul and Saint Peter, in their day, we may certainly pay to their memory now. And we may surely use any innocent means in doing this.

Pictures and images of Christ, of Mary, of the apostles, and of the martyrs, are intended simply to excite devotion by bringing up before the mind a more concentrated and lively history of the persons and scenes represented. Prose, poetry, and painting, are only signs or mediums of thought and fact. These different modes of representation have each their peculiar advantages. It is by a combination of them all that the best representation can be had in many cases.

For this reason we see works of art and science, as well as of biography, constantly illustrated by drawings, plans, and pictures. By the use of prose a more exact and full description can be given, while that of poetry is more vivid, and that of painting more touching. When we look upon an image or painting of the crucifixion, it at once brings to our recollection, by the power of the association of ideas, all the remembered incidents of our Lord's passion. The word cross is but a sign, and only brings up the same emotions as the image or picture of the same thing represented.

In the Old Testament, we are told that the dead man was instantly restored to life when he touched the bones of the prophet.[38] So, we are assured that miracles were wrought by handkerchiefs and aprons from the body of Saint Paul.[39] We are also told that the shadow of Saint Peter and the hem of our Lord's garment had this effect.[40] From these examples we see that God, of old, did make use of such means to show His power and love, and He certainly may do so now.

11. Testimony of the Fathers and the early Church

I shall put passages together that relate to the invocation of the saints, their relics and images, leaving the reader to distinguish one from the other.

In an account given of the martyrdom of the holy Ignatius, Bishop of Antioch and disciple of Saint John, it is related:

> He was thrown to the wild beasts at a spot close to the temple; and so was speedily carried into effect the desire of the holy martyr Ignatius, according to which is written, "the desire of the righteous shall be granted." For thus he was a burthen to none of his brethren from the trouble of gathering up his remains; a consummation in correspondence with a wish which he had previously expressed in his Epistle. The harder parts alone were left, and these were gathered up and carried to Antioch, where they were wrapped in a linen cloth, and deposited with the brethren of that Holy church – a treasure rendered invaluable by the Christian graces which had adorned the martyr's life....
>
> And now we make known to you the day and the time at which this event occurred; that at the season of his martyrdom we may gather together and collect a portion of the spirit which animated this courageous champion and martyr for Christ.

The same holy martyr in his Epistle to the Trallians, says, "my spirit saluteth you, not now only, but when I shall have gone to God." Observe how explicit this is.

In a letter of the Church of Smyrna giving an account of the martyrdom of the holy Polycarp, they say:

> And so we afterwards gathered up his bones, more valued than stones of much price, and purer than gold, and laid them in a fitting treasure

> house. Thus assembling, as we may, in joy and triumph, the Lord shall grant us to celebrate the birthday of his martyrdom, both to the remembering of them who wrested *before* in the cause, and the training and preparing of those that shall come *after*.

That the Christians who were the disciples of the apostles were in the habit of meeting together and celebrating the martyrdom of a saint over his relics, (which they esteemed of so much value,) is shown by the foregoing extract. It is also shown by the account of the martyrdom of Ignatius in which they say:

> And now we make known to you the day and time at which this event occurred. That at the season of his martyrdom we may gather together, and collect a portion of the spirit which animated this courageous champion and martyr of Christ

It will be remembered that the bones of the holy martyr had been deposited with that Church. The foregoing extracts may be found in the first volume of the *Oxford Tracts*.

Saint Justin Martyr says:

> But both God and the Son who came from Him, and taught us these things, and the host of other good angels that follow and resemble (him or them), and the prophetic spirit, we venerate and adore, honoring in reason and truth, and freely delivering to every one who wishes to learn, even as we have been taught.[41]

Saint Clement of Alexandria says:

> The perfect Christian also prays together with the angels, as being already the equal of angels; nor is he ever out of the holy guardianship; even though he may pray alone, he has the chair of the holy ones standing by.[42]

Tertullian says:

> You may begin from parables: when is the lost sheep sought for by the Lord, and carried back upon his shoulders? Let the very pictures of your chalices come forth, if even in them the interpretation of that animal will clearly shine forth, whether it portrays the restoration of a sinner that was a Christian, or a Gentile.[43]

From this authority, it is clear that it was usual, in the time of Tertullian, for images of Christ returning with the lost sheep upon his shoulders to be engraved upon chalices used in the celebration of the Eucharist.

Also Eusebius says:

> And it is no wonder that they of the Gentiles, who were formerly benefited by our Savior, should have done this, when we have learnt that the images also of the apostles, Peter and Paul, and even of Christ Himself, are preserved in paintings.[44]

The foregoing are testimonies from the second century. Another class of testimony of a very ancient date consists of the inscriptions upon the tombs of the saints whose bodies repose in the Catacombs. These inscriptions are certainly before the general persecutions ceased in 315 A. D. "Every part of Rome," says Bishop Wiseman,

> is undermined with the catacombs, in which the bodies of saints and martyrs were deposited after their deaths. The tombs are even some of them yet sealed up and unbroken; some with inscriptions on them, or perhaps a palm branch rudely sculptured, to show that there repose the martyrs of Christ. We have phials, adhering and fastened to the covers of the tombs, in the walls of the catacombs, in which are sponges, or sediment, still tinged with the color of blood. Indeed the very instruments of martyrdom are constantly found in the tombs.
>
> Certainly these were men who knew Christianity, who fully appreciated what was due to Christ, for whom they died, who were fully convinced that nothing on earth was to be preferred before Him, and that no creature could pretend to one particle of the honor reserved by Him to Himself! Surely we cannot want purer or more satisfactory witnesses to what Christ instituted than they who shed their blood to seal the truth; we cannot want teachers better imbued with the spirit of His religion, than those who were ready to lay down their lives to defend it!
>
> Let us see what was their belief regarding their brethren, when they deposited them in the tombs and sealed them up, and inscribed on them their regrets and hopes. Nothing is more common that to find on them a supplication, a prayer to the saints or martyrs to intercede for the survivors with God....
>
> "Sabbatius, sweet soul, pray and entreat for thy brethren and comrades."
>
> "Atticus, thy spirit is in bliss; pray for thy parents."
>
> "Jovianus, may you live in God and pray."
>
> "Anatolinus made this monument to his well-beloved son who lived seven years. May thy spirit rest well in God, and thou pray for your sister."

"Pray for us, because we know thou art in Christ."

> These are, most of them inscriptions on the tombs of martyrs, whose bodies were deposited therein during the very first centuries of Christianity, when men were ready to die for their faith of Christ.

I give only the English translations of the original Latin, as given by the Bishop. Refer to the thirteenth of his *Moorefield Lectures* for the original Latin.

In the third century, we also have many examples. In the account of the martyrdom of the saints Perpetua and others, it is stated that Saturnus the martyr asked of Perdeus "the ring on his finger and having plunged it in his wound, returned it to him, leaving him that pledge as an inheritance, and a memorial of his blood."

Origen who wrote in A.D. 216 says:

> And no wonder if a saint sanctify, by the word of God and prayer, the food of which we partake, when even the garments with which he is clothed are holy.
>
> The handkerchiefs and aprons of Paul derived so much holiness from his purity, that when applied to the bodies of the sick, they drove away diseases, and restored health. And of Peter what shall I say, the very shadow of whose body leave with it so much holiness, that whosoever, not he, but his shadow only touched, was at once relieved from every ailment....[45]
>
> But not the high priest [Jesus Christ] alone prays with those who pray sincerely, but also the angels who rejoice in heaven upon one sinner who is penitent, more than upon ninety-nine just who need not penitence, as also the souls of the saint who have already fallen asleep.

In this extract it is clearly stated that the angels, and the saints who fallen asleep, pray with those who pray sincerely. For proof, Origen refers to the Book of Tobias and to Maccabees. He then refers to the New Testament in this way:

> But one of the principle virtues, according to the Divine Word, is charity toward our neighbor. We must needs think it is felt by the departed saints, toward those who are struggling in life, more exceedingly than by those who are yet in human infirmity and are but struggling together with those who need aid. Not here only is it fulfilled in those who love the brethren. "If one member suffer, all the members suffer with it; and if one is honored all members rejoice

> with it."(1 Cor 12:26) For it is also suitable to the love of those who are out of this life to say "The care of all the churches: who is weak, and I am not weak? Who is scandalized, and I am not on fire? (2 Cor 11:29) [46]

In this extract, it is very clearly stated that the love of the brethren spoken of by Saint Paul is more perfect in the saints in glory than it is in the saints on earth. Moreover, that it is suitable for those in glory still to say with Paul, "The care of all the churches… is still on us"

Origen also says:

> If we wish that there be a multitude of those whom we desire to be kindly disposed toward us, that "the thousand times a hundred thousand stand before Him, and thousands of thousands minister to Him."(*Cf.* Dan. 7:10) They who regard as relatives and friends those who imitate their piety toward God, cooperate in the salvation of those who call upon God, and pray sincerely, appearing to them, and thinking that they ought to obey, and as though by some compact to come for the benefit and salvation of those praying to God, to whom they also pray. For they "are all ministering spirits…."(Heb. 1:140 Jesus has taught us not to despise the little ones in the Church, saying, "their angels always see the face of my Father who is in heaven.[47]

Saint Dionysius of Alexandria says,

> They who are about to struggle in the sacred conflict of suffering for righteousness, have angels bringing aid to them from heaven. [48]

Saint Cyprian wrote about 248 A.D. In a letter to Camilius, who was then in exile, he says:

> Let us be mutual mindful of each other, of one heart and mind. Let us ever on either side pray for each other, by mutual love lighten our burdens and difficulties. And if one of us shall by the speediness of the Divine vouchsafement, depart hence the first, let our love continue in the presence of the Lord. Let not prayer for our brethren and sisters cease in the presence of the mercy of the Father.

In another place he says:

> Endure with courage, proceed spiritually, arrive happily; and then remember us when virginity shall begin to be honored in you.[49]

We find further examples in the fourth century. Eusebius says:

> For the brethren there [at Jerusalem] venerate, according to a derived custom the throne of James, the first who received from Christ and

the apostles the episcopate of the Church of Jerusalem, which has been preserved to this day. They point out clearly to all, what veneration, both they of old and the men of our days preserved, and still preserve toward holy men, on account of their love of God....

Who can doubt that the places which have been honored by the bodies of the martyrs, and have preserved the memory of their glorious death, belong to the Church....

Hence, it is our custom also to go to their tombs, and offer up prayers beside them, and to honor their blessed souls. Those things are laudably practiced by us....

of which may we found worthy by prayers and intercessions of all the saints.[50]

Saint Cyril of Jerusalem says:

Let us not foolishly disbelieve, as though this had not happened. For if handkerchiefs and aprons, which are external, when they touched the bodies of the sick raised up the infirm, how much more should the body itself of the prophet raise the dead....

We then commemorate also those who have fallen asleep before us, first, patriarchs, prophets, apostles, martyrs, that God by their prayers and intercessions may receive our petitions.[51]

From the *Apostolical Constitutions*:

Wherefore even the very relics of those who live with God are not without honor. For even Eliseus the prophet after he had fallen asleep, raised up a dead man who was slain by the pirates of Syria. For his body touched the bones of Eliseus and he rose and lived again. Now this would not have happened unless the body of Eliseus was holy.[52]

From the Martyrdom of Saint Vincent of Saragossa:

There might you have seen the multitude that had stood round, emulously kiss the feet of the saint, touch with pious curiosity the wounds with which the whole body was lacerated, receive in linen clothe the blood, as with sacred veneration, to be a future benefit to their posterity.

Saint Hilary of Poitiers says:

We owe more to your cruelty Nero, Decius, and Maximinian, (than to Constantius,) for through you we conquered Satan. Everywhere was the holy blood of the martyrs received. Their venerable bones are a daily testimony, while the evil spirits halt at them, while maladies are expelled, while wonderful works are seen….

So those who would fain stand, neither the guardianship of saints, nor the defenses of angels are wanting….

Not therefore, the nature of God, but our infirmity needs their intersession. For they are sent on behalf of those who shall inherit salvation. Not that God is ignorant of anything we do, but our infirmity stands in need of the ministry of spiritual intersession in order to supplicate and to merit.[53]

Celsus says:

Thus, Job the just is exhibited as about to pray and petition for the sins of his three friends, and the proof of his fear and faith is sealed by attesting voice of the Lord. When therefore, in the day of thy liberation, thou shalt first present thyself before the face of Christ… by the mercy of the Lord, then bear in mind thy child Celsus.[54]

Saint Ephraim of Syrus says:

God dwells in their relics. Thence have they ability to work every kind of miracle. O God that dwellest in the just, to thee be glory, and may thy mercy be upon us….

For the grace of the Holy Ghost that performs all miracles is ever present with their holy relics….

Accept, O Lord the supplication of thy servant, by the intercessions of the saints who have been well pleasing to thee….

Blessed are they that suffer in the Lord, for the delights of Paradise await them. Of which may we be all partakers by the intercessions of all those who have been well pleasing to our Lord Jesus Christ.[55]

Saint Gregory Nazianzum says:

Such is the veneration of truth that a little dust, or some small relic of old bones, or a small portion of hair, or shreds of rag, or a stain of blood, are enough to have the same honor as the whole body…[56]

I am persuaded that he (Saint Cyprian) now (guards the flock) more effectually by his intercession than he did formerly by his teaching, by so much as he is nigher unto God.[57]

Saint Basil says:

> It will be a good action on your part to send martyrs' relics to this country, since according to your account, the prosecution in your parts, even now, makes martyrs unto the Lord…
>
> Of the holy spiritual powers that have their places in heaven, some are called eyes – from being entrusted to watch over us; others ears – from receiving our prayers.[58]

Saint Ambrose says:

> Let others hoard up silver and gold and tear it from the hidden veins. We gather up the nails, and these are not few, that have pierced the martyrs. We gather up their victorious blood, and the wood of the cross. These (relics) we have not been able to refuse to the request of the pious widow. Receive ye therefore, those gifts of salvation which now are deposited under the sacred altars…
>
> Whilst we were translating them, [the remains of Saint Gervase and Saint Protase] a blind man was restored to sight….
>
> May Peter who wept so effectually for himself, weep also for us, and turn toward us Christ's benignant countenance….
>
> Then angels – who have been given to us for our protection – are to be invoked in our behalf; the martyrs – whose patronage we seem to have a claim to a kind of pledge derived from the body – are to be invoked.[59]

Saint Siricius, who was Pope from A.D. 384 to A.D. 399, says:

> Very many of our brethren assembled with us at the relics of the holy apostle Peter, through whom both the apostolate and episcopate took its rise.[60]

Saint John Chrysostom says:

> The place that received that slaughtered body, small and confined as it is, is more revered than ten thousand royal chambers, and more precious than kings themselves. "And his sepulcher shall be glorious."(Is 11:10) And what is more strange still, this has not befallen Him (Christ) only, but the very same has happened to His disciples. For the men that were dragged and led about, the men that were despised and bound in fetters, the men that suffered countless hardships, are since their death, more honored than kings. And now learn hence. In that most regal city, Rome, both kings and consuls, and generals, leaving every thing else, hasten to the tombs of the fisherman and the tentmaker [Peter and Paul]….

> May we then also be enabled to become companions of the saints by the prayers of those saints, and the grace and goodness of our Lord Jesus Christ.[61]

Saint Jerome says:

> You say that Virgilantius again opens his fetid mouth, and casts his most vile filth against the relics of the holy martyrs. And that he calls us, who admit relics, cinder-worshippers and idolaters, who venerate dead men's bones. The miserable man whose state is to be bewailed with torrents of tears…
>
> But we worship not, we adore not, I do not say relics only, but not even the sun and moon not, not angels, not archangels, not cherubim, not seraphim….
>
> Lest we serve the creature rather than the creator, who is blessed forever more. We honor the servants, that the honor given to the servants may redound to the Lord who says, "He that receiveth you,receiveth me."

Addressing Virgilantius he asks: "who thou madman has ever adored martyrs? Who has thought man a God?[62]

As we have seen, the first to charge the early Christians with idolatry, because of the honor paid to the relics of martyrs, were the unbelieving Jews who witnessed the martyrdom of Polycarp. In 380 A.D. the sophist Eunapius made the same charge. The charge was also made by Vigilantius, as the above extract shows. It was also made by Faustus. It was a common charge found in the mouths of infidels and the worst class of heretics.

The above extract from Saint Jerome exactly expresses the faith of the Catholic Church. It makes the clear distinction between subordinate and supreme honor. Saint Jerome also has this to say of another martyr:

> The day will come wherein thou wilt return a conqueror to thy country, wherein thou wilt traverse the heavenly Jerusalem, the brave man crowned. Then too wilt thou pray for me who spurred thee on to conquer.[63]

He also invoked the prayers of Saint Paula in the close of his life of the saint.

Saint Athanasius says that we ought to recite and sing the Psalms exactly as the words are written, "that the holy men who have communicated the words as ministers, recognizing their own words, may pray for us."[64]

Saint Gregory of Nyssa says:

> Do thou (Ephraim) that art standing at the divine alter, and art ministering with the angels to the life-giving and most holy Trinity, bear us all in remembrance, petitioning for us the remission of sins, and the fruition of an everlasting kingdom.[65]

Saint Epiphanius of Salamis says:

> Holy indeed is the body of Mary; but she is no God....
>
> Let no one make an oblation unto her name, for that ruins his soul. Nor on the other hand, let him behave madly by insulting the holy Virgin....
>
> We are not to honor the saints beyond what is due, but to honor their Lord....
>
> But neither Elias is to be adored, though still living; nor John....
>
> Be Mary in honor; but be the Father, Son, and Holy Ghost adored – let no one adore Mary....
>
> Though Mary be most excellent and holy and honored, yet she is not to be adored.[66]

These extracts related to an obscure sect of female heretics in Arabia, called Collyridians, who offered a kind of twisted cake in sacrifice to the blessed Virgin.

Pope Saint Damasus says, "Be favorable, I beseech thee, glorious martyr, to the prayers of Damasus."[67]

In the fifth century, the great Saint Augustine says:

> Of the martyrs, the justice is perfect because in their passion itself, they were perfected. For this cause, prayer is not offered for them in Church. For the other faithful departed we pray. For martyrs we do not pray for they departed so perfect as to be our advocates, not to be our clients. Neither are they this in themselves, but in Him to whom they cleaved – perfect members of the Head....
>
> A most delightful picture is this, when you behold Saint Stephen being stoned, you behold Saul holding the garments of those who cast the stones... with him whom thou didst stone though reignest with Christ. You both there behold each other, you both hear my discourse, both pray for us....

> But the Christian people unite in celebrating with religious solemnity the memories of the martyrs, both to excite to an imitation of them and to be associated with their merits, and aided by their prayers. Yet, although in places dedicated to the martyrs, to none of the martyrs do we raise altars. For in the places of their holy bodies, what prelate standing at the alter ever said, "we offer to thee Peter, or Paul, or Cyprian?" What is offered, is offered to God, who crowned the martyrs, whom he crowned in the place dedicated to their memory. From the admonition furnished by those very places, a greater affection may arise to make our love keener, both toward those whom we are able to imitate, and toward Him by whose help we have that ability.
>
> We therefore, worship the martyrs with that worship of love and of fellowship with which, even in this life, holy men are worshipped, whose hearts we feel are ready to endure a similar death for evangelical truth. But we worship the martyrs more devotedly as it is the safer after their conflicts are overcome. Also with more confident praise do we exalt those who are already triumphant in a happier life than those still engaged in battle in this life. With that worship which in Greek is called *latreia* (in Latin it cannot be expressed in one word) as it is a kind of service properly due to the Divinity, we neither worship, nor teach to worship, other than the one God.
>
> Whereas to this worship pertains the oblation of sacrifice – whence they who offer this also to idols are declared guilty of idolatry – we do not in any wise offer, or teach to be offered, anything of this kind either to any martyr, to a holy soul, or to any angel. Whoever falls into this error he is reproved by sound teaching, either that he may amend or be avoided.[68]

It will be seen by attentive examination of this extract that the distinctions now made by the Catholic Church were made by this great writer. The first extract proves that prayers were offered for the dead, but not for the martyrs who needed them not.

I will close this list by the following extract from this great and distinguished saint. There perhaps never lived a brighter example of piety and ability since the days of the apostles.

> We celebrate on this day the erecting of a place to the memory of Saint Protasius and Saint Gervasius, the martyrs of Milan. Not the day whereon it was erected here, but we on this day celebrate the day on which the death of his saints was. Through Ambrose – that man of God, precious in the sight of God – of which the great glory of the martyrs I was also a witness. I was there. I was in Milan. I knew the

> miracles done. God testifying to the precious deaths of saints, that through those miracles that *death* might be not only precious in the sight of God, but also in the sight of men.
>
> A blind man, very well known to the whole city received his sight. He ran; he caused himself to be led; he came back without a guide.... Not to all does God bestow health through the martyrs, but to all that imitate the martyrs does he promise their immortality.[69]

Were these great and noble men imposters and idolaters? They were the witnesses upon whom Dr. Paley relied to prove the truth of Christianity! I have passed over many authorities for want of space.

That the Catholic doctrine was the universal doctrine of the Church in the very first ages of Christianity, there would seem to be no doubt. The fact is certain, that angels are ministering spirits, as Saint Paul says. The saints in glory are as the angels, as we are told by Christ; and as the angels are such ministering spirits, it is very strange that they cannot aid us by their prayers, while this assistance can be given us by our brethren on earth. What substantial difference there can be between the principles of the two cases it is difficult to perceive?

---

[1] Session. xxv.

[2] Heb 16:22.

[3] Matt 22:30.

[4] Matt 18:10.

[5] Heb 8:3-4.

[6] Luke 15:7-10.

[7] Rev 8:3-4.

[8] Nicholas Wiseman, *Moorfield Lectures*, vol. ii, p. 87.

[9] *Cf.* Matt 5:44

[10] Jas 5:16

[11] As quoted in Milner's *End of Controversy*

[12] 1 Tim 2:5

[13] The whole Epistle may be found in the first volume of the Oxford Tracts, from which this extract is taken.

[14] T, viii., lib. 20, n21 *Contra Faustum.*

[15] Matt 22: 35-39.

[16] Bryant. *The Immaculate Conception, a Dogma,* Preface, xiv.

[17] *Cf.* Luke 1; Jer 1:5.

[18] I have been struck in reading the New Testament that there is no express eulogy pronounced upon any of the persons mentioned, not even upon Christ Himself. We are not told anything of the personal appearance of Christ, or of his apostles. The sacred writers seem to be wholly absorbed with the sublime subject they treat. Would this have been so in a forged narrative?

[19] Bryant, *op. cit.* p. 63.

[20] *Ibid.* p. 47.

[21] *Cf.* Saint Gregory, *Orat. In Nat Christi*; Saint Augustine *De Virg* 1 iv. Cited in note to Bishop Kendrick's translation of the Four Gospels.

[22] *Cf.* Jn 2.

[23]. Cited in note to Bishop Kendrick's translation.

[24] *Contra Hæres, Noët.*, n.7.

[25] Bryant. o*p. cit.*. Bryant says, " This remarkable document was first regarded by some with suspicion, in consequence of the Latin copy only being known. But since the Greek original has been found in the Bodlëian Library, and published by Chareles Woog, a Protestant writer, all doubt has ceased. Baconius proves this letter to be genuine; and so does N. Alexander in his *Ecclesiastical History* Vol. 1. M. Edvoy, Professor of History and Antiquities at Leipsie, follows the same opinion in some learned dissertations which he published in 1784-51. Abdias Babilonicus also adds the weight of his name to its authenticity; and the celebrated Marcelli has inserted it, as authentic and true, in his Calendar of the Church of Constantinople, under the date of November 30.

[26] *Advers. Haeres.*, lib. v, cap. xix, p. 879.

[27] *Hom. 1 De B. V. Maria.*

[28] *Sermo. De Conceptione.*

[29] Lib. 1 *De Carne Christi.*

[30] Tom. 5; *Orat. Ad Dei Gen.*

[31] Orat 4, *in S. Delp. et Simeone.*

[32] *Sermo.* 22, in Ps. 118.

[33] *Lib. De Natura et Gratia* cap. 23.

[34] Session. xxv.

[35] Session. xxv.

[36] Jn 13:34; 15:12,17.

[37] James 3:23.

[38] *Cf.* 2 Kings 13:21.

[39] *Cf.* Acts 19:11,12.

[40] Matt 19:20; Acts 5:15.

[41] *Apol.* i. n.6.

[42] *Strom.* 1. vii ., p. 879.

[43] *De Perdici.,* n. 7, p. 559.

[44] H.E.L. vii., c. xviii.

[45] T. iv., L. ix., *Com. In Ep. Ad Rom.* 666.

[46] T. i. *De Oratione*, n. xi.

[47] T. i. *Contra Celsus,* 1. viii., n. 34, p. 766, 767.

[48] *De Martyrio.* p. 40.

[49] *Cf.* Ep. lvii. *Ad Cornel.* p. 206; *De Habit. Virg*, p. 362.

[50] *Cf.* H.E.L. vii. c. xix; *Vita Constant 1 ii, c. xl*; *Præp. Ev.*, L. xiii., c. xi., p. 633; *Comm. In His. in fine*, t, ii., *Nov. coll. Monte.*

[51] *Catech. Myst.* xviii. n. p. 16; *Ibid.* v. n. ix. p. 328.

[52] *Apostolical Constitutions* is an ancient manuscript of uncertain authorship. Codices exist in various languages. Here Burnett quotes from Book VI Canon 30 – Editor.

[53] *Cf.* Contra *Constantius Imp. n. 8; Tract. in Ps.* lxxiv. *n.5,6. p. 454; Tract.* cxxix. *n. vii. p. 494.*

[54] *Præf. De Jud. Incud. Ad Virgil, Ep. Galland,* t. iv. p. 440.

[55] *Cf.* T. ii., *Gr. in Vit. B. Abra.,* p. 19; T. ii., *Gr. Encom. in Glorios.* M. M. p. 308; T. i. *Gr. De Poenit.* p. 153; T. i. *Gr. Confess. seu Precat.* p. 226, *de Virtute, cap.* ix.

[56] T. ii., *Carm. Iamb.* xviii. p. 216.

[57] T. i. *de St. Cypriano,* p. 288.

[58] T. iii., P. ii *Ep. clv.* P. 354; T. i. *Hom. In Ps.* xxxiii., n. 11. p. 219.

[59] T. ii. *Exhort. Virgin,* 7-10, 15.; T. ii. Ep. xxii.,*Class i., Sorori Seræ*, col. 874 – 8; T. i. *Hexæm.*, 1. v., c. 25, n. 90. p. 114; T. ii. *De Videris*, c. ix., n. 54,55. p. 200.

[60] *Epis. per Afric.*, col. 1028, t. ii. Labb.

[61] T. i. *Contra Gent. Et Jud. Quod Christus sit Deus*, n.8, 9, 10. p. 695 –8.; T. ii. *Hom.. S. Ign. M.* , n. 5. p. 716,717.

[62] T. ii. *adv. Vigil;ant..*, n.1, 4 – 6. col. 387 – 91.

[63] T. i. Ep. xiv. *Ad Heliador.* n. 3. p. 29.

[64] T. i. n. 31. p. 1001.

[65] T. iii. *De Vita Ephraim.* P. 616.

[66] T. i. *Adv. Hæres Collyrid.* .. p. 1061 –5.

[67] *Carm.* xx.

[68] See – T. v. serm.. cclxxxv., n. 5, col. 1685; *Serm..* cccvii., n. 5, col. 1689; T. iii., lib. xx., n. 21, *Contra Faustum,* col. 544 –6.

[69] T. v. Serm. clxxxvi., n. 4,5. in Natal.M.M. *Pro. et Ger.*, col 1689.

CHAPTER VIII

BARRIERS TO TRUTH

1. General misrepresentation of Catholic doctrines

That fair and candid controversialists may often misconceive each other's meaning is not surprising. This arises from the general poverty, and uncertain character, of language, and often from a want of certainty and clearness in the statement of a position. Writers, who have confused conceptions of the subject they discuss, or of the positions they lay down, will necessarily use confused language.

In quoting from an author, who did not understand distinctly what he intended to state, or who uses inappropriate and loose language, it may be very difficult to avoid the appearance of unfairness. Quotations must have their practical limits; and it is not always easy to know, in every case, where these limits are to be found. So much of an author should be quoted as to show his true position in reference to the single point regarding which quotation is made. It cannot be expected that the reasons for his position can be quoted, unless these reasons are examined. If, therefore, he states a general principle, and then states a qualification or limitation to be taken out of, or annexed to, this general principle, the exception to the general principle ought to be given; provided the point, to prove which the quotation is made, requires it.

If I quote an author for a given purpose, I need only quote so much as that purpose fairly requires. The quotation may also prove other matters not then under discussion; but the reader must keep in view the matter the writer has in his mind' eye when making the quotation. Every writer upon moral and philosophical subjects must have learned the practical difficulty of sometimes apprehending the true meaning of an author, and of representing him correctly. Mistakes of this kind are to be anticipated, to a certain extent. It must also be conceded, that the fairest and most impartial writers are sometimes improperly accused of unfairness.

But after making every fair and just allowance for the general poverty and uncertainty of language, and the natural frailty of the human mind, I am compelled to say, that in all my reading and observation, I have never met with the same amount of gross, bitter, and continued misrepresentation, as I have found on the part of Protestant controversialists, when writing upon the subject of the Catholic faith. Any calm, careful, and diligent reader, who will take the authors on both sides, and fairly compare them together, can readily see that I am correct upon this subject, and in this opinion.

2. Reception of Dr. Milner's work

In reading Dr. Milner's *End of Controversy,* I could not but remark the amount and character of the misrepresentations. The candid James Brown, in his letter to the author says:

> The whole of your letters have been read over in our society, and they have produced important though diversified effects on the minds of the members….
>
> With respect to certain other members of our society, I am sorry to be obliged to say that, on this particular subject – I mean the arguments in favor of your religion – they do not manifest the candor and good sense which is natural to them, and which they show on every other subject.
>
> They pronounce, with confidence and vehemence, that Dr. Porteus' charges are all true, and that you cannot make any rational answer to them; at the same time that several of these gentlemen, to my knowledge, are very little acquainted with the substance of them. In short, they are apt to load your religion, and the professors of it, with epithets and imputations too gross and injurious for me to repeat, convinced as I am of their falsehood.
>
> I shall not be surprised to hear that some of these imputations have been transmitted to you by the persons in question, as I have declined making my letters the vehicle of them. It is a justice, however, which I owe them, to assure you, reverend sir, that it is only since they have understood the inference of your arguments to be such as to imply an obligation on them of renouncing their own respective religions, and embracing yours, that they have been so unreasonable and violent. Till this period, they appeared to be nearly as liberal and charitable with respect to your communion as to any other.

In his thirty-second letter, the learned divine mentions a portion of these misrepresentations and they are surely grievous enough.

3. Unfair statements in theological dictionaries

So strong is that feeling of violence and prejudice that even in theological dictionaries and other works, whose professed purpose is historically to state the true tenets of different bodies of professed Christians, we can very seldom find anything like a fair statement of the Catholic faith. The only theological dictionary compiled by a Protestant that did give a fair and just statement of the Catholic faith, so far as my examination has gone, was one by an English author, the just and impartial Bellamy.

The Oxford Tracts also give generally a fair representation of the particular tenets of the Catholic Church, discussed by them. But the *Encyclopaedia of Religious Knowledge*, so confidently quoted by Mr. Campbell as impartial, is one of the most inaccurate works I saw, in all that relates to the Catholic system. No man, I apprehend, can read the article upon the Catholic faith, and from it form any tolerably accurate idea of its true character.

4. Doctor Spring

Among the Protestant writers whose works I examined, I found Dr. Spring, in his Dissertation, to whom I have often referred, one of the most extreme. He charges the Catholic Church with a complication of evils enough to ruin any cause, if true. He says, among other things: "Rome cannot endure discussion. The only safety of her wicked system is to keep the world in darkness."

The learned divine, Dr. Spring, goes on to say that: "Romanism is to a great extent the religion of Infidels." He charges the Church with:

> [Finding] fault with none, whose faith, be what it may, is sufficiently effective to reach their purses in support of its claims....
>
> The Faith of Rome must be received implicitly or nor at all....
>
> I pity the poor Catholic. He believes he knows not what....
>
> But it is a fact that no Romanist will deny, that the Popes of Rome, as a body of men, have been a dishonor to human nature....
>
> The Romanists have altered and amended, and so mistranslated the Bible, as to render it conformable to their own standard....
>
> The religion of Rome is a cruel religion....
>
> The Romish church is the bitterest foe of the people....
>
> I do not know a system of folly, or impiety, which, as a religious system, can be compares with that which this prolific principle of error has produced....

After making these and many other charges against the Catholic Church, the learned author winds up with this bold and indignant figure:

> But no; it is the incarnate spirit of darkness roaming over the world, seeking whom it may devour, laying waste its valleys and its hills, and drenching them with the blood of its slain.[1]

But not only were the charges themselves most grievous, and often contradictory, but some of the most revolting circumstances that a prejudiced and diseased imagination could conceive, are brought in to heighten the picture. "Her crimes," he says, "are plotted at the altar of mercy."[2]

5. Doctor Wiseman's contrasting position

As I read Protestant and Catholic writers together, I soon found the charge that "Rome cannot endure discussion" denied by the latter. One of the works read by me at the same time I read this dissertation of Dr. Spring's, is the volume containing the *Moorfield Lectures* of Dr. Wiseman, in the thirteenth lecture of which I found this language,

> We are anxious not to shrink from inquiry, but to court it; we throw open our places of worship to all men; we publish our books of prayer and instruction before the world; we submit the least of our children and their catechism to examination; we invite all to inspect our schools and present the masters and their scholars to their interrogation; all that we write and read is at the command of the learned; and, if in our power, we would open our breasts, and ask them to look even into our hearts – for God knows we have nothing to shade, nothing to conceal – and then let them read our belief, as written on its tablets in the simplest and plainest terms. No attack can any longer be allowed by any sensible, reasonable, generous, or liberal-minded man, except through calm and cool investigation, based entirely on the correct statement of our doctrines, and conducted exclusively, not by vague quotations from the word of God, but by arguments clearly and strongly addressed to his understanding.[3]

6. Mr. Campbell

The first work I read, in the course of my investigations into the truth of the Catholic system, was the debate between Campbell and Purcell. I was a member of the same church with Mr. Campbell and had the utmost confidence in him. All my partialities were in his favor. And yet I must say, I was mortified when I read the debate in question, because of the extreme bitterness of the charges he made, and the manner in which he shifted his positions, and the objectionable character of many of his main assumptions, inferences, and deductions. The reading of the debate did not make me a Catholic, as I thought I saw grounds of objection not met by Bishop Purcell; but I could not but see that Mr. Campbell had fought with all sorts of weapons, and had addressed too many of his arguments to mere ignorance and prejudice.

For example, he says in reference to the doctrine of Transubstantiation:

> But the priest can bring down the divine Savior from heaven, and offer him body, soul, and divinity, as often as he pleases, and have the people adore both him and the miracle in his hand!![4]

In this extract it is substantially assumed that, in the contemplation of the Catholic theory, the change in the elements is produced by the miraculous power of the priest, and that the priest is adored as well as the miracle. In all my investigations I could never find such a doctrine. The change is held to be produced by the words of Christ, "This is my body," in the same way that the words of Christ produce the effect intended when He said, "Thy sins are forgiven thee" – "Be thou clean" – "Thou art loosed from thine infirmity" – "Lazarus, come forth." The Catholic Church holds that Christ has promised, that when these words are used in the administration of the Eucharist, He Himself, by His own Word, will produce the change. And that any adoration was allowed to the priest, I could never find any proof, except the statement of Mr. Campbell.

It seemed a little remarkable that Mr. Campbell should have made this misrepresentation, when his own church had been made the victim of one based on a similar ground. Mr. Campbell maintains, "Christian baptism is for the remission of past sins."[5] As pardon is something done *for a man* and not by him; and as this pardon was a consequence that followed baptism; and as this baptism was administered by an Elder of Mr. Campbell's communion, it might *improperly* be said that this remission was the act of the administrator of baptism – not an act of Christ.

Now, if I remember correctly, it was erroneously objected to the Disciples, that they claimed the power to remit sins in baptism. They did not claim any such power. They did, and still insist, that upon the performance of certain precedent specified conditions; Christ does remit sins in baptism. The performance of these conditions is the act of men, and the remission is the act of our Lord.

So it is with regard to the Catholic doctrine in reference to the change of elements. The precedent conditions are performed by the priest, and are his act. The change is the act of Christ. The change in the Eucharist, in contemplation of the Catholic theory, is no more the act of a sovereign power than the remission of sins in baptism. They are both held alike to fulfill the permanent provisions of a pre-existing law.

7. Historical misrepresentation

A very common mode of misrepresentation among Protestant writers was the assumption of an historical fact contrary to the genuine facts of history. A notable example of this may be found in the late work of Dr. Edward Beecher, *The Papal Controversy Exposed.* I have not seen the work, and quote only from a review of it:

> The Pilgrim Fathers of New England, and the other Protestant founders of this great nation, came to this continent soon after the Reformation had shaken the European world, to lay the foundation of a new order of things, by erecting a new social system upon the great principles of civil and religious liberty.

If the Pilgrim Fathers and other Protestant founders, came with the intention to lay the foundation of a new order of things, and did so, embracing both civil and religious liberty, we are at a loss to find any competent historical proof of that fact. But all history of the times shows the contrary, even their own historians. Charles Marshall, a Protestant, in his lecture before the Irish Social and Benevolent Society of Baltimore, delivered in 1855, very truly says:

> It was the settled principle of the English Constitution that the government must take religion under its protection. That the church established by law was the only church that good subjects should support, and that a refusal to conform to the legalized religion of the land, was an offence against the government, which the government might and should punish by the infliction of personal pains and penalties, or by a denial of civic and political privileges. This idea was flourishing in full vigor at the time of the settlement of America. It was one of the abuses imported by the colonists.
>
> The right of government to interfere with religious matters at all was not questioned even by dissenters who suffered most from its exercise. They only maintained that government was giving its

> support to the wrong form of worship. That their peculiar dogmas were those which deserved, and should receive, the fostering aid of the law.

I mention this instance to show, that men occupying high literary positions at the present day, are so careless or prejudiced, as to misrepresent the facts of history when they write against the Catholic Church. I do not make the extract for the purpose of instituting any comparison between Protestants and Catholics in respect to persecution. They both have erred. I believe the Puritan Fathers, and other Protestant founders of our country, acted from honest, though mistaken views. I believe they were governed by these reasons, in brief:

1. They believed their religion the only true form of Christianity.

2. They believed in the right and duty of civil government to protect it, and to prohibit others.

3. They believed religious error and dissention a great evil.

4. They believed the dissenters from them, if successful, would prohibit their form of religion.

5. They, therefore, thought that self-protection, and the best humanity, required the suppression of dissent in its inception.

This system of general misrepresentation has been confessed by many of the most candid Protestant writers. Thus the Rev. Mr. Nightingale, says:

> From diligent inquiry it has been ascertained that party spirit and prejudice have thrown the most undeserved obloquy upon the religion and practices of the Roman Catholics; – in scarcely a single instance has a case concerning them been fairly stated, or the channels of history not grossly, not to say wickedly, corrupted.[6]

"Even the illiberal Mr. Ulix," says Archbishop Hughes, "says that the Catholic religion is calumniated cruelly." Hume declares that "Protestants seemed to have thought that no truth should be told of the Papists." The learned Grotius reproaching the Protestant ministers on this head, received for reply, "that they found it necessary for the public good of the Reformed Religion."[7] And Vossius himself, in the same correspondence, writes, that when he reproved the ministers of Amsterdam, they admitted the iniquity of the proceeding; "but," added they, "if we leave off such language, our people will soon leave us."

8. Causes of this system of misrepresentation

Several questions naturally arise under this state of fact. What causes originally led to this system of general misrepresentation? What causes continue it even to the present day? Is it done with the calm and deliberate intent to create and foster that "contempt prior to examination," which can and will resist any amount of argument and proof whatsoever? Or does it continue from an ignorance of the Catholic doctrine?

That this system of injustice had its origin mainly in a want of integrity, I have no doubt; and that, in many instances, it is still continued from the same motive I am forced to believe. In most cases its continuance arises from a real ignorance of the Catholic faith and its history, and from such a prior disgust, as prevents a fair examination.

In the beginning and during the progress of what is called the Reformation, many of the most unprincipled men, from a variety of motives, put themselves at the head of that movement. Such men are ever disposed to lead any new commotion that promises them any gratification of their passions. Alison, the distinguished Protestant historian, in his *History of Europe*, has this language:

> The great sin of the Reformation was the confiscation of so large a portion of the property of the Church for the aggrandizement of temporal ambition, and the enriching of the nobility, who had taken part in the struggle. When the great convulsion broke out, nearly a third of the whole landed estates, in the countries which it embraced, was in the hands of the Roman Catholic Church. What a noble fund was this for the moral and religious instruction of the people, for the promulgation of truth, the healing of sickness, the assuaging of suffering. Had it been kept together, and set apart for such sacred purposes, what incalculable and never-ending blessings would it have conferred upon society. Expanding and increasing with the growth of population, the augmentation of wealth, the swell of pauperism, it would have kept the instruction and fortunes of the poor abreast of the progress and fortunes of society; and prevented, in a great measure, that fatal effect, so well known in Great Britain in subsequent times, of the national church falling behind the wants of the inhabitants, and a mass of civilized heathenism arising in the very heart of a Christian land. Almost all the social evils under which Great Britain is now laboring, may be traced to this fatal, and most iniquitous spoliation, under the mask of religion, of the patrimony of the poor, on the occasion of the Reformation.

And the learned historian may well call this confiscation, "The great sin.... This most iniquitous spoliation of the patrimony of the poor, under the mask of religion." From these great and unquestioned historical facts, two conclusions plainly follow:

1. That they were truly the leaders to whom the plunder was distributed. This is a test, simple and conclusive.

2. That the love of plunder and pure intentions are never found in the same breast at the same time. They are too incompatible to exist together.[8]

It is, then, clear to my mind, that the motives of the leading spirits who did, in fact, control and govern that movement generally were interested and mercenary. And from this it is also evident that the sincere who participated in it were forced to yield to the bold, the forward, and the unprincipled. We see a noted example of this, in the dispensation granted by Luther, Melancthon, and others, to Philip, the Landgrave of Hesse, to have two wives at once.

These being the characteristics and motives of the leaders of the Reformation, they would necessarily labor to vindicate and sustain themselves; and, in doing so, the only question they would ask, would be this: *"How shall we do so most successfully?" Success, not right,* would be, with them, the leading impulse.[9] And not only so, but they would naturally make up in bitterness, false accusation, and crafty evasion, what they truly lacked in argument and fact. An act of gross injustice is certain to be vindicated by calumny and slander. The victim must be degraded, to justify the oppressor; and this is but the result of the "despairing necessities of falsehood."

It was very natural, therefore, to resort to this system of vindictive and bitter crimination and crafty evasion. The taking of property that did not belong to them, but really had, for ages before, belonged to others, was so plain and palpable a violation of the principles of eternal justice, that nothing could extenuate it, even in appearance, but the utmost delinquency on the part of the plundered victim. The most vindictive, bitter, and relentless animosity will always be found with those who themselves have grievously wronged others, from mercenary motives.

In this way the "channels of history," as Mr. Nightingale truly says, were originally "*grossly,* not to say, *wickedly,* corrupted." Or, in the language of another distinguished writer, (if I can quote from recollection correctly,) "modern history has been one grand conspiracy against truth." Speaking of Bishop Burnet's History, Dr. Johnson said: "Burnet's History of his own times is very entertaining. The style, indeed, is mere chit-chat. I do not believe that Burnet intentionally lied; but he was so prejudiced, that he took no pains to find out the truth. He was like a man who resolved to regulate his time by a certain watch; but will not inquire whether the watch is right or not."[10]

This system of misrepresentation created in the minds of the great mass of Protestants that sort of credulity which is the sure and never-failing mark of prejudice, namely: *a predisposition* to believe any and every thing horrible and absurd in the doctrines and practices of religious opponents, upon the mere reiteration of bold assertion. This prejudice extended to all classes; and grew up with the ministers, as well as with the members. The ministers and writers among Protestants have preached and written for this class of hearers and readers generally. And it is a melancholy truth, that those preachers and writers who have been most bitter and uncharitable, have generally been the most popular, and the most honored and patronized. This tribute to prejudice and bitterness has naturally called into prominent activity too many preachers and writers of that reckless character; and those again have reacted upon their readers and hearers.

By such means, and such instruments, prejudice is still kept up; and prejudice is ever unreasonable. It always reverses the rules of logic and reason, and loves a smart sophism much better than a sound argument. Starkie laid down by in his treatise on evidence, that

> the more atrocious the nature of the crime is, the more repugnant it is to the common feelings of human nature – the more *improbable* it is that it has been perpetrated at all.

In violation of that great rule of law and right reason, this unfortunate state of mind will believe a charge the more readily, because of its unnatural atrocity and absurdity, and the improbability of its being committed by such *numbers,* and under *such circumstances.* Consequently, when the Tales of Maria Monk were published, they were read and believed with eagerness by too many Protestants, and even by Protestant ministers.

Had such a mass of vilification been published against any other body of professed Christians, no one would have believed it. This *eagerness* to hear and believe such stories and calumnies is the sure test of a diseased state of mind. You may take two persons, one impartial, and the other prejudiced, and you may inform them of a charge against the members of an imposing party or Church, imputing very base misconduct, and the impartial man will require proof, clear and strong, in proportion to the enormity of the offense, and will believe it with *regret,* while the dupe of prejudice will *jump* to a conclusion of guilty, with a joy and alacrity in proportion as the offense is grievous, and the evidence doubtful; especially when the charge is of some *secret crime,* that requires a *smart* man to find it out. And I have often remarked, in the course of my reading and observation, that charges of dark, secret, and unnatural crimes are most readily believed by prejudiced persons in every grade of life.

It is this prejudice on the part of too many Protestant writers and readers, which prevents them from examining Catholic authorities for Catholic doctrines. They blindly follow others who have gone before them.

But another reason which prevents even just and unprejudiced Protestants from consulting Catholic standards for Catholic tenets, is the melancholy fact that these misrepresentations of the Catholic system are too often found in the works of Protestant writers of distinguished ability, of great personal purity, and official dignity. It is as if these eminent men had first carefully built up such a reputation, that they might give the more permanence and force to their misrepresentations. In their eminent stations they had been scrupulously just and gentle to all the world besides; as if reserving all their injustice and bitterness for one single object – the Catholic Church. As examples, I will mention two eminent Bishops of the Church of England, Porteus and Watson, whose extreme and bitter misrepresentations of the Catholic faith were, indeed, surprising. It is not at all strange, when such men make such statements, that they should be implicitly believed.

9. The role of naiveté

This general *continuance* of misrepresenting the Catholic faith, and the history relating to it, is mainly the result of a true ignorance of what they are. This is not only shown to be true by the fact that such misrepresentations exist too generally to be the result of a calm and deliberate predetermination among the majority of Protestant writers of the present day, to commit so grievous a moral wrong, not to say crime. But it is very conclusively proven by a circumstance stated by Bishop Hughes, in his letter to Mr. Breckenridge, dated March 25, 1833.[11]

> Since your allusion to Bishop Kendrick has led me into this episode, I may as well close it with a little incident which occurred to myself last spring, and does not, therefore, depend on "information." I happened to go into the session-room of the General Assembly, and found the Bishop engaged in settling a question which I soon discovered to be *interesting* viz., whether baptism, administered by a Catholic priest, is valid! A committee, it seems, had been appointed to draw up a report, which was being read when I entered. The committee had decided in the *negative,* and in support of this decision, reported a variety of reasons, with two of which I was particularly struck. One was that they (Catholic priests) baptize in Latin; as if infants were not quite as well acquainted with *this language* as with any other. The second was, that they (Catholic priests) baptize with *oil* – a discovery reported on the authority of a certain doctor, I think, of Maryland. It was listened to with great but *silent* solemnity – although there were at the moment *five baptismal fonts,* in as many Catholic churches, within half a mile of where the Assembly was sitting; and though it is known to all the world that the Catholic baptism is, and ever has been, with water. I retired from the presence of these 'Teachers in Israel,' revolving in my mind the words of our Blessed Redeemer: "If in the *green* wood they do these things, what shall be done in the dry?"

Another remarkable case occurred in Campbell & Purcell's Debate. A Catholic priest had been excommunicated in Philadelphia some years before, and some mischievous wag had copied the obscene curses found in Sterne's *Tristram Shandy*, and had them published in a newspaper as the curses pronounced against the expelled priest. Mr. Campbell was deceived by this trick, and *seriously* read Sterne's curses, as a grievous charge against the Catholic Church.

I have said that in the beginning and during the progress of the Reformation, many unprincipled men put themselves at the head of that movement; and that such men necessarily adopted that line of self-justification which, in the nature of the case, would be most *successful.* And while a greater proportion of the unprincipled men was found among the early writers of the Reformation, it is undoubtedly true, that many of the same character have lived and flourished since, and still live and flourish;

"Without the care of knowing right from wrong,
Always appear decisive, clear, and strong;
Where others toil with philosophic force,
Their nimble nonsense takes a shorter course,

Flings at your head conviction in a lump,
And gains remote conclusions at a jump."

Then, again, there is a large class of Protestants, who, while they will not themselves positively and affirmatively propagate these misrepresentations of the Catholic faith, will still wink at them and take no care, and make no effort, to prevent or correct the wrong. They are entirely *passive,* while they see the grossest injustice done, and seem to satisfy their consciences, as Pilate did his, when he washed his hands and declared himself innocent of the blood of Christ. But is such conduct just? Is it not the bounden duty of all good men to affirmatively oppose falsehood, and *prevent* injustice, when in their power? Will such morality stand the stern and rigid test of the great Judgment?

10. Reflections

This system of misrepresentation of Catholic doctrines, practices, and intentions, so general among Protestant writers, gave rise, in my mind, to very serious questions. Why did success originally require such a line of argument? Why did truth require such a support? Why was such a course preferred in support of an alleged true system? And why is it still necessary? Are bad arguments more effective than good! Is misrepresentation better in a good cause, than candor and truth! If the doctrines really held by Catholics were so false, erroneous, and absurd, did they need exaggeration to cause their rejection? Does the grossest error, or error of any kind, require to be darkened beyond its real demerits, to make it hated and despised? And is it necessary to prepare the human mind for the reception *of truth that* it should first be filled with falsehood? Do you sow *weeds* before you sow good grain? Is it necessary to inculcate charity, that you should first give a proof of its absence, in the party who inculcates it? And if you wish to put down falsehood, is it necessary, by your own act, to show its *utility and necessity?*

True, it is a practical rule with too many to use falsehood against alleged falsehood, according to the common maxim, that you must oppose the Devil with fire. But is this Christianity? Is it true philosophy? On the contrary, is it not the doctrine of revenge, the practice of savages, the chief maxim of morality among wolves and tigers? And if you wish to vanquish the Evil Spirit and his bad cause, had you not better fight him with something the opposite of that which he uses himself? Had you not better oppose evil with good?

Does not this *necessity* arise from other causes? Is it because there is a unity, a force, a beauty, in the Catholic system that renders it logically impregnable? Is it because it is so conformable to the truth of Christianity, *just as it is*, and not as the passions interests, and pride of men would make it, that the Catholic theory is so much misrepresented and despised? Why is it that every proud innovator upon a permanent system – every wild fanatic – every demagogue in religion – every sect, and the broken fragments of every sect, from Simon Magus to the present time, have one and all been down upon the Old Church?

It is true, it is an exclusive system. Every *true sys*tem must be so. It is a system of humility, of penance, and of self-mortification and restraint. And these features are exceedingly distasteful to human nature. The Catholic does claim to be the sole true Church; not a mere part and parcel of it. She acts as if she was such. She is as exclusive as truth – as stubborn as fact. She has no compromise to make – none to offer – none to accept. Like an immovable mountain, you must go to her. She adapts not her faith to suit changing circumstances, or the whims of men, or the temper of the times. Her terms are the same to all.

If the great Napoleon sins at the head of his victorious legions, he is excommunicated. If the mighty Henry VIII did labor for her, and did great service in her cause, and, therefore, did deserve her thanks; and presuming upon his claims and influence, asks a divorce from his lawful, injured, and innocent wife, his request is peremptorily refused, whatever may be the consequences. Gratitude does not demand the sacrifice of truth. Her friends must be content with justice. They can obtain no more. The true faith cannot and must not be sacrifice for individuals, however great.

She teaches that Christianity cannot be improved – that the Church, being the work of Christ, cannot be reformed. If a man is proud, he cannot go to confession. If he be fond of luxury, the fasts of the Church will appear exceedingly absurd and oppressive. In short, if he enters her confines, he must make great *present* sacrifices. He must merge his individual religious importance in that of the Church, as one whole. And this constitutes the true distinction between the impulses of immediate self-interest and holy love for the *cause.* She also teaches that salvation and glory are found at the *end* of the journey, and not along the path of travel. She also teaches this alleviation, that "He is worthy for whom we should do this;" and that heaven is worth these sacrifices, and cannot be gained without enduring great crosses.

Are not these characteristics of the Catholic Church the true cause of that *inexorable necessity* which forces her opponents to fight with any weapons they find most *available,* and, therefore, to resort to this ungenerous system of misrepresentation and abuse? True it is, she does claim *superiority over all others.* And this claim would necessarily wound their pride. This is natural. It was so of old. From the very nature of this *exclusive* system, it must arouse this peculiar kind of resistance. It stands opposed to too many darling wishes and impulses not to incur this most bitter and unrelenting opposition.

11. Catholicism is exclusive

It was so with Christianity in the beginning. "Now the first thing that strikes us," says Dr. Paley,

> is, that the religion they carried with them was *exclusive.* It denied without reserve the truth of every article of heathen mythology, the existence of every object of their worship. It accepted no compromise; it admitted no comprehension. It must prevail, if it prevailed at all, by the overthrow of every statue, altar, and temple in the world. It will not easily be credited that a design so bold as this could in any age be attempted to be carried into execution with impunity.[12]

While it must be readily confessed that Protestants and Catholics hold more doctrines in common than did the Heathens and Christians in the first ages of Christianity, still the Catholic Church is equally exclusive. She cannot sanction a mixed system of truth and error. She requires the genuine, and refuses the debased coin. She too "accepts no compromises" – she "admits no comprehension." And the fact that Protestants consider themselves Christians, while they are regarded by the Catholic Church as heretics, is, of itself, the more calculated to produce this system of opposition.

This rigid and consistent adherence to her faith – this intolerance, as it is called, is the ground of great complaint on the part of Protestants. "The faith of Rome," says Dr. Spring, "must be received implicitly, or not at all."[13] And Dr. Spring is right herein. Her faith must be implicitly received. I believe that is always the case with conscientious truth. If she is the true Church, she is certainly *right* in this. If she is not the true Church, and erroneously claims to be such, she still has the sense to be consistent; she has still one great and indispensable mark of truth.

Protestantism is not exclusive. Its leading principle, from which all others logically and necessarily flow, is studiously adapted to flatter individual pride, and indulge the will. Its soft and flexible gum-elastic character admits of infinite modifications, without any efficient checks, and easily conforms itself to the prevailing sentiment of each succeeding age. Progress and Reform being its leading ends, it never finds rest, so long as the human mind loves novelty, and seeks excitement in change. This flexibility is fully shown by the great and continual shifting from the doctrines of the early Reformers. Under such a theory it is very true, as Pope says:

"Manners with fortunes, humors turn with climes,
Tenets with books, and principles with times."

Is it not most wonderfully surprising that the Catholic Church, with all her alleged superstitions, corruptions, errors of faith, absurd doctrines, whimsical practices, and austere observances, with the superadded and accumulated mass of distortion and exaggeration of these alleged evils, still cannot be put down – cannot be confuted – and will maintain her pre-eminence in the Christian world? There is something most marvelous in all this. God must have concerned Himself in this matter. And as Blanco White says:

> If the mass of Christians must submit to the decision of another authority, by whatever name it may be called, the Church of Rome can fear no rival. You may raise doubts against supremacy. But how very few minds of a pious character will not be overpowered by the preeminence of Rome in the Christian world?[14]

And Mr. White, though a decided Protestant, might well say what he did. True, you may "raise doubts" against any thing. You may raise doubts against Christianity. The Christian religion is not so plain as to be wholly free from doubt in unwilling minds. I cannot conceive what merit there could be in faith, what room there would be left for the fair exercise of humility, if the proofs of Christianity were so overwhelming as to demonstrate its truth to all men. There is ample proof to satisfy the honest, patient, and diligent inquirer, while there is enough of doubt to perplex the proud and suspicious – the dishonest and the selfish – the thoughtless and the negligent – and especially those prevaricating

"Philosophers who darken and put out
Eternal truth, by everlasting doubt."

So it is with respect to the Catholic system. You may raise doubts and cavils over many points; and the less you know of the system, the more these cavils you can raise. You may interpose bold, brief, and sophistical positions, inferences and deductions; but after all, they cannot weigh against the clear, great, and decisive principles and facts that sustain it. After all the bitterness with which she has been assailed; and after all the cavils and objections that human wit, sharpened by interested animosity, or habitual prejudice, has been able to raise, or may be yet able to raise, who would not, *at last,* rather die in the communion of this old calumniated, suffering, and yet invincible Church? Old House of God, I love thee! And the reason why, I have told, and will tell.

12. Protestant theory of the alleged errors

One of the most deep and serious questions that arose in my mind was this: How and when did these alleged, absurd, unscriptural, and disgusting errors get into the Church? In my investigations I began at the beginning, and considered the Church as it came from the hands of the apostles. By the consent of all parties, the apostles did their duty, and taught all the truth, no more. They left the Church in the hands, and under the government, of those officers they themselves had personally instructed and appointed.

That they generally made good and worthy appointments, I had no doubt. That those they appointed were properly instructed, I could not question. The Church left by them needed no improvement, and certainly did know her faith.

In contemplation of the Protestant theory, each member had been carefully taught the right of private interpretation in the last resort, and each member knew that those most grievous errors, as alleged, were contrary to the known faith, daring innovations upon the truth, and degrading invasions of private rights.

She was spread over the entire Roman Empire; and numerous Churches existed as branches, of *the church*, in all of which the faith, once delivered, had been carefully taught and deposited. It was in the best days of Roman literature, when those arts best calculated, in their nature, to develop the reasoning facilities, were most fully cultivated, and most generally diffused. And this state of things continued until the destruction of the Roman Empire in the West, by the Goths, Vandals, and other barbarous hordes in the fifth century.

THE TRUE CHURCH

The first three centuries were days of general persecution, with intervals of rest; while in the fourth, the Church was alternately protected and oppressed by the Roman Emperors; and in the fifth, her sufferings were extreme. It was in those suffering ages that the "seed took root amongst the stones and thorns, and sprang beneath the axe, and blossomed in the blast" – it was then that "the Circus flowed with blood, but the immortal Spirit walked the red surge and foam, and led the sinking to eternal rest" – and it was then that twelve millions of martyrs laid down their lives,

"And lift their raptured looks on high,
As though it were a joy to die"

for the sublime faith of Christ. In short, the Church arose, and continued for the first five centuries, in an enlightened country, came well instructed, widely diffused, and yet perfectly united, from the hands of the apostles.

In my investigations concerning the truth of Christianity itself, I met with no line of argument more conclusive and unanswerable than Leslie's *Short and easy Method with the Deists.* The essence of that argument may be briefly stated thus:

1. There now exists a certain book, which states that at a time and place therein mentioned, certain great, notable, and visible public facts occurred. It states that at the same time and place, a certain association of men was organized, and certain visible observances instituted in this association to be known to, and kept by all the members, and to continue from that time forward

2. This great association of men still exists, and we know the fact these observances are still kept up.

Now to prove the fact that these observances, and this organization began at the time and place mentioned, we will assume that they were organized and instituted at some time and place, for the association is now in being, and these ordinances are now observed. The organization of this body, and the institution of those observances, are plain matters of historical fact, and can be known; and whenever they did take place, the fact must have been known, from the very nature of the case.

Can any one show that this organization, and the institution of these visible observances, were commenced at any *other* time? If they originated at one time, and the book stated they originated at another and a different time, then there would be a positive contradiction, and the falsehood must be known. Suppose this association did not exist, and the observances were not instituted by the persons, and at the time and place stated, and the book should have been forged at a *later* date, still stating the *pre-existence* of those alleged *notorious visible facts,* would not all men at once say? "This book is false upon the face of it; for it states as *past events,* things that no one ever heard of, and all our own experience is in direct and palpable conflict with the alleged facts recorded in this book. This whole thing is new, and not *old,* as stated; and, therefore, must be false. Where is the body of men that ever did keep these observances? Who has heard of them before? Who has ever heard of this book before? These alleged facts were of such a character as to attract the earnest attention of all men. Who can believe that they could have existed, as alleged, and no one know it?"

Inconsistency is a sure mark of falsehood, and is understood as such, by all men of every country,

"By saint, by savage, and by sage,"

this knowledge, and the disposition to use it, is found in the humblest minds, and at an early age, even in children. To weigh and compare one part of a theory with another is the natural result of the faculty of reason. If the inconsistency be plain and palpable, it will never be overlooked, and never sanctioned, unless some great motive exist to produce the result. If the inconsistency be merely theoretical, requiring a process of laborious and rational deduction to detect it, or if it be immaterial, then it may escape detection and exposure among the great mass of men.

Dr. Paley, in his *Evidences of Christianity*, says:

> The success of a religion founded upon a miraculous history, shows the credit that was given to the history: and this credit, under the circumstances in which it was given, *i.e.* by persons capable of knowing the truth, and interested to inquire after it, is evidence of the reality of the history, and by consequence, of the truth of the religion....
>
> But it will be said, is one religion could make its way without miracles, why might not another? To which I reply, first, this is not the question. The proper question is not whether a religious institution could set up without miracles, but whether a religion or a change of religion, founding itself in miracles, could succeed without any reality to rest upon. I apprehend these two cases to be very different....

THE TRUE CHURCH

> One would imagine, to hear some men talk, or to read some books, that the setting up of a religion by dint of miraculous pretences, was a thing of every day's experience; whereas I believe, that except the Jewish and Christian religion there is no tolerable well-authenticated account of such thing having been accomplished.

It is evidently true, that the bare *success* of a religion, without regard to the *character* of the proofs upon which it *assumes* to rest, or the means used to attain this success, or the circumstances attending the propagation of the theory, is no evidence of the entire truth of the system itself. All religions have prevailed to a greater or less extent; and the truth is undeniable, that they assume to rest upon *different* grounds, appeal to different classes of proof, were propagated by different means, and under different circumstances; while they all agree in *some* great leading features. These facts, when justly considered, would seem to lead clearly to these conclusions:

1. That man, by a law of his own nature, impressed upon him by the Creator, is a religious being. From this law he knows that he is a subordinate being – that there exists a Supreme Intelligent Cause – and that the natural relation existing between the Creating and the created Intelligence, entitles the former to the adoration and obedience of the latter. This knowledge of his duty, derived from this law of his nature, though limited as it is, is still sufficient to put him upon *inquiry,* and makes the duty of further inquiry, obligatory. It is a well known principle of law, applicable to certain classes of cases, that when a party is entitled to notice of certain facts, and has not notice of them in full, but has sufficient notice to put him upon inquiry, by a reasonable use of which he may know all the facts he has a right to know in reference to the alleged matter, then the law presumes full notice, and treats the party accordingly.

2. That man, without a special revelation, could never know his full duty, and his true destination.

If, then, a system of religion should be proposed, embracing the first great truth above stated, it will necessarily attract the attention of men, and lead to investigation. If the theory *assumes* to be only based upon reasoning, or *secret* miracles, the efficient *means* of contradiction are not given by the *theory itself;* and where one exists, or another is proposed, at the same time, the choice must rest between bald, desolate Atheism, or cold, vague Deism, on the one hand, and the system already existing, or the one proposed, on the other. As man cannot, without a direct revelation, arrive at all the features of the true religion, he is compelled, from the nature of the case, *to take the best offered, or reject all.* And as it must be a very bad religion, that is not better than infidelity, and that contains less of truth in it, the natural religion of the human heart and mind will generally take the lesser evil of the two.

But, on the contrary, if a *new* religion, or any material *change* of a received religion, be proposed, and such religion or change be based upon visible miracles, or upon any *other* simple and easily understood basis, the natural law of consistency will induce all to compare the system or change proposed with the grounds *assumed* for it to rest upon. *The means of detection are given in both cases alike, and will be used in both.* If, therefore, the grounds, *as given* be false, or the thing proposed be inconsistent therewith, it must, and will, in most cases, be rejected. The human mind loves consistency; this love is one of its simplest impulses; and when referred for proof to that which is either plainly false or clearly inconsistent with the theory to be established, will uniformly turn away, and seek truth in some other quarter, unless some other very powerful and tempting motive overrule this natural result.

From the admissions of all parties – from the language of the Scriptures, and the testimony of the Fathers, *the faith once delivered was to remain unchanged to the end of time.* And no sentiment is more often and continuously reiterated and affirmed than this: that nothing *new* was to be *added,* and nothing taken away.

The Church, as it came from the hands of the apostles, was firmly grounded in this very plain and important fundamental position. And it was not only grounded in the position itself, but each member did know what was taught – what were his recognized and established rights – what observances were in the Church and uniformly kept by all – and what doctrines, ordinances, and practices, were *claimed* as coming from the apostles. And with this plain and obvious rule in the mouths of all the *teachers,* and of all the *lay members,* and with this knowledge in the memories and minds of all, what a strange unaccountable falsehood it was, in the face of this plain principle, and of these simple and known facts, to assert and insist that these *new*, absurd, glaring, and unscriptural tenets, and oppressive ordinances, had, always existed in the Church – had come down from the apostles – were *old*, and not *new* – if it be true, as Protestants contend, that these daring innovations upon an admitted unchangeable faith, were introduced into the Church by fraud, covin, and deceit. And if these alleged errors were introduced into the true Church, in their true garb, *as new,* how perfectly inconsistent they were with the known faith, and the plain established rule!

That these alleged errors were of a character to arrest the immediate attention of all, and to give the most serious shocks to the entire system, is clear, not only from their own nature, but from the strong and violent denunciations they receive from Protestants themselves. If errors at all, they were certainly great and important. They made a change in the system, as palpable and important, as can well be conceived: a change that made as great a difference between the old and the new theory, as is the difference between *fallibility and infallibility* in the Church. And the alleged change was not only manifest and plain, but the means of detection, confutation, and resistance, were known to, and within the reach of, all the members.

Under the Protestant view, this well-instructed, widely diffused, and united suffering Church, went with rapid strides from the pure faith once delivered, into the most grievous errors; and by the absurd change, involved herself in still more intense suffering and disgrace.

She gave up the great fundamental right of private interpretation in the last resort, without a struggle; and in lieu thereof admitted the wicked principle of actual governmental infallibility in the Church. For a mere communicative and intelligible Eucharist, she received the absurd dogma of the Real Presence. For Christian liberty, she obsequiously received humiliating and degrading confession. In place of rational religion, she prayed to saints, honored their relics, and her children foolishly received the sacrament of Extreme unction when they died.

Not only did she add to the faith the most grievous errors, and oppressive and nonsensical observances, but she actually mistook for permanent powers those mere temporary gifts intended for the days of the apostles alone. Consequently, when they departed, the church at once forgot their words, or the apostles forgot to tell her, that Extreme Unction and miracles were to cease. She seems to have been suddenly seized and stupefied with a monomania to assume doctrines, and powers, and practices, unwarranted by the Scriptures which all understood – wholly incompatible with her received teaching – inconsistent with her plainest maxims – and oppressive upon her children.

Why did she do so? What unaccountable delusion could so deceive her? The same reasons existed then against these errors, if errors at all, as exist now. The same permanent code of law then existed as now, and the same objections would have been urged. The Christians of those days had the same impulses of human nature, and must have entertained the same opposition to injury and oppression.

For Mr. Campbell has well said:

> the moment that B propounds his synopsis with the slightest air of authority, in the way of exacting obedience or acknowledgement, at that moment there is something in human mature that whispers to A, who is this brother B? A fallible like my self? A great man he may be, but he is fond of his own opinions and prides himself upon his superiority. I will not lay a victim upon his altar, nor burn incense at his shrine; I too am a man, and will yield to non the right to dictate to me.[15]

And human nature, my old friend and ancestor, what have you to say? Are you guilty or not guilty? Did you know your rights? Did you know the law? Had you any instinct – any faith—any courage? Were you asleep? Or waking did you willing, and without a murmur, and against all your impulses and your rights, surrender to brother B? If so, why did you do it? Tell us if you please "old soldier, who put the knapsack on your back?" and how it was done? Tell us gentle bird, who caught and caged you? Tell us pale and wasted prisoner, who put those shackles on your limbs, and that rope around your neck? Tell us sighing patriot, who drove the iron of despotism into your soul, and made you a slave? And why did you not die in the last ditch? Why did you not cry aloud and spare not? What commotion did you make? What resistance did you offer? And if you did offer any, where is the proof of the fact to be found?

Has history entirely neglected you? Your delinquency has certainly been very great if these charges against you are true. You followed dictation so blindly – surrendered so easily – abandoned your rights and those of truth so promptly – abjured your faith so readily – and suffered yourself to be bound and manacled, hand and foot, with a spirit so craven, that you deserver not commiseration. "Who is there to mourn for Logan? No one"

True it is that some of your children, while they darkened your memory and aspersed your character, woke up after some thirteen or fifteen centuries of sleep and assumed to reassert your abandoned rights,

"And things Unknown, proposed as things forgot."

13. The alleged errors would be easily opposed by early Christians

Upon the basis that these alleged errors were truly such, the Christians of that period when they were introduced, had less difficulties in their way than had modern Protestants. They were in good condition – their path was plain – their sky was clear. To oppose these alleged errors, they were not forced into the melancholy position of a practical abandonment of Christ's promises to His Church. They were not forced to admit in affect, that the gates of Hell had prevailed against her. They were not bound to sustain their position by bringing against their predecessors charges of high crime against God and His Christ.

It was not necessary for them to assume that for eight hundred years Christendom, both lay and clergy, were drowned in idolatry and heresy. They were relieved from the unavailing and fruitless search among the silent records of the past for ancestors for their faith. It was not incumbent upon them, either to abandon all visible connection with the apostles, or to supply the defective records of history, and refresh the memory of past ages by mere construction of the law, which had been promulgated before the alleged historical events are assumed to have happened.

Their invention would not be put to the torture for the purpose of discovering some new plausible theory of the Church reconcilable with their anomalous position. In reference to the nature, powers, and purposes of the institution, there was no necessity to assume so many contradictory and perplexing theories.

In short, they were not compelled to assume that Christianity had been a practical failure. They were not compelled to assume that its tendency and effect, as attested by experience of a series of ages, was, with scarcely an exception, to stupefy the human mind – to destroy human virtue – and to render its professors fit subjects for impostors and victims.

They not only had no such difficulties in their way, they had advantages the advantages of plain simple tests of truth that the reformers did not have. Until the alleged errors were introduced into the church, she was pure and untainted. She must have been aware of this state of the case. All preceding ages were with her in sentiment from the beginning. The *precedents* of all the past sustained her. They were for, and not against her. How, then, could a plain and grievous innovation in faith or observances be introduced, and her teachers not know it? To condemn such an error, or such a practice, it was only necessary to recur to their memories. Their past and present experience – the simple testimony of recollection – was sufficient at once to mark the error. If *new* it was *false.* And this act of memory was a test in possession of all. It was simple and certain. Even a child can remember; and the most simple-minded individual can know what he has seen and heard all his life. A man can also know whether be *believes* a certain doctrine. He may not be certain that the doctrine is true; but among the simple matters of fact which he can know, is the fact whether he *believes it to be true.*

It is upon this plain testimony of memory and experience, that Leslie's argument in answer to the charge, that the Scriptures were forged in ages *after* the rites were said to have been instituted, is based. And he insists, with unanswerable power, that the fabricators of this alleged forgery could never have made the Jews to:

> believe, *in spite of their invariable experience to the contrary,* that they had received these books long before from their fathers, had been taught them when they were children, and had taught them to their own children; that they had been circumcised themselves, had circumcised their families, and uniformly observed the minute detail of sacrifices and ceremonies; that they had never eaten any swine's flesh, or other prohibited meats.

Is not this line of argument equally applicable to the case in hand? In the case of the Jews, the difficulty was to convince them, *contrary* to their positive experience, and the simple testimony of their memories, that they had long possessed a book, claiming to be ancient, but, in fact, then for the first time introduced, and had long actually believed and practiced the doctrines, and kept the observance therein mentioned. In the case of the alleged Catholic errors, the insuperable difficulty was, to make the Christians believe that *they had always held doctrines then first promulgated and never heard of before, and had always kept observances that no one in the Church had ever seen performed.* In such a case, the gray-haired and venerable members of the Church, in every part of the world, would have risen up as one man, and said: We have been members of the Church for many years – we never heard of such a doctrine – we never witnessed such a practice. *It is new, inconsistent, and false."*

For the sake of illustration we will take the doctrine and practice of Confession. It is a *doctrine* not flattering to human pride – not palatable to human nature. *The practice* is equally repugnant to that "something in human nature" referred to by Mr. Campbell; and this practice is remarkably plain, and easily understood and remembered. How, then, were the Christians persuaded to submit to both the doctrine and practice of that which was not only false in itself, but contrary to the universal and fundamental rule to reject all innovations upon the known and established faith? How were they made to believe, contrary to their invariable experience, that these things had always been in the Church? How was human nature so completely overcome? That which shocked all common sense – falsified all experience, and yet claimed to be old and familiar – that which was new, repugnant, arrogant, oppressive and disgusting, was palmed upon the universal Church without difficulty or resistance! How could this be possible? If this could have been done, what could not have been done? Can we fix any limits at all to human imposition, or to human credulity?

We of the present day know that we possess some memory and mind. Is there any reason why we should substantially assume the entire oblivion of these faculties in our Christian ancestors?

Suppose that all the Elders, with one exception, among the disciples, were to rise up and with one united voice and effort endeavor to introduce Infant Baptism among them, upon the ground that it had been a practice with them from the beginning. Suppose that they should each continuously assert this to the day of the death of the last one of them. Could they convince a single individual they were right?

Suppose they sought to introduce it upon the ground that it never had been the faith and practice of their Church, but that it should have been – that in this respect, they had before erred in construing the Scriptures. Perhaps then they might, even contrary to their former teaching, convince some members. This would be consistent with the basis of private interpretation in the last resort; and consequently of the continued reformability of thc Church.

You might as well attempt to establish a religion assuming to found itself upon visible miracles, when, in fact, there were no miracles, as to hope to introduce *new* doctrines and observances *as old and well known*? In both cases the thing proposed is wholly inconsistent with the recognized basis upon which it assumes to rest, and in direct contradiction to the plainest tests of truth – the evidence of all our senses in the one case and of our memory and positive experience in the other.

14. The alleged errors were additions to the deposit of faith

There was another weighty reflection that forced itself upon my mind, which was this: That these alleged errors were *additions* to the faith, not *subtractions* from it. In the view of Protestants the following tenets are held to be pure *additions* to the faith once delivered, namely:

1. The Infallibility of the Church,

2. The Primacy of St. Peter,

3. The Sacraments of Confirmation, Penance, Matrimony, Extreme Unction, and Holy Orders,

4. The doctrines of Traditions, Transubstantiation, Purgatory, Invocation of Saints, Prayers for the Dead, and the continuance of miracles in the Church, and

5. In the view of those who reject Infant Baptism, and baptism by pouring or sprinkling, these were also pure additions.

In reference to one or two of the sacraments mentioned above, a portion of the Protestant world agreed with the Catholic Church.

This list of alleged errors is certainly very formidable; and the crimes therein stated are grievous enough, and their alleged introduction sufficiently inconsistent in a Church always, at all times, and in all places *claiming* only to teach that which had always been received in one unbroken and continuous line of succession from the apostles. Such a mighty mass of imposition, if imposition at all, is, *under the existing circumstances,* entirely without any parallel in human history.

I must say that the peculiar character of these alleged errors, being mere alleged *additions*, made it the more difficult to understand how they could get into the Church. The admitted and undeniable fact that the Church had lost none of the original deposit of faith – that if she had added more she had at least preserved all – to my mind proved her vigilance and integrity. Had she been either negligent or corrupt she would have lost some doctrines, particularly such as were above human comprehension and such as required humiliating sacrifices.

Her alleged innovations, however, did not run in the line of negligence, but in that of vigilance. Ever wakeful and honest in preserving all that was left to her, she is assumed at the same time to have been equally wakeful and dishonest in the addition of absurd and false doctrines and oppressive ordinances. There were in the Church, according to this theory, vigilance and honesty to *preserve*, and at the same time, vigilance and dishonesty to *innovate.*

Dr. Paley says in his *Evidences of Christianity:*

> In the moral, as in the natural world, it is change that requires a cause. Men are easily fortified in their old opinions, driven from them with great difficulty.

And the learned divine might have well added, that this change is still the more difficult when produced by additions, than when the effect of mere negligence. *Affirmative* change is the more difficult. And when this affirmative change is inconsistent with the plain and well understood basis upon which the system itself assumes to rest, and when it is *against,* not only the old opinions and received maxims of individuals, but also their interests, and their acknowledged rights, then, indeed, the difficulty becomes insurmountable.

If you ask a person to rise earlier and do more work in the day than he has been accustomed to, you will be apt to incur very strong opposition, and very forcible reasons will be required to produce the change. But, on the contrary, if you require *less,* you will scarcely offend him. He will most readily sleep later, and do less work.

If the Church could make any change in the faith, I should always expect to find it in the negligent loss of some mystery above reason, or of some humiliating doctrine and practice. It certainly is the impulse of human nature, to get to heaven with as little sacrifice as possible! Whatever is above reason, or apparently repugnant to it, and whatever is painful to our pride, or asks a sacrifice of any kind, would be most apt to be lost by either a corrupt or negligent Church. To omit a doctrine or practice requires no *affirmative* act. It requires nothing but *inaction.* Negligence will bring this about. You do not shock men by requiring them to believe and practicc that which they never did before. All you do is to let their faith, by slow degrees, die out.

When we look to the history of ancient heresy, we shall find that it *generally* consisted in denials and rejections of received doctrines. Hymenaeus and Alexander denied all future resurrection. The heretics mentioned by St. Ignatius, denied the reality of Christ's body. The Arians denied His divinity. The Novatians denied the efficacy of repentance. The Manichaeans forbid marriage, and prohibited meats, and denied the supremacy of the one God.

When we look into the principal tenets of the Reformers, we shall still find the same general characteristic. Their alleged Reformation consisted in *denials and rejections* of received doctrines and observances. There were very few, if any, doctrines that they alleged had been lost. The Catholic Church only required *too much.* Whether these denials and rejections by Protestants be heresy or not, they certainly run in the most natural and usual line of error.

15. The impossibility of the alleged errors not causing dissension

The most insuperable difficulty with me, was to understand how a Church, so well instructed – so well grounded in the true faith – always acting upon the plain principle that no *additions* could be made to the faith, and *nothing lost* – a Church so vigilant that nothing was, *in fact*, lost – could be so far deluded and deceived, as not only to surrender her rights, her faith, and her integrity, but to do so *with such an entire and easy unanimity as to cause no dissensions in the Church?* If these alleged errors possess anything like the enormity attributed to them by Protestant denunciation then it is clear beyond a doubt, they must have caused a mighty rent in the Church, or she must have lost her integrity, and each and all of her members must have been slaves before they were made so by these alleged errors.

That the Church was vigilant to guard the deposit of faith is not only shown by the conclusive fact that she lost none originally given, but it is shown by the history of the Church itself. Saint Clement, Bishop of Rome, in the first century, by his Epistles and messengers, healed the divisions at Corinth. Saint Ignatius says to the Trallians:

> I exhort you, therefore, (yet not I but the love of Jesus Christ,) to use only Christian nourishment, and to abstain from the strange herb, which is heresy.

The works of the Fathers are full of proofs of this vigilance. We have the most full and minute lists of heretics, including even the most obscure sects. Yet we never hear of any divisions caused by the introduction of this great mass of alleged error. The very animated discussions in the Church, at an early day, as to the time of celebrating Easter, shows her care and anxiety to preserve unity, even in matters of discipline. The time when each heresy arose, by whom it was introduced, and its distinctive characteristics, are all given. What is still more remarkable is the fact that these sects agreed with the Catholic Church in most of the doctrines condemned by Protestants, and separated from the Church upon grounds conceded by Protestants to have been erroneous. The topics that were discussed, and which led to divisions and heresies during the first five centuries of the Christian era were entirely different from the questions arising between Catholics and Protestants, except the fundamental right of private interpretation in the last resort, without which there would exist no dissent.

"The three most ancient topics of controversy," says Dr. Paley, "were the authority of the Jewish constitution, the origin of evil, and the nature of Christ.[16] The learned author goes on to say:

> The Millennium, Novatianism, the baptism of heretics, the keeping of Easter, engaged also the attention and divided the opinions of Christians at and before that time, (by the way, it may be observed, that such disputes, though on some accounts to be blamed, showed how much men were in earnest upon the subject....

In speaking of the heretics of those times, Dr. Paley says:

> I think there is no reason to believe that the numbers of these bear any considerable proportion to the body of the Christian Church.

There were then, no disputes between the heretics of those ages and the Catholics about matters in difference between Protestants and Catholics, with the exception of the rule of Faith. Yet, "men were in earnest upon the subject." We then know the questions, and the persons who raised them in the ancient Church. If as Mr. Campbell says, "Taylor and others have shown that all the abominations of Popery were hatched in the second century," and that the "Nicene [creed] was a symbol and exponent of the faith of the whole world at the beginning of the fourth century," how shall we account for the extraordinary insensibility of the Christians of those days? How such a moral phenomenon and such silence could exist, under such circumstances, I pretend not to understand.

That the Catholic doctrines were held by the universal Church of the first five centuries, and were not in general denied even by those heretics, whose doctrines Protestants themselves cannot stand, (except as to the Rule of Faith,) would seem to be clear beyond all reasonable doubt. Even those who would deny the justice of this conclusion, must still concede the unquestioned fact, that these Catholic doctrines, now disputed by Protestants, were held and maintained by the greatest and most widely known Fathers and martyrs of those days, as well as by the councils of the Church. Why, then, were there no discussions, no divisions, no denials by others, if those doctrines were new, disgusting, revolting and false? We know that Origen and others put forth certain opinions of their own, upon a few points, and these were promptly resisted, and put down. Why was this vigilance not exercised in resisting the introduction of the alleged Catholic errors?

That the alleged introduction of those supposed errors caused no divisions in the Church is equally clears from history. In the second century Saint Irenæus says:

> And neither do the churches founded in Germany, nor those in Spain, in Gaul, in the East, in Egypt, in Africa, nor in the regions of the middle of the earth, believe in a different faith....
>
> The whole Church has one and the same faith throughout the whole world as we have explained above.

For further proof, I must refer to the quotations from the Fathers already made to show the unity of the Church. How then did these alleged errors get into this universal and united Church?

That a universal combination among all the clergy, so widely scattered over the world, could have been entered into, cannot be supposed. It is utterly impossible! Every one of them would have been, at the same time, without any integrity whatever.

But suppose it possible, how did the well-instructed laity come to yield up their Christian liberty as well as the true faith. Had they all lost their memories?

To introduce these alleged errors at once was surely impossible. To introduce them gradually, without producing intense commotions and divisions, would seem equally incredible. Dr. Priestly did contend that the Divinity of Christ, never dreamed of, as he supposed, in the days of the apostles, crept in as an opinion a short time afterwards, waxed strong, until it was finally enacted into an article of faith in the Council of Nice A. D. 325.

I must confess I could not understand this silent and gradual process. It was so *silent* and gradual as to awaken no attention, and yet so efficient as to make you understand and believe those false doctrines. It did not make you forget the well-known universal rule, that nothing new was to be introduced, but it made you entirely overlook the plain fact, that these alleged errors were new additions, never heard of before. By the magical and mysterious efficiency of the gradual silent process, it is substantially assumed that the suffering, vigilant, universal, and united Church actually mistook these innovations for her old tenets, contrary to the simple testimony of her memory. It was certainly a very remarkable oblivion of memory, on part of so many intelligent and sincere persons, who "were," as Dr. Paley well says, "in earnest upon the subject."

How this process could be so silent as to escape detection entirely and, at the same time, so efficient as to introduce successfully such alleged errors, I could not perceive. How the change could be so gradual as not only to escape notice, while going on, but also to be unknown and unfelt after it was accomplished, I could not tell. Can you cut a man's arm off so gradually that he will not feel it? Can you do this so imperceptibly that he will not know, *after it is done,* that he has lost an arm? And can you make him believe that he never had but one? Can you introduce a viper into my house so secretly that I will never know it? and so gradually that when I do find him out, I will not know him? Can you so gradually change a man's view from Infidelity to Christianity, that he will not perceive the change during its progress, and not know it after his conversion?

As to introducing them first in the shape of *opinions,* and then afterwards adopting them as articles of faith, I could not well understand how this could be; especially in reference to those tenets *contradictory* of the existing faith. For example, I could not understand how the Church, holding, as an article of faith, that Christ was not God, could tolerate even the *opinion* that He was God. Certainly, if I am required to believe in the absence of all divinity in Christ, I cannot be allowed to hold the precise opposite, even as an opinion.

If it be the established faith that Christ is not present in the Eucharist, I cannot see by what semblance of reason the Church would permit any member to believe the contrary. In short, I cannot form any conception of that theory which would require members to hold a certain doctrine as an article of faith, and, at the same time, permit them to hold its opposite as an opinion. Nor can I understand how the human mind could contain these opposites, and believe them both, at the same time. I can well understand how, in reference to matters of discipline and speculative opinions, the Church allows her children to hold *either* side of the question, *as a matter of opinion;* but I cannot understand how she could *require* her members to believe one thing as a matter of faith, and, at the same time, allow them to disbelieve it.

It would certainly be most surprising, that the introduction of these alleged errors, even in the shape of opinions, created no dissension or discussion in the Church. And still more surprising, that when they were changed from that shape, all were required to believe, as faith, what before all had been required to disbelieve as heresy; and yet this state of case produce no discussions and no divisions.

This silent creeping and gradual process, if true, completely answered and upset Leslie's line of argument. And if once conceded to be practicable, it would prove that all the doctrines and practices of the *Jews* could have been so gradually introduced, that they would not have known it. I could have no confidence in the solidity of this attempted explanation. It was too weak and doubtful to rely upon. A Church starting right, and upon the basis of an *unchangeable faith,* and remaining so vigilant as to forget nothing, could not possibly be thus entrapped and deceived.

If a few ministers had attempted to introduce them at any time, all the other clergy and all the lay members would have opposed them, and they would have been either put down, or the introducers expelled from the Church. There could never have happened such a universal and wholesale apostasy, so silently and smoothly accomplished, that no one opposed it, and no divisions followed. Not all could have slept at their posts, nor could even a majority. Nor could many have been dishonest in those days of trial and suffering. "Their integrity was insured by the insults they suffered." So long as one single honest and vigilant bishop, priest, or layman remained anywhere in the Church, these alleged errors would have encountered his stern opposition; and his opposition would have aroused that of others.

We have accounts of many heresies, and it is most remarkable we have non of these alleged errors, if they be in fact, heresies. The Church would have felt and recorded the shock. Such a mighty mass of error would have left certain and clear evidences of its introduction and effects.

The march of a mighty army through a cultivated country leaves visible desolation behind. The travel of a monster along a dusty road, or through a swamp, will leave a visible track. In both cases the trail is plain, and it can be easily followed. And the introduction of great and grievous errors into such a Church, would always arouse opposition, too strong to be ever overlooked or forgotten.

16. The alleged colossal change and immutability of the Church

Another reflection arose in my mind as to the state of case supposed by Protestants. The Church is conceded to have started right. She then held the true faith, no more, no less, in her widely extended but united communion. She had hundreds of thousands in her ranks, of all conditions, dispersed over the wide world. She was particularly grounded in the plain and intelligible principle, universally acknowledged and understood, that nothing new was to be added to the faith of the Church, and nothing lost. Whatever the faith was, it was one and indivisible – complete and entire – a single unit – and was to remains so to the last day and the last man.

This Church, universal, united, and grounded in such fixed sentiment, is supposed to have become suddenly possessed of the most daring and reckless spirit of innovation. The Apostle John had scarcely been in his grave before the very men appointed by the apostles, even the holy martyrs for the faith – those valiant and devoted souls who faced a heathen world, bearing the cross to the nations, and sealing their ministry, like the apostles, with their voluntary blood – are supposed to have been led away by this most strange and unaccountable delusion. And while the Church was proclaiming everywhere *"nothing new,"* she was introducing these alleged errors. Then, after accomplishing the ruin of the her own faith, like a sinking ship, she settled down – gave up all this fell spirit of innovation and insisted that her faith was *unchangeable,* as she had always done. With this difference, however, that before the faith was supposed to have been corrupted, she was mistaken, but that since that melancholy event happened, she is right in her assertion of immutability, and the complaint now is, that she is not reformable at all. So she is at he same time accused of an innovating spirit for evil, and a conservative spirit for the same. Her creed is alleged to have been changeable enough for the introduction of error, but wholly unchangeable for its correction.

For such a history, it would be as if some great and far-seeing mind had deliberately surveyed the Christian Church, when in its purity. Then having clearly perceived, in advance, what additions the system would bear, and the members endure, and marked with logical precision and consistency, the precise point to which these errors could, with safety and success, proceed, and, after having maturely surveyed the whole ground, set about to accomplish these mighty changes. Either he succeeded himself, or his successors and disciples did in his stead so that when all this was accomplished, the Church rested from her labor of innovation, and stands thenceforward firm upon her usurped territory.

It is one of the peculiarly aggravating circumstances in her case, that she boldly and continually asserted that her faith was fixed and unchangeable, while in the very act of changing it in the most palpable and glaring respects. And having hypocritically accomplished this, she, with wicked inconsistency, sanctified and fixed these alleged changes permanently in the Church, upon the very same ground of immutability. And not only so, but while in the very act of making these alleged additions to the faith, she was herself claiming an infallibility never heard of before, and, at the very time, giving to all the most conclusive proofs that she did not possess it. She was guilty, according to the Protestant theory, of the gross inconsistency of declaring, with one and the same breath, that her creed was unchangeable – that she must change it – and that she was infallible in making changes in a fixed and immutable system.

Notwithstanding her alleged monstrous errors, her palpable innovations, and her grossly inconsistent conduct, she has succeeded in keeping in her communion the overwhelming majority of all professed Christians in all ages since she began. So effectually has she covered up these alleged errors, and concealed the existence of the supposed true Church, in past ages, that the finger of time points not to them, and the page of history is silent. And not only so, but she has succeeded in making all her children, numerous as they are, and have ever been, and widely dispersed, believe in her alleged pretense of infallibility, and love and adhere to her in proportion as she is supposed, by her enemies, to have been wicked, inconsistent, and oppressive. And so intense is this love and this reverence, that when her alleged errors are depicted in the vehement and glowing colors of supposed light and truth, and her assumed delinquencies are portrayed in strains of vindictive denunciation,

"And hung on high to poison half mankind,"

her deluded children love her the more, and cleave to her as the friends of old Paul did to him, only the more closely for these things. For by some awful and mysterious influence – by some subtle logic – she binds her children with cords too attenuated to be perceived, and too strong to be broken. And truly, in the contemplation of the Protestant theory, she has been, and is,

"The glory, jest, and riddle of the world."

In proportion as Protestantism degrades the Old Church, by these criminations, it claims for itself a position so sublime, that the distance between the two is as great as human delinquency on the one hand, and faith and fidelity on the other could well make it. For if the Old Church wantonly and wickedly corrupted the faith of Christ under all the advantages she possessed, and the Protestants have restored it under all the difficulties in their way, the distance between the two must be very great. There must in the very nature of the alleged fact, be the greatest criminality on one hand, and the sublimest virtue on the other. Surely, Protestantism does assume to occupy a "painful pre-eminence" – a position that must be attained through mighty crimination, and by wading thorough the moral slaughter of the Christian world.

17. The Old Church must consider Protestants to be heretics

After making these charges of errors so gross – of wickedness so general – of conduct so inconsistent – arising from motives so impure, Protestants complain loudly of the Old Church because she insists, as she always insisted, that Christ never did organize, or intend, but one Church. That therefore, she cannot abandon the faith by acknowledging any Protestant communions as parts of the true Church of Christ. Her intolerance, as it is called, in regarding them as heretics, professing an erroneous faith, is bitterly condemned by them. But under the state of case I do not know what else the Old Church could do. If not guilty of these diversified and grievous charges, she could not, with any self-respect or with regard to the truth, plead guilty.

If Protestants have placed themselves in a false position by a denial of the truth, they have no right to expect the Old Church to do the same thing, and become false to her mighty trust, and to her uniform profession, out of mere kindness to them. If she is guilty then she is wholly unworthy of the communion of Protestants. For this plain alternative must ever come up in the minds of all sincere and reflective persons: either the Catholic Church was guilty of fundamental error, or there was not just cause for the Reformation! As one or the other alternative must be true, there is grievous error somewhere.

Under such circumstances can any fair and just man, upon reflection, expect that the Old Church could make so gross a sacrifice of the faith, (which she has so long maintained,) as to acknowledge, as true sisters, those who lay charges so extensive and grievous against her door? What self-respect – what sincerity – what consistency could she claim, were she to sacrifice her ancient faith in that way? She cannot do it. The gates of hell would at once prevail against her if she did.

While she and her children can hear and bear with patience and charity, the oft reiteration of these charges, and pray for those who make them she cannot deceive them by pleading guilty, when innocent. This would be betraying the cause of Christ, and ruining herself, without doing them the slightest good, except to afford them a mere passing gratification. There can be but one of two courses for her to take. If she be guilty she should acknowledge the fact ands abandon her errors. If not guilt, she must maintain her integrity and her faith, and hold those as heretics who dispute them.

18. Adequate motives for the alleged additions

Another question arose in my mind. What adequate and efficient motives could have existed to produce these alleged additions to the faith? Men are not "wickedly wise" without motive. The motive must bear a due proportion to the wickedness of the act and the difficulties to be overcome in its accomplishment. Protestants have been sensible of this reasonable position. Hence, their controversialists impute to the Catholic clergy the most ambitious, sordid, and unworthy motives.

While their theory imputes to the clergy such a mass of wickedness it at the same time imputes to the laity motives precisely opposed. The theory assumes this exact state of case: unbounded ambition and corruption in the clergy, and a base abandonment of their dearest and plainest rights on the part of the laity. In short, the theory imputes the most criminal delinquencies to both clergy and laity. While it imputes so much ambition and corruption to one class, it assigns to the laity other vices equally fatal to the truth.

It must be obvious to the reflective mind that ingenious, active, restless malice, suspicion and prejudice, can impute a plausible improper motive to every good and virtuous act. There is scarcely a single virtuous act that man can perform that will not allow this. It arises from the plain fact that known good and virtuous actions merit, and will receive, the admiration and applause of good men. As the love of fame is inherent in the bosoms of all men, to a greater or lesser extent, such a motive can always be assigned with some plausibility to ever action however disinterested.

In substance, Protestant writers allege that Catholic theory gives more importance to the clergy in the government of the Church than the Protestant theory. They contend that this constitutes the motive that led to the introduction of these alleged additions to the faith.

It must be obvious that the wise founder of any government will keep in his eye the necessary powers to attain the end intended to be reached by its organization. If he gives too little power, his government fails from weakness. If he bestows too much, and that is unchecked, it may lead to abuses and consequent suffering. After all that can be said about liberty and tyranny, freedom and oppression, the just conclusion must be at last reached: that the *proper* measure of power and authority must be given to every government. To accomplish a great end proportionate powers must be conferred.

It must be conceded that in the Catholic theory the clergy, as a collective body of men, are relatively more important than in the Protestant theory. If this importance was not checked and counterbalanced by other opposing influences, it might be said with some plausibility, that there did exist such a motive. But while it might thus be said of the clergy, it must at the same time, be said of the Catholic laity, that they had an equally strong opposite motive. The impossibility of introducing these alleged errors against the settled faith and maxims of the Church, and the dearest rights and plainest impulses of the laity, would be obvious.

When we come to examine these alleged additions and calmly estimate their true character, it will be seen that they, in themselves and abstractly considered, do increase the importance of the clergy collectively. It will be seen that they at the same time, impose such additional sacrifices and labors as constitute a complete counterbalance. A reward may be tempting but the sacrifice necessary to attain it may be proportionately discouraging!

The law of evidence will not allow a witness to testify in favor of the party who calls him when the witness has a direct and immediate interest in the result of the suit in favor of the party whose witness he is. If however, the witness be interested both ways, so that if the party who calls him gain or lose the case the witness will still be substantially in the same condition – the law holds him counterpoised and permits him to testify.

If then, these alleged errors offer inducements on the one hand, and impose proportionate or greater sacrifices on the other, where is the motive for their alleged introduction? As to the laity, they had the most powerful motives to oppose. Because the introduction of these alleged errors would, diminish their privileges, increase their burdens, while at the same time the true faith was sacrificed.

It would seem eminently just in itself, to suppose that Christ intended to accomplish some great and mighty end by the organization of the Church. Those great functions must, in the nature of the case, have been bestowed upon the governing power of the institution. At the same time, such sacrifices and labors would be imposed as to constitute efficient checks to abuses.

The honor of being regarded as the immediate and chosen apostles of the Son of God was certainly a very great. It did bring to the apostles, in the minds of their brethren, the greatest love, veneration, and respect. "And they all wept sore, and fell on Paul's neck and kissed him – sorrowing most of all for the words which he spake, that they would see his face no more."[17]

While our Lord bestowed such powers and honors, He at the same time imposed such labors, responsibilities and perils, as constituted a most overpowering motive on the other side, if the system He established was untrue. The rose, indeed, was sweet, but the thorns were sharp!

It would seem to be the true theory of every government to impose great responsibilities with great powers –that those to whom the governing power of the Church is entrusted, should, in the nature of the system, be required to make greater sacrifices, perform more arduous labors than the laity, would seem a sentiment just in itself. And is this not so in the Catholic theory? As we have seen, the Catholic clergy make greater sacrifices than the Protestant. The difference between the two classes in this respect is great and obvious.

While I considered the alleged motives imputed to the Catholic priesthood, I also looked into those that could be urged against the Protestant clergy. I must confess that I could not find a doctrine or practice that increased their labors or sacrifices or diminished their enjoyments as compared to the Catholic theory. The exception was that of administering baptism by immersion. This applied to but a very small proportion of them, and was in itself but a slight increase in labor. While their labors and sacrifices were not increased by the Protestant theory, they were relieved from the onerous duties and sacrifices incumbent upon the Catholic clergy.

It is true that while their collective relative importance was diminished by theory, their individual privileges, and sometimes their individual importance, was increased in practice. The only checks imposed by the fundamental rule was the discretion of the preacher and his ability to procure hearers and followers. These obstacles could be readily overcome by the ambitious and talented.

The Protestant clergy having been forced to adopt the rule of private interpretation in the last resort, and therefore to deny all government in the Church, they still insist upon the possession, in mere form, of such powers. While they maintain the theory itself for the purpose of attack and self-justification they, at the same time, awkwardly and inconsistently endeavor to maintain the opposite principle of government in the Church.

In comparing the motives that could be plausibly alleged to produce the two clerical and doctrinal theories this case occurred to me: suppose a worldly-minded individual to seek the ministry simply as a profession. Suppose him to have a choice of a place either in the Catholic or Protestant ministry; which would he prefer? That he would always prefer the Protestant I could not doubt, so far then as worldly motives may be supposed to operate, I could have not hesitation in arriving at the conclusion that they are much more powerful in the Protestant than in the Catholic theory.

19. The alleged additions would have led to powerful divisions

That these alleged additions to the faith of the Church were held and universally believed in the Church of the first five centuries I could have no doubt. Even if this could possibly be disputed, the same insuperable difficulties against their introduction must have occurred whenever they are alleged to have arisen.

It did seem to me that the attempt to restore the alleged pure faith and to abolish these alleged errors led to palpable divisions and discussions, at and since the alleged Reformation. From the nature of the case, the same must have happened whenever they were introduced. No other case, to my mind, was conceivable upon any rational basis whatever. I could just as readily believe that the Scriptures themselves were forged. That they, and all the alleged notable and miraculous facts upon which the system of Christianity assumes to rest, could have been palmed upon the first Christians as true, when they were in fact false. The widely-dispersed Church must have powerfully felt the shock and given us powerful demonstrations of its sensibility had this mighty mass of alleged error been imposed upon the universal and united Church contrary to her fixed and fundamental maxims.

To my apprehension, the Protestant theory, when calmly and thoroughly examined, will be found to be a formidable attack upon the truth of Christianity itself. Most of their leading arguments to refute the Catholic theory will be found in the mouths of Infidels. Put the main arguments of Protestants and Infidels side by side and examine them closely. They will be found to be based essentially upon the same erroneous principles. Their logical and inevitable tendency leads at last to the same result: a denial of the truth of Christianity itself.

20. Unity as an attribute of the true Church

It has been said that the continued unity of the Catholic Church constitutes but a flimsy argument in her favor. The idea intended to be conveyed by this objection is, that the professors of other religions, Mohammedan and Heathen, have continued united in their false theories; and that, therefore, continued unity is no argument to prove the truth of any religion. For if we say it does in one case, it does in the others, and this would prove all true. I have put the objection in its strongest and clearest form.

This objection, at first view, would seem to be very plausible. But conceding, for the sake of the argument only, that this unity has continued to exist among the professors of other religions, as well as among Catholics, and to the same extent; what, then, are the true and legitimate deductions from such conceded premises? I apprehend that these results must follow:

1. That, in the matter of *religion,* men are so deeply and vitally concerned, that among the great mass of its professors, the faith *once* delivered, is always preserved, and safely transmitted from generation to generation. And that, for example, the Mohammedanism of today, is the Mohammedanism of the beginning. It proves the safe *transmission* of religion, even though false, as it was in its *original state.*

2. That the unity of the great body of professed Christians in the Catholic Church proves, in the same way, the safe transmission of the religion of

Jesus, as it was by Him delivered; and, by consequence, is a most powerful argument to prove her to be in the right.

For whether a system of religion be true or false in its *origin,* the fact that the great mass of its professors have, for a long course of ages, continued united in the same faith, is a very strong proof of their vigilance, sincerity, and consistency. These qualities will be found in those who do safely transmit a religious theory, purporting to be *permanent* in its *original form;* while these qualities will not always be found in those who seek to vary or change such a system. If the theory originally promulgated assumes to be incomplete, and therefore, improvable and variable, changes in the system would be compatible with its original basis. But where the system, as in Christianity, assumes to be perfect and unchangeable from the beginning, this unity does constitute one of the most powerful arguments to prove which is the true Church.

It seemed to me that unity was one of the leading duties of Christians. That duty arose not only for the reason, to show evidence which is the true Church; but that it was a powerful argument, even with Infidels themselves. Our Lord certainly so considered it, when He prayed so fervently for the union of His followers, "that the world might believe that the Father had sent Him." So did Saint Paul and Saint Peter, when so earnestly warning their brethren against heresies and divisions.

I supposed that this continued unity was, at least, one very powerful argument, for the explicit reason, that in the contemplation of Christ, this unity was always to be found in the true Church. If this continued unity was always to be found in the true church, its being found in the Catholic Church, as I supposed, is surely one strong argument in her favor. This conclusion was made overwhelming to my mind, by the fact, that this unity, contemplated by the Divine Lawgiver, cannot always be found elsewhere; for this reason, that those who have adopted the opposite of her fundamental rule, in different ages since the beginning of the Christian era, have uniformly severed and divided, until reforms became interminable.

As unity is an attribute of the true Church, and one of the leading duties of Christians, were an intelligent stranger seeking for the true Church, would he expect to find it among those who do not possess this attribute, and have not done their duty in this great and essential respect? Would he expect to find a *discordant true church* or a *changeable* true Church? In his examination, I suppose, he would begin at the beginning, and first examine the fundamental rule of each party; and if he found that one party, under its fundamental rule, was full of discords and variations, his common sense would tell him there was something radically wrong there. And he would naturally say to himself: "one of two things is true; either Christianity has changed, or the true Church is not here." But were he to examine the other rule, and find that all who adhere to it do possess this unity, and at all times have possessed it, he would as naturally say: "one of two conclusions is true; either this is the true Church, or the promises of Christ have failed. For the true Church must always profess the *true,* and, therefore the *same* faith, and possess this *same* unity."

The state of unity assumed, in reference to the professors of false religions, is not borne out by the facts of history. The Mohammedans have long been divided into at least two parties. Mohammed was not a very competent legislator, and left his system very imperfect in some respects. Though these divisions have occurs among them, they do not, in fact, bear any proportion to the alleged changes in the Christian Church. And not only so, but they have not been produced so silently and gradually, as to leave no trace behind. The history of these divisions, when and how they arose, and by whose agency, is very well preserved.

So that the truth of history, as I understand it, is substantially this: there has been a greater unity in the Catholic Church than in the Mohammedan, or any other, so far as we have the means of knowing. At the same time those divisions have not been so great as the *alleged* divisions and errors in the Catholic Church. In other words, the alleged inconsistent changes in the faith of the Catholic Church have been greater than those actually introduced into any of the anti-Christian Churches of the world.

We may take either view of the historical fact, and the argument from the continued unity of the Catholic Church, is, indeed, a very powerful one. If it be true, that one large portion of mankind united in the profession of one religion, and another large portion in the profession of a different theory, for many ages together; then it does show, that when a system is *once established,* which purports upon its face to be *permanent* in the same form, and to continue without addition or subtraction, it cannot be changed by a wholesale addition of the most disgusting, oppressive, and inconsistent errors, without incurring the most strenuous resistance, and without leaving the most palpable historical evidences of the struggle behind.

THE TRUE CHURCH

Macaulay, the brilliant English Protestant historian, has a well-known passage, in which he speaks of the wonderful sagacity of Rome, and concludes that she is the masterpiece of human wisdom. That she is a masterpiece of wisdom, there can be no doubt; and the only question is whether it is human or divine. If human, it is the most wonderful of all human institutions. But whether human or divine, that wisdom is just what we should expect to find in the work of Christ. We should naturally expect the same unity, consistency, and durability, in any true system. And where we do not find all these qualities, we may safely conclude that the true Church is not there.

There is certainly something most extraordinary in the history of this venerable old institution. If she ever did possess an innovating spirit, and did once taste the sweets of its novelties, how completely has she cast it aside, and abandoned that which was so bewitching to her enemies! Has Protestantism done this?

The very admission of the attribute of reformability in a Church, makes reforms interminable. For how can truth be reformable? And how can the true Church be reformable? How can the true Church admit that she is reformable contrary to the fact? Would she admit a falsehood?

To admit that a church may be the true Church, and yet not know it, would be equally erroneous. What sort of Church would that be that did not know herself? Whenever a Church conceded that she can only say she *thinks* she is right, but if not right now, that her theory permits her to reform her faith, she admits to an infirmity that never can be found in the true Church.

It would seem clear that no Church that ever did change her faith, or that admits it to be reformable at all, can be the true Church of Christ, the pillar and ground of the truth. Who can form any conception of such a thing?

Upon the supposition that the Catholic Church is not the true Church, how can we account for the fact that she has withstood all the storms of time, while so few traces remain of the numerous sects that arose before the Reformation? If she was false as well as they, why did she not share their fate? How did she happen to possess so much unity, so much wisdom, and so much tenacity of life, while they, numerous as they were, vanished, one after another from the map of existence? Why could none of them possess the human wisdom mentioned by Macaulay? Those of them which composed the alleged chain of Protestant succession, why did they flourish and fall. Did the true Church possess less wisdom, less permanency, less tenacity of life, than the false Churches? Out of so many enemies how did it happen that the Roman Church still stands while they are gone? She is found at all times, and in all places.

It is very true that the Old Church during the long course of her career has had her enemies and trials without and within. These enemies have been numerous and powerful, and the trials so severe that it may be said that to all appearances she was gone. History tells many a sad tale of her sufferings. But the most remarkable feature in this sad but glorious history is that these formidable, and to human appearances irresistible enemies could never proceed beyond *almost,* and never did reach *entire* destruction. This has always been the fate of the Church – *trials, sufferings, and triumphs.*

It was so in the beginning. Judas betrayed his Master, Peter denied Him, and the rest forsook Him and fled, and He was crucified and buried. The religion of Jesus, the despised Nazarene, was, to all human appearances, exterminated. Even the apostles lost faith for the moment. The Jews thought they had made sure work of it. They sealed the sepulcher, and put a guard over it to prevent even the pretense of a resurrection. But Christ would, and did, rise again.

So it has ever been with His Old Church. Her entire destruction has often been threatened, but it has not yet been accomplished. Her grave has often been dug, in imagination, and her enemies have so often supposed that she was dead and buried; but still she would *rise again.* At the very moment when she was thought to be the weakest, she was, in fact, the strongest. Wonderful vitality! Glorious invincibility! Her enemies could die. She could not.

And since the alleged Reformation, her destruction has been often *threatened,* but only threatened. It is always in the power of her enemies to threaten. A few years after the dawn of that event, the Turks made renewed and mighty efforts to conquer Europe; and Luther, at the time, advised his followers to refrain from opposing the Turks, until the Papacy should be destroyed. Under these circumstances, every thing seemed suspended upon the fate of one battle. The great battle of Lepanto was fought between the Mohammedans and Catholics, and the Turks were vanquished.

THE TRUE CHURCH

When the followers of Luther, under the Landgrave of Hesse, rebelled against the government of Charles V. the battle of the Elbe declared in favor of the Emperor. Afterwards the great Gustavus, that thunderbolt of war, whose career threatened the entire destruction of the Catholic Church, was slain at the battle of Lutzen, and the Church again triumphed. Still later, and during the French Revolution, it was thought the days of the Church were numbered, and the notes of triumph were already sounded. But Napoleon appeared, and the Church rose again. And when this great man oppressed the Church, others put him down. And so it has ever been in the history of this Old, but invincible Church. Difficulty after difficulty – trial after trial – she has always met and overcome.

These stern and gloomy trials – but glorious triumphs – only increase our faith in the stability of this mighty Old Church. Is there any virtue without temptation? any fidelity without a trial? any victory without a struggle? Must not the true Church fight, if she would reign? And if she fights, must she not bleed? And if she expects to gain *great* victories, let her trials be severe. So much the better. Let her "come up through great tribulation," *but let her come up.* She has always done it. Will she not still do it? Is she not able?

These trials – these threatened exterminations – give Catholics no uneasiness. They have faith – unwavering faith – in the promises of Christ. If the Church be not protected by Christ let her fail. And if she had not been so protected, she would have failed long ago. If she is the work of Christ, she must and will live on, though her trials and sufferings be still more severe. Let them come so she but gains the victory. Her old martyr, the holy Ignatius said:

> Fire and the Cross, the assaults of beasts, the rending of my bones, the laceration of my limbs, the crushing of my whole frame, dire tortures of Satan, let them come upon me, so that I but go to Christ.

I confess that I love a Church that has overcome all these trials. Her sufferings have been intense. So they should be. Shall the true Church have a primrose path on *earth,* and also a golden path in *heaven.* Will not her glory be in proportion to her sufferings and trials? Her victories in the past but assure me of her victories in the future. The good ship that has triumphantly rode out many a severe storm, and is yet staunch and tight, is the more to be trusted. The veteran soldier that has fought on many a battlefield, wears honorable scars, and is yet strong and vigorous, is but the more reliable. And the Church expects trials, and would not escape them if she did not expect them. It is her vocation, her business, to meet and overcome them. Let her fulfill her duty – the very purpose of her creation.

21. Conclusion

In his debate with Mr. Rice, Mr. Campbell says:

> Catholic parents do their work more faithfully than most of the Protestants, and the consequence is, it is generally more difficult to convert a Romanist to any Protestant profession, than a Protestant to the Roman persuasion.[18]

If it be true, as stated, that "Catholic parents do their work more faithfully, than most of the Protestants," it does show their greater sincerity, faith, and devotion. And these are most commendable traits in the Christian character. The exertions of a parent to instruct his children in the religion he himself believes will bear a just proportion to the fixedness and importance of his own faith.

The greater difficulty of converting a Catholic than a Protestant, does not arise solely, or mainly, from the cause assigned by Mr. Campbell, but from others. The great Dr. Johnson said:

> A man who is converted from Protestantism to Popery may be sincere; he parts with nothing; he is only superadding to what he already had. But a convert from Popery to Protestantism gives up so much of what he has held as sacred as anything that he retains; there is so much *laceration of mind* in such a conversion, that it can hardly be sincere and lasting.

And the biographer himself adds: "The truth of this reflection may be confirmed by many and eminent instances, some of which will occur to most of my readers."[19]

There certainly is a great deal of truth, though not the whole truth, in this reflection. The convert from the Catholic Church seems conscious that he is embracing an inferior and lower grade of faith, and adopting a colder and more suspicious estimate of human veracity. He cuts himself loose from the holy ties that bound him to the suffering martyr-Church of old. He severs all connection with the apostles, except that *hidden* one, which is supposed to be buried in the darkness and silence of the dim distant ages of the past. He leaves the sweet communion of saints, which combines the children of the true faith everywhere, in every age, in one holy brotherhood. What are the heroic martyrs and saints of old to him?

They are now become "mystics and visionaries." What to him is now the great and universal Church of the mighty past? "The Man of Sin." Who were the clergy of the Old Church – that Church which won the world to Christianity? To him they are now become impostors, who betrayed the faith of Christ. And the laity, who were they? Simple dupes. In short, to him what is the Christian past – a blurred and blotted page for evil, and a practical blank for good? It is a melancholy view of Christianity – a humiliating estimate of human veracity – a mighty accusation against humanity itself. No wonder it produces so much *"laceration of mind."*

But it is not so with the convert to the Catholic Faith. He is conscious that he has embraced a higher grade of faith, has been brought into closer and holier communion with the unseen world, and has adopted a more just and charitable estimate of human veracity. He has taken a step towards the Celestial City, from the low murky valleys of discord, where the fogs of error love to dwell. He shakes hands with the brethren of every kindred, name, and tongue. He worships with the people of every nation. He joins his prayers with those who speak the varied languages of earth. On every shore, in every land, beneath every sky, and in every city, he meets his brethren of the universal Church. He is at home everywhere, and bows down with the millions who have worshipped, and still worship, at the same altar, and hold the same faith.

But the convert not only joins the brethren of every kindred. He looks back over the pages of past history, and ascends by a plain, visible, and unbroken chain to the apostolic day. He has no chasms to leap, no deserts to cross. At every step in this progress he finds the same Old Church – the same faith – the same worship still pre-eminent in the Christian world. He sees the rise and fall of empires and sects; but the same Old Church always pre-eminent. The records of the past are with him. He has the sanction of antiquity. Time tells for him a glorious story. He meets with myriads of brethren all along the slumbering ages. The old martyrs and saints are his brethren. He claims companionship with them. Their memories are beloved by him. And Blandina, the poor slave, but noblest of martyrs, was his sister. And old Ignatius, and Polycarp, and Justin, and Irenaeus, are also his brethren. And she, the humblest of the humble – the purest of the pure – the stainless Virgin Mother of his Lord, whom all generations call "blessed," is revered by him as the noblest of creatures. And the old apostles – the noble and the true – the holy and the just – the despised and persecuted – they, too, are his brethren. In short, the saints and martyrs of the olden time, held the same faith, worshipped at the same altar, and used the same form of worship that he does. He venerates and loves their memory, admires their virtues, calls them brethren, and asks their prayers in heaven. He has no accusations to bring against them – no crimes to lay to their charge.

Besides all this, his faith is sustained by a logical power, and a Scriptural proof, that cannot be fairly met and confuted. It is sustained by every plain and luminous principle upon which society and government are founded. His reason, his common sense, the best feelings of his nature, thc holiest impulses of his heart, all satisfy him beyond a doubt, that he is in the right.

It is not at all surprising, then, that it is so difficult to convert a Catholic to Protestantism when in the vigor of life; and so difficult, that it never has been done, at the hour of death. For there is no known instance where a Catholic changed his faith upon a dying bed; while thousands of Protestants have done so. If a Catholic can live a faithful member of his Church, he can always die in it. In that awful hour – that honest hour –

"When all the blandishments of life are gone.
When tired dissimulation drops her mask,
And real and apparent are the same;"

when eternity, with all its mighty consequences, rolls up its endless proportions before the dying vision – Ah! then, no Catholic asks to change his faith! Oh! give me the last sacraments of the Church! Let me die in her holy communion! Let me be buried in consecrated ground! Let my brethren pray for me!

But there is still another most weighty consideration with him. He examines carefully the doctrines of his Church. From the first to the last article of faith, they are as consistent with each other as truth itself could be. There is no discrepancy – no contradiction. The whole theory, in all its parts, is perfectly consistent with itself. He finds few, if any, to deny this entire consistency of parts with the whole. He knows that every part of a true system must be consistent with each, and with all. No one truth jars with another. There can be no enmity, no discord, in a true system. But he knows it is exceedingly difficult to find this consistency and harmony in a theory of pure error; and still more difficult to find it in a mixed theory of truth and error. And he cannot understand how the alleged additions to the faith could have been made, and so *nicely fitted to the true system, as to be perfectly consistent with it.* He finds it conceded that his Church has the fundamental truths of Christianity, and that her faith is consistent throughout; and he cannot see how this consistency could be found between the alleged added errors and the old truths; and he is forced to conclude, that a theory so consistent in all its parts and admitted to contain many truths, must be true in every particular.

I will close this work in the words of that distinguished French writer, La Bruyère:

> If my religion be false, it is, I must own, the most artful snare that could possibly be devised. It is impossible to avoid falling into it and being caught. What majesty, what magnificence, in its mysteries! What coherency, what connection, in all its doctrines! What sound reasons! What candor! What innocence of morals! What an invincible and overwhelming body of evidence is given successively, and for three whole centuries, by millions of the most learned and most considerate persons then in the world, and whom the conviction of one and the same truth supported in exile, in fetters, at the approach of death, and under the most cruel torments.

---

[1] Gardener Spring. *A Dissertation on the Rule of Faith.* p. 39, 5, 63, 71, 74, 86.

[2] *Ibid.* p. 85.

[3] Nicholas Wiseman *Moorfield Lectures* p.110, vol. 2.

[4] A. Campbell and J. Purcell, *A debate on the Roman Catholic religion.* p 292.

[5] *Ibid.* p. 47.

[6] Joseph Nightingale. *The Religions and Religious Ceremonies of All Nations.* p. 65.

[7] Letters to Vossius.

[8] It is well laid down in Starkie, and other authors on the Law of Evidence, that there are some circumstances *conclusive* in their nature. For example, the body of a female was found in her bed, and so disposed as to lead at once to the conclusion that she committed suicide. This was the first impression until they discovered the bloody print of a right hand upon the back of her right hand.

A father was found dead in his bed. Suspicion attached to his blind son, until it was observed that the murderer had left the bloody prints of his hands on the wall in feeling his way out of the room at night. This could not have been the case with a blind man to whom day and night were alike.

[8] It would seem that no one but an Atheist could *consistently* be a hypocrite. For under every theory of a future state of rewards and punishments, hypocrisy is considered a serious sin. Our Lord denounced it in the most severe terms: "Woe unto you Scribes and Pharisees, hypocrites." Homer puts into the mouth of one of his heroes (as translated by Pope; and if I can quote him correctly) these strong lines:of all until they discovered the bloody print of a right hand upon the back of her right hand.

A father was found dead in his bed. Suspicion attached to his blind son, until it was observed that the murderer had left the bloody prints of his hands on the wall in feeling his way out of the room at night. This could not have been the case with a blind man to whom day and night were alike.

[9] It would seem that no one but an Atheist could *consistently* be a hypocrite. For under every theory of a future state of rewards and punishments, hypocrisy is considered a serious sin. Our Lord denounced it in the most severe terms: "Woe unto you Scribes and Pharisees, hypocrites." Homer puts into the mouth of one of his heroes (as translated by Pope; and if I can quote him correctly) these strong lines:

"Who dares to think one thing and another tell
My soul detests him as the gates of hell."

[10]Cf. James Boswell. Life of Johnson.

[11]J Hughes and J Breckenridge, Hughes-Breckenridge Controversy. p 70.

[12] William. Paley, A View of the Evidences of Christianity.

[13] Gardener Spring, op. cit. p39.

[14] Cited in Fletcher's Notes to Fenelon's Letter on the Use of the Bible.

[15] A. Campbell and N. Rice, Campbell Rice Debate on the Holy Spirit. p. 764.

[16] William. Paley, op. cit. The learned divine then gives a short account of the heretics to show these topics. He mentions Basilicans A.D. 120, the Valentinians A.D. 125, the Carpocratians a little later, the Sethians A.D. 150, the Montanists A.D. 156, the Marcasians A.D. 160, Heromgenes A.D. 180, Prexius A.D. 196, Artimon A.D. 200, Theodatus A.D. 200, Tatian A.D. 172, Paul of Samosata A.D. 246, the Sabellians A.D. 246, Novatians A.D. 251, the Donatists A.D. 328, the Arians about A.D. 300, the Priscillianists A.D. 378, the Pelagians A.D. 405. The learned divine mentions Origen A.D. 216, as the author of some new opinions, which were condemned by the Bishops of Rome and Alexandria.

[17] Acts 20:37.

[18] A. Campbell and N. Rice, Campbell Rice Debate on the Holy Spirit. p. 3I7.

[19] James Boswell in 1769.

PART 2

INDEX

D

O

P

R

FUTURE TITLES

Other titles that Solas Press will publish in the present series

The Theory of American Government by Peter H. Burnett

This book was published in 1861 under the title *The Theory of American Government: With reference to the Present Crisis.* Burnett, one of the architects of the states of Oregon and California, a student of the Supreme Court, and a philosophic lawyer was troubled by the operation of the Federal government in the 1860's. In this book he identifies the theoretical underpinnings of a successfully functioning democratic society. His vision of the American nation rested on a rational, pragmatic base.

In this short work, Burnett provides a window into the mind-set behind American governance in the 1860's. He also raises theoretical issues that are of continued interest.

Recollections and Opinions of an Old Pioneer by Peter H. Burnett

This book was first published in 1880. It is a valuable accounting of the early constitutional and political history of Oregon and California. In addition, his stories on a variety of topics are appealing as well as informative.

The Love of God by Peter H. Burnett

This book was first published in 1884 under the title *Reasons Why We Should Believe in God, Love God and Obey God.* With this book, Burnett in his *mature* years looks at the greatest controversy of the day –evolutionary theory. He brings to his task the ability to analyze the logic of arguments and to evaluate evidence. As with Phillip Johnson in *Darwin on Trial* a century later, Burnett leans to the juridical approach to the topic. He divides the work into four parts, the existence of God, evolution, the old dispensation and the new dispensation.

TESTIMONIALS

19th Century

Orestes Brownson. American Philosopher and essayist –(*The Path which led a Protestant Lawyer to the Catholic Church*) is the work not of priest, nor of a professional theologian, but of a clear headed, strong minded lawyer, who has not suffered the law to make him forget his soul, or to stifle his conscience. Is written in a clear, forcible and unpretending style, in a straightforward earnest manner, and is not to be judged as a mere literary performance, but as the grave utterance of a man who has something to say, and is pressed by an internal necessity to say it.

What strikes the reader at a glance in this remarkable volume is its perfect honesty and sincerity. As you read it you feel that the eminent jurist is honestly retracing the path and detailing successive steps, by which he actually came into the Church; and it has a high psychological value aside from its positive and conclusive arguments for the objective truth of Catholicity or the divine foundation and constitution of the Catholic Church.

The whole tone and character of the work inspires confidence in the author, as a fair minded man, as a candid judge, and as one who be as incapable of knowing deceiving others as of deceiving himself. He has evidently inquired earnestly and honestly for the truth for his own mind, and he gives the results of his inquiries for precisely for what he found them worth to himself….

20th Century

James Sullivan, S.J. Saint Louis University Editor of an abridged version of *The Path which led a Protestant Lawyer to the Catholic Church.* –The editor takes great pleasure in acknowledging his gratitude to Judge Burnett for the invaluable aid his book has been to him in his dealings with many sincere and intelligent non-Catholics….

Testimonials continued

21st Century

Cornelius Buckley, S.J. Historian and author of (among others) *Ignatius of Loyola: The Pilgrim Saint.* —*With* steel clean logic and crystal clear style the 19th century Peter Burnett has written what can be read as a kind of contemporary commentary on *The Catechism of The Catholic Church.* Anyone interested in apologetics will find this work invaluable.

Avery Cardinal Dulles S.J. –Peter Burnett, applying the principles of Anglo-American law to Scripture and the Fathers of the Church, produced a remarkably full and impressive apologia for the Catholic faith. Too little remembered in our day, the work has more than historical interest. Many issues treated in it are still lively topics of controversy. Together with Orestes Brownson another great convert and autodidact, Burnett stands in the first rank of 19th century American Catholic apologists.

Most Reverend William J. Levada, Archbishop of San Francisco. –Since I have been privileged to serve the Church both in Oregon and in California, I took a particular interest in the career of this remarkable man. His (Burnett's) work is a *tour de force,* and stands as a worthy predecessor to many fine works of Catholic apologetics being authored by lay people of our time.

Stan Fabian Parmisano, O.P. Author of *Mission West.* –First because of the worth of the book in and for itself: a splendid instance of the genre "apologetics," defending with heart as well as mind, with courtesy, authority, close and careful reasoning, the truth of the Catholic Church.

Joseph Pierce. Highly acclaimed literary biographer of Chesterton, C.S. Lewis and others. –As an Englishman fairly recently arrived in the United States I found myself enthralled by this defence of the Catholic Church by a convert from the days of the 'wild west'. Burnett's *apologia* published a few short years before Cardinal Newman's more famous *Apologia pro vita sua* enabled me to understand the relationship between Mother Church and Uncle Sam more clearly. *The True Church* shows how the romance of Rome could transform the romance of the old West.

Msgr. Francis Webber. Archivist, Author of *Encyclopedia of California's Catholic Heritage 1769-1999.* –He (Burnett) was as the title of one of his books indicates "An Old Pioneer." But he was more than that – he was a man of destiny. Catholics, Protestants and Jews all owe much of their California heritage to this first American Governor of the State!